The Hindi Public Sphere

The Hindi Public Sphere 1920-1940

Language and Literature in the Age of Nationalism

FRANCESCA ORSINI

OXFORD
UNIVERSITY PRESS

OXFORD
UNIVERSITY PRESS

YMCA Library Building, Jai Singh Road, New Delhi 110 001

Oxford University Press is a department of the University of Oxford. It furthers the University's objective of excellence in research, scholarship, and education by publishing worldwide in

Oxford New York

Auckland Bangkok Buenos Aires Cape Town Chennai
Dar es Salaam Delhi Hong Kong Istanbul Karachi Kolkata
Kuala Lumpur Madrid Melbourne Mexico City Mumbai Nairobi
São Paulo Shanghai Singapore Taipei Tokyo Toronto

with an associated company in Berlin

Published in India
By Oxford University Press, New Delhi

First published 2002

ISBN 019 565084 0

Typeset in Naurang
by Guru Typograph Technology, New Delhi 110 045
Printed in India by Roopak Printer, Noida
Published by Manzar Khan, Oxford University Press
YMCA Library Building, Jai Singh Road, New Delhi 110 001

To
Alok and Rajul

Acknowledgements

First of all I should thank all the people in India who made this research a living and relevant, as well as a most exciting and enjoyable, enterprise. They include:

In Allahabad: Dr Mushtaq Ali for having shared with me his doctoral work and introducing me to all the survivors of that epoch; Ramādatt Śukla, Ṭhakurprasād Miśra and the late Thakur Śrīnāth Siṃh; the librarian and assistants of the Hindī Sāhitya Sammelan library for patient assistance and photocopying; the Warden of Sarojini Naidu's Hostel for allowing me to stay twice in such a 'period' ambience, and Roly and Vandana for delightful company there; Ashok Saigal for letting me see whatever was left of the Chand Press (now *Rock Street Journal*); Amrit Rai and Sudha Chauhan, who are sadly no more, for their warm hospitality; Alok and Rajul Rai, Raghoo Sinha, Arvind and Vandana Mehrotra, Sara and Aslam for making Allahabad into something of a second home.

In Varanasi: Dr Dhīrendranāth Siṃh and Dr Anand Krishna for guidance and more information than I could gather; the Āryabhāṣā Pustakālay for being the treasure it is (and the boisterous librarian who insisted on telling everyone I was 'Sonia Gandhi kī bahin' despite my murderous glances); the family of Pravin and Navin Sharma for their unexpected and generous hospitality and the many interesting discussions on 'Bhārtīy saṃskṛti'; Ratnaśaṅkar Prasād for showing me his house and his father's heirlooms.

In Delhi: Purushottam Agrawal, Krishna Kumar, and Alok Rai (yes, again) for sharing many ideas and reading my very first draft; the staff at Jawaharlal Nehru University and the Nehru Memorial Museum and Library; Nora, for her friendship and unfailing hospitality; the teachers of the Central Institute of Hindi, for having inadvertently prompted several years ago many of the questions raised in the book.

In London: my supervisors, Dr Amrik S. Kalsi and Dr Sudipta Kaviraj, for their perfect balance of encouragement and criticism; the SOAS and India Office libraries, for having most of the books I needed and many, many more.

My heartfelt thanks also to Pramod Singh, Rachel Dwyer, Frances Wainwright, Lucy Rosenstein, Veena Naregal, Pragati Mahapatra and Sanjay Sharma, Eivind and Sudeshna Kahrs, and many more friends who 'shared the load'. To Pankaj Mishra, for reading an earlier draft and to Vasudha Dalmia for her most timely and valuable comments. Peter Kornicki read the manuscript at several stages and saved it from many pitfalls. Finally, I should thank all the protagonists and actors of this book, for taking such vivid shape in front of my eyes and letting me live with them for several years. My only hope is to have done justice to them in this work.

FRANCESCA ORSINI

Contents

Note on Orthography

Hindi words that have become part of the English language like Brahmin or Pandit have been written without diacritical marks. For Hindi proper names and when citing directly from Hindi, the transliteration followed by R.S. McGregor in his *Outline of Hindi Grammar* (1972) has mostly been used. When citing from secondary sources, the author's usage has been retained, hence possible discrepancies.

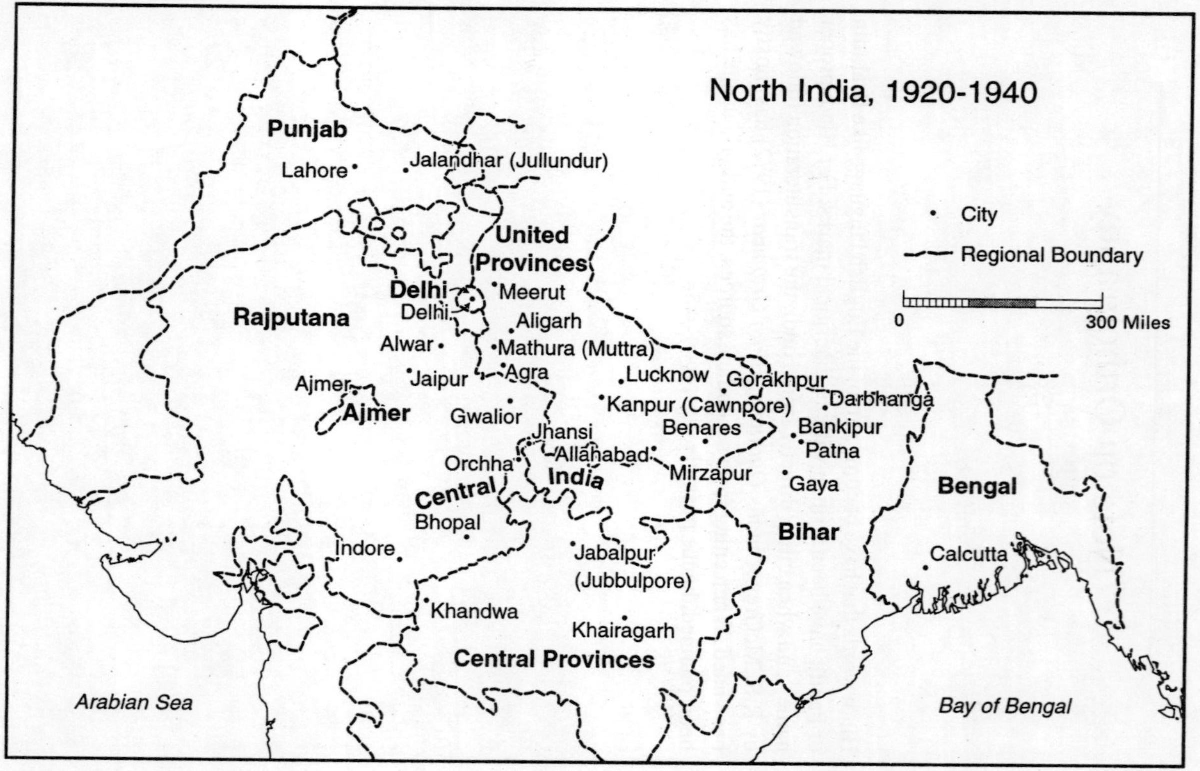
North India, 1920-1940
City
Regional Boundary
0
300 Miles
Punjab
Lahore
Jalandhar (Jullundur)
United
Provinces
Delhi
Delhi
Meerut
Rajputana
Aligarh
Alwar
Mathura (Muttra)
Jaipur
Agra
Ajmer
Ajmer
Lucknow
Gorakhpur
Darbhanga
Kanpur (Cawnpore)
Gwalior
Jhansi
Benares
Bankipur
Patna
Allahabad
Orchha
Mirzapur
Gaya
Central
India
Bengal
Bhopal
Bihar
Indore
Jabalpur
(Jubbulpore)
Calcutta
Khandwa
Khairagarh
Central Provinces
Arabian Sea
Bay of Bengal

The Hindi Public Sphere

When editor Devīdatt Śukla changed out of his mirzai-lungi into a kurta, a well-creased dhoti and pump-shoes to go to his office, when fellow litterateurs switched from colloquial gossip to pure Hindi at a literary venue, when poet Maithilīśaraṇ Gupta invoked Vedic Aryans as 'our ancestors', and when the word 'national' (*jātīy, rāṣṭrīy*) was attached to every field of discourse and activity (*national* education, *national* literature, *national* language), different aspects of the same process were in action. From the first half of the nineteenth century, under the influence of British ideas and institutions, many educated Indians started evolving codes, institutions and a language to express the need for new concepts like 'unity', 'progress', and a 'common cultural heritage'. Public spaces for argument and debate were established and codes evolved by which people acknowledged that they were entering spaces that were common and public. These spaces transcended, while incorporating, people's social being.

Devīdatt Śukla (1888–1970), like many others, had first entered this space through education and the press. At 16 when he was in the sixth form, he encountered his first newspaper, the Calcutta weekly *Bhāratmitra*. Soon his small circle of school friends began sharing newspapers to keep abreast of political movements in Bengal. Later he himself became part of the world of print as editor for a prestigious publishing house, the Indian Press.[1]

The Hindi Area: Geographical, Social, and Linguistic Boundaries

Print-languages create boundaries, but the world Devīdatt Śukla lived in was a multilingual one: English, Urdu, Hindi, local dialects, and the

[1] Devīdatt Śukla, *Sampādak ke pacchīs varṣ*, Allahabad, Kalyan Mandir, 1956, p. 3.

distant influence of Bengali marked overlapping but distinct levels of language use along social, cultural, and urban–rural faultlines. Even Indian-owned English and Hindi newspapers from the same area reveal two socially different audiences.[2]

Geographically, the Hindi area extended from the princely states of Rajputana (present Rajasthan) in the west to Bihar in the east, and from Punjab and Garhwal in the north to the Central Provinces and Berar in the south [map]. The North-Western Provinces of Agra and Oudh (later renamed the United Provinces of Agra and Oudh, abbreviated here to UP), and especially the cities of Allahabad and Benares, were at the centre of the 'Hindi heartland'. It was an area previously under the Mughals and their successor states. Bihar apart, its colonization was late and piecemeal: the North-Western Provinces were annexed in 1805, the Nerbudda (Narmada) territories of Central India in 1819, Oudh (Awadh), Punjab and parts of Garhwal only after 1857. Large tracts remained nominally under Indian rule with British paramountcy. The English-educated, bilingual middle-class of Calcutta had no real equivalent in north India, where local traditions of learning remained strong among educated families, both Muslim and Hindu. Over this wide geographical area, the public use of Hindi was unevenly distributed.

Socially, the importance of Persian, the court language of the Mughal empire and of most successor states, had ensured the continuity of a Hindu–Muslim class of Persian-educated gentry, officials and law professionals that was predominantly urban. Their language of communication was called 'Hindi' i.e. the language of Hind, written in the Arabic

[2] 'The British-owned Anglo-Indian newspapers,' recalled Jawaharlal Nehru, 'were full of the doings of high officials; English social life in the big cities and in the hill stations was described at length with its parties, fancy dress balls and amateur theatricals.' (Nehru, *An Autobiography*, Delhi, OUP, 1998 (1936), p. 48.) The Indian-owned *The Leader* (Allahabad, edited by Liberal politician C.Y. Chintamani) would mix the items typical of the English newspapers with detailed discussions of national conferences, government bills, and market reports; editorials were perfect examples of parliamentary idiom, while regional news came under the somewhat disparaging rubric 'Mofussil'. Advertisements for banks and goods tried to captivate readers with capital and saving power; those for English schools appealed to the socially mobile. By contrast, Hindi newspapers addressed a popular and highly politicized audience, in the case of *Vartamān* (Kanpur, ed. R. Avasthī) the specific audience of factory workers; their format and style were those of a tabloid, with big and captivating headlines ('Bolshevik government in China', 'Prostitutes work magic on judge'), international news about workers and a special eye for local communist activities and communal disturbances. See *The Leader* and *Vartamān*, 2 January 1925.

script, until in the late eighteenth century John Gilchrist and other Orientalists popularized the names 'Hindustani' and 'Urdu' in order to spread the notion that there were actually two different languages, one for Hindus and one for Muslims.[3] Irrespective of the names, the thriving Urdu press and the publishing market in Urdu and Persian in the early nineteenth century testifies to the prominence of this mixed urban group, and Urdu remained the dominant vernacular in Punjab, Delhi, and Awadh (Oudh) well into the twentieth century.

The use of Khari Boli Hindi, which would later become modern standard Hindi, was more uneven. As a spoken language identical to Hindustani, it was the lingua franca of the bazaar over the whole of northern and central India, and the mother tongue of a relatively small area around Meerut in western UP. It was also the mother tongue of merchant castes like the *pāchiyā* (western) Agrawals who had spread all over northern India from UP and who used it for long-distance trade communication. Braj Bhasa rather than Khari Boli was the universally acknowledged medium for poetry, but the survival of some specimens of Khari Boli prose from before 1800 have been taken to suggest that it too had some functions as a written language, especially beyond the pale of the highly educated.[4] In the nineteenth century, Khari Boli Hindi rather than Braj Bhasa or Avadhi, in Devanagari script, instead of Kaithi or Mahajani, came to be regarded as 'standard Hindi', mainly through the agency of Fort William College and missionary textbooks. The story has already been told and need not be repeated here (cf. 1.1).[5] The self-conscious adoption by the educated Hindus of northern India of Khari Boli Hindi as their public language in the second half of the nineteenth century marked the upsurge of a cultural movement that Urdu intellectuals could not comprehend. The champions of Hindi belonged to small zamindar or even peasant families whose fathers and grandfathers had sometimes diversified into

[3] Shamsur Rahman Faruqi, *Early Urdu Literary Culture and History*, Delhi, OUP, 2001.

[4] See Rāmvilās Śarmā, 'Gadya aur padya meṁ kharī bolī 1800 ke pahle', *Bhārtendu yug aur hindī bhāṣā kī vikās paramparā*, New Delhi, Rajkamal Prakasan, 1975.

[5] R.S. McGregor, *Hindi Literature of the Nineteenth and Early Twentieth Centuries*, Wiesbaden, Harrassowitz, 1974; Shardadevi Vedalankar, *The Development of Hindi Prose in the Early Nineteenth Century (AD 1800–56)*, Allahabad, Lokbharati Publications, 1969; Lakṣmīsāgar Varṣṇey, *Ādhunik hindī sāhitya kī bhumikā*, Allahabad, Hindi Parishad, 1952; Christopher King, *One Language, Two Scripts. The Hindi Movement in Nineteenth Century North India*, Delhi, OUP, 1994; Vasudha Dalmia, *The Nationalization of Hindu Traditions. Hariśchandra and Nineteenth Century Benares*, Delhi, OUP, 1997; Alok Rai, *Hindi Nationalism*, Delhi, Orient Longman, 2001.

teaching, law, the lower echelons of government service or the army; they could be from families that still served local landowners and worked as village clerks (*patwaris* and *kanungos*); or they could be scholarly or priestly Brahmins, educated in Sanskrit, who performed ritual duties in the village and sometimes taught at village schools (*pāṭhśālās*); and finally they could belong to Agrawal and Khatri merchant families. It was these higher and middle castes, of once-diverse linguistic competencies, that compacted around Khari Boli Hindi. They produced the first wave of activism and created institutional spaces for Hindi in the form of periodicals, literary and public associations and textbook writing. The spectrum hardly widened after 1920: over half of the Hindi literati, men and women, were Brahmins, including a few Bhumihars, while the rest were Kayasthas, Agrawals, Khatris, and Thakurs.

This was the nascent Hindi public sphere that Vasudha Dalmia has brilliantly outlined in her book on the most important figure of this generation, Hariśchandra of Benares (1850–85).[6] In many ways, my work in this book is a continuation of hers in following the development of the Hindi public sphere beyond those pioneering beginnings in cities like Benares, Allahabad, Agra, and Patna. It was in competition with the already established Urdu (Hindi in the Arabic script with a growing predominance of Arabic vocabulary) and developing Urdu institutions. Scripts in different alphabets justified the divide between Hindi and Urdu and helped coalesce separate linguistic and cultural identities and competing vernacular public spheres in the same region (see 1.1 and 2.1).

Finally, the colonization of north India in the course of the nineteenth century brought along with it not only English, the new elite language, but also English-educated Bengalis as government servants and professionals who settled in administrative centres all the way from Bihar to Punjab. Distinctively urban and anglicized in clothes and lifestyle, often highly educated and at the forefront of public sphere activities, Bengalis appeared very much the direct model to imitate. Not only were they quite bilingual in English and Bengali, they had also been successful in nurturing their mother tongue equally with English and using it to spread 'modern knowledge', *naī vidyā*. The spread of education (also among women), and the growth of the press, theatre, and literature in Bengal testified to their 'advanced' state and made the Hindi area appear distinctly 'backward' by comparison.

[6] Dalmia, *The Nationalization of Hindu Traditions.*

It was on this fragmented and contested terrain that Hindi took shape as a print language, that Hindi organizations spread the public use of Hindi, and that Hindi writers asserted their authority. Especially in the years between 1920 and 1940 Hindi gained much ground and was indeed able to stake its claim as the national language of the whole of India. Yet it could not discard the linguistic hierarchy that saw it as a competing vernacular below English, and in the process it had alienated Indo-Persian cultural traditions.

Language, Literature, and Nationalism

To indicate the larger community which they claimed to belong to and simultaneously aspired to create, Hindi intellectuals used two terms: *rāṣṭra*, which stood for 'nation' in a political sense, and *jāti*, which was used to indicate a common cultural identity. Nineteenth-century Hindi writers thus envisaged the public as a cultural community whose contours and essential features had to be extricated from the many layers and splinters of social reality with its diverse cultural and religious traditions. Linguistic divides added special nuances to the importance of language and literature in this discourse.[7] In nationalist terms, language and literature were the means to define and communicate the agenda for progress, and were themselves metaphors for the jāti/nation: the strength of literature showed the strength of the nation, the life of the language was the life of the nation. It was the 'we' (*ham*) of the jāti that was to speak as the subject of language and literature, transmitting its essential values. In the context of the Hindi/Urdu and English divide, Hindi was singled out as the bearer of the peculiar values of Indian tradition and the means to reach out to and unite the whole (Hindu) population (see 2.1 and 2.2). In order to perform these reformist duties, the existing varieties of language and literature had to be redefined, in Hindi as in other languages.

The redefinition of Hindi from the perspective of the 'public' began in the second half of the nineteenth century and was formalized in the early twentieth century primarily by Mahāvīr Prasād Dvivedī (1864–1938). What did this redefinition consist of? Nineteenth-century writers like Hariśchandra and his circle, while embracing the aim of unity and reform, had actually drawn on *all* the resources of the language and the

[7] General studies on language and nationalism include: Benedict Anderson, *Imagined Communities*, London, Verso, 1983; and Paul Brass, *Language, Religion and Politics in North India*, Cambridge, Cambridge University Press, 1974. On nationalism and literature, see also Sudhir Chandra, *The Oppressive Present. Literature and Social Consciousness in Colonial India*, Delhi, OUP, 1992.

various literary traditions in their own creative writing—they used the colloquial *spoken* language and concrete metaphors in a way that retained the *particularity* of language use, so that the caste, region, and profession of every character showed in their language,[8] displaying an attitude to realism similar to that of the ancient Romans.[9] A generation later Mahāvīr Prasād Dvivedī did exactly the opposite, and exhorted other writers to do so too. By purging print-language of colloquialisms, regional usages and 'Urdu' words, by privileging abstract over concrete words and making Sanskrit loanwords the rule, and by fixing syntax along regular subject–object–verb lines, Dvivedī 'standardized' Hindi into a sober written language. Only such a standard language was fit for discussing 'public' matters, for creating literature, and for representing the jāti: in short, for serving the many purposes of a modern nation. The 'Indianness' of such a language was expressed with a metaphor analogous to that of 'Mother India': Hindi (feminine, as all languages) was the 'daughter' of Sanskrit and the 'elder sister' of the other Neo-Indo Aryan languages, while Urdu was the quarrelsome 'co-wife'.[10]

Not only was modern Hindi effectively reshaped by this discourse, but also views of the past and of literary tradition were filtered through it in the literary canon that was formed by literary associations and the school curriculum.

The Literary System: An Approach

The serious reformist literature that formed the staple of Mahāvīr Prasād Dvivedī's journal *Sarasvatī* and that we find in Hindi literary histories, was only part of the literature produced and enjoyed at the time. It can therefore provide only a partial picture of the Hindi world of that period, only one side of the coin. To gain a more comprehensive and critical view we need to enlarge our range of vision in order to set reformist

[8] A striking example is Hariśchandra's play *Premjoginī* (1874–5), set in Kāśī (Benares): characters in the first and second acts speak particularized and colloquial forms of Hindi, in the fourth act even Marathi; pure Hindi is used in the third act to wax on the public face of Kāśī; *Bhārtendu samagra*, ed. H. Śarmā, Benares, Hindi Pracharak Samsthan, 1987.

[9] See Erich Auerbach, *Mimesis: The Representation of Reality in Western Literature*, Princeton, Princeton University Press, 1953, chapter two.

[10] For plays elaborating on this metaphor in the context of language controversy, see Christopher King, 'Forging a New Linguistic Identity: The Hindi Movement in Benares', in S. Freitag, ed., *Culture and Power in Benares*, Berkeley, University of California Press, 1989.

literature in its proper institutional context. The commercial production and transmission of literary genres and the popular political press and pamphlets with their wider reach need to be borne in mind. So does the ubiquitous presence of oral traditions. The object of this study is thus not Hindi literature *stricto sensu*, but rather the Hindi literary system as a whole, and especially what semioticians and sociologists of literature call 'institutional arrangements', i.e. the places and mechanisms of production, transmission, and fruition. These will allow us to draw a picture of the Hindi literary sphere in all its variety of traditions, tastes, audiences, and modes of transmission (see 1.2), to explain the rich diversity of literary output in the period between 1920 and 1940, and to piece together the different shades of public opinion. Literary sources, journals in particular, will be interrogated to unravel ideas and discourses about language, history, society, and politics in Hindi public opinion.

Institutions, especially the press, schools and publishing, are to me particularly important. Inspired by exotic England (where 'even coachmen read newspapers'), the agenda of progress and the 'public' was able to take root in colonial north India, on such different and unlikely terrain, because educated Indians created institutional spaces for it. These spaces were both concrete and discursive. The press, education and schools, literary genres, associations, and political activities were all spaces where language, ideas, literary tastes, and individual and group identities were reshaped, both consciously as well as by the dynamics and momentum of each medium. Its institutional grounding in journals, associations, universities, and schools allowed the literary and historical discourse of Hindi–Hindu to become hegemonic, with a hold on the social transmission of knowledge, despite the presence of dissenting voices and different agendas.

Also, institutions create actors. If, for example, the idea of writing as 'service' (*sevā*) to literature, to the people, and to the nation provided writers with a new identity, it was institutional spaces like the press, publishing houses, literary associations, and the education system that directed their activities and defined their social positions. The literary association created the figure of the scholar–activist like Śyāmsundar Dās; the press and print market created those of the independent writer, the journalist, and the editor like Mahāvīr Prasād Dvivedī and Devīdatt Śukla; and schools created that of the nationalist-minded teacher. At the same time, such actors came to these institutional spaces bringing their own diverse backgrounds, attitudes, and beliefs. All these were reflected in their opinions and tastes, and in the ways in which they interpreted publicity and moved in the public sphere. The focus of this book on ordinary textbook writers, teachers, journalists, writers, and activists is thus a conscious choice, for they best represent the horizon and expectations of the age.

The many and important changes in the Hindi literary sphere during the 1920s and 1930s can be said to be, in some form or other, different effects of publicity. There was the publicness of the 'jāti', the imagined community which transcended the social world as one knew it: much of the activism and discourse around Hindi refers to this potential community. Then there was the publicity of print, which did away with authorial or other control on who would read what, and gave the writer multiple audiences, both the close-knit literary community expected to read his or her work, and the invisible and open-ended audience of the jāti. Everything about literature was now open to public discussion in the pages of journals, with questions of style, taste, criticism, and popularity invariably related to the 'welfare of the people', *lokhit*. Anyone could write to a journal and make his or her voice public. Invested with a new freedom and sense of purpose, writers directly confronted 'the public' through their works. While poets in Braj Bhasa largely spoke to a tradition, writers who chose Khari Boli were aware that they were addressing a wider and more differentiated audience. They moved in an increasingly commercial literary market, and they often viewed creative writing as a form of social critique and indirect political action. The effects of publicity on the literary sphere can thus be summarized as *openness* (e.g. to criticism), *transferability* and *expansion* (of discourses, ideas, initiative, and participation to new subjects and groups), and *plasticity* (of ideas, tastes, and identities). At the same time, public activism worked effectively for the *institutionalization* and *consolidation* of Hindi language and literature. The result was modern Hindi culture as we know it.

The Public Sphere

Although the focus of this book is the Hindi literary sphere, its transformation mirrored more general processes of expansion, institutionalization, and consolidation in the larger public–political sphere. The period covered in this book stretches from the spectacular expansion of the nationalist movement with the mass campaigns under the leadership of Gandhi in 1919–20, to the institutionalization of the Congress party in the

1920s and 1930s, and finally to its consolidation as a ruling party with the provincial Congress governments of 1937–9, almost on the eve of Independence.[11] A general model that encompasses the literary, social, and political phenomena as well as activities, institutions, actors, and discourses is thus required. Jürgen Habermas' concept of 'public sphere' is attractive for several reasons. First of all, it was the European (in particular, English) public sphere that Hindi and other Indian intellectuals had in mind while evolving their own vision of progress and the modern nation. Secondly, the striking differences between the European public sphere as described by Habermas and the Hindi public sphere of the early twentieth century may establish the specificity of the European (English) case and that of colonial India, and measure the distance between the Indian vision and reality.

Habermas' definition of 'public sphere' stems from his analysis of the development of bourgeois society in seventeenth- and eighteenth-century Europe, in which 'private citizens [came] together as a public' to discuss matters of 'public concern' or 'common interest' and to criticize and put pressure on the absolutist state.[12] In traditional feudal society the ruler was the public and represented his status and rights 'before' the people. The people partook of the spectacle from their place in the hierarchically ordered feudal structure. With the transition to an impersonal state, the growth of a bourgeois economy and the emergence of the private realm of the bourgeois family, Habermas argued, private citizens came together as a 'public' in an intermediary sphere of social institutions like the club, journals and periodicals.[13] These citizens, in the free and rational exchange of ideas (especially with the lifting of censorship laws), formed public opinion and created a *language, codes* and

[11] See Gyan Pandey, *The Ascendancy of the Congress in Uttar Pradesh: 1926–34. A Study in Imperfect Mobilization*, Delhi, OUP, 1978; Sumit Sarkar, *Modern India, 1885 to 1947*, Delhi, Macmillan, 1983.

[12] Jürgen Habermas, *The Structural Transformation of the Public Sphere*, Cambridge, MIT Press, 1989 (original German edition 1962), p. 27. The present exposition owes much to Nancy Fraser, 'Rethinking the Public Sphere: A Contribution to the Critique of Actually Existing Democracy', in C. Calhoun, ed., *Habermas and the Public Sphere*, Cambridge, Massachusetts, MIT Press, 1992, pp. 109–42.

[13] For example, the individual subjectivity nurtured in the bourgeois family could produce and respond to a literature that valued individual endeavour, intelligence, and feelings, such as, for example, the eighteenth-century English novel. The classic study is Ian Watt, *The Rise of the Novel*, Harmondsworth, Penguin, 1979 (first published in 1957).

practices to express it. The spread of literacy in the previous centuries led to an 'accumulation of socio-cultural change' with the growth of urban culture, the press, and commercial publishing.[14] The 'general public' these citizens spoke of was actually quite limited and consisted mainly of the bourgeoisie and the titled gentry, yet in its self-understanding this literary sphere was 'the public' and was accessible to all. Also, despite exclusive claims on the practice of reason by the bourgeoisie, 'the virtue of *publicness*' and 'the liberal desideratum of reasoned exchange also became available for nonbourgeois, subaltern groups, whether the radical intelligentsia of Jacobinism and its successors or wide sections of social classes like the peasantry or the working class . . . [T]he *positive values* of the liberal public sphere quickly acquired broader democratic resonance, with the resulting emergence of impressive popular movements, each with its own distinctive movement cultures (i.e., form of public sphere)'.[15]

Media, publics, and the critical functions they expressed first developed around innocuous literary concerns, giving rise to a sort of 'republic of letters'.[16] Reason became the universal standard for criticism and, soon enough, critical debates moved from questions of taste to questions of the state, i.e. to political matters, for example requiring that information about state functioning be made accessible so that state activities would be subject to critical scrutiny and to the influence of public opinion. Such debates fostered a public discussion on the rules and functions of the state, crystallized citizenship ideals, and also gave rise to the more abstract idea that actions were rationally acceptable only after they had been subjected to the process of public judgement. This held great democratic potential: as a critic of Habermas has suggested, it implied that 'public concerns' were not necessarily an *a priori* set of concerns; rather 'what will count as a matter of common concern will be decided precisely through discursive contestation' among participants.[17] Public

[14] Geoff Eley, 'Nations, Publics, and Political Cultures', in Calhoun, pp. 290 ff.

[15] Ibid., p. 304.

[16] As Peter Uwe Hohendahl remarks, this literary public sphere was actually rooted in aristocratic court circles and only gradually freed itself from their influence; Hohendahl, *Institution of Criticism*, Ithaca, Cornell University Press, 1982, p. 53. This work also contains an interesting discussion on the debate over taste and the evaluation of literature between German Neo-classicists and Romantics, in which 'popularity' (*Volkstümlichkeit*, i.e. closeness to popular lore) became an issue; cf. 2.3 in this book.

[17] Fraser, 'Rethinking the Public Sphere', p. 129.

opinion becomes, then, the result of such discussions, a consensus about the common good.[18] Habermas could thus abstract a general definition of the 'public sphere':

> By the 'public sphere' we mean first of all a realm of our social life in which something approaching public opinion can be formed. Access is guaranteed to all citizens. A portion of the public sphere comes into being in every conversation in which private individuals assemble to form a public body. They then behave neither like business or professional people transacting private affairs, nor like members of a constitutional order subject to the legal constraints of a state bureaucracy. Citizens behave as a public body when they confer in an unrestricted fashion—that is, with the guarantee of freedom of assembly and association and the freedom to express and publish their opinions—about matters of general interest. In a large public body this kind of communication requires specific means for transmitting information and influencing those who receive it.[19]

Essential to this notion of public sphere is the existence of a common language of debate. Further, respect for rational–discursive arguments means that in this space opinions, expressions, and actions take on a certain plasticity: existing norms, beliefs, and social relations can be questioned and become consciously impermanent. The existing world, and one's own identity, take on a new mobility and flexibility. Common agendas and institutions can be set up and resources and publics mobilized to implement them. This common horizon and space gives rise to a public activism which is not necessarily constrained by the existing limits of participation: it can set itself extraordinarily ambitious goals, since theoretically everyone can be included. While even Habermas has conceded that in this form the public sphere was always at best an ideal, and critics have pointed out its serious exclusions in terms of gender and class, yet as an ideal we can imagine how powerful and attractive it must have been for Indian nationalists, eager to create their own public idioms and institutions and, especially at the dawn of the 1920s, to involve the whole populace in the anti-colonial struggle.

The Hindi Public Sphere: Peculiar Features

The public sphere as outlined above can be said to involve discursive and institutional spaces, a common language, a set of procedural principles (e.g. respect for reasoned argument and open debate), some activism,

[18] Ibid., pp. 112–13.

[19] Jürgen Habermas, 'The Public Sphere', *New German Critique*, 3, 1974, p. 49 quoted in Eley, 'Nations, Publics, and Political Cultures', p. 289.

and the awareness of a public 'out there'. Therefore, that *critical* voices and new subjects should engage in public debate is only to be expected: included in this book are the voices of writers, women, and peasant leaders. In matters of language, there were writers who rejected 'pure Hindi' and its historical discourse, believing instead that Hindi ought to be inclusive and amenable to the widest possible political community. In literature, there were writers who warned of the cultural and moral strait-jacket such a 'purity' imposed over a composite and ebullient literary reality. Women questioned men-made family relations and individual roles, while socialists and peasant leaders argued that *svarājya* had no meaning without changed economic and social relations. For these critical voices, 'public' meant an open space in which to question the status quo from particular points of view, and 'Indian' meant a plastic identity that had to take into account the differences on the ground.

Yet one recurrent feature of the Hindi literary and political sphere of the 1920s and 1930s is an attitude to public matters, to public media, and to the 'public' that I call *normative*, for it was based on the assumption that there is one, and only one, tenable position, which constitutes the norm. Despite engaging in debate, litterateurs and politicians who held this view tended to see differences of opinions as a deviation from the norm and as harmful to unity. This normative attitude was apparent, for example, in ideas of śuddh or 'pure' Hindi, of the Indian jāti as culturally homogeneous, of 'rural harmony', of the harmony of Indian society, of how literature ought to be, and of the nature of the Indian woman. Institutions like the press and the education system were, in this view, means of propagating the normative ideal.

Choices in matters of language mirror attitudes to the political sphere.[20] 'Pure Hindi' mirrored, and brought into being every time it was used, an (ideal) community of serious, equal, educated, and public-minded Indian citizens, *without any visible marker* apart from education and familiarity with the cultural tradition: differences of caste and status were thus pushed outside (written) language. Similarly, according to this normative attitude only matters which appeared under the jātīy or 'national' guise were fit to be discussed. Anything which appeared particular or heterogeneous was, as a consequence, not part of the 'public'. This of course does not mean that it disappeared: only, that it did not become part of the public self-definition of what is 'Indian'.

[20] For a similar argument concerning English, see John Barrell, 'The Language Properly So-called: The Authority of Common Usage', in *English Literature in History, 1730–80. An Equal, Wide Survey*, London, Hutchinson, 1983.

Critics of Habermas have—rightly—pointed out his blindness to the exclusions that the bourgeois public sphere meted out to women, who were relegated to the private sphere of the household, and to subaltern groups.[21] Exclusion was also implicit: women and members of the subaltern classes could be kept out of the ostensibly equal discursive interaction by, for example, protocols of style and decorum in public interaction 'that were themselves correlates and markers of status inequality', or by bracketing status 'as if' it did not exist when in fact it still counted.[22] In the Indian public sphere exclusion was both explicit and implicit. Language, to take one example, worked as an explicit faultline in the case of English, and not surprisingly it became one of the symbols of colonial inequality.[23] But Hindi itself could be implicitly exclusive, both of Indo-Persian culture and, in a largely illiterate region, of uneducated speakers who had not mastered 'pure Hindi'. The question of exclusion is raised several times in this book, especially in connection with women and peasants and the issue of authority: the case of women, for example, shows that in fact in the 1920s women began to defy exclusion by claiming simultaneous access to the literary and the political spheres. Women's journals espoused the notion, inherent in the principles of the public sphere, that points of view could differ and that norms had to be negotiated with the parties involved. They held up issues of domestic and caste practice to public scrutiny and extended women's sphere of activity (*kāryakṣetra*) to include new and public roles. In this, one can argue, journals were much more effective than women's associations, which were intrinsically restricted to the elite and 'emancipated' women who could take part freely in their proceedings. At the same time, this expansive movement was undercut by implicit exclusions, or rather self-censorship, as moral respectability became the requisite for public access.

One may note that the socially subordinate Hindi middle class that constituted the bulk of the Hindi public sphere bears little resemblance to the ascending and self-confident bourgeoisie of Habermas' account, or even to the Bengali *bhadralok* in the 'middle' between the English elite

[21] In revolutionary France, 'a specific, highly-gendered bourgeois male discourse . . . depended on women's domesticity and the silencing of public women, of the aristocratic and popular classes': Joan Landes, *Women and the Public Sphere in the Age of the French Revolution*, Ithaca, Cornell University Press, 1988, p. 204; see also Eley, 'Nations, Publics and Political Cultures'.

[22] Fraser, 'Rethinking the Public Sphere', p. 119.

[23] For an evaluation of English newspapers in India as catering to an 'artificial', elite audience, while Hindi newspapers address the real nation, see B.V. Parāṛkar's speech, quoted in 1.3.1; also 5.1.

and the subaltern masses.[24] The shrillness of Hindi's demands and the grandness of its aspirations may be related to the ambition and frustration of a 'subordinate elite'. Compared to Bengal, only very few scions of landed or moneyed families, or highly placed government servants, were actively involved with Hindi. Even the few exceptions did not display the kind of 'cultural bilingualism' we find in the Bengali bhadralok, at ease in both the English and the 'vernacular' world. The important task of translating ideas, literary forms and sensibilities back and forth between English and the 'vernacular', of mediating class and cultural differences, was thus left in Hindi to usually obscure and overworked salaried practitioners. Teaching and journalism, the two most likely avenues for Hindi literati, were generally poorly paid and involved a condition of submission, to the education department or to the owners of the school or the newspaper. It is a sign of the times that resignations and disputes were far from infrequent. Working in 'national institutions' was a welcome, if unstable, alternative. As a consequence, Hindi intellectuals, especially if born in a village, often led remarkably peripatetic lives. Links with the land were hardly severed: often the family stayed back while the lone intellectual tried his luck in the large provincial centres of Allahabad, Benares, Lucknow, Kanpur, Jabalpur, Delhi, and of course Calcutta and Bombay. Most of the Hindi literary people mentioned in the pages of this book were involved in the nationalist movement at some point in their lives, a few became full-time Congress activists, but only a handful gained positions of power in the party and became leaders of national importance (see Biographies in the Appendix).

Finally, in Habermas' study the development of a public sphere was shown to be directly connected to the emergence of the private sphere of the bourgeois family as an economic and affective unit. The 'private', in the gendered division of roles, was the sphere of woman, and also the secluded and sheltered space in which individual personality was reared and individual feelings, tastes, and thoughts cultivated. Public and private have in fact become complementary notions and are generally mentioned together. Yet this hardly seems to be the case in colonial India, however much the nuclear family and reformed housewife appeared as powerful ideals. Even in an ostensibly 'private' genre like the novel, which in the 1920s and 1930s delighted in the expression of individual, especially romantic, feelings and moved towards psychological

[24] Cf. Partha Chatterjee, *The Nation and Its Fragments,* Princeton, Princeton University Press, 1993.

introspection, morality (*maryādā*) and duty to the family and to the community are consistently depicted as being higher and more pressing necessities than the aspirations of the individual or the couple. Realistic novels of this period show literally *no place* for a private language of feelings and for private aspirations in the family or elsewhere.[25] Indeed the fictional worlds of the novels themselves, the extraordinarily popular 'social romances' that originated in these decades, seem to have been the only place (perhaps with films?) where private feelings could be securely indulged.[26]

What seems to exist, I would suggest, is not a twofold dichotomy of public and private, but a three-layered one of public, private, and what, for want of better term, one may call 'customary'. 'Public' refers to the spaces of interaction, reflection, and self-representation outlined above. 'Private' indicates the voice of the individual that generally rises in opposition to or defiance of public or customary expectations (see e.g. the 'right to feel' in 4.3). Finally, 'customary' refers to those sets of practices, beliefs, and relations that constituted the social world outside the purview of the 'public'. When Devīdatt Śukla recalls with grateful surprise that the publishers he worked for treated him, a mere employee, with respect; when off-hand remarks on someone's caste occasionally erupt; when discrepancies arise between social reformers' exhortations and their personal choices (for example in matters of marriage or commensality); or when claims for active and equal participation by subaltern subjects are met with disbelief or hostility, we realize that the space occupied by public discourse was by no means total and did not coincide with the world of social and cultural practices. As we shall see, caste as *varṇa* was part of 'public' discourse in Hindi, castes as jātis were not (see 3.3). In the case of women, the discourse redefining Indian 'woman' as essentially superior to both western women and Indian men was a 'public' discourse, and so were the codes in dress and behaviour that

[25] See e.g. Premchand's novels, especially *Gaban* (Embezzlement, 1931), where the newly married couple can express their real desires and beliefs only in their thoughts: even dialogues between them involve a complicated social play of dissimulation. Madhav Prasad has made a very convincing argument about the self-imposed denial in Hindi films of that quintessential seal of privacy, the kiss, as symbolic of the ideals of the bourgeois nuclear family kowtowing to the higher, feudal values of community, represented by the extended family; Madhava Prasad, 'Cinema and the Desire for Modernity', *Journal of Arts and Ideas*, 25–6, December 1993, pp. 71–86.

[26] For one example, see my 'Reading a Social Romance: Pāṇḍey Becan Śarmā Ugra's *Cand hasīnoṁ ke khutūt* (1927)', in V. Dalmia and T. Damsteegt, eds, *Narrative Strategies*, Delhi, OUP, 1999.

educated women adopted when moving out in the open. The letters and literature expressing women's emotions and aspirations, their exploitation and the indifference of their families remained 'private'. 'Customary' refers to the actual realm of the household and of 'common sense' (see Chapter 4). The fact that this book is concerned specifically with the realm of the public does not imply a blindness to other dimensions.

The book will thus chart the institutional spaces and the actors which together formed the Hindi literary sphere (Chapter 1) and the political sphere (Chapter 5), and analyse some of the discourses that circulated and were reproduced through the media, the education system, and other means (Chapters 2 and 3). The strategies needed by new voices to access the Hindi sphere will be examined in a separate chapter on women (Chapter 4).

The Period: 1920–1940

The two decades between 1920 and 1940 saw a continuation of the processes in the literary and political spheres that had started in the second half of the nineteenth century. Yet the quantitative expansion—of literary and political actors, of public spaces and institutions, of the print market and of literary and political audiences—in the 1920s brought about a qualitative leap. New subjects raised critical voices that could not be ignored, and at times created real counter-publics; the openness and scope of Hindi literary media allowed bold experimentation, new genres, and the existence of independent writers; also, the potential public of nineteenth-century efforts seemed finally to actually be there. A powerful tension emerged, which will be highlighted throughout the book, between *normative* tendencies, which developed into a kind of Hindi establishment and sought to consolidate their grip on institutions and harness the public to their cause, and *critical* voices which believed they could influence public opinion through the media. Language and literature bear prominent marks of this tension. It was an exciting and heady time for those involved, many of whom were taking on a public role for the first time. In Hindi this is known as the 'golden age' of modern Hindi literature and it was a period of truly extraordinary literary creativity in all fields: in poetry with Chāyāvād, in fiction with Premchand (1880–1936) and a host of other writers, in literary criticism with Rāmchandra Śukla (1884–1941) and the other critics who shaped the way we read Hindi literature to this day.

CHAPTER 1

Language and the Literary Sphere

Reviewing in 1926 a quarter of a century of Hindi efforts, the veteran writer from Bombay, Lajjārām Mehtā (1863–1931), remarked with satisfaction on the great change since the time when the English elite used to laugh Hindi off and Hindi supporters worked in the 'age of Urdu' (*urdū kā zamānā*). Thanks to the support of national leaders the goal of Hindi as national language seemed nearer, and now the day seemed not far when

> the public drum [i.e. authority] of Hindi will resound from one corner to the other [of the country], and Indians speaking different languages, while improving their own languages, will perform worship (*ārtī*) for Hindi with clasped hands and bowed heads, and Hindi's younger sister, or, if anyone objects to that name, Hindi's elder sister, Urdu, will sacrifice herself standing at her side, and the language of the Raj, English, with all its pomp and pride, with its genius and terror, will garland Hindi with flowers.[1]

Between the second half of the nineteenth century and 1920, the linguistic economy—the hierarchical, functional and cultural arrangement of languages—had changed dramatically in north India. Literary writing in Hindi, as in other Indian languages, had also changed significantly. How is one to account for such dramatic changes, and how should one analyse them? One of the main premisses of this work is that new discourses, tastes, genres and literary figures could emerge only thanks to new

[1] Apart from 'a couple of languages of Madras [sic!]', Mehta continued, all Indian languages originate from Sanskrit; thus a simple language with a reservoir of Sanskrit words was the Hindi style Mehtā suggested for the national language. All will agree to this, he concluded, apart from Muslims in the United Provinces and Punjab; Lajjārām Mehtā, 'Bhāratvarṣa kī rāṣṭrabhāṣā', *Mādhurī*, IV, pt. 2, 5, June 1926, p. 620.

institutional contexts. Journals, school and textbooks, literary and other voluntary associations, and literary publishing were the institutions which provided the spaces, the arena, for a new public-minded activism. They shaped language and literary production, and emphasized certain linguistic styles and literary tastes at the expense of others. They also encouraged a sense of the Hindi reading public that was more open-ended and self-conscious at the same time.

Our investigation into the Hindi public sphere therefore begins with a survey and analysis of these institutional changes which made possible the discourses and works I discuss later in the book. By introducing the main actors, journals, institutions, places, and concepts mentioned in the course of the book, this chapter also provides a context. The first section examines the historical background to the rise of a community consciousness around language. This consciousness differed substantially from that in precolonial practices. In the second section, an overview of the stratification and variety of literary practices and tastes supports the argument that while old practices and tastes largely survived, they were affected by the new ways in which literature was transmitted, through journals and schools. The concept of 'literary saṃskāra' (acquired taste) is suggested as an analytical tool to explain the stratification of tastes in the light of the different modes of literary apprenticeship and transmission. The rest of the chapter explores the main arenas in which Hindi literature came to be produced, transmitted, and consumed—the journals and the education system—and the way in which an older form of (oral) literary transmission, the poetry-meeting, adapted to the changed literary system.

1.1. A Question of Language

निज भाषा उन्नति अहै सब उन्नति को मूल
बिना निज भाषा-ज्ञान के मिटत न हिय को सूल।

> Progress in one's language is the source of all progress;
> if you know not your own language your heart cannot be pure.[2]

Language was one of the essential concerns of Indian reformers in the nineteenth century, a basic constituent of their discourse of progress and reform. Establishing Hindi as a public language and compacting a group

[2] Bhārtendu Hariśchandra's famous couplet in the verse speech 'Hindī kī unnati par vyākhyān' (1877), in *Bhārtendu samagra*, p. 228.

identity around it were themselves products of this concern. The idea that a nation 'has' one language—Bhārtendu's *nij bhāṣā*—which belongs simultaneously to the individual and to the community, covers all spoken and written practices and, finally, acquires the seal of recognition by becoming the language of the state (*rājbhāṣā*) and of the nation (*rāṣṭra-bhāṣā*), was itself new. This idea, engrained as it was in European assumptions about national unity,[3] was problematic when applied to the Indian context, and to the Hindi context in particular, as colonial officials were quick to realize in their taxonomic zeal. And yet it was to have a powerful appeal for Indian reformers: although proficient in and regularly using more than one language, they still looked up to 'one country, one language' as to an ideal and a goal.

Extensive research has already been done on linguistic change in nineteenth- and twentieth-century India.[4] Scholars agree that the impact of print, the influence of the English language, of colonial linguists

[3] For a comparative account, see Anderson, *Imagined Communities*. For a discussion of this problem, D. Washbrook, "To Each a Language of His Own': Language, Culture, and Society in Colonial India', in P.J. Corfield, ed., *Language, History and Class*, Oxford, Blackwell, 1991.

[4] A useful and comprehensive account is C. Shackle and R. Snell, *Hindi and Urdu since 1800: A Common Reader*, SOAS, London, 1990. Other works include: Jürgen Lütt, *Hindu-Nationalisms in Uttar-Pradeś 1867–1900*, Stuttgart, Klett, 1970; J. Das Gupta, *Language Conflict and National Development: Group Politics and National Language Policy in India*, Berkeley, University of California Press, 1970; Kerrin Dittmer, *Die Indischen Muslime und die Hindi–Urdu Kontroversie in den United Provinces*, Wiesbaden, Harrassowitz, 1972; Brass, *Language, Religion and Politics in North India*; Bernard Cohn, 'The Command of Language and the Language of Command', in R. Guha, ed., *Subaltern Studies IV*, Delhi, OUP, 1985, pp. 276–329; A. Rai, *A House Divided: The Origin and Development of Hindi–Urdu*, Delhi, OUP, 1991; David Lelyveld, 'The Fate of Hindustani: Colonial Knowledge and the Project of a National Language', in P. Breckenridge and van der Veer, eds, *Orientalism and the Postcolonial Predicament*, Philadelphia, University of Pennsylvania Press, 1993; King, *One Language, Two Scripts*. For the role of pro-vernacular colonial orientalists: Tej K. Bhatia, *A History of the Hindi Grammatical Tradition*, Leiden, Brill, 1987; C.A. Bayly, *Empire and Information*, Cambridge, Cambridge University Press, 1996, Chapter 8. For the role of Fort William College in providing the initial framework and spur to the linguistic and literary re-definition of the two vernaculars, see R.S. McGregor, 'Bengal and the Development of Hindi, 1850–80', in *South Asian Review*, 5, 2, 1972, and Sisir Kumar Das, *Sahibs and Munshis: An Account of the College of Fort William*, Calcutta, Orion Publications, 1978. For a thorough review of nineteenth-century developments in Hindi: Dalmia, *The Nationalization of Hindu Traditions*, Chapter 4. For an interesting discussion of the difficulty in establishing a standard form for Urdu: J. Majeed, ' "The Jargon of Indostan": An Exploration of

and policy makers, and missionary efforts in education were all factors helping to crystallize new standard forms of vernaculars and a new consciousness of language as a community marker.[5] These standard languages, in turn, inspired the growth of journals and of a new kind of 'useful literature' aimed at the progress of the self and the community. Although it is difficult to ascertain in what proportions each of those factors was responsible, and although print, for example, stimulated first of all the reproduction of works and genres belonging to the earlier manuscript and oral traditions, we may safely say that print, colonial rule, and missionary efforts together brought about crucial changes in the linguistic economy of north India in the nineteenth century. Khari Boli Hindi emerged as the main print language of prose over its regional variants, as a means of mass education and, gradually, of literature. With the demise of Mughal paramountcy and with colonial inconsistencies in language policy, there began a long-drawn out controversy between defenders of Persian-Urdu and supporters of Hindi and the Devanagari script: while the former argued for continuity and the pre-eminence of Urdu as the language of administration and of the Indo-Muslim literate ecumene, the latter emphasized the scope for change under the 'just and neutral' European rulers (and a return to an earlier era, 'before' Muslim rule, when, they claimed, Hindi was widely used as an administrative language). These two phenomena brought about sweeping changes both in the nature and in the uses of Hindi. Hindi became a culturally loaded language (see 2.1), and several public institutions were formed for its advancement and propaganda. Education and the press were identified as the two main avenues of activism, as will become clear in the course of this chapter. Since several monographs already exist on the subject, this section will merely cover the elements in the process of language change that are relevant to our study.

Firstly, we should recall that the notion of a *nij bhāṣā* which expressed at the same time the individual and collective language identities relating to a particular place (like French or English or German), and covered both

Jargon in Urdu and East India Company English', in P. Burke and R. Porter, eds, *Languages and Jargons. Contributions to a Social History of Language*, Cambridge, Polity Press, 1995.

[5] For comparable processes in Oriya and Bengali, see Pragati Mahapatra, 'The Making of a Cultural Identity: Language, Literature and Gender in Orissa in Late Nineteenth and Early Twentieth Centuries', unpublished Ph.D. thesis, University of London, 1997; and Anindita Ghosh, 'Literature, Language and Print in Bengal, *c.* 1780–1905', unpublished Ph.D. thesis, University of Cambridge, 1998.

written and *spoken* styles, was itself new. While awareness of the existence of Hindi (Hindavi/Hindui) as a (spoken?) language goes back to the thirteenth-century poet Amir Khusrau, literacy and literary, administrative, sacred and spoken 'languages' were considered separate issues. Linguistic diversity, multilingualism, and diglossia were the norm. As David Lelyveld remarks:

> Languages were not so much associated with place as with function, and in many cases the naming of a language—for the directors of British census operations and more elaborately for the *Linguistic Survey of India*—was problematic. People didn't have languages; they had linguistic repertoires that varied even within a single household, let alone the marketplace, school, temple, court or devotional circle. These codes of linguistic behaviour took on the same characteristics of hierarchy that other sorts of human interaction did. . . .[6]

Even a cursory glance at the material printed in north India in the second half of the nineteenth century supports this view, with books printed in Urdu, Persian, Arabic, Khari Boli Hindi, Avadhi, Braj Bhasa and Sanskrit, and a substantial number of bilingual publications: primers, phrase books, grammars, dictionaries, commentaries, etc. The bilingual texts each reflects a different purpose and a different audience: glossaries in Urdu of Arabic and Persian, Persian grammars and letter writers speak of apprenticeship in Persian scribal culture; Urdu translations of Persian historical texts and Sanskrit dramas speak of their vulgarization for a mixed, Urdu-literate public; Hindi translations of Sanskrit works and Sanskrit–Hindi dictionaries speak of an effort at cultural continuity; and early Hindi editions of popular Urdu genres such as the play *Indarsabhā* by the Lucknow courtier Amānat speak of the search for an extended popular audience.[7] This diversity and diglossia survived even in the age of separate Hindi and Urdu paths. Yet the process of standardization and monolingual transmission gained momentum and ate away at the mixed Indo-Persian reading public. As C.R. King has shown, the number of Persian and Arabic publications fell drastically between 1868 and 1925; Urdu publications increased in absolute numbers but were gradually eclipsed by Hindi (Devanagari) publications, mainly educational texts: by 1925 Urdu books amounted to just one-sixth

[6] Lelyveld, 'The Fate of Hindustani', in *Orientalism and the Postcolonial Predicament*, p. 202.

[7] See the *Catalogues of Books Printed in the North Western Provinces*. These were quarterly publications covering the years 1873–5. Originally printed in Allahabad, they can now be found in the Oriental and India Office Library Collections at the British Library, London.

of Hindi publications, and after 1900 even decreased in absolute numbers of copies.[8] It is against this background of multilingualism that the process of language standardization and the rise of language movements must be viewed. Although standardization of literary languages like Braj Bhasa had already begun, what was now demanded was a standard *written* and *spoken* form. Inconsistencies and variations in spelling and grammar persisted in Hindi throughout the nineteenth century and into the twentieth, yet the need for a standard, public language that would cover the whole of north India emerged as a public issue and a pressing need among Indian literati.

The influence of the English language over the process of standardization still needs to be studied in detail. Whether it was the printed page and its genres or English that brought about notable changes in syntax, for example, with longer and more complex sentences, remains to be ascertained. Macaulay's famous Minute of 1835 settled the dispute about a language for the education of Indians in favour of English; but certainly well before this, English had begun to exert its influence both as the model for Indian languages to imitate and as the new language at the top of the language hierarchy, with political as well as cultural connotations. As one scholar puts it: 'The concept of modernity in literary history was also related to the relation each Indian language and literature developed with English. Sanskrit and Persian literary models were labelled as traditional and medieval, and those found in English, irrespective of any period, as modern.' While British scholars and provincial officials were busy finding out which was *the* vernacular of each province, the one language that would serve as a channel of communication between foreign rulers and Indian masses, the old service classes and new intellectuals were busy refashioning their linguistic repertories into standard vernaculars: Indian languages, too, were construed in terms of bounded linguistic communities, each with its own 'natural language'.[9] While a certain degree of linguistic readjustment, and hence competition, had in the past, too, customarily followed each change of political rule,[10] the

[8] King, *One Language, Two Scripts*, tables pp. 38–9 and 43–5. King gives absolute numbers of copies, which tend to favour textbook production, as the books with largest editions were primers.

[9] Sisir Kumar Das, *History of Indian Literature*, vol. 8, New Delhi, Sahitya Akademi, 1991, pp. 30–1.

[10] For this particular 'bilingualism' of local elites *vis-à-vis* changing outside rulers in the case of Surat, see Douglas Haynes, *Rhetoric and Ritual in Colonial India: the Shaping of a Public Culture in Surat City, 1852–1928*, Berkeley, University of California Press, 1991.

novelty was that now language was linked to community identity, at a time when a new community history was also being written (see 3.1).

Together with standardization came diversification. The difference in script between Urdu (Persian) and Hindi (Devanagari) coalesced with the difference in literary and religious traditions and made language a 'multi-congruent' symbol of separate cultural and religious identity.[11] For both British officials and Indian intellectuals, Hindi and Urdu became languages in this objectified form, 'public languages' to be used in print, in the network of government schools, in public meetings, associations, and so on. Even religious orators helped in developing standards of Hindi and Urdu by using them to preach throughout north India to Hindu and Muslim audiences.[12] Where earlier several linguistic repertoires existed, one standard was now being developed to comprise spoken and written, mundane, literary, and religious usages in an unbroken continuum.

Colonial policies concerning language tried to apply rational, European standards and categories: first of all, in advocating the use of the vernacular as the language of education and administration, and then in trying to define the best or 'true' script and style and encouraging their use. At the same time colonial authorities were weary of alienating existing allies: hence most changes in language policies were partial and permissive rather than prescriptive. Policies regarding the official language for public employment, legal use, and education were themselves inconsistent and changed repeatedly throughout the nineteenth century.[13] The most patent inconsistency regarded the use of the term Hindustani: according to different linguists and administrators, each drawing upon his restricted personal experience and different practical or literary examples, it could indicate either Urdu or Hindi. It has repeatedly been stressed that, far from being a neutral arbiter, British administration exploited the tensions between Indian languages, in our case between Hindi and Urdu, to pursue a policy of *divide et impera*. By

[11] For the concept of 'multi-congruent' symbol, see Brass, *Language, Religion and Politics*.

[12] Noteworthy in this respect was the use of Urdu by preachers like Sayyid Ahmad Barelvi and Shah Muhammad Isma'il, who toured north India in the 1820s, and the adoption of Khari Boli Hindi by Dayānanda Sarasvatī in the 1870s; Lelyveld, 'The Fate of Hindustani', p. 203.

[13] Early supporters of the wide use of Hindi rather than Urdu included J.R. Ballantyne, principal of Benares Sanskrit College, and M. Kempson, Director of Public Instruction in the Province from 1861 to 1877; McGregor, *Hindi Literature of the Nineteenth and Early Twentieth Centuries*, pp. 71n., 74.

distinguishing the two languages in education but not in administration, they 'fostered a Hindi-speaking elite by providing Hindi speakers with employment in the educational system, and simultaneously favoured an Urdu-speaking elite by retaining Urdu as the only official vernacular for many years'.[14] This point has become a commonplace among Hindi intellectuals who place the responsibility for language conflict and for Hindu–Muslim animosity squarely on colonial shoulders. This is largely true, no doubt, whether we take colonial policy makers to be shrewd machinators or to be following ill-suited and contradictory notions of their own. What cannot be denied, however, is the reality of conflicting interests and cultural competition between Indo-Persian and Hindu elites, in which language became a multi-congruent symbol, and a means to advance or defend one's position in the hierarchy. Thus, while it is true that colonial policies conditioned the shaping and genealogy of Hindi and Urdu, it is also true that the ideologues of both languages took as 'official authority' the views of colonial officers who supported their own views and claims.

More importantly, by accepting public petitions, testimonies, and addresses from Indian experts and associations before official commissions of enquiry, British administrators encouraged educated Indians to act as spokesmen and representatives of public opinion. Also, with their centralized system of education and the regular publication of official data regarding publications, education and the census, they fostered a culture of statistics and in doing so helped identify education and publications as key areas of competition.

It is important to remember here that the definition of language was controversial even within Hindi.[15] People like Śiva Prasād Siṃh 'Sitāre-Hind' (1823–95), the influential official and compiler of textbooks from

[14] King, *One Language, Two Scripts*, p. 54.

[15] See for example the early controversy within the Nāgarī Prachāriṇī Sabhā between Śyāmsundar Dās and Pandit Lakṣmīśaṅkar Miśra, who was president between 1894 and 1902 and resigned in disagreement over the policy of linguistic differentiation. As he wrote in a letter to the Hindi Sub-Committee of the UP Education Department in May 1903, 'For ordinary purposes, such books as are not technical and which are intended for the common people [an] attempt should be made to assimilate the two forms into one language, which may be called Hindustani, and may be written either in the Persian character or in the Nagari', quoted in C.R. King, 'The Nagari Pracharini Sabha of Benares, 1893–1914: A Study of the Social and Political History of the Hindi Language', unpublished Ph.D. Thesis, University of Wisconsin, 1974, p. 312. Also Lala Sītārām objected that in Benares it was fashionable to sanskritize Hindi, hence the view of the Sabhā was not representative of the literary activity of the province;

Benares, favoured the independent 'progress' of Hindi, acknowledged its cultural separateness from the Perso-Urdu tradition, but objected to 'cleansing' it of words of Persian origin. Those like Lakṣmaṇ Siṃh (1826–96), the Hindi translator of *Śakuntalā* (1863), on the other hand felt differently:

In my opinion Hindi and Urdu are two different languages. Hindi is spoken by Hindus and Urdu by Muslims as well as Hindus well versed in Persian. Hindi abounds in Sanskrit forms of expression and Urdu has abundance of Persian and Arabic words and phrases. It cannot be said that Hindi cannot exist without Urdu words and idioms, and I am not prepared to give the name of Hindi to any linguistic form which abounds in such an alien mode of expression.[16]

Their different stances were due not only to the background and the literary genres each turned to, but also to their public positions. Both had had a colonial education and were part of the colonial administration—Śiva Prasād in the education department, Lakṣmaṇ Siṃh as a deputy collector—but Śiva Prasād was possibly more aware of and sensitive to Urdu and British opinion, while Lakṣmaṇ Siṃh, writing from Etawah, had only the Hindi public to address. It is remarkable how Hindi activists fought with the weapons of rationality not only against internal variants (Kaithi, Braj Bhasa), as Christopher King has shown, but also about the style of Hindi, as if it could be defined positively once and for all.

A new, important correlative of these debates concerning language assertion was the institutional spaces in which they occurred: Hindi journals and voluntary associations, animated by the new figure of the literary activist.[17] Literary associations in particular formed autonomous institutions for public intervention; they provided local focuses for propaganda and literary activities, pooled financial and human resources for campaigns and publications, and fostered interaction between Hindi literary people. Associations inspired them with a sense of public

---

UP Education Department, Proceedings of the Provincial Textbook Committee of Allahabad, 2, August 1902, p. 37, quoted in K. Dittmer, *Die Indischen Muslims*, p. 114.

[16] Preface to his translation of *Raghuvaṃśa* (1878), quoted in Das, *History of Indian Literature,* vol. 8, p. 143.

[17] Before the founding of the Nāgarī Prachāriṇī Sabhā of Benares (1893), nineteenth-century Hindi associations were mostly the work of one or a few individuals, often with the support of some local British officer: e.g. P. Gaurīdatt's Devanāgarī Prachāriṇī Sabhā (Meerut, 1882), Babu Totārām's Bhāṣā-Saṃvarddhinī Sabhā (Aligarh, 1877) and Allahabad's Nāgarī-Pravārddhinī-Sabhā (1876); McGregor, *Hindi Literature*, pp. 72 ff.

purpose (*sevā*), linking the language issue with other issues of community interest like education, and with exclusively Hindu symbols like cow protection. They were looked upon favourably by British officials, who at times were directly involved in their activities.[18] The role of the Nāgarī Prachāriṇī Sabhā of Benares (1893) is illuminating in this respect.[19] Founded by some young students of Queens' Collegiate School in Benares, most of whom were to have lifelong careers in education, it defined its goal as the 'progress of the Nagari language' (i.e. of Hindi in Devanagari script):

(a) The chief duty of members of this Sabha will be to *learn* the Nagari language, *to use the same language in conversation and correspondence*, and to advance its cause among the circle of their friends. b) Members of this Sabha will translate books from other languages into the Nagari language themselves, or have others to translate them. c) Members of this Sabha will frequently write articles on the subject of the progress of the Hindi language for publication in Hindi newspapers.[20]

Noteworthy is the notion that even Hindi speakers must 'learn' the proper, standard form of Khari Boli Hindi and endeavour to use it in conversation, correspondence, and public writings: a language style was to be created that would be fit for proper discourse and polite intercourse. From these rather modest beginnings, the Sabhā developed an impressive agenda. It became an important producer of Hindi textbooks and readers, and a publisher of edited Hindi classics. It undertook an important and long search for old manuscripts throughout north India that would provide the basis for subsequent literary histories. It built up the premier Hindi library in the province, with the help of a government grant. It became the centre of a network of Hindi scholars and associations, both locally and throughout north India, with distinguished British orientalists like George Grierson and Edwin Greaves among its members. It was also directly instrumental in promoting the public use of Hindi by putting pressure on the provincial government for the use of Hindi in the courts, education, and public notices. For a few years it even employed Hindi letter writers to write petitions free of charge outside the *kachehri* in Benares and spread the use of Hindi in the law courts.[21] As

[18] E.g. M. Kempson, Director of Public Instruction of the North West Provinces from 1861 to 1877 and a former Head of Bareilly College, supported the activities of Bareilly Tattvabodhinī Sabhā; ibid., p. 74.

[19] See King, 'The Nagari Pracharini Sabha'.

[20] Statement of 1893, translated, ibid., p. 282, emphasis added.

[21] King, *One Language, Two Scripts*, p. 162.

will become clear in the course of the chapter, the Sabhā was to acquire great authority in the Hindi literary sphere and play a very important role in the creation of the Hindi literary curriculum.

As previous studies have pointed out, early efforts at the self-definition of Hindi implied in fact a threefold process of separation from Urdu, standardization and historicization. The claim of absolute autonomy for Hindi was coupled with the cultivation of vocabulary, and phonological and grammatical features that were alternative to Urdu.[22] While Hindi's claim will be discussed in the next chapter, it is important to outline here the climate of competition and animosity that surrounded Hindi assertiveness in the nineteenth century. The ground for contestation was established in the 1830s, when vernaculars were introduced in place of Persian at the lower levels of the judiciary, fixing a territorial homeland for each of them;[23] but the real Hindi–Urdu controversy erupted only in the late 1860s, when the question of 'which is the true vernacular of the province?' was thrown up again in the context of colonial educational efforts. Articles, pamphlets, and even plays were written to support either view: on the Hindi side, Śiva Prasād argued in favour of the adoption of Hindi in Nagari script in courts and in schools.[24] His memorandum, like Madan Mohan Mālavīya's pamphlet thirty years later, dwelt on the periods before and after 'Muslim conquest' in order to show that Hindi had been the 'language of the country' before that invasion. The heterogeneous linguistic repertories of the whole of north India were construed into a homogeneous natural language, and its cultural referents and relationships with the other Neo-Aryan languages of India were laid down once and for all. Further occasion for extensive and fervent

[22] See e.g. Dalmia, *The Nationalization of Hindu Traditions*, p. 148.

[23] On the one hand this threatened the vested interests of clerks and officials employed thanks to their exclusive knowledge of Persian, on the other it threw open the question of which vernacular was the proper or most widely used one in the area. Although the Nagari script was initially introduced in the Central Provinces and Kaithi in Bihar, the move failed to affect the status quo, favourable to the Persian script, and in the absence of vocal pro-Nagari public support an Urdu abounding with Persian words and expressions remained the court language in the North-Western Provinces as well. The merely permissive, and not prescriptive, introduction of Nagari in the Central Provinces in 1839–40, for example, did not effect a replacement, since most Kayastha clerks refused to give up their monopoly; see King, *One Language, Two Scripts*, p. 62.

[24] In a memorandum for private circulation titled *Court Characters, in the Upper Provinces of India* (1868). For a discussion of it, see King, 'The Nagari Pracharini Sabha', pp. 106 ff.

public debate, in print and at public meetings, was provided in 1882 by the Hunter Commission which toured the North-Western Provinces and the Punjab 'to review the progress of education in India'. More than a hundred memoranda with tens of thousands of signatures were presented at various places, and witnesses included the most prominent literary activists of the time, like Śiva Prasād, Bhārtendu Hariśchandra, and Sir Syed Ahmad Khan. Although the Hunter Report of 1883 did not accept Hindi grievances, the campaign inspired by it activated Hindi supporters, and public associations in defence of Nagari mushroomed all over north India, the most important of all being the Kāśī Nāgarī Prachāriṇī Sabhā.[25] Intense lobbying by the Sabhā with pro-Nagari officials in the Education Department between 1895 and 1900 resulted in the permissive introduction of Nagari in courts in 1900. Again, it was mostly a symbolic victory: proceedings and writs continued to be written in Persianized Urdu for at least the next four decades. During the campaign, however, Hindi in the Nagari script was successfully turned into a question of Hindu cultural self-assertion, and the united Muslim–Kayastha community of Urdu was shaken. Within the Hindi sphere, the success of the pro-Nagari campaign strengthened the position of those who championed maximum differentiation of Hindi from Urdu in style, and an aggressive Hindi–Hindu cultural policy. Crucially, an independent, voluntary association like the Nāgarī Prachāriṇī Sabhā had successfully staked its claim to be the expert on Hindi in relation to the government and the broader Hindi community, and to decide the cultural faultline of Hindi, namely by excluding Urdu lexicon as 'foreign':

> Having examined all the various viewpoints, our principle is this: as far as possible, no words from *Persian, Arabic or other foreign language* should be used for which an easy and current Hindi or Sanskrit word is available, but those words from foreign languages which have become fully current, and for which no Hindi word exists or the substitution of a Sanskrit word for it means that a flaw of difficulty in comprehension is possible, those words should be used. In summary, the very first place should be given to pure Hindi words, the next to easy

[25] One of the first activities of the Sabhā was to campaign for the official recognition of Nagari at a provincial level: Rādhākṛṣṇa Dās toured the western districts of the province, Śyāmsundar Dās Allahabad and Lucknow, and Mālavīya contributed with his pamphlet, his vast influential contacts, and his leadership abilities. The campaign started reaping results when the Vaishya Conference (est. 1891) and even the Kayastha Conference (est. 1887) passed a resolution in favour of Nagari in 1899, and submitted a memorandum to this effect to the Governor, Antony MacDonnell; Śyāmsundar Dās, *Merī ātmakahānī*, Allahabad, Indian Press, 1957, pp. 19 ff.

and current Sanskrit words, the next to ordinary and current words from Persian and other foreign languages, and the very last place should be given to non-current Sanskrit words. Difficult words from Persian and other foreign languages should never be used.[26]

Since many of the writers and scholars associated with the Sabhā were pandits and scholars who knew Sanskrit well, 'their judgement as to which were easy and which difficult Sanskrit words must have been inclined to be lenient in favour of admitting Sanskrit words'.[27] Their saṃskāras (see 1.2), as well as their aim of creating a 'high' language, resulted in a sanskritized Hindi far from current speech.

The linguistic economy of nineteenth-century north India was thus in a state of flux. Print and colonial policy pressed the need for a standard vernacular to be used as public and print language. While Urdu appeared the most immediate candidate and was in fact the first to benefit from the print revolution, other forces were at work as well. Educational efforts (and textbooks) and the demise of 'Muslim rule' awakened expectations of a greater scope for Hindi in its standardized, Khari Boli guise, as the potential public language of the Hindu majority. Writers within and without the education department, like Śiva Prasād Siṃh and Bhārtendu Hariśchandra, were among those influential in envisaging new possibilities and uses for Hindi as a language of public communication and literature and for the spread of 'useful knowledge'. Literary associations and journals were particularly effective in making language a 'community' issue, drawing agendas, pulling people together and trying to re-compact social groups along linguistic lines. Hence the Hindi–Urdu controversy of the late nineteenth century was not only a competition between old service elites and new groups, a competition for jobs and status; it was also a struggle for cultural self-assertion in which new cultural symbols were being created. Whereas Urdu supporters denied Hindi's existence, resented any assertion of it as a threat to their own existence and pristine glory, and deemed it a vulgar and demotic idiom, Urdu was dismissed by Hindi supporters as a spurious offspring

[26] Dās, *Merī ātmakahānī*, p. 72; quoted in King, 'The Nagari Pracharini Sabha', p. 309, emphasis added. 'Moderate though they appeared', King remarks, 'in practice these principles could and did lead to highly-Sanskritized Hindi' (ibid., p. 310). Despite the objections already mentioned, this statement was important because it influenced official guidelines: it was quoted for example by one of the Hindi members of the Provincial Textbook Committee as evidence; see Dittmer, *Die Indischen Muslims*, p. 114.

[27] King, 'The Nagari Pracharini Sabha', p. 310.

of Hindi in a foreign (Persian) guise, all the more hideous since it reminded them of centuries of 'enslavement' by alien Muslim rulers.[28] Thus language as a symbol tied in with the writing of a 'national history'.

The self-definition of Hindi against Urdu drew new and rigid linguistic boundaries. While most Hindi writers of the nineteenth century were proficient in Urdu, at critical junctures their advocacy of Hindi as public and written language would become exclusive and create a hiatus between their *public* and *private* uses of language. Although privately they would read Urdu, Persian, and English, publicly they would dismiss them in favour of Hindi. In fact, writing and reading Hindi became a self-conscious choice, which began to imply one's loyalty to one's own culture—as much as writing Urdu became a sign of disloyalty. In addition, the spread of Hindi literacy and formal Hindi education in the early twentieth century brought about a change in the social transmission of language, as it bred unfamiliarity with Persian and Urdu. Numbers played in favour of Hindi. What Hindi activists could not alter, with their policy of polite pressure and cooperation with colonial authorities, was the subordinate status of Hindi in relation to English. It was only when Hindi acquired the political support of Congress leaders, and of Gandhi in particular, that this subordinate status could at least be questioned (see 5.4). Further, the expansion of Hindi as a public language in education and the press suggested to Hindi activists that the Hindi sphere had actually become autonomous and could aspire to eventually replace the English-speaking one. It also highlighted a tension that will surface again and again in the course of this book: while most of the activities of literary associations aimed at forming a 'high' standard for Hindi as a language of modern, civilized, literary, and even erudite expression on every subject on a par with English, the claim that Hindi was 'the language of the people' remained intact. This claim which saw Hindi as a 'low' idiom, the language of simple and pure rural India and of Hindu religiosity, positioned it against Urdu, which was projected as the language of a debauched and tyrannical elite, and against English, the language of imperialist rule. With Gandhi, village India became the hallmark of India's moral superiority over modernity and foreign rule, and Hindi was upheld as the 'language of the people'.

[28] For a symbolic identification of Hindi in Devanagari characters as the virtuous Hindu wife and of Urdu as a disreputable courtesan, see the svāṁg discussed by Christopher King in 'Forging a New Linguistic Identity: The Hindi Movement in Benares, 1868–1914', in Freitag, *Culture and Power in Benares*, pp. 179 ff.

1.2. Diversity in the Hindi Literary Sphere

The 1920s are generally viewed as the 'golden age' of modern Hindi literature, when a galaxy of talents such as the Chāyāvād 'Romantic' poets, novelist and short story writer Premchand, and critic Rāmchandra Śukla brought poetry, fiction, and criticism to 'maturity'. The flourishing of the arts at this time is widely acknowledged to be connected with the nationalist movement, generally under the rubric of the 'influence of Gandhi'. Literary histories so far have tended to accept this as a fact, a natural step in the linear evolution of Hindi literature. Such an approach is based on the belief in the sudden appearance of individual genius and in a linear, unproblematic relationship between culture and politics: in a nationalist era, *of course* every artist was nationalist, we are told. But were all writers nationalist in the same, Gandhian way? And was their 'maturity' all of the same kind?

One of the striking features of writing in this period is in fact its variety, which is actually of two kinds. First, there is variety in literary traditions and forms of transmission: courtly, devotional and popular, and manuscript, oral and mixed. Some of them appeared together in the unified linguistic and literary field created by print and publicity: the printed page of the journal, the public forum of the literary association, the canon-setting textbook. Others continued their mixed written-oral transmission, now at the margins of the world of print. Second, we find a great variety of literature in printed form: literary, educational, and commercial. Premchand's ground-breaking novels of social realism appeared together with scores of historical romances, social dramas, and chapbooks of ballads from the folk tradition. Traditional love poetry in Braj Bhasa coexisted in the same journals with the didactic poetry of the Dvivedī poets, the strikingly new diction and voice of Chāyāvād poets, samples of Urdu verse and folk-songs collected from the field.

The two kinds of variety, that of literary traditions and transmission and the variety of content within literature in print, are clearly linked to each other. Editions of Braj Bhasa poetic 'classics' were collated on the basis of manuscripts; collections of folk-songs drew upon an ongoing oral tradition. Yet the obvious argument for continuity, for print supplementing rather than supplanting orality and pre-existing traditions, should not blind us to the structural changes in the literary system.[29]

[29] Cf. Stuart Blackburn, 'The Tale of the Book: Print and Storytelling in Nineteenth Century Tamil', in R. Dwyer and C. Pinney, eds, *Pleasure and the Nation: The History, Politics and Consumption of Public Culture in India*, Delhi, OUP, 2001.

Institutions such as the press and publishing, literary associations, and the education system all helped reshape the production, transmission, and consumption of literature; they reshaped the participants in these processes, the audiences, tastes, and opinions in ways that will be analysed in the course of this book. It is precisely the aim of this and of the following chapter to show how institutional changes in the transmission of literature (and of knowledge in general) affected the ways in which different kinds of genres were produced, appreciated, and evaluated. This is not to suggest that 'institutions' such as the press or the education system were independent of the social and economic changes that were taking place in north Indian society. What I do suggest is that institutions carried a momentum of their own, and that those people who exercised a degree of control over them, for example over the school curriculum, came to command a considerably greater cultural authority than is warranted by their place in literary histories, or in histories *tout court*.

Why did a particular kind of diversity exist in a particular historical epoch; why did common historical circumstances give rise to very different attitudes; and to what extent does the predominant focus on new literary trends obfuscate our perception of how older tastes continued to exert their influence? These are the questions which form the basis of this section. Rāmchandra Śukla's new way of evaluating literature on the basis of its social relevance did not supersede the system of classification and evaluation of literary artefacts based on *rasa* and *alaṃkāra*. His aesthetic conservatism and preoccupation with social order sit badly with the Chāyāvādīs' urge to break free of social norms, and with Premchand's less-than-holy attitude towards the hierarchical order of Hindu society—yet they were all products of the same epoch.

The literary sphere which Hindi writers entered in the 1920s and 1930s had expanded considerably compared with the previous decades: the rise of a popular press, fuelled by the expansion in 'vernacular' education and by events such as World War I, the resultant economic crisis and the new nationalist drive towards popular politicization, contributed to the growth of a publishing market and literary public wider than ever before. This expansion finally validated the notion, current since the mid-nineteenth century but so far not borne out by reality, that writers were the 'vanguard of the people', dependent on the general public both for their authority and ther livelihood (2.2). The dynamics of the expansion and consolidation of Hindi language and literature in the public sphere of north India will be examined in the next two sections of this chapter, while the following chapter will discuss some of the qualitative consequences this quantitative change had in the institutional spaces in which literature was situated. In order to situate these changes in the context of existing practices and tastes, this section presents a kind of geographical overview of the literary activities and institutions in the area. This overview, superficial and limited though it is, will give us some initial coordinates along which we can place the developments and actors mentioned in the course of the book. It also shows the extent to which new tastes did not snuff out existing ones but required readjustments and often entailed inner tensions and contradictions that are the hallmark of this age of change. It was over these diverse and unruly developments that critics at the beginning of the century, from Mahāvīr Prasād Dvivedī to Rāmchandra Śukla, tried to impose a uniform, reformist agenda. It is their tastes and their approaches to literary history that resulted in the prevalent view of the 'golden age' of Hindi literature mentioned above. The reality was more composite and diverse.

1.2.1. The Literary Sphere

Diversity in the Hindi literary sphere of the early twentieth century needs to be retrieved from the straitjacket of nationalist historiography, itself a product of the period. This diversity carries a particular historical significance, poised as it is between oral and literate traditions and the new print culture, the nationalist call and the lures of the market, the exigencies of canon building, and the exhilaration of modernity. Its proper appreciation is long overdue.

A synchronic view of the Hindi literary sphere of Benares at the turn of the century reveals the extent of this diversity. There was, firstly, a group of *rīti* poets collected around Jagannāth Dās Ratnākar (1866–1932), the last great representative of the genre, and loosely organized in a 'society of poets' (*kavi-samāj*) by Jīvanlāl Gosvāmī of the Vallabhite Gopal Mandir. The main activity of this unofficial group of *rasiks* (connoisseurs) was poetic riddles (*samasyā-pūrtis*) in Braj Bhasa (see below 1.3.3), following a well-established tradition of merchants' involvement with Braj Bhasa poetry, both devotional and erotic.[30] Although samasyā-pūrti was mainly an impromptu, oral practice, the kavi-samāj also published riddles and their solutions in printed form 'for entertainment' (*vinodārtha*).[31] Ratnākar's regular and informal circle of friends also

[30] See Rāykṛṣṇadās, '*Prasād kī yād*', unpublished manuscript, p. 33.

[31] Jagannāth Dās (Ratnākar), comp., *Samasyāpūrti, arthāt kāśī kavisamāj ke dvādaś adhiveśanoṁ par jo pūrtiyāṁ kāśīstha tathā anek deś deśāntar ke kaviyoṁ kī kī huī paṛhī gaī thīṁ*, pt. 1, Benares, saṃvat 1951 (1894).

included Bālmukund Gupta (1865–1907), a survivor of Bhārtendu's circle, and popular novelists like Kiśorīlāl Gosvāmī (1865–1932), Harikṛṣṇa Jauhar, and Devkīnandan Khatrī (1861–1922).[32] Another younger group of poets collected around Lala Bhagvān Dīn (1876–1930), also a master of samasyā-pūrtis, a connoisseur of Urdu and Braj Bhasa poetry, and author of a popular book of patriotic poems in Khari Boli, *Vīr pañcaratna* (1918). Whereas Ratnākar belonged to the old service class and was secretary to the Maharani of Ayodhya, Bhagvān Dīn, though only informally trained in literature, was a salaried literary person. He taught Persian at Annie Besant's Central Hindu School and later became Hindi lecturer at Benares Hindu University in 1924. He also ran free Hindi literature classes to prepare candidates for the Hindī Sāhitya Sammelan examinations.[33] Among his disciples were Viśvanāth Prasād Miśra, the future scholar, and Murārelāl Keḍiyā, treasurer of the Nāgarī Prachāriṇī Sabhā, amateur archaeologist, collector, and organizer of *ex tempore* Braj Bhasa poetry sessions (*paṛhant kavi sammelan*) in the streets of Benares that lasted all night. Younger poets assembled at the informal Chāyāvād haven of Jayśaṅkar Prasād (1889–1937) in Gobardhan Sarai. Among them was Kṛṣṇadev Prasād Gauṛ ('Beḍhab Banārsī'), who wrote humorous poems, edited satirical journals, and taught English literature; there were also Vinodśaṅkar Vyās, Rāmnāthlāl 'Suman', and Śāntipriy Dvivedī who were the first to write positively about Chāyāvād in the controversy around it (see 2.2) and contributed to the journal *Jāgaraṇ*.[34] At the grander *salon* of Rāykṛṣṇadās (1892–1980) at Ramghat, poets, scholars, painters, musicians, art dealers, and others assembled regularly for almost half a century.[35] The old Carmicheal Library, the Nāgarī Prachāriṇī Sabhā and later Benares Hindu University provided venues for regular literary (and general) conversation and for learned talks, poetry sessions, grand annual meetings, and other literary events. Benares' role as an education centre, of Sanskrit as well as Hindi and western education, ensured the presence of a young literate audience for books and literary events. Also, enterprising Khatris and Kayasthas had made Benares into a centre of commercial publishing in Hindi since the late nineteenth century, at a time when the book trade in the rest of the province was predominantly centred around Urdu and Persian. Rāmlīlās,

[32] See Madhureś, *Devkīnandan Khatrī,* New Delhi, Sahitya Akademi, 1980, p. 13.

[33] See 1.4 and Appendix.

[34] Rāmvilās Śarmā, *Nirālā kī sāhitya sādhnā,* vol. I, Delhi, Rajkamal Prakasan, 1969, p. 122.

[35] Interview with Dr Ananda Krishna, Rāykṛṣṇadās' son, Benares, August 1992.

Rāmkathās, music and poetry programmes at temples or in private houses, under the patronage of the Maharaja or of the numerous wealthy merchants, marked the festive calendar of the city. A few local amateur drama groups, travelling Parsi and folk theatre companies, and the first films provided entertainment to a wide spectrum of townsmen, usually on the esplanade in front of the Town Hall.[36] While each genre of entertainment—literary or otherwise—had its own aesthetic world, its rules and practitioners, traditional and modern forms coexisted and audiences overlapped. 'Elite' intellectuals freely took part in festivals and so-called popular forms of entertainment; indeed, the cultivated eclecticism we find in Bhārtendu Hariśchandra in the nineteenth century, and in Rāykṛṣṇadās and Jayśaṅkar Prasād in the twentieth, was a trademark of Benares.

By comparison, the Hindi literary scene in Allahabad, of which Bālkṛṣṇa Bhaṭṭ (1844–1914) had been a brave pioneer with the journal *Hindī pradīp* (1877–1910), was strongly influenced by the growth of the city as a centre of western education, journalism and publishing, of provincial administration and nationalist politics.[37] The presence of the University, the High Court, government offices and the Civil Lines gave the city a genteel outlook, while the 'Town' resounded with the usual bustle of the bazaar, and the area near the *saṅgam*, Daraganj, had a strong presence of river paṇḍās and small printer-publishers. In 1922 Allahabad University became a residential teaching institution rather than just an examination board, and some of the oldest and most prestigious colleges of the province, Muir Central College (1872) and the Kayastha Pathshala (1873), were merged into it. With its imposing buildings and hostels, its professors and students, the University was a stronghold of English and only slowly made some allowance for 'vernaculars'. Indeed, even when Hindi literature was first introduced in 1923, it was taught in English like all the other subjects! The Hindi lecturers, Dhīrendra Varmā (1897–1973), Rāmśaṅkar Śukla 'Rasāl' (1898–1980) and Rāmkumār Varmā (1905–?), played an active role in the literary institutions of the city,

[36] The amateur Nāgarī Nāṭak Maṇḍalī, established in 1909 by relatives of Bhārtendu Hariśchandra, produced either his or other historical plays much in the style of Parsi companies. A split gave birth to the Bhārtendu Nāṭak Maṇḍalī; see introduction to Dhīrendranāth Siṃh, ed., *Jānakīmaṅgal nāṭak*, Benares, Nagari Pracharini Sabha, 1996.

[37] Karine Schomer, *Mahadevi Varma and the Chhayavad Age of Modern Hindi Poetry*, University of California Press, Berkeley, 1983, reprint Delhi, OUP, 1998, pp. 135 ff.

whether in the independent Hindī Sāhitya Sammelan or in the government-sponsored Hindustani Academy, and published regularly in the Hindi press. Kavi-sammelans became a regular feature at colleges and hostels: the Sukavi Samāj encouraged young talents and provided them with a weekly forum for recitation and discussion. Sumitrānandan Pant (1900–77), Rāmkumār Varmā, Mahādevī Varmā (1902–87), and Ānandīprasād Śrīvāstava were among the many new poets who flourished in the protected atmosphere of the University. In the late 1930s and 1940s the University became a base for Progressive and Marxist writers and critics.[38] Another literary circle, the Rasik Maṇḍal, preserved the taste for Braj Bhasa poetry in a more private form. Once a week the group of *rasiks*, including Rāmprasād Tripāṭhī, 'Rasāl', and Rāmnārāyaṇ Chaturvedī, would meet in a private room near the Chowk and delight in samasyā-pūrtis.[39]

The role and development of publishing houses will be discussed in Section 1.3.2. With the Indian Press and Rāmnārāyaṇ Lāl taking the lion's share of textbook production, Allahabad emerged at the turn of the century as one of the main centres of Hindi publishing in the province, rivalling the earlier monopoly of the Nawal Kishore Press of Lucknow. Smaller publishers like Rāmnareś Tripāṭhī's Hindi Mandir or the Hindi Press took advantage of the growth of higher literary studies in Hindi and produced readers and anthologies. Allahabad had the biggest concentration of newspapers in the province, both in English and in Hindi: in English, apart from the Anglo-Indian *Pioneer* (1867), there was the *Leader*, launched by Madan Mohan Mālavīya (1861–1941) and edited by C.Y. Chintamani (later a Birla concern), Motilal Nehru's *Independent* and Sacchidananda Sinha's *Hindustan Review*. In Hindi Mālavīya had launched *Abhyuday* (1909) and *Maryādā* (1910), managed and edited by his nephew Kṛṣṇakānt Mālavīya (1883–1941). The *Leader* group brought out *Bhārat* (1928), the Indian Press published *Sarasvatī* (1900), the famed literary journal, and *Bālsakhā* for children (1917).[40] A former employee

[38] Progressive critics, all university graduates, centred around the Progressive Writers' Association (1936) and included Śivdānsiṃh Chauhān, Amṛt Rāi, Prakāśchandra Gupta, and Rāmvilās Śarmā. Amṛt Rāi and Chauhān took over Premchand's journal *Haṁs* after his death, Gupta edited *Nayā sāhitya*. Pant's journal *Rūpābh* (Kalakankar, 1938–9) provided a space for Progressive criticism.

[39] Śrīnārāyaṇ Chaturvedī, *Manorañjak saṃsamaraṇ*, Allahabad, Indian Press, 1965, p. 96.

[40] There were attempts at other journals, too, but rather short-lived; see Mushtaq Ali, 'Hindī sāhitya ke itihās meṁ ilāhābād kā yogdān, iṇḍiyan pres ke viśiṣṭ sandarbh meṁ', unpublished Ph.D. thesis, University of Allahabad, 1989.

of the Indian Press, Rāmjīlāl Śarmā, (1876–1931) published two more children's magazines, *Vidyārthī* (1913) and *Khilaunā* (1924). Allahabad also pioneered women's journalism with *Gṛhlakṣmī* and *Strīdarpaṇ*, both established in 1909, while in the 1920s the Chand Press brought out *Chāṁd* (1922, see 4.2) and the political weekly *Bhaviṣya* (1919).

Allahabad therefore provided the Hindi literati with plenty of opportunities for employment and interaction. Yet Allahabad highlights the paradox of Hindi: although a centre of Hindi press and literature, and of Hindi politics with Madan Mohan Mālavīya and P.D. Ṭaṇḍon (1882–1962), the Hindi literary sphere remained quite separate from the English one. Across the geographical and social divide between the University area and Civil Lines on one side, and the Town and Daragaṁj on the other, contacts were occasional and rather guarded, mediated mainly through personal acquaintances. Even in the main centre of nationalist politics, Nehru's residence Anand Bhavan, Hindi remained a slighted and largely alien presence. Yet, within the Hindi world, the Hindī Sāhitya Sammelan and newspaper offices supplied meeting places for genteel academics, educated students, enterprising writer–publishers, salaried intellectuals, and traditional literati.

Lucknow had long been a stronghold of Indo-Persian culture and flourished in the nineteenth century as a centre of Urdu journalism and book publishing.[41] The early Hindi scholars and writers who lived there, such as the Miśra brothers (Śyāmbihārī, Śukdevbihārī, and Gaṇeśbihārī), and Rūpnārāyaṇ Pāṇḍey (1884–1958), had to work with the journals and publishers of Allahabad. It was only in the 1920s that Hindi acquired some public space in Lucknow, when members of the Nawal Kishore family branched out into Hindi: Biṣṇunārāyaṇ and Dulārelāl Bhārgava started *Mādhurī* (1922), *Sudhā* (1927), and the literary publishing house Ganga Pustak Mala (see 1.3). These attracted noted writers such as Premchand, Kṛṣṇabihārī Miśra, Rūpnārāyaṇ Pāṇḍey, Nirālā, Ilāchandra Jośī (1902–82), Mātādīn Śukla, and Badrīnāth Bhaṭṭ (1891–1934). Badrīnāth Bhaṭṭ (see 1.2.2) became the first Hindi lecturer at the newly established Lucknow University (1922), which was created out of Canning College (1864)—the taluqdars' college—King George's Medical College, and Isabella Thoburn College for girls. Among the new writers who assembled around Nirālā in Lucknow were Amṛtlāl Nāgar (1913–1985) and Rāmvilās Śarmā (1912–2000), then a student of English at the University.

[41] See Nazir Ahmad, 'Development of Printing in Urdu, 1743–1857', unpublished M.Phil. thesis, School of Library Archive and Information Studies, University of London, 1976.

An industrial and business city, Kanpur could hardly be called a literary centre, despite the presence of Pratāpnārāyaṇ Miśra (1856–95), a prolific editor and novelist of Bhārtendu's time, and of poet Rāy Devīprasād 'Pūrṇa' (1868–1915).[42] In Bhagavatīcharaṇ Varmā's words:

> In those days, the whole culture in Kanpur was dominated by Kanaujiya Brahmins. Business was mostly in Kanaujiya Brahmins' hands, and they were everywhere—in the cloth-market, in banking, in the grain-market. Besides, most zamindars of the Kanpur district were Kanaujiya Brahmins. They went hunting, robbed and masterminded highway robberies. After the Brahmins came the Khatris, who were purely businessmen. They were not many in number but controlled very big business firms. Marwaris had just started then to establish their position as industrialists.[43]

Viśvambharnāth Śarmā 'Kauśik' (1891–1942), one of the leading short-story writers of the period, was one such absentee Kanaujiya zamindar; while the personality emerging from his stories is very much that of a moralist, we know from recollections of his friends that he was a connoisseur of literature, music, bhang (cannabis), and humorous conversation.[44] His informal circle of literary friends included, among others, young Varmā, Ramāśaṅkar Avasthī and the poet Bālkṛṣna Śarmā 'Navīn' (1897–1960). Young Varmā, Avasthī, and Navīn became attracted to the publicist and activist Gaṇeś Śaṅkar Vidyārthī (1891–1931) and worked for his journals *Pratāp* (1913) and *Prabhā* (1920). The Pratāp office became the most important literary and political meeting place in Kanpur, and Vidyārthī the centre of a widespread network of Hindi writers, both within Kanpur [Mākhanlāl Chaturvedī (1886–1964), Gayāprasād Śukla 'Sanehī' (1873–1972)] and outside it [Vṛndāvanlāl Varmā (1889–1973), Maithilīśaraṇ Gupta (1886–1964)].[45] With the growth of denominational schools in the 1920s, Kanpur also became a sizable educational centre, and colleges held literary events.[46] Although Kanpur had no local

[42] A famous advocate, and a strong supporter of *sanātan dharma*, Moderate Congressman and Braj Bhasa poet, he edited several *rasik* journals with samasyāpūrtis, like *Rasikmitra*.

[43] Bhagavatīcharaṇ Varmā, *Atīt ke gart se*, Delhi, Rajkamal Prakasan, 1979, p. 19.

[44] Ibid., p. 26.

[45] See Appendix for biographies.

[46] Apart from the government Christ Church College and the Technological Institute, a Dayanand Anglo-Vedic school and college was established in 1919, and a Sanatan Dharma Commerce College in 1921; see editorial note in *Mādhurī*, II, pt. 1, 3, October 1923, pp. 384–8.

theatre company in the early twentieth century, the concentration of labourers, artisans, traders, and professionals provided an ideal audience for touring Parsi companies, which often came to perform. In the 1920s a Kanpur style of popular *Nauṭaṅkī* theatre was developed by Śrīkṛṣna Khatrī, a former wrestler and tailor, who turned Nauṭaṅkī into a more commercial performance, introduced modern or overtly nationalist historical plots, and changed its musical style. The chapbooks of his plays were printed locally and sold widely.[47] Although there was no organized or sponsored cultural life as such, temples would host all-night musical events attended not only by the educated public but also by the substantial numbers of artisans and workers who peopled the city.

The cities mentioned so far give a picture of the worlds encountered by the literary people who moved to them. By contrast, the literary sphere of a small town in central India at roughly the same time provides an example of the environment most Hindi literary people were born into and experienced in their early years, the substratum under the later experiences of their often peripatetic lives. The recollections of Khairagarh by Padumlāl Punnālāl Bakhśī (1894–1971), teacher, editor, and writer, can be taken as a fairly typical example of the background and experiences of many Hindi intellectuals. First of all, the court was at the centre of town life: all inhabitants depended on the Raja in one way or another for their livelihoods. Since the Raja was a patron of music and of Hindi literature, the local cultural life reflected his tastes. There were three groups of literary practitioners. The first was one of illiterates, who provided aesthetic enjoyment to common people through bhajans and songs. During the rainy season, accompanied by a drum, they would sing verses from the popular heroic epic *Ālhā,* resounding with *vīr-rasa*, heroic sentiment. Another group of illiterate or semi-literate bhajan singers sang songs which carried the signatures of Sūrdās, Tulsīdās, and Kabīr but were really the creation of anonymous poets. A third group consisted of educated literature lovers that included some *vyākhyātās* (orators) and poets. Bakhśī recalled listening in his childhood days to recitations in the local temple ranging from Tulsīdās' retelling of the Rāmāyaṇa story to Braj Bhasa devotional and courtly poetry that had achieved 'classic' status, as well as Keśav Dās' *Rāmchandrikā* and Bihārī's *Satsaī.* The Raja himself composed poetry (or had it composed by various poets): a

[47] See Kathryn Hansen, *Grounds for Play. The Nautanki Theatre of North India*, Berkeley, University of California Press, 1992, p. 247.

couple of poetry collections were published in his name.[48] The local Victoria School and Danteśvarī temple also hosted performances by visiting scholars and poets. Some of the headmasters of the Victoria School were respected scholars, and the school provided a new forum for literary activities. The meetings of its Debating Society, lasting whole afternoons, involved not only teachers and students but many cultured people of the town as well; among the audience, and impressed by the seriousness and dignity of the speakers, was young Bakhśī.[49] Ārya Samāj śāstrārthas (disputations) by visiting preachers were also public performances of a kind.

Over these oral forms of literary entertainment and apprenticeship, literate children like Bakhśī superimposed literary tastes acquired at school or through contact with the printed word. Bakhśī's main source of Hindi *literary* education was, as for many others, the literary magazine *Sarasvatī,* while popular novels like Devkīnandan Khatrī's *Chandrakāntā* (1891) and *Chandrakāntā Santati* (1894–1905) bridged the chasm between the oral world of the *Ālhā* and that of private reading. The translation of Bankimchandra Chatterjee's essays, published in Hindi by the Hindi Grantha Mala of Bombay, and journals like *Bhāratmitra* and the *Hindī kesarī* gave Bakhśī his first political education and the urge to contribute to that public medium himself.[50]

Even this brief survey will have given an idea of the stratified literary tastes of the time. To take the case of poetry, which shows the greatest stratification, if we were to draw a map of the poetic genres practised in the Hindi literary sphere at this time, we would have to include first of all Braj Bhasa poetry, kept alive in the traditional (*rīti*) literary education, in informal circles and in specialized journals. Printed editions of 'old' Hindi (i.e. mainly Braj Bhasa) poetry from the fifteenth to the eighteenth centuries, and manuals of poetry composition ensured the visibility of Braj Bhasa even in print. As we shall see in the following sections, the school curriculum, literary prizes and kavi sammelans all testify to the ongoing familiarity with the conventions of traditional poetry and to its

[48] P.P. Bakhśī '*Smṛti*', in *Merī apnī kathā*, Allahabad, Indian Press, 1972, pp. 19 ff.

[49] Young Bakhśī, who did not understand the content of the debates, wondered 'इन वक्ताओं में ज्ञान की वह कैसी गरिमा होगी जिसके कारण इतने लोग यहां मन्त्रमुग्ध बैठे हैं।' [God knows what prestige the knowledge of these speakers must have for so many people to listen to them so enraptured.] Ibid., p. 23.

[50] While studying at Allahabad University, Bakhśī later became acquainted with contemporary European and Bengali literatures and introduced them in *Sarasvatī* when he was the editor between 1921 and 1928; ibid., p. 43.

renewed status as 'classic' in the early twentieth century.[51] The extraordinary fortune and importance of Tulsīdās' *Rāmcharitmānas* in printed form as a focus of both religious and cultural identity is a particular example.[52] Devotional poetry in Braj Bhasa and Avadhi also continued to circulate orally through *bhajan-maṇḍalīs*, in temples, and through public and private ritual singing. Second, there were the didactic Khari Boli poets of the Dvivedī generation, all still active and enjoying great respect in the literary world. Their patriotic poetry was unfailingly published in journals and reprinted in textbooks, and they were often called upon to preside over literary gatherings and poetry meetings. One of them, Maithilīśaraṇ Gupta, was hailed as the first *rāṣṭrakavi* (national poet) in the 1930s (cf. 3.1). In fact, a lot of patriotic poetry in Khari Boli and Braj Bhasa was recited at poetry meetings and printed in newspapers, journals, chapbooks, and textbooks. Many lesser-known local poets produced nationalist versions of bhajans, Ālhās, *svāṁgs* that bridged the gap between printed and aural poetry, and between literate and illiterate audiences, and performed an important cultural and political role. Finally, exposure to the poetic diction of Rabindranath Tagore and a sudden turn to individual imagination produced a new poetic idiom in Khari Boli with Chāyāvād, a refined poetic sensibility that spoke through striking new metaphors and played upon well-known ones in an individual voice. Although greatly appealing to the ear, Chāyāvādī poetry needed nevertheless to be read for the meaning to be understood. It

[51] Published Braj Bhasa poets after 1900 include Ratnākar, Nāthūrām Śaṅkar Śarmā, Rāy Devīprasād 'Pūrṇa', Śrīdhar Pāṭhak, Lala Bhagvān Dīn, Ayodhyāsiṃh Upādhyāy 'Harioudh', Gayāprasād Śukla 'Sanehī', Satyanārāyaṇ 'Kaviratna', Viyogī Hari, and Rāmśankar Śukla 'Rasāl'. About half of them wrote in Khari Boli, too; see Appendix. Many other amateur poets, whose verses appeared from time to time in Hindi journals and who took part in poetry meetings, testify to the ongoing popularity of Braj Bhasa poetry even in the 1920s and 1930s; see 2.2 and 2.3 in this volume.

[52] For the changing status of Tulsīdās' text through the four centuries of its life and its popularity in printed form in the nineteenth and twentieth centuries, see Philip Lutgendorf, *The Life of the Text: Performing the Ramcaritmanas of Tulsidas,* Berkeley, University of California Press, 1991. Tulsīdās himself became an important cultural hero for Hindi intellectuals of the early twentieth century, as one who had 'saved' Indian (Hindu) religious culture in an age of foreign oppression; cf. P. Lutgendorf, 'The Quest for the Legendary Tulsīdās', in W. Callewaert and R. Snell, eds, *According to Tradition: Hagiographical Writing in India*, Wiesbaden, Harrassowitz,1994; and my own 'Tulsīdās as a Classic', in R. Snell and I. Raeside, eds, *Classics of Modern South Asian Literature*, Wiesbaden, Harrassowitz, 1998.

also required familiarity with a great deal of sanskritized vocabulary. It was thus mostly educated and young poets, among them several women, who in the pages of various journals enthusiastically adopted the alluring style of Prasād, Pant, Nirālā, and Mahādevī.[53]

Despite the centrality of print, oral poetic genres and literary transmission did not disappear. The large numbers of pamphlets of bhajans, religious and patriotic songs, and theatre chapbooks intended for oral recitation bear witness to the successful adaptation of these genres to the world of commercial publishing. But orality lost some of its earlier prominence in the literary system and in literary transmission. When literature came to mean something in printed form, it included as a category either 'modern' writing written *for* the printed page, or the old Braj Bhasa and Avadhi texts formalized in a canon. For the literate and mostly urban intelligentsia, oral literature was recuperated with a nostalgic and almost ethnographic meaning: it was the voice of the 'simple village folk', as in the case of Rāmnareś Tripāṭhī's pioneering collection of *Grām-gīt* (3 vols, Allahabad, Hindi Mandir, 1930), or what one had heard in the village as a child. Oral poetry also continued to work as a subtle influence in contemporary poets: such is the deliberate use of folk-song patterns in Mahādevī Varmā's *Nīrjā* (1934) and in Nirālā's *Gītikā* (1936),[54] and the almost universal presence of Tulsī's *Mānas* in the form of quotations, references, or allusions.

At the same time, the growth of Benares, Allahabad, Lucknow, and Kanpur as centres of education and the press points towards an unmistakable process of urban concentration, which intensified in this period. This, together with the growth of institutions like journals and publishing houses, and the widening impact of formal education, contributed to the making of a *unified linguistic and literary field.* Different generations of writers, coming from different backgrounds, shared the same linguistic and literary space in journals and literary meetings; they were thus exposed to comparison and to mutual criticism (1.3, 2.2, and 2.3). At the same time, as school education and public debates on the kind of poetry suitable for the age began to make an impact (2.2), it became increasingly difficult to accept and accommodate the existing heterogeneity of tastes. In an environment where heterogeneity was a reality for most writers and readers, this had implications beyond the familiar need for neat categories: it meant that only certain trends and tastes were acknowledged in

[53] Other early experiments included Rāykṛṣṇadās' prose poems (*Sādhnā*, 1919, and *Praval*, 1928).

[54] Schomer, *Mahadevi Varma*, p. 243.

public discourse as part of one's identity, while other tastes were to be enjoyed beyond the pale of critical consciousness. Yet the reality was that readers and writers remained able to switch effortlessly from the aesthetic world of one genre to that of another.

1.2.2. Literary Saṃskāras

The 1920s were thus a period of intense change and experimentation that took place without the demise of earlier genres. The same was true of individual writers and readers, very receptive of new styles and yet strongly rooted in the old. Poets ventured on new ground in Khari Boli and still wrote and enjoyed Braj Bhasa and Urdu. It was not just a question of language: each poetic tradition had its own ethos, very different in the case of Braj Bhasa and Khari Boli. In an age where cultural uniformity was becoming a public ideal, the ideal could not but clash with reality.

Yet it is precisely their familiarity with various literary traditions and their openness to change that makes creative writers of this period so eclectic, flexible, and exciting. Their appropriations of the new can by no means be considered a passive act of influence, nor should their tensions be criticized (or shamefully hidden) as contradictions. While critics were busy choosing, dictating, and excluding, it was as if creative writers such as Nirālā were trying—both for themselves and for their readers—to contain all the worlds they were aware of in a single, difficult embrace.

How is one to pick up the threads and explain this diversity within individual writers and readers? Instead of seeing it as a process of influence, or a linear evolution (e.g. from Braj Bhasa to Khari Boli, from non-realism to realism), the notion of saṃskāra may be fruitfully adopted to explain how different tastes overlapped. The word saṃskāra itself carries several layers of meaning in Sanskrit and Hindi. It means primarily: (a) to polish, refine; (b) refinement of the mind and behaviour, hence the making of culture; (c) rite of passage; (d) the effect of previous actions on the mind and behaviour; (e) influence; (f) idea.[55] Generally saṃskāra thus indicates an active change or an aspect of a layered mind. The expression 'literary saṃskāra', current in Hindi, suggests a taste, an inclination *and* its source, i.e. whether it is inherited from one's family, local traditions and tastes, or is acquired through education and contact with the outer world and with literary trends; the expression suggests a taste

[55] According to *Bṛhat Hindī Kos*, Benares , Jnanmandal, 1989, p. 1178.

which settles upon other tastes according to one's individual experience of life.[56] The notion of saṃskāra thus emphasizes the creative process of acquiring and combining tastes. It also highlights the importance of the medium of transmission. This helps us avoid misleading simplifications such as 'traditional' and 'modern': not all that was inherited was traditional, not all that was acquired was modern. The Sanskrit saṃskāra was one of 'tradition'. Yet that of a pandit trained in the master–disciple, *guru–śiṣya*, system was radically different from that acquired by, for example, the poet Mahādevī Varmā at Allahabad University. Even if the content might be roughly similar, and also the sense of belonging to an ancient culture, Mahādevī's saṃskāra was filtered through a strongly individual and selective mind and had a touch of vindication, for here was a woman acquiring and commenting upon an overwhelmingly male-dominated tradition. Both aspects come across in her scholarly and reflective essays.[57] Literary saṃskāras often did not come from formal schooling. In the case of the poet Nirālā, the son of a Brahmin army officer from Unnao working *pardeś* ('abroad') in a princely state in Bengal, literary taste came first from reading Braj Bhasa and Sanskrit kāvya, which imprinted in him a sense of beauty. He then discovered Tagore's poetry and, almost at the same time, Tulsīdās, who became for him a kind of literary alter-ego. In the absence of a formal education and with his informal poetic training, his further reading was largely haphazard: he gradually absorbed Vidyāpati, other Braj Bhasa 'classics', and the Bengali Vaisnava poets; he read intensely the other poets who were, like him, dubbed 'Chāyāvādī', coming to the English Romantics only in his 30s. Although not formally trained in Urdu, he read Urdu poets (in Devanagari?) and even experimented with Urdu metres and ghazals in *Belā* (1943).[58] Each area of intensive reading became a saṃskāra and was reflected in his own tastes and composition.

If we link, rather summarily, saṃskāras to social groups we find that, among the traditionally literate groups, family saṃskāras for Kayasthas and other service groups[59] would consist of a taste for Persian classics,

[56] It is in the first sense that the word *saṃskāra* is used, for example, by Sumitrānand Pant in his Introduction to the poetry collection *Pallav* to give a negative connotation to the stultified taste for Braj Bhasa; S. Pant, *Pallav*, Delhi, Rajkamal Prakasan, 1963 (first ed. 1926), p. 21; cf. 2.2 here.

[57] Mahādevī Varmā, *Śṛnkhalā kī kaṛiyāṁ*, Allahabad, Bharti Bhandar, 1942; *Sāhityakār kī āsthā*, Allahabad, Lokbharti Prakashan, 1962.

[58] See Rāmvilās Śarmā, *Nirālā kī sāhitya-sādhnā*, vol. 1.

[59] Most of the Hindi intelligentsia well into the first decades of the twentieth century belonged to these classes (e.g. Miśra brothers, Harioudh, Śyāmsundar Dās,

for Indian poets in Persian and Urdu such as Ghalib (1797–1869) or for the Urdu novels of Ratannāth Sarshār (c.1845–1903) and Abdul Halīm Sharār (1860–1926). The Urdu saṃskāra was a largely secular one, as the eclectic nature of the Urdu press and publishing testifies (cf. 1.3).

For educated Brahmins, family saṃskāras would include any Sanskrit tradition of knowledge and Sanskrit literary classics; these would facilitate the appreciation of Braj Bhasa courtly (rīti) poetry. The taste for Braj Bhasa poetry, whether devotional or courtly erotic, widely spread also among merchant families, was acquired through direct contact with a master and flourished in small circles of connoisseurs or along sectarian lines. Thus we find that several Hindi poets were sons of amateur Braj Bhasa poets and were trained by uncles, grandfathers, or family friends. Depending on family circumstances, any combination of these tastes could be found. A study of manuscript circulation would go a long way in telling us which Braj Bhasa texts were actually the most widely circulated and were part of literary apprenticeship.

As mentioned above, familiarity with Tulsīdās' *Rāmcharitmānas* and the songs (*padas*) of Kabīr, Sūrdās, and Mīrābāī was available to all, literate and illiterate, through oral recitation, bhajans, exposition, etc. In addition to these family saṃskāras, print and schooling introduced the influential models of English and Bengali. The essays and novels of Bankimchandra Chatterjee (1838–94), the poetry of Rabindranath Tagore (1861–1941) and later the novels of Sharatchandra (1876–1938) are mentioned as influential and mind-opening texts by many Hindi writers of this period. Hindi poets like Pant, Prasād, and Nirālā freely borrowed entire verses from Tagore, exposing themselves to charges of plagiarism.[60]

Literary Khari Boli was itself an acquired saṃskāra for the majority

---

and Premchand). One of the foremost Urdu literary monthlies, *Zamānā* from Kanpur, was edited by one such Kayastha, Munshi Dayānārāyaṇ Nigam.

[60] Nirālā was at the centre of a long controversy in 1924, carried in the pages of the journals *Manormā* (Allahabad), *Prabhā*, and *Matvālā*. When Pant, in the introduction to his collection of poems *Pallav* (1926), criticized Nirālā's use of Bengali blank verse, Nirālā accused Pant (whose friend he was, after all, and whose poetic talent he acknowledged), of the same 'sin' he had been accused of: with scores of examples he showed how Pant himself had freely drawn upon Tagore. Here are just a few: गन्ध-मुग्ध हो अन्ध-समीरण। लगा थिरकने विविध प्रकार (Pant) and तोमार मदिर गन्ध अन्ध वायु बहे चारि भिते (Tagore); नीरव-घोष भरे शंखों में (Pant) and नीरव सुरेर शंख बाजे (Tagore); मेरे आंसू गूंथ (Pant) and गेंथेछि अश्रुमालिका (Tagore); गाओ गाओ विहग-बालिके। तरवर से मृदु-मंगल गान (Pant) from Wordsworth's 'Then sing ye birds, sing, sing a joyous song'; Nirālā, 'Pantjī aur pallav', in *Mādhurī*, September 1927, now in *Nirālā rachnāvalī*, vol. 5, Delhi, Rajkamal Prakasan, 1992, pp. 176–7.

of writers and readers of the period. It came via formal education and contact with the printed word, both for those from traditionally literate families and those who were the first in their families to acquire an education, and it was a means of identifying with a wider community, regional and national, at the same time. Thus it often implied a step into the evolving public sphere, as the example of the Bhaṭṭ family of Gokulpura (Agra district) shows. In two generations they moved from being Sanskrit and Hindi pandits to professional Hindi writers and teachers. Rāmeśvar Bhaṭṭ was a noted Hindi and Sanskrit scholar and one of the major Tulsī commentators of his time. His first step in the new public sphere involved becoming professor of Sanskrit and Hindi at Agra College and establishing his own press in Agra. In an interesting overlap of public and private roles, it is said that he used to bring proofs from the press to school and correct them himself; he also produced, for the Indian Press of Allahabad, commentaries on Tulsī's *Vinay patrikā* (1913) and on the *Mānas* (*Amṛtalahirī*, 1926).[61] After retirement he went back to his village. His sons, instead, probably through his contacts, became fully part of the Hindi public sphere. Kedārnāth Bhaṭṭ regularly wrote children's books for the Indian Press. Badrīnāth Bhaṭṭ (1891–1934), after a brief spell at the Indian Press, where he edited the children's journal *Bālsakhā* and contributed regularly to *Sarasvatī*, moved further away to Lucknow. There he became the first Hindi lecturer of Lucknow University. He published several humorous plays for the best Hindi publishers and became a stable figure in the Hindi establishment.

Writing and reading Hindi could mean different things for people with different saṃskāras. For Brahmin pandits it meant entering a modern public sphere and accepting a wider medium. For the Urdu-educated it meant espousing a sense of identification with a broad Hindi–Hindu community and accessing a larger and growing public. For the English-educated it could mean adhering to the nationalist project, the desire to communicate with a wider public and possibly to act as interpreters between the local and the outside worlds. For women it was a public voice they had hitherto lacked. In any case, Hindi was an acquired, sometimes a chosen, public voice which, even in the case of the Bhaṭṭ brothers from Gokulpura, required some rearticulation of identity.

Print, schooling, journals, networks, and meetings brought together men and women from remarkably different backgrounds, each with different family saṃskāras. Centralized education and the press also

[61] Ali, 'Hindī sāhitya ke itihās meṁ', p. 120; see Appendix.

produced new, common saṃskāras (cf. 1.3 and 1.4). But what happened when literary saṃskāras and inherited tastes confronted the new sense of linguistic identity and nationalist ideas about literature? Few had any doubts that the nation 'needed' certain kinds of literature and did not need others (cf. 2.2). Inevitably this involved excluding some tastes. Questions of publicity and tradition underlay discussions about the 'vulgarity' and licentiousness of certain literary traditions. Erotic poetry which was fine within a circle of connoisseurs was not acceptable in a public medium (cf. 2.2); yet should a whole rich poetic tradition be discarded for this reason?[62] We can identify four kinds of reactions to this problem. In the first instance, the weight of one's saṃskāras was too strong to permit a rejection; thus one made a distinction between public and private tastes and indulged in 'improper' tastes—such as for Braj Bhasa poetry with erotic overtones—only in safe circumstances: this was the case with poet Ayodhyāsiṃh Upādhyāy 'Harioudh', short story writer Viśvambharnāth Kauśikh, and a score of others. This involved only a compartmentalization. Another reaction was that of critic Rāmchandra Śukla, who reinterpreted literary traditions on the basis of the *Zeitgeist* of his age. Each age had a dominant taste, he maintained, erotic courtly poetry had been acceptable in the age of decadent princely states, but now historical circumstances required a different taste. Other 'socially useful' literature of the past would provide a model. A third kind of reaction was that of Nirālā, who tried to accommodate 'improper' and heterogeneous tastes with the argument that moralistic criticism would narrow the scope of literature in a deeply harmful way. A fourth kind of reaction, rather an exceptional one, was that of Premchand, who, much like most Progressive Writers of the 1930s, set little store by the literary saṃskāras of the past.

It is the interplay between inherited family saṃskāras and those each person acquired during his/her particular experience within the shared literary field that accounts, I would argue, for the striking variety of tastes and expressions within the literary sphere, within individual actors, and among audiences. The shared cultural ethos that institutions transmitted, along with the weakening of alternative modes of literary transmission and the polarization between 'high' and commercial literature, palpably altered literary saṃskāras and literary production in the

[62] The dilemma was, of course, not peculiar to Hindi. Debates over 'vulgarity' were crucial to the making of modern literary discourse in most (all?) Indian languages; cf. Ghosh, 'Literature, Language and Print' and Mahapatra 'The Making of a Cultural Identity'.

following generations. Internal differences, of course, remained, but then diversity became of a different kind.

1.2.3. Literary Publics

The diversity of literary genres and traditions present in the overview outlined above attests to the existence of a diversified Hindi reading and listening public. Delineating a reading public is a difficult topic and requires groundwork which, in the case of Hindi, is unfortunately yet to be done. Catalogues of publications and library inventories and records would provide important information on reading publics; we need a study of the circulation and production of manuscripts and comparative research on Hindi and Urdu publications and journals in order to signal reading habits and changing tastes. Works on oral genres need to be integrated into our picture of literary publics, too. Here I can only advance some suggestions on the basis of evidence from the contents of journals, changes in the Hindi book market, and the discussion so far.

The overall expansion in the numbers of journals, of copies printed and of publishers, and the diversification in book production suggest a distinction between traditionally-literate and newly literate publics (cf. below 1.3.2). The traditionally-literate public, comprising mainly pandits, munshis, and literary-minded merchants, was mostly oriented toward poetry, both in Braj Bhasa and Khari Boli, and toward serious journals and scholarly publications. The polemics between supporters of poetry 'within rules', whether in Braj Basa or in Khari Boli, and those of '*svacchand*' (spontaneous) poetry, and between critics and readers of novels, was both a generational one and one of old versus new saṃskāras. In fact, the large numbers of textbooks and of journals and publications directed at juvenile readers signal the emergence of a new literate public, whose saṃskāras were mostly formed by print and who were more eclectic and open to novels, foreign literature, and new literary trends. Familiarity with Braj Bhasa remained, to an extent because of its large presence in the school curriculum (cf. 1.4), but the interest and creative urge clearly lay elsewhere: Mātādīn Śukla, Vinodśaṅkar Vyās, and P.P. Bakhśī can be taken to represent the cream of this young and sophisticated public, who wrote even dialogues in literary Khari Boli and appreciated Chāyāvād. The audience for Chāyāvād is known to have comprised mostly college students (both boys and girls), who might have come into contact with the English Romantics and with Tagore, and who could relate to the intensely personal tone and the invocations to the sublime.[63] The boom in 'social romances' in this period can also be attributed to the emergence of a newly literate public, for whom literature was more an entertainment than a serious cultural or academic pursuit. Romantic or sensational social novels (see 4.3) blended the values of social reform with emotional nurture and excitement in melodramatic plots mostly about love. Section 1.3.2 on Hindi publishing will offer more on the popular readership of Hindi.

A similar expansion of publications specifically aimed at women signals a growth in female readership substantial enough to be considered a special market. Here, again, more study is needed, for data on school attendance by girls cannot be taken as direct evidence, since they represented only a section of women readers, and women's attitudes to reading were severely determined by their husbands' families. Factors like the price of books, physical access to them, and leisure time to read all need to be taken into consideration before we venture into generalizations about women's readership. What cannot be denied is a substantial growth and diversification of material directed at women: apart from educational books, there were the cheap books, booklets, and pamphlets printed in large numbers by the Gita Press of Gorakhpur (est. 1926) and by the Arya Samaj. The hugely successful journal *Chāṁd* (1923) projected the image of a curious, restless, and questioning female readership, eager consumers of political news, social analyses, sophisticated poetry and sensational fiction (cf. 4.2 and 4.3).

The fact that part of the Urdu-literate public was turning to Hindi is signalled by the greater, if short-lived, presence of Urdu in Hindi journals, and by the success of Hindi editions of Urdu poetry.[64] Starting from the early 1920s snippets of Urdu poetry started to figure in Devanagari script on the pages of Hindi journals (e.g. in *Chāṁd* and *Mādhurī*) in the form of 'garlands' or selections of verses, and collections of popular ghazals were printed more often in Devanagari than in the Perso-Arabic script, thus transmitting the taste for Urdu poetry to the wider public of

[63] The intense poems on 'Tum aur maiṁ' (You and me) by Nirālā, Gulāb Rāi, etc. were turned into parodic doggerel by critics, e.g. in 'Tū tū maiṁ maiṁ' [the verse of the parrot] by Rāmcharit Upādhyāy, in *Chāṁd*, IX, pt. 2, 3, July 1931, p. 337.

[64] As a result of the same tendency, writers like Rajinder Singh Bedi, Krishan Chander, Khwaja Ahmad Abbas etc. are considered to be Hindi writers but are generally not included in the syllabus. In the 1960s again Balvant Siṃh used to edit a magazine called *Urdū sāhitya* which published Urdu works in Devanagari.

new Hindi literates. Couplets, *shers*, were part of the cultivated individual's repertoire of verses put to memory to be recited on the right occasions and as such they appear also occasionally in Hindi novels.[65] A single couplet could evoke the whole ethos inherent in Urdu poetry (for example love and disenchantment about the present world), just as the mere use of Braj Bhasa evoked the *nāyak–nāyikā* ethos. At a more popular level, ghazals appeared on records, in popular theatres (e.g. the Kanpur school of Nauṭaṅkī),[66] in films and in the variety programmes that preceded them. This popularity was not enough to secure the literary transmission of Urdu poetry in the Hindi sphere: literary transmission was based upon an extensive knowledge of Persian and Urdu, both excluded from the Hindi literary curriculum, which only included Muslim poets who wrote in Hindi (Avadhi and Braj Bhasa). Witness the gap which continued to exist between the secular and sophisticated audience of Urdu poetry-meetings, the *mushairas*, and the audience of contemporary Hindi kavi sammelans (see 1.3.3).

The unprecedented variety of printed literature in the 1920s conceals another variety, that of literary traditions and ways of transmission. Both reflect the actual expansion of the Hindi reading audiences and of the groups involved in the public sphere. Hindi literature in the early twentieth century was not something first encountered at school, nor was it as clear and well-defined an entity as it is now. Poetry was something heard from other poets, at poetry meetings, and learnt from manuals. Bhajans and religious verses were commonly heard at home, in temples, and at special recitations and performances. Yet poetry was increasingly becoming something one read in journals, libraries, in books and textbooks. Traditional and modern tastes differed so much as to seem mutually exclusive. Yet, although each genre evoked a different ethos and required its peculiar kind of literary participation (*rasāsvādan*, to use the traditional term), writers and readers were eclectic enough to switch—so to speak—between modes of response. This remains partly true even now, though occasions for alternative modes of transmission are fewer.

This account of the Hindi literary sphere, mapping the persistence of different and layered literary tastes in urban and rural audiences, shows nonetheless the emergence of two processes which were to alter the existing picture quite drastically. The first was a realignment of earlier literary styles under the impact of print and the activity of Hindi

[65] E.g. Pāṇḍey Bechan Śarmā Ugra's *Chand hasīnoṁ ke khutūt* (1927).

[66] See Hansen, *Grounds for Play*, Chapter 7.

associations (see 1.3 and 1.4). In the print-media, certain genres, as well as linguistic styles, became prominent, while others became marginal or changed their nature. In journals, genres and styles coexisted, but essays, Khari Boli poems, and short stories became central, while old Braj Bhasa poets become objects of study (classics), and popular forms like seasonal songs almost disappeared (1.3). Saṃskāras connected with print and public self-representation became central and acquired a wider (potentially universal) currency; others did not disappear but remained, so to speak, in the background, in the personal and private rather than the public domain. A similar realignment took place within the audiences; since print circumscribed literature as that which appears in printed form, it also circumscribed the audience more sharply into a literate one, while at the same time declaring itself to be potentially open to all through formal education or self-education. The consequences of this realignment in the transmission, evaluation, and hierarchy of literature will be discussed in the following chapter.[67]

Implied in this process of realignment was in fact a selection and this is the second process. Selection concerned both the literary traditions of the past and the literature of the present; it also demarcated 'high' literature from low-brow *sāṁgīt*, *qissās*, and detective novels (1.3.2 and 1.4). Debates on what constituted the Hindi linguistic and literary tradition and on what modern Hindi language and literature should be like had been an essential feature of Hindi public discourse from the nineteenth century onwards. What was peculiar about the 1920s and 1930s was that such a process of selection was actually carried through by literary scholars in the literary curriculum for schools, at the same time as a vibrant new literature was coming to the fore.

1.3. Arenas of Literature: Journals, the Publishing Industry, and Poetry Meetings

Despite the variety of literary practices, traditions, and tastes outlined so far, it is possible, and indeed legitimate, to speak of a Hindi literary sphere. First, because writers, publicists, and readers perceived it as

[67] As Aijaz Ahmad has argued: 'Because of this privileging of print in a predominantly non-literate society, the social weight in the very process of literary production has shifted towards the leisured class and the professional petty bourgeoisie, away from the alternative modes of preservation and transmission which do not involve print and are then involved also in modes of evaluation rather differently from those of print culture.' Aijaz Ahmad, 'Indian Literature', in *In Theory. Classes, Nations, Literatures*, London, Verso, 1992, pp. 254–5.

such and, second, because the very institutions of the literary sphere, what we call here arenas, threw in their lot together. But what was the nature of the 1920s literary sphere? Writers of this generation, coming from diverse backgrounds and equipped with different degrees of formal education, or none at all, and with varied literary saṃskāras, entered a literary world in which old practices and rules were (at least partly) no more in force, where publicity and commercialization forced them to take up new lifestyles and wonder how they could combine a public role and their actual status, their own tastes and those of the public. This Hindi literary world was itself part of a vernacular public sphere which, though interacting with writing in English and other Indian languages, was mostly sorting out its own public, its own possibilities, its own strengths and weaknesses. How much then was Hindi literature of the 1920s and 1930s shaped by institutional changes in the media of literary production and transmission? And how did literary people take to these changes? I examine here the development of the three main media—journals, books, and poetry meetings (kavi sammelans). In these 'arenas' writers, poets, and scholars made their thoughts and work public, and came face to face with Hindi literati of different tastes and persuasions and with Hindi audiences. The first two media were a direct product of modern print-culture, while poetry meetings were a traditional form of literary entertainment which acquired new dimensions with the spread of nationalism and of Hindi activism.

1.3.1. Journals

It is hard to overestimate the centrality journals acquired in Hindi literary life in these decades. Most, if not all, of the Hindi literature of the 1920s and 1930s appeared first in journals, and the great majority of Hindi writers were, at least partly and at some time in their lives, professional editors. Already nineteenth-century pioneers of Hindi had grasped the importance of journals as a medium to foster the use of Hindi as a public language, to circulate ideas and initiate discussion on matters of social and cultural reform, and to make literature travel beyond the closed circle of connoisseurs-friends to a not-yet-too-clearly defined 'Hindu-Hindi readership'. In fact all writers of Hariśchandra's circle, from Hariśchandra himself in Benares to Bālkṛṣṇa Bhaṭṭ in Allahabad, from Pratāpnārāyaṇ Miśra in Kanpur to Bālmukund Gupta in Calcutta, founded at least one journal. The avowed purpose of these often one-man efforts was not commercial but to 'serve Hindi', yet, despite their high literary quality, they languished for lack of readership since in the nineteenth century a reading public for such publications existed only in Urdu. These early Hindi journals were nonetheless very important as early expressions of a political critique of colonialism, for setting the agenda for Indian patriotism and, significantly, for developing Hindi as a language of supple and argumentative prose and for developing the essay as a pliable genre.[68]

Hindi associations in the late nineteenth century also brought out their own journals, weaving a network of scholars and cultured notables across the whole Hindi area. The most important of them, the *Nāgarī prachāriṇī patrikā* (Benares, 1896 as quarterly, monthly from 1907 to 1920), despite its declared aim of providing a forum for Sabhā members and other Hindi writers to express their opinions, remained a scholarly enterprise. It appeared sporadically, and its very limited circulation mirrored the limited appeal of its activities. The importance of the journal was partly scholarly—essays concerning mostly the pre- or non-Muslim heritage and the scientific and literary traditions of the West were published in Hindi for the first time—but it also had a larger significance. It clearly contributed to the definition of a high register of written Hindi, as its policy statement of 1896 made amply clear:

> Articles, reports, etc., written and published by the Sabha itself will use pure Hindi words, i.e., neither big Sanskrit words nor words from the Arabic and Persian languages. Essays coming to the Sabha for publication from elsewhere will not be accepted by the reviewing committee if they are filled with Persian and Arabic words.[69]

Only at the turn of the century, under Mahāvīr Prasād Dvivedī's editorship (Allahabad, 1903–20), did a commercially viable miscellaneous journal, the *Sarasvatī*, appear in Hindi. Backed by a powerful publisher–owner, Chintamani Ghosh of the Indian Press, *Sarasvatī* single-handedly ushered in a new era in Hindi literature and helped move the centre of Hindi journalism from Calcutta to the United Provinces.[70] Dvivedī set the standard in many ways, and the main features of *Sarasvatī* exemplify the impact of the journal form on Hindi language and literature. First, it was

[68] See Brajratna Dās, *Bhārtendu maṇḍal*, Benares, Sri Kamalmani-Granthamala-Karyalay, 1949. For journals as a discursive sphere in Hariśchandra's time, see the excellent discussion, with numerous examples, in Dalmia, *The Nationalization of Hindu Traditions*, Chapter 5.

[69] Quoted in King, 'The Nagari Pracharini Sabha', p. 318.

[70] See Box 1.1 here.

central to Dvivedī's agenda that a grammatically fixed, standard print language should be unequivocally established. Already Bhārtendu, who claimed to be a 'master' (*āchārya*) of Hindi, had indicated 1873, the year he launched *Hariśchandra's Magazine*, as the beginning of a new era for (Khari Boli) Hindi. But whereas Bhārtendu, an eclectic experimenter, had kept his definition of the print language fairly loose, Dvivedī took a rather more stern and normative view on the matter. The standard language he relentlessly imposed on all contributions to *Sarasvatī* was a high register with regular syntax and word order, elaborate subordinate clauses and a preference for abstract nouns and nominal verbs. The same regular syntax, considered fit for the expression of abstract ideas in an objective manner, was applied to both prose and poetry, while it was left to adjectives to convey sentiment. Second, *Sarasvatī* was a miscellanea of 'useful knowledge' and 'useful literature': it comprised articles and creative pieces on historical and contemporary issues of public interest. At the same time, the choice of subjects and of language revealed Dvivedī's strong opinions about what kind of literature was fit for the times (cf. 2.2): only Khari Boli poetry and short stories on historical or reformist themes were accepted. For example, he commissioned a team of 'Dvivedī poets' to illustrate with poems reproductions of Ravi Varma's historical and mythological paintings; Maithilīśaraṇ Gupta's *Bhārat-bhāratī* can be considered a typical example of the poetry Dvivedī approved of (cf. here 3.1). By exercising such rigid screening and censorship of the material to be published in terms both of language and content, and by reviewing regularly and extensively publications in Hindi, Dvivedī demonstrated the potential of the journal as an *educational* and *standardizing* medium. He was famous for the stinging sarcasm he directed at works that did not meet his standards, and he could be equally harsh against Braj Bhasa poetry and Chāyāvād, which he rejected as 'useless' and harmful to Hindi literature.[71] Dvivedī thus embodied the figure of the editor-arbiter before the figure of the professional critic existed, and used the journal as a means to spread 'standard' norms and values in the Hindi public sphere.

Jayśaṅkar Prasād's venture *Indu* (Benares, 1909–), by contrast, broke new literary ground by introducing Khari Boli and Braj Bhasa poetry that *Sarasvatī* would not publish. Yet its self-consciously sophisticated outlook speaks more of the desire of two 'rasiks' (connoisseurs), Prasād (1889–1937) and Rāykṛṣṇā Dās (1892–1980), to 'publicize' their own

[71] Under the pen-name 'Sukavi kiṃkar', *Sarasvatī*, May 1922.

tastes and the results of their experimentations than of any organized project. The journal brought out a few 'rays', i.e. issues, and then withered. By contrast, when *Mādhurī* came out from Lucknow in July 1922 under the editorship of Dulārelāl Bhārgava, 'adorned with varied topics, related to literature, illustrated' (*vividh viṣay-vibhūṣit, sāhitya-sambandhī, sacitra*), it had immediate impact on the literary sphere. As a competitor said, it 'created a sort of revolution in Hindi journalism . . . until then nobody knew that such a large magazine could be brought out in Hindi'.[72] It was not only a question of size and presentation (it was over a hundred pages long, with plenty of colour plates, several columns, and all the most famous Hindi writers and poets as contributors). *Mādhurī* differed from *Sarasvatī* in one crucial respect: its openness. Without the moralist and reformist mould Mahāvīr Prasād Dvivedī had cast *Sarasvatī* in, without a definite agenda and with a more commercial orientation, it opened its pages to a much greater variety of voices and styles. It tried to reflect contemporary public opinion rather than mould it. In fact, though in outlook *Mādhurī* did not differ substantially from its predecessor,[73] it showed how openness alone made all the difference. *Mādhurī* became the forum for discussion and literary production in Hindi. As had been the case with *Sarasvatī*, essays on literary or topical subjects, mostly by learned contributors, took up half of the journal, along with political news and comments by the editor, fixed columns on literary and general news, short contributions, book reviews, etc. The emphasis was on the wide-ranging nature of the reading material offered, and more on information than on edification. This apparently minor shift brought about a very significant change and allowed *Mādhurī* to become an open venue for different tastes and opinions, from Braj Bhasa to the latest experimentations in Khari Boli. Notes, articles, and contributions by unknown names were welcome. Both renowned scholars and newcomers could tackle the same topics and addressed the same public solely on the strength of their arguments. In this way, both acquired a public voice and a role that transcended their individually defined identities, becoming members of the discursive public sphere; readers were implicitly invited to make up their own minds between the different opinions presented. When the contributor's opinion differed considerably from that of the

[72] Devīdatt Śukla, at the time assistant editor of *Sarasvatī*, admits that his own journal had to increase the number of pages, plates, and columns in order to keep pace. Śukla, *Sampādak ke pacchīs varṣ*, p. 20.

[73] In the introductory statement to the first issue, Dulārelāl Bhārgava acknowledged *Sarasvatī* as his model.

editor, the latter could choose to publish along with it a short note if he considered it worthwhile or exciting reading nonetheless. It was this openness, the variety of the information the journals provided, and their participatory nature that made them the most important supplement or substitute for schools as a source of cultural and political education.

The other great appeal of *Mādhurī* lay in creative writing, mostly poems and short stories, which took up the other half of every issue. Here, again, Bhārgava was more catholic than Mahāvīr Prasād Dvivedī in his tastes. Braj Bhasa poems appeared along with Khari Boli ones, whether by established 'Dvivedī poets', fiery nationalists such as Gayāprasād Śukla Sanehī 'Triśūl' (1883–1972), 'Ek bhārtīy ātmā' (Mākhanlāl Chaturvedī), Lochanprasād Pāṇḍey and others, or by new voices such as Badrīnāth Bhaṭṭ, a very young Bālkṛṣṇa Śarmā 'Navīn' (1897–1960) and Bhagavatīcharaṇ Varmā (1903–81); there were also the controversial Chāyāvādīs: some of Nirālā's first poems, 'Tum aur maiṁ' and 'Adhivās', appeared in early 1923 and Prasād's play *Janmejay Kyā Nāg-yajña* in December 1922. Braj Bhasa poetry featured regularly, not only in scholarly articles and commentaries by the foremost Hindi scholars: an additional column on Braj Bhasa poetry and poets, 'Kavi charchā', started in January 1925, bearing witness to its enduring popularity and the ongoing process of canonization. Short stories, universally acknowledged to be what made journals sell, were practically created as a genre by these journals. *Mādhurī* supported this trend, enlisting regular contributions from authors who had acquired a loyal readership: Premchand, Viśvambharnāth 'Kauśik', and Sudarśan. Indeed, short stories by unknown authors were also readily published, and they were the first contributions to command payment. As a rule, short stories and novels followed different courses of publication. Although at the turn of the century some periodicals appeared carrying only novels in instalments, novels published in journals in the 1920s were surprisingly few. Short stories always appeared in periodicals first, while novels were mostly sold to a publisher, possibly an indication that a distribution system that could ensure continuity of reading was yet underdeveloped.[74]

Journals like *Mādhurī* were thus vital in providing an opening, legitimacy, and publicity for new writers. They also reflect a literary sphere

[74] The only novels *Sarasvatī* serialized were translations from Bengali; *Chāṁd* was more enterprising and serialized among others Premchand's *Nirmalā* (1925–6) and *Pratijñā* (1927), and G. P. Śrivāstava's *Dil kī āg urf diljale kī āh* (publ. 1933). *Sudhā*, Bhārgava's next venture after *Mādhurī*, serialized Vṛndāvanlāl Varmā's *Kundalī cakra*, Kauśik's novel *Mā* (1929) and Nirālā's first novel, *Apsarā* (1930). Among the separate journals publishing novels in instalments and catering to the low-brow

in which variety was accepted and novelty was not only tolerated but encouraged: in this way, the originality and literariness of contemporary Khari Boli poetry were legitimized. At the same time, the taste for Braj Bhasa poetry, though not of the most erotic kind, was also validated in the public arena (cf. 2.2). The team of literary scholars Mahāvīr Prasād Dvivedī had collected around *Sarasvatī* was drawn to the new, more glamorous and financially rewarding journal: among them were the Miśra brothers, Rāmchandra Śukla, Gulābrāī, and occasionally Dvivedī himself. At the same time, *Mādhurī* gave space to the younger generation of poets and graduates like Kṛṣṇadev Prasād Gauṛ (1895–1965), Mātādīn Śukla and Paraśurām Chaturvedī, who sympathized with and defended the new literature. Altogether, they made *Mādhurī* the foremost forum in Hindi for literary discussion.

It was journals, more than public associations, that carried controversies and created news. With literary reviews slowly developing, they also provided an on-line commentary on the literature that was being produced. To writers (and therefore readers) coming from varied schooling experiences and literary saṃskāras, magazines like *Mādhurī* thus provided a common and thorough literary grounding. As we have seen, they were enormously influential in validating and encouraging new tastes while accommodating earlier ones. Finally, it was the growing centrality of journals that shifted the main medium of literary transmission from orality to print. Even poems recited at kavi sammelans acquired a longer lifespan through publication. While earlier poems were recited and *dīvāns* were printed, now journals ensured a more piecemeal and continuous publication in print. In fact, literature in journals had a peculiar semi-permanence. Journals, available privately or in libraries even in rural areas, travelled further and faster than books, but they also disappeared more quickly, since few libraries kept old files; only at times were journals a prelude to a more permanent existence as books, yet literary material in journals aimed at something more than the provision of entertaining reading matter. Beside the declared aim of 'filling the *sthāyī bhaṇḍār* [treasure] of Hindi', they fostered a lively discursive literary sphere, where contributors referred to other contributors and poets responded to other poets in a uniform, public space.

---

market were Kiśorīlāl Gosvāmī's *Upanyās* (1900), Gopālrām Gahmarī's *Jāsūs* (1900), and Devkīnandan Khatrī's *Upanyās lahrī* (1902), still running in the 1920s with an average of 500 copies. See my 'Detective Novels: A Commercial Genre in Nineteenth-century North India', in V. Dalmia and S. Blackburn, eds, *New Literary Histories for South Asia* (forthcoming).

The expansion of journals in the 1920s went hand in hand with their commercialization. A large investment required sales of at least 2000 copies to break even, hence more attention was paid to the technical aspects of advertising and distribution. *Sarasvatī* had counted on the network of government and affiliated schools and public libraries throughout the Gangetic plain, thanks to the excellent rapport between the Indian Press and the Education Department. An expensive enterprise like *Mādhurī* needed both a big initial investment, and especially managerial skills. While the former could be provided by a publishing house or by making the journal a limited company, the latter depended on the new figure of the editor–entrepreneur. *Sarasvatī* belonged to the Indian Press, *Mādhurī* to Nawal Kishore, *Viśāl Bhārat* to the Ramananda Chatterjee group which published *Modern Review* and *Prabasi*. *Chāṁd*, started with private capital, turned into a press and publishing house—Chand Karyalay—and was made into a limited company in 1932. The daily *Āj*, founded by the nationalist millionaire Babu Śivaprasād Gupta through a company, Bharat Samachar Samiti, was said to have incurred a loss of Rs 40,000 in the first year, a loss no lone editor could have faced; it was incorporated with Jnanmandal, Śivaprasād Gupta's publishing house, and converted into a limited company in 1940.[75] Dulārelāl Bhārgava and Rāmrakh Siṃh Sahgal of Chand Press were representatives of the new wave of editors who had managerial flair. Dulārelāl Bhārgava in fact provides the best example of a literary entrepreneur in this period: with *Mādhurī* he created a new sense of competition among Hindi monthlies by loud self-publicity, by continuously increasing the number of pages, columns and illustrations, improving paper quality, and offering extra features like special issues: in a word, by making continuous innovation a value. Other journals had to follow suit in order to remain competitive, and the old one-man ventures could hardly afford it. Further, enterprising editors such as Dulārelāl Bhārgava and Rāmrakh Sahgal tried to increase distribution by employing local sales representatives and by distributing their journals at railway stalls through an agreement with A.H. Wheelers, the bookseller. They also fostered a strong emotional link

[75] B.V. Parāṛkar (1880–1955), the editor of *Āj*, remarked in his presidential speech at the first Editors' Conference at the 16th Hindī Sāhitya Sammelan meeting in Brindaban in 1925 that the time of the owner–editor was gone. Though the need for capital inevitably narrowed down the editor's freedom, 'progress can only happen through commercial means. . . . Now capitalists [invest] out of patriotism or indirect interest, later when success comes they will invest out of interest, and it will be a tough time for editors and for the independence of news'; quoted in *Sammelan patrikā*, XIII, 4–5, 1925, p. 237. See Viśvanāth Prasād, 'Jñānmaṇḍal', n.d.

with their readership through aggressive self-publicity in the pages of their own journals. One peculiar form of self-publicity Bhārgava introduced (and Sahgal took up) was the regular publication of appraising comments (*sammati*) on the journal and its publications by leading literary people, other journals, and noted personalities.[76] Advertising was also actively pursued, generally at the front and the back: *Mādhurī, Sudhā, Chāṁd, Sarasvatī*, and *Āj* carried several pages of advertisements for small consumer items, testifying to the fact that the vernacular public had started to be acknowledged as a consumer market (Illustration 1.1).

Another factor in the greater commercial viability of journals in the 1920s was the symbiosis between periodical and 'stable' (*sthāyī*) literature. *Sarasvatī* once again had shown the way and most of the important

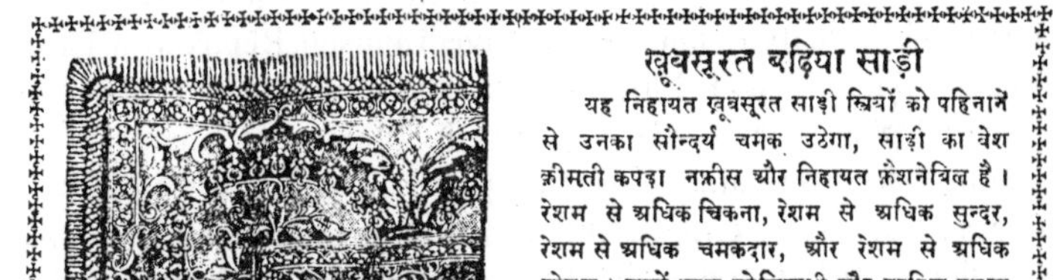

Illustration 1.1

Hindi periodicals followed suit. Journals were either launched by book-publishing houses or else their publishers branched out into book publishing themselves. The symbiosis between periodical and 'stable' literature is easily explained: books enhanced and confirmed the success

[76] See advertisements in the second issue.

of poems, short stories, or novels already familiar to the public through journals. They also multiplied the profit, since the same material could be used twice—and with no additional cost when the editor–publisher bought the rights of the work, as Dulārelāl Bhārgava did. Journals meant publicity, since they could carry large advertisements for the books published by the publishing house (Dulārelāl Bhārgava even had his own book praised in his own magazine!), and both journals and books could use the same channels of distribution. The habit of subscribing to a journal or a publisher, becoming a *sthāyī grāhak*, was strongly encouraged: beside creating a sentimental link between the publisher and the reader, it provided financial security to the former and concessional rates to the latter.

Journals and publishing departments could share not only the material, but also manpower, thus creating the first professional class of salaried intellectuals in Hindi. After Dvivedī himself, Rūpnārāyaṇ Pāṇḍey, Śivpūjan Sahāy (1893–1963), Navjādiklāl Śrīvastava (1888–1939), Devīdatt Śukla, Banārsīdās Chaturvedī, Mākhanlāl Chaturvedī and Mātādīn Śukla were among the first professional literary editors.[77] To take *Sarasvatī* as an example, M.P. Dvivedī worked also as literary advisor to the publisher, suggesting titles, writers and employees, and was the first ever Hindi editor to receive a pension from his employers. Later, Devīdatt Śukla, who joined the Literature Department of the Indian Press in 1918, was asked to assist in editing the house's children's journal *Bālsakhā*, read the proofs of *Sarasvatī*, and translate articles for it as well as several books for the Indian Press. Premchand, who in 1927 was offered the editorship of *Mādhurī* by Babu Biṣṇunārāyaṇ Bhārgava (at Rs 200 per month, the highest pay for an editor at the time), was entrusted as well 'with the task not only of preparing textbooks for the Nawal Kishore Press but also of getting them prescribed in syllabi, and . . . had to do a lot of travelling, to Benares or to Kanpur, to Patna or to Naini Tal'. In 1931 he was moved to another branch of the publishing house, the Book Depot.[78] Journals required both stable, salaried staff who sat in the office and occasional or fixed contributors who sent in their work by post and came to the office for occasional meetings. Dulārelāl Bhārgava in particular introduced the practice of regularly paying contributors and for the first time allowed writers to think that they might actually earn a living

[77] See biographies in the Appendix.

[78] See Amrit Rai, *Premchand: A Life*, Delhi, Oxford University Press, 1991, pp. 230 and 266.

from freelance writing. In practice, the question of monetary remuneration remained a thorny one. Only large journals could afford salaried staff and paid contributors; and actually, most occasional writers were content to see their articles in print (Illustration 1.2). Besides, demanding money for *sāhitya-sevā*, service to literature, could appear improper. Throughout his life, Jayśaṅkar Prasād considered that payment for any of his writings defiled his pure devotion to Sarasvati, the goddess of learning. Poems were not paid 'by column' like the rest, 'They have no price and cannot be paid by page,' cunningly argued D. Bhārgava in an editorial note, and concluded laconically: 'कविता पर पारिश्रमिक देना एक जटिल समस्या है' (to reward a poem is a complex matter).[79]

On the other hand, for the new impecunious Hindi intelligentsia writing had become a means of survival, however meagre and however tinted

Illustration 1.2. The poor editor is surrounded by what are now clearly recognizable as 'writer types'. 'Print our essays, which usher in a new age', they say, 'I've got a cupboard full of them and I'm going mad', is his reply.

Source: *Mādhurī*, III, pt. 1, 5, December 1924, p. 663.

[79] *Mādhurī*, II, pt. 1, 4, November 1923, p. 512.

with nationalist passion. Poor remuneration jeopardized the possibility of maintaining a dignified living standard adequate to the public status of a 'writer' (cf. 2.3).[80] Journals attracted Hindi literati, whether as stable staff or as occasional contributors, and tended to shift the centre of literary production from villages and courts to towns. They also induced a shift in literary training and recognition: the editor became the *ustād* or *guru* who passed or failed one as a writer; to have published in *Sarasvatī, Mādhurī, Prabhā,* etc. became the mark of recognition. Editors' offices became symbols of this shift and of the poignant ambiguity between literary work as *sevā* (i.e. dedicated service) or as *naukrī* (clerical work). The 'professional' atmosphere of the office could feel unpleasantly impersonal for the traditional literary person: in 1923 Śivpūjan Sahāy left the Matvālā office in Calcutta, where the atmosphere was congenial but the pay insignificant, to go and work for Dulārelāl Bhārgava's *Mādhurī* for much higher remuneration. Yet the business-like atmosphere was so disturbing that he quit shortly after and went back to Matvālā.[81] When Kiśorīdās Vājpeyī, already well-known as a grammarian, decided to quit teaching and work 'among the gods' (i.e. among editors), he was appalled by the office-like (*daftarī*) reception at *Sudhā*'s office and left immediately. The working atmosphere at Chand Karyalay, though equally 'European' and professional, was tempered by the familial and protective attitude Sahgal and his wife had towards the staff.[82] The complete trust Chintamani Ghosh (and later his son Harikeshav Ghosh) had in Mahāvīr Prasād Dvivedī is well known. Dvivedī, always very sensitive about hierarchy, was deeply moved, since this trust concealed the fact that Dvivedī was only an employee; he termed the publishers' attitude towards him as one of personal *kṛpā* (favour). Devīdatt Śukla, who worked at the Indian Press for 26 years, from 1919 to 1945,

[80] Once questioned by Banārsīdās Chaturvedī on the subject in 1930, Premchand replied that to that time, writing (130 stories and seven novels between 1921 and 1932) had earned him from Rs 50 to Rs 80 a month—a meagre sum for the best and most popular Hindi fiction writer; quoted in Robert O. Swan *Munshi Premchand of Lamhi Village,* Durham, Duke University Press, 1969, p. 28. This conclusion has been questioned by later critics, who point to Premchand's liberality and disastrous management of his press as the causes of his financial problems.

[81] Rāmvilās Śarmā, *Nirālā kī sāhitya sādhnā,* vol. 1, p. 83.

[82] Devīdatt Śukla recalls the awe the first glimpse of the Indian Press office inspired in him; *Sampādak ke pacchīs varṣ*, p. 9. In fact, his experience is fairly indicative of that of a Hindi literary publicist; see biography in the Appendix. See also Kiśorīdās Vājpeyī, *Sāhityik jīvan aur saṃsmaraṇ,* Kankhal, Himalay Agency, 1953, pp. 8–13.

recalled his joyful surprise at finding that the publishers behaved towards employees more like family elders than masters.[83]

BOX 1.1

The Hindi Political Press

The expansion of miscellaneous journals and of the reading public must be set in the context of the general expansion and growth of the Hindi press, especially the political weeklies and dailies. While Urdu newspapers flourished in the nineteenth century, the only Hindi daily launched in the North Western Provinces was more the result of an experiment than of existing demand (*Hindosthan*, 1883). The concentration of Marwari capital and of Bengali publishing made Calcutta an early centre of the Hindi press and attracted a sizable community of 'expatriate' Hindi literary people with a high turnover. Here emerged some successful political weeklies, and the first dailies with World War I: *Bhāratmitra* (weekly, 1878, then daily), *Hindī baṅgvāsī* (1890), *Calcutta samāchār* (daily, 1914–18), *Viśvamitra* (daily, 1916), *Svatantra* (daily, 1920–30), with eminent editors like Bālmukund Gupta, Lakṣmīnārāyaṇ Garde, Ambikāprasād Vājpeyī, and B.V. Parāṛkar. In north India, the torch-bearers were *Hindī pradīp* (1877–1910) in Allahabad and *Bhārat jīvan* (weekly, 1884) in Benares.

But it was only between 1910 and 1920 that political weeklies, and dailies after 1920, grew in every town into real focuses of political activity, and often of factionalism, attracting activists and writers. Among them were: in Allahabad *Abhyuday* (weekly, 1907) and *Maryādā* (monthly, 1910–21, ca. 1500 copies) launched by M.M. Mālavīya; later the radical *Bhaviṣya* (1919, daily in 1920, ed. Sundarlāl), soon forced to close down, and the weekly *Bhārat* (1928, daily in 1933) edited by V.N, Tivārī for the Leader Press. In Kanpur G.Ś. Vidyārthī's *Pratāp* (weekly, 1913, daily during World War I and after 1920) and *Prabhā* (monthly, 1920, 3000 copies in 1921), and the dailies *Vartamān* (1920, ed. R. Avasthī) and *Ādarś* (1921, 4000 co. in 1921) acquired a popular edge, as did *Sainik* (ed. K.D. Pālīvāl, weekly 1925, daily 1935) in Agra. Benares grew into a centre of the nationalist press with *Āj* (daily, 1920, ed. B.V. Parāṛkar), *Jāgaraṇ* (weekly, 1929), and *Haṃs* (monthly, 1930, both

[83] D. Śukla, *Sampādak ke pacchīs varṣ*, p. 10.

ed. Premchand). In Lucknow, Hindi dailies emerged only after the Hindu–Muslim riot of 1924. *Ārtī* (1924) and *Ānand* (1924) eroded the common readership of the Urdu *Hamdam*;[84] in Delhi and the Punjab Hindi newspapers like the short-lived *Dainik Vijay* (daily 1918, 7000 copies), *Arjun* (daily, 1923), and *Navyug* (1931) were run by Ārya Samājists, often from Gurukul Kangri. Other locally important nationalist newspapers were active in Almora (*Śakti*, 1918), Garhwal (*Viśāl Kīrti*), Hathras (*Bhārat bandhu*), and Gorakhpur (*Svadeś*, 1919, ed. D.P. Dvivedī); in the Central Provinces there were *Karmavīr* (1924) in Jabalpur, the Gandhian *Tyāgbhūmi* (1927) in Ajmer; in Bihar *Bihār bandhu* (1874), *Paṭaliputra* (1920), and the socialist *Jantā* (1937).[85] Table 1.1 list important periodicals in UP between 1921 and 1937.

Table 1.1. Important periodicals in UP, 1921–1937

		1921	1926	1930	1935	1937	price p.a. Rs annas
English							
Independent	D	4000	–	–	–	–	
Leader	D	3600	7500	14,000	15,000	14,500	20.0
Pioneer	D	7000	16,000	12,000	8,500	19,000	24.0
Urdu							
Hamdam	D	4500	2000	2500	5000	1000	18.0
Medina	Bi-weekly	12,500[a]	6000	6500	7500	8000	6.0
Zamana	M	2000	1600	1500	500	1000	5.0
Hindi							
Abhyuday	W	6000	3000	3000	2500	6000	3.8
Āj	D	2000	3000	5000	5000	6000	12.0
Bhārat	Bi-weekly	–	–	9000	5500	5000	20.0
Bhaviṣya	W	2000	–	11,000	–	–	
Chāṁd	M	–	6000	15,000	6,500	5000	6.8
Haṃs	M	–	–	1500	2000	1000	6.0
Hindī kesarī	W	3600	700	3000	5000	300	2.4

[84] See *Mādhurī*, III, pt. 1, 4, November 1924, p. 571.

[85] Bibliography: in English only R.R. Bhatnagar's informative but unwieldy *The Rise and Growth of Hindi Journalism* (Allahabad, 1951) is available; in Hindi, K.B. Miśra, *Hindī patrakāritā* (1968) is valuable for Calcutta journalism; Brahmānand's *Bhārtīy svatantratā āndolan aur uttar pradeś kī hindī patrakāritā* (1986) is a comprehensive survey and a history of the nationalist movement through the Hindi press. Comparative charts on subscriptions to and numbers of Hindi and Urdu newspapers are available in Bhatnagar, *The Rise and Growth*, pp. 368 ff.

Mādhurī	M	–	6000	4000	2000	2000	6.8
Pratāp	W	9000	7500	16,000	14,000	1000	3.6
	D			5000	12,000	1000	10.0
Sainik	W	–	1000	4500	7000	5000	3.00
Sarasvatī	M	4000	3200	3500	2500	5000	6.8
Śakti	W	1000	1500	–	1000	1200	2.8
Sudhā	M	–	–	7200[b]	2000	2000	12.0
Svadeś	W	3500	1200	–	–	–	
Vartamān	D	8000[a]	2500	4000	4000	2500	12.0

[a]1922 [b]1928
Source: 'Statement of Newspapers and Periodicals published in the UP' (Government Press, Allahabad) for the relevant years.

Part of the political press expanded by lowering prices and increasing sales. In a general shift from being journals of ideas to journals of news, Hindi newspapers widened their appeal and paid more attention to the popular public of Hindi. This is what G.Ś. Vidyārthī's *Pratāp* and B.V. Parāṛkar's *Āj* did: they gave voice to local concerns through a network of local stringers rather than relying on English news agencies. This important move contributed substantially to opening and widening the Hindi public sphere (cf. 5.1) and showed an awareness that the Hindi public was intrinsically different from the more elite English one. In the editors' eyes, it was also more genuine: the lives of Hindi readers were 'true', those of English-educated Indians were 'artificial'. 'Hindi newspapers ought to mirror their lives instead of aping English papers,' argued Parāṛkar, who in his daily *Āj* did just that:

हमारे पाठक किन-किन श्रेणी के हैं उनकी रहन-सहन कैसी है उनकी जीविका के साधन क्या हैं उनको जीवन-संग्राम के किन-किन कठिनाइयों से सामना करना पड़ता है उनका आमोद-प्रमोद क्या है उनकी रुचि कैसी है वे क्या सोचते हैं और क्या चाहते हैं इन बातों का हम सम्पादकों को बिल्कुल पता नहीं रहता। . . . इन बातों का हम पता लगाया करें लोगों को वही समाचार दें जो वे चाहते हैं और उनके जीवन-संग्राम में सहायक बनने का प्रयत्न करें तो हमारे पत्रों का प्रचार देखते-देखते बढ़ जायगा। . . . हम जब तक साधारण समाज को न अपनाएंगे और अपने पत्रों को उसके प्रतिबिम्ब न बना सकेंगे तब तक न हमारी उन्नति ही होगी और न हम प्रकृत देश की सेवा कर सकेंगे।

We [Hindi] editors completely ignore facts like what classes our readers belong to, how they live, how they earn their living, what are the difficulties they face in the battlefield of life, how they enjoy themselves, what are their interests, and what they want. If we found out about them and gave our

> readers the news they want, and if we turned ourselves into their helpers in the struggle for life, our newspapers would become more popular in no time at all. . . . Until we adopt the common folk and we turn our newspapers into reflection of them we shall not progress and serve the real [*prakṛt*, as opposed to *kṛtrim*] nation.[86]

The expansion of Hindi journalism and publishing after 1920 marked the coming of age of a modern Hindi literary industry concentrated in a few big towns; at the same time, it created a *unified literary space* through a network of distant contributors and regional distribution. Thanks to the growing interest in news generated by World War I and by the first nationalist mass campaign, Hindi journals and the political press reached beyond the pale of the highly literate and formally schooled public; through periodicals and print language, this more mixed reading public received a common cultural and political education. At the same time, journals became more open to the diversity of tastes and voices present in the Hindi literary sphere and became show-cases for contemporary writing. In fact, whether monthlies, weeklies or dailies, whether political or social or religious in inclination, all Hindi periodicals of this period featured literature in some form. This helped popularize the names of contemporary writers and highlight the social relevance of literature. Although not a highly remunerative or secure job, journalism became an important avenue for nationalist-minded Hindi intellectuals, and possibly the only source of remuneration for the first professional writers.

The growth of big literary magazines in the 1920s should not lead us to conclude that small or one-man journals disappeared from Hindi journalism; indeed, quite the contrary. The fact that there is hardly a writer of the period who did not contribute to or to launch a magazine, and the host of small-to-medium-sized journals which printed between 500 and 2000 copies in provincial towns like Mirzapur, Etawah, Gorakhpur, Khandwa, Jabalpur, Indore, and Ajmer, bear witness to the fact that publicity had multiplied and that there was finally a real Hindi-reading public (Illustration 1.3). Although larger ventures set the pace, scholarly, local, or one-man journals survived to provide local venues for expression—often at great financial cost for the editor–owner.[87] The overall

[86] B.V. Parāṛkar, Speech at the Sampādak Sammelan, *Sammelan patrikā*, XIII, 4–5, pp. 233, 235.

[87] Premchand's well-known financial troubles in running *Haṃs* and *Jāgaraṇ*

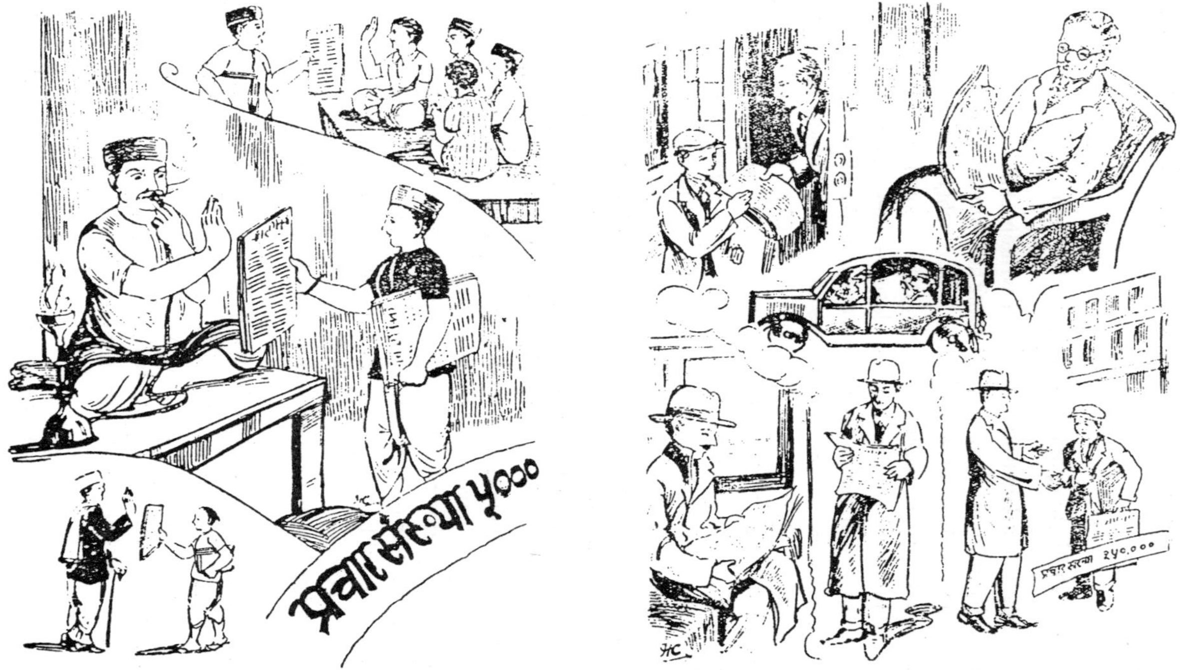

Illustration 1.3. 'Even coachmen in England read newspapers', complained the Hindi press. Here the contrast between indifferent Indians and eager readers abroad is supported by publication figures: 5000 copies are considered a success in India, while 150,000 are commonplace abroad.

Source: *Chāṁd*, XVI, pt. 2, 6, May 1939.

spectacular growth of the Hindi press in this period shows the tremendous importance attached to the medium. At this important historical juncture it was journalism that made Hindi writers aware of their public voice and authority.

1.3.2. Publishing and the Literary System

The history of publishing in Hindi still waits to be written. Only a handful of monographs exist on some important publishing houses in north India, and although valuable in themselves they cannot shed light on the many questions connected to print, reading, and writing. Accounts of nineteenth-century Hindi literature, for example, describe these publishers as heroic, public-minded pioneers, but what is one to make of the quick spread of printing presses even in small towns all over north India between the 1820s and 1840s? What did they print? As Chris Bayly has observed, what is striking about printing in India is not (only) that it spread so late, when the technology was long known to Europeans in their coastal enclaves, but that it suddenly spread so rapidly between 1820 and 1840, and not only at the hands of the modernizing elites.[88] Was publishing seen as a commercial business after all? Who were the professional printers? Can they be distinguished from the publishers? What we need is a study of publishing as an industry and as a market. Such a study, I will argue here, would shed a different light on the literary system as a whole, for even oral genres got printed, in fact got printed first. Literary histories, by contrast, have so far included only texts and authors of an either educational or reformist character. What about cheap, popular publications? The question of distribution and sales is still unexplored, and we have little idea of how books, collections of poems, and stories circulated. This, together with an eye for the different prices of books and chapbooks, would in turn help us understand the audience such publications catered to.

A study of Hindi publishing would necessarily have to be one of Hindi *and* Urdu publishing, for they were part of an osmotic literary system. They had different traditions, of course, partly reflected in their different publics divided by education and script, but these in fact had to interface in the new world of print. Not only did linguistic allegiance shift from the

---

indicate both the need for commercial acumen and the writer's resilient dream of having his own magazine, his own platform to speak from.

[88] Bayly, *Empire and Information*, pp. 238 ff.

mid-nineteenth century onwards, translations (or, rather, transliterations) from one language to the other were readily undertaken whenever it was felt that there was a market on the other side.[89] Finally, certain genres, especially of fiction, like detective, social and historical novels, first took root in Urdu and later caught on in Hindi;[90] others, like the booklets of *ghazals* printed in great numbers and with large print-runs were, by the 1930s, published almost exclusively in Nagari script.[91] The number and print-runs of Urdu literary publications declined significantly by 1935 (see Table 1.2): literary and miscellaneous publications continued to appear but the popular market definitely belonged to Hindi. Should we deduce that elementary literacy, along with elementary education, switched script, or that we have here two different publics?

From 1868 onwards provincial education departments started compiling lists of publications, in English and Indian languages, registered according to the Registration Act of 1867. These catalogues, preserved in the Oriental and India Office Collections of the British Library in London, make wonderful sources; they have been used by some scholars in recent years[92] and they are the basis of my observations here. Christopher King has used them to write about patterns of publishing, but while

Table 1.2. Urdu publications in UP, 1915–1940

		1915	1920	1925	1930	1935	1940
Fiction[a]	titles	52	56	93	56	19	19
	copies	63,300	53,250	138,400	47,900	16,300	13,500
poetry	titles	78	104	143	166	64	31
	copies	79,700	96,000	126,500	200,900	68,000	31,400
education	titles	80	45	90	110	74	43
	copies	119,500	178,400	72,500	113,350	66,100	71,200
overall titles		334	331	472	556	306	203

[a]Fiction and drama.

[89] Thus, *qissās* were printed in Hindi from the 1860s; the Purāṇas, Rāmāyaṇa versions and compilations, Devkīnandan Khatrī's *Chandrakāntā* (published by his son in both Hindi and Urdu) and textbooks were also printed in Urdu; *Statement of Particulars Regarding Books and Periodicals Published in the United Provinces of Agra and Oudh,* quarter ending on March 1915.

[90] E.g. social novels by Pyārelāl, Ratannāth Dar, and Śambhu Dayāl Saxenā appeared in Urdu from (at least) 1914, while they caught on in Hindi a decade later; ibid.

[91] See *Statement of Particulars Regarding Books and Periodicals Published in the United Provinces of Agra and Oudh* for the year 1935.

[92] Frances Pritchett, *Marvelous Encounters. Folk Romance in Urdu and Hindi,*

his tables show the overall numbers of copies, I have indicated the number of titles and of copies only in the case of those genres relevant to an assessment of the reading public: fiction, drama, poetry, and educational books (Tables 1.2 and 1.3).

The situation in the 1870s in Oudh may serve as a point of comparison: while Urdu was then definitely the lingua franca of publishing and Persian was still a relevant language, Hindi publications were limited in number and range. They comprised religious books (Rāmāyaṇa, *Sūr Sāgar, Prem Sāgar, Hanumān chālīsa*, etc.), a few textbooks and educational books, almanacs and the odd Nagari version of well-known *qissās* (stories).[93] Data from the Benares region would probably provide a somewhat different picture, but it is evident that publications in Urdu, and indeed in Persian, were more eclectic in nature: they included Hindu, Muslim and Christian religious texts, translations of Persian histories and literary texts used for educational purposes, literary works, Urdu ghazals, books of useful knowledge, and translations of government laws.[94] By the turn of the century, small religious publishers in Hindi had cropped up almost everywhere, often at pilgrimage centres, producing devotional and ritual texts of low printing quality in huge numbers.[95] Benares and Calcutta were the main centres for religious books of all kinds and for popular publications.[96]

Delhi, Manohar, 1985; King, *One Language, Two Scripts*; Ghosh, 'Literature, Language and Print'; Priya Joshi, 'Culture and Consumption: Fiction, the Reading Public, and the British Novel in Colonial India', *Book History,* 1, 1, 1998.

[93] *Catalogue of Books printed in Oudh during the quarter* . . ., for the years 1873 and 1874.

[94] Famously, it was the profitable monopoly on the publication in Urdu of the Indian Penal Code (*Tazkirāt-i Hind*) in 1861 that started the fortune of Munshi Nawal Kishore; 30,000 copies were printed and purchased by the government at Rs 3 per copy, which Nawal Kishore set aside for scholary publications in Persian, Arabic, and Urdu; Syed Jalaluddin Haider, 'Munshi Nawal Kishore (1836–95). Mirror of Urdu Printing in British India', *Libri,* XXXI, 3, September 1987, p. 232.

[95] Ved Sansthan, Ajmer was the main centre for Ārya Samāj publications, while Brahmanand Ashram in Pushkar sold millions of copies of its *Brahmānand bhajanmālā,* and the Ramakrishna Mission in Nagpur published Ramakrishna and Vivekananda literature. Other centres in U.P. were Mathura (with Shiksha Bharati, Shyamkashi Press, etc.), Gorakhpur (Gita Press) and Benares—which had a tradition of both Sanskrit and Hindi publishing. In Bombay Khemrāj Śrīkṛṣṇadās had the greatest stock of religious titles, followed by the Nirnay Sagar Press and Vipul Trust. Most of this information is drawn from K. Berī, 'Hindī prakāśan kā itihās', typewritten article by courtesy of the author, n.d., pp. 16 ff.

[96] E.g. Mahāvīr Prasād Poddār's Hindi Pustak Agency, Mūlchand Agravāl's

Table 1.3. Hindi publications in UP 1915–1940

		1915	1920	1925	1930	1935	1940
Fiction[a]	titles	105	119	186	169	283	184
	copies	149,000	173,200	287,900	253,700	480,200	241,400
Poetry	titles	371	338	585	1014	1048	650
	copies	674,400	613,600	1,146,600	2,506,600	2,281,750	877,900
Education	titles	127	141	176	342	257	211
	copies	314,700	625,600	646,200	871,600	514,850	540,100
Overall titles		870	939	1365	2039	2095	1548

[a] Fiction and Drama.

Table 1.4. Overall numbers of titles published in UP, 1915–1940

	1915	1920	1925	1930	1935	1940
Urdu	334	331	472	556	306	209
Hindi	870	939	1365	2039	2095	1548
English	164	137	301	289	313	230
Polyglot	469	271	401	447	518	218
Sanskrit	73	51	84	92	153	86
Persian	2	ca. 7	16	8	6	–
Arabic	4	–	7	–	3	2

Source: 'Statement of Particulars Regarding Books and Periodicals Published in the United Provinces of Agra and Oudh', for the relevant years.

It was in fact religious books and the profitable and growing market for textbooks that made the fortune of the first big publishers in Hindi such as Nawal Kishore (1858) in Lucknow, Khadgvilas Press in Bankipur (Patna, 1880) and the Indian Press in Allahabad (1884).[97] The case of the Indian Press well exemplifies the nature of Hindi publishing at the

Popular Trading Co., Nihalchand Berī's Nihalchand & Co. and the Narsingha Press published both religious and popular publications. Several Hindi publishers, like Nihalchand Berī and R.S. Varman, fluctuated between Calcutta and Benares; ibid.

[97] The Nawal Kishore Press, the largest early publisher in the United Provinces, published mostly Urdu books, translations of religious books (Quran, Upaniṣads, Purāṇas) and Hindi translations of Persian and Urdu romances. The Khadgvilas Press of Bankipur, near Patna, was the pioneering literary publisher in Bihar; it published Bhārtendu's books, the earliest translations of Bengali novels and theatre chapbooks of *Mudrārākṣasa* and *Satya Hariśchandra* 'which sold by tens of thousands'; Kṛṣṇachandra Berī, *Hindī prakāśan kā itihās*, p. 4. Information on the Indian Press comes from Mushtaq Ali, 'Hindī sāhitya ke itihās meṁ ilāhābād kā yogdān'.

turn of the century. Its founder, Babu Chintamani Ghosh (1854–1928), a Bengali, was a self-made man, a pioneering editor, and a patriotic reformer in the spirit of the times. He realized the potential of educational publishing, and thanks to his contacts in the education department and to the literary expertise and skills of Mahāvīr Prasād Dvivedī and Śyāmsundar Dās, he became the foremost publisher in north India for school textbooks, anthologies, readers, biographies, and other reading books for schoolchildren in English and Hindi.[98] The literature department published almost exclusively translations from Bengali: contemporary Hindi literature was practically absent.[99] However, the Indian Press was crucial in establishing high printing standards for Hindi publications. Chintamani Babu was particularly fond of character-building biographies (43 titles between 1909 and 1940), 'useful literature', religious books for both adults and children and quality illustrations.[100]

The view from the bazaar gives a different and more composite picture. After all, in both Hindi and Urdu entertaining publications outnumbered educational ones. As the 1920s marked a big change, it will be

[98] In fact, thanks to Śyāmsundar Dās, the Indian Press struck a very advantageous deal to publish educational books prepared by the Nāgarī Prachāriṇī Sabhā; in 1928 it entered an agreement with the Sabhā to print all its publications, and a special branch of the Press was opened in Benares to deal with the work. The agreement lasted until 1940, when the Sabhā revoked it, suspecting mismanagement of funds by Śyāmsundar Dās. Publications included all the Sabhā series: the 'popular' Manorañjan pustak-mālā, the historical Devīprasād-aitihāsik-pustak-mālā and Sūryakumārī pustak-mālā, the Nāgarī-prachāriṇī-granthamālā for critical editions of Hindi 'classics', and the dictionary *Hindī śabdasāgar*; Ali, 'Hindī sāhitya ke itihās meṁ', pp. 442 ff. See also Dās, *Merī ātmakahānī*.

[99] Translations of Bankimchandra, Tagore, R.C. Dutt, Charu Chandra, Prabhat Kumar Mukhopadhyay, Sharatchandra, etc. were done mostly by employees of the Press such as Janārdan Jhā, Lallīprasād Pāṇḍey, and Rūpnārāyaṇ Pāṇḍey, the most prolific of all. In order to understand the stature of the Indian Press, it suffices to note that it was Tagore's publisher until he retrieved the rights for his own press at Santiniketan, and it published Ramanand Chatterjee's *Prabāsī* and *Modern Review* until Chatterjee moved back to Calcutta. For a complete list of publications and a history of the press, see Mushtaq Ali, ibid. For a list of English and Bengali novels translated into Hindi, see Gopāl Ray, *Hindī-upanyās-koś*, Patna, Grantha Niketan, vol. 1, pp. 362 ff.

[100] The large illustrated edition of the *Hindī Mahābhārata* (transl. from Bengali by Mahāvīr Prasād Dvivedī, 1908) became a prized household book. In the *Bālsakhā pustak-mālā* (a series of children's books), *Mahābhārata, Bhagavadgītā, Śrīmad Bhāgavat* for children were also published; *Bāl Rāmāyaṇa*, reprinted in a new edition in 1920 at 8 annas, sold 12,000 copies in one year.

useful to start from 1915. By then Hindi had already overtaken Urdu for numbers of publications and copies, and Urdu seems no longer to have been considered a vehicle for Persian, as the decline of bilingual publications shows. Yet Urdu publishing was still growing, and was a more eclectic field than Hindi, with significant numbers of new titles and genres and of books of non-fiction on various subjects. It reflects a 'mature' reading public that sustained a literary publishing market, took an interest in political affairs, and was not averse to novelty in poetry and fiction. A closer look at Hindi publications shows, first of all, that the categories of classification need to be questioned: for example, dramatic stories in verse and prose, *sāṁgīt*, were classified sometimes as drama, sometimes as verse, and sometimes as fiction. When we collapse these categories, we see that the *market* for publications in 1915 was made up of about 50 per cent of short collections of songs, bhajans, and retellings of the Rama and Krishna stories; 30 per cent of sāṁgīt (verse ballads and dramas), qissā, and Ālhā, tales in verse, ballad, or dramatic form; about 10 per cent of the early fictional spin-offs of these verse creations and of the commercial novels of Devkīnandan Khatrī and Kiśorīlāl Gosvāmī (cf. 3.2), and the last 10 per cent of secular poems in Braj Bhasa and Khari Boli: seasonal songs such as *phāg, chaitī, kajlī, bārahmāsā, jhūlanā*, compositions in the well-known metres and forms of the rīti tradition, *savaiyā, kavitta* (classified as 'erotic'), and ghazal, qawwali, *chappaī*. Selling for a few annas, sometimes for a few paise, these books were printed throughout the region and show that it was largely the oral genres of songs and story-telling, catering to well-established tastes and requiring only elementary literacy and limited literary saṃskāras, that constituted the literary market.[101] Publishers of all these genres were in fact confident enough in their audience to run editions of one or two thousand copies—even in the case of unknown authors; yet these are totally absent

[101] E.g. the twelve-page *Baṛā gopāl gārī*, on the marriages of Ram and Krishna, published by Baijnāth Prasād at the Shri Lakshmi Venkateshvar Steam Press in 15000 copies for 3 paise each was constantly reprinted until at least 1940. The same publisher also printed religious chapbooks (15,000 copies of a collection of Krishna *līlā* were printed), *lāvanī*, qissā, and was based in Benares and Darbhanga. A rough count of Hindi publishers, booksellers and printers mentioned in the 1915 and 1920 *Catalogues for U.P. and Bihar* gives a number of ca. 250, with the greatest concentration in Benares (31), and others spread over Agra, Aligarh, Hathras, Allahabad, Bareilly, Bijnor, Brindaban, Bulandshahr, Dehra Dun, Etawah, Faizabad, Farrukhabad, Gorakhpur, Jhansi, Kanpur, Lakhimpur, Lucknow, Mainpuri, Meerut, Moradabad, Mathura, Bhagalpur, Chapra, Darbhanga, Gaya, Muzaffarpur, Patna-Bankipur, and Ranchi.

from literary histories. By contrast, the few publications of the 'serious' authors who, like Śrīdhar Pāṭhak and Maithilīśaraṇ Gupta, made it into literary histories appeared few and far between. Generally speaking, although original works in Hindi had the same print-run (of 1000–2000) as the genres mentioned above, they were more expensive; on the other hand, novels running along well-tested tracks cost 4–8 annas, and qissās 1 anna or even less.[102] Thus a second or third edition was crucial in bringing the price down: this was Maithilīśaraṇ Gupta's fortune, for example, for his historical–mythological poems did find an audience and were reprinted regularly in cheap editions until the 1940s.[103]

The other striking point about Hindi publications in 1915 is that poetry was the medium for almost everything: apart from literary enjoyment (*rasāsvādan*), verse was the vehicle for religious discourse and controversy, social reform, women's uplift, and political awakening. By contrast, in the case of Urdu, prose fiction was already the medium of public discourse.[104] Finally, the politicization of the Hindi public with World War I was borne out by the publishing market, too, with a book like Sheokumar Singh's *Europe kī laṛāī* (1914), selling at 4 annas, running into three editions and selling 12,000 copies within a year![105]

After 1920 the situation changed in many ways, both in terms of a general expansion in the numbers of titles and copies and of diversification in the market. Within fiction, new genres such as thrillers, romantic novels, and detective stories captured a share of the commercial market, first in Urdu and subsequently in Hindi, too. In Hindi, apart from the usual fare of *jāsūsī upanyās* (detective stories), translations of 'social' and 'historical' novels from Bengali and Urdu, original historical, social, and even political novels started to appear. Drama showed a similar trend, with more historical and original literary plays and satires published alongside sāṁgīt, and even a drama series, Nāṭak Granthamālā,

[102] Sāṁgīt generally sold for 1 or 2 annas, qissās, ghazal, bhajan, and song collections for 1 anna or 6 paise; a translation of the *Mysteries of Paris* sold for 4 annas in 1918, while the translation of a Bengali novel, part of the Upanyās Grantha-mālā published by Sheo Ram Das Gupta, sold for Rs 1 and 4 annas in its first edition.

[103] His poem *Raṅg meṁ bhaṅg* (1909, pp. 31) was in its 8th edition of 2000–4000 copies in 1920 and sold for 4 annas.

[104] See e.g. Muhammad Husain's *'Ilm kī devī* (The goddess of learning, 1915), in favour of *pardā* among Muslim women.

[105] All details are taken from the *Statement of Particulars Regarding Books and Periodicals Published in the United Provinces of Agra and Oudh* for the year 1915.

published by Sheo Ram Das Gupta in Benares. The plays by Agha Hasra Kashmiri (1879–1935), Arzu, and Haridās Maṇik also became popular at this time and were simultaneously published in Urdu and Hindi. Collections of selected songs from different dramatic plays also started to appear as a separate item, attesting to the impact of commercial theatre and foreshadowing the publication of film songs.[106] In poetry, too, historical–patriotic poems started circulating in book form (Maithilīśaraṇ Gupta was by no means alone; cf. 3.1), while print-runs for religious and popular poetry swelled to 5000–10,000.[107] Overall we can say that the popular market diversified its production, embracing new commercial genres in poetry, fiction and drama, while literary and nationalist books started finding a market.[108]

Journal editors were crucial in making some space for modern literature in the market place, for when they branched out in the book market they consistently published literary books; Dulārelāl Bhārgava's Ganga Pustak Mala in Lucknow was perhaps the most successful attempt and made a very significant difference to the Hindi literary sphere. Beside the standard 'useful literature'—biographies, history, children's and women's books[109]—Bhārgava created a remarkable catalogue of contemporary Hindi literature, comprising novels, short stories, drama, poetry, essays, and literary criticism.[110] With his selection of both 'high-brow' and popular writers, the use of thick 'antique' paper and cloth binding, a rāj saṃskāraṇ (royal edition) along with a sādhāraṇ saṃskāraṇ (ordinary

[106] See e.g. *Rāginī thiyeṭar*, compiled by Master Bachcha Lal for Sheo Ram Das Gupta, 4th edition 1925, 5 annas (1000 copies).

[107] See e.g. Rādheśyām, *Śrīrāmkathā*, Bareilly, 5th ed. 1920, 3 annas (4000 copies), and *Bhajan ratnāvalī*, published by Gullu Prasad Kedar Prasad, Benares, 1925, 3 annas (15,000 copies).

[108] A distinction should be made within the 'popular' market between those genres that carried over into print from pre-print traditions, and those, like detective novels, which were born with print, and which I have termed 'commercial'.

[109] In the series Mahilā-mālā and Bāl-vinod-vāṭikā.

[110] His catalogue of authors and titles is truly impressive: it included Premchand's *Raṅgbhūmi* (in 1925, paid the record sum of Rs 1800), the play *Karbalā* and several collections of stories; also Viśvambharnāth Śarmā 'Kauśik', Chatursen Śāstrī, Bhagavatīcharaṇ Varmā, Vṛndāvanlāl Varmā, Pāṇḍey Bechan Śarmā 'Ugra', Nirālā, Govindvallabh Pant, Badrīnāth Bhaṭṭ, Rūpnārāyaṇ Pāṇḍey, and Pratāpnārāyaṇ Śrīvāstava, etc., in a word all the best Hindi writers. Bhārgava took care to include also works by older writers like Bālkṛṣṇa Bhāṭṭ, Mahāvīr Prasād Dvivedī, Śrīdhar Pāṭhak, Kṛṣṇabihārī Miśra. Translations of Molière, Galsworthy, Gorky, and Alexander Dumas were published, too.

edition) and aggressive advertising, Bhārgava identified and captured both the sophisticated audience (and library circuit) and the new Hindi middle-brow readership. Backed once again by business innovations, he recognized the swelling tide of Hindi and managed to keep a purely literary concern afloat.[111] By 1930, a host of small literary publishers existed, such as Ganga Pustak Mala in Lucknow, Bharti Bhandar in Benares and Hindi Pustak Bhandar in Laheriasarai (Darbhanga), who were committed to publishing quality literary books by the new poets, playwrights, novelists, and short story writers.

A major factor in the expansion of Hindi publishing and reading in the post-1920 period, with significant peaks in 1920 and 1930, was the boom in political publications. They were brought out by three different kinds of publishers. First, there were newspapers like *Abhyuday, Pratāp, Āj* and *Chāṁd* which branched out into book publishing and brought out political books and cheap tracts, collected speeches and biographies of nationalist leaders, and collections of the articles and nationalist poems published in their newspapers.[112] Sasta Sahitya Mandal in Ajmer (est. 1926) was another important publisher of cheap nationalist books.[113] A special mention should be made here of Babu Śivaprasād Gupta,[114]

[111] Maithilīśaraṇ Gupta had also proved successful in publishing his own works from his village near Jhansi. Rāykṛṣṇadās established Bharti Bhandar (1927) in Benares as a cooperative publishing house to give a higher royalty—25 per cent—to writers, but he had to sell it in 1935–6 to the Leader Press in Allahabad, a Birla concern. Also in Benares Premchand founded his Hans Karyalay, and Vinod Śaṅkar Vyās the Pustạk Mandir (1930–50).

[112] For example V. N. Tivārī's articles published in *Sarasvatī* in favour of Hindi in the Hindi–Hindustani controversy, quoted later here (5.4), appeared also in booklet form, distributed free by the Indian Press in 10,000 copies in 1939. Pamphlets and books put out by the Pratap Press included the translation of Gandhi's prison account, nationalist poems by 'Triśūl', Vidyārthī's book on the Princely states and booklets on Russia and communism.

[113] Sasta Sahitya Mandal was a Gandhian publishing venture established by Ghanshyamdas Birla and Jamnalal Bajaj in 1926, managed by Haribhāū Upādhyāy, editor of the Gandhian paper *Tyāgbhūmi*; it published mainly translations of Gandhi's and Tolstoy's works, of historical and 'useful' books and biographies; all information is taken from publication lists in journals.

[114] During a long world tour, Śivaprasād Gupta had been impressed by the excellent and cheap publications he found abroad, and once back in India he drew up a long list of titles and subjects inviting Hindi writers to write books on them in keeping with 'scientific standards'. These included biographies of patriots from all over the world; critical editions of classics, and books on history, sociology, political science, science, handicraft, religion, and philosophy. He then suggested popular

whose publishing concern, Jnanmandal (1917), and newspaper *Āj* became centres for serious and scholarly books on history and political science: they provided Hindi readers and students with nationalist-inspired political and historical analyses, and several Hindi scholars, politicians, and publicists with the chance to work on seminal subjects.[115] For its breadth of scope, nationalist vision and partial freedom from commercial compulsions, Jnanmandal presented a unique case and a particularly precious opportunity for the Hindi public sphere.[116] Second, there were commercial booksellers and publishers who branched out into nationalist songs and sāṁgīts. Third, the Catalogues of Publications show an impressive amount of self-produced and locally-printed miscellaneous nationalist tracts, pamphlets, speeches, stories, drama, songs, bhajans, Ālhās, many of them given away free or almost free, which speak of a more direct use of print for intervention in the political sphere.[117] The Sharda bill or Child Marriage Restraint Act provoked a flurry of *Śārdā bil nāṭak*, poems, and tracts both in favour and against it, and translations of the bill into Hindi and Urdu.[118] During the Non-cooperation and Civil

---

English books for translation, and drew up a list which included the Home University Library series, science primers, Jacks People's Books series, Temple Encyclopedic Primers, important books on history such as Bury's *Greece*, Rhys Davis' *Early Buddhism*, V. Smith's *Early History of India*, MacDonnell's *History of Sanskrit Literature*, Lecky's *Democracy* and *Civilisation*, basic texts of European philosophy, physics, chemistry, botany.

[115] Among the writers associated with Jnanmandal were Chāvīnāth Pāṇḍey, a Congress activist, Padmasiṃh Śarmā, Rāmdās Gauṛ, Sampūrṇānand, Janārdan Bhaṭṭ and Mukundīlāl Śrīvāstava. Among the books published were: Śrīprakāś, ed., *Svarājya kā sarkārī masvidā* (2 vols.), Chandraśekhar Vājpey, *Yūrop ke prasiddh sudhārak* (1920), Lakṣmaṇnārāyaṇ Garde, *Jāpān kī rājnītik pragati* (transl., 1921), Prāṇnāth Vidyālaṃkār, *Rājnītiśāstra* (1922), Sampūrṇānand, *Antarrāśtrīy vidhān* (1924), Hariharnāth, *Saṃsār ke vyavsāy kā itihās* (tr. 1924), Ambikāprasād Vājpeyī, *Chīn aur Bhārat* and the seminal *Samāchārpatroṁ kā itihās* (1953), on nineteenth-century journals in Hindi; list of publications available from the publicity list at Jnanmandal Press, Benares.

[116] Despite generous funding, poor distribution brought huge losses every year. In the end, Jnanmandal survived thanks to its academic and educational publications.

[117] This phenomenon was more visible from an earlier stage in Bihar; see, for example, in 1920 *Kisānoṁ ko matadhikār milā*, a free tract translated and published in 5000 copies by a Swami Vidyānand containing the appendix of the Franchise Committee report on peasants' enfranchisement.

[118] Among the publications condemning it: Sajjād Ali, *Islāmī naqqārā*, published by the author in Moradabad (2nd ed. 1930, 1000 copies for 1 anna each); and Lachmī Nārāyaṇ Śarmā, *Śārdā śatrañj*, a farce contemplating the evil consequences of the

Disobedience movements, nationalist poems and songs swamped the market (240 titles in 1930 alone);[119] for example, one collection titled *Rāṣṭrīy ḍaṅkā athvā svadeś khādī* (National kettledrum or svadeś khādī), compiled and published by one Chandrikā Prasād Jijñāsū, was printed five times adding up to 30,000 copies in 1930![120] Nationalist publications swelled in Urdu, too, although several tracts against the movement and against peasants' activism were also published.[121] The picture that emerges is not one of centralized Congress propaganda 'mobilizing' the people, but of a strikingly diffuse intervention in, and controversy over, political affairs through print.[122]

Finally, the market for Hindi textbooks expanded into a veritable industry during this period; this made the fortune of several Hindi publishers such as the Indian Press, Ram Narayan Lal, Nandkishor & Bros. (see 1.4), and many smaller ones. It was a continuous expansion in terms of titles, copies and print-runs, while Urdu textbooks expanded in terms of titles but not of copies (see Table 1.2) Apart from the textbooks themselves, an industry mushroomed in 'keys' (to the textbooks), reading books and juvenile books in general: several booksellers and publishers launched series aimed specifically at children and youth, like the Indian Press' Bālsakhā Pustakmālā, Ram Narayan Lal's Bālakopyogī Pustakmālā, Rāmjīlāl Śarmā's Sadvichār Granthamālā and the Śiśu Pustakmālā, all in Allahabad, the Bāl Manorañjanmālā from Darbhanga (Bihar), and many, many others. While publishing textbooks allowed small Hindi literary publishers to survive, it also strengthened the dependence of the Hindi book-market on the education system—making Hindi literature a kind of subsidized department.[123]

Act published in Benares in 1930 (100 copies, 2 annas). Among the publications in favour: the poems *Rupye kā lobhī bāp* by Rām Dās Pāṇḍe (Gorakhpur, 3rd edition 1929, 6 paise, 8000 copies!), and Rādhākṛṣṇa Premī's *Śārdā bil qānūn urf bāl-vivāh* (Patna, 1930, 1 anna, 5000 copies); and Līlāvatī Devī and Haṁsmukhī Devī's pamphlet *Bhārat meṁ bālvivāh kī bhīṣaṇtā*, published by the authors in Bulandshahr in 1930 (1 anna, 1000 copies).

[119] For example, Premchand's nationalist stories were published in 1930 in 5000 copies at a price of 2 annas and 6 paise; *Catalogue of Publications* for the year 1930.

[120] Ibid.

[121] See e.g. the tract *Kisānoṁ kī nek mashvirā* by one Chaudhuri Muhammad Māsūd, asking cultivators to remain loyal to the British government, and published by the author in Bara Banki in 1930 (free, 500 copies).

[122] Cf. Gyan Pandey, 'Mobilization in a Mass Movement: Congress "Propaganda" in the United Provinces', *Modern Asian Studies*, IX, 2, 1975, pp. 205–26.

[123] This is a thorny question which still troubles the Hindi publishing world; several

By 1940, then, the Hindi publishing market had expanded and diversified: popular and commercial genres of poetry, drama, and fiction still formed the largest share of the market; another share comprised educational books; while devotional and educational songs commanded the largest print-runs.[124] Literary publications by contemporary authors also acquired a small but significant share of the market; print-runs seldom exceeded 2000 copies, but some writers like Premchand, M. Gupta, and J. Prasād were continuously reprinted. A small but well-established readership for modern Hindi poetry, drama and literary fiction, and for translations of world classics such as Tolstoy and Dumas had thus certainly come into being.

The growth of literary publications did not alter the general balance between readers of popular and of literary publications, however: the 184 'poetry' titles in 1925 had grown only to 189 in 1940, and the breakdown in terms of popular genres, both religious and secular, and literary genres remained roughly the same (see Table 1.5).

Table 1.5. Hindi 'Poetry' titles 1925–1940

	1925	1940
Religious and devotional	70	64
Sāṁgīt, seasonal songs and ghazals	67	69
Didactic and topical (in Khari Boli)	23	22
Nationalistic	15	16
Literary (new style in brackets)	9 (2)	18 (11)
Total	184	189

What we can assume, then, is a Hindi readership divided between those who could buy *Sarasvatī* and books at Rs 2–3, and those who bought bhajan, sāṁgīt, *kajlī*, and nationalist songs for a few annas. It remains to be seen whether the balance changed at all after Independence.

This imbalance between the flourishing and ubiquitous popular literature and the few and stunted 'serious' publications must have struck

factors seem to contribute to it: low literacy and hence a limited readership despite the enormous potential; an inadequate system of distribution, which makes literary books difficult to get outside the main urban centres; and the complete dichotomy between 'good literature' (studied at school) and literature for entertainment. All these factors already prevailed in the 1920s and 1930s.

[124] See for example the 6-annas and 4-annas detective series published in 500 copies by K.N. Bhargava of Bhargava Bhushan Press, Benares, R.L. Burman in Calcutta, and Harikrishna Jauhar of Hindi Press, Benares.

Hindi writers and intellectuals of the 1920s and 1930s. It certainly explains why reformers anxiously pleaded with the Hindi public to read serious literature (cf. 2.2 and 2.3). It also underlines, from a different angle, the centrality of journals for introducing and supporting contemporary writers. As the case of Dulārelāl Bhārgava's Ganga Pustak Mala shows, journals were successful in creating a space for modern literature in the market place; they managed to form a reading public for Khari Boli books out of former Urdu readers and newly educated groups. However, this space hardly amounted to the commercial success that would have enabled contemporary writers to acquire the wider cultural authority that stems from mass popularity (cf. 2.3 and 5.4). Nor did writing generally bring wealth sufficient to ensure social status. Thus the cultural capital acquired by writing in journals and publishing literary books was not spendable in the wider public sphere; the exceptions were nationalist writers and university professors. In the case of the former, their cultural capital came from their political role and the popularity they acquired through newspapers and poetry meetings (cf. 1.3. and 1.3.3); in the case of the latter, it came from their institutional role, which will be discussed at length in Section 1.4.

The picture the Hindi publishing world presents is thus one of inner division within the Hindi public. This division became even more apparent and problematic when old tastes and new aspirations, and old and new audiences came face to face in the mixed arena of poetry meetings.

1.3.3. Kavi sammelans

The institution of the kavi sammelan, or poetry meeting, offers a particular demonstration of how existing literary tastes and aural transmission adapted to the twin aspirations to publicity and to the world of printed literature. Also, compared with journals and publishing, the kavi sammelan was an arena where poets confronted concrete and localized audiences which reacted according to their own saṃskāras and participated vocally. At the same time, it was a unique opportunity for poets to experience the power of popularity. The development of this arena and contemporary discussions about its potentialities and problems therefore offer us a direct insight into the impact of publicity on the Hindi literary sphere.

A kavi sammelan is a highly formal poetic reading in which poets take turns to recite or sing out their poems to the audience, who repeat the refrain. As such, it is modelled on the Urdu mushaira and on Braj Bhasa courtly poetic contests, at which poets would recite new poems or even extemporize in front of a patron and a selected audience. Mushairas were agonistic poetic encounters at which poets were called upon to present their work by reciting it aloud to one another and to an audience of connoisseurs. Most mushairas involved poets composing poems on the same theme and metrical scheme; matters of protocol were taken very seriously, with senior poets asked to recite last, and audience response was essential.[125] In the course of the nineteenth century, mushairas had successfully turned from courtly ritual to highly sophisticated urban gatherings. At Braj Bhasa poetry readings at courts (*darbār*), one way of testing excellence and favouring competition among patronized (*āśrit*) poets was samasyā-pūrti, i.e. a set 'problem' (samasyā) or fragment of verse to which poets had to provide a 'solution' in the form of a full poem (pūrti). The best poems would be rewarded immediately by the prince or patron, and the custom persisted even when the competition was taken out of the court into a public place: there, the wealthy in the audience would reward the successful poet with gold and silver medals or cash.[126]

Traditionally, kavi sammelans had been a means to entertain and educate a select circle in poetic sophistication and the enjoyment of *rasa*. It was typically the erotic, or *śṛṅgāra,* mood of courtly or pastoral dalliance crystallized down the centuries around Rādhā–Kṛṣṇa lore that prevailed.

The limited subject-matter and the highly stylized set of metaphors ensured immediate communication between the poet and his audience. In fact, much of the pleasure lay in the subtle play of combining well-known metaphors, giving a sudden twist to a familiar scene, that has been recognized as a characteristic feature of much 'traditional' poetry, in India as well as elsewhere. Needless to say, it was a highly self-referential system.

In the new public sphere of Khari Boli Hindi, kavi sammelans predictably underwent several changes. These were a shift from the court to the public arena, from erotic subjects to rousing nationalist themes and experimental poetic metaphors, and from the circles of connoisseurs to

[125] Munibur Rahman, 'The Musha'irah', in *Annual of Urdu Studies*, 3, 1983, pp. 75–84; and Frances W. Pritchett, *Nets of Awareness: Urdu Poetry and Its Critics,* Berkeley, University of California Press, 1994, pp. 70 ff.

[126] Nothing is known about samasyā in Sanskrit texts, at least up to Rājāśekhar's time, wrote Rāmśaṅkar Śukla 'Rasāl', Hindi lecturer at Allahabad University, a specialist in *rīti* poetry and a Braj Bhasa poet himself, nor in Hindi texts until the recent *Kāvya-prabhākar* (1905) by Jagannāthprasād 'Bhānu' (1859–1945). But many anecdotes of Raja Bhoja's time spoke of its popularity in medieval Sanskrit literature. In Hindi too, samasyā-pūrti started flourishing around the sixteenth century, both at courts and in the main towns in small circles of poets and connoisseurs (kāvyapremīs); R. Śukla 'Rasāl', 'Samasyā-pūrti', *Mādhurī*, VIII, pt. 2, 1, February 1930, pp. 47–56.

more open-ended audiences of students, political activists, and the general public, the *jantā*. Circles of rasiks did publish the poems recited at their meetings, but they were now not the only ones. The self-referential system was broken, and the audience could no longer recognize and anticipate images, words, and moods. In the public arena, rousing political poems, elusive poems of novel taste and the expectations of the popular public provided contrasting aims. The change in poetic language, from Braj Bhasa to Khari Boli, signalled a change in orientation: at mixed Braj Bhasa and Khari Boli kavi sammelans, Braj Bhasa poets were given a samasyā, and Khari Boli ones a theme. In Dvivedī's time these were often 'social' themes such as 'untouchable' or 'widow'. During nationalist campaigns the themes were 'khadi', 'charkhā' (spinning wheel), 'martyr', and the like.[127]

Hindi kavi sammelans became increasingly popular from the 1920s onwards: they became the typical 'cultural programme' at annual functions of schools, colleges, and hostels. They were indispensable features at the annual meetings of literary associations and at Congress sessions.[128] Large meetings in public halls or under makeshift tents (*paṇḍāl*) for paying audiences, with Hindi poets from all over north India, joint Hindi–Urdu kavi sammelans and even all-India kavi sammelans were organized by the Hindī Sāhitya Sammelan to mark the growing catchment-area of the potential 'national language'. Kavi sammelans became part of their countrywide Hindi propaganda and a public show of the strength and unity within the Hindi community. For literary people, they became a major indicator of their public, political role. The new political importance of Hindi kavi sammelans is underscored by the fact that at such large gatherings it was nationalist poems in Khari Boli, the same that appeared copiously in the nationalist press, which usually carried the day. Even minor Khari Boli poets like Mādhav Śukla, Sohanlāl Dvivedī, and Śyāmnārāyaṇ Pāṇḍey became small-scale celebrities thanks to their fiery nationalist poems at kavi sammelans. Sohanlāl Dvivedī acquired scores of fans, and when he recited aloud his poem on Gandhi:

न हाथ एक शस्त्र हो।
न साथ एक अस्त्र हो।
न अन्न नीर वस्त्र हो।
हटो नहीं डटो वहीं।
बढ़े चलो बढ़े चलो।

[127] Harivaṃs Rāy 'Bachchan', 'Kavi-sammelan: ek siṃhāvalokan', in A. Kumār, ed., *Bachchan rachnāvalī*, vol. 6, Delhi, Rajkamal Prakasan, 1987, p. 447.

[128] For the importance of Hindi kavi sammelans for Hindi propaganda in the

No weapon in his hands,
No weapon beside him,
No food, water or cloth.
Do not retreat, resist,
Move ahead, move ahead . . .

a contemporary wrote that 'the thousand-strong audience in the *paṇḍāl* joined in with the poet at the refrain 'Move ahead, move ahead.'[129] In this way, a kind of poetic accompaniment to the national movement was being written and disseminated through the kavi sammelan, which became an important 'place' of nationalist identification. The major nationalist poets such as Gayāprasād Śukla Sanehī 'Triśūl', Maithilīśaraṇ Gupta, Mākhanlāl Chaturvedī, and later Subhadrākumārī Chauhān, Dinkar and Bālkṛṣṇa Śarmā 'Navīn', were often called upon to attend kavi sammelans.[130] As young Rāmnāthlāl 'Suman' observed then, 'Since usually people's taste veers more towards nationalism, this kind of poet has become more and more famous,' so much so that 'any author of nationalist doggerel can be honoured—is indeed honoured—more than the author of the finest verse of śṛṅgāra rasa.'[131] Those poems might not have stood the test of time, but they had that unique virtue of modernity: *sāmāyiktā*, timeliness. This potential to attract a different, untrained mass public, to whom patriotic messages could be conveyed, was quickly recognized, and it changed the function and outlook of kavi sammelans substantially.

Yet the majority of poems recited at kavi sammelans were in Braj Bhasa and reproduced the self-referential system of courtly darbārs.[132] Indeed, it was through kavi sammelans that Braj Bhasa poetry regained momentum, exposure, and popularity, once more a proof of how resistant and engrained a poetic saṃskāra it was. Especially at minor kavi sammelans with mostly local and amateur poets, samasyā-pūrti remained the easiest and most practised option, and śṛṅgāra rasa the favoured mood. Why was Braj Bhasa poetry so popular in this Khari Boli age, wondered an editor. The reason, he suggested, had to do with the familiarity of the

---

Punjab, see 3rd Annual Report of Punjab Provincial Hindī Sāhitya Sammelan by Jaychandra Vidyālaṃkār, in *Sammelan patrikā*, XII, 10, pp. 444.

[129] Amṛtlāl Nāgar, *Jinke sāth jīyā*, Delhi, Rajpal and Sons, 1973, p.124.

[130] E.g. Sanehī, *Pratāp*'s 'house-poet', presided over a poetry-meeting at Allahabad University's Hindu Hostel in 1922; L. Vājpeyī presided over the annual Nāgarī Prachāriṇī Sabhā meeting in Agra in 1925.

[131] R. Suman, 'Hamāre kavi aur unkī rachnāeṁ', *Sammelan patrikā*, XI, 9, pp. 391–2.

[132] See editorial note on 'Kavi sammelan', *Mādhurī*, IV, pt. 1, 3, September 1925, p. 414.

audience with this poetic style. Samasyā-pūrti was already a tradition in Braj Bhasa, and in terms of content and of style Braj Bhasa poetry corresponded to, and competed with, Urdu mushairas.[133]

However, structural changes were at work here, too. Earlier, poetic samasyās had been a 'brief and pleasant' test of a poet's talent and skill in a circle of connoisseurs. For the poet trained in strict poetic rules, this was a means to stir creativity: though restrictive, a *samasyā* allowed enough freedom to exercise the imagination. On the other hand, in public kavi sammelans in the twentieth century, samasyā-pūrti was no longer a test: samasyās were set, announced, and printed in advance. Catering now to a general audience, easy samasyās or a general theme were only meant to arouse expectations and generate entertainment.[134] As such they were part of the successful pattern of mixed oral-printed transmission noted above for chapbooks and booklets of seasonal songs and 'erotic' poems. Something similar happened in the case of the nationalist poems: their popularity at kavi sammelans and high sales went hand in hand. When *Haldī ghāṭī*, a long nationalist poem on Maharana Pratāp and Rajput valour by Śyāmnārāyaṇ Pāṇḍey, appeared in 1938, his inspiring public recitations made the book an instant success. It was reprinted several times and even won the prestigious Dev Puraskar (see 2.3).

New poetic tastes like Chāyāvād, by contrast, did not fare so well with the general audience of kavi sammelans. Meaning was often deliberately obscure, vocabulary laden with long and difficult Sanskrit compounds, metres strikingly unfamiliar:

> They were weird not only in their diction but also in their attire. The people (*jantā*) watched and listened dumbfounded. . . . People thought they were creatures from another world who had descended on to earth and disappeared again after uttering some mystery.[135]

Kavi sammelans in schools and colleges provided a more receptive audience and favourable platform for Chāyāvād poets. It was at the Jain Hostel in Allahabad in 1921 that the student Sumitrānandan Pant recited a poem in public for the first time to immediate recognition.[136] Also in Allahabad, young Mahādevī Varmā, who had started attending kavi sammelans of samasyā-pūrtis as a representative of her school, later kept away from public gatherings and recited her new poems in the protected

[133] Ibid.

[134] Rasāl, 'Samsayā-pūrti'.

[135] 'Bachchan', 'Kavi-sammelan: ek siṃhāvalokan', p. 448.

[136] Śukla, *Sampādak ke pacchīs varṣ*, p. 23.

environment of a smaller, sophisticated circle like the Sukavi Samāj.[137] Not surprisingly, delivery was the single most influential element for the success of recitals of Chāyāvād poetry, much of which was meant to be sung anyway. Rāmkumār Varmā and Bhagavatīcharaṇ Varmā were the most popular, the former for his soft diction, the latter for his powerful delivery. Even Nirālā could occasionally carry the audience along thanks to his good singing and booming voice despite the obscurity of his verse.

All in all, public kavi sammelans seemed to be an excellent venue for showing the richness and maturity that Hindi had reached, and it is not surprising that the Hindī Sāhitya Sammelan should have organized larger and larger ones. Its 14th annual meeting in Delhi in February 1924 featured the first Hindi–Urdu kavi sammelan, blessed by a telegram from Gandhi. Presided over by Dvivedī-poet Nāthūrām Śaṅkar Śarmā, it featured both Braj Bhasa and Khari Boli poets: among others, Harioudh, the Miśra brothers, Padmasiṃh Śarmā, Jagannāth Prasād Chaturvedī, 'Sanehī' (whose poem 'Svadeśī' won acclaim), Rāmnareś Tripāṭhī, Mākhanlāl Chaturvedī, and Rūpnārāyaṇ Pāṇḍey; practically the entire Hindi establishment attended, including Puruṣottam Dās Ṭaṇḍon, Rāmdās Gauṛ, Seth Kedarnath Goenka and Śrīnārāyaṇ Chaturvedī (see Appendix). Urdu poets Maulana Arif Hasbi, Maharaj Bahadur 'Barq', and Latif Hussein also recited their poems. The joint session was perhaps instrumental in drawing a full house even in a city still largely indifferent to Hindi. In fact, the poets were so many that a second day was required.[138]

Later attempts at even grander meetings encountered significant problems. First of all, it became evident that to break the Braj Bhasa–*śṛṅgāra* (erotic) mould was not easy. This was apparent at the next attempt, the all-India Hindi kavi sammelan organized for the 16th Hindī Sāhitya Sammelan session at Brindaban in November 1925. What was meant as an occasion for young poets to meet their celebrated peers from all over India, bridging differences and forging a sense of unity of purpose, turned out to be a disappointment.[139] In Braj, Braj Bhasa poems reigned; only a few showed nationalist feelings, but most poems were of śṛṅgāra,

[137] In fact, Mahādevī was especially invited to give the weekly meetings of the Sukavi Samāj social respectability, so that other young women poets would be allowed to attend. 'During the few years of its existence, it provided the young poets with an audience of their peers that could appreciate and comment with sophistication on their current writings;' Schomer, *Mahadevi Varma*, p. 145.

[138] See reports in *Sammelan patrikā*, XI, 7–8, pp. 346–7; and *Mādhurī*, II, pt. 2, 2, February 1924, pp. 270–1.

[139] *Sammelan patrikā*, XIII, 2, pp. 76–8.

'which we are now sick and tired of hearing', and when an overly bold poem in śṛṅgāra rasa was recited, the small group of women heroically present in the audience walked off offended by its 'vulgarity'. This painful incident led the reviewer to observe that 'it lacked the seriousness and organisation proper to an All-India Hindi kavi sammelan'.[140] Once again, it was nationalism that acted as a sort of bridge between the popular and the literary audience. At the Kanpur Congress of December 1925, a triumphant kavi sammelan was held for four days, partly in the Congress paṇḍāl itself, with the concerted effort of all literary people in the city, first and foremost Gayāprāsad Śukla 'Sanehī'. This time, Khari Boli and Braj Bhasa poems were kept in different sections. The proceedings, part of the Congress *melā* (fair), included many speeches and poems; the majority of the Hindi literary world of the time attended, and the audience amounted to about 4000.[141]

Such a display of unity should not induce us to believe that kavi sammelans in Hindi had actually negotiated a common literary ethos between the high-literary and popular audiences, or between courtly and popular Braj Bhasa and 'public' Khari Boli. Indeed, the danger of holding huge kavi sammelans was brought home ten years later after the disastrous proceedings of the all-India Rāṣṭrabhāṣā Kavi Sammelan held in Lucknow in April 1936.[142] The experience highlighted the tensions that emerged when a sophisticated arena was opened indiscriminately to the general public, and when different tastes and expectations clashed. The traditional system of Braj Bhasa poetic training, exercise, and correction placed authority in the hands of patrons, scholars, and peers. In the arena of the public kavi sammelan, there was no such test or check: popular taste became the bottom line and recognition came into the hands of the general public. And it was one thing to recite subtle śṛṅgāra poems for a small circle of connoisseurs, it was quite another to recite them in front of a large, paying audience in a paṇḍāl, where there could be problems of order and control. In the 1936 meeting, the price of entry tickets was

[140] Reported in *Mādhurī*, IV, pt. 1, 5, November 1925, p. 701. Years later, at a meeting of the local Nāgarī Prachāriṇī Sabhā branch in Ballia, Rāhul Sāṅkṛtyāyan remarked that now that women were coming out in the literary sphere, self-control (*saṃyam*) and refinement (*suruchi*) were indispensable. Quoted in *Chāṁd*, XV, pt. 1, 3, January 1937, p. 380.

[141] Report in *Mādhurī*, IV, pt. 2, 1, January 1926, pp. 126–8.

[142] Mahādevī Varmā, 'Kis aur?', editorial in *Chāṁd*, XIV, pt. 2, 2, June 1936, pp. 109–13 and pp. 175–9; cf. Schomer, *Mahadevi Varma*, pp. 235 ff.

kept extremely low (1 anna) with the aim of attracting vast crowds and calling it '*virāṭ*' (huge), thus proving Hindi's popularity. There were no restrictions on the noisy public or the excited poets' effusiveness, and no proper order, sound, or seating arrangements; the respectable public and good poets avoided the show altogether. By the time Mahādevī Varmā, the appointed president, arrived, the scene had already become chaotic, with people shouting because they could not hear and poets struggling with each other for precedence. Mahādevī left immediately without saying a word; clearly, the new fashion of appointing women convenors had failed to check uncouthness, indeed had enhanced it.

This appalling Hindi kavi sammelan looked even more embarrassing in comparison with the Urdu mushaira organized the following night. The same paṇḍāl was well arranged, with seats and loudspeakers and flowers, tickets sold for Rs 9, Rs 2, or 8 annas, and invitations assured the presence of city notables and of the literary community. The secretaries had prepared in advance a printed booklet (selling for 8 annas) with a list of the poets, a selection of the poems, and photographs of Jawaharlal Nehru and Sarojini Naidu (who presided). The President of the welcoming committee stuck to the order; since it was a 'national mushaira', there would be no samasyās and everyone read poems of their own choice; poets like Jigar, Asghar, and Bismil Ilahabadi won great acclaim. After the Hindi kavi sammelan Premchand was heard saying 'God knows when Hindi people will learn their manners' ('हिन्दी वालों को मालूम नहीं कब तमीज़ आयेगी').[143] Urdu mushairas were successful, an exasperated Mahādevī argued later, because (1) the subjects and metres of the poems were well known to the public, too, who could immediately enjoy them; (2) each *bhāva* (emotion, idea) was completed in a couplet, which the audience repeated; and (3) the poems were checked by the poets' ustads beforehand, and no faulty, poor, or obscene poem was allowed to be read.[144] In other words, they followed a well-tested pattern, addressed a cultivated, civilized audience, followed a scrupulous ritual and did not attempt indiscriminate popularization. In Hindi, mass-oriented kavi sammelans worked only with nationalist poetry, otherwise they risked

[143] Editorial note in *Chāṁd*, XIV, pt. 2, 2, June 1936, p. 175.

[144] M. Varmā, 'Kis aur?', p.109. Bachchan recalls how the early Hindi kavi-sammelans tried to forge a distinctive idiom for the same ritual: they would shout '*sundar*' or '*atisundar*' instead of '*khūb*', '*bahut khūb*' or '*vāh! vā!*' in appreciation, and '*punarvād*' instead of '*mukarrar irshād*'; this lent an apparent artificial tone to the proceedings; Bachchan, 'Kavi-sammelan', pp. 447–8.

degenerating into unruly, squalid affairs. The issue of popularity was obviously a controversial one (cf. 2.4).

Later developments show mass kavi sammelans turning more and more into bawdy gatherings. Modern, complex Khari Boli poetry, with rarefied contents, new metres, or no metre at all, confronted audiences with a poetry that was not part of their saṃskāras, did not aim at entertainment, and could not inspire immediate identification. In the words of a critic, its audience was perforce 'constrained within the narrow limits of the schooled public'.[145] This dilemma was partly solved by the phenomenal success of Harivaṃśray 'Bachchan' (1907–), whose *Madhuśālā* (1935) bridged different saṃskāras and appealed to both sophisticated and popular audiences by combining the Perso-Urdu tradition of wine and love with an easy diction in Khari Boli and the flowing rhythm of *rubāī* quatrains.[146]

The expansion and commercialization of Hindi literature in the 1920s seemed to be a sign of strength to contemporaries, and the discursive notion of a 'Hindi public' seemed to be taking on a concrete reality. Journals and publishing houses provided contemporary writers not only with avenues of publicity, but also with institutional occupations, roles, and audiences. Besides, literary journals worked as institutions of the literary sphere in that they fostered literary genres, determined tastes, and gave a new order on the printed page to the variety of tastes present in the Hindi literary system. The self-confidence and sense of common purpose that the pages of these journals exude is so great that if we were to look at only books and journals, we would believe in the existence of an autonomous and self-sustained Hindi public sphere. Hindi nationalism, as we shall see in the next chapter, at least formally denied the prominence of English and promised that Hindi was well on its way to succeeding it as the public language of the whole of India (2.1).

Yet tensions of several kinds also emerged in the transition to open

[145] Ibid., p. 52.

[146] A witness to the first recital in the Shivaji Hall of BHU recalls how 'young and old, all started swinging (*jhūmnā*). I myself felt inebriated . . . to sway in the wave of the sound, to swing in the ecstasy of intoxication and at the end of every fourth line, when the word '*madhuśālā*' came up, to repeat it along with the poet, and every listener was feeling the same.' There were not that many students among the audience that day, but from the same evening lines from *Madhuśālā* were on from every student's lips; 'They were crazy about it'. 'Manorañjan', 'Madhuśālā kā sarvapratham sammelan: ek saṃsmaraṇ', in D. Śaraṇ, *Bachchan jī kā jīvan tathā vyaktitva*, Kanpur: Sahitya Niketan, 1967, pp. 57–8.

access and popularity. There was a palpable contradiction between the acknowledged social importance of literature and the low and insecure status of the professional writer, and between the avowed independence of writers and their new dependence on the market and popularity (2.3). Between the urge to widen the appeal of Hindi literature and the active pursuit of high literature, whether 'useful' or purely artistic, arose another tension. The former led certain journals and publishers, especially political ones, to popularize their idiom; it also led to those massive Hindi kavi sammelans. The latter urge was expressed in the literary curriculum (see 1.4) and in the trend towards sophistication that reflected the linguistic and literary saṃskāras of the editors themselves and of the schooled, cultivated public. Finally, openness was not welcomed by all: critics and editors-arbiters tended to perceive it as chaos (cf. 2.2) and to deprecate critical voices as irresponsible attacks on the normative project.

1.4. Hindi Education and Literature

Education was, together with the press and publishing, the most important arena in the making of the Hindi public sphere right from the start. As we saw at the beginning of the chapter, education was the first 'public issue' around which, from mid-nineteenth century onwards, Hindi intellectuals tried to rally support in the community. Education and the law courts became symbolic places where the flag of Hindi had to be hoisted in order to gain recognition as a public language. Education was in fact considered a vital terrain by most Indian colonial intellectuals, sensitive both to the dangers of cultural colonization and to the effectiveness of a modern, centralized system of education. The activities and views of Hindi intellectuals reveal that they were keenly aware of its importance both as an *institutional* and a *discursive* space. By institutional space I mean the space schools occupied and created: the often imposing public buildings and the space for public interaction, which for girls was the first one outside the home. Schools often became local centres of literary and political activity visited by national leaders and leading poets, and the classroom provided a space for politicization outside the curriculum. Schools hosted the institutional figure of the teacher or headmaster, both important occupational outlets for intellectuals. They were institutions that created their own momentum: they grew, expanded, and acquired patrimonial property, a name and a tradition. They also created, through the students, an important section of the Hindi reading public.

But education also created a discursive space: it was a way in which ideas and perceptions about society, modernity, culture and the 'differences' between India and the West could be spelt out. Thus colonial intellectuals invested practices within the classroom with a national(ist) agenda: 'national education', unitary, standard, and for all, was to lift Indians out of their present backward and subjected state to a rank equal to that of the most advanced nations in the world. The textbook especially came to be seen as a primary medium to instil, together with 'useful knowledge', feelings of duty towards the nation (*deś-sevā*) and a common, 'national' identity. Hindi intellectuals perceived themselves to be ideally placed to transmit cultural identity, for, unlike their English-speaking counterparts, they had profited from modern ideas without being 'corrupted' by English or western ways. This discursive space thus allowed a grand agenda for education to be discussed repeatedly in the face of huge practical hurdles such as widespread illiteracy, lack of funds and infrastructure for mass education, and the punitive hierarchy of the colonial education system.

This section outlines the activities and developments in the field of Hindi education in both the institutional and discursive sense: the growing institutional space for Hindi both within the colonial education system and the alternatives to it, and the saṃskāras that textbooks written by Hindi literati produced and transmitted. Krishna Kumar has written authoritatively on the centrality of the textbook in Indian colonial education: the centralized education and examination system, he has argued, divested teachers of authority and initiative and made textbooks the sole focus of instruction. The lack of other reading material for both students and teachers, both chronically impoverished in vernacular schools, further accentuated this dependence. In this context, the importance of textbooks and the curriculum in shaping children's notions of knowledge and of their official cultural identity cannot be overestimated:

> What is considered worth teaching to the young is selected out of the available body of knowledge and then represented in teaching materials, such as textbooks. In the Indian context, textbooks are not just one of the materials used for teaching; most of the time, they have been the only material that the teacher could use. Hence the importance of how knowledge is represented in textbooks. In the context of language teaching, the textbook is all that the children are expected to be able to read.[147]

[147] Kumar, *The Political Agenda of Education*, New Delhi, Sage, 1991, p. 131; this section owes much to his chapter on Hindi school literature, 'Quest for Self-Identity'. Teachers did not fare very differently. According to a survey of Etawah district in

Since Hindi literati were almost solely responsible for the production of Hindi textbooks, it is their choice of language and materials that we shall analyse.

The 1920s were a period of great expansion, activity, and change in the field of Hindi education. Hindi finally became an established language in education during this decade, the medium of instruction for most subjects in the lower forms, and a subject taught in high schools, colleges, and universities.[148] This quantitative expansion translated into a qualitative change; it was read as a sign that a Hindi public sphere had finally come into its own and could provide a uniform means of reproducing knowledge at all levels, from the bottom to the top. It also marked the success of independent activism on behalf of the community and of the constant pressure Hindi literary associations and Hindi literati exercised on the colonial government and the education department. Moreover, the general move to 'vernacularize' education to a certain extent created its own momentum and had significant repercussions on the development of the Hindi literary sphere. As Krishna Kumar put it:

> The teaching of Hindi at college level, and the subsequent starting of Hindi departments in universities in the first quarter of this century made a major contribution towards the success of the Hindi literati's cultural agenda. Syllabi and anthologies were required to teach Hindi in colleges. Preparation of a syllabus meant the systematization of available knowledge, its codification in a formal way. Once codified as syllabus, the knowledge would gain legitimacy from the university's name and from the rigour and reputation of its examination.[149]

1929, of 702 teachers who answered the survey questionnaire, 306 read no newspapers and 40 no books, while religious books were the first choice for private study. 'It is evident from the above that most of the teachers are suffering from intellectual starvation' concluded the author. S.N. Chaturvedi, *An Educational Survey of a District*, Allahabad, Indian Press, 1935, pp. 232 ff.

[148] It was not a plain victory, though: it was in fact one thing for Hindi to find a place in the curriculum, it was quite another for it to become the teaching medium for all subjects. The fact that Hindi was used as a teaching medium for all subjects only in the lower classes and that it became problematic to teach non-literary subjects in Hindi at the higher levels is symptomatic of the orientation of Hindi efforts, and of the difficulty of making Hindi a complete medium of instruction. The issue was much debated, but with little consequence; was it because, as it was generally argued, proper scientific textbooks, books and good translations in Hindi were in short supply? Or was it due to a lack of interest in, and familiarity with, such subjects on the part of Hindi pandits? (with only the exception of Rāmdās Gauṛ). The matter deserves separate study.

[149] Kumar, *The Political Agenda of Education*, pp. 129–30.

Hindi as a subject largely involved the teaching of Hindi literature. This meant formalizing a Hindi literary canon, something an association like the Nāgarī Prachāriṇī Sabhā had been working on for decades. Only, their linguistic and cultural choices now carried the stamp of official recognition, a good twenty years before political independence. This syllabus was reproduced in large numbers of publications for the student market (cf. 1.3). This invested textbooks—and the professors and writers who compiled them—with additional literary authority, exceeding that normally vested in syllabus makers; in the absence of a wide market for contemporary literature, the professors could, thanks to their role as textbook compilers, exercise critical judgements that were much more widely influential than those of critics in journals. Similarly, their exclusions, unless later corrected, have meant that certain authors and books have completely disappeared from the history of Hindi literature. Finally, the linguistic and literary saṃskāra transmitted by Hindi textbooks and readers increasingly became the only legitimate one, to the exclusion of those transmitted through informal channels. Because of the freedom with which a compact group of scholars and activists was able effectively to run Hindi education, we shall be able to speak in the following pages of a 'Hindi establishment'.

In a sense, we can see journals and textbooks in this period working at opposite ends: the journal expanded and validated varied and new literary forms and experiments, the textbook codified some as the only legitimate forms, and downplayed the others by excluding them. For all these reasons, textbooks figure in this study as important instruments in the attempt of the Hindi establishment to shape public language and the public sphere.

1.4.1. Primary Education and Hindi Textbooks

This is not the place to give a history of education and textbook writing in Hindi.[150] A few observations on the framework of the colonial education system and on nineteenth-century developments will be enough to place the efforts and aspirations of Hindi scholars and activists in a

[150] See 'Bāl-sāhitya kā nirmāṇ aur uskā vikās' by Jagannāthprasād Singh, *Mādhurī*, XI, pt. 1, 3, October 1931, pp. 367–71, for contributions of the Agra School Book Society (1833), Calcutta School Book Society, Allahabad Mission Press, Orphan Press Mirzapur, etc. Also his 'Prārambhik śikṣā kī hindī pustakeṁ', *Sarasvatī*, November 1911.

context.[151] First of all, the remarkable official output right from the early nineteenth century of policy documents, correspondence, despatches, reports, statistics, regular enquiries, and laws could give the impression that educating Indians was one of the priorities of colonial rule. Colonial budget allocation alone would be able to correct such an impression. What such a mass of material certainly indicates is a general policy towards a centralized, comprehensive and standardized system of instruction, inspection and examination, and the local concern of individual officials for the advancement of the region they helped administer: most nineteenth-century institutions seem to be the result of a combination of general guidelines and individual initiative, and Hindi was no exception.[152] Second, while official documents constantly emphasized the importance of mass education and the vernaculars, only fitful and limited attempts were made in that direction, mainly for lack of funds and infrastructure to cope with a task of such magnitude. James Thomason's 'Complete Scheme of Vernacular Education' (1846) was first rejected, then accepted in a revised form, put into action in 1850 in trial districts,

[151] Studies on colonial policies and enterprises in education have multiplied in recent years; general surveys include S. Nurullah and J.P. Naik, *A History of Education in India During the British Period*, Bombay, 1951, M.L. Bhargava, *History of Secondary Education in UP*, Lucknow, 1958, and A. Basu, *The Growth of Education and Political Development in India, 1898–1920*, Delhi, 1974; on missionary education, see Gauri Viswanathan, *Masks of Conquest*, New York, Columbia University Press, 1989; on Hindi education in particular, see Kumar, *The Political Agenda of Education*, King, *One Language, Two Scripts*, Dalmia, *The Nationalization of Hindu Traditions*; textbooks are discussed also in Vedalankar, *The Development of Hindi Prose in the Early Nineteenth Century*, D. Siṃh, *Ādhunik hindī sāhitya ke vikās meṁ khaḍgvilās pres kī bhūmikā*, Patna, Bihar Rastrabhasa Parisad, 1986 and Ali, 'Hindī sāhitya ke itihās meṁ ilāhābād kā yogdān'.

[152] 'The general policy in respect of direction and inspection led to a highly centralised and bureaucratic system of supervision and control. The institution of grant-in-aid system and payment of grants on the results of examinatons conducted by the Inspectorate, further strengthened this type of educational administration. The prescription of curriculum by the Calcutta University and the compulsory affiliation of all institutions to it enforced rigid control over the subjects to be studied and allocation of time to each subject. Control of contents and methods was enforced through control of textbooks and their sale through governmental agency'; M.L. Bhargava, *History of Secondary Education in UP*, Lucknow, Superintendent Printing and Stationery, 1958, p. 238. Krishna Kumar has discussed at length the parallel loss of authority of the schoolteacher within the centralized system, where the curriculum, examinations, timetables and retribution were all in the hands of others; *The Political Agenda of Education*.

and shelved five years later. The 1857 Rebellion brought schooling to a standstill for two years, and subsequent despatches and acts, while reiterating the aims of general education in the vernacular, actively undermined them by concentrating efforts and funds in favour of higher education and English. In fact, the rapid expansion of higher education from the 1880s, which made the University Entrance Exam the threshhold and English the principal subject of instruction in the classroom, resulted in a neglect and even decline of vernacular intermediate education. Such disparity within the same system was mirrored concretely in the glaring difference between the few well-organized government schools and the poorly funded and ill-kept private ones; it ran like a dividing line through teachers' salaries, school fees, library stocks, school attire, students' performance, etc. This disparity encouraged mobility from the vernacular to English both in the case of students and of schools and associated English with 'progress' and the vernacular with 'backwardness'. It should not come as a surprise if such a system inspired Hindi activists with feelings of neglect, inadequacy, and emulation. And, of course, rejection.

Even when criticizing it, the attitudes of Indian leaders and intellectuals towards English education were at best ambivalent. As others have already pointed out, English education was criticized on moral grounds because it lacked religious instruction or actively upheld Christianity, a criticism reworked in countless articles, stories, and pamphlets on the evil effects of western education. English education was also deemed to be too expensive for India, hence inadequate for the education of the masses, indeed for education as a whole.[153] However, most Indian writers on the subject looked favourably at the potential the centralised system offered for spreading knowledge and values. As Tagore put it in 1919, 'We say that the only thing wrong in our education is that it is not in our absolute control; that the boat is sea-worthy, only the helm has to be in our own hands to save it from wreckage.'[154] Control was crucial if education was to fulfil its nation-building role. 'All progressive (*unnatiśīl*) nations build their own civilization and its several constituents according

[153] For a damning critique of English education and of western modernization, see M.K. Gandhi's *Hind Swaraj* (1907), new ed., Cambridge, Cambridge University Press, 1997.

[154] Rabindranath Tagore, 'The Centre of Indian Culture', 1919, in *Towards Universal Man* (Bombay, Asia, 1961, p. 204), quoted in Kumar, *The Political Agenda of Education*, p. 117.

to their own ideals', wrote an editor on the subject of 'national education'.[155]

If the 'administrative control of institutions was perceived by Indian social leaders as a tangible expression of the colonizers' grip on the indigenous culture,'[156] the efforts of colonial intellectuals to counteract it took two forms. Either they sought to 'Indianize' education by preparing textbooks with a different cultural content and by pressing for the use of the vernacular, or they founded independent educational institutions. Noteworthy in north India in this respect were the schools founded by the Ārya Samāj and those established during the nationalist movement, the so-called 'national' schools. Such independent schools became, as we shall see, important symbolic 'places' and rearing grounds for nationalists. In all of them Hindi figured centrally as the 'national language.' In practice, such schools often differed little from government schools: self-management, religious instruction, spinning, and constructive work were the only features peculiar to them.[157] A few set their own curriculum, wrote and published alternative textbooks and provided symbolic 'Indian' alternatives in education (see below). All in all, the first avenue, that of influencing the school curriculum and the education department 'from within', proved to be the safer and more feasible option, especially as the scope of Hindi education within the public system increased. Also, the reformist and self-improving aims of Hindi writers and publishers often partly coincided with those of concerned officials in the colonial administration.

Nineteenth-century Hindi textbooks for primary and middle schools were largely the result either of missionary activity or of direct commissioning by education officials (the Education Department of Oudh was set up in 1864).[158] William Kempson and Śiva Prasād Siṃh in Benares, A.W. Fallon, George A. Grierson, and Bhudev Mukhopadhyay in Bihar were key figures at this stage. Their support for Hindi as the 'language

[155] 'Rāṣṭrīy śikṣā', editorial in *Chāṁd*, VII, pt. 2, 6, October 1929, p. 630.

[156] Kumar, *The Political Agenda of Education*, p. 116.

[157] *General Report on Public Instruction*, quinquennium 1917–22, p. 51.

[158] By 1870–1 there were 20 government high schools in the province and 35 English middle schools and Tahsili schools, in which instruction 'to a fairly high standard was given in the Vernacular exclusively'. Government schools had an ernolment of 11,500 students, aided schools 16,200; this was before the expansion in University education diverted funds and attention from these 'feeder' institutions; Bhargava, *A History of Secondary Education*, p. 32.

of the people' encouraged them to write, translate, and commission textbooks. Śiva Prasād's textbooks on arithmetics, history, and his *Hindi Selections* (1867, renamed *Guṭkā*) were used all over north India for decades. Bhudev Mukhopadhya, who came to Patna as Director of Public Instruction in 1877, established his own Branch Bodhoday Press to print textbooks and collaborated with the Khadgvilas Press of Bankipore (Patna), virtually giving the latter monopoly over textbook production in Bihar at least until 1930. The anthology compiled by the Khadgvilas Press manager Sāhabprasād Siṃh, *Bhāṣā-sār* (1881), remained until 1936 the prescribed textbook in High School and Intermediate examinations in Bihar.[159] Like Śiva Prasād Siṃh's *Guṭkā*, *Bhāṣā-sār* did much to popularize and keep in print the writings of nineteenth-century Khari Boli writers that had appeared in journal or book form; indeed, such-textbooks initiated the process of canonization of modern Hindi literature.

This osmosis between British and Indian officials and private writers and publishers was the beginning of a trend that was to become dominant when Textbook Committees transferred to private publishers and authors the task of preparing textbooks for the regular curriculum.[160] Among the first publishers to jump at this opportunity were the Indian Press of Allahabad, which gained an almost complete monopoly in UP, Macmillan Co. of Calcutta, and Khadgvilas Press in Bihar.[161] Primers, elementary readers, and textbooks on arithmetics, geography and history guaranteed their publishers large print-runs and continuous publication, indirectly

[159] Siṃh, *Ādhunik hindī ke vikās meṁ kaḍgvilās pres kī bhūmikā,* pp. 250 ff.

[160] Formed in 1894, the UP Textbook Committee superseded previous similar committees for each educational division of the province. Its duties were to select textbooks for government schools, to recommend changes in prescribed textbooks, to make suggestions for the creation of new books, and to make lists of books for school prizes and for school libraries. The work was mainly done by sub-committees: the Hindi Sub-Committee initially did not include any Hindi native speaker! Still, a few Hindi literati worked in other branches of the Department, bridging the gaps between the policy of the Committee and the wishes of Hindi associations. King, 'The Nagari Pracharini Sabha', pp. 297 ff.

[161] The writers were often teachers or officials of the education department itself, who would naturally find it easier to have their books prescribed by the Textbook Committee. Thus, among the first writers of textbooks we find Lala Sītārām, Deputy Collector, and Mr Mackenzie of the Indian Education Service, who later became Director of Public Instruction in UP. The other main writers were: Rāmjīlāl Śarmā, who initially worked for the Indian Press and later started his own press and two children's journals, Pt. Rāmdīn Miśra, Lala Bhagvān Dīn, Babu Rāmlochanśaran 'Bihārī', Pt. Rāmlochan Śarmā 'Kaṇṭak', Śyāmsundar Dās, and Mahāvīr Prasād Dvivedī.

financing other 'serious' publications. In this way private publishers and their writers acquired the means to prepare textbooks according to their own linguistic and cultural tastes. The Committee became the object of unofficial pressure from publishers, literary associations, and their members in the education department. Hindi intellectuals became even more involved in, and sensitive toward, education. They realized that the 'right' ideas could be instilled early and deep by circulating them in the public sphere through textbooks. In fact, the first generations of Hindi literati mostly found employment in the education department or in areas connected with it. Thus their loyalties were divided between the department and its policy, and cultural agenda of Hindi propaganda. To gain control over Hindi textbook production was a 'soft' way to pursue the latter without endangering the former, at least until the whole climate changed after 1920. Schools were a low-status institution within the colonial administration, and vernacular schools even more so. 'The role of language teaching as a means of spreading religio-cultural consciousness was far too subtle', Krishna Kumar has argued, 'to be acknowledged by the bureaucracy of the education department as a contradiction in its "secular" policy.'[162]

This situation partly changed in the 1920s when the UP Municipalities Act (1916) and the UP District Boards Act (1922) gave the Boards, which were responsible for the administration of most vernacular schools, elective chairmen who were also the chief executives in charge of local vernacular schools. The education department continued keeping tight control over the curriculum, examinations, the recognition and inspection of schools, and grants-in-aid; even so, when the municipal elections of 1922–3 put Congressmen in control of municipal boards in Lucknow, Allahabad, Kanpur, and Benares, former non-cooperators could exercise some power and undertake some initiatives within the official system of education.[163] Although the extent and nature of their initiatives require further study, Congressmen seem indeed to have taken some

[162] Kumar, *The Political Agenda of Education,* p. 135.

[163] The chairman of the district board controlled, among other things, the appointment, leave, punishment, dismissal, and transfer of teachers; the arrangements for opening new schools; and the supply of furniture to the schools; however, limited financial means usually curbed radical initiatives. As a result of the Montagu-Chelmsford reforms of 1919, two Indians became in 1922 ministers in the new elected UP cabinet (C.Y. Chintamani and Jat Narain, and after they both resigned, Rai Rajeshwar Bali and Jwala Prasad Shrivastava). None of them was from a Hindi background, and all in all they showed limited interest in education. K.P. Kichlu was chief inspector of vernacular education from 1920 to his retirement, and 'his office

steps in both institutional and discursive directions. In Allahabad, for example, the second municipal election in 1921 returned Puruṣottam Dās Ṭaṇḍon (1882–1962) as chairman of the Board and Saṅgamlāl Agravāl as chairman of the education committee: together they implemented a scheme for a national Hindi-medium college for women, the Prayāg Mahilā Vidyāpīṭh (see 4.1). Similarly, in the 1923 election in Benares, Dr Bhagvān Dās, the noted philosopher and father of Congress leader Śrīprakāś, was elected chairman of the Board. Sampūrṇānand became the dynamic chairman of the education committee, and in that capacity he acted against a previous decision taken by the education department, that of banning some textbooks Rāmdās Gauṛ had written for 'national' schools. Although Sampūrṇānand was not empowered to lift the ban, he could commission new textbooks. Because Gauṛ's 3rd and 4th reader were used in municipal schools, Sampūrṇānand claimed that after the ban 'the need arose for books that might take their place, i.e. which would teach patriotism, love for freedom, self-reliance, self-control, self-sacrifice and other such qualities along with the other useful subjects'.[164] Mukundīlāl Śrīvāstava (BA and Hindī Sāhitya Sammelan graduate), the editorial director of the nationalist publisher Jnanmandal, was appointed to compile them. Predictably, the new readers contained much nationalist literature, with passages by Gandhi, nationalist poems by poets like 'Triśūl' and M. Gupta, and biographies of Tilak and C.R. Das.[165] In this way, a partly nationalist syllabus came to be taught within government schools, albeit only at primary level, and teachers were brought in direct contact with politics. When the Benares municipal board was dismissed for mismanagement in 1933, Premchand protested that the education department of the board was probably one of the best of the province, and education was not

> as lifeless as in the schools managed by the government bureacracy [*naukarśāhī*]. Moreover, no one has tried as much as the muncipality of this town to teach children, beside knowledge, the sorrowful state of the country, its political subjection, and to make them the future reformers of the country, and their teachers true masters.[166]

---

dealt directly with district boards and municipalities in matters concerning vernacular education'; Bhargava, *A History of Secondary Education*, p. 153.

[164] This and the following information are taken from his introduction to Mukundīlāl Śrīvāstava's *Hindī kī chauthī pustak*, Benares, Jnanmandal, 1925.

[165] See ibid.

[166] Premchand, 'Śrī rāmeśvar sahāy sinhā', *Jāgaraṇ*, 14, May 1933, quoted in *Vividh prasaṅg*, vol. 2, Allahabad: Hans Prakasan, 1980, p. 528; cf. 5.1, here.

The two aspects in which Hindi literati could most make their mark in primers were the choice of language and cultural content. When Chintamani Ghosh, the founder of the Indian Press, picked up Mahāvīr Prasād Dvivedī from his obscure job as a telegraph clerk and appointed him the editor of the Press' Hindi journal and its foremost literary advisor, he did so after Dvivedī brought out a critique (printed as a booklet in 1899) of the Indian Press' *Third Hindi Reader* (*Hindī śikṣāvalī,* 1889) by Dīndayāl Śarmā and Lala Sītārām (1858–1938).[167] He did so with good reason. In his rigorous and sarcastic analysis, Dvivedī had pointed out faults in grammar, syntax and idiom, and the improper choice of didactic and poetic passages (all in Braj Bhasa), and of passages from the *Manusmṛti*. His sure sense of language and of what he considered proper moral instruction, his appeal to reform, and his blend of loyalism and patriotism must have appealed to Chintamani Ghosh, who felt very much along the same lines.

इस पुस्तक को हमने सद्यान्त पढ़ा परन्तु इसमें ऐसा कोई पाठ हमको न मिला जिसमें अंग्रेज़ी राज्य की प्रशंसा अथवा कथा होती। नादिरशाह का वृत्तान्त है, भारतेश्वारी विक्टोरिया का नहीं। बाबर की कथा बड़े प्रेम से वर्णन की गई है, किसी वाइसराय की नहीं। जिसके राज्य में हम लोग सुख से शयन करते हैं, जिसके राज्य में हिन्दी पाठशालाएँ नियत हुई हैं, और जिसके राज्य में आज किताबें लिखने का सौभाग्य हमको प्राप्त हुआ है, उसका अथवा उसके किसी प्रतिनिधि का परिचय लड़कों को दिलाना क्या कोई अनुचित बात थी?

I have read this book from beginning to end and could not find any lesson which contained some praise or description of English rule. The story of Nādirśāh is there, but not that of empress Victoria. Babar's story has been lovingly told, but there is nothing about a Viceroy. Wouldn't it have been appropriate to introduce pupils to the reign in which we sleep peacefully, which has established Hindi schools, and for which we have now the good fortune of writing Hindi books [and introduce them] to any of its representative figures?[168]

In the primer Dvivedī produced for the Indian Press in 'everyday language' (*rozmarrā kī bolī*),[169] the emphasis was all on moral instruction, with lessons on the good boy (lesson 7) and the bad boy (8), and on

[167] Dīndayāl Śarmā was at the time Assistant Inspector of Schools in the Allahabad division, and Babu Sītārām BA was Deputy Collector and a veteran Hindi writer in the public service; for Sītārām's career, see biography in the Appendix.

[168] *Criticism on the Hindi Reader No III by Mahavir Prasad Dvivedi*, Jhansi, 1899, p. 33. Noteworthy here are both the loyalism, not surprising among patriots of the time, and the need Dvivedī felt to introduce children to the contemporary predicament.

[169] M.P. Dvivedī, *Hindī kī pahlī kitāb*, Allahabad, Indian Press, 1911 edition, but probably 1903, title page.

how children should not wear jewellery (9). All animal stories, according to the Indian tradition, carried a lesson, in this case a very moral one (the donkey was a model of hard work, the parrot of a student learning by rote, monkeys as examples of bad behaviour, etc.). Children were told to obey and love their parents, to make good use of their time and to be enterprising. For example, they were told not to consider office employment as their only aim nor to look down on commercial occupations:

नौकरी करके कभी कोई अमीर नहीं हुआ। अमीर होने के लिए बैपार चाहिए . . . हम लोग बैपार करना नहीं जानते यह अफ़सोस की बात है . . . नमक मिर्च मसाला तेल तक बेचने में शरम न करना चाहिए। बैपार बनियों ही के लिए नहीं है- सभी के लिए है।

No one ever got rich by working in an office. Business makes one rich . . . It is a pity that we do not know how to do business . . . There is no need to feel ashamed of selling salt, pepper, spices or even oil. Business is not only for baniyās, it is for all.[170]

Simple natural and physical descriptions of nature, a poem in praise of education and a final one on God who is presented as a well-meaning creator without sectarian specifications, concluded the book. In terms of language, Dvivedī dutifully respected the Indian Press' wish to conform to the policy of the education department of keeping the language of Hindi and Urdu textbooks the same, the only difference being that of script.[171]

The fierce public debates in the province over the proper language of education forced the government to undertake an official enquiry and accept a compromise solution. After the Piggott commission of 1912–13, the government reiterated its policy of a 'common language' but at the same time ordered separate supplementary readers in Hindi and Urdu, which came into use in 1916. The decision amounted to an admission that its policy of a 'common language' had failed, and gave leeway to the introduction in the school curriculum of a more sanskritized Hindi, of passages with more definite and elaborate cultural content, and of Hindi literature. In a word, it gave a great boost to textbook production.[172] It also

[170] Ibid., p. 21.

[171] See e.g. the letter (dated 16.5.1903) from the government of U.P. to the Director of Public Instruction, confirming a policy dating from 1876: 'Several recently published school books have been expressly designed to give a practical effect to the principle that the common language of the educated classes in N.W.P. is one and the same, whether it be written in the persian or nagri letter . . .'; quoted in King, 'The Nagari Pracharini Sabha', p. 298.

[172] Ibid., p. 472.

showed that Hindi enterprises in the public sphere, and a different political environment, could compel the government to take a more compliant stance.

Rāmjīlāl Śarmā's *Bālvinod* (part 5 for the 5th class), first published by the Indian Press in 1910, shows this shift. If compared with Dvivedī's primer, its cultural content was much more wide-ranging: passages on moral values (piety, diligence, thrift, hygiene) were interspersed with stories from India's glorious past (with poets such as Tulsīdās and Kālidāsa, and rulers such as Śūdraka and Yudhiṣṭhira but also Ahalyābāī), and with stories from other countries of the world (Portugal, Russia, Japan, Italy). Geography and religion merged in the passage on 'The history of queen Ahalyābāī', which opened with: 'Those who have travelled even once to Kāśī, Prayāg and Vṛndāvan . . . must have noticed the monuments left by queen Ahalyā.'[173] These 'prose sections' were accompanied by 'poetry sections', which included a large selection of moral couplets, descriptive passages from Tulsī's *Rāmcharitmānas* and the episode of Rāma's bow, a few Braj Bhasa couplets by Girdhar and Vṛnd, and a poem on *Bhāratvarṣa*. All in all, *Bālvinod* was more of a reader and offered the child educated through the medium of Hindi the same format as an English textbook, with its Victorian engraving, its emphasis on moral instruction, and some of its 'adventurous' quality.[174] Significantly, it ignored the British presence in India to concentrate either on India's glorious past or on modern Indian reformers. Finally, it introduced the child to Tulsīdās, the hero of the Hindi literary tradition, and used Hindi poetry to convey both moral instruction and a sense of community.

[173] Rāmjīlāl Śarmā, *Bālvinod*, pt. 5, Allahabad, Indian Press, 1910, p. 25. The second part of the prose section included a similar miscellany of Indianness, modernity, adventures from the world, and moral values: ancient Indianness in the shape of the Nala–Dāmāyantī story and new Indianness in the shape of Vidyāsāgar's biography and Bālkṛṣṇa Bhaṭṭ's classic essay on 'conversation'; modernity in the form of passages on the art of printing; adventures in the form of Robinson Crusoe's story and other stories from around the world, and moral values with five out of the thirteen passages on physical and moral education.

[174] If we look at Śarmā's parallel textbook for girls, *Bālābodhini*, part 5 (Indian Press, 1912), we find a consistent simplification. No mention is made of the world outside, and only Indian stories are presented: no Robinson Crusoe, no Portugal, no Russia. There were common passages (on Kālidāsa, on Ahalyābāī), but in the version for girls history is turned into stories, with no dates and no historical perspective. The book, half the size of the one for boys, contains much the same poetry and the same percentage of moral tales, though of course geared towards making good daughters, wives, and mothers.

Religion as such was not present, but was subsumed in a 'secular' cultural message. Moreover, both in the textbook for boys and that for girls, the language was far from the 'rozmarrā kī bolī' of Dvivedī's book of 1903 and reflected the growing pressure of Hindi activists to make the language of Hindi textbooks distinct from Urdu. The same public language of polite and serious discourse that had been shaped in journals was thus now replicated in textbooks; competence in this language became the mark of 'having an education' and a prerequisite for white-collar employment.

After 1916, Hindi rose slowly but steadily in the education system: it became a compulsory subject up to the high school leaving examination in 1922 and an optional subject in intermediate colleges in 1927. Again, more and more literary readers, anthologies, and students' editions had to be prepared, giving rise to a veritable industry. This change went hand in hand with the building of the Hindi literary canon in the first Hindi university departments (see 1.4.2). The process of setting the syllabus and choosing and preparing course books took up the greater part of the 1920s. By the 1930s the curriculum was ready, and could be reproduced, transmitted, diluted, splintered and slightly altered for countless readers in the higher primary and secondary grades. Compiling textbooks provided a side income for lecturers, but more importantly, in this way their values, choices, and opinions acquired much wider currency, reaching pupils far greater in number than those who would actually make it to university. This, in turn, enhanced their intellectual authority, and their status as inheritors of a Hindi intellectual tradition. It was in fact thanks to the likes of Śyāmsundar Dās (1875–1945), Harioudh, Bhagvān Dīn, Rāmdās Gauṛ, Rāmchandra Śukla, Pītāmbardatt Baṛathvāl (1902–44), P.P. Bakhśī, and Kāmtāprasād Guru that the works of Hindi intellectuals from the nineteenth century onwards were compacted into a common corpus of literary passages.

Anthologies of the nineteenth century, like Śiva Prasād's *Guṭkā* and Sāhabpratāp Siṃh's *Bhāṣā-sār*, had been miscellaneous collections of passages deemed suitable for instruction, either written for the purpose or drawing upon translations and articles that had appeared in journals; later school readers became more literary and less dependent on translations.[175] Moreover, anthologies for high schools and intermediate

[175] See, e.g. Ayodhyānāth Śarmā and Sadguru Saran (both professors at the Sanatan Dharma College in Kanpur), *Sāhitya-kusum*, in 3 parts, for classes 4 to 6 of vernacular schools, expressly produced according to the curriculum set by the education department in 1916, Kanpur, Gautam Press, n.d. Since Śarmā was member

colleges started to include histories of the Hindi language and literature, and arranged selections in chronological order, establishing a tradition of modern classics along with that of medieval poets. They became the means by which the idea of Hindi as a language with a separate linguistic tradition and cultural identity could be spread authoritatively. The prose section of *Hindī-bhāṣā-sār* by Lala Bhagvān Dīn and Rāmdās Gauṛ (1916, 4th augmented edition 1927), for example, traced the development of modern Hindi prose back to Munśi Sadāsukhlāl, and included Urdu writers like Nazīr Ahmad and Ratannāth Sarshār. This allowed the authors to argue that language was not determined by script, and that Hindi had two styles, 'pure' (*śuddh*) and 'mixed' (*miśrit*), 'also called Urdu' (p. 9): in other words, that (a) Urdu had filiated from Hindi and was not actually a separate language, and that (b) Hindi prose had not developed only under the patronage of Fort William college (with the customary Lallūjī Lāl), but also independently.[176]

Prose always meant almost exclusively non-fiction, with only the occasional short story, since novels were deemed too entertaining to be included. Whereas poetry selections for the lower forms included more patriotic poetry (M. Gupta, 'Triśūl', 'Ek bhārtīy ātmā', i.e. Mākhanlāl Chaturvedī), anthologies for the higher classes emphasized the unbroken line from the medieval 'Hindi' (i.e. Avadhi, Braj Bhasa) tradition to modern Braj Bhasa and Khari Boli poetry, with a few 'daring' incursions into Chāyāvād.[177]

Long historical introductions and biographical notes were an attempt to bring in some critical analysis and to change the customary method of teaching, which involved giving only the meanings of words and explanations of phrases and of figures of speech.[178] However, these methods

---

of the UP Board of High School & Intermediate Education, his reader was sure to be adopted. See also Kālidās Kapūr (Headmaster of Kalicharan High School, Lucknow), *Hindī-sār-saṅgrah* for classes 4 and 5, Allahabad: Agraval Press, 1933; Harioudh and Girijādatt Śukla 'Girīś', *Sāhitya-mālā* for classes 5 and 6 (illust.), Benares, Nandkishor and Bros, 1932.

[176] B. Dīn and R. Gauṛ, *Hindī bhāṣā sār*, prose section, Prayag, Hindi Sahitya Sammelan, 1916, 4th edition 1927, pp. 2–3.

[177] See e.g. Keśavprasād Miśra and Pītāmbardatt Baṛathvāl (both lecturers at BHU), *Padya parijāt*, Benares, Nagari Pracharini Sabha, 1931; Kāmtāprasād Guru, *Padya samucchaya*, Allahabad, Indian Press, 3rd ed. 1934—both for high school classes. Quite innovatively, *Padya parijāt* included poems by Prasād, Pant, Nirālā, and Rāykṛṣṇadās.

[178] Śyāmsundar Dās, foreword to *Hindi Prose Selection* for classes 9 and 10 of High schools, Allahabad, Indian Press, 1929, p. 1.

must indeed have remained the norm, judging by the 'keys' (*kuñjīs*) and answer books for the textbooks and the exams, by the appendices on metre and rhetoric in the anthologies, and by the kinds of questions future teachers were asked in Hindī Sāhitya Sammelan examinations. Selections were treated as independent, self-sufficient texts which students had to memorize, to 'translate' into their own language or into the standard language used for examinations, and to interpret in one, set way—the notorious *bhāvārth* and *vyākhyā* which are still the examinee's lot today.

The expansion and rise of Hindi in the curriculum took place under the influence of Hindi literary experts and brought them to a position of intellectual authority even in colonial times. Unlike journals, education was an arena in which their choices in terms of language and literature encountered no challenges. The standard language, the 'pure' Hindi of literary reformers, became the language of education and the mark of school proficiency. As Krishna Kumar has pointed out, this choice of language in education, which excluded spoken varieties and labelled Urdu words as 'foreign', was not without consequences. It involved 'an exacerbation of syntactical complexity and a Sanskritization of vocabulary. These tendencies, in turn, strengthened the reproductive role of education. Only children of upper-caste backgrounds could feel at home in a school culture where the language used was so restrictive.'[179]

It was not only a question of language: literary texts from the past and from the present were also forced and arranged into neat categories and assigned only 'useful' or character-building meanings; it was this which constituted the Hindi literary canon. Once students became teachers they would, in turn, reproduce the same linguistic and literary saṃskāra. Literature as entertainment and as the adventurous discovery of one's environment and of other worlds, as a variety of possible experiments through language, seems to have had little room in this.

1.4.2. The Hindi Curriculum in Universities

To establish Hindi as a university subject was one recurrent aspiration voiced in Hindi journals of the 1910s and 1920s.[180] For all the emphasis on Hindi as the medium of mass education, clearly to establish Hindi at the top of the education system was equally, if not more, important for Hindi supporters. This was seen as a way to 'Indianize'

[179] Kumar, *The Political Agenda of Education*, p. 142.

[180] See e.g. 'Deś-bhāṣā meṁ śikṣā', *Sammelan patrikā*, III, 7–8, February–March 1916, p. 205.

universities, those 'domains of English'; the predominance of English in colleges was a sign of systematic denationalization. As a Hindi editor lamented: 'Our nation is being formed, there is no doubt about it, but it will not be a Hindu nation, it will be an English nation like Canada and New Zealand.'[181] Hindi at university level would prove that the language and its literature were fully developed, and establish its authority as much as possible on a par with English. The creation of Hindi departments was thus a question of status; it also involved codifying a literary canon according to institutional requirements. While the first university to hold MA examinations in Hindi was Calcutta, the first full-fledged Hindi departments were all in the United Provinces: initially at Benares Hindu University (BHU) in 1922 (a good six years after the university was founded), followed by Allahabad University in 1926, Lucknow, Agra, etc.[182]

In fact, when BHU was finally inaugurated in 1916 after ten years of relentless fund raising tours by Madan Mohan Mālavīya, Hindi supporters were hopeful that this champion of Hindi would make it the first university with Hindi as the medium of instruction. Never before had so much money been collected for a public institution, and no other university could count so many departments. 'The BHU was a community project, not a gift of the administration as Allahabad was. It quickly became the mint where the modern cultural coinage of the north Indian plains was stamped and approved for circulation . . . The name of BHU was supposed to wash away the associations of Macaulay and his legacy from one's education.'[183] So much greater then was the disappointment and puzzlement of Hindi supporters when they discovered that English would still be the medium of instruction and that there was to be no Hindi department either. Several public appeals were made, especially by the nationalist millionaire Babu Śivaprasād Gupta, who had donated generously to the

[181] See the editorial note in *Mādhurī*, III, pt. 2, 2, March 1925, p. 276.

[182] The fact that Calcutta was the first university to introduce Hindi as a subject was a source of no small embarrassment for Hindi intellectuals of the United Provinces. Since the provision of Indian languages, and Bengali in particular, as main subjects had been in place there since 1916, the introduction of Hindi seems to have been mainly a question of funds and endowments. Hindi teaching started on a small scale in 1922 after a donation by Ghanshyamdas Birla. Lala Sītārām, the retired Hindi scholar of the UP education department, was approached by the Vice-Chancellor, Sir Ashutosh Mukherjee, and prepared 6 volumes of *Hindi Selections*, which the publisher, the Indian Press, presented to Calcutta University as a gift; quoted from *Bhāratmitra* in *Sammelan patrikā*, VI, 12, June 1920, pp. 280–3.

[183] Kumar, *The Political Agenda of Education*, p. 129.

University: he wrote several open letters to *Bhāratmitra*, presented motions at the Jhansi Provincial Hindī Sāhitya Sammelan and the Bhārtīy Sāhitya Sammelan in Jabalpur, and eventually decided to found a national university single-handedly, Kāśī Vidyāpīṭh, where higher instruction would all be in the 'national language'.

Mālavīya's arguments had been threefold: firstly, BHU was not a provincial university (like Allahabad) but a national one, which was to cater to students from all over India; secondly, India was not yet ready to accept Hindi as its national language in practice, though that was the common aim; third, and this was kept confidential, BHU, despite being an independent institution, needed government aid, and the condition of the then Education Secretary, Sir Harcourt Butler, was that instruction should be in English.[184] In his presidential speech at the UP Provincial Hindī Sāhitya Sammelan in Moradabad in 1920—with both Mālavīya and Gupta present—Padmasiṃh Śarmā responded scathingly to these arguments:

हिन्दु विश्वविद्यालय जैसे सफ़ेद हाथी के पालन पोषण में गरीब पबलिक का लाखों रुपया नष्ट करने से देश और जाति को क्या लाभ पहुंचा यह ज़रा गर्दन झुकाकर सोचने की बात है। गरीब क़ौम को ऐसे तिलायी चर्खों की ज़रूरत नहीं है। इसके लिए देशी काठ के करघे गुरुकुल महाविद्यालय ऋषिकुल जैसी संस्थाएँ ही कहीं मुफ़ीद हैं जो यथाशक्ति राष्ट्रभाषा का प्रचार कर रही हैं। हिन्दू विश्वविद्यालय से हिन्दी का बहिष्कार इतना न अखरता यदि यह जाति की न होकर सरकारी संस्था होती।

We ought to bow our heads in shame and think what good has accrued to the country and the community (*jāti*) by wasting lakhs belonging to the poor public to feed a white elephant like the Hindu University. A poor nation has no need for such foreign machines. Institutions like the Gurukul university and the Rishikul, which are trying their utmost to propagate Hindi, are much more useful. The exclusion of Hindi from the Hindu University would not feel so bad if it were an official institution instead of a community one.[185]

The appointment of the first two Hindi lecturers, Rāmchandra Śukla and Lala Bhagvān Dīn, at BHU in 1921 marked the belated recognition of public opinion. It also signalled an important step: both lecturers were well-known literary figures but with no university qualifications. Both belonged to the Kāśī Nāgarī Prachāriṇī Sabhā: after thirty years of voluntary activity in the public sphere, the foremost association of Hindi literati had come to occupy a seat of official literary authority. The

[184] Quoted in *Sammelan patrikā*, VIII, 10, May–June 1921, p. 235.
[185] Quoted in *Sammelan patrikā*, VIII, 6, p. 98.

scholars and activists had become professors. With the appointment as the head of the Hindi department a few months later of Śyāmsundar Dās, one of the Nāgarī Prachāriṇī Sabhā founders, the creation of a Hindi establishment was complete. Nonetheless, despite being leading authorities in the Hindi literary sphere, Hindi lecturers at BHU soon found out that they were still suffering discriminatory treatment within the university and were being paid less than their colleagues, so engrained was the English vernacular hierarchy in education, even within a 'community' institution.[186]

The appointment of the Nāgarī Prachāriṇī Sabhā scholars was an important step also in terms of canon formation, as they brought into the standardized curriculum the expertise and scholarly achievements of the Sabhā critical editions. One of the main problems facing Śyāmsundar Dās in organizing the courses was the lack of course books: good editions of Hindi classics, notably by the Sabhā itself, were by now in print but not easily available. Nothing, moreover, existed for subjects such as linguistics and literary criticism, and almost nothing on the history of the Hindi language and literature. On the strength of their publishing experience with the Sabhā and with pioneering zeal, the three teachers produced what would become the standard manuals and critical editions for decades. Lala Bhagvān Dīn, an expert on rīti poetry as well as a skilful poet himself, wrote commentaries and works on traditional poetics.[187] Śyāmsundar Dās wrote on literary criticism and on the history of the

[186] Both Rāmchandra Śukla and Bhagvān Dīn had been initially appointed at a lower salary than any other lecturer (Rs 60 per month); despite Śyamsundar Dās' protests, he, a professor, was paid at the rank of an assistant-professor, something which made him wonder about the sincerity of Mālavīya's feelings towards Hindi; see Dās, *Merī ātmakahānī*, pp. 207, 210. By comparison, salaries at Allahabad University in 1927 were Rs 800 to 1250 per month for professors; Rs 450 to 850 for readers; Rs 250 to 450 for lecturers, and Rs 150 for junior lecturers. Salaries in aided primary schools in 1922 were Rs 10 for untrained teachers, Rs 14 for trained teachers, and Rs 20 for schoolmasters, *Quinquennial Report on Public Instruction in the United Provinces of Agra and Oudh*, for the years 1922–27, p. 14, and 1917–22, p. 78.

[187] Bhagvān Dīn wrote commentaries on Keśavdās (*Keśav-kaumudī*, Benares, 1923–4), Bihārī (*Bihārī-bodhinī*, Benares, 1925–6, and *Bihārī aur Dev*, Benares, 1926), Tulsīdās (*Tulsī-pañcharatna*, 1928; a commentary to the *Ayodhyākāṇḍa* and the *Kiṣkindhākāṇḍa* in 1926–7, and to *Kavitāvalī* in 1931–2 with Viśvanāth Prasād Miśra). He had written *Alaṃkār-mañjuṣā*, a treatise on poetic tropes, in 1916; in 1927 he added another, *Vyaṅgyārtha-mañjuṣā*, and a translation of the Sanskrit text *Anyokti-kalpadruma* in 1931–2. Cf. Appendix.

Hindi language.[188] And Rāmchandra Śukla's output was truly impressive.[189]

To take a brief look at the syllabus: the Entrance examination paper on Hindi poetry included extracts from Chandbardāī, Kabīr, Sūrdās, Tulsīdās (56 out of 104 pages for him alone), Bihārī, Keśavdās, and only one modern work, Maithilīśaraṇ Gupta's revivalist poem *Bhārat bhārtī* (cf. 3.1). The emphasis thus was heavily on medieval Hindi, and modern literature ended with the earnestly reformist Dvivedī age; fiction, as well as contemporary poetry, had no part in the curriculum. The tension between the canonical and the contemporary is, of course, not peculiar to Hindi. But with modern Hindi being a tradition 'in the making', choices made in academia had immediate reverberations in the literary sphere. They made the issue of literary authority all the more irksome for contemporary experimentators, particularly in the absence of widespread popularity as a counterbalance (cf. 2.2 and 2.4).

Literary criticism, according to the syllabus, involved some description of the historical context and a redefinition of rasa in psychological terms. However, in reality it consisted largely of an admixture of moral judgements and traditional Braj Bhasa poetics. The literary past of the region was ordered in a nationalist narration; it was a literature which had had a glorious, martial beginning with the *rāsos* in Rajasthan, had come to a cultural and literary climax with Sūrdās and Tulsīdās during the Bhakti period, the flame being kept alight even in the dark age of Muslim

[188] Dās compiled a textbook on criticism while teaching (*Sāhityālochan*, 1922, see 2.2); he then compiled a similar course-book on linguistics (*Bhāṣā-rahasya*, Indian Press 1935, augmented edition as *Bhāṣa-vijñān* in 1938) with the help of Padmanārāyaṇ Āchārya. The section on the development of Khari Boli was also published in English in the 'Bulletin of the School of Oriental and African Studies' at Grierson's behest; Dās, *Merī ātmakahānī*, pp. 222 ff.

[189] Having worked until then on Nāgarī Prachāriṇī Sabhā projects, Śukla now edited a large number of classic texts: with Lala Bhagvān Dīn and Brajratna Dās, the three volumes of *Tulsī granthāvalī* (1923), the complete works of Jāyasī (1924), Sūrdās's *Bhramar gīt* (1925), and Bhārtendu's works (1928). To these should be added his important works on aesthetics: *Chintāmaṇi* (1939 and 1945) and the essays of *Ras-mīmāṃsā* (1922, but published together in 1949). His history of Hindi literature (1923–9, rev. ed. 1940), originally a preface to the monumental dictionary of the Nāgarī Prachāriṇī Sabhā, has remained the standard text on the subject, a landmark in terms of periodization, historical characterization, and critical treatment of single authors. His admiration for Tulsīdās and the 'golden age' of medieval Hindi literature and his mistrust of contemporary developments (especially Chāyāvād) set the tone of the atmosphere at BHU (cf. 5.2).

occupation; it had declined then into unhealthy and useless eroticism during the rīti period and started ascending again along a reformist path in the nineteenth century. This was, in a nutshell, Śukla's historical account, barely questioned in Hindi scholarship since, apart from Hazārīprasād Dvivedī's rehabilitation of Kabīr, and Nāmvar Siṃh's attempt at discerning a 'progressive', popular Hindi tradition.[190]

Allahabad University, the first official university in the province, had a different history altogether. Originally an examining body, it was reorganized in 1921 as a teaching University through the Allahabad University Act. Colleges in other parts of the province and in neighbouring areas were disaffiliated and new teaching universities were formed in Lucknow (1921), Agra (1925), and Nagpur. By 1937 the University comprised about a 100 professors and 1500 students, out of whom a 1000 lived in eight hostels. One of them, Holland Hall (est. 1900), was modelled on Oxbridge colleges. Teaching was—and still is—mostly geared towards law and the administrative services, though with due attention to the Arts (English literature, Sanskrit, Arabic, Persian, philosophy, history, etc.), and by all accounts the atmosphere was definitely genteel. In contrast with BHU, the Hindi department in Allahabad University had nothing against contemporary literature. In fact, with Sumitrāṇandan Pant, Rāmkumār Varmā, Mahādevī Varmā, Bagavatīcharaṇ Varmā, Harivaṃśrāy 'Bachchan' and later Dharmvīr Bhārtī, Jagdīś Gupta and many others among its students and teachers, Allahabad University was definitely in the vanguard on the literary front.

Even so Hindi was a latecomer there, too. Despite the efforts of Vice-Chancellor Gaṅgānāth Jhā, a Sanskrit scholar, Hindi teaching started only in 1923, with the appointment of Dhīrendra Varmā, a Sanskrit graduate from the university.[191] In 1916 Gaṅgānāth Jhā had proposed at a Senate meeting that instruction in *deśbhāṣa* be made compulsory for

[190] See Nāmvar Siṃh, *Dūsrī paramparā kī khoj*, New Delhi, Rajkamal Prakasan, 1982, where the critical climate at BHU during Hazārīprasād Dvivedī's time is vividly recaptured. The subject requires a much broader discussion, which would demand a separate study.

[191] As a student of Muir Central College, Dhīrendra Varmā had lived at the Hindu Boarding House, with Acharya Narendra Dev, Paraśurām Chaturvedī, Sumitrānandan Pant, and Bābūrām Saxenā as hostel mates. Dhīrendra Varmā and Bābūrām Saxena were both students of Gaṅgānāth Jhā; Saxena and Paraśurām Chaturvedī were later employed in the University, too. Among Varmā's students were Mātāprasād Gupta, Hardev Bāhrī, Lakṣmīsāgar Vārṣṇey, Brajeśvar Varmā, and Raghuvaṃś, all familiar names in Hindi literary historiography.

Matriculation, but his proposal was rejected. A Hindī Pariṣad was then founded in 1922 by Dhīrendra Varmā on the pattern of other students' societies. Setting up debating competitions, poetry meetings, and essay-writing competitions, it 'helped a lot in creating feelings of respect, sympathy and affection towards the mother-tongue Hindi in the "English" atmosphere of the University'.[192] In fact it was part of the success of the society that a full fledged Hindi department was created. Lectures started in 1924 with five students, and in 1926 Urdu and Hindi formally became degree subjects—as French, German, and Italian already were.[193] As mentioned earlier in the chapter, in the beginning Hindi was taught in English (!) like all other subjects, and Hindi journals could not help wondering how two '*Hindī-premīs*' and active members of the Hindī Sāhitya Sammelan like Dhīrendra Varmā and Devīprasād Śukla could abide by such a rule.[194] The rule later changed (though theses were written in English until 1947), and Allahabad's Hindi department, initially small and with few students, became the second centre for Hindi studies. After Dhīrendra Varmā and Devīprasād Śukla, other Arts graduates from the University were appointed as lecturers: Rāmśaṅkar Śukla 'Rasāl', the first D.Litt. in Hindi from Allahabad (in 1937), and the poet Rāmkumār Varmā, also a student of the department.[195] This meant that Hindi students and lecturers at Allahabad either were or grew quite familiar with the English-speaking world, and could move freely between the English and Hindi spheres, something very few Hindi literati could yet do. Moreover, as a product of the university system and not of associationism, the Hindi department in Allahabad had less of a Hindi tradition and identity to pursue and uphold. Rather, it was more oriented towards mapping the field of Hindi literature and literary criticism in a modern fashion: the history of the Hindi language, Hindi linguistics, comparative literary criticism, and research methodology were all part of the curriculum and became trademarks of the department.[196] Nor did Hindi lecturers in Allahabad share any of the alienation from Urdu that their colleagues in

[192] 'Introduction' to *Pariṣad nibandhāvalī*, pt. 1, 1929.

[193] *Sammelan patrikā*, XIII, 7–8, 1926, p. 205.

[194] *Sammelan patrikā*, XIII, 9, 1926, p. 382.

[195] Interview with Rājendra Kumār Varmā, former student of Dhīrendra Varmā and Head of the Hindi Department in Allahabad, Allahabad, July 1993.

[196] Among the works written and used as course books by the members of the department are: Dhīrendra Varmā's *Hindī bhāṣa kā itihās* (1933), *Hindī bhāṣa aur lipi* (introductory chapter of the former, published separately in 1935), *Brajbhāṣa vyākaraṇ* (1937), *Aṣṭachhāp* (1938); Rāmkumār Varmā's *Sāhitya-samālochnā* (1929), *Kabīr kā rahasyavād* (1930) and *Hindī-sāhitya kā ālochnātmak itihās* (1939).

Benares had: Raghupati Sahāy 'Firāq', one of the most distinguished Urdu poets of the day, was a colleague in the English faculty, and both Hindi and Urdu lecturers took part jointly in the founding and subsequent activities of the Hindustani Academy (see 2.3).

Graduates from Benares and Allahabad gradually spread to colleges and departments all over the Hindi area, carrying with them the literary curriculum the two departments had set up for Hindi literature. Smaller universities more or less followed the curriculum set by Benares and Allahabad and used the same course-books.

By 1940, then, at the end of the period under survey, Hindi literature had established its credentials as a subject worthy of research and teaching at the highest level of education, and Hindi scholars in the universities had become central figures of authority and symbols of Hindi enterprise.[197]

1.4.3. Hindi in Ārya Samāj Institutions

Although the centralized education system made the influence of public institutions particularly pervasive, autonomous institutions were important as well. Their cultural impact was perhaps more indirect but they were like laboratories for symbolic alternatives in education. I noted earlier that autonomous schools included institutions which broadly followed the government curriculum but were managed by Indian bodies and had a few Indian features, and also some that were completely independent of the government system. The schools founded by the Ārya Samāj comprised both and were in fact the earliest and most important enterprises of the kind in north India.

The Ārya Samāj had been from the start one of the most vociferous critics of the moral dangers of English education as a vehicle for conversions to Christianity. Dayānand Sarasvatī himself had been sensitive to the use and potential as a community language of Hindi, which he called *āryabhāṣā*, the language of the Aryans. He had also switched over from Sanskrit to Hindi as the medium of preaching after meeting Brahmo Samāj leaders in Bengal in 1872, and the Ārya Samāj had been very active in Nagari propaganda at the end of the nineteenth century. The fifth of the 28 basic norms of the Ārya Samāj, established in Bombay in 1875,

[197] So much so that Hindi journals argued that the government was insulting the Hindī Sāhitya Sammelan by not taking its advice while appointing Hindi lecturers and teachers: instead of selecting only University graduates it should consult with the Hindī Sāhitya Sammelan (as some Princely States did); see editorial notes in *Mādhurī*, IV, pt. 2, 4, May 1926, pp. 562–4.

read: 'प्रधान समाज में वैदोक्तानुकूल संस्कृत और आर्यभाषा में नाना प्रकार के सदुपदेश की पुस्तक होगी,' [In the main centre there will be several books in Sanskrit and in āryabhāṣā.][198] Hindi in its sanskritized form 'became part and parcel of the movement's vision of a reformed Hindu society in which Vedic ideals would be practised.'[199]

Education, as a synonym for progress, āryabhāṣa, and Vedic ideals became the germ of Ārya Samāj propaganda, and met with a good reception among the Hindu community in the Punjab and in western UP. In fact, the first Dayanand Anglo-Vedic (DAV) college that opened in Lahore in 1886 managed to be completely independent of government aid thanks to some brilliant experiments at fund-raising from the community; by 1893 it was officially recognized.[200] Over the next twenty years, a successful network of DAV schools and colleges, now affiliated to the government system, covered the whole of Punjab and also several places in the United Provinces: Kanpur, Dehradun, Benares, Lucknow, Anup Shahar, Meerut. DAV schools were the first autonomous attempts at Indian western-style education in the area. Instruction was in English and followed broadly the government curriculum, although some of the textbooks were written by Ārya Samāj members and 'Vedic' (i.e. religious) instruction was imparted. Thus, DAV schools combined the advantages of western education with a revivalist and patriotic spirit. As Kenneth Jones put it: 'Aryas recognized the new world's demand for English literacy and sought that literacy within a milieu of revived Hinduism.'[201] Hindi was introduced as a compulsory subject by Lala Hansraj, and though it did not become the medium of education as in Ārya schools for girls (see 4.1), the success of these schools among the entire Hindu community popularized Hindi throughout the Punjab as the symbolic Hindu language. According to Lajpat Rai's autobiography, it was the Hindi–Urdu controversy of the 1880s which wedded him 'to the idea of Hindu nationalism'. Despite a heavily Islamicized father and an Urdu education, he began to make pro-Hindi speeches even before he learnt the Devanagari script![202]

[198] Quoted in Lakṣmīnārāyaṇ Gupta, *Hindī bhāṣa aur sāhitya ko ārya-samāj kī den*, Lucknow, Lucknow University, 1960, p. 26.

[199] Kumar, *The Political Agenda of Education*, p. 128.

[200] Techniques such as the *āṭā* fund, rag fund, *paisā* fund were later used in the nationalist movement; see Kenneth Jones, *Arya Dharm, Hindu Consciousness in Nineteenth Century Punjab*, Berkeley, University of California Press, 1976, pp. 81 ff.

[201] Ibid., p. 69.

[202] Quoted in Sarkar, *Modern India*, p. 127.

The official orientation of DAV schools, however, came under attack early on from more radical educationists in the Samāj like Lala Munśīrām of Jallandhar (later Svami Śraddhānand, 1856–1926), who advocated a radical alternative to the English education system. Munśīrām and the Ārya Pratinidhi Sabhā split from moderate or 'College' Āryas over the issue, and in 1898 he started collecting funds for his school modelled on the ancient Hindu universities.[203] The Gurukul he founded on the banks of the river Ganges near Hardwar (1900, 1902 in Kangri) was to be a model of true Indian education, with the explicit aim of turning a few children into *brahmachārīs*. Students and teachers lived together in a simple and wholly dedicated environment. The place, especially at the time of its annual festivals, became a favourite pilgrimage spot for nationalist leaders and Hindi literati, who came to breathe for a few days the air of ancient India. As one teacher put it: 'The Gurukul does not belong to the Ārya-Samāj alone, nor to the Ārya jāti alone, nor to Punjab alone: it belongs to Bhāratvarṣa.'[204] Although the school grew—a Mahāvidyālay department was opened in 1907, and in 1921 the Ārya Pratinidhi Sabhā turned it into a chartered university—the Gurukul never provided the kind of practical alternative to government schools that DAV schools did. The curriculum was too markedly different from that of government schools, though other Gurukul branches in Brindaban (1911), Kurukshetra, Indraprastha, Vaidyanath (Bihar), and a few other places in the Punjab followed it.[205] The Mahāvidyālay founded in Jvalapur near Hardwar by

[203] 'We are just like an ungrateful man who is feeding sweets to other people while his own mother is starving. In other words, to abandon one's own language and rely on another for writing literature is a complete sin. The institutions which use Hindi for this [literary] purpose are following their *dharma* and are worthy of praise', wrote Rāmchandra Śarmā MA, quoted from *Ārya jagat* in *Sammelan patrikā*, XII, 3–4: 1924, p. 161.

[204] Ibid.

[205] Teaching lasted 14 years, 10 in the school and 4 in the Mahāvidyālay, which was divided into a Vedic department, an Arts department, and a department of Ayurveda. Graduates from the Vedic department were called Siddhānthālaṅkār and studied comparative religions apart from Vedic scriptures; they later became preachers or teachers themselves. Arts graduates studied western philosophy, history, Maths, English, and Hindi, and were called Vidyālaṅkār. Graduates in Ayurveda studied comparative medicine and received 'nothing short of government medical training'. Of the 125 graduates by 1925, 10 had become journalists, 15 were Ārya preachers, around 30 were teachers; none had joined the civil service, as could be expected; Satyavrat, 'Gurukul kāṅgṛī', *Mādhurī*, III, pt. 2, 5, May 1925, pp. 635–42. Yaśpāl studied here before moving to the DAV college in Lahore, to terrorism, and to Hindi literature.

Pandit Nardev Śāstrī in 1907 provides a similar example of education free from western influences: 'यह महाविद्यालय अंग्रेज़ी के वातावरण से रहित है। यहाँ आते ही प्राचीन ऋषि आश्रम का साक्षात दर्शन होता है।' 'This University is devoid of the environment of English. As soon as you arrive here you have *darśan* [a vision] of the ancient seers.'[206] Teaching focussed even more on the Vedas, on ancient Indian philosophy, and on ancient and modern Sanskrit literature; graduates usually became Ārya Samāj preachers, teachers, or Ayurvedic doctors.

Because Hindi was the medium of instruction in such institutions, a large number of textbooks in Hindi had to be written for all subjects, such as Acharya Rāmdev's history textbook *Bhāratvarṣa kā itihās*, and readers for the lower classes in the sanskritized āryabhāṣā. This kind of Hindi was not immediately accessible to Urdu- and Persian-educated Punjabis, even if they were affiliated to the Ārya Samāj.[207] However, despite being ill-equipped for the task linguistically, Ārya Samāj Punjabis made efforts to write Hindi text books. Bhavānīprasād of Bijnaur, the compiler of the *Āryabhāṣa pāṭhāvalī*, observed in his introduction that another reason why other textbooks could not be used to teach Hindi at the Gurukul was that Hindi 'textbooks used by the education department are written in a language which is neither Urdu nor Hindi, and they lack a classical language to support them'.[208] It is interesting to note that in the later 1923 edition of the *Āryabhāṣā pāṭhāvalī* the author proudly remarked that textbooks for government-aided vernacular schools were now written in 'polished Hindi' and contained examples of poems and essays by distinguished Hindi authors.[209] Four years later, in the preface to the 5th edition (1927), he was 'overjoyed at seeing that the polished style of āryabhāṣa shown in this reader is now universally approved and established' (p. 10). By the 1920s, a sanskritized Hindi, like that of the Gurukul textbook, which systematically proposed a 'high' register and excluded colloquial expressions, had become the accepted language of Hindi education. For example, in the passage 'Billī' ('Cat', pt. 1), the

[206] Quoted in Gupta, *Hindī sāhitya ko ārya-samāj kī den*, p. 125.

[207] Padmasiṃh Śarmā mentioned in several letters to Dvivedī his displeasure about the impure language (Urduized, with Punjabi influences) of Lal Devrāj's textbooks for the Ārya Kanyā Mahāvidyālay, which were used in other ĀS schools; see Baijnāth Siṃh, *Dvivedī yug ke sāhitykāroṁ ke kuch patr*, pp. 97–8. It was possibly for this reason that Śarmā left the Gurukul for the Mahāvidyālay in Jvalapur.

[208] Bhavānīprasād, *Āryabhāṣa pāṭhāvalī*, Kangri, Gurukul Press, 6th ed. 1927; Introduction to the first edition (1909), p. iii.

[209] Ibid., pt. 2, p. 9.

word used for 'white' was *śvet* and not *safed*, 'angry' was *kruddh* and not *nārāz*, 'tongue' was not *jībh* but *jihvā*, 'clean' not *sāf* but *svacch*: whenever possible, even common Perso-Arabic words were dismissed as 'foreign', and words of Sanskrit origin which had changed significantly in common usage (*tadbhava*) were replaced by Sanskrit words (*tatsama*). The effect of this change from a colloquial to a higher register was one of defamiliarization. The passage 'Din aur rātri' was a typical exercise in 'translation' into a *tatsama* vocabulary:

रात्रि होते ही सब पशु और पक्षी विश्राम करते हैं। हमको भी अधिक रात्रि गए तक जागना उचित नहीं है अन्यथा प्रातःकाल उठने में विलम्ब होगा और इससे अगले दिन कार्य में बाधा पड़ेगा। इसलिए रात्रि को दस बजे से पूर्व ही सो रहो।

[As soon as *night* descends all *animals* and *birds* have *rest*. It is not proper for us, either, to wake *too long* into the *night*, *lest* we are *delayed* in getting up *in the morning* and our *activity* the next day is *impeded*. Therefore go to sleep *before* ten o'clock at *night*.] (words in italics are unfamiliar words used instead of familiar ones in the original Hindi.)[210]

In terms of content, too, the *Āryabhāṣa pāṭhāvalī* resembled Dvivedī's 'useful' and moralizing model, and indeed several passages were taken from his textbooks and many poems from *Sarasvatī*; beyond the 'orthodox' versus Ārya divide, the broad cultural orientation of both schools was the same. Children seem to have been regarded as wild things ever ready to stray, needing to be controlled, domesticated, and ordered.[211]

Overall, education in the Gurukul could not be called entirely 'traditional', in the sense that it reworked traditional and new subjects, old rituals and new concerns, into an ostensibly 'ancient Indian' framework. Hindi literature figured only marginally in the curriculum. The literary saṃskāra imparted there was again a mixed version of a traditional one, the progeny of Sanskrit poetics and a reformist spirit.[212] The only Hindi literary scholar of note directly associated with Gurukul education was Padmasiṃh Śarmā, who taught for some time at Kangri before moving to the Gurukul Mahāvidyālay in Jvalapur. A scholar of Sanskrit and

[210] Ibid., p. 34.

[211] Cf. the daily life of the Gurukul brahmachari as described in the poem 'Hamārā gurukul', where every moment of the pupil's life is disciplined, and devotion to the masters repeatedly emphasized; ibid., pt. 2, pp. 102–4.

[212] At a literary meeting there Premchand, on a visit to the Gurukul, could not help remarking that 'most of the poems were ridiculous; but I'll praise the courage of the *brahmachārīs* who were not in the least shy of reciting their inchoate poems'; Premchand, 'Gurukul kāṅgṛī meṁ tīn din', in *Mādhurī*, VI, pt. 2, 3, April 1928, pp. 364.

connoisseur of Braj Bhasa (cf. 2.2) he was a close friend of Mahāvīr Prasād Dvivedī, with whom he shared the reformist spirit and a scholarly outlook.

Although at first the Gurukul avoided political involvement, the spiritual and patriotic atmosphere provided an alternative to the colonial system, and its agenda for education and culture easily turned nationalist in a political sense. Thus Gandhi, who sent his own son to the Gurukul, remarked about Śraddhānand: 'We met each other in 1915 at the favourite Gurukul and with each meeting we came closer and knew each other better. His love of ancient India, Sanskrit, Hindi was remarkable. He was undoubtedly a non-cooperator before non-cooperation was born.'[213] In fact, Śraddhānand and the students became actively involved in the Non-Cooperation and Khilafat movements, and even launched a nationalist daily from Delhi, *Vijay*.[214] He later became one of the initiators of the militant movement for *śuddhi*, and was killed by an enraged Muslim in 1926.

The impact and importance of the Ārya Samāj educational institutions should be judged not in terms of their direct influence on Hindi literature, which was after all meagre, but in terms of their broader cultural influence. They were crucial in the construction of an Indian past rooted in the 'Āryan myth'. The relationship between modern Hindus and Vedic *ṛṣis* was made apparent and alive in the independent, pure, and disciplined enclave of the Gurukuls, which offered to contemporary Indians almost a *tableau vivant* of what education must have been like in ancient India (cf. 3.1). The cultural ideal represented physically by the Gurukuls appealed powerfully not to the Ārya Samāj alone, but to a very wide section of the Hindi intelligentsia and of nationalist leadership, who saw in them a symbol of the living force of 'Hindu tradition'. This appeal will be analysed at greater length in the third chapter.

1.4.4. Hindī Sāhitya Sammelan Examinations

Another interesting educational experiment, independent and yet practical and not completely severed from the government system, was that of the Hindi literary examinations set up by the Hindī Sāhitya Sammelan.

[213] Quoted in Shraddhanand, *Inside Congress*, Bombay, Phoenix, 1946, p. 7.

[214] Ibid., p. 46. The paper was edited by his son, Indra Vidyāvāchaspati, who served the Gurukul as teacher, principal, and vice-chancellor between 1912 and 1920. Later he became the editor of the important nationalist daily *Arjun* (later renamed *Vīr Arjun*) in Delhi.

The scheme, set up in 1915, was perhaps the most far-reaching and successful enterprise of the Sammelan. A committee formed after the 5th Hindī Sāhitya Sammelan meeting in Lucknow in 1914, much before Hindi was studied at any university, had prepared a scheme for Hindi proficiency examinations to be submitted to the provincial government. According to the proposal, the examinations would be administered and marked by the education department: in a word, the Hindī Sāhitya Sammelan was putting its expertise at the service of the government, while advancing its own claim as an alternative think-tank.[215] Government did not follow up the proposal, and the Hindī Sāhitya Sammelan began implementing it on its own. At first meant only to train teachers in officially recognized and aided schools, the scheme was later opened to the general public and succeeded in fulfilling several needs of the fast-growing Hindi public sphere.

These examinations offered a cheap alternative to University degrees in Hindi at a time when Hindi teachers were in great demand; much of the primary and secondary school curriculum had been converted to the vernacular, but trained teachers were rare. Apart from new teachers, there was a need to retrain old ones in the vernacular, and there were few official training colleges. Candidates for Hindī Sāhitya Sammelan examinations could prepare cheaply at home, even while keeping their jobs, and sit for examinations in the growing number of centres. According to the original scheme, the first examination was to include seven papers testing knowledge of medieval and modern poetry and prose, including grammar, rhetoric, and the rules of prosody, with unseen passages and essays and translations from and into Sanskrit. The actual examination consisted of three papers on Hindi literature and several others. The curriculum was broadened to include, among other subjects, history, geography, mathematics, English, hygiene and, after 1925, religion, politics and, only for women, home science. The high proficiency was based on a similar pattern but with a much wider syllabus. The *uttamā* examination could only be taken in literary subjects (Hindi or Sanskrit) with some extra papers. The degrees accorded (*sāhitya-viśārad* and *sāhitya-ratna*) were halfway between the traditional titles (*upādhi*)

[215] See *Sammelan patrikā*, II, 10, 1914, p. 276. The committee included Rāmdās Gauṛ, Rāmnārāyaṇ Miśra, Śyāmsundar Dās, Puruṣottam Dās Ṭaṇḍon, the Miśra brothers, and several other 'founding fathers' of both the Nāgarī Prachāriṇī Sabhā and the Hindī Sāhitya Sammelan. Thus, it was not a completely anti-colonial scheme until Independence, as the former director of the Sammelan maintained: interview with Prabhāt Śāstrī, Allahabad, July 1993.

granted by patrons and literary institutions, mere marks of prestige, and the degrees of the official education system, which were of practical value. Several Hindi literati started adding the title *viśarad* or *sāhitya-ratna* after their names as had earlier happened only with degrees like BA and MA. In fact, as the examinations became more and more popular, the degrees earned greater acceptance both with Congress boards and ministries and with the government Board of Secondary Education.

The *Sammelan patrikā* regularly carried news about individual teachers who had obtained jobs or higher wages after passing Hindī Sāhitya Sammelan examinations; they also advertised vacancies for teachers with Sammelan degrees. By 1940 the proud editor could announce that the UP Board of Intermediate education had recognized the *madhyamā* examination as on a par with the Intermediate examination; the Bihar government followed suit and recognized *prathamā* as equivalent to the High school examination, madhyamā to Intermediate and uttamā to BA, affording candidates the same job opportunities. In central India, the governments of the Central Provinces and of Jodhpur, Jhalabar, and Chattarpur states offered higher wages to teachers with Sammelan degrees.[216] The authority and endeavour of the Hindī Sāhitya Sammelan were thus acknowledged by a colonial government unable to fufil the task of training teachers on a large scale.[217]

Hindī Sāhitya Sammelan examinations provided a safe and useful way of showing one's commitment to the national language and consequently to the nationalist cause. The success of the scheme thrilled the Hindi intelligentsia and seemed to offer convincing evidence that Hindi was indeed being accepted as the national language. Initially most of the examination centres were in the United Provinces and Bihar, but by 1939 there were hundreds of centres all over India.[218] Yearly reports with

[216] See e.g. *Sammelan patrikā*, XXVII, 8–9, June–July 1940, p. 16.

[217] Punjab University in Lahore launched Hindi proficiency examinations that were popular with teachers in aided schools, but their impact was limited because they were not open to candidates from other provinces. Allahabad University set up Hindi Proficiency examinations only for teachers of the province. The syllabus at Lahore included grammar, rhetoric, M.P. Dvivedī's *Sacitra Mahābhārata*, the *History of India* by the Miśra brothers and by Marsden, Bhārtendu's plays and *Vīr Abhimānyu* by Rādheśyām Kathāvāchak, *Premsāgar,* and the usual Hindi classics: Tulsī's *Rāmāyaṇa*, Bihārī, Dev, Bhūṣaṇ, Keśavdās, and among the moderns only Maithilīśaraṇ Gupta; see *Mādhurī*, II, pt. 2, 1, February 1924, pp. 96–7.

[218] In 1939, 562, according to the *Hindī-sāhitya-sammelan ke hindī-viśvavidyālay kī parīkṣāoṁ kī vivaraṇ-patrikā*, saṃvat 1995–6 [1938–9], Allahabad, 1939; the names are given on pp. 82–99.

figures and statistics highlighted the continuing spread of the scheme as well as the path yet to cover; itinerant preachers sent by the Hindī Sāhitya Sammelan contacted principals to establish new examination centres even in small townships.

In short, the examinations provided the Sammelan with a much-needed focus for Hindi propaganda, which had so far remained quite abstract. The whole undertaking fed perfectly into its centralizing strategy, which had suffered so far from a certain lack of means and ideas. Examinations became also a profitable business: although very cheap to take,[219] they paid handsomely since all examiners were volunteers. In particular they gave a boost to the textbook industry, since Hindī Sāhitya Sammelan course books, critical editions, and anthologies were sure to run into several large editions. This attracted a kind of publishers and booksellers' lobby which struggled to control the Sammelan in order to get their books accepted, thus thwarting other activities and democratic management.[220]

Thanks to the single, centralized curriculum, the Hindī Sāhitya Sammelan could exert great cultural influence as an agency which exercised judgement and decisions on what Hindi literature was and how it should be read. This makes the syllabus of the examinations all the more interesting, for we can see what kind of literary curriculum Hindi literati (for many were called to take part in drawing up the syllabus and to be examiners) wished to set up and transmit, whether it differed from that of official institutions, and which literary saṃskāra candidates would derive from it.

The prathamā examination tested language proficiency and a general knowledge of rhetoric and of literary selections. Whether in language or literature, candidates were tested on their ability to 'translate' passages from complex (*kliṣṭa*) Hindi (with words like *sāṅgtā* and *pratigrah*) into plain (*saral*) Hindi, to explain their meaning (bhāvārtha), and to be able to name and explain figures of speech. The candidates were also asked to correct mistakes in grammar and in metre and to make sentences with particular words, proverbs, and compounds.[221] No creative or intellectual effort was required or invited. Literary proficiency meant knowing

[219] Fees were Rs 2.50 for prathamā, Rs 6 for madhyamā, Rs 11 for uttamā and journalism in 1938; ibid., p. 2. The income the Hindī Sāhitya Sammelan derived was Rs 7101 in 1936, Rs 22,321 in 1942. See *Sammelan patrikā*, XXIV, 3 and XXX, 10.

[220] See Vājpeyī, *Sāhityik jīvan aur saṃsmaraṇ*, pp. 106 ff.

[221] Exactly the kind of examination I had to take at the Central Institute of Hindi in New Delhi seventy years later!

metres and rhetorical figures and possessing a stock (*bhaṇḍār*) of literary passages mostly from Bhakti poets, conveniently packaged and explained in the anthologies and commented editions brought out by the Sammelan. To know Hindi meant being able to use a 'high', sanskritized register in addition to the one for daily use, and to accept the cultural presumptions and social relations inscribed in passages like these:

सरस्वती भी धन्य है जो उनके मुखकमल के सम्पर्क का सुख अनुभव करती हुई ऐसे महात्मा के प्रसन्न गंभीर मानस में राजहंसी सी वास करती है।

अकेली गंगा है। लम्बी चौड़ी वासनाओं का निवास उस स्थान में नहीं। आकाश पाताल को एक करनेवाले विचारों का वहाँ प्रवेश नहीं होता।

ब्राह्मण लोग हिन्दू जाति के अगुए हैं। इसमें कुछ संदेह नहीं कि बहुत से ब्राह्मणों ने पढ़ना लिखना छोड़ दिया है। परन्तु यह समय की गति है। उनका प्रभूत्व ज्यों का त्यों बना है।

[The goddess Sarasvatī is fortunate, for she dwells like a royal *haṃsa* bird in the blissful and profound lake of the mind of such great spiritual souls, and experiences the joy of contact with their visages.

The Ganges is unique. It has no place for wide and large desires. Thoughts which bring the sky and the netherworld together cannot penetrate there.

Brahmins are the leaders of the Hindu community. Undoubtedly, many of them have stopped studying, but this is a consequence of the times. Their authority (*prabhūtva*) is undiminished.][222]

As for the texts chosen, they were almost exclusively drawn from the Braj Bhasa and Avadhi traditions: recent trends in Khari Boli poetry, drama, and prose were completely absent.[223] Only in the uttamā paper on

[222] The first Hindī Sāhitya Sammelan examination paper for 1915; *Hindī sāhity sammelan kī parīkṣāoṁ kī vivaraṇ-patrikā*, saṃvat 1982, Allahabad, Hindi Sahitya Sammelan, 1915, p. 7.

[223] See Badrīnāth Bhaṭṭ's review article 'Sammelan-parīkṣāoṁ kī pāṭhya-pustakeṁ', in *Mādhurī*, I, pt. 2, 3, *Sammelan-aṅk*, pp. 289–91. The initial syllabus for the prathamā examination included selections from Jāyasī's *Padmāvat,* Tulsīdās's *Ayodhyākāṇḍa,* the *Sūrsāgar, Sabhā-vilās* and Keśavdās's *Rāmchandrikā*. For the modern texts: Harioudh's *Priyā-pravās,* Śrīdhar Pāṭhak's *Śrānta-pathik* and *Kaśmīr-suṣmā* and the Hindi translation of Kālidāsa's *Meghadūta* by Raja Lakṣmaṇ Siṃh, of *Mṛcchakaṭika* by Lala Sītarām, and of *Mudrārākṣasa* by Hariśchandra; Lallūjīlāl's *Premsāgar*, three early Hindi novels (*Sau ajān aur ek sujān, Parīkṣāguru,* and *Kahānī ṭheṭh hindī kī),* Bālmukund Gupta's essays, Ś. Dās's *Hindī bhāṣa kī utpatti*. In other words, almost all that had been written in Hindi until then, barring contemporary literature. The syllabus for the high proficiency examination included the second half of all the works for the first examination, plus eleven cantos of *Pṛthvīrāj rāso*, Bihārī and Keśavdās, Miśra-bandhu's shorter history of Hindi literature and other collections of essays.

modern literature were some Chāyāvādī poets included by the end of the 1930s, tellingly, along with Rāmchandra Śukla's stinging critique of Chāyāvād in the essay 'Mysticism in Hindi poetry' (Hindī kāvya meṁ rahasyavād)![224]

Broadly speaking, the saṃskāra of Hindi literature that was thus transmitted was similar to that in the university and high-school syllabi, and so was the canon. Literature considered worth the name was mainly literature of the past, along a national chronology. The few moderns present were those who had marked the birth of modern Hindi (e.g. Lallūjī Lāl, Insha Allāh Khān, Śrīnivās Dās, Bhārtendu), those who had achieved the status of 'modern classics' like Maithilīśaraṇ Gupta and Harioudh, and those who, although experimenting, had not subverted the literary order (Sumitrānandan Pant, Rāmkumār Varmā). Literary history meant a sound period classification according to the 'scientific' principles laid out by Rāmchandra Śukla; it also involved placing authors and texts in neat categories and trends: each category 'contained' a particular kind of poetry, whose characteristics mirrored the characteristic people's attitude (*lokapravṛtti*) of each epoch (cf. 2.2). The modern period was called the 'age of prose', but prose meant mainly essays and didactic novels; among Premchand's novels only *Godān* (1936) was selected, and not the more widely acclaimed and problematic *Sevāsadan* (1919), *Premāśram* (1921) or *Raṅgbhūmi* (1925), and certainly not the kind of fiction that was popular.

Looking back at the main processes concerning Hindi education in the two decades, we can see how the centrality of education was not only on the discursive level. To transmit a sense of cultural identity (see 3.1) and the right values for the nation in the making, education was crucial for the Hindi intelligentsia. Hindi scholars and literary associations were largely successful in their task, in so far as it involved carving a niche for themselves and their agenda in the colonial education system: in fact, the Hindi curriculum in the government system and in independent enterprises was substantially the same, because the experts behind them were the same. Hindi scholars and associations were not so successful in 'vernacularizing' knowledge, that is in bringing about a wholesale transformation of the knowledge imparted in the education system. Despite

224 The paper on modern poetry included Rāy Devīprasād 'Pūrṇa' as the only representative of modern Braj Bhasa poetry, a few Dvivedī poets, and contemporary works awarded the Maṅgalāprasād prize, like Viyogī Hari's *Vīr satsaī*, M. Gupta's *Sāket*, S. Pant's *Pallav*, J. Prasād's *Jharnā* and *Āṁsū*, and Rāmkumār Varmā's *Chitrarekhā*; *Vivaraṇ patrikā, uttamā parīkṣā*, 1938–9, p. 6.

the brave attempt of the Hindī Sāhitya Sammelan exams and of individuals like Rāmdās Gauṛ, scientific subjects remained the domain of English, and the same was true for the social sciences at the higher level. This might have had something to do with their limited resources, the hierarchical nature of colonial education, and the huge practical difficulties that made education generally quite a limited affair in north India in this period. It was also connected with the saṃskāras, the normative attitudes, and the social and cultural conservatism of the scholars associated with Hindi education: after all, education was for them a means to establish their own cultural values and the status of Hindi in the education system, not to bring about a wholesale change in the system and in society.

The teaching of Hindi literature, whether in government or in independent schools, provided an institutional setting for the historical vision of the Hindu jāti that was fashioned in nationalist discourse (cf. 3.1.); in the lower classes it even included contemporary nationalist poetry. It followed the reformist and normative attitude of Hindi critics towards contemporary literature (cf. 2.2). Literature for education, both in the form of textbooks and of prescribed texts, certainly provided a boost to the publishing industry, but in the absence of a self-reliant literary market it also helped turn Hindi literature into a kind of subsidized industry. Hindi literature became part of a 'textbook culture' which severed the texts from their living contexts; it also discouraged a critical disposition by giving texts one meaning only and expecting a set answer for each question. What was left for students was to read selected passages from the prescribed texts with the help of commentaries and 'keys', and to memorize critical definitions (*sthāpnāeṁ*) as factual knowledge, without questioning the values and assumptions underneath them. The transmission of literary knowledge through education thus ensured the acquisition of a 'pure' linguistic and cultural identity. The success of the Hindi intelligentsia in imposing such a syllabus was dense with other, cultural and political consequences, both during the nationalist struggle and after Independence: Hindi education became a 'secret door' through which cultural nationalism could enter the colonial system, but it also imposed a rigid linguistic and cultural ideal that was to survive undisturbed even in independent India.[225]

The central hypotheses of this chapter are, first, that the new literature, whether reformist, patriotic, or original, was but one strand among a

[225] Kumar, *The Political Agenda of Education*, p. 145.

variety of tastes and literary traditions still in vogue; and second, that the existence and expansion of modern Hindi literature was itself the product of the particular institutional spaces in this period, and that it is therefore necessary to turn to the institutions themselves to explain the variety and changes in literary output and transmission. Having shown here the arenas where linguistic and literary saṃskāras were made and transmitted, we may now qualify and develop these hypotheses.

If we compare the arenas and their role in the public sphere, we can therefore argue that *journals* created their own authority as spaces for public debate conducted in the name of public opinion; they were vehicles for both normative and critical understandings of the public sphere. They were also the only space for new literary experiments.

Textbooks and education were the products of the active and successful influence of reformist scholars and literary associations. Despite being critical of English and of much of 'western modernity', they broached a consensual and normative approach towards Indian culture and society and disdained critical ('anarchic') tendencies in contemporary Hindi. Nevertheless, the teaching of Hindi in schools allowed students to read and understand the complex diction of Chāyāvād and the rather more accessible social and historical fiction that became increasingly popular in the 1920s. The *book market* remained largely dominated by popular religious and secular publications, a sign that both reformist and experimental tastes had by no means become dominant (cf. 2.3).

It was nationalism and mass politicization that brought these three spaces closer together and allowed a significant amount of overlap, in a way covering up the considerable gaps. Authors and publishers of popular genres started in the 1920s to bring out nationalist versions of bhajans, sāṁgīt, plays, etc. along with the traditional fare. Popular publications and cheap pamphlets also became more topical, signalling a greater awareness of the popular public towards contemporary events. The 1920s also saw the great expansion of the political press in Hindi, run by intellectuals but aimed at the popular public: this was embodied not only in the style of writing, more accessible and closer to spoken, idiomatic language, but also in the openness to new subjects and issues (cf. 5.2). Moreover, it was the political press that made certain Hindi literary figures, mainly nationalist poets, popular with the larger public. Their poems were regularly printed even in political dailies and were acclaimed at poetry meetings. The political movement brought about an even closer identification of public debate and writing in journals (sāhitya-sevā) with political work and deś-sevā, service to the country.

Thus creative writing came to be seen as another way of doing political work: not only Premchand's stories of demonstrations and *satyāgraha*, even Nirālā's poems to the gathering clouds (*Bādal rāg*) were considered effective calls for mobilization (cf. 5.1). The Gandhian movement also inspired a great faith in the potential for the expansion of the Hindi sphere and in the leading role of the independent intellectual therein.

Underneath this picture of unity and strength, cracks and tensions remained which reveal the structural limitations outlined above, not to speak of those represented by English and Urdu. For all the emphasis on Hindi's popularity as a source of strength (e.g. *vis-à-vis* Urdu), popularity for example remained a problematic and controversial issue for Hindi literati, both with regard to the evaluation of the market and to political authority (2.3). As we shall see, popularity as a value clashed both with the normative view of the public and with the sophisticated aspirations of contemporary poets. Similarly, critical openness became a controversial issue in as much as it brought to the surface new subjects and new demands. Whether in the case of women or of peasants, the transition from being objects of debate to subjects of discourse and activities was a turbulent and contested one. Finally, the concept of saṃskāra will allow us to entangle the different and conflicting, sometimes self-contradictory, strands in intellectuals and activists of this period, and to make sense both of their diversity and of their urge for unity and consensus.

CHAPTER 2

Language, Literature, and Publicity

The institutional spaces described in the previous chapter allowed us to recreate the world in which Hindi literati moved and worked, and which provided them with horizons, boundaries, and the urge to overcome them. This context is necessary in order to understand their formulations on the issues of language and literature that are the subject of this chapter. Language and literature, we have seen already, had been at the centre of intense arguments and discussions about the progress and reform of the country since the nineteenth century: 'The progress of one's language is the root of all progress,' Hariśchandra had said. In the context of Hindi we have seen how such arguments were instrumental in creating a cultural identification with the language, over a wide geographical area and in opposition to English, to Urdu, and to earlier multiple linguistic saṃskāras. The growing support for Hindi, and its politicization in the 1920s on the wave of Gandhi's nationalism, changed the context of the language issue quite dramatically: suddenly the question of a national language (*rāṣṭrabhāṣā*) appeared plausible, even urgent. What had been thus far a provincial contest between scholars of Hindi and Urdu now became a matter of national politics. This suited the rhetoric and aspirations of Hindi intellectuals and activists very well. Yet it also posed new and ultimately intractable problems, as the controversy between Hindi and Hindustani in the 1930s shows (cf. 5.4). How did the nationalist perspective influence Hindi debates on the notion of language and literature and on the role of the writer? And how did Hindi intellectuals react to the new publicity of the literary sphere, which transformed their roles and the way their work was evaluated? These are some of the questions raised in this chapter.

2.1. The Nationalist Discourse of Language: *Mātṛbhāṣā-deśvyāpak bhāṣā-rāṣṭrabhāṣā*

Necessity has enlightened [our] fellow nationals on the importance of a national language. The wave that arose in their hearts spread and went on to engulf the whole country. . . . All the farsighted intellectuals of the country welcomed this thought. Everyone acknowledged the need for a national language. It is a source of pride for us that the honour (*pad*) has been given to our mother tongue [i.e. Hindi].

[. . .] [the national language] is worship of the goddess Sarasvatī. There is no difference between rich and poor here, no need for the hussle of B.A.s and M.A.s. The door is open to all those whose hearts are filled with feeling and love for their mother. They can all bring their offerings. There is no love for the moderns nor hate for the ancients here, no flattering the rich nor scolding the poor—all are worshippers of Mother Sarasvati, all have come to lay their loving offerings at the feet of the Mother. All have but one aim, one interest; it is a blissful state which those who are sensitive can feel. Thus, when we enter the temple of the Mother, we see her worshippers embracing each other, discarding all external differences. Hindus, Muslims, Parsis, etc., all play the same tune, all sing the same song: the words uttered in Bihar are heard in Sindh.[1]

Hindi's claim to be the national language of India was an ideological construct. In the passage quoted above, the existence of an Indian language that would communicate with the entire, multilingual, nation and hold it together is presented both as a historical 'necessity' and a direct product of nationalist feelings. At the same time, this language is endowed with more than mundane, practical qualities: to use and value it 'is to worship the goddess Sarasvatī' and tap a source of mystical bliss. The issue of the national language is thus embedded in a rhetoric of an all-inclusive religious community along devotional (Bhakti) lines. Just as the path of devotion is open to all and is both a means and an end, so the national language is presented as the means to create a national community open to all and conferring a sense of unity. Sarasvatī, the rather stern goddess of learning in the Hindu tradition, the goddess all poets and scholars invoke, here takes on an ampler presence as the 'Mother' of all Indians irrespective of their religion and social position, essentially a metaphor for Mother India. Consensus is elicited, through a common rhetorical device, by presenting it as already accomplished: 'All farsighted intellectuals of the country,' indeed 'everyone', has acknowledged

[1] Chatursen Śāstrī, 'Rāṣṭrabhāṣa aur sanskṛtajña', *Sammelan patrikā*, IV, 4, December 1916, pp. 145–6. Chatursen Śāstrī was at the time editor of the monthly *Śārdā*; in the 1920s he became a popular novelist and was sometime editor of *Chāṁd*.

the need for Hindi to be the national language, and all devotees, 'Hindu, Muslims, Parsis play the same tune.' Who could be opposed to such a picture of blissful unity but some ill-willed spoilsport?

Although the rhetoric of 'the progress of one's language' existed in each Indian language, Hindi's fate was peculiar in as much as it had, since the nineteenth century, been considered India's potential national language by some scholars and political leaders (see following pages). In the light of the subordinate status Hindi had in its own provinces and of the contest with Urdu highlighted in the previous chapter, this destiny was particularly fraught with difficulties. In fact, notwithstanding the firm belief in the metaphor of the 'Mother's temple', the path to actual recognition was not as smooth as the rhetoric suggested. Each step towards establishing the mother tongue Hindi as a public language, in the local boards, in the education system, in the Legislative Assembly and in the Congress itself, proved to be controversial. Compromise formulations emerged in the 1930s when it became clear that political consensus was hard to realize, and even within Hindi there were more open-ended notions of language than that pushed for by Hindi literary associations and scholars (cf. 5.4.1). But first, let us consider the dominant formulation.

Mahāvīr Prasād Dvivedī's importance in establishing and popularizing the standard form of modern Hindi has already been discussed. What is relevant here is that, on the strength of a rational–logical argument, he also helped establish an ideological construct which linked the issue of nij bhāṣā with that of rāṣṭrabhāṣā. Certainly, he was not the only one to do so; but the authority he enjoyed in the early twentieth century, the eloquence of his rhetoric and the clarity of his arguments make him an ideal model. Dvivedī started editing the journal *Sarasvatī* in 1903, when the Hindi–Urdu contest of the nineteenth century was raging in the foreground. His first task was thus to convert Urdu-literate Hindus to their 'mother tongue' and to spur English-literate Hindus to acknowledge their duty towards the improvement of nij bhāṣā: 'We request all scholars of English to grant us the favour, after considering the condition of their society and country, of writing useful articles in their own language. If they do not know how to write it they need not feel ashamed: if they really do not know how they only have to learn! Please fulfil your duty!'[2] It is worth remembering that the use of the term 'mother tongue' marked already an ideological step: the form of Khari Boli used in print was hardly

[2] M.P. Dvivedī, 'Hindustāniyoṁ ke aṅgrezī lekh', *Sarasvatī*, September 1914, quoted in Bhatnagar, *The Rise and Growth of Hindi Journalism*, p. 332. Worth noticing is the shift from the exhortative to the imperative mood.

anybody's mother tongue at the time, except for people in the area around Delhi and Aligarh and for groups who had moved eastwards and southwards from there, e.g. Agarwals and Khatris. In Dvivedī's terms, 'mother tongue' indicated a standard vernacular that mirrored one's cultural and religious identity. Its status as a print language gave standard Khari Boli this position in an area where various dialects of Hindi prevailed, while the 'mother' metaphor helped identification between mother tongue and motherland. The use of Hindi could appear thus as a duty and a service to the nation. Echoing Hariśchandra, Dvivedī had said in 1903:

> The progress of dharma and of the country rests on propagating the mother tongue and on the growth and enrichment of national literature. To strive and work for the progress of Hindi therefore is presently the first and foremost duty of every patriot (*deśhitaiṣī*) and rightful man.[3]

And as chairman of the welcome committee of the XIII Hindī Sāhitya Sammelan meeting in Kanpur in 1923, he said:

> A man's mother tongue is as important as his mother and motherland are. . . . One who does not respect his language, who does not love it and does not enrich its literature, can never improve the state of his country. His dream of *svarājya*, his vow of improving the country and his praise for patriotism are quite shallow.[4]

Dvivedī's 'mother tongue' became the basis for arguing several further points, namely: that Hindi was the real language of the province ('our language is Hindi!'[5]); that despite regional variants, it was one language, i.e. the mother tongue of all Hindus who lived in the United and Central Provinces, Bihar, Rajputana, Punjab, and the various states in central India, whether they acknowledged it or not;[6] and finally, that

[3] Dvivedī, 'Deśvyāpak bhāṣā', *Sarasvatī*, November 1903, quoted in Gauṛ, *Sarasvatī aur rāṣṭrīy jāgaraṇ*, p. 97.

[4] Quoted in *Sammelan patrikā*, X, 8–9, 1923, p. 301.

[5] Dvivedī, 'Hindī śikṣā ke vistār kī mahattā', *Sarasvatī*, April 1915, quoted in Gauṛ, *Sarasvatī aur rāṣṭrīy jāgaraṇ*, p. 332.

[6] Dvivedī dismissed all suggestions that Hindi covered a spectrum of sub-languages as dangerous provocations: he reacted angrily to Grierson's classification in the Linguistic Survey: 'The clerks of the government have now diminished the sense of vastness of our language by cutting it into several pieces. They have divided it into Western Hindi, Eastern Hindi and Bihari Hindi. They have gone even further: they have divided Hindi and Hindustani in two more parts. . . . Hindi, Hindustani and Urdu have been made into three different languages. God only knows how these two

Urdu's position as court language was not 'natural' but the result of a political privilege that had lost its historical rationale.[7] Thus Dvivedī argued in favour of a historical change in the linguistic status quo in 'objective' terms. The notion of mother tongue provided the basis for belittling Hindus educated in other linguistic repertoires, and heterogeneous spoken varieties: all were recompacted in a homogeneous community. Similarly, the 'objective' need was sufficient to argue for Hindi as national language. This was first couched in terms of a *lingua franca* spread throughout the country (*deśvyāpak)*:

> The existence of a common language has a peculiar influence and very strong effects. It creates in the hearts of people a longing to be one. They long for their whole country to be one, they strive for its improvement and look upon the country's welfare as their own good. . . . Without a common language there can never arise true national pride, there can never be national unity. Only Hindi can attain the status of country-wide (*deś-vyāpī*) language.[8]

Nationalist rhetoric and 'objective' reasoning came together in his authoritative statements, which presented arguments uncompromisingly as facts:

> Hindi *is* the language of the people of Hindustan. It is easy to speak, to write and to understand. It covers a wide area from Punjab to Brahmadesh. Punjabi and Bengali are very similar to Hindi. Even in Marwar, Central India, Madhya Pradesh, Berar and Gujarat there are very many Hindi speakers. Maharastrians are not unfamiliar with it.[9]

But Hindi, especially Dvivedī's Hindi, was no longer merely the *lingua franca* of bazaars throughout the country: now the language, standardized in print form, was called upon to perform much wider functions. In order to don the loftier mantle of 'national language', the flexible colloquial Hindi had to be superseded by a culturally more legitimized

---

languages—Hindustani and Urdu—differ!'; Dvivedī, 'Apnī bhāṣā kī bāt', *Sarasvatī*, July 1914, quoted in Bhatnagar, *The Rise and Growth of Hindi Journalism,* p. 332.

[7] 'The importance Urdu has acquired is solely due to government favour. If the government had not enhanced it as the language for courts and offices, Urdu would amount to very little in the British Raj' replied Dvivedī to Azghar Ali Khan, a member of the UP Textbook Commission who had argued against the introduction of separate Hindi textbooks on the ground that there was no such language as Hindi; M.P. Dvivedī, 'Kyā hindī nām kī koī bhāṣā nahīṁ?', *Sarasvatī*, December 1913, p. 707.

[8] Dvivedī, 'Deśvyāpak bhāṣā', p. 27.

[9] Ibid., emphasis added.

language: 'pure Hindi' (*śuddh Hindī*). As textbooks showed, even at its popularizing best, Hindi propaganda emphasized proficiency in the *written*, sanskritized style, even for the least educated (1.4).

The step from lingua franca to national language immediately brought up the question of Hindi's subordinate status in its own province: subordinate in relation to English and, in the minds of the Indo-Persian elite, to Urdu as well. How could Hindi reach the 'highest honour' under such circumstances? Once again, Dvivedī solved the problem on the rational–discursive ground by rejecting all other claims (for Urdu, Bengali, and of course English) and by presenting an opinion as an acknowledged fact.[10] In this way, thorny questions like that of the script could also be easily solved: 'In India we need not only one language but also one script, and this script can only be beautiful (*sarvāṅgasundar*) and comprehensible Devanagari. On this point not only all Hindus of the country but many intelligent Muslims and Englishmen agree.'[11] At this stage the issue of script, so charged with symbolic overtones, was still thought of as one that could be solved on paper, or by scholarly gatherings like the Ek-lipi Vistār Pariṣad of Calcutta (1905, see below), of which Dvivedī was a member, and which reduced the contest to a 'scientific' assessment of the inherent qualities or faults of each script. The fact that Sanskrit itself had been written in very many scripts over the centuries was conveniently forgotten. Mahāvīr Prasād Dvivedī's stance shows how a normative approach sought to 'solve' the issue by mere strength of argument in the enclosed public sphere of Hindi journals. And because what was really at issue was a *written* language, it was scholars (pandits) who undoubtedly enjoyed the last word on the matter: their scholarship allowed them to decide for the people (jantā) on whose behalf they were arguing.

The arguments Dvivedī used were to be heard again and again from Hindi campaigners until 1950. But rationality and scientificity, useful tools when persuading British administrators and mustering authority in the Hindi literary sphere, proved less successful when dealing with the claims of other languages in the political sphere. Hindi supporters tried to use them nevertheless, and to dismiss other claims on the 'neutral' ground of scientific arguments and experts' committees. But now there

[10] 'Everybody knows that Bhāratvarṣa needs a common, country-wide language, because there can be no unity without it, and no progress without unity. Everybody acknowledges, too, that only Hindi can be that language: it is the language of mutual exchange'; ibid.

[11] M.P. Dvivedī, 'Roman lipi ke prachār se hāniyāṁ', *Sarasvatī*, April 1913, p. 248.

was no 'neutral' arbiter and no 'neutral' ground. What was needed was a new formulation and the willingness to negotiate and reach a broader agreement in the public sphere, an agreement that would be cultural as well as political. However, the hard-line literary associations on both the Hindi and Urdu sides decided to leave little ground for inner debate and for mutual compromise. Our discussion of literary saṃskāras and of institutional authority may help explain why: why alternative, critical formulations failed.

2.1.1. Hindi's Lineage

History emerged as one of the most contested sites in the language controversy between Hindi and Urdu. While Urdu supporters dismissed Khari Boli Hindi as a 'new' and artificially created language,[12] Hindi claimed greater antiquity and the advantage of 'Indianness' over Urdu's 'foreignness'. Literary history was directly invoked too: already in its first annual report of 1894, the Nāgarī Prachāriṇī Sabhā had dwelt upon the origins of Hindi. In its historical outline, the fate of Hindi was shown to mirror closely that of the 'Hindu nation'—united, fallen and now resurgent (cf. 3.1). The 'Indianness', naturalness, and antiquity of Hindi were emphasized so as to downplay Urdu as an artificial and foreign language, derived from a spoken (i.e. inferior) style of Hindi. Christopher King summarizes the position:

> Hindi had existed as long ago as the reign of Raja Bhoja [XI century], but since no works had come from that time to the present, the *Pṛthvīrāj Rāso* [XII century] served to mark the origin of Hindi. . . . The Muslim invasion of India, which came just about the time of the creation of this work, prevented further progress of Hindi. Muslims, seeing that they could not settle in India unless they knew Hindi, and realizing that Sanskrit-mixed Hindi presented difficulties, created Persian-mixed Urdu. Though Hindi poetry flourished even after the beginning of Muslim rule and the rise of Urdu, and was sometimes patronized even by Muslim rulers, Hindi prose language languished because it was considered to be of little significance. Sanskrit continued to be the most important language of prose. A few books on subjects such as religion, medicine, astrology and the like appeared during this period, but their language was either Braj Bhasha or such a bad Hindi

[12] E.g. the statement by Dr Tara Chand, Principal of the Kayastha Pathshala, secretary of the Hindustani Academy and leading spokesman for Hindustani, that 'Hindi is 135 years old'; Tara Chand, 'Some Misconceptions about Hindustani', pamphlet printed at the Leader Press, n.d. but around 1939, p. 5; courtesy of Harimohan Malaviya.

that they could not even be considered literature. Prose received greater attention with the coming of English, however, and Lallu Lal created some of the first works in Hindi prose (such as *Prem Sāgar*) under Dr Gilchrist.[13]

Hindi is presented here as the pre-eminent language of India, without further specifications: the linguistic identity constructed in the present is projected backwards in history for the sake of one, national community. All that was needed was to expand the range of languages covered by the term 'Hindi'; as King has argued, 'The Sabha's usage of the term "Hindi" expanded as it moved towards the past, and contracted as it moved towards the present. To give Hindi a glorious past, one had to include all of its elder sisters, but when one came to the present, only the youngest sister—Khari Boli Hindi—received attention.'[14] Although Muslim conquest had obstructed its progress, the superiority and resilience of Hindi (i.e. of Hindus) was proved by the facts that Muslim rulers had had to learn it in order to survive and govern, that Hindi (Braj Bhasa) poetry had held sway even at their courts and that Sanskrit had retained its high status. Urdu was but the bastard daughter of Hindi and Persian, and now Hindi, after the end of Muslim rule and the coming of the British, had received a new impulse and could resume its progress.

If in the nineteenth-century controversy Urdu supporters had maintained that Hindi did not exist as a separate language, now it was the turn of Hindi supporters to say that Urdu was no more than an offshoot of Hindi. This view of the origin of the two languages, and the assimilation of all medieval literary languages under the blanket term 'Hindi', informed Hindi literary historiography and Hindi textbooks alike. Like 'Parsi Gujarati', Urdu was 'mixed Hindi', different from 'pure Hindi' only in lexicon—argued Lala Bhagvān Dīn and Rāmdās Gauṛ. Therefore they included in their anthology of Hindi prose for Sammelan and college students pieces originally in Perso-Arabic script by Urdu authors.[15] Inśā

[13] King, 'The Nagari Pracharini Sabha', p. 316.

[14] Ibid., p. 318. See for example Ayodhyāsiṃh Upādhyāy Harioudh's Presidential speech at the first All-India Indian poetry meeting in Kanpur, December 1925; quoted in *Mādhurī*, IV, pt. 2, 2, February 1926, p. 147.

[15] Bhagvān Dīn and Rāmdās Gauṛ, eds, *Hindī bhāṣā sār*, p. 9; cf. 1.4.1 here. The authors included were Munshi Sadāsukhlal, Inśā Allāh Khān, Nazīr Ahmad, and Ratannāth Sarshār. Munshi Sadāsukhlal was appropriated as the first Hindi prose-writer: though his 'Surāsur nirṇay' was written in the Shikasta script, 'Munshiji wrote in the common language spoken by educated Hindus from Delhi to Prayag', and though a scholar of Persian and Arabic, he did not use 'foreign words'; ibid., pp. 2–3.

Allāh Khān's *Rānī ketakī kī kahānī* (1803) was included to 'make our Muslim brothers reflect on how a famous Muslim citizen of Lucknow, an able writer of Urdu and Persian and a favourite and court poet of Nawab Saadat Ali Khan, could consider writing a book in Hindi. Did he consider it worthless and dead, or was it rather a source of pride for him to be able to write a book in that language?!'[16] Once all pre-modern forms of Hindi were assimilated under the same term, the presence of Muslim poets in the Hindi tradition and of Hindi as a public language in Muslim courts until Akbar's time was held up as proof of 'how former Muslim poets had adopted Hindi with unshakable love. . . . Their hearts, unlike those of contemporary Muslims, were not marred by narrow feelings'.[17] If only Muslims were acquainted with history, ran the argument, they, too, would realize the high status Hindi was accorded in Muslim courts and by Muslim poets in the past! Later, the more Aurangzeb 'tried to crush Hindi, the more Hindus loved it and sheltered it in the temple of their hearts'.[18] The history of Hindi scholars and teachers as portrayed in textbooks closely followed the history of the Aryan–Hindu community in M. Gupta's poem *Bhārat-bhārtī* (3.1): poetry and scholarship supported each other. Accordingly, Hindi, the direct descendant of Sanskrit, had been downgraded from its position of hegemony during Muslim rule; the end of Muslim rule was the beginning of its new rise, which would culminate in its acceptance as the national language in independent India.

The notion that the two languages were in fact one informed a different historiography. In the attempt to overcome the hostility between scholars, activists, and associations on both sides, scholars of Urdu and Hindi were invited to give public lectures under the aegis of the Hindustani Academy on subjects concerning Indo-Muslim culture (cf. 3.1.1). Padmasiṃh Śarmā (1877–1932), for example, tried to downplay the cultural difference between Khari Boli Hindi and Urdu by disproving the antiquity of their separate names: they were merely different names for the same language:

Our Hindi was and is but one language, but because of the different names Hindi and Urdu it came to acquire two separate forms. Its worshippers shaped two different forms out of it according to their own inclination and culture, and established them as idols. Languages usually bind countries with the thread of unity, of nationality (*jātīytā*); unfortunately here the opposite is happening. One and the

[16] Ibid., pp. 6–7.

[17] M.A. Vaśiṣṭh, Hindī-prabhākar, 'Hindī sāhitya aur musalmān kavi', *Chāṁd*, X, pt. 1, 2, December 1931, p. 275.

[18] Ibid., pp. 274–5.

same language is becoming, on the basis of false names, the cause of terrible sectarian division.[19]

Unlike Chatursen Śāstrī's quote at the beginning of this section, blind worship is here presented as a source of confusion and division rather than of unity. Padmasiṃh Śarmā minced no words arguing that the Persian and Arabic saṃskāra of poets and scholars had really turned Urdu into a foreign language: Hindi words had gradually become so discredited that Urdu poets living in north India could assert that they did not even know Hindi. Even Urdu scholars eager to rectify such a view were themselves unable to use Hindi words.[20] Implicit in Śarmā's judgement was the view that the literati's literary and historical saṃskāras were most responsible for the growing distance and unfamiliarity between the two languages: a true national perspective required that such saṃskāras be transcended in favour of a more comprehensive and neutral view. His lectures ended with an appeal for unity in the familiar terms of the 'division within the family' (*kuṭumb kā baṭvārā*), the *bête noire* of every Indian family. Himself a scholar, he believed that scholarly consensus under the institutional arbitration of the Hindustani Academy could bring about a solution.[21]

Tara Chand, professor of Urdu at Allahabad University and an active member of the Academy, put forward a similar argument in support of Hindustani.[22] In the public sphere of journals, Premchand was one of the most eloquent supporters of Hindustani: that hybrid language was for him the symbol of what Hindi rāṣṭrabhāṣā needed to *become*. In the new national perspective, Hindi needed to change and become as elastic in terms of grammar and vocabulary as the language of the Delhi–Meerut

[19] Padmasiṃh Śarmā, *Hindī, Urdū, Hindustānī*, Allahabad, Hindustani Akademi 1932 (3rd ed. 1951), p. 36.

[20] Ibid., p. 81.

[21] Ibid., pp. 150–1.

[22] In the pamphlet 'Some misconceptions about Hindustani', Tara Chand refuted the 'Hindi tradition' of the Hindī Sāhitya Sammelan and treated modern Khari Boli separately from the medieval neo Indo-Aryan dialects. Instead, he used 'Hindi' in the meaning given it by Muslim poets from the thirteenth century; he traced back a literary tradition in Hindustani to the sixteenth and seventeenth centuries and maintained that Urdu was just the literary form of the speech known by the names of Hindustani, Khari Boli, or Dehlavi, while phonetically and morphologically it was identical to modern Hindi. In practice he rejected the Hindi–Urdu divide and the emergence of a separate Hindi identity. See also his article 'Hindustānī kyā hai?', *Chāṁd*, XVII, pt. 1, 1, June 1939, pp. 36 ff.

area had been, a crucible of people and cultures.[23] More pragmatically, Dhīrendra Varmā, also an active member of the Hindustani Academy and head of the Hindi department in Allahabad University, argued that Hindi or Hindustani could at most become the official language (*rājbhāṣā*) of India: it could aspire to replace English as the state language but not to unite what was essentially a diverse culture. Moreover, in their obsession with rāṣṭrabhāṣā, Hindi campaigners had forgotten Hindi's own frailties and subordinate status in the Hindi heartland.[24]

While for some supporters of Hindi's claim, like Gandhi and Premchand, Hindi had to transcend its present cultural faultline in order really to become the language of all Indians, for Hindi activists and associations, as well as for Hindi politicians like Madan Mohan Mālavīya and Puruṣottam Dās Ṭaṇḍon, Hindi was predestined to be the national language *because* it was culturally the language of the Hindu nation (cf. 5.3 and 5.4). The discourse on rāṣṭrabhāṣā as the life-spirit of a community that we found in Mahāvīr Prasād Dvivedī was retroactive. As in the historical poem *Bhārat-bhārtī,* the fact that India was not united and did not have a national language was itself proof that it once had had one and had lost it: Hindi was that language. The multilingual past, an essential feature of India, was denied, downplayed, and misrepresented in the triumphant majoritarian drive for one national culture.

2.1.2. Public Support for the Claim

Public support for Hindi's claim to national status shifted in interesting ways in the nineteenth and early twentieth centuries as the idea of 'the vernacular language of Hindustan' moved from colonial and missionary circles to the Indian public sphere.[25] In Indian circles, support had first come from religious associations and, not surprisingly, from Bengali scholars already in the nineteenth century, such as Bhudev Mukhopadhyay and Keshab Chandra Sen.[26] At the beginning of the century there was, at least on paper, the will to imagine Hindi as the rāṣṭrabhāṣā of India and to put Devanagari forward as the national script. A scholarly consensus

[23] Premchand, 'Hindī, urdū aur hindustānī', in *Kuch vichār*, Benares, 1939, pp. 101–13.

[24] Dhīrendra Varmā 'Hindī rāṣṭrabhāṣā banāne kā moh', *Sarasvatī,* July 1938, pp. 2–4; see also his earlier book *Hindī-rāṣṭra yā sūbā hindustānī* (Allahabad, Leader Press, 1930) in which he questioned several nationalist assumptions.

[25] Cf. Lelyveld, 'The Fate of Hindustani'.

[26] See Siṃh, *Ādhunik sāhitya ke vikās meṁ,* pp. 251–2.

took concrete shape in the form of the Ek-lipi Vistār Pariṣad (Society for the Propagation of One Script) of Calcutta. Its first aim was 'to urge and increase the use of the Sanskrit script (Devanagari) everywhere and especially for all Indian languages', and members were requested to fulfil the aim by printing books in various Indian languages using Devanagari, by lobbying for the use of Devanagari in schools, in the press and in public associations, and by putting pressure on the government, on local rulers, and on Indian and foreign scholars. Members of the Society included government officials, inspectors of schools, university professors, writers, scholars, advocates, and a few Indian rulers, mostly from Bengal and north India but also from other parts of the country, and both Hindus and Muslims. Chandrakanta Tarkalankar was its distinguished president, Justice Shardacharan Mitra the secretary, and among the eminent members were Rabindranath Tagore, Edwin Greaves, the Maharajas of Ayodhya, Darbhanga and Kalakankar, Sanskrit professors from several prestigious Calcutta colleges, Mahāvīr Prasād Dvivedī, Lala Sītārām, and the founders of the Nāgarī Prachāriṇī Sabhā. A Devanagari Conference, organized by the Pariṣad in Baroda in 1909 and hosted by the Maharaja, was presided over by R.C. Dutt and R.G. Bhandarkar, with mostly non-Hindi-speaking scholars among the participants.[27] As Svami Śraddhānand recalled in his opening speech at the XIV Hindī Sāhitya Sammelan meeting in Delhi in 1924, 'The English Vice-President of the Ek-lipi Vistār Pariṣad once said in a speech that the Devanagari script should be publicized throughout the world since there is no other complete script. A Muslim Vice-President said that Indian Muslims should transcribe the Quran into Devanagari.'[28] When the issue came out of the secluded closet of the associations into the public arena, however, scholarly consensus proved to be of little use, yet Hindi campaigners could still hark back to it in order to uphold their claim.

The claim had found further institutional support in nascent religious reform associations and in the voluntary associations of Hindus that mushroomed in towns all over north India in the late nineteenth century. As already mentioned, the fifth rule of the Ārya Samāj established Hindi (called āryabhāṣā) as the public language of the Samāj; Dayānanda Sarasvatī himself started using it for public preaching in the 1870s (1.1). His translation of the Vedas into Hindi was termed by Lajpat Ray 'the boldest act of his life'.[29] The Punjabi Hindu service groups which formed

[27] See *Ek-lipi vistār pariṣad—niyamāvalī*, Calcutta n.d.; from the Āryabhāṣā Pustakālay, Benares; see also *Mādhurī*, I, pt. 2, 2, March 1923, p. 239.

[28] Quoted in *Sammelan patrikā*, XI, 7–8, p. 275.

[29] See Gupta, *Hindī bhāṣā aur sāhitya ko āryasamāj kī den*, p. 26.

the Ārya Samāj, had been traditionally Urdu educated; their gradual adoption of Devanagari and Hindi, that too in a sanskritized version, no doubt helped the identification between language and religious identity. Even when Punjabi or Urdu remained the languages of intercourse among Punjabi Ārya Samājists, Hindi was publicly upheld as the āryabhāṣā. The fact that the Ārya Samāj was the sole force behind Hindi propaganda in the Punjab could not but strengthen in the eyes of other groups the notion that Devanagari, Hindi and Hindu were one. Similarly, propaganda in support of Hindi and the Devanagari script figured as one of the aims of local Hindu Sabhās such as the Prayāg Hindū Samāj of Allahabad (1880), where Madan Mohan Mālavīya first emerged as a champion of both Hindi and cow-protection; according to Jürgen Lütt, the mobilization in favour of Hindi and against Urdu was the first expression of a Hindu self-awareness.[30] In the 1920s, the revived Hindu Mahasabha, the political expression of the coming together of Ārya Samāj and Hindu members within Congress, included Hindi propaganda 'in cooperation with the Hindi Sahitya Sammelan' as one of the points of its 1925 programme.[31] Thus support for Devanagari and Hindi fell squarely within the purview of the defence of 'Hindu interests' as envisaged in the revived slogan 'Hiṇdi, Hindu, Hindustan.'

The birth of the Hindī Sāhitya Sammelan out of the Nāgarī Prachāriṇī Sabhā in 1910 marked an important change in strategy. The Sabhā had remained solidly loyalist and had pushed for the gradual recognition of Hindi within the framework of the colonial state and its agencies, the judiciary and the administrative and education systems. The Sammelan instead formed a bridge between Hindi intellectuals and Congress politicians at a time when several of the latter, like Tilak and Gandhi, were starting to realize the importance of Hindi as a political language. The first 'Conference on the National Language and National Script' was organized under the aegis of the Ārya Samāj in Lucknow in December 1916; it coincided with the annual Congress session, at which for the first time an array of nationalist leaders took an explicit stand on Hindi rāṣṭrabhāṣā. Gandhi presided, Annie Besant, M.M. Mālavīya, Śraddhānand, Ramaswamy Iyer, Śyāmsundar Dās, Satyadev Parivrājak and P.D. Ṭaṇḍon spoke, and Tilak and others sent messages of support. The conference resolved that 'in order to increase unity in the country and to spread nationalist feelings, it is necessary to make use of a national script and

[30] Lütt, *Hindu-Nationalismus*, pp. 37 ff; on the Prayāg Hindū Sabhā, see Bayly, *The Local Roots of Indian Politics*, pp. 105 ff.

[31] Craig Baxter, *The Jana Sangha*, Pennsylvania, Pennsylvania University Press, 1969, p. 14.

national language for all matters concerning the country as a whole, and for this only Devanagari and Hindi are appropriate.'[32] Much of the subsequent efforts of the Sammelan would be directed at Congress rather than at the colonial government, in the attempt to make Congress leaders stick to this resolution. Yet the consensus on Hindi among nationalist leaders before 1920 concealed different agendas. What Mālavīya, Tilak, and Lajpat Rai shared was a cultural affiliation to Hindi as the essentially 'Indian' language because of its Hindu core; Gandhi's support instead was for Hindi as the language of *svadeshi*, the antithesis to English, and he considered Hindi to be the *spoken* language of village India that transcended divides of literacy, script, region, and religion. For this reason, he later rejected Hindi as too identified with Hindu interests and supported Hindustani (cf. 5.4).[33]

What Hindi activists and institutions had not realized at this stage was that the vocal support of a broad political movement and that of the government were of a different nature. While the latter carried, despite obvious practical limitations, the letter of the law and official authority, the former was subject to the pressures of different claimants and to political considerations. The support of national Congress leaders assured Hindi activists and supporters that Hindi's rise to the honour of being the national language was only a matter of time, and yet they seemed exasperatingly prone to procrastination. During a speech in Kanpur in April 1917 on his Home Rule League tour of the province, Tilak expressed grief at being unable to deliver the speech in Hindi. To the correspondent of the popular Calcutta paper *Bhāratmitra*, Tilak said that there was no longer any doubt that Congress proceedings should take place in the 'national language', i.e. Hindi; however, this could not happen just yet. When the correspondent suggested that all Congress representatives should learn Hindi, Tilak again agreed in principle but refused to consider the language issue as a matter of urgency. What one could do was make propaganda, he said, thus delegating responsibility to Hindi associations. Mālavīya's stand was also temporizing, as the choice of English as the medium of instruction in BHU showed (cf. 1.4). The special Congress session held in Nagpur in 1920 declared Hindi–Hindustani the

[32] Resolution quoted from *Abhyuday* in *Sammelan patrikā,* IV, 5, January–February 1917, p. 180. Similar resolutions were passed the following year at the Āryabhāṣā Sammelan for the Annual festival of Gurukul Kangri, and at the second Rāṣṭrabhāṣā Sammelan in Calcutta in December, presided over by Tilak; quoted in *Sammelan patrikā,* IV, 8, April–May 1917, pp. 252–3 and V, 7, February–March 1918, p. 158.

[33] See Lelyveld, 'The Fate of Hindustani'.

national language of India, and a resolution presented by P.D. Ṭaṇḍon at the special Congress in Kokonada introduced a change in the Congress rules according to which proceedings were to be held in the national language 'as far as possible'. 'We have reached very near to our aim', wrote the *Sammelan patrikā*; 'we should accept this statement provisionally, and after a while, we believe, the words "as far as possible" will be removed and Hindi-Hindustani will be the language of Congress.'[34] All the greater was their surprise when Gandhi and several other national leaders withdrew or qualified their support in the following decade and Hindi was termed narrow and communal.

The first problems with political support arose when Congressmen started taking concrete steps to introduce Hindi in constitutional venues. Using Hindi as a symbolic protest against, and as a reversal of, English had positive connotations, but nationalist leaders quickly realized that it also aroused strong Muslim objections: in the local boards and provincial councils the language issue was discussed heatedly. For example, in February 1917, when C.Y. Chintamani, the *Leader* editor and liberal politician, not known to be a Hindi supporter, asked in the UP Legislative Council that all court clerks and judges learn Hindi in accordance with the 1900 Resolution, British and Muslim members objected and the controversy spilled over into the press. The proposal appeared to be a step towards decolonization: at the UP provincial Hindī Sāhitya Sammelan Conference in Sitapur in October, which took place at the same time and in the same tent as the UP Political Conference, Chintamani was publicly thanked, and at the Political Conference the atmosphere got so heated that every speech in English was greeted with derision and with cries for Hindi. As the reporter for the Bombay newspaper *Śrīveṅkateśvarsamāchār* remarked, 'People have realized that it has become difficult to function without Hindi.'[35] This marked a historic shift in the public perception of Hindi from 'You cannot function with Hindi' to 'You cannot function without Hindi' (from हिन्दी से काम नहीं चल सकता to बिना हिन्दी के काम नहीं चल सकता). On the other hand, the proposal was decried by Muslim publicists as proof of Hindu aggression. After 1920, when former Non-Cooperators were elected to local boards, they began to exercise direct pressure on language policy, and Muslims regularly petitioned against it.[36] Babu

[34] *Sammelan patrikā*, XI, 5, 1924, p. 206. The same resolution was to be repeated at several other Congress meetings, itself a sign that its implementation was taking longer to materialize.

[35] Quoted by *Sammelan patrikā*, V, 2, October–November 1917, p. 41.

[36] See the petition presented by a *Representation of the Muslims of the United*

Śivaprasād Gupta and Sampūrṇānand in Benares, and P.D. Ṭaṇḍon and Babu Saṅgamlāl Agravāl in Allahabad, the most vociferous supporters of Hindi on the boards, did manage to introduce Hindi in municipal and district board offices. However the 'nationalist' move again proved to be divisive, and Congress politicians in office discovered that they now had varied public opinions to care about. By then there existed a consensus in the Hindi public sphere over the need to introduce Hindi in public administration; Urdu objections appeared unwarranted both on 'scientific' and on majoritarian grounds, and compromise unnecessary. The problem deepened. The difference in script between Hindi and Urdu became an insurmountable hurdle and divided loyalties along the lines of the religious communities. For example, in February 1925 a Muslim League meeting in Allahabad issued a protest against the use of Hindi instead of Urdu in the local boards' offices; the Nāgarī Prachāriṇī Sabhā reacted by warning all Hindu Sabhas, Sanatan Dharma Sabhas and Ārya Samāj branches about it.[37] In 1924 a committee was appointed by the Benares Municipal Board to decide in which script the Hindustani proceedings should be written; all Muslim members insisted that they be written in both scripts, while a Hindu member was driven to the point of saying that English would be better than such squabbles. Śivaprasād Gupta decided to make the debate public and wrote an open letter to all Hindi newspapers suggesting a compromise: the language would be called Urdu and the script would be Devanagari.[38] Fairly typical of Hindi opinion was the reply of the editor of *Mādhurī*, with its uncompromising stand communicated through reasoned argument. Revealing a kind of Hindu majoritarianism, he said that there could be no doubt about the script, and to call the language Urdu would be a great mistake, losing ground one had already conquered.[39]

Language, the binding element of identification and a powerful symbol of nationalism for the Hindi public sphere, proved therefore to be a divisive element in the political sphere, long before the Self-respect Movement in Tamil Nadu rejected Hindi as a symbol of Aryan

---

Provinces (India) to the Indian Statutory Commission, July 1928, Allahabad, p. 30; quoted in Dittmer, *Die Indischen Muslims*, p. 194.

[37] *Sammelan patrikā*, XII, 8, March 1925, pp. 379–80.

[38] See Śivaprasād Gupta, 'Ek lipi kā praśn', *Sammelan patrikā*, XI, 4, 1924, pp. 129–32.

[39] Editorial 'Ek lipi kā praśn aur bābū śivaprasād gupta', *Mādhurī*, II, pt. 2, 1, February 1924, pp. 128–9.

imperialism.[40] In the United Provinces especially, Hindi became a double-edged weapon for Congress. When Saṅgamlāl Agravāl, Mālavīya, Ṭaṇḍon, and others spoke in Hindi in the Legislative Assembly it was a powerful symbol of independence, for it was used against the British; but internally, structural divisions could not be overcome: whenever resolutions concerning the script were raised or enforced they touched cultural faultlines and created public animosity. Above all, Hindu members were now supposed to protect the interests of Hindi and Muslim members those of Urdu, with little or no space for compromise positions. When a motion on Hindi failed to pass at the Benares municipal board in 1926, the Hindi press (*Āj, Hindī kesarī, Bhāratmitra, Pratāp, Abhyuday*) sprang up in arms as a body to accuse the Hindu members of treason, and spoke of it as a question of shame for the entire Hindu community.[41]

Hindi had enjoyed wide scholarly support, spearheaded cultural activism, and found an effective formulation in nationalist terms. But it now came up aganst political and cultural opposition. The potential divisiveness of the discourse of Hindi, which Hindi rhetoric had tended to mask, became apparent. When Congress began insisting on the compromise formula of Hindi–Hindustani, Hindi activists could not bear to see the efforts of a quarter of a century jeopardized. Once again they tried to shift the question from the political arena to the 'neutral' ground of rationality by having experts decide which 'style' of Hindi would be best suited for the national language. In doing so, they were trying also to reach a national solution to the provincial contest with Urdu. The 'defence of Hindi' which took place in associations and the press in the 1930s manifested a wider and more complex conflict of authority: while seeking out political influence and support in Congress, Hindi supporters and associations fought from their institutional positions and their authority as 'Hindi experts', which they had acquired within colonial government (cf. 5.4). Instead of evolving a new discourse and arriving at a broad consensus in the struggle against English, they rehearsed old arguments from the Hindi–Urdu controversy. In the process they tightened the cultural boundaries of the language and their control over language even within the Hindi public sphere, treading further along the path of exclusion.

[40] See Sumathi Ramaswamy, 'Battling the Demoness Hindi: The Culture of Language Protest in Tamilnadu, 1937–67', in S. Freitag, ed., *Culture as a Contested Site: Popular Participation and the State in the Indian Subcontinent* (forthcoming).

[41] See *Sammelan patrikā*, XIII, 7, February 1926, p. 231.

2.2. Changing Concepts of Literature

Illustration 2.1. Poetry, the fair damsel, is vied for by different poets: the mystical poet calls her up to the infinite sky, the erotic poet sitting on the right invites her to a merry party, and the nationalist poet calls her to duty on the left. Source: *Mādhurī*, VIII, pt. 1, 1, August 1929.

[Earlier] literature was not created for the common people. Poets and playwrights were honoured only at the courts of a few literary-minded rajas and wealthy men, therefore neither did poets worry about the influence of their works on the common people nor did critics feel the need to evaluate these works from the social point view.[42]

Once the 'people' (*lok, jantā, jāti*) were accepted as a central and overarching category, everything from language to literature, from society to politics, had to be thought out again. The debates on the meaning of

[42] Kālidās Kapūr, 'Samālochnā', in *Sāhitya-samikṣā*, an early attempt at a new kind of literary criticism; Allahabad, Indian Press, 1929, p. 14.

literature that started to take place in Hindi journals from the end of the nineteenth century show writers, scholars, and critics grappling with the category of '*lok*', 'people': as in English, the word indicates both a single collectivity ('the English people') and particularly the lower rungs of society (*lok-sāhitya* translates as folk literature). Therefore, linking 'literature' and 'the people' had wide-ranging and important implications for the way writers and intellectuals interpreted their role and the function of literature and criticism. This is directly relevant to our discussion of the public sphere in Hindi, for in discussing 'literature' and 'the people' intellectuals were both theoretically and practically coping with publicity and its implications. For example, such debates highlight the fact that once norms were questioned in the light of what were perceived as the needs of the time, new guidelines and concepts could emerge only after public contestation. This, in turn, raised the question of authority, for if everyone could question norms, who was going to set them afresh? By the 1920s, the sheer variety of contemporary literary practices gave a peculiar edge to this theoretical discussion. Also, in the new, open literary sphere such debates and formulations had a direct impact on contemporary writers: praise or rejection from influential editors and critics meant a lot to poets and their self-esteem. The diversity of positions in the debate, conducted in the public venue of journals, reflects partly the different saṃskāras of Hindi literary people and also the selective use of western criticism of Indian literary sources. Sanskrit definitions were compared to those of ancient Greek thinkers as well as Shaftesbury, Burke, Hume, Winckelmann, Lessing, Herder, and Kant in order to prove that aesthetics had a place in Indian philosophy, too.[43] It has been argued that orientalists working on India consistently used an all-inclusive Enlightenment conception of literature covering works in all branches of knowledge. At the same time, they operated with European concepts and the developing tools of philology, which led them to concentrate on Sanskrit and its early textual tradition. Moreover, orientalists also used the Romantic notion of literature as the expression of the 'national spirit' of a people.[44] Echoes of all these concepts will be found in the debate. What was new about it was first of all the perspective of *lokruchi* (interest of the people) and *lokdharma*: the 'people' were put firmly centre stage. This raised two questions: first, how to interpret the literary traditions of

[43] See e.g. 'Bāṇa', 'Saundarya-śāstra', *Mādhurī*, II, pt. 2, 1, February 1924, p. 9. See also 'Kavitā, sadāchār aur nīti', *Mādhurī*, IV, pt. 1, 3, September 1925.

[44] Vinay Dharwadker, 'Orientalism and the Study of Indian Literatures', in Breckenridge and van der Veer, *Orientalism and the Postcolonial Predicament*, pp. 158–85.

the past in the light of this concept.[45] In one of the earliest modern books to be written about the medieval Hindi poets, the Miśra brothers' *Hindī navaratna* (1911), there was unease about presenting devotional and courtly poets together, as Karine Schomer has observed. In the introduction, devotional poets were termed 'poets with a message', while the courtly poets 'had no important message, but expressed themselves beautifully'. Furthermore, while rīti poets were all referred to simply as *kavi*, the bhakti poets were given religious appellatives: '*Gosvāmī* Tulsīdās', '*Mahātmā* Kabīr.'[46]

The second question was: what kind of literature was needed now? The oft-used metaphor of the *bhaṇḍār* (treasure-house) reflected a preoccupation with the present state of Hindi literature and a sense of collective enterprise, but underlying it was also a selective attitude: every work published contributed to 'filling the bhaṇḍār,' but only works of a certain kind were suited for this role. The question itself implies a yearning toward a single definition analogous to the yearning for a single language: now *one* common standard was sought in place of the earlier multiplicity of tastes. The question 'what literature is needed now?' also reflected the need to bring some order to the eclectic and changing literary scene, especially with its new experimentations and the commercial market. Debates centred on poetry, partly because it was here that the most radical changes were taking place and partly because this was the literary form with the highest pedigree, where the heritage from the past was most significant and challenging. Debates on fiction (cf. 2.3) reflect similar concerns and attitudes, but partly because of the relative newness of the novel form and partly because of the towering presence of Premchand, they did not display the same degree of friction.

For the sake of clarity, we can broadly reduce the positions in the debate on literature to three: that of rationalist reformers like Mahāvīr Prasād Dvivedī, that of defenders of tradition (i.e. Braj Bhasa) such as Padmasiṃh Śarmā, and that of modernists such as Ilāchandra Jośī. Since mainstream Hindi criticism was formed by a sort of compromise synthesis of these three, this section will serve to identify its different sources. Once again, literary saṃskāras will assist us in understanding the genealogy of each position.

Traditional literary training in Sanskrit and Braj Bhasa involved texts and manuals of rhetoric and poetics and the analysis of literature in terms

[45] For a similar dilemma in Urdu literature, see F. Pritchett, *Nets of Awareness*,1994.

[46] Schomer, *Mahadevi Varma*, p. 57n.

of *rasa, alaṃkāra, dhvani, chand*, etc.[47] But scholars like Mahāvīr Prasād Dvivedī, Śyāmsundar Dās, and Rāmchandra Śukla had also read and translated English rationalist and utilitarian thinkers and found in them a conception of the social function of literature which suited their reformist attitudes.[48] These were the tools they had at their disposal when rethinking literary tradition and contemporary literature, and also in their critical practice: what they did was to try and accommodate Sanskrit and utilitarian poetics. Dvivedī's public stance on literature first appeared in *Sarasvatī* as a radical critique of Braj Bhasa ('Nāyikā bhed', June 1901), and with new rules for the poet ('Kavi kartavya', July 1901). Like many contemporaries, Dvivedī believed that traditional poetry in Braj Bhasa, with its samasyā-pūrti, its figures of speech (ālaṃkāra) and erotic themes (śṛṅgāra), was outdated and immoral. He rejected Braj Bhasa as a poetic language, arguing, like the Romantics and the colonial Education Department, that the language of poetry should not be different from that of speech and prose. He also rejected the erotic content of rīti poetry and called instead for poems on history and the great figures of the Indian past, and didactic or descriptive compositions on nature and on moral values.

> The best poetry is that which tells of the aims of life and the ways to make it meaningful (*sārthak*) in the most enchanting language; which gives man good instruction and shows the path to progress and seeks to render his heart liberal and sympathetic. [The best poetry] is that which expresses high thoughts, exerts a good influence on heart and mind and gives teachings that are necessary and useful for the age in such a way that man grasps them very quickly.[49]

In fact, literature to Dvivedī meant all kinds of useful knowledge, and its aim was not only, or not primarily, to entertain but to inform and

[47] For a discussion of these terms see Edwin Gerow, *A Glossary of Indian Figures of Speech*, Le Hague, Mouton, 1971, and by the same author *Indian Poetics. A History of Indian Literature*, vol. 5, fasc. 3, Wiesbaden, Harrassowitz, 1977.

[48] Rāmchandra Śukla translated Edison's *Essay on Imagination* in *Nāgarīprachāriṇī patrikā*, IX, 1905, and J.H. Newman's 'Literature', from *The Idea of a University*, in *Sarasvatī*, June 1904. M.P. Dvivedī translated Herbert Spencer's *Education* (1861) as *Śikṣā* (Indian Press, 1910), as well as J.S. Mill's essay on Liberty; cf. Siṃh, ed., *Dvivedīyug ke sāhityakāroṁ ke kuch patr*. The exact nature and extent of the impact of western rationalist thinkers on these great Hindi literary reformists is yet to be reassessed, after the enthusiastic appraisal by Rāmvilās Śarmā in *Mahāvīr prasād dvivedī aur hindī navjāgaraṇ*, New Delhi, Rajkamal Prakasan, 1977, and *Rāmchandra śukla aur hindī ālochnā*, New Delhi, Rajkamal Prakasan, 1973.

[49] Dvivedī, 'Ādhunik kavitā', *Sarasvatī*, March 1912, quoted in Bhatnagar, *The Rise and Growth of Hindi Journalism*, p. 332.

to educate. The shift was not only in *taste*, but in the whole idea of poetry. For that, Dvivedī rejected the more recent tradition of Braj Bhasa and looked further back to Sanskrit: its bhaṇḍār of literature was to be the model for Hindi. As an editor, Dvivedī actively enforced his ideal in a variety of ways. As we have seen, he inspired and commissioned poets to write along these lines, as he did with Maithilīśaraṇ Gupta for *Bhārat-bhārtī* (cf. 3.1), he rejected poems he deemed unsuitable and he wrote copious reviews of, and comments on, contemporary works. In this way he became for Hindi the most influential critic and arbiter of taste of the early twentieth century. Also, he showed how a public medium such as a journal could be used as a means to lay down and spread standard norms and values in the public sphere (cf. 1.3.1).

Such a rethinking of literature in the light of contemporary needs was expressed in explicit terms in a series of articles on 'literature and nationalism' by, among others, Veṅkateś Nārāyaṇ Tivārī (1890–1965), one of Dvivedī's early contributors, himself an editor and a Congress politician. In these articles Tivārī typically drew upon Sanskrit and European theorists to express modern concerns over the function of literature: he quoted the definitions of western critics such as Saint-Beuve, Matthew Arnold, and Carlyle in order to underline the link between literature and life, and literature and society. His argument was based on the premises that Hindi literature was currently in a state of anarchy because of confusion over the meaning of the word 'literature', and that Hindi *rāṣṭrabhāṣā* needed a literature worthy of such status. He then distinguished the broad meaning of 'literature' as anything serious written in a given language from the narrow one of literature as poetry, 'which arises from the unbroken power of imagination and charms humanity, adorned by the jewels of language'.[50] Whereas Sanskrit literature had developed fully, Hindi thus far had limited itself to the second definition only. By considering literature only as an 'aesthetic utterance' (*rasāt-makaṃ vākyaṃ*), Hindi had killed its soul. For what mattered in literature was not the language (*bhāṣā*) but the meaning or feeling (*bhāva*): to this end, Tivārī adopted Saint-Beuve's definition of the classic as that of the writer *tout court*:

A classic is a writer who has expanded the human mind, who has literally increased man's treasury and inspired man to move a step ahead, who has

[50] V.N. Tivārī, 'Sāhitya aur rāṣṭrīytā', pt. 1, *Sammelan patrikā*, V, 8–9, March–May 1918, p. 163.

discovered an uncontested moral truth or has reached an eternal passion that was hidden in the human heart.[51]

A writer worthy of the name had therefore to be a seer (*draṣṭā)* and to inspire noble feelings. Here entered the question of nationalism: since every nation found expression in its own literature, and since its literature expressed the essence of its nationality, Hindi literature had to be judged from this perspective.[52] This meant that Hindi writers had to produce 'pure literature worthy of being offered like a garland of flowers at the feet of Mother [India]' and that 'bad saṃskāras must need be uprooted without mercy'.[53]

A similar blend of Sanskrit poetics and utilitarian attitudes towards literature became the mainstay of literary theory in the curriculum. *Sāhityālochan* (1922) by Śyāmsundar Dās, which became the standard manual of literary criticism, attempted to blend Sanskrit poetics with modern preoccupations concerning the social and nationalist function of literature.[54] Despite the traditional title, it was more or less a translation of William Hudson's *Introduction to the Study of Literature*, but with some telling departures from the original.[55] For instance, the second chapter on 'Sāhitya kā vivechan', 'The study of literature', closely followed Hudson's categories in discussing *uddeśya* (aim), *sāhitya-darśan* (poetics), *sāhitya aur vijñān* (literature and science); yet on one telling point Śyāmsundar Dās modified the original. And what for a sarcastic reviewer was an incorrect translation is in my opinion a self-conscious adaptation to the Indian concept of rasa. Whereas Hudson had put the writer's feelings (bhāva) at the centre of the creative process, the Hindi professor of Benares Hindu University put the focus on the reader's feelings, according to the rasa theory: 'A piece of literature appeals to us only when it activates in us the same resources of sympathy and imagination as went into its making,' which Dās translated as: 'काव्य मनुष्य के

[51] Ibid., p. 164.

[52] V.N. Tivārī, 'Sāhitya aur rāṣṭrīytā', pt. 2, *Sammelan patrikā*, V, 10, May–June 1918, pp. 220–3.

[53] Tivārī, 'Sāhitya aur rāṣṭrīytā', pt. 1, p. 162.

[54] Published by Rāmchandra Varmā for Sahitya-Ratna-Mala-Karyalay, Benares, the book was compiled especially as a course book for MA students. A revised edition is still in print and used in the university syllabus.

[55] William Hudson, *Introduction to the Study of Literature*, London, Harrap, 1910. In his Introduction, Dās admitted using ideas and materials from other works, refashioned in Hindi in his own words.

हृदय को तभी अपनी ओर खींच सकता है जब उसमें अनुरागजनक और कल्पना की वही सामग्री हो जो पाठक श्रोता या द्रष्टा के हृदय में विशेष रूप से जागृत रहती है।' [Poetry appeals to the human heart only when it displays the same elements of sympathy and imagination that are especially alive in the heart of a reader, a listener or a viewer.][56] And because the critic was the arbiter of what people's feelings should be, both author and reader were denied authority and independence.

This creative attempt to combine new (western) notions about the meaning and function of literature with terms and analytical categories of Indian poetics, a blend that would become the mainstay of literature teaching, was therefore implictly normative. Much like nineteenth-century Russia, the centrality of the people, though flaunted, actually only served to validate the nationalist credentials of intellectuals and did not translate into any direct involvement by the people. Besides, this attitude translated into a prescriptive, rather than descriptive, approach to contemporary literature. The emphasis on feelings (bhāva) and on the nation became a means to uphold a moral view of literature that disparaged critical or cross-cultural experiments as 'un-Indian.' As Puruṣottam Dās Ṭaṇḍon, the leader of the Hindī Sāhitya Sammelan and Congress politician, wrote:

> The immortality of national glory (*kīrti*) depends on national literature. National wealth and national literature are mutually dependent. [. . .] Great literature cannot be created by narrow feelings (*saṅkuchit bhāva*). No literature can become immortal and worthy of the whole nation's respect if it contains scores of texts *full of different opinions*. . . . Scholars who write disparate texts to spread controversial opinions or particular social beliefs may succeed in their aim, but their works cannot help to produce pure literature (*viśuddh sāhitya*).[57]

However, an entire poetic sensibility like that of Braj Bhasa could not be swept away single-handedly, as the lasting popularity of samasyā-pūrti in poetry meetings and of Braj Bhasa songs in print testifies (cf. 1.3.3). Although even sympathetic critics could not help deploring the fact that modern Braj Bhasa poets seemed to disregard contemporaneity altogether—they were deemed incapable of representing it and of introducing new themes into their poetry—Braj Bhasa poets and connoisseurs nevertheless defended a tradition polished over centuries.[58]

[56] Dās, *Sāhityālochan*, quoted by Hemchandra Jośī in *Mādhurī*, IV, pt. 2, 3, April 1926, p. 292.

[57] P.D. Ṭaṇḍon, 'Jātīy sāhitya', in *Ṭaṇḍan nibandhāvalī*, Wardha, Rastrabhasa Prachar Samiti, 1970, pp. 74–6; emphasis added.

[58] See editorial on 'Ḅrajbhāṣā aur samay kā pravāh', in *Mādhurī*, IV, pt. 1, 3, September 1925, pp. 414–15. For a passionate defence of Braj Bhasa and a critique of

By comparison contemporary literature appeared clumsy and chaotic. Pandit Govind Nārāyaṇ Miśra's speech on 'Hindī sāhitya kī vartamān daśā' ('The present condition of Hindi') at the 10th Hindī Sāhitya Sammelan meeting in Patna in 1920 voiced this defence in vehement terms. Under the influence of English education, he argued,

> We have abandoned the main definition of Literature, i.e. *vākyaṃ rasātmakaṃ kāvyaṃ* [from the *Sāhityadarpaṇa*]. We have forgotten it, we have forgotten rasa and all the other [elements of poetry]. And this is the reason for the decay of our literature. People have forgotten the old poetry and love the new poetry in Khari Boli, and this is the reason for the ruin (*satyanāś*) of our literature.[59]

The reaction centred around the notion of rules and literary authority. The defenders of Braj Bhasa expressed anxiety at the impossibly wide notion of literature and perplexity about who would now set standards for and assess literary works. The speech of the noted critic and scholar Padmasiṃh Śarmā at the 6th UP Hindī Sāhitya Sammelan in Moradabad in October 1921 best expresses this view and the bewilderment of a traditionally trained critic with regard to contemporary trends. The joy at the swift progress of Hindi was spoilt at the sight of the language corrupted and the elegance (*sauṣṭhava*) of its literature destroyed, Śarmā said. He objected to the new meaning of the word 'literature' which included Ayurveda, mathematics, and geography, and said:

> Earlier by literature one meant a particular code (*śāstra*) related to the art of *kāvya* containing alaṃkāras, rasa, dhvani etc., which discriminated between its qualities and errors—as in the *Sāhityadarpaṇa*. Moreover, earlier literature used to rule over language, poetry over grammar and the literary scholar was the highest authority in deciding if a word was correct. But now ever since Bolshevism, like the sweep of time, has turned literature into a unified democracy, a rebellion (*gadar*) has erupted in the realm of language! Anything which anyone may write in any style on any subject is called 'Literature'. Every writer is completely free to write the way he wants. There is no obligation (*pābandī*) to follow any rule (*qāydā-qānūn*), in fact there is no rule to follow![60]

The 'law-and-order' metaphor expresses well the exasperation of traditional literati with the new 'democracy of literature', which upset the hierarchy of authorities and genres (cf. 2.3).

---

contemporary Hindi, see 'Ṣāhitya meṁ sannipāt' by Kaviratna Pandit Ramāśaṅkar Miśra Śripati', a poet who often appeared in *Mādhurī*; *Mādhurī*, X, pt. 1, 1, August 1931, pp. 96–100. Interestingly, much of the blame is put on the market, where literary people are said to have sold their souls, principles and strength of character; cf. 2.3.

[59] Quoted in *Sammelan patrikā*, VII, 8, December 1920, p. 225.

[60] Quoted in *Sammelan patrikā*, VIII, 6, October 1921, p. 100.

उन्हें शौके इबादत भी है और गाने की आदत भी।
निकलती है ऋचाएँ उनके मुँह से ठुमरियाँ होकर॥

They feel religious and they like to sing:
spouting Vedic *ṛcās* like *ṭhumrīs*.

Whereas 'ancient literary scholars set special metres for each particular rasa, nowadays everyone makes fun of the rules and uses whatever metre for whatever rasa', Śarmā remarked.[61] As a scholar educated to a strict poetic code, he had little sympathy for the experiments with metre that Khari Boli poets were conducting all the time.[62] P. Śarmā's reaction was: 'कोई फ़ारसी बहरों की लहरों में पड़ा बह रहा है, कोई बंगला से पयाल और मराठी से अभंग मांगा जा रहा है मानों हिन्दी छन्दों का दिवाला निकल गया है!' [Some are flowing away along with Persian bahars, others are borrowing pāyal from Bengali and abhaṅga from Marathi, as if Hindi metres had gone bankrupt!][63] A close associate of Mahāvīr Prasād Dvivedī, Śarmā was ready to make allowance for Khari Boli poetry only if it established new rules and then followed them.

What the new Chāyāvādī poets vindicated instead was the poet's individual right to experiment and break existing norms. But what was to them the justified expression of a poet's genius appeared to traditional literati as unacceptable presumption and a prelude to anarchy. That the sense of wonder and sublime inspiration from within that a young Chāyāvād poet like Bhagavatīcharaṇ Varmā expressed could be enough qualification for poetic status was unprecedented:

कौन हो तुम अग्नि-शिखा की ज्वाल ?
तुम्हारा सुधा-पूर्ण गायन-
मधुर, कोमल शिशु-का-सा हास-
कल्पना के सुख का सागर !
तुम्हारा है अनुपम उल्लास-

Who are you, light of a flame?
Your sweet singing
like a baby's soft laughter—
a joyful ocean of the imagination!
Your delight is incomparable![64]

[61] Ibid., p. 106.
[62] For metric experiments in Khari Boli and Chāyāvād's 'liberties' with grammar and metre, see Schomer, *Mahadevi Varma*, Chapter 3, and Raykṛṣṇadās, *Prasād kī yād*, pp. 44 ff.
[63] P. Śarmā's speech, *Sammelan patrikā*, VIII, 6, October 1921, p. 106.
[64] Bhagavatīcharaṇ Varmā, 'Kavi', in *Mādhurī*, V, pt. 2, 2, March 1926, p. 179.

In an important early defence of 'free' (svacchand) poetry, Chāyāvādī poet Sumitrānandan Pant compared the narrow world of Braj Bhasa to the spacious one of Khari Boli. Using highly metaphorical language, Pant criticized Braj Bhasa conventions for having narrowed the world of poetry, which now had to be open and receptive.

Most Bhakti poets spent their entire life going from Mathura to Gokul, the river [Yamuna] of their narrowness flowing in-between: some remained on its banks, some were washed away by the stream, and those who struggled hard and crossed the river reached only up to Dwarka: here the whole expanse of the world ended for them!

Illustration 2.2. The young Chāyāvād poet, called Mr Bombast, recites a symbolist poem full of high-sounding words which sounds less than appealing to the audience's ears.

Source: *Chāṁd*, IX, pt. 2, 3, July 1931, p. 318.

Braj Bhasa poets had not explored the (national) space beyond Braj and emotional space beyond that of devotion to God or the various moods of the heroine: 'Those excellent poets could not go beyond that three-foot long world that went from her tip to her toe.' Using another spatial metaphor, Pant argued that Khari Boli did not have the beautiful and ornate temples Braj Bhasa had, but it had 'spacious avenues', a market for novelties and 'consumer goods' (*upbhogya padārth*) from all over the country and abroad, and its parks were full with all sorts of new flowers.[65]

Hence, it was not only the notion of poetry as a 'criticism of life' that questioned Braj Bhasa aesthetics. New ideas flowing in either through Rabindranath Tagore or from Europe attacked both the Braj Bhasa tradition and the uninspiring poetry of Dvivedī's generation. Also, from the mid-1920s onwards Ilāchandra and Hemchandra Jośī, Sumitrānandan Pant and Kṛṣṇadev Prasād Gauṛ quoted Maeterlinck, Yeats, and Croce to question the stranglehold of English literature and English criticism on the mind of Indian critics and to uphold the notions of individual genius, originality and 'mysticism' in literature.[66] With Chāyāvād, the free rein of the poet's individual imagination was also interpreted in terms of freedom from intellectual colonization. New authorities were upheld:

> English is a language of traders and selfish scientists. It has produced Shakespeare and Wordsworth, but could not produce Rousseau. It produced a Salisbury, but not a Saint-Beuve. It lacks that purity and truthfulness of soul. . . . What I mean is that mad genius (*paglī pratibhā*), which is the soul of literature, could not prosper on English soil . . .

wrote Hemchandra Jośī in 1926.[67] He further eulogized the idea of art for art's sake, which was exactly what Hudson, Dvivedī, Śyāmsundar Dās and Rāmchandra Śukla all despised.[68] However, even Hemchandra Jośī was careful to translate the concept into a suitable Sanskrit definition: *L'Art pour l'Art* was a higher concept than (Arnold's) 'Art as criticism of Life' because it translated *niṣkāma kalādharma*—practising art with no expectation of reward *à la Bhāgavadgītā*. *L'art pour la vie* translated

[65] Sumitrānandan Pant, 'Praveś' to *Pallav*, Delhi, Rajkamal Prakasan, 1963 (first ed. 1926), pp. 9–18.

[66] I use 'mysticism' (*rahasyavād*) here in the ambivalent sense it has in Hindi, where *rahasyavādī* means both mystical and mysterious.

[67] H. Jośī reviewing *Sāhityālochan* in *Mādhurī*, IV, pt. 2, 3, April 1926, p. 291.

[68] Śyāmsundar Dās had quoted Hudson saying: 'From time to time we hear more than enough of "art for art's sake". But this vague and shadowy doctrine is, so far as the art of poetry is concerned, brought into contempt by the rank and standing of those who inculcate it; for it is for the most part associated with minor poets and dilettante critics'; Hudson, *Introduction*, p. 120. To them Jośī replied that *'l'Art pour l'Art'* was an important concept, of which Hudson and his like could not understand the greatness precisely because they were English; Jośī, 'Sāhityālocan', p. 291.

jīvanopyogī kalā and was hence a lowlier form. If Hudson had been Kṛṣṇa, continued Jośī, he would have told Arjun:

बेटा कौरवों को मारो-काटो उनका राज्य जीतो। उसके बाद हम और तुम मिलकर मज़ा करेंगे। ज़िन्दगी का उद्देश्य ओल्माइटी दाल्लर अर्थात सर्वशक्तिमान डालर जोड़ना है। जिससे मनुष्य छोटी उमर में भोग-विलास से छक जाय।

Son, kill the Kauravas and win their kingdom. After that we shall have fun together. The aim of life is to amass the 'Almighty dollar', so that a young man will enjoy sensual pleasures to the full.[69]

As this parody shows, both the colonial and reformist notions of 'useful literature' could be ridiculed and exposed as materialistic, and hence as a lowlier ideal. India's tradition of selfless art mirrored India's spiritual superiority over Britain. Second, it showed a receptivity to a different kind of modernity, a modernity which valued individual freedom and originality.[70]

This was the kind of modernity Chāyāvād embraced. From the criticism it drew it is clear that it represented not just one more poetic trend, but a concept of literature and literary order, so to speak, that was deeply subversive of both Braj Bhasa poetics and Khari Boli reformism. Since the debate over Chāyāvād has been the subject of extensive study both in Hindi and English, there is no need to rehearse it here.[71] Chāyāvād poetry was deemed to be 'useless' because it did not adhere to the notion of socially useful and didactic poetry; and Chāyāvād poets were generally accused of destroying the planned development of Hindi with their eclectic, unrestrained, unmetred poetry. The Head of the Hindi department at BHU, Śyāmsundar Dās, thundered:

आजकल जो हिन्दी-कविता की भंयकर बाढ़ आ रही है, उसमें न जाने कहाँ-कहाँ का कूड़ा-करकट चला आ रहा है। अंगरेज़ी और बंगला में जब मनमाने छन्दों में कविता ढाली जाती है, तब हिन्दी में क्यों न बेसुरी रागिनी छेड़ी जाय। ऊँची कविताएँ आजकल वही कही जाती हैं जिनकी वर्णन शैली बड़े पेचीदा हो, साधारण-सी बात कहने के लिए जिनमें ब्रह्माण्ड की छान-बीन कर डाली गई हो, या जिनमें अलौकिक और अनिर्वचनीय भावों की दुहाई दी गई हो। छायावाद और समस्यापूर्ति से हिन्दी

[69] Ibid., p. 300.

[70] See an article by Ilāchandra Jośī on literary talent, in which genius is placed well above society and its norms, whereas talent paves the way to worldly success and fame; I. Jośī, 'Pratibhā aur uskā vikās' in *Mādhurī*, VI, pt. 2, 6, July 1928, pp. 773–80.

[71] For a contemporary discussion of the criticism of Chāyāvād, see Govarddhandās Tripāṭhī, 'Āj kī Hindī aur uskī kavitā', *Chām̐d*, XV, pt. 1, 3, January 1937; for an excellent discussion in English, see Schomer, *Mahadevi Varma*, Chapter 4.

कविता को बड़ी हानि पंहुच रही है। छायावाद की ओर नवयुवकों का झुकाव है और ये जहाँ गुनगुनाने लगे कि चट दो-चार पद जोड़कर कवि बनने का साहस कर बैठते हैं। इनकी कविता का अर्थ समझना कोई सरल काम नहीं। . . . पूज्य रवीन्द्रनाथ का अनुकरण करके ही यह अत्याचार हिन्दी में हो रहा है।

God knows what horrible rubbish is entering the kind of Hindi poetry which deluges us today. If poetry in English and Bengali can be moulded in arbitrary metres, why shouldn't graceless rāginīs start in Hindi, too? Nowadays high poetry is only that which has a very contorted descriptive style, which searches the whole universe to say the simplest thing, and which worships supernatural feelings that defy description. Chāyāvād and samasyā pūrtis are doing great harm to Hindi poetry. Our youth favours Chāyāvād and they only have to hum something and jot down a couple of verses straight away in order to consider themselves poets! To understand their poems is no easy task either . . . This is the disgrace that is happening in Hindi by aping the venerable Rabindranath.[72]

Looming behind such criticism was the fear, one that Padmasiṃh Śarmā echoed above, that a new kind of anarchy might be setting in; that with their eccentric behaviour and declaration of individual freedom, Chāyāvād poets were ushering in a dangerous disrespect for *all* norms and authority. In fact, much of the critical vocabulary of Chāyāvād poets and enthusiastic critics referred to 'breaking' norms and conventions and bringing about a revolution.[73] Favourable critics argued that Chāyāvādī poetry had to be read more carefully: it expressed a new sensibility and required a new kind of sympathetic (*sahṛday*) reading. Instead of calling it imitation or plagiarism of Rabindranath Tagore, they preferred to interpret their own rahasyavād (mysticism) as a call for the expression of individual experience and of nationalist consciousness. Mysticism in modern literature was not of a religious kind and need not be so, *pace* Rāmchandra Śukla's dismissal in 'Kavitā meṁ rahasyavād': 'Mysticism-Chāyāvād is that which expresses the force of the heart thanks to which man can experience the immense in a limited, the infinite in a finite form.'[74] What Chāyāvādī poets had opened up was a space for the

[72] Quoted in Kṛṣṇadev Prasād Gauṛ, 'Chāyāvād kī chānbīn', *Mādhurī*, V, pt. 2, 6, July 1927, p. 791. In his humoristic column 'Ḍubejī kī chiṭṭhī', short story writer Viśvambharnāth Śarmā 'Kauśik' wrote several parodies of Chāyāvād poetry. Once he wrote that to compose a Chāyāvād poem was as easy as to cook *khichṛī*: all you needed was to open a dictionary, choose 5 to 10 kilograms of words, add some verbs without caring for metre or rhyme, and there was your poem ready; *Chāṁd*, IX, pt. 1, 1, November 1930, p. 155.

[73] See e.g. Nāmvar Siṃh, *Chāyāvād*, New Delhi, Rajkamal Prakasan, 1955.

[74] Gauṛ, 'Chāyāvād kī chānbīn', p. 787; also Rāmnāthlāl Suman, 'Vartmān hindī

imagination and for an inner, private world which their readers shared. It was an emotional and intellectual space, vast, sublime, and passionate, that may not necessarily have existed in real life, just as the poets' poetic 'I' was patently different from the autobiographical person. Chāyāvādī poetry and attitudes became popular with the young, educated public and the new generation of critics. With time, it was accommodated in the canon as one more literary trend (cf. 1.4).

In this section I have focused on debates over poetry because they were more numerous and reflected engrained tastes and critical attitudes. Debates over fiction, as we shall see in the next section, lacked both a substantial theoretical background and critical categories (2.3.3). Besides, Premchand's towering example showed how social or political aims could successfully be combined with entertainment and with literary and imaginative value. Pre-empting the criticism of the 'rasik samāj' of connoisseurs, he stated:

यह भी मानना पड़ेगा कि गत शताब्दियों में पाश्चात्य देशों में जितने सुधार हुए हैं, उनमें अधिकांश का बीजारोपण उपन्यासों ही द्वारा किया गया है।

We have to admit that the seeds of whatever reforms have taken place in western countries in the last few centuries have been sown by novels.[75]

The theoretical debates on the nature of literature reveal a great sense of contemporaneity. In the age of nationalism, they were concerned with bringing in a new system of values, a shift in perspective and authority, and attempted to defend either a tradition under attack (Braj Bhasa) or a new subjective sensibility (Chāyāvād). Although they involved scholars, poets, connoisseurs, and students in the public venues of journals, literary associations, and university departments, ultimately it was university professors—the new experts and authorities—who synthesized the different positions held by Braj Bhasa supporters, by Khari Boli reformist intellectuals, and by modernists, into a set of theoretical assumptions (*sthāpnāeṁ*). Outlined below is the normative synthesis by the quintessential critic–professor, Rāmchandra Śukla.[76]

First of all, the crucial relevance of literature for society and of society for literature was now an established fact. Literature was responsible to the people and aimed at changing and improving their tastes (lokruchi).

---

kavitā aur chāyāvād', *Mādhurī*, VIII, pt. 1, 1, August–September 1928, and Nanddulāre Vājpeyī, 'Vartamān hindī kavitā', *Mādhurī*, VI, pt. 1, 6, January 1928.

[75] Premchand, 'Upanyās rachnā', in *Mādhurī*, I, 4, October 1922, p. 358.

[76] Rāmchandra Śukla, *Chintāmaṇi*, 1st part, Allahabad, Indian Press, 1939.

Second, each period had a peculiar, pervasive *yug-dharma*, 'the ideal distillation of people's tastes', which both literature and society had to grasp.[77] Third, literature was a mirror which opened the eyes of society, thanks to the 'divine sight' each poet is endowed with, something testified to by the almost magical hold poetry can have on human beings. This power, which is a power of the heart over the mind, was partly a gift and partly the result of the poet's selfless asceticism (*sādhnā*).[78] Implied in the notion of the artist as a *sāhitya-* and *samāj-sevī* (dedicated to literature and to society), who incarnated the virtues both of a *tapasvīn* (ascetic) and of a *karmayogī* (selfless worker), was a notion of self-control that tempered the individualism of the Chāyāvādīs. Thus the poet's discipline consisted of studious reading, cultivation of 'a wide intelligence', reflection on contemporary society and its problems, and the company and advice of older, more experienced scholars. Only then could he enter the 'field of literature, and even then with no freedom to burst into a reckless and arbitrary wailing' (*bedhaṛak manmānā vilāp*).[79]

What we see here is a peculiar tension between the crystallizing of a notion of the writer as the vanguard and moral leader of society, which bestowed great authority upon him, aligned with a subtle form of control, as if only a restrained, norm-abiding, and selfless individual had the moral right to be called a writer. This, indirectly, bestowed even greater authority on the critic, who became the appointed judge of a writer's behaviour and would discriminate between those who wrote good poetry and those who burst into 'reckless and arbitrary wailings'.

The debate was directly affected by the structural changes in the field of literature which had placed writers, scholars, and connoisseurs with different saṃskāras in direct contact with each other and with the new, anonymous, and global public of printed media. The fact that 'people's tastes' and 'individual freedom' were central issues bears witness to the change of perspective. The two clashed famously in the literary sphere of the 1940s, when Progressives were pitted against Experimentalists. The Marxist orientation of Progressivist critics made them search for an interpretation of Hindi literary history in terms of structure–superstructure that differed from, but did not question, Rāmchandra Śukla's framework. In a way Progressivist critics took over Śukla's mantle in stressing the social usefulness of literature. Experimentalists, on the other hand,

[77] Sāgar Prasād Rāy 'Sāhityālaṃkār', 'Sāhitya meṁ lok-ruchi tathā yug-dharma', *Chāṁd*, XVII, pt. 1, 1, June 1939, p. 52.

[78] Śukla, *Chintāmaṇi*, p. 227.

[79] Ibid.

claimed that the 'authenticity of individual experience' was the only valid point of departure for good poetry and rejected political engagement.

From my point of view, sensitive to the institutional space and impact of discourses, it is important to underline the power of Rāmchandra Śukla's synthesis in normalizing literature for the curriculum. Literary history followed the history of the jāti in its rise, fall, and revival; teaching literature involved a text-based treatment of a few representative authors from each epoch in a simplified historical context. For textual analysis the traditional tools of Sanskrit poetics continued to be used, perpetuating the deeply embedded notion of codified poetry. Both (expurgated) rīti texts and Chāyāvād compositions figured in this canon, their differences, and the profound implications of such differences, ignored and unaddressed.

2.3. Publicity and the Evaluation of Literature: Prizes, Popularity, and Criticism

Forms and standards of evaluation provide excellent measures by which one can assess the impact of publicity on writers and on the literary sphere. In the light of structural changes in the literary system and the notion of literature, in literary transmission and education, the forms and sites of evaluation reflect issues of cultural values and intellectual authority. What were the standards and the expectations critics and writers placed upon the different forms of public evaluation, whether prizes, reviews, or popularity among readers? Who had the authority to exercise evaluation? What were their values and norms? These questions are inextricably linked on the one hand to the changes in the figures of the writer and the professional editor–critic, their professionalization and self-conscious cultural and political roles, and on the other, to the way the Hindi book market was taking shape (1.3). Popularity, i.e. high sales, became of crucial, and ambiguous, importance as an index of a writer's worth. If this fulfilled the writer's urge to reach out to the highest number of people and exert influence through print, it also required the new—elusive, felicitous, cultivated, and despised—skill of capturing and complying with the tastes of the anonymous reading public. Was this, then, a sell-out, at a time when readers' tastes urgently needed refining and uplift? Was lack of popularity and recognition actually a heroic struggle to teach readers and critics to know better? These were the questions that made the evaluation of literature a critical issue.

Before the advent of print culture, the judges of a writer's merit had been his patrons, fellow poets, scholars, and connoisseurs. Patronage depended on personal ties; criticism was conducted either through poetic contests or commentaries, both internal to the system of literature. With the spread of print culture and the print market, the norms and authority on the basis of which literature was evaluated had now to emerge from the new literary sphere and contend with the reality of the market. All the changes examined in this section—the shift in patronage and the establishment of literary prizes, the impact of the market and the ambiguous value of popularity for the independent writer, and finally public evaluation in journals through criticism and book reviews—are aspects of the same transformation.

2.3.1. Prizes and Patronage

In the nineteenth and early twentieth centuries, court patronage was still being extended to Braj Bhasa poets and to scholars of Sanskrit and Braj Bhasa in the courts of Benares, Orchha, Rewa, and Chattarpur among others. Some Hindi scholars and poets were employed in these courts as dignitaries, secretaries, or officials; among those who worked in the protected but strongly hierarchical court environment were Jagannāth Dās Ratnākar in Ayodhya, and Śukdevbihārī Miśra and Gulābrāī in Chattarpur.[80] In addition, the colonial government had emerged as a patron, indeed the first patron, for prose in modern Khari Boli at Fort William College (1800), where textbooks were prepared to instruct junior civil servants in Indian languages.[81] Later in the century, provincial governments and education departments patronized Hindi and Urdu by heavily subscribing to journals they deemed worthy and by purchasing textbooks and reading books on 'useful subjects'. Some of the first 'novels' in Urdu and Hindi were written in direct response to government prize-giving schemes, such as Nazīr Ahmad's *Mir'āt ul-urūs* (1869), Pandit Gaurīdatt's *Devrānī jeṭhānī kī kahānī* (1870), and Śraddhārām Phillaurī's *Bhāgyavatī* (1877).[82] Many a nineteenth-century Hindi journal in the

[80] See biographies in Appendix.

[81] See Cohn, 'The Command over Language and the Language of Command', pp. 276–329; also King, *One Language, Two Scripts*, and McGregor, *Hindi Literature of the Nineteenth and Early Twentieth Centuries*.

[82] For the prize scheme by the government of the North-Western provinces for meritorious books in 1868, see Amrik S. Kalsi, 'Realism in the Hindi Novel in the Late Nineteenth and Early Twentieth Centuries', unpublished Ph.D. thesis, Cambridge University, 1975, pp. 25–6; and C.M. Naim, 'Prize-Winning *Adab:* A Study of

United Provinces survived because of these official subscriptions, small in number but steady. The provincial government also subsidized literary activities like the search for Hindi manuscripts and public libraries. Through prizes and purchases, the colonial government emerged not only as a major supplier of jobs for Hindi literati, especially in the education department, but also as a potential patron of modern Hindi literature.

Apart from the colonial government, early Hindi literary associations also looked to the princely states for patronage. The Nāgarī Prachāriṇī Sabhā, for example, strove hard to acquire a number of royal 'protectors' (*saṃrakṣaks*, i.e. patrons) as well as grants from the provincial government for its search for old Hindi manuscripts, its monumental Hindi dictionary, a *pukka* building and library, using somewhat different arguments to woo each.[83] With the colonial government it argued in the idiom of progress and scientific work; with royal patrons it used the traditional language of community service and meritorious acts. In his memoirs, Śyāmsundar Dās, the leading organizer of the Sabhā, recalled with some bitterness his strenuous pursuit of royal patronage.[84] He realized that while royal patronage was arbitrary and fickle, colonial patronage was institutional and ostensibly 'impartial', with set rules and judging committees, and that a special authority derived from it. This was the kind of authority that Hindi associations aimed to acquire for themselves, and as they became institutions in the Hindi literary sphere they also assumed a similar role as 'impartial' patrons.

One of the main avenues of patronage for the Sabhā became awarding literary prizes. At first literary people themselves started endowing prizes and medals *through* the Sabhā, usually in their own names or in memory of a deceased relative.[85] Merchant families with philanthropic ambitions followed suit.[86] Such prizes continued the colonial enterprise

---

Five Urdu Books Written in Response to the Allahabad Government Gazette Notification', in Barbara Metcalf, ed., *Moral Conduct and Authority*, Berkeley, University of California Press, 1984.

[83] See King, 'The Nagari Pracharini Sabha of Benares'.

[84] Dās, *Merī ātmakahānī*, pp. 123 ff.

[85] Rāmnārāyaṇ Miśra endowed a Channūlāl Puraskār of Rs 200 for books on science in 1916; Jodhsiṃh Mehtā of Jodhpur a yearly prize of Rs 200 for the best historical book; Jagannāth Dās Ratnākar endowed Rs 1000, which yielded a prize of Rs 200 every three years for the best poetry collection in Braj Bhasa, and M.P. Dvivedī endowed the Dvivedī *svarṇa padak* (gold medal); *Nāgarī prachāriṇī sabhā kā vārṣik vivaraṇ*, Kāśī Nāgarī Prachāriṇī Sabhā, for the years 1920 and 1921.

[86] R.B. Baṭukprasād Khatrī endowed a Baṭukprāsad prize of Rs 200 in 1922 for the

of financing books on useful subjects; at the same time they displayed the independent authority of the Hindi public vested in the associations. By doing so Hindi associations asserted that they knew what kind of books 'Hindi needed' and that it was their 'duty' to mark them out: only now, instead of 'in absence of' a market, these prizes were given 'in spite of' the commercial market.

Over the years, literary associations became sites for recognition. The Nāgarī Prachāriṇī Sabhā started publishing in its annual report a list of the best books of the year; when it started in the 1910s, the list included practically all the new Hindi books of the year, but as numbers increased rapidly the list became more exclusive. Rather than suggesting books for good reading, the association now formally recognized the better books. And when two prizes suddenly raised the cash award to unprecedented levels, this trend gained even greater resonance. The Maṅgalāprasād Paritoṣik (1921) and the Dev Puraskār (1927), awarded by the managing committee of the Nāgarī Prachāriṇī Sabhā, carried a more than symbolic sum of Rs 1200 and Rs 2000 respectively, along with the Sītārām Seksariya Puraskār (1930) of Rs 500 for the best book by a woman writer; these were announced with great pomp at the annual meetings of the Hindī Sāhitya Sammelan and created a stir before and after the announcement.[87] While the Maṅgalāprasād prize reflected a '*bhaṇḍār* building' intention and was given mostly to serious books on history, philosophy, literary criticism, or science, the Dev Puraskār was a purely literary prize.[88] They became seals of recognition in the Hindi literary community.

Even government patronage for Hindi and Urdu literature came to be vested in a semi-official association, the Hindustani Academy of Allahabad (1927), run mainly by Indian teachers of Allahabad University.

---

best Hindi drama or novel and (Raja) Baldev Prasād Biṛlā endowed a similar prize in 1931 for the best books on religion and ethics; *Nāgarī prachāriṇī sabhā kā vārṣik vivaraṇ*, for the years 1921 and 1934.

[87] They were endowed by Babu Gokulchand of the family of Raja Motīchand of Benares in memory of his younger brother, and by Raja Bīrsiṃhjū Dev of Orchha, himself a Braj Bhasa poet and of the family which had patronized Keśavdās.

[88] Among the recipients of the former were literary scholars Padmasiṃh Śarmā (for his commentary on Bihārī's *Satsaī, Sañjīvan bhāṣya* in 1922), Rāmchandra Śukla (for *Chintāmaṇi*); historians G.H. Ojhā, Satyaketu, and Jaychandra Vidyālaṃkār, philosophers Sudhākar (for *Manovijñān*), Gaṅgāprasād Upādhyāy (for *Astitvavād*), Hindī Sāhitya Sammelan activist Viyogī Hari and the authors of a book on anatomy and one on photography! See *Gṛhalakṣmī*, XIV, 2, April–May 1923, pp. 137–8.

Continuing the pattern of official patronage, but this time in Indian hands, the Academy each year awarded cash prizes for the best books in Hindi and Urdu, and published quality books (mostly translations or scholarly books) for no profit.[89]

Thus, by the 1930s, traditional patronage had largely made way for an interesting admixture of traditional and modern patronage, with aristocratic, mercantile, or industrial patrons using the agency of the major Hindi associations. Instead of the traditional *vidā* (cash on departure), where the amount was at the whim of the patron, the poet or writer was now given a payment by the publisher and could publicly win a literary prize; interestingly, both were called by the same name: *puraskār*, i.e. reward. As the case of the Hindustani Academy shows, Hindi intellectuals had also made an indent in the new royal patronage, that of the colonial government.

Prizes became a new form of recognition within the literary sphere, especially when awarded for purely literary works. In fact, only rarely was a prize awarded to the first work of an unknown author, or to someone outside the Hindi establishment, perhaps the only case being that of Jainendra Kumār's novel *Parakh* in 1931. Prizes reinforced the authority of the awarding institution apart from strengthening the self-avowed role and right of the institution and of the critic to shape the outlook of modern Hindi literature and to choose what people ought to read. However, this fell short of the power of choosing what people actually preferred to read, and this is what emerged as a source of tension for the Hindi literati.

2.3.2. Popularity and the Market

The pattern of the Hindi publishing market sketched in the previous chapter (1.3) showed that while the market for Hindi books expanded significantly in the early twentieth century, new literary works gained a small share of it only slowly and with difficulty, and circulated mainly through journals. The market for Hindi publications was dominated either by secular and religious songs, chapbooks of semi-oral genres, or

[89] Among the authors rewarded were Premchand (for *Raṅgbhūmi*) and Jagannāth Dās Ratnākar (for *Gaṅgāvataraṇ*) in 1929, Rāmnareś Tripāṭhī and Jayśaṅkar Prasād (for *Skandagupta*) in 1930, Rāmchandra Śukla for his *Hindī sāhitya kā itihās* and Jainendra Kumār (for *Parakh*) in 1931, and Maithilīśaraṇ Gupta for *Sāket* in 1933; see *The Report of the working of the Hindustani Academy, United Provinces, Allahabad (1927–1939)*, Allahabad, 1939, pp. 12–14.

by the new commercial genres of detective, 'social', and 'historical' fictions. The other sizeable shares of the market were taken by educational books and by overtly nationalist publications. In short, 'serious' or 'high literary' books had to be rewarded with prizes or be introduced into the school syllabi in order to achieve a circulation and sales.

When a class of professional Hindi literati with high reformist and nationalist ideals emerged, they realized that journals accommodated serious writing but that the market for their books was too small, in fact insignificant when compared with the market for religious or low-brow literature. A tension developed then between the perceived ideal and status of writers and their actual financial condition. Writing was considered a form of sevā, selfless service, which could not be valued in terms of money, and yet clearly the dignity and social standing of a writer could hardly be maintained if he lived like a pauper.

Attitudes to the market were thus ambiguous. On one side, the present predicament was explained as the corruption of the market and was contrasted with a past ideal, when poets had been free to practise high art. As Braj Bhasa poet Ramāśaṅkar Miśra wrote: 'What we call by the name of literature are the mature and faultless ideas a good poet expresses clearly and well through his poetic voice or through words, and then places in front of the world in the form of poetry. Full of the nine *rasas*, mature with lustre and charm.' To this ideal, realized in the golden past of Kālidāsa, Chandabardāī, Nānak, Kabīr, Tulsīdās and Sūrdās, and even in the more recent past of Bhārtendu, Devīprasād 'Pūrṇa', and Śrīdhar Pāṭhak, Miśra juxtaposed the literary market of the day. He compared, for example the lofty titles of the past—*Raghuvaṃśa, Kumārasambhava, Mālatīmādhava, Kādāmbarī*—with those of the present, which themselves suggested a pervasive malaise: *Apsarā, Vhyabhichār, Pāp kī aur, Gorī, Camelī* (two are by Nirālā): 'The same country which could not restrain its pride at the literature of yesterday has now to lower its head in shame at the attitude and ambition of modern sāhitya-sevīs.' The change appeared total to him: it was no more the age of the *Gītā*, but of Bengali translations, and the 'pride, heroism, generosity and self-sacrifice of earlier literary figures has been ransacked by capitalists'.[90] The market thus figured as a corrupting force for all: writers, publishers and critics, who lost their dignity and soul to it:

> Nowadays [writers] do not sit down to study their own soul but to study the sales of the market. They do not gauge their own force but the capital of the publishers,

[90] 'Kaviratna' Ramāśaṅkar Miśra 'Śrīpati', 'Sāhitya meṁ sannipāt', *Mādhurī*, X, pt. 1, 1, August 1931, pp. 96–8.

and they write and contract books they think will win prizes. . . . And if writers accept everything from [publishers], from 10 annas to 5 rupees per page, from insults to the promise of publishing their photograph, from the threat of a punch to rewards of a thousand rupees, where will they get enough courage to rebel against publishers?[91]

Hindi writers could not produce great literature because they earned too little and were too dependent on editors and sales, he argued: they never reached that point of financial security, self-respect, and independence that would allow them not to write for the market.[92] The tyranny of the market was even greater than that of the patron.

On the other hand, the market was seen as a purveyor of wealth and, through wealth and popularity, of status and recognition. The pitiful condition of the serious Hindi writer became even more evident when editors and journalists started comparing their financial situation with that of writers abroad. Clearly, the market had two sides to it: it could and did humiliate Hindi writers, even as it prized and raised to stardom their English counterparts. Figures of Rs 8 or 10, even Rs 4 or only Rs 2 per form for Hindi translations were compared with the figures which Walter Scott, Charles Dickens, Edward Gibbon, and Thomas Macaulay earned in sterling for their works and which were repeated with fascination and wonder.[93]

The market signified popularity. Popularity and sales potentially conferred wealth, status, and authority. Yet serious and experimental writers *shared the same space* with cheap publications, and it was clearly to the latter that the lion's share went. So, while traditional poets like 'Śrīpati' were inclined to consider popularity as a loss of integrity, more dispassionate critics recognized it as a value and argued that popular

[91] Ibid., pp. 97–8. Dulārelāl Bhārgava objected tongue-in cheek that many Hindi writers did not accept remuneration in the name of sāhitya-sevā; that sāhitya-sevā was both a profession and an addiction, so that poets usually did not even notice financial strains; finally, literary work, especially poetry, could not be valued in money! Bhārgava, 'Kavitā ke liye puraskār', *Mādhurī*, IX, pt. 2, 4, May 1931, pp. 568–71 (cf. 1.3.1).

[92] If one were to ask this question of Premchand, of critic Avadh Upādhyāy, of Maithilīśaraṇ Gupta, and even of Mahāvīr Prasād Dvivedī, they would probably choose to remain silent, the only way to maintain dignity, concluded Ramāśaṅkar Miśra. The point here is not whether Miśra was right or whether his were unrealistic expectations, but his feeling of frustration for the predicament of Hindi writers.

[93] Ibid., Cf. Rāmkṛṣṇa Garg Śāstrī, 'Puraskār carchā', *Mādhurī*, X, pt. 1, 4, November 1931, pp. 458–62. Only Premchand, Rāmdās Gauṛ, Mahāvīr Prasād Dvivedī, and a few others could dictate their price and get as much as Rs 20 per form; see *Mādhurī*, IX, pt. 2, 4, May 1931, p. 568.

writers possessed a keener understanding of the needs of the public and a real inner strength.[94] Finally, the market was not so problematic for all writers: some continued to ignore it, like Jayśaṅkar Prasād; some took advantage of it and, for example, made translation a profitable and respectable career, like Rāmchandra Varmā and Rūpnārāyaṇ Pāṇḍey; some managed to strike a balance between good and popular writing, like Premchand and Bhagavatīcharaṇ Varmā; and finally some chose to titillate readers and be unashamedly popular, like Bechan Pāṇḍey Śarmā 'Ugra', G.P. Śrīvāstava, Dhanīrām Prem, Chatursen Śastrī and others.

The debate over popularity is closely connected in Hindi with the boom in 'social novels' in the 1920s and 1930s, and in novels as a whole (cf. 4.3). The controversy around Pāṇḍey Bechan Śarmā Ugra's *Chocolate* (1927) illustrates the tension popularity and success in the market aroused, especially for the reformist agenda of the Hindi intelligentsia. The 'problem' with (and reason for the success of) 'social novels' was their ambiguity: they combined the avowedly serious and indeed reformist aim of 'exposing' contemporary social evils with melodramatic plots and morbid romances. 'Ugra' specialized in a kind of sensational fiction, in which social critique became a pretext for exploring the most morbid aspects and taboos of Hindu society such as homosexuality, the abduction of girls into prostitution, Hindu–Muslim love, and the like.[95] The advertisement for *Chākleṭ* (*Chocolate*), a collection of short stories

[94] In his obituary of Marie Corelli, who was widely translated and very popular in India, Rāmchandra Ṭaṇḍon, himself a prolific critic and translator of contemporary European literature, tempered criticism with admiration. He recalled the adverse (and just) criticism she had faced, the many editions her novels went into and her strengths. She had understood that 'in modern times, most readers read novels to placate their curiosity, not for character-studies or particular subtlety' (p. 35), and had exploited that curiosity with exotic settings, powerful descriptions and melodrama. He also recalled her many distinguished admirers (including Queen Victoria) and her inner, spiritual strength: *Mādhurī*, III, pt. 1, 1, August 1924, pp. 31–7. Among the translations of her novels were *Śaitān kī śaitānī* (*Sorrows of Satan*, 1926), *Pratiśodh* (*Vendetta*, 1927), *Prem-parīkṣā* (*The Treasure of Heaven*, 1929), *Premikā* (*Thelma*, 1936); Rāy, *Hindī upanyās koś*, vol. 1, pp. 183 ff.

[95] See *Chand hasīnoṁ ke khutūt* (*Letters of beautiful ladies*, 1927), *Chakleṭ* (*Chocolate*, i.e. homosexual, 1927), *Dillī kā dalāl* (*The tout of Delhi*, 1927), *Budhuā kī beṭī* (*Budhuā's daughter*, 1928), *Śarābī* (*Drunkard*, 1930), etc. He published in the Calcutta journal *Matvālā*, edited by Mahāvīr Prasād Seṭh, and for the Seṭh's own publishing house, Bisvin Sadi Pustakalay, Mirzapur. For a lively account of the 'Matvālā maṇḍal' see Rāmvilās Śarmā, *Nirālā kī sāhitya sādhnā*, vol. 1, pp. 76 ff.

'exposing' the social evils connected with male homosexuality, expresses clearly the complexities of the genre while proudly announcing its success.

> It contains stories of Ugrajī which will make you hold your breath. In this book, an extensive and penetrating guide into the frightening effects of growing homosexuality in our society, you will find such a vivid depiction of the atrocities committed by respectable and well-to-do scoundrels that after reading it even the most innocent boys will recognize those fiendish beings as soon as they see them and will be able not only to escape their enticements, but also to save the country, which is dangerously moving towards self-destruction because of the addictions of such sinners. The best proof of the utility and need for such a book is that its first edition sold out in only two months. Printed on good antique paper, the price of this 216-page-book has been kept to only Re 1 in view of its propaganda value.[96]

Ugra's books were popular even with contemporary writers, not least for his unique frankness and vigorous language full of humour, but their popularity enraged the guardians of morality in Hindi literature. Banārsīdās Chaturvedī (1892–1981), the editor of *Viśāl Bhārat*, the Calcutta monthly belonging to the same group that published *Modern Review* and *Prabāsī*, launched in 1928 a sustained campaign against '*ghāsleṭī sāhitya*' (obscene literature) aimed expressly at *Chocolate*.[97]

Chaturvedī was an expert campaigner and sent his indictment along with a copy of the book to Gandhi himself for an opinion (*sammati*), knowing that Gandhi's support would lend immense weight and authority to his campaign. At first, without reading the book, Gandhi added a short note supporting Chaturvedī's statement. As Chaturvedī revealed only many years later, after reading the book Gandhi was taken in by the ostensible reformist aim and sent Chaturvedī a disclaimer. Chaturvedī, however, did not disclose the disclaimer in order not to spoil his campaign, which raged for several years, confessing his deception only in 1950.[98] The controversy around *Chocolate* shows militant criticism deployed aggressively to uphold normative values and to 'protect' the public from 'unhealthy' influences. Whatever the result of such campaigns, the critics' hostility towards popular novels and, by extension, towards

[96] From the advertisement printed in the first edition of *Dillī kā dalāl*, Mirzapur, Bisvi Sadi Pustakalay, 1927, p. 3.

[97] E.g. Chandragupta Vidyālaṃkār, 'Ghāsleṭ sāhitya', *Viśāl bhārat*, II, pt. 2, 3, September 1929.

[98] See the preface to the new edition of *Chākleṭ*, Calcutta, Tandon Bros., 1953.

entertainment per se, produced a lasting rift between the literature that was enshrined in the canon and subsidized through it, and that which survived thanks to popularity. Although Ugra, G.P. Śrīvāstava and other popular novelists remained, along with Premchand and Devkīnandan Khatrī, the most widely read writers of their day, reading their books was almost a crime for students. University departments, literary associations, and authoritative journals backed this hostility by excluding such fiction from their canon and, indeed, from the histories of Hindi literature. Outside the canon and the curriculum, books popular only in the market had a short lifespan.[99] With an eclectic and layered literary sphere, and in the absence of universally accepted literary values and of a sizeable audience for serious literature, the balance between critical acceptance and popularity remained a fine and difficult one.

2.3.3. Reviews and Criticism

Finally, criticism offers an interesting perspective from which to view people engaged in applying to the literary field the notions of literature discussed in the previous sections. What was expected of practical criticism, and what forms did it take? These questions help us bring into sharper focus the impact of publicity on the Hindi literary sphere, the normative and critical attitudes of experts and writers in the face of the variety of literary forms and the commercial market. Critic and reviewer Kālidās Kapūr attempted to take stock of the situation in the essays and reviews collected in the volume *Sāhitya-samālochnā* (1929). The points raised by his declaration of intent will guide us into what is necessarily a summary treatment of an important and vast subject.

First of all, the new notion of literature as a social act required a change of direction in criticism:

> Wherever literature existed in the country, its critics existed alongside it. But their manner of criticism was suited only to their time. Literary works then were not meant for the general public (*sādhāraṇ jantā*). Since poets and playwrights were esteemed only in the courts of a few literary-minded rajas and *raises* [the wealthy], neither did poets care about the influence their works may have on the people nor did critics feel the need for a social outlook (*dṛṣṭikoṇ*) in order to evaluate those works. As a consequence, the ancient Sanskrit critical system only comprised *alaṃkār-bhed*, prosody (*piṅgal*), discrimination of the qualities or faults of language, metaphors, and observance of rules.

[99] Superseded by the new generations of commercial fiction by Gurudatt, Gulśan Nandā, and others, the 'social novels' of the 1920s and '30s, despite their intrinsic qualities and historical value, were forgotten and are not even available in print.

However, now that literature was meant for the 'common people', criticism had to change accordingly. A new kind of 'social criticism' was needed that would be sensitive to the social and historical background of literary works. In practical terms, Kapūr envisaged criticism as an exercise in tracing the effects of the historical and social conditions, and of the writers' psychology, on their work; the characteristics of new works would emerge after comparing them with old and foreign works and becoming aware of similarities and differences. Criticism as the analysis of metre and of figures of speech had only limited scope in this scheme.[100]

Second, Kapūr expressed the need for the professional figure of the critic–reviewer, like in England. In Hindi, editors had thus far fulfilled this function, but they could not be experts on everything. Moreover, their attitude thus far had predominantly been one of welcoming anything written in Hindi as an 'expansion' of the literary field, so that reviewing meant more or less simply publicizing new works. Professional critic–reviewers in England, conversely, were led by a sense of duty (*kartavya*) and enjoyed authority among readers: 'people base their views on their criticism' (*uskī ālocnā par hī jantā apnī rāy kāyam kartī hai*). The time had come for 'established literary servants' (*pratiṣṭhit sāhitya-sevī*) and 'expert scholars' (*viśeṣajña vidvān*) in Hindi as well to exercise selective judgements and open their 'third eye' on harmful books; this would mean facing the ire of 'dissatisfied writers' and the 'indifference of the people', but here lay the dharma of the critic.[101] Finally, Kapūr appealed to readers and pointed at the dilemma that his brand of taste-refining criticism faced in the existing literary market. He acknowledged that readers expressed 'collective judgement' (*sammilit samālochnā*) in a way that overrode any individual criticism:

यह समालोचना आप यों प्रकट करते हैं कि अमुक पुस्तक हाथोंहाथ बिक रही है या प्रकाशक की अलमारियों में शोभा दे रही है। आपकी रुचि पर हमें फ़ैसला सुनाने का कोई अधिकार नहीं है।

The expression of your judgement is the fact that a book may sell like hot cakes or adorn [only] the publishers' shelves. We have no right to judge your taste.

Still, Kapūr urged readers to exercise discrimination: after all, literary taste is a means of determining the social condition of a given society, and 'our future generation will evaluate our social condition accordingly'.[102]

[100] Kālidās Kapūr, *Sāhitya-samālochnā*, Allahabad, Indian Press, 1929, pp. 14–18.
[101] Ibid., pp.18–20.
[102] Ibid., p. 20.

Kapūr's comprehensive discussion of literary criticism proves especially useful if set against the trends that are visible in the literary field. New literature required scholars and critics to develop principles of practical criticism for genres without an Indian critical tradition, for example. This applied both to the new Chāyāvād poetry and to the novel. Yet, the diversity of literary saṃskāras and notions of literature (2.2) and the temptations of the normative attitudes each notion implied, at times explicitly, at times implicitly, together produced a practical criticism that was deeply agonistic. Opposing camps fought, each championing one poetic taste and denigrating all others. So much so that when Śukdevbihārī Miśra, one of the Miśra brothers and at the time editor of *Mādhurī*, wrote positively about Chāyavād, he had to publicly justify his positive and sympathetic (sahṛday) criticism because all other 'old' literati like him were violently opposed to it; he also had to specify that this was his personal opinion and not that of his brothers. Paradoxically, a critic who tried first to understand the nature and intentions of the author, and could admire different trends at the same time, had to defend his position![103] The new literature faced criticism which was not impartial from the start, whether favourable or hostile, and acknowledgement of the existence of different tastes remained on an abstract level.[104]

A second phenomenon that characterized practical criticism in Hindi was its taxonomic urge. In the case of new and original literary works and genres, this subordinated serious and close examination (as Kapūr advocated) to the categories in which they were supposed to fit. With the implicit assumption that everything new must come from elsewhere, models in English or Bengali literature always had to be found for new poems and novels in Hindi. As is often the case in literary criticism, description turned into prescription. In the case of novels, English novels provided the categories ('social', 'historical') with all the relevant characteristics; Bengali novels by Bankimchandra, Tagore, and Sharatchandra were also seen as models because they had successfully adapted the

[103] See 'Rāybahādur paṇḍit śukdevbihārī miśra aur paṇḍit sumitrānandan pant', editorial note in *Mādhurī*, VII, pt. 2, 5, May–June 1929, pp. 716–17.

[104] For an early acknowledgements of the fact that images, symbols and values were bound to be different in foreign poetry, see 'Kāvya meṁ sadāchār aur bhāvnā', *Mādhurī*, VII, pt. 1, 5, January 1929, pp. 956–7 and Paraśurām Chaturvedī, 'Kavitā par paristhiti kā prabhāv', *Mādhurī*, II, pt. 1, 1 and 3, October and December, 1923, pp. 191–5 and 329–34. This could easily take the shape of essentialist views on different national traditions, rather than the acknowledgement that different systems of images, symbols and values could exist within the same literary world.

genre to Indian soil. This could be used positively, as when Jainendra Kumār was acclaimed as Hindi's Sharatchandra. But when no model could be found for Premchand's novel *Premāśram* (1921), the reviewer saw it as a fault of the novelist rather than of his own approach:

> When reading the novels of Bankimchandra, the critic acquainted with English literature can say at once that they are historical novels in Scott's fashion. One may call the novels of Rabindranath 'social novels' and find English equivalents for them: George Eliot, Thackeray, Dickens. Premchand's novels, instead, do not fit into any of these categories.[105]

The cultural politics of this attitude, which saw Hindi at the bottom of a hierarchy that placed English (or French, or Russian, etc.) at the top and Bengali right below it, is evident in the case of Hemchandra Jośī, then a young and sophisticated graduate in Berlin: the weight of his Bengali and foreign saṃskāras is apparent in his strong denigration of the novel. To critics who had 'dragged in' great names from other literatures to compare with *Premāśram*—Sharatchandra was said to have mentioned even Rabindranath—Jośī replied:

> Impossible! What is there in *Premāśram*? There is not one character which can do honour to literature. Not one sentence which will leave a mark on your heart. Not one chapter without gross mistakes. I could not even figure out to what category of novels it belongs. Is it naturalistic? Emotional? Philosophical, Or a mixture of all of them?[106]

The comparison with 'Ravi babu' was a 'sacrilege'; whereas *Premāśram* was condemned to a transient success, Josī predicted, '*Gorā* gives us as much pleasure today, and Shakespeare's *Hamlet* is still as new'.[107]

Finally, this kind of practical criticism, exercised in the open pages of journals, easily fell prey to sensationalism: one kind of Hindi literary criticism was to 'expose' apparent plagiarizers of foreign novels. These unsavoury 'scoops' came in fact to dominate reviews of novels; they certainly increased the sales of journals and the fame of reviewers, but had deeply negative effects on writers and did little to develop the practice of balanced criticism.[108]

[105] Kālidās Kapūr, 'Premāśram', review in *Mādhurī*, I, 4, October 1922, p. 365.

[106] Quoted in the reply by Janārdan Jhā, 'Sāhitya-kalā aur premāśram', *Mādhurī*, I, pt. 2, 5, May 1923, p. 500.

[107] H. Jośī, 'Premāśram aur sāhitya-kalā', *Mādhurī*, II, pt. 1, 3, December 1923, p. 341.

[108] Such is the case, for example, of Avadh Upādhyāy, a mathematician with literary ambitions linked with the Hindī Sāhitya Sammelan, who made it his goal to

As Kapūr admitted, popularity was one judge that critics would be hard pressed to dismiss. *Premāśram*, a commercial success as well as the recipient of the prestigious Maṅgalāprasād prize, attracted many reviews.[109] To a certain extent, the problem of its categorization did force critics to rethink their categories and consider the novel on its own terms. One feature of the novel critics marvelled at was its apparent lack of all the qualities that make a novel interesting: its characters were ordinary people and the plot centred on problems related to the land and the zamindari system. 'Who cares about Sukkhū Caudhrī, Balrāj, the winter crop, jobs and socialism . . . What is there in *Premāśram?* How can Dukhran Bhagat, Manohar, free labour (*begār*) and rural conflicts between Ghaus Khān and Qādir Miān entertain?' wrote one reviewer.[110] Moreover, in *Premāśram* contemporaneity was treated as an asset: though never mentioned directly, nationalism and the peasant campaign of 1920 were implied in the political awakening of the villagers and in the personality of the 'good zamindar', Premśaṅkar. Did this perhaps mean that it would be of no importance in fifty years' time—and hence was no great art?[111] It was an issue-based novel, with credible characters, and had a message to give, wrote Janārdan Jhā in his balanced review: 'When literature's aim is to preach the welfare of the people (*lokhit*) there is nothing wrong if it contains elements of propaganda. In fact, its decorum (*maryādā*) increases instead of diminishing.'[112] Reviewers were further puzzled by the fact that *Premāśram* had no hero or heroine: the ideal couple of the novel, Premśaṅkar and his wife Vidyā, were not the real protagonists,

---

'expose' Premchand. In 1926 he persuaded Devīdatt Śukla to publish in the otherwise impeccable *Sarasvatī* a series of slanderous articles on Premchand, then at the peak of his fame. Upādhyāy 'demonstrated' that in *Raṅgbhūmi* (1925) Premchand had plagiarized *Vanity Fair,* and in *Premāśram* Tolstoy's *Resurrection.* The articles, 'which all read with great gusto' were discontinued only at Premchand's personal request, but soon afterwards Upādhyāy started reviewing Premchand's *Kāyākalp* (1926), again claiming that it plagiarized *The Eternal City.* Through a practically amateur reviewer, the editor had not only increased the journal's popularity but had also been able to air his own personal dislike for Premchand as a novelist; see Śukla, *Sampādak ke paccīs varṣ*, p. 33.

[109] For a complete analysis of these reviews see Vīr Bhārat Talvār, *Kisān, rāṣṭrīy āndolan aur premchand: 1918–1922. Premāśram aur avadh ke kisān āndolan kā viśeṣ adhyayan*, New Delhi, Northern Book Centre, 1990, pp. 225–37.

[110] Janārdan Jhā, 'Sāhitya kalā aur premāśram', p. 504.

[111] Śrīdhar Pāṭhak, quoted by Hemchandra Jośī in 'Premāśram aur sāhitya-kalā', p. 341.

[112] Jhā, 'Sāhitya-kalā aur premāśram', p. 504.

who were instead Gyānśaṅkar and his sister-in-law Gāyatrī, far less ideal characters.[113]

The taxonomic urge of reviewers and their overriding concern with the 'people's tastes' were accompanied by unease about the popular market and by the notion that the critic's duty was to exercise exclusive judgement and that his/her authority overrode that of writers and readers (2.2). This translated into the already familiar diffidence towards novels: an uneasiness about defining the status and function of the genre, and the attempt to distinguish serious novel writing from writing for the low-brow market.[114] One crucial way forward suggested was to 'keep to Indian ideals' and to *maryādā* (decorum, mortality).[115] This would circumscribe the danger of western influence and provide emotionally inspiring and faultless models of 'Indian culture'. In his enthusiastic review of Jainendra Kumār's first novel, *Parakh* (1929), Avadh Upādhyāy remarked that it 'maintained Indian ideals to quite a good extent'. To do so, he said, was particularly important when writing about love and marriage, because India and the West had different ideals—in fact, the West was still seeking one. Girls in the West were always ready to 'sacrifice' themselves on the altar of love (i.e. lose their virginity) and thereafter commit suicide: if in western literature there are so many examples of lovers taking their lives, there must be some truth in it, he concluded. For Indian writers to copy these plots was inexcusable, for love does not have the same place in 'Hindu life' as it has in 'western society'. In India marriage is a religious (*dhārmik*) act and a moral necessity, in order to fulfil one's duty in life.[116] In a similar vein, at the First All-India Galpa-Sammelan in Meerut (April 1937), Premchand's widow, Śivrānī Devī, said: 'Strangers reading our stories will think that people here have nothing else to do but love-dalliances (*prem-krīṛā*). The country is deep into all kinds of crises, and here we are happily inebriated with sensuality.'[117] What is at issue here is not so much realistic depiction in accordance with the locale and characters of the novel, as proper self-representation on the basis of essentialist views of 'Indian culture'. Here, again, the critic wanted to lead and discipline the novelist and to

113 Kapūr, 'Premāśram', p. 366.

114 Pratāp Nārāyaṇ Śrīvāstava, 'Upanyās aur hindī ke vartamān upanyās-lekhak', *Mādhurī*, VIII, pt. 2, 1, February 1930, pp. 20–4.

115 See also Kālidās Kapūr, 'Upanyās-sāhitya', an article lamenting the absence of such novels in Hindi, in *Maryādā*, pt. 22, 6, March–April 1921, pp. 327–8.

116 A. Upādhyāy, 'Parakh', *Sudhā*, IV, pt. 2, 4, May 1931, pp. 471–7.

117 Quoted in an editorial note in *Chāṁd*, XV, pt. 2, 2, June 1937, pp. 209–11.

warn, or preach to, the reader—thus treading on moral(istic) rather than literary terrain.

It is important to note that novelists themselves tried to establish respectable credentials and put forward models for analysing the novel. Both Premchand and Pratāp Nārāyaṇ Śrīvāstava upheld entertainment as a right, in fact as a duty, for the novelist. 'Novel writing is considered "light literature" because it entertains the reader', wrote Premchand, 'but it takes as much mental toil for a novelist to write a novel as for a philosopher to write a book on philosophy.'[118] A novel's aim is to entertain while giving a message: most social reforms in modern Europe had been ushered in by novels. As for the constitutive elements of a novel, those by which it should be judged, Premchand mentioned subject, plot, and 'spice' (*masālā*); the marks of a good plot are simplicity, originality, and interest; masālā includes experience, self-study, insight, curiosity, observation, and imagination.[119] Pratāp Nārāyaṇ Śrīvāstava regarded realistic novels as the highest product in the historical progression of the genre, i.e. after romances and idealistic novels; the qualities novels should have were characterization, compact language (*bhāṣā-sauṣṭhava*), style, psychology, and interesting events.[120] This understanding of the novel went hand in hand with a strong valorization of the social function of the creative writer. As Premchand put it, 'Writers are generally the creators of their age. They have a strong aspiration to free their country and their society from suffering, injustice and illusions (*mithyāvād*)'. Formerly at the service of the rich and powerful, 'today we, the educated, cannot look indifferently at injustice' in the present age of 'struggle for life' (*jīvan-saṅgrām*).[121] This led Premchand the reviewer sometimes to speak harshly against what he perceived to be 'harmful' or 'useless' works, such as J. Prasād's historical play *Skandagupta*, on which he passed the famous judgement: 'इन गढ़े मुर्दों को उखाड़ने से कोई फ़ायदा नहीं' [There's no point unearthing buried corpses].[122] But while overall Premchand, like other writers, was readier to evaluate a work on the basis of its intrinsic logic and strengths, professional critics and reviewers appeared on the whole little concerned with interpretation and literariness and at same time ruthless in exercising negative judgements according to their own normative views.

[118] Premchand, 'Upanyās rachnā', *Mādhurī*, 1, 4, October 1922, p. 354.
[119] Ibid., pp. 355–7.
[120] Śrīvāstava, 'Upanyās', pp. 20–7.
[121] Premchand, 'Upanyās rachnā', p. 355.
[122] Review in *Mādhurī*, VII, pt.1, 4, October 1928, quoted in K.K. Goyinka, *Premchand kā aprāpya sāhitya*, Delhi, Bhartiy Jnanpith, 1988, p. 450.

What we see at work then is a process by which the tendency to publicize and encourage the production and reading of Hindi literature was regularly undercut by exclusions and prohibitions and warnings about what not to read and write. The authority and freedom for writers to explain the world in their own way and for readers to accept it or reject it, which came with the openness of publicity, was constantly undermined by normative concerns. Literary criticism in Hindi, for example, developed under several compulsions: first, the literary saṃskāras of critics, both in terms of notions of literature and of critical practice (rasa and alaṃkār, taxonomy, etc.); second, their cultural saṃskāras and preoccupations with 'Indian culture', which made them view novelty only in terms of 'foreignness'; finally, the overall orientation of literary authorities towards lokhit and nation-building, which implied a paternalistic attitude towards readers and a normative one towards writers, and linked to that suspicions about the market and popularity, particularly about 'light' genres such as the novel. Under such circumstances, it is not hard to understand why a new kind of practical criticism (*samālochnā*) was slow to develop. In poetry, which was clearly divided into 'camps', the play was somewhat overt. To develop general rules of interpretation was difficult because tastes were so diverse: Khari Boli poetry of the Dvivedī school could not be evaluated in terms of figures of speech since it valued plain diction, and the rasa theory worked only up to a certain point with elusive Chāyāvād poetry. In practice, the taxonomic urge went hand in hand with the continuing critical tradition of rasa and alaṃkāras, firmly ensconced in examination practices. In reviews of novels, the taxonomic attitude was combined with an eye for 'lokhit'.

Publicity was thus a double-edged sword: some publicized their ideas as normative only to see them challenged critically. Others challenged critically established views or habits only to discover that the dominant opinion was normative. On the one hand, public exposure increased the sense of self-importance of Hindi writers and put them face to face with the public, so much so that many could reject the traditional system of patronage and live as independent individuals. On the other hand, writers and intellectuals faced unprecedented challenges to their ideals and their very sense of self-importance as new forms of evaluation became dominant. The main challenge was that of the market, i.e. of popular taste, which valued entertainment above everything else. The second challenge was that of criticism in print, which often tried to impose rigid demands and took the form of strong personal attacks by unsympathetic critics. Thus independent writers could find themselves in a peculiar situation, pressed between an unresponsive market and the demands of a literary establishment that did not look favourably upon literary experimentation or entertainment. Thanks to wider publicity and greater mobility, independent writers could count on mutual support and appreciation, and also enjoyed some popularity and status, but they remained largely excluded from the process of building and transmitting a literary tradition in Hindi. It was once again the scholars in literary associations and in education who, thanks to their strategic position as Hindi experts, could pursue their cultural agenda and force it upon the public.

CHAPTER 3

The Uses of History

3.1. The Engagement with History

When a jāti, lost in darkness, forgets its history, when it forgets its great men and their lofty ideals, and follows the path to decadence, fulfilling only its base, worldly desires, then its destruction is only a question of time. A fallen jāti can only be saved by hearing and reflecting upon the story of its ancestors. . . . This is precisely what we can see now in Bhāratvarṣa. From one corner of the country to the other, waves of national consciousness (*jātīytā*) are spreading all over, and with them a devotion to history has arisen in its inhabitants, who have started to worship their forefathers with devotion and love, and who in their hearts feel strongly inclined to listen to their sacred stories (*pavitra kathāeṁ*).[1]

Veṅkateś Nārāyaṇ Tivārī (1890–1965), the Hindi journalist and Congressman from Allahabad, gives a fair idea of early-twentieth century Hindi intellectuals' concern for history: history was meant to remind the modern inhabitants of India that they belonged to a common, if vaguely defined, national community (jāti) and it was to provide meaning to this common bond by retelling the 'sacred stories' of its great men. To take an interest in history meant to 'worship one's ancestors', and it was this spirit of worship and devotion that was supposed to inspire modern Indians to patriotic consciousness and activism. The passage suggests a history and a nation that were already 'there' and a consensus that, as we have seen, was part of the 'normative' attitude (see Introduction) to the public. Yet historical discourse was not a given. It, too, was shaped by the encounter of western—colonial and orientalist—and Indian forms of knowledge, and by the developing institutions and concerns of the public sphere. In fact, history figured prominently in the making of cultural nationalism: history taught in colonial schools became a focus for

[1] Veṅkateś Nārāyaṇ Tivārī, 'Bhagvān buddhadeva', *Sarasvatī*, January 1910, quoted by Gauṛ, *Sarasvatī aur rāṣhṭrīy jāgaraṇ*, p. 10.

debate and reaction; historical research, especially on ancient India, was cultivated by literary associations, and journals popularized their findings and made history a topic of public debate; finally, literature found in history a rich reservoir of stories that perfectly fitted its aims to uplift and inspire, and were gripping, too. In this way, poems, novels, and plays were very effective in spreading a nationalist historical consciousness, a true historical saṃskāra.

By the early twentieth century the framework and features of the nationalist discourse on history had been worked out in Hindi, as in other Indian languages. The terrain was largely defined by orientalist historiography, and although Hindi historians engaged critically with it and reshuffled it according to their own preoccupations, basic issues such as 'what is history', 'whose history', and what constitute 'valid' historical sources were shared. The history of India thus fashioned was of great consequence in the twentieth century: it evolved into a very successful rhetoric for political mobilization; other histories, e.g. that of literature, were grafted on to this stem; finally this history helped crystallize modern 'Indian' identity as being essentially the same as modern 'Hindu' identity. Literature and education were crucial in disseminating this historical discourse, and debates in journals throw light on its concerns. Since history, as Tivārī wrote, was meant to inspire a collective sense of pride (or shame), poems, biographies, and 'historical stories' (*aitihāsik kahāniyāṁ*) were even more effective than actual historical studies. They form the material of this chapter.[2] Gail Omvedt has pointed out how, in the case of Marathi historiography, critical and conflicting views helped shape, by reaction, the dominant discourse on Shivaji and the Marathas.[3] No such 'alternative' historiography seems to have emerged in Hindi, but the dominant discourse of Indian history was sometimes used

[2] Apart from original studies by Munshi Devīprasād, Gaurīśaṅkar Hirāchand Ojhā, Viśvambharnāth Reu, Kāśī Prasād Jaiswāl, and others on ancient India, historical publications in Hindi mainly included compilations from English sources, like Śyāmbihārī and Śukdevbihārī Miśra's series of books on Indian, German, Russian, English, and Japanese history for the Indian Press, Allahabad, between 1908 and 1912 (cf. Ali, 'Hindī sāhitya ke itihās meṁ ilāhābād kā yogdān', pp. 383–5); there were also endless retellings of 'historical stories', especially for schoolchildren, like Dvārkāprasād Chaturvedī's *Aitihāsik kahāniyāṁ*, for the Manorañjan Pustak-Mālā of the Nāgarī Prachāriṇī Sabhā, and Devnārāyaṇ Mukhopādhyāy's *Mere deś kī kathā* (Indian Press, 1938), and of course poems, plays and novels.

[3] Gail Omvedt, *Cultural Revolution in a Colonial Society*, Bombay, Scientific Socialist Education Trust, 1976.

against the grain by some critical voices among women and lower castes, as we shall see.

How inextricably the history we tell is linked to linked the history we believe in has become arrestingly evident for contemporary Indians. Many scholars have noted that the secular veneer applied to official institutions after Independence through the idea of 'composite culture' clashes with the construction of national(ist) history, with its neat categories of 'Aryan', 'Hindu', and 'Muslim' periods. Some have even argued that modern textbooks of Indian history present, by avoiding or downplaying conflicts in the past while leaving nationalist categories untouched, a confusing and contradictory picture to Indian children and make them turn to the rawer, black-and-white categories of nationalist history, on which fundamentalist groups can liberally draw.[4]

Before analysing the public discourse on history in the Hindi sphere of the early twentieth century and the material it produced, it may be useful to look at how the field itself was constituted and transformed.[5] Different genres of writing the past, and of keeping account of it, had existed in India when orientalists set about writing the 'history of India' in the nineteenth century. There was the tradition of Persian chronicles and histories written by court historians at Muslim and subsidiary courts: to modern historians they appeared to be the most objective and reliable; translated in great number, they became the standard references for the 'Muslim period' of Indian history.[6] Then there were the genealogies and stories contained in the Purāṇas, the compendia of myths and ancient stories which were being printed both in Hindi and Urdu by the mid-nineteenth century. Narratives and genealogies (*khyāt, vārtā, vaṃśāvalī*) of Rajput clans had been produced by specialist groups of Chāraṇ and Bhāṭ (bards) for rulers and their courts and preserved in their books;[7]

[4] Krishna Kumar, *Learning from Conflict*, New Delhi, Longman, 1996.

[5] These brief points owe a lot to discussions with Norbert Peabody; *kṣepaka*, faulty transmission and misguided speculations are of course mine.

[6] See Alexander Dow's *History of Hindostan* (1770), drawing upon Persian sources, the eight volumes of *History of India as Told by Its Own Historians*, brought out by H.M. Elliott and J. Dowson between 1867 and 1877 and Briggs' translation of Farishta, the Urdu translation of which was published by Nawal Kishore in the nineteenth century, all of which are quoted extensively by Hindi historians; and Munshi Devīprasād's translations of Al-Biruni and *Ain'-e Akbari*.

[7] Norman P. Ziegler, 'Marvari Historical Chronicles: Sources for the Social and Cultural History of Rajasthan', *Indian Economic and Social History Review*, 13, 1976, pp. 219–50.

praśasti (praise-poems) were composed by court poets to suggest continuities with some heroic past; vārtās (stories) and the hagiographical literature of religious sects circulated among those affiliated to them; merchants' private family histories were added generation after generation and preserved together with the accounts; finally, one may add the anthological compendia of poets and of Sufis (*tazkirās*). Other records included those of patrons kept by pandits in pilgrimage temples and the oral narration of folk epics like that of Pābūjī in Rajasthan and of Ālhā and Ūdal in north India. That these compositions told different histories is obvious, for the concerns and subject axes of each genre were different, and so were their settings and audiences: court, devotees or family. In the nineteenth century, this fragmented field was partly transformed and unified by orientalists and by the shift from court, sect, and family to print and the public sphere. Hindi historical writing of the late nineteenth- and early twentieth-centuries was very much the product of this double shift. Not that printing meant widespread publicity and circulation right away: the first printed genealogies in Rajasthan, like *Vīr-vinod* and *Vaṃś bhāskar*, seem to have been hardly available beyond the court for which they were produced.[8] A similar argument could be made for the hagiographies of sampradāy (sects), caste histories and vaṃśāvalīs: the first, when printed, would be used only by literary historians, while the latter two, affected by colonial publicity and written with an eye to land settlements or the value of philanthropy, still maintained a specific and limited focus.

Tod's *Annals and Antiquities of Rajasthan* (1829) was immensely influential in shaping modern Hindi historiography and historical consciousness and was translated into Hindi probably as early as the 1880s.[9] It exemplifies well how Indian sources went through a process of translation and transformation before being presented again before Indian audiences. In putting together a history of Rajasthan through a history of the Rajput clans, Tod had drawn heavily on bardic chronicles, thus making them widely available in print and outside their original space for the first time; at the same time he expressed a strong rationalist distrust of their language and their historical validity, preferring Sanskrit sources to vernacular ones whenever available. He took over from vaṃśāvalīs one of their primary concerns, the continuity of lineage.

[8] Oral communication by John D. Smith, May 1998.

[9] D. Siṃh's otherwise thorough monograph of the Khadgvilas Press does not mention it, but G.H. Ojhā quotes a 'Khadgvilas Press edition' in his *Rājputāne kā itihās*.

However, he shifted their preoccupation with the *origin* of the clans and their connection with the founders of the solar and lunar dynasties (and with the ancient empires of Mauryas and Guptas) from questions of legitimacy to one of chronology: accordingly, he advanced *theories of origin* and set the lineages in a *geographical and chronological order*, filling in the empty spaces. In order to arrive at 'historical truth' he also introduced the principle of validating the chronicles in the light of other sources. In some ways, as with his emphasis on the ascribed status of Rajputs, on the purity and continuity of lineage, Tod was but following the language of descent and kinship already dominant in Rajasthani geneaologies.[10] In others, as in the difference between stories and historical truth, and in providing a gazetteer, a complete picture, he was moving sharply away from the tradition of the bards. Further, by writing in English and with the authority of his research, he offered the stories of Rajput valour to an eager Indian audience in search of historical heroes.[11]

The influence of orientalist scholarship on nineteenth-century Indian constructions of the past, whether of Aryan superiority or of heroic Rajput resistance, has been the subject of intensive and brilliant scholarly work in recent years and need not be repeated here.[12] In the context of Hindi, before moving to Hindi historical writing of the 1920s and 1930s, we need only mention two points. First, we should note the intense antiquarian interests of the new intellectuals writing in Khari Boli Hindi. For example, when trying to widen and modernize the historical tradition of the Vallabhan sect he belonged to, Bhārtendu Hariśchandra, as Vasudha

[10] Norbert Peabody, 'The King is Dead, Long Live the King!: on Karmic Kin(g)ship in Kota', in S.C. Welch, ed., *Gods, Kings, and Tigers: The Art of Kotah*, Munich, Prestel-Verlag, 1997; Dirk H.A. Kolff, *Naukar, Rajput and Sepoy: the Ethnohistory of the military labour market in Hindustan, 1450–1850*, Cambridge, Cambridge University Press, 1990.

[11] Cf. Norbert Peabody, 'Tod's *Rajast'han* and the Boundaries of Imperial Rule in Nineteenth-Century India', *Modern Asian Studies*, 30, 1, 1996.

[12] The story of how colonial Indians became obsessed with history, of how history became a 'source of nationhood', and how Indian intellectuals contested European rationalistic and colonial histories of India has been variously told by recent scholars, with special reference to Bengali intellectuals: e.g. Ranajit Guha, *An Indian Historiography of India: A Nineteenth-Century Agenda and Its Implications*, Calcutta, K.P. Bagchi, 1988; Tapan Raychaudhuri, *Europe Reconsidered*; Sudhir Chandra, *The Oppressive Present*; Partha Chatterjee, *The Nation and Its Fragments*; Sudipta Kaviraj, *The Unhappy Consciousness: Bankimchandra and the Formation of Nationalist Consciousness in India*, Delhi, OUP, 1994.

Dalmia has brilliantly shown, followed with great interest the contributions to the Asiatic Society and antiquarian journals; he translated and publicized their findings in his own journals and also published, translated, abridged, and collated any kind of 'historical' material he could lay his hands on: inscriptions, chronicles, and documents from a private merchant collection. He also wrote on the 'origin' of the Khatris 'from the Śāstras', a universal chronology (*Kālachakra*) and genealogies of various Rajput and Muslim dynasties; he wrote biographies and drew horoscopes of eminent Indians and Europeans, and attempted 'histories' of Maharashtra, Udaipur, and Bundi.[13] All this now constituted history, the history of India that needed to be written, provided it was based upon sound historical sources and filtered through the rational mindset of the scholar.

Second, parallel to this antiquarian interest, more popular historians in Hindi largely followed European footsteps in relying heavily on Arabic and Persian sources. As they did with European texts, they read these, too, against the grain from the point of view of the 'atrocities' perpetrated on the 'Hindu jāti' and in search of 'Hindu resistance': the first history textbook in Hindi, Raja Śiva Prasād Siṃh's *Itihās timirnāśak* (3 pts., 1864–74), is a case in point.[14] Only in the early twentieth century did historians like G.H. Ojhā (1863–1947) contest the blind faith in the historical veracity of Muslim accounts by pointing to some glaringly improbable details that had filtered through in European works by Dow, Gibbon, Morris, James Mill, Price, Elphinstone, and even Hindi books like Śiva Prasād's.[15] Yet, even Ojhā was uncomfortable with the historical style of Rajasthani bards, to which he preferred Sanskrit texts like the Purāṇas and hard historical evidence such as inscriptions and coins. Thus, although he was extremely familiar with bardic texts, Ojhā, deeply influenced by Tod and himself involved in writing genealogies, mentioned khyāts and vaṃśāvalīs only collectively and anonymously, and only edited and published one of them, Muṃhṇot Naiṇsī's *Khyāt*, whose historical veracity was more easily proved. Even during the intense

[13] Dalmia, *The Nationalization of Hindu Traditions*.

[14] Only in the third part, published in 1874, did Śiva Prasād, who had published his own abridged version of the Manusmṛti in the anthology *Guṭkā*, attempt to write more extensively on ancient India drawing on the epics and other Sanskrit texts.

[15] One specific detail was the presence of precious jewels inside the *mūrti* (image) of the temple in Somnath, a *linga*, which Mahmud of Ghazni looted and to which Firishta appended a story that had been quoted by all the historians mentioned above; Ojhā, *Rājputāne kā itihās*, vol. 1, Ajmer, Vedic Karyalay, 1925, pp. 264–5.

twentieth-century search of the Hindi tradition for 'heroic' poems of vīr-rasa—to invalidate accusations of decadent eroticism—Hindi scholars were cautious about considering them as historical sources and preferred to value them as literary creations, manifestations of nationalist spirit in the past.[16]

3.1.1. A National History of India in Hindi

The impact of orientalist categories and the shift to the public sphere are both crucial factors in understanding Hindi historical writing in the colonial period. Articles, reports, and findings by the Asiatic Society and the Archaeological Survey were eagerly discussed along with the works of major orientalists; articles on history, a regular feature of Hindi journals, never failed to quote them and indeed engaged critically with them, so much so that Hindi historiography can be seen as part of an ideal dialogue between the incipient patriots and their colonial models.[17] It was however a fractious dialogue, for although Indian historians studied and absorbed the European rationalistic conception of history, their historical enterprise was radically different.[18] They absorbed the notion of history as the story of a people, i.e. a national history rather than a drama played out between kings and gods; they also saw history writing as a

[16] Conversely, Captain Pogson had had no qualms about translating Lālkavi's poem on the Bundela king of Panna Chatrasāl, *Chatraprakāś*, as *History of the Boondelas* (1822). Lālkavi became, with Bhūṣaṇ, a court poet of Śivājī and Chatrasāl, very much the centre of scholarly patriotic interest in vīr-rasa: the Nāgarī Prachāriṇī Sabhā of Benares published the *Chatraprakāś* in 1904 and *Bhūṣaṇ granthāvalī* in 1907.

[17] Indeed, it had been so since the time of Hariśchandra and his circle; see e.g. Chandra, *The Oppressive Present*, Chapter 1; in the twentieth century, historical essays appeared in every issue of the *Nāgarī prachāriṇī patrikā*, *Sarasvatī*, and *Maryādā*; they were regularly read out at meetings of the Nāgarī Prachāriṇī Sabhā and the Hindī Sāhitya Sammelan, and the annual Sammelan meetings featured a special *Itihās pariṣad*. In fact, G. H. Ojhā's first work was a biography of Colonel Tod (1902), while his notes on the translation of Tod's work remained unpublished; cf. Śyāmsundar Dās, *Hindī ke nirmātā*, vol. 2, Allahabad, Indian Press, 1941, p. 10. R.C. Dutt's *History of Civilisation of Ancient India* and his historical novels were read in Hindi as early as the 1880s, and so were Bankimchandra's essays and his *Ānandamaṭh*; see Gopāl Rāy, *Hindī upanyās koś*, vol. 1, pp. 306 ff.

[18] 'If judged in rationalistic terms, their efforts often fell far short of the European ideal of constructing a reliable account of the people's past; in some other ways, in giving an imaginative unity to it, they went far beyond'; Kaviraj, *The Unhappy Consciousness*, p. 108.

collective enterprise, something the historian did on behalf of the community. As Partha Chatterjee has argued, although relying on British histories, Indian historians denied British rule the honour of being the culmination of India's history. This they did first by shifting the subject from a British to an Indian 'we', with an emphasis on the Aryan ancestors, and second by viewing history as a secular play of power, where conquest did not necessarily bestow moral superiority on the conquerors.[19] The subject that furnished the axis to this historical narrative gave a new meaning both to medieval history and to the British conquest. Muslim invasions and kingdoms became a 'narrative break', usually the result of a series of 'betrayals', and British rule was just the prelude to national resurgence: both were equally 'alien'.

The main issues of historical debate in Hindi journals and books reveal how much history was seen as a community enterprise contesting European 'authorities' while in fact moving on the latter's terrain. At an annual meeting of the Hindī Sāhitya Sammelan in Dehradun in 1924 the nationalist millionaire Śivaprasād Gupta even advanced a resolution on the need for an Indian history of India.[20]

> The nation which does not have an authentic history of its own is not a living nation. . . . The history textbooks which are taught in Indian schools and colleges are extremely misleading and unreliable. Our heroes like Śivājī are called 'looters'! Our Vedas are called ballads of herdsmen and peasants! Can such books be called histories? Can any scholar and dispassionate historian say that such historical books contain a true picture of life in ancient India?[21]

Education was once again a crucial field of struggle and activism (cf. 1.4). But since the colonial education system, the goal of much of Hindi efforts, was barred and in fact was hostile to nationalist histories, enterprises in this field had to be internal to the Hindi public sphere and aimed, for example, at independent schools like those of the Ārya Samāj.[22] Although Śivaprasād Gupta's project was not carried out, his

[19] Chatterjee, *The Nation and its Fragments*, pp. 83 ff. The moral superiority and military invincibility of the British was implied in history textbooks for Indian schoolchildren such as Edmund Marsden's *A History of India* (1900), translated into Hindi by Rāmchandra Prasād as *Bhāratvarṣa kā itihās,* Macmillan, 1920, for the 5th and 6th classes of vernacular schools.

[20] He suggested launching a public fund of Rs 1 lakh, and a committee composed of Śivaprasād Gupta himself, Narendra Dev, G. H. Ojhā, P.D. Ṭaṇḍon, and Rāmkaraṇ Siṃh Asopā of Jodhpur was formed to finalize the project.

[21] See *Sammelan patrikā*, XII, 4–5, pp. 216–17.

[22] Jaychandra Vidyālaṃkār, 'Bhāratvarṣa kā ek rāṣṭrīy itihās', *Mādhurī*, V, pt. 1,

resolution was recalled at later meetings, and several articles and books appeared along the same lines, some of which form the basis of the discussion below.

The first contentious issue concerned the beginning of Indian history, which also involved establishing India's original claim to historicity and the use of Indian sources. Vincent Smith[23] had set the beginning of Indian history in the Buddhist period, with Alexander's campaign and the Indo-Bactrian and Indo-Parthian states, when the first 'historical' (i.e. Greek) sources could be found. But this meant pushing the whole Vedic period into prehistory or myth, 'as if *they* [the Greeks] had brought history, civilization, etc. into this country', wrote Ārya Samāj historian Jaychandra Vidyālaṃkār. On this very ground he condemned even the *History of India* by Lala Lajpat Rai. Though written especially for national schools at the time of Non-Cooperation, it closely followed Smith's chronology and classification. In order to write a true national history of India, argued Jaychandra, one needed to reframe the whole of accepted knowledge, and this involved basic issues of belief and identity.

> For European scholars, Rāma and Sītā, Kṛṣṇa and Duṣyanta are mythological figures—does Lalaji think so, too? When does the history of India begin; did Duṣyanta and Bharata, Rāma and Lakṣmaṇa, Kṛṣṇa and Arjuna exist historically or not? These are very important questions for our nation (jāti) and our history.[24]

What is evident here is the need to preserve the status of the *Rāmāyaṇa* and *Mahābhārata* as the two most meaningful histories (*itihāsa*) and also to ground them in historical 'truth'.[25] Even though more research

---

2, September 1926, p. 167. Jaychandra, who offered to realize Śivaprasād Gupta's project, taught at Ārya Samāj schools and 'national' institutions like Lahore's National College (where Bhagat Singh and Sukhdev were among his students) and Patna's Bihar Vidyāpīṭh; for details, see biography in the Appendix. Other Ārya Samāj historians included Acharya Rāmdev, the Vice-Chancellor of Gurukul Kangri, and Satyaketu Vidyālaṃkār, who was also awarded the Maṅgalāprasād prize.

[23] Whose *Oxford History of India* (1904) and *The Oxford Student's History of India* (1908) were the standard reference books.

[24] Jaychandra Vidyālaṃkār, 'Bhāratvarṣa kā ek rāṣṭrīy itihās', p. 167.

[25] In fact, though the *Rāmāyaṇa* is technically a *kāvya* and not an *itihāsa*, Hindi historians enthusiastically upheld its historical truth. 'The search for a counter-history was facilitated by the traditional absence of a distinction between mythology and history', Sudhir Chandra has suggested. 'So, both literary and quasi-historical classics of the past—the Ramayana, the Mahabharata and the Purāṇas, for example—came to be seen as more than repositories of the community's myths, wisdom and traditions; they were seen as containing a history and a meaning relevant in providing the

was needed, conceded Jaychandra, genealogies in the *Mahābhārata* and the Purāṇas could provide standpoints for pre-Buddhist chronology and should be considered historical sources. This was exactly what G.H. Ojhā did. While lamenting the fact that genealogies in the Purāṇas and other texts of historical interest lacked any kind of dating, he nevertheless started 'fixing' dates for various Rajput lineages on the basis of Purāṇic genealogies, geographical names and accounts in the *Mahābhārata*, and cross-checking references there and in other Sanskrit literary and genealogical texts with inscriptions and references from Greek historians and Chinese travellers.[26] Through painstaking work he was able to assert, in a series of books on 'ancient royal lineages' (*prācīn rāj-vaṃś*), that medieval Rajput clans were the direct descendants of the original solar and lunar dynasties, and that their kṣatriya status was beyond doubt.[27]

After assessing the arguments [*dalīl*] of scholars who do not consider the Rajput jāti to be kṣatriya, we have proved [*sapramāṇ*] that Rajputs today are the descendants [*vaṃśdhar*] of those Aryan kṣatriya people who ruled India thousands of years ago. The Aryan kṣatriya jāti ruled not only over India but also over the whole of Central and Western Asia and beyond, and Aryan civilisation was well known there, too. That same Aryan kṣatriya jāti ruled Rajputana before and after the *Mahābhārata* up till now. With changes over time it was natural for Rajput customs and lifestyle to change somewhat according to historical and geographical conditions [*deśkāl*], but many ancient customs of the Aryans can be still found among them.[28]

Although contesting Tod and Vincent Smith on the issue of the 'foreign' and non-kṣatriya origin of the Rajputs, Ojhā nevertheless followed Tod in using chronologies, now 'scientifically' cross-checked, to weave a tapestry of names, dates, events, and dynasties in pre-Muslim India; this history linked the hazy but all-important world of the epics to the historical empires of the Mauryas and Guptas and to clans still existing and (almost) ruling even now. The outcome was, thus, a continuous history,

---

raw materials for reconstructing India's past. They were histories'; Chandra: *The Oppressive Present*, p. 57. Cf. Kaviraj, 'Imaginary History', in *The Unhappy Consciousness*, pp. 107–57.

[26] Ojhā, *Solāṅkiyoṁ kā prācīn itihās*, Ajmer, Vedic Karyalay, 1907.

[27] An earlier enterprise in the same direction was Kavirāy Śyāmaldās' *Vīr-vinod*, first printed in woodblock in 1880 and then reprinted in type in the early twentieth century. I owe the reference to Norbert Peabody, and a glimpse of this truly extraordinary work to John D. Smith.

[28] Ojhā, *Rājputāne kā itihās*, vol. 1, p. 303.

and also a 'classical' polity and culture which references in temples, inscriptions, Sanskrit literature, and stories about glorious kings and generous patrons were expected to flesh out. In a similar vein, comparatively recent understandings of Rajput clans as closed castes were projected back into the millennial past along the same principle of historical continuity. Then, as now, they had been part of the same jāti, the subject of 'our' history. Contemporary reviewers saluted his 'unquestionable' (*akāṭya*) arguments and his 'measured, bold and fearless' refutation of English historians.[29]

The motif of the 'Aryan age', the original golden age, thus acquired a precise historical foundation, being *mirrored faithfully* in the Vedas, Brāhmaṇas, the epics, and the Śāstras; it also acquired powerful contemporary relevance: it could be evoked with daunting immediacy through poems like *Bhārat-bhārtī* (see below) and by the Ārya Samāj gurukul (cf. 1.4).[30] Even the discovery of the Indus Valley civilization could be used to counteract colonial historians: since excavations in the Indus valley linked the Indus civilization with the Sumerians, 'it is therefore demonstrated that India is really the original teacher (*ādiguru*) of all the civilizations in the world'.[31]

The motif of the original golden age of the Aryan jāti, once accepted—and it was accepted, with the help of western orientalists, by all Hindi authors—framed its own historical questions, as also their answers. The first question concerned the onset of decadence: if 'ours' had been such a splendid civilization, how could 'we' be invaded and subjugated by 'Muslim' attackers? (Afghans, Turks, and Iranians were all collapsed into the one category.) Dates and opinions differed according to whether decadence had been the consequence of inner weakness and conflict or of alien invasions. According to one Prof. 'Indra', decadence had started in 1192 with Pṛthvīrāj Cauhān's defeat at the hands of Shahabuddin Ghuri.[32] In Maithilīśaraṇ Gupta's poetic vision, decadence had started much earlier with the Mahābhārata war, i.e. when the perfect harmony of

[29] 'Extracts from Opinions on Fasciculus I of the History of Rajputana' appended to the second volume of *Rājputāne kā itihās* (1926).

[30] See e.g. Uma Chakravarti, 'Whatever Happened to the Vedic Dasi? Orientalism, Nationalism and a Script for the Past', in K. Sangari and S. Vaid, eds, *Recasting Women*, New Delhi, Kali for Women, 1989.

[31] Janārdan Bhaṭṭ, 'Bhārtīy purātattva meṁ naī khoj', *Mādhurī*, III, pt. 2, 2, March 1925, p. 149.

[32] Prof. 'Indra' (probably a pen-name), 'Prācīn bhārat meṁ rājnītik svādhīntā', *Mādhurī*, IV, pt. 2, 2, February 1926, p. 186.

the Aryan–Hindu polity had begun to be marred by inner conflict.[33] *Bhārat-bhārtī*'s poetic answer was that history follows a cyclical pattern: thus after the heights reached by ancient India there could only be decline and decadence. In fact, decadence was itself a proof of the earlier glory:

> उन्नति तथा अवनति प्रकृति का नियम एक अखण्ड है।
> चढ़ता प्रथम जो व्योम में गिरता वही मार्तण्ड है।
> अतएव अवनति ही हमारी कह रही उन्नति-कला।
> उत्थान ही जिसका नहीं हुआ उसका पतन ही क्या भला? ॥६॥

> Rise and decadence are a natural law:
> It is the sun which rises first in the sky then falls.
> Thus decadence itself speaks of our past progress.
> How can anyone fall without having risen first?[34]

In both cases, the existence of a Hindu/Indian nation deriving directly from the Aryan past and incorporating all regional kingdoms was implied. For historians like Ojhā (and K.P. Jaiswal), bent on reconstructing 'ancient India' in its pristine purity, the arrival of foreign rulers who maintained cultural distance marred the 'pure' model of Aryan–Hindu polity. As Partha Chatterjee has argued, 'The theory of medieval decline fitted nicely with the overall judgement of nineteenth-century British historians that "Muslim rule in India" was a period of despotism, misrule and anarchy—this, needless to say, being the historical justification for colonial intervention.' This theory fitted also with prejudices about Islam as 'essentially' cruel, fanatical, bigoted, warlike, and dissolute.[35]

Already in the first Hindi 'nationalist' history textbook, Śiva Prasād Siṃh's *Itihās timirnāśak* (3rd part, 1873), it is clear that by making this jāti/nation the subject of history it became easy for Hindi writers to combine the memory of 'Turk' attacks with an instrumental reading of the bombastic accounts of Muslim court historians. Reading them against their grain, along with British histories, Hindi writers could construe the period starting with the Afghan invasions as a Dark Age of dreadful religious wars, as the beginning of political slavery and, consequently, of decadence. Not all agreed. A contemporary reviewer, probably Hariśchandra himself, remarked that in relying too heavily on Elliot's compilation of Muslim historians, Śiva Prasād had given a biased view

[33] Gupta, *Bhārat-bhārtī, Atīt khaṇḍ*, stanzas 195–6, Cirgaon, Sahitya Sadan, 1991 (original ed. 1912), see 3.1.2 here.

[34] Ibid., stanza 6, p. 12.

[35] Chatterjee, *The Nation and Its Fragments*, p. 101.

of the period. 'It is a dreadful catalogue of the violence and oppression practised by Delhi kings on their subjects.' Whereas European historians praised the Mughal rulers for their just rule, Śiva Prasād only saw faults in them; in fact, they were ahead of their times and far more enlightened and tolerant than the European rulers of the period. Whatever the truth of Śiva Prasād's assertions, it was wrong to write them down in school textbooks, for children would then be brought up in a spirit of bigotry and hatred.[36] Yet it was Śiva Prasād's view that gained currency in the incipient nationalist construction of history.

Closely connected to the issue of the beginning of decadence and the reasons for defeat, was the question of history after the 'defeat'. Had 'we' been defeated completely? As other scholars have pointed out, the framework of the weakened nation as the subject of history allowed the history of the Muslim period to be reinterpreted as a history of resistance. Prof. 'Indra' argued in a long article on 'Political independence in ancient India' that Hindu defeat had never been complete: Muslim rulers, both during the Sultanate and in the Mughal period, had constantly to fight against Hindu rajas, hence their victory was never total or final. Iltutmish had fought against the rulers of Malwa, Babar against the Hindu rulers of Ranthambor, Malwa, and Kalinjar and so on.[37]

किसी भी मुसलमान-बादशाह का राज्य ऐसा नही गुज़रा जिसमें उसे हिन्दुओं के साथ लड़ना न पड़ा हो। भारतवासी सामाजिक तथा धार्मिक दृष्टि से पूरी तरह से स्वाधीन रहे। विदेशियों और भारतवासियों के सदियों तक चलते हुए राष्ट्रीय युद्ध में अंतिम विजय भारतवासियों की हो चुकी थी जब एक और विदेशी शक्ति बीच में कूद पड़ी।

There was never a Muslim sultan who did not have to fight with Hindus. Indians (*bhāratvāsīs*) always remained completely independent from the social and religious points of view. In the national war that went on for centuries between foreigners [i.e. Muslims] and Indians, the last victory would have belonged to Indians if another foreign power had not intervened.[38]

The complex relationships between the Muslim overlords in Delhi and local rulers, chieftains, and governors, both Hindu and Muslim, were thus revisited in a drastically simplified manner according to the two

[36] Review in *Hariśchandra Magazine*, February 1874, quoted in Dalmia, *The Nationalization of Hindu Traditions*, pp. 330–1.

[37] For a catalogue of wars between Mughal and Hindu rajas, see Ojhā, *Rājputāne kā itihās*, vol. 13, pp. 274–5.

[38] Prof. 'Indra', 'Prāchīn bhārat meṁ rājnītik svādhīntā', part 2, *Mādhurī*, V, pt. 1, 3, October 1926, p. 326.

overlapping axes of religion and nationhood. In his essay, Indra was explicit that by bhāratvāsī one should read 'Hindu', and by 'foreigner' 'Muslim'. It was the 'people' (*prajā*) who had not accepted foreign subjection and had risen, he argued. Although they had not objected to different Indian rulers, 'they could not bear domination at the hands of *mlecchas*, that was real subjection for them. Then their 'natural will for independence arose'. In the end, Sikhs, Mahrattas, Jats, once again as many parts of 'us', had defeated 'them'.[39] Further, although Aryans had been a jāti, a nation-community, they did not become a rāṣṭra, a nation state, until they encountered the 'other'; just as the sense of independence comes from tasting subjection, 'Indra' argued, a national sense can only emerge out of an encounter with the 'other'.[40] 'Therefore, although the seven-centuries-long war looks like a Hindu–Muslim war, it was in fact a war of Hindustanis against foreign invaders.'[41] A more circumspect view was taken by Ojhā:

> Śivājī showed that his primary aim was to arouse a feeling of unity among Hindus in order to destroy Muslim rule in India and establish a Hindu kingdom by organizing Hindus on a jātīy basis. He actually aroused a kind of enthusiasm in the Maratha jāti, but because the foundations of Śivājī's empire were not based on the solid rock of national [rāṣṭrīy] sentiment but on shallow sand, illness and mutual division and enmity quickly began to spread in the vast [*virāṭ*] body politic of the Marathas. Each individual tried to tread upon the other to advance his own interests. Ignorant of the tolerant and elevated sentiments needed to establish an empire, the Maratha jāti believed that the formula to rule is the pursuit of one's own interests by looting, injustice and oppression. As a result, the third intelligent and *nītinipuṇ* [politic, prudent] jāti which came from over the sea annihilated its power and snatched the kingdom of India from it.[42]

Identities, too, were reframed from this national perspective. While pre-nineteenth-century sources show that Rajputs believed they shared to some extent their worldview with Muslim warriors,[43] now the line between them became impermeable. Rajput relationships with Sultans and Mughals were reframed in terms of either 'treason' or 'glorious resistance': Rajput rulers who had cooperated and served as Mughal commanders were now seen as traitors, while those who kept fighting, like Maharana Pratāp, became national heroes. At the time of the Mughals,

[39] Ibid., pt.1, p. 182.
[40] Ibid., p. 185.
[41] Ibid., pt. 2, p. 328.
[42] Ojhā, *Rājputāne kā itihās*, vol. I, pp. 274–5.
[43] Peabody, 'The King is Dead, Long Live the King!'.

wrote the editor of *Chāṁd*, Rajputs had shown little love for national independence and most of them had become Mughal generals, happily fighting their own 'brothers' and even a national hero like Śivājī. 'With what words can we address those who made their sisters and daughters the servants of cow-eating Yavanas for the sake of their own fleeting wealth and pomp? We are writing these lines not with ink but with our own tears.'[44]

While political subjection might have been complete, most writers upheld the view that there had been important areas, like religion and society, which had remained independent. If the lack of national sense and national unity among Hindu rulers had brought about subjection, it had been the people who had kept national identity alive by refusing to convert and to abandon their customs. The upsurge of Bhakti devotionalism in north India, and especially the celebration of the virtuous king Rāmachandra as the supreme god by Tulsīdās in the sixteenth century, acquired a connotation of cultural resistance that coloured much of the Hindi assessment of the 'Bhakti movement' (see 3.3). Sufi poets who had used Indian folk stories to tell spiritual allegories were similarly taken as examples of the power of attraction of Hindu culture. In this perspective, Indo-Muslim cultural forms presented a dilemma and were more ambiguous to assess, as were 'good' Muslim rulers. The figure of Akbar presented the most interesting paradox, and it is noteworthy how Indian histories of India juggled in their perceptions of him: on the one hand, Akbar was the paradigmatic 'good ruler' who promoted tolerance and cohesion between the Hindu and Muslim communities; he had raised Hindus to the highest offices of state and had prized Indian literature, knowledge, music, and art. On the other hand, this policy could be viewed as a clever ruse, a *kūṭnīti*, while his war against Maharana Pratāp and Rani Durgāvatī placed him squarely in the role of the villain (see 3.2).

Finally, historical judgement of the Muslim period was directly linked, in English as in Indian historiography, with that of British rule. Here the question was: were we 'freed' by the British? At stake here were the notion of British superiority and the assessment of contemporary times. Yes, British conquest was a liberation, wrote Maithilīśaraṇ Gupta, following British historians like Vincent Smith in maintaining that India had been saved from a state of chaos after Aurangzeb's death.[45] Yes, wrote G.H. Ojhā in his *Itihās*, for British rule had brought peace and prosperity

[44] 'Vartamān rājputānā', editorial in *Chāṁd*, 'Rājputānā aṅk', X, pt. 1, 1, November 1931, p. 5. See 3.2 here for the actual aim of this critical attack.

[45] Gupta, *Bhārat-bhārtī, Vartmān khaṇḍ*, stanzas 243–7, p. 91.

after Maratha exactions and Pindari looting. No, objected others like 'Maṇḍan Miśra', arguing that regional kingdoms had in fact been quite prosperous, popular, and attentive to the needs of their subjects. Quoting reports of Indian and European travellers, he remarked that regional rulers *had to* pay more attention to their prajā, their subjects, citing in support the examples of Alivardi Khan in Bengal, Nawab Saadat Ali Khan in Awadh, the Holkars and Scindias in Malva, the Marathas in Poona, the Nizam in Hyderabad, and Haider Ali in Mysore. The overall situation was not as bad as it had been depicted, especially when compared with contemporary Europe, ravaged by the Seven-year War and the French Revolution. The absence of 'central' rule could not be called anarchy; the economy and trade had prospered, fairs circulated both goods and religion, and a village economy ensured Muslim and Hindu interdependence.[46] This stand was in tune with the fictional revisitation of recent local rulers like Rani Lakṣmībāī as model nationalist rulers (see 3.2), and with the indictment of early British governors for their ruthless and unjust annexation policy.[47]

It has been argued that much of the hostility towards, and 'othering' of, Muslim rule in colonial India was the result of a 'transferred hostility': since colonial intellectuals could not directly vent their hostility against the British, they transferred it onto Muslims.[48] However true the first part of this argument may be, the second part does not necessarily follow. What we have seen here is a more complex process by which certain categories—of chronology and identity—were absorbed from European historiography and reinterpreted by Indian intellectuals. These categories provided a framework for Indian history as the history of the Aryan-Hindu jāti and produced their own historical questions and explanations. Sanskrit and vernacular texts, Muslim chronicles and British

[46] Maṇḍan Miśra, 'Britiś-sāmrājya ke pūrva bhārat', in *Mādhurī*, IX, pt. 2, 1, February 1931, pp. 47–54.

[47] See e.g. Chaturvedī Pandit Dvārkāprasād Śarmā's biographies of Robert Clive and Warren Hastings, which cost him his government job; Udaynārāyaṇ Tivārī, 'Bhaiyā sāhab paṇḍit śrīnārāyaṇ chaturvedī', in V. Miśra, ed., *Hindīmay jīvan. paṇḍit śrīnārāyaṇ chaturvedī*, Delhi, Prabhat Prakasan, n.d.?

[48] Sudhir Chandra has argued that the narrative of oppression and of the fight for nationhood could have either Muslim and/or British rule cast in the role of the enemy: the and/or nexus was left lax, so that the identification of Muslims as British and vice versa could or could not be activated, often depending on the context and occasion of the narrative. See Chandra, *The Oppressive Present*, pp. 116 ff. However, this did not leave much space for more positive images and notions of Muslim participation in Indian history, which could only be exceptions.

histories could then be used as historical documents to provide the answers.

From the time of the Khilafat movement and after the great riots of the 1920s, Gandhi and Gandhians became wary of anti-Muslim historical statements, and the Hindi textbooks prepared by the Gandhian association for Hindi propaganda in the South (Dakṣiṇ Bhārat Hindī Prachār Sabhā) show an attempt at presenting Mughal rulers in a more positive light.[49] On the scholarly and semi-official level, the Hindustani Academy in Allahabad tried to bridge the widening gulf between Hindi and Urdu and Hindu and Muslim versions of Indian history by promoting lectures on Hindu–Muslim relations and interdependence under the Sultanate and the Mughals.[50] This rapprochement was easier among the elite united by a common Indo-Persian cultural background, and most Hindi journals continued to view such initiatives with some suspicion, as strategic moves to construct a fake history of communal harmony. 'Good Muslims' were accepted as exceptions, but the subject of 'our history' remained Hindu.

What the articles and works discussed here certainly show is that by the second and third decades of the century, Indian historians could weave into their narrative certain strands critical of British policies which had already emerged in the nineteenth century, and view the transfer from Muslim to British rule as another chapter in the history of subjection. The motives behind colonial historiography could be 'exposed', as 'Maṇḍan Miśra' had done in the article mentioned above, and a critical history of British rule became the accepted nationalist historiography, exemplified by Pandit Sundarlāl's banned *Bhārat meṁ aṅgrezī rājya* (1929) (cf. 4.2). As we shall see later, the categories of the Indian history of India became available to other subjects seeking their own self-assertion. These categories, and the dominant mood of Hindu heroism, also acquired a direct political relevance. Popular self-assertion by some lower castes (touchable *śūdras*) in the public sphere of religious

[49] See Avadhnandan and Satyanārāyaṇ, *Hindī kī dūsrī pustak*, Madras, Hindi Pracar Pustak Mala, 18th ed., 1939, pp. 19–21. Cf. Pandey, *The Ascendancy of the Congress in Uttar Pradesh*, pp. 148 ff.

[50] Between 1928 and 1933, Abdulla Yusuf Ali, G.H. Ojhā, Gaṅgānāth Jhā, Maulana Syed Sulaiman Nadvi of the Shibli Academy of Azamgarh, Tara Chand, Mohammad Amin Abbasi of Calcutta, Dr Bhagvān Dās, Maulana Abdul Haq, Padmasiṃh Śarmā, and others were invited to give lectures on subjects like 'Contributions of the Hindus to Muslim Culture' and 'Contributions of the Muslims to Hindu Culture'; see *The Report of the working of the Hindustani Academy, United Provinces, Allahabad (1927–1933)*, pp. 11–13.

processions, festivals, popular entertainment, and martial activities (*akhāṛās*) in urban areas in the 1920s took place in the name of kṣatriya identity. Their active participation in the Rāmlīlā festival as 'the army of Mahāvīr', as well as the growing Bīr worship, the formation of *yādav akhāṛās* and related performing arts such as Nauṭaṅkī, gave the belief in Lord Rām a contemporary significance and a martial and militant edge, and they progressively merged in Hindu revivalism and in direct involvement in local communal conflicts.[51]

We now turn to a literary text that was crucial in popularizing this version of Indian history and making it relevant to the interpretation of contemporary India. It also shows how literature contributed to the making of a unified historical saṃskāra which became a substratum even for 'secular' intellectuals; this was Maithilīśaraṇ Gupta's long poem *Bhārat-bhārtī* (1912).

3.1.2. *Bhārat-Bhārtī* and the Interpretation of Indian History

हम कौन थे क्या हो गये और क्या होंगे अभी
आओ विचारें आज मिलकर ये समस्याएँ सभी।
यद्यपि हमें इतिहास अपना प्राप्त पूरा है नहीं
हम कौन थे इस ज्ञान को फिर भी अधूरा है नही॥

Who we were, we are and we shall be,
Come, let's ponder over it together.
Though we do not have our full history
we still know fully who we were.[52]

Maithilīśaraṇ Gupta (1886–1964),[53] the first poet to turn wholeheartedly to Khari Boli as a poetic language, can be described as a quintessential reformist Dvivedī poet (cf. 2.2); his view of poetry, choice of themes, use of language and sense of history were largely shaped by Mahāvīr Prasād

[51] Nandini Gooptu, 'The Political Culture of the Urban Poor: the United Provinces between the Two World Wars', unpublished Ph. D. thesis, Cambridge University 1991, pp. 122 ff. See also the articles by Freitag, Coccari, Hansen, and Marcus in Freitag, *Culture and Power in Benares*.

[52] The 37th edition of the work is used here, published by Gupta's own concern, Sahitya Sadan, in Cirgaon, Jhansi, 1991, *Atīt khaṇḍ* stanza 14, p. 14.

[53] For a brief evaluation, see McGregor, *Hindi Literature in the Late Nineteenth and Early Twentieth Centuries*, pp. 109–10; also the special issue of *Ālochnā*, New Delhi, October–December 1986.

Dvivedī, his mentor. When Maithilīśaraṇ Gupta started writing *Bhārat-bhārtī* at the age of 26 in 1911, he was already an established poet, with *Raṅg mem bhaṅg* (*Valour and Adversity*, 1909) and *Jayadrath vadh* (*The killing of Jayadrath,* 1910) published; he was also a regular contributor of historical poems to *Sarasvatī*. The pride in, and glorification of, ancient India coupled with a strongly reformist attitude toward the present condition of the country were at the centre of Dvivedī's agenda. Most historical poems published in *Sarasvatī* were hymns to India as the land of the Aryans, like 'Āryabhūmi' by Dvivedī himself (April 1906); or they reworked figures from the Epics and the Purāṇas in a historical and national framework: for example, Dvivedī commissioned poems to accompany colour plates by Raja Ravi Varma.[54]

Gupta's *Bhārat-bhārtī*, a long poem (702 stanzas) on the past glory and present disarray of India, modelled on Altāf Husain Hālī's *Musaddas* (1869),[55] was serialized in *Sarasvatī* and was a resounding success on publication. It soon became a modern classic and one of the very few works of contemporary Hindi poetry to enter the Hindi university syllabus (cf. 1.4.2).[56] Since the poetic qualities of the text are scant—rhyme often the only element to distinguish it from prose—the success and ensuing status of the book can only have arisen from its content and from the historical juncture at which it was published. It was in fact the first full-scale poetic elaboration of the debates on the Indian history of India mentioned above, a fitting example of how literature could provide a nationalist answer to colonial views of Indian history. The narrative inflation of a previous poem by Gupta, 'Pūrva darśan' (Vision of the past, 1910), *Bhārat-bhārtī*, like Hālī's *Musaddas*, was ambitious in scope, reformist in aim, and argumentative in attitude. Like the *Musaddas, Bhārat-bhārtī* represented a self-conscious attempt at a new kind of poetry, with new themes and a new function. In his Introduction of 1869, Hālī had justified his 'dry, insipid, plain and simple poem', which contained 'only historical material or translations of Quranic verses or of Hadith or an exactly accurate picture of the present state of the [Indian

[54] Later collected in *Kavitā kalāp*, Allahabad, Indian Press, 1909.

[55] Gupta was presented a copy of the *Musaddas* by Raja Rāmpāl Siṃh of Kurri Sidhauli together with a letter urging him to write something similar for the Hindus. Gupta eventually used Hālī's poem and another *Musaddas* inspired by it, Kaifī's; see the poet's introduction to *Bhārat-bhārtī*, pp. 9–10. For other Urdu poems inspired by Hālī's *Musaddas*, see Shackle and Majeed's edited translation, Delhi, Oxford University Press, 1997.

[56] By 1930 it had run into ten editions, the tenth consisting of 4000 copies.

Muslim] community', by saying that it had not been composed 'in order to be enjoyed or with the aim of eliciting applause, but in order to make my friends and fellows feel a sense of outrage and shame'.[57] Similarly, Gupta stated in his Introduction that 'everything can be achieved with industry (*udyog*). But for industry you need enthusiasm (*utsāh*). Poetry is an excellent means of stimulating that enthusiasm, that mental spur'.[58] Whereas Hālī's *Musaddas* had marked a watershed in the Urdu poetic tradition and had itself commented and reflected on it, *Bhārat-bhārtī* perfected what had been in place from the late nineteenth century—the trends of reformist poetry and the motif of past glory versus present 'sad state' (*durdaśā*).[59] The lamentation over the glorious past and the doleful analysis of the present were enhanced by arguments, historical evidence, stories, dramatic scenes, monologues, and notes from a number of heterogeneous sources grounding the poem in putative historical, scriptural, and factual truth; *Bhārat-bhārtī*'s notes quoted the Vedas, Upanishads, and Śāstras, European history books, R.C. Dutt's *Civilization of Ancient India*, newspaper items, traditional stories, and so on. While making use of 'factual' and historical sources, poetry could, through its greater freedom in imaginatively choosing and arranging material and through creating connections and correspondences, achieve much more than historical writing. Both Hālī's *Musaddas* and *Bhārat-bhārtī* were, for example, able to convey a stronger sense of the vast tide of history and of Indian Muslim or Hindu subjecthood. Hālī's poem conveyed in fact three senses or images of the historical process: a cyclical image of tidal forces, a nostalgic one of the capricious vicissitudes of fortune, and an image of linear progress.[60] The same complexity is apparent in *Bhārat-bhārtī*: the strong emphasis on decline and the opposition between past and present were counteracted by making decline part of a vast cyclical process and, echoing the Purāṇas, it inscribed historical time in the much wider span of aeons and yugas. Further, linear progress and reform took the place of the eschatological conflagration. The relativity of historical time becomes apparent if we look at the allocation of stanzas: the Aryan golden age was given by far the greatest attention (180 stanzas), and even in the narrative of decadence, the pre-Muslim period (26) took up more space than the Muslim age (15); this was further downplayed by the counter-narrative of Hindu resistance (5); British history was telescoped (4) and figured only as a time of transition

[57] Translation in Shackle and Majeed, *Hālī's Musaddas*, pp. 96–7.

[58] Gupta, *Bhārat-bhārtī*, p. 8.

[59] See Chandra, *The Oppressive Present*.

[60] Shackle and Majeed, *Hālī's Musaddas*, p. 74.

to the present. Already in its structure, then, *Bhārat-bhārtī* was able to convey positively the sense, which historians could only debate about, that Muslim India had only been an interlude, an almost insignificant episode in the *longue durée* of Indian time.

The other way in which poetry could be more eloquent than historical writing was in the construction of the subject of history. Hālī had addressed Indian Muslims as a community; furthermore, by placing them in a long line of descent from the Arabs and as part of a pan-Arab cosmos, he had sought to loosen ties with Indian Persianate culture.[61] In *Bhārat-bhārtī*, too, the subject ('we') of history is posited uncompromisingly from the beginning; the direct filiation of 'us' from the Vedic 'ṛṣis' is repeated time and again in the poem, and the development of Aryan civilization is presented under the headings of 'our origin', 'our ancestors'. The perspective, too, is clearly national; heroes of the past are taken indiscriminately from all regions and kingdoms of India; heroes of the present include leaders, rulers, artists, and scientists from all over the country (*Bhaviṣya khaṇḍ,* stanzas 123–30).[62] Equally importantly, the same projection works for the readers, too: the small audience of the Hindi-educated is addressed in the poem and represented *as if* it were the nation. In this way, actual readers are invested with a garb and a role that transcend their particular identities. The real barriers that existed among the Hindi-educated and separated them from other audiences within the nation are overcome discursively: literature becomes thus the site where an undivided national consciousness can be 'retrieved' and reworked. This has, according to Gupta, as much to do with the power of poetry as with the power of history telling: both can revive a dead nation.

संसार में कविता अनेकों क्रान्तियाँ कर चुकी।
मुरझे मनों में वेग की विद्युत्प्रभाएँ भर चुकी।
है अन्ध-सा अन्तर्जगत कवि-रूप सविता के बिना।
सद्भाव जीवित रह नहीं सकते सु-कविता के बिना॥
मृत जाति को कवि ही जिलाते रस-सुधा के योग से।

[61] Ibid., p. 31.

[62] The impressive list mentions Rammohan Roy and Dayanand Sarasvati, Tilak and Madan Mohan Mālavīya, Rajendralal Mitra and Debendranath Tagore, the Maharajas of Darbhanga and of Mysore, the painters Abanindranath Tagore and Ravi Varma, the musicians Paluskar and Satyabala, Rabindranath and the sculptor Mhatre, Gokhale and Gandhi as signs of hope for the future; interestingly, R.C. Dutt's *Mahārāṣṭra jīvanprabhāt* is one of two novels mentioned as rays of hope. Mālavīya is the only person of Hindi background mentioned, praised with the Maharaja of Darbhanga for founding BHU.

How many revolutions has poetry brought about in the world!
As if injecting withered minds with an electric charge;
The inner world is blind without a poet's light,
Goodness cannot survive without good poetry.
Only poets revive a dead nation with the nectar of rasa.[63]

'Our history', the history of India, is the history of the Hindus in Gupta's poem. Community and nation cannot but overlap when the all-important tie is the one that links the imagined Hindu community of the present to the Aryan 'ancestors'. Non-Hindus can only be foreigners or seek to merge in the mainstream.[64] Puruṣottam Agravāl calls this Gupta's '*baddhamūl saṃskāra*' (rooted assumptions); he observes that though Gupta sincerely desired unity and a truly national consciousness, his saṃskāra led him to view the Indian nation as coterminous with the Hindu jāti. This vision was partially altered when the poet came under the influence of Gandhi and his idea of a universal 'human jāti', but would resurface regularly every time he wrote about his saṃskāra, as in the poem *Hindū* (1927–8).[65] We may add that it was poems like *Bhārat-bhārtī* that helped create this saṃskāra by fusing a historical sense with a particular view of present society. It is precisely the 'uncriticized' gap between saṃskāra and nationalist ideology which enabled poets like

[63] *Bhaviṣya khaṇḍ,* stanzas 97–8, p. 182.

[64] The millennial history from the first invasions of the Śakas to the arrival of the first Muslim invaders takes less than 20 stanzas (out of the 253 of *Atīt khaṇḍ*): Buddha, Jīna, Śaṅkara, Vikramāditya, Bhoja are only the bright stars of a darkening sky. The section on Muslim rule is also surprisingly short, only 20 stanzas, and clearly less important than that on Hindu civilization. We find here all the *topoi* of the Indian history of India: 'we' summoned the Islamic horde; Jaychandra's selfish betrayal; the rule of the 'Yavanas' was mostly destructive (the longest section goes under the heading '*atyāchār*', persecution), with a few good exceptions like Akbar (explained logically, since a whole community cannot be bad and keep completely apart from the whole—Hindu—society, p. 87) but with Aurangzeb as a dark epilogue. Set against 'Yavana' rule are examples of Hindu pride: Maharana Pratāp, the collective sacrifice (*jauhar*) of Rajput women, Śivājī. Once again, the end of Yavan rule is caused by the end of a cycle (*Atīt khaṇḍ,* 242, p. 90): 'अन्यायियों का राज्य भी क्या अचल रह सकता कभी? आखिर हुए अँगरेज शासक राज्य है जिनका अभी॥ संप्रति समुन्नति की सभी हैं प्राप्त सुविधाएँ यहाँ॥ सब पथ खुले हैं भय नहीं विचरो जहाँ चाहो वहाँ॥' [Can an unjust rule last forever? Finally the British became rulers and they still rule. Hence all means of progress are there, all routes are open, you can go anywhere you want without fear.] *Atīt khaṇḍ,* stanza 243, p. 90.

[65] Puruṣottam Agravāl, 'Rāṣṭrakavi kī rāṣṭrīy chetnā', *Ālochnā*, New Delhi, October–December 1986, pp. 127–36.

Gupta, his many readers, and Hindi nationalists in general to subscribe later to a secular, broad-minded ideology while retaining a sense of identity and history based on the exclusive and unquestioned notion of Hindu subjecthood voiced in the poem.

Let us now turn to the poem itself. Divided into three parts, *Bhārat-bhārtī* seeks to answer the question of 'who we were, are and shall be'. Existing identities are evidently insufficient to answer that question, and the answer has to be sought in the Vedic past and nowhere else. The first two parts are descriptive, as if the ancient Aryans were 'out there' and what was required was only an act of description. Opposition and continuity connect past and present, the latter subtly subverting the former. For if the truth is that 'we' have declined from the glory of our ancestors, the fact that 'we' derive from them itself belies the notion that decline is absolute. Also, the relationship between past and present symbolizes the relationship of history to nationalism: the past, like history, provides the model, a blueprint that will bring unity and order into the present. The third part, concerning the future, is hortatory and follows the path charted by the previous two: since history is cyclical, if 'we' rise from the present decadence it will only be to become what we were. There is no need to imagine a future different from the past. Centuries of Indo-Muslim history, with its many dimensions and the necessity for pragmatic and ideological compromises, could be brushed aside as if they had never happened.

As in Hālī's *Musaddas,* the first two parts of the poem present a stark contrast; everything was good and pure in ancient India, while everything is bad, very bad, in modern India—'*Hā, hāy!*' [Alas!] is the common refrain. Past and present are in fact complementary, and the glorified vision of the past sets the agenda for the present. The section on the past starts uncompromisingly with '*hamārī śreṣṭhtā*', our excellence: India, the land of the Aryans, was the seat of creation, the 'pride of the earth', the 'land of the ṛṣis'. Quotations from Manu, the Purāṇas, Tod, Sir Walter Raleigh, the Gospels, and the Quran all prove India's antiquity and excellence. Antitheses, like a refrain, compare ancient Aryans to the rest of the world: when others went around naked, we built palaces which touched the stars; when others roamed in jungles eating meat, we practised agriculture (*Atīt khaṇḍ*, stanza 47).[66] India has given knowledge, science, philosophy and even religion to the world: 'संसार को पहले

[66] This was of course a common-enough line in Hindi journals and in literature from the time of Hariśchandra's *Bhārat durdaśā*. The note accompanying the first line quotes a Mr D.A. Brown, who in the *Daily Tribune* of 10.2.1884 wrote: 'After

हमीं ने ज्ञान-भिक्षा दान की। आचार की व्यापार की व्यवहार की' [We were the first to introduce the world to knowledge, to civilized manners and to business.] (*Atīt khaṇḍ*, stanza 45). Also, 'We first preached to the world, we first inhabited the world, we civilized Greece' (stanza 191); even Jesus was a disciple of the Hindus, and Japan learnt from India (stanzas 67–8). What is important here is not the originality of this view of Hindu superiority, but its typicality and wide currency: these passages from the section on the past were invariably the ones included in the school syllabus (cf. 1.4), and similar views were aired in all seriousness in prestigious Hindi magazines.

The description of the Aryan forefathers is predictably one of perfection; along with general virtues, Aryan men, women and children are endowed by Gupta with exactly the qualities he thought modern Hindus lacked and needed: independence, selflessness, self-control, and maturity in 'behaviour, commerce, science' (stanza 45). Much space is devoted to the ancient Hindus' excellence in world sea- (and air!) trade, in science ('we knew all the world's secrets', p. 29), in education, and in literature in the wide sense of the word, that is in all branches of human endeavour. Above all, the Aryan community had all the marks of a nation, namely unity of language and of feeling:

> थी एक भाषा एक मन था एक सबका भाव था।
> सम्पूर्ण भारतवर्ष मानो एक नगरी थी बड़ी
> पुर और ग्राम-समूह-संस्था थी मुहल्लों की लड़ी।
>
> All had but one language, one mind, one feeling,
> The whole of Bhāratvarṣa was like a big town:
> Cities and villages like a net of *muhallas*.
>
> (*Atīt khaṇḍ*, stanza 73)

In a historical 'glimpse' (*jhalak*) of ancient India, with a backdrop of temples and buildings, the poet leads us through the daily routine of Aryan men, women, and children. The land of India, 'the image of Brahmā', the 'giver of life', 'endowed with knowledge and glory', the poet assures us, is still the same; only 'we' have changed. Although the point is not overemphasized, we find it again at the onset of the second section: buildings and ruins are signs and reminders of the past. Temples speak, though where once children chanted, now owls cry and warn Hindus of impending disaster.[67] Gupta dwells particularly at length on

objective examination we have to admit that the Hindus are the true creators of world literature, religion and civilisation'; Gupta, *Bhārat-bhārtī*, p. 26n.

[67] *Atīt khaṇḍ*, stanzas 143 ff., pp. 65 ff; *Vartamān khaṇḍ*, stanza 6, p. 96.

education, comparing it to the present system in order to criticize English education; in the past, education was imparted to both boys and girls, first at home by their parents (after all, mothers were educated, too), then at gurukuls, where education was free and teachers were respected. The idyllic and moving view of children chanting the Vedas recalls the reports of enthusiastic visitors to Ārya Samāj gurukuls.[68] English education, on the contrary, is alienating, morally and intellectually harmful, since it hides from Hindus the truth that they were the jagadgurus; furthermore, it teaches 'free thought' instead of the Vedas (*Atīt khaṇḍ*, stanza 148).[69] Unlike traditional Indian education, English education is for sale, does not inculcate self-respect, and leads only to badly paid clerical jobs, or to begging:

> हा! आज शिक्षा-मार्ग भी संकीर्ण होकर क्लिष्ट है
> कुलपति-सहित उन गुरुकुलों का ध्यान ही अवशिष्ट है।
> बिकने लगी विद्या यहाँ अब शक्ति हो तो क्रय करो
> यदि शुल्क आदि न दे सको तो मूर्ख ही मरो!॥
>
> Ah, the path of education is but narrow and crooked today,
> Only the memory of those Gurukuls and teachers is left!
> Knowledge is for sale, if you can buy it, good,
> If you cannot, you can die illiterate!
>
> (*Vartamān khaṇḍ*, stanza 138, p. 126).

Worth noticing is Gupta's description of kingly power in ancient India: after eulogizing the heroism of the ancient kings, the Aryans' wonderful weapons, and the conquest of South East Asia, he states that 'we' resorted to violence only for self-defence. Valour, the ideal of selfless action, and the essentialist view of India as 'peace-loving' come together.[70] The power of the ruler was 'naturally' limited by the paternalistic ideal of the king as 'father to the people' (*prajā-pālak*). Society was perfectly ordered according to the four varṇas, its building blocks; competition and conflict were absent.

[68] 'आधार आर्य्यों के अटल जातीय-जीवन-प्राण का। है पाठ कैसा हो रहा श्रुति शास्त्र और पुराण का। हे राम! हिन्दू जाति का सब कुछ भले ही नष्ट हो। पर यह सरस संगीत उसका फिर यहाँ सु-स्पष्ट हो॥' [(it was) the basis of the national life of the Aryans: how the Śruti, the Śāstras and the Purāṇas are chanted!Oh Rām, may everything be destroyed of the Hindu jāti, but may this melodious music resound here clearly!] *Atīt khaṇḍ,* stanza 175, p. 72.

[69] 'Free thought', one of the *bêtes noires* of Hindi reformist thinkers, is glossed here as 'unrestrained thought, blabber', ibid., p. 129.

[70] 'Where did we ever light the flame of war? We travelled everywhere but never caused revolutions'; *Atīt khaṇḍ,* stanza 137, p. 63.

The motif of order–strength against disunity–weakness is an important explicatory one in Gupta's vision.[71] Decadence, for example, is explained as the result of inner flaws, i.e. of straying from the Aryan ideal. With a kind of sin of hubris, 'our' self-pride blocked our resources of truthfulness and humility, and the seeds of hatred, envy, and self-interest began eating at Hindu/Indian society from within. The Mahābhārata war was the product of this process and marked the beginning of decadence; the Muslim conquest was only a step further in the decline.[72] By situating the motor of decay very early on, on moral grounds and completely within the community (i.e. not as a consequence of foreign invasions), Gupta managed to send a particular message to his audience: if decadence was a moral process of disorder, so is progress a moral process of unity and order. History ought to teach Hindus that the key to progress lay not in historical circumstances but in their inner unity, purity, and strength, in returning to the ideals of the past. This view of history thus contained a normative attitude toward modern society (cf. 3.3), providing the ideal types and the duty/dharma that would bring about progress and order.

In the *Vartamān khaṇḍ*, the second part of the poem, the contemporary state of poverty, famine, agricultural, and industrial stagnation, ignorance and social ills was explained by Gupta in terms of social disorder: people were not abiding by their duty. Thus Gupta was especially harsh on the wealthy and their offspring, the failed leaders of society. A monologue by an arrogant and self-contented raīs indifferent to the fate of his fellow countrymen[73] is followed by a strong comment on the lack of public sense and sense of nationalism (jātīytā) and on the conspicuous consumption and indifference towards education of rājā-raīs [the wealthy and feudal lords] (*Vartamān Khaṇḍ* 108–32). The same holds for the other sections of society grouped, according to their roles, as reformers,

[71] In Hālī's poem the contrast between chaos and order is posited in a different way: chaos is what comes before order, as in the Jahiliyya before Muhammad brought unity and order among Arab tribes. 'The link between the order the Prophet brings to the Arabian peninsula and the order the British bring to the Indian subcontinent is reinforced by the overlap in the depiction of the Arabs of the Jahiliyya and contemporary Indian Muslims, particularly aristocrats, who have yet to avail themselves of the benefits of 'European' progress'; Shackle and Majeed, *Hali's Musaddas*, p. 78.

[72] *Atīt khaṇḍ,* stanza 195, p. 98.

[73] तुम मर रहे हो तो मरो तुमसे हमें क्या काम है?। हमको किसी की क्या पड़ी है नाम है धन-धाम है। तुम कौन हो जिनके लिए हमको यहां अवकाश हो। सुख भोगते हैं हम हमें क्या जो किसी का नाश हो। [What do I care if you are dying? Why should I care, I have name and fame. Who are you that I should spend time on you? I am content. Who cares if someone else is ruined?] *Vartamān khaṇḍ*, stanza 107, p. 120.

preachers, religious specialists (*sādhu, mahant*), the four varṇas and finally women and children (177–247).

In the *Vartamān khaṇḍ*, the poet abandoned the earlier lyrical elegiac style for an argumentative, prosaic tone; indeed, were the rhyme absent, this could be one of the many articles on *Bhārat durdaśā* coming straight from Dvivedī's pen. Dvivedī's influence is apparent, first of all, in the emphasis on the need for economic independence, on the state of agriculture, and on the importance of education. Gupta's criticism of contemporary India is merciless: education is insufficient and harmful; literature, whether poetry or fiction, is useless, impure (when not downright vulgar) and indifferent to its real duty; associations are only cradles of division and unrest; religion is in the hands of unscrupulous mahants (priests) while sadhus (ascetics) have forgotten the ancient ideals of the Vedic seers.[74] The final verdict on contemporary (Hindu) society is a familiar list of 'social evils': mismatched unions between old men and child brides, the sale of brides or bridegrooms, corruption, unnecessary litigation in court, addiction to liquor, inner divisions, adultery, family quarrels, hypocrisy, lack of self-support. Gupta's indictment of India's economic, social, religious, and cultural bankruptcy and his agenda of reform, much along the lines of Dvivedī's *Sarasvatī*, acquire here historical depth and a unifying logic: economic stagnation, social chaos, and cultural confusion are the result of lack of unity and forgetfulness of the ancestors; social evils are corruptions of originally good principles. Thus the appeal for radical reforms in the second and third sections is voiced as an appeal to the four castes and to the 'natural leaders' of society to return to the purity of the *varṇāśrama* system (cf. 3.3). Once again, the future does not have to be imagined differently from the past. Whereas Hālī in the 1860s had been fundamentally ambiguous about the relationship between the model of the past and the blueprint of progress ('carrion progress', pp. 73 ff.), for Maithilīśaraṇ Gupta the formula could be worked out: technological progress, industry (udyog), and the orderly ideals of the Aryans.

In all this, British rule appears as the very paradox of modernity. On the one side it is presented as the avenue to progress and opportunities, in full accordance with the colonial view: safety, civic amenities, good administration, rail, telegraph, hospitals, and schools.[75] This possibly explains why the nationalism of *Bhārat-bhārtī* was considered outdated by the 1920s, as nationalist poems took an outspoken anti-British

[74] *Vartamān khaṇḍ*, stanzas 157–200, pp. 130–9.
[75] *Atīt khaṇḍ*, stanzas 243–7, pp. 90–1.

stance.[76] But British rule also appears ruinous and alienating in that it suppresses economic svadeśī and the cultural ideal of the forefathers: economic dependence on foreign goods is seen as a sign of both physical and psychological subjection. The polemic is here directed at the modern cityfolk, who take pride in buying foreign goods and are westernized to the point of not believing in God—in a word, who have stopped being Indian.[77]

Bhārat-bhartī ends with an exhortative section, very much modelled on the *Vartamān khaṇḍ*. Gupta's appeal is first to Hindu society as a whole, and then to the *leaders* of every group—raīses, mahants, pandits, the four castes, religious leaders, students, youth, the wealthy, poets, and finally women and children, reminding each of their dharma. The message, in short, is two-fold: adapt to the new times, to technology, but, above all, remember your cultural origin and follow the footsteps of your forefathers (*Bhaviṣya khaṇḍ*, stanza 35). The view of history in *Bhārat-bhārtī* comprises a normative vision of a society that is articulated in different, compact, and complementary groups, where conflicting interests and ideas are only an effect of cultural confusion and do not reflect any real disharmony. It will be enough for each group to 'progress' along the dharma of its forefathers for the whole society to progress harmonically.

The rationalist agenda of Mahāvīr Prasād Dvivedī is thus enmeshed with an idealized view of the past; devotion to this history becomes an unquestioned source of identity, clearly defined but open-ended enough to be attractive and amenable to a wide variety of subjects. In her study of political mobilization among the urban poor between the wars, Nandini Gooptu has shown how the lower castes mobilized along two different trajectories. 'Clean' or 'touchable' lower castes, such as Kalwars (oil-pressers) and Yādavs (milkmen), who had been able to acquire wealth and education in the colonial economy, pursued the well-trodden path of 'sanskritization', claiming affiliation to one of the upper castes. At the same time they discovered that they could gain advantages and influence in administrative institutions by portraying themselves to the British as

[76] See Rāmnāth Lāl 'Suman', 'Vartamān hindī kavitā aur chāyāvād', in *Mādhurī*, VII, pt. 1, 1, August–September 1928.

[77] The tone is that of sarcastic tirades in Bengali against the westernized Babu, but here the reproach is directed primarily against rich traders, the raīses, who should ideally be entrepreneurs and civic reformers and lead the country on the path of economic self-reliance and social progress; *Vartamān khaṇḍ*, stanzas 106–22, pp. 120–3.

economically and socially 'backward castes' in need of special rights. For them Aryan ancestry and the nationalist historical saṃskāra became the perfect vehicles of self-enhancement and they identified enthusiastically with the chauvinistic and aggressive historical discourse that set Hindus against Muslims in perennial combat. They were in fact the protagonists of the popular assertion of 'kṣatriya', martial, Hindu prowess in the public sphere of religious processions, festivals, popular entertainment (Nauṭaṅkī), and wrestling activities (*akhāṛās*). Local bands such as 'the army of Mahāvīr', i.e. Hanuman, Rama's monkey attendant played a prominent role in the communal riots of the 1920s. Conversely, untouchables moving into the urban centres of north India in the late nineteenth and early twentieth centuries found that, while there were occupational opportunities for them in the public and private sectors, access to education, to better living facilities, and to more diversified employment was still largely barred, for social attitudes had hardly changed. In this context of greater expectations and thwarted economic and social improvement, they turned to devotional sects inspired by the medieval Bhakti *sants*, who had preached an egalitarian spirituality and the absurdity of caste distinctions, as a means of self-assertion.[78] Their reaction to the nationalist discourse of history was quite different, as we shall see. For them, to accept the Aryan past of caste order and unity as an ideal was impossible, for it would have validated their inferior status. Thus they contested it and brought forward a different construction of the past. Although the impact of this critique, and of the movement that advanced it, was ultimately local and transient, it nevertheless shows the dynamics of publicity at work in the field of historical imagination. In other words, the consensus that the nationalist discourse of history implied was easily achieved on the discursive level of literature, but in the public and political spheres it was open to interpretation and criticism by subjects who objected to the role and status bestowed upon them.

3.1.3. Critiques: History in the Hands of Other Subjects

The narrative framework for history articulated in *Bhārat-bhārtī* was a powerful one. As we have seen, Indian historians, borrowing categories and tools from European historiography, had been able to subvert its meaning and construct a powerful nationalist identity. The same categories and tools were also available to other subjects in the public sphere, and were used, for example, by untouchable ideologues and Ārya

[78] Gooptu, 'The Political Culture of the Urban Poor'.

Samāj-educated women. Both used the nationalist narrative for their own ends: the former by pushing the discourse of origins a step further and arguing that Śūdras were in fact the original inhabitants of India; the latter by deploying the notion that women were highly educated and active in Vedic times and thereby arguing for their empowerment in contemporary India. Rather than establishing a counter-historiography, both subjects worked within the existing framework and only disputed their own place in it. In doing so, Ādi Hindu ideologues and Ārya Samāj-educated women implictly demonstrated the impact and great elasticity of the nationalist narrative of Indian history and its categories.

Although there was in Hindi nothing like the widespread and comprehensive critique of Hindu religion and history mounted by Jotirao Phule in Marathi in the nineteenth century, the terms of the critique developed by the fledgling Ādi Hindu movement of the 1920s in the United Provinces are remarkably similar. This movement was the political expression of a Bhakti revival among urban untouchables, and as part of its critique of caste society it also presented a critique of the nationalist discourse of history. In the 1910s, their spiritual leaders were in fact associated with the Ārya Samāj, which was then preaching the inclusion of untouchables in the Aryan fold through 'purification' rites, śuddhi (cf. 3.3), in order to prevent their conversion to Christianity or Islam. By the 1920s, when they saw that caste distinctions were maintained even within the Ārya community, they parted ways. What the untouchable ideologues, Swami Achutanandand and Ram Charan, retained from the Ārya Samāj was the notion of the forcible imposition of religion—in the case of the Ārya Samāj, Islam—and projected it backwards to the Vedic age in order to argue that Aryan invaders had forcibly imposed Vedic Hinduism on the original inhabitants of India, the Ādi Hindus. Untouchables were thus the original, ancient inhabitants of India, the Ādi Hindus, and Bhakti was their religion, i.e. the original, egalitarian religion of India. Similarly, the notion of the golden Vedic age was transformed into a golden Ādi Hindu age. Ādi Hindu leaders claimed that there had been ancient Ādi Hindu kingdoms with capital cities, forts, and a thriving civilization; the Aryans then invaded the country and conquered them variously by brute force, repression, cunning, and treachery. Being righteous, good, and free of deceit, Ādi Hindus were no match for the sly Aryans, even though they were courageous.[79] Ādi-Hindu ideologues retained the basic categories

[79] Ibid., pp. 97–100. For an assessment of J. Phule's enterprise, see Omvedt, *Cultural Revolt in a Colonial Society*; and Rosalind O'Hanlon, *Caste, Conflict and Ideology: Mahatma Jotirao Phule and Low Caste Protest in Nineteenth-Century Western India*, Cambridge, Cambridge University Press, 1985.

and mainstream narrative of Indian history but turned it on its head, with the Aryans taking the part of the foreign oppressors and untouchables that of the indigenous nation striving for freedom.

This vision pushed the Ādi Hindu movement into what was to the nationalists a provocative loyalism to British rule. As the *de jure* untouchable member of the UP Legislative Council, J.P. Gavai, said at an Ādi Hindu Sammelan held at Allahabad in December 1927: 'We do not need svarājya, because it will not resolve our situation. The experience of ancient Hindu rule proves that with svarājya we shall be even more enslaved.' One of the motions passed at the meeting urged the government to amend passages in the classical social code (the *Manusmṛti*) that were offensive to Ādi Hindus.[80] The political expression and impact of the movement was sporadic and limited, and the relationship between the Congress and untouchables in UP towns remained ambiguous. As is well known, Gandhi refused to consider untouchables as separate from Hindu society, while his Harijan uplift programme had little impact on caste Hindus.

Similarly, women educated at Ārya Samāj institutions and acquainted with its view of Indian history used the historical categories and narrative of decline to critique prevailing attitudes towards women. They argued that Hindus had subverted the original Aryan ideal of gender equality: whereas Vedic women were respected and educated on a par with men, Manu's famous *śloka* which declared that a woman always belonged to someone else, be it father, husband, or son, had led to subsequent misinterpretations and, eventually, to the present disempowered status of women. After Manu, Buddha, Śaṅkara, and all of Hindu culture had considered women to be on a par with animals, not with humans. 'Leafing through the pages of history, one's heart burns, boils, bursts with the fire of revolution' wrote Suśīlādevī Vidyālaṃkār.[81] Present attitudes and practices could thus be castigated as deviations from the original model.

The Pre-Aryan and Aryan idyll, then, could actually become an effective argument for empowerment in the hands of certain subjects, like

[80] The editor of the Hindi journal which reported the proceedings, while visibly worried by the consequences of a separate movement of untouchables as subjects and not objects of reform, commented favourably on this last issue. Interestingly, however, he put the blame for the passages against women and untouchables not on Manu himself, but on his later Brahmin commentators; besides, he urged that the amendments be carried out by a group of 'reasonable, pious and just' scholars, and not by the government, thus pre-empting the possibility of anything of the kind happening; editorial in *Chāṁd*, VI, pt. 1, 4, February 1928, p. 430.

[81] S. Vidyālaṃkār, 'Ārya saṃskṛti aur striyāṁ', *Chāṁd*, XV, pt. 2, 5, September 1937, pp. 462–7.

women and some lower castes. What is noteworthy is how this paradigm of Indian history survived despite critiques from other subjects. Just as it could accommodate both faith in British rule (as in *Bhārat-bhārtī*) and the complete rejection of it, as in the case of the later historians, this paradigm could also accommodate partial shifts in points of view and meaning without destroying the general framework. In fact, this view of history became, especially in the Hindi area, the foundation for the whole discourse on language and a common historical saṃskāra for men of quite different political persuasions, from Mālavīya's Hindu Right politics to Gaṇeś Śaṅkar Vidyārthī's radical nationalism and even Narendra Dev's socialism (see 5.2 and 5.3). It also circulated widely, across the Ārya Samāj–*sanātanī* divide, as the nationalist history of India. The example of *upadeśaks* and *prachāraks* (preachers) like Svami Satyadeva Parivrājak and Devīdatt Dvivedī, who were originally affiliated to the Ārya Samāj but acted independently on a variety of nationalist issues, from Hindi–Devanagari to svadeśī, from temperance to cow protection, and from śuddhi to caste reform, shows how this historical view gained currency across sectarian affiliations and crossed the literacy divide.[82] In fact, the Aryan–Hindu myth was accepted even by writers like Nirālā and Vidyārthī who took a strong and active stand against communalism in the 1920s and 1930s, though they did not go to the Arya Samaj extreme of claiming that the Aryans had invented everything, from the aeroplane and rocket to the telephone. However, rather than dubbing this whole historical discourse as communal, an exercise that is both simplistic and unproductive, I have tried here to see how it was historically engrained in the colonial encounter, in the transformations of the public sphere, and in the formation of nationalist identity. I would argue that it took a self-conscious effort for individuals to alter or overcome this historical discourse, and generally speaking, alterations were mostly partial.

Fictional literature had several advantages over academic history in that it could, to use Kaviraj's words, 'utter what history could not spell'.[83]

[82] For an overview of Satyadev Parivrājak's long and chequered career, see Appendix; Satyadeva, Pandit Jīvānand Śarmā 'Kāvyatīrth', and Rājārām Śarmā were appointed by the Nāgarī Prachāriṇī Sabhā between 1912 and 1916 for Nagari propaganda: their speeches in villages, caste sabhas, temples, etc. ranged from education to religion to nationalism, and crossed the divide between urban and rural publics; for an example of the confluence of issues and the rhetoric style of a preacher, see Devīdatt Dvivedī, *Bhārat kī varṇavyavasthā aur svarājya*, published by the author with an introduction by Pandit Sundarlāl, Fatehpur, 1929. The role and cultural synthesis of these preachers deserves separate study.

[83] Historical narratives were a 'continuation of history, uttering what history could

It could, as we shall see in the following section, determine the meaning of events by choosing their order: thus defeats could be downplayed as temporary setbacks or even valued as instances of heroic resistance, while temporary victories could become the foretaste of future triumphs. Even more importantly, as *Bhārat-bhārtī* showed, fiction writers and poets could take advantage of the 'conceptual indeterminacy' concerning the subject, the 'we' of history, and the meaning of jāti. In this way the Indian nation could gradually emerge as the Hindu nation out of the Vedic past, include regional powers, heroes and communities, decide how to interpret Muslim 'exceptions', and single out figures or events for the contemporary 'Indian' audience to identify with.[84]

3.2. History as a Mirror

So far we have seen how a nationalist narrative of Indian history was created out of a selective use of western and Indian sources and categories, and how it identified ancient (Hindu) India as a powerful fulcrum of identity. While ancient Indian history provided an ideal of excellence, medieval history compelled historians and writers to grapple with a more painful and problematic past: a past that was, according to their narrative, full of decadence, defeat, division, and subjection. By another identification, that subjection mirrored the present under colonial rule. To find self-respect and dignity in that painful past meant to find self-respect and dignity in the present. But how could one find pride in defeat? And how could one learn from it? Once again, fictional narratives, rather than scholarly history, offered imaginative ways to answer these questions. They could 'work through' certain painful knots and still offer positive identifications by qualifying defeat, imagining resistance, introducing fictional characters and investing defeated heroes with a nationalist halo.[85] This is exactly what historical dramas and novels did, drawing on a range of *vīr-vīrāṅganās*, local or folk heroes or heroines, celebrated for centuries in folk epics, songs and drama, and also of more recent

---

not spell. . . . Novels had a deep internal relation to historical works. For they helped spell the same ideas only in a different manner or style: they tried to spell, as much as serious history sought to do, a self-respecting relation with the community's past'; S. Kaviraj, *The Unhappy Consciousness*, p. 111.

[84] 'Fiction writers used the fuzziness of this idea of community to give their audience a community which had not existed before, by conceiving gradually a community called the nation, or selecting the appellation of the nation for one of these communities'; ibid.

[85] Kaviraj, *The Unhappy Consciousness*.

lineage. At this particular juncture these figures acquired a nationalist resonance and became part of the master narrative of nationalist history.

History thus became available for a different kind of use. In the hands of popular writers, it became a reservoir of backdrops, scenarios, characters, and situations; a kind of general grid that underpinned romantic and heroic exploits. So much so that 'historical novel' came to mean in Hindi little more than costume drama, where black-and-white characters, heroism, fervid imagination, and diffuse nationalist pride took the place of local traditions or historical verisimilitude. As Kiśorīlāl Gosvāmī (1865–1932), one of the first practitioners of the genre, wrote in the preface to *Tārā vā kṣatrakulkamlinī* (1910): 'In my novels, I have given precedence to imagination over history; at places, the history has been altogether set aside for the benefit of the imagination. Therefore the reader should understand my intention clearly; it is a novel, not history.'[86] The predominance of the imagination possibly had something to do with the fact that historical novels were geared to impressionable juvenile audiences, which in our eyes enhances the importance of the historical saṃskāra these narratives disseminated.[87]

In this section I shall juxtapose some examples of nationalist vīr-vīrāṅganā fiction with a quite different enterprise—one of the very few novels which, directly dealing with an Indian vīrāṅganā against British rule, was the outcome of personal research and historical reflection: Vṛndāvanalāl Varmā's *Jhānsī kī rānī lakṣmībāī* (*Lakshmibai the Queen of Jhansi,* 1946). Although published after 1940, I have chosen it because it was the product of decades of personal quest and tried to work through some of the questions thrown up by the nationalist engagement with Indian history.

3.2.1. Narratives of Heroism

Narratives of male and female heroism in Hindi in this period stood at the crossroads of several genres and concerns.[88] *Vīr-rasa* (heroic) literature

[86] Translated and quoted by Kalsi, 'Realism in the Hindi Novel', p. 118n.

[87] In reviewing Rāmchandra Miśra's *Prempathik* (1926), Premchand remarked: 'This is a historical novel. It shows the period of Maratha–Muslim conflict, which was a wonderful if brief period of Indian renaissance (*bhārtīy punarutthān*). Our literary taste changes together with our age. Historical novels are a favourite in adolescence (*kaiśor*), when our imagination soars to the sky, and common, mundane things appear dull, lifeless and devoid of wonder. We hope that our youth will read with pleasure this tale of heroism (*vīr ras kī kathā*) and will dream to become another 'Mādhav' [the hero of the novel]. Quoted in G. Rāy, *Hindī upanyās-koś*, vol. 2, p. 126.

[88] See Kathryn Hansen, 'The Vīrāṅganā in North Indian History. Myth and Popular

was considered, in the reformist view, one of the necessary features of a national literature. Narratives of heroes and heroines were seen as the most appropriate means of carrying the message of valour, virility, and strength. That Hindi literature in the centuries of 'Muslim rule' had been a literature largely of śṛṅgāra (erotic love) was taken as both a cause and a consequence of political subjection: too effeminate to think of war, rulers had turned to worldly and decadent pleasures. The few examples of vīr-rasa were interpreted as marks of nationalist awareness, and in the search for Hindi manuscripts, such texts were greeted with enthusiasm and taken as proof that a literary tradition of vīr-rasa poetry had in fact existed. Thus one Bhāgīrāthprasād Dīkṣit traced the tradition of heroic poetry in Indian literature from the Vedic period onwards; it was the prominence of vīr-rasa during that time that had resulted in the Aryans colonizing America, Java, Bali, Egypt, Bukhara, and even Mexico; but as soon as śṛṅgāra set in, decadence followed, as the degeneration from Sanskrit to Prakrit and Apabhraṃśa proved. The eighteenth and nineteenth centuries were a golden era after centuries of darkness, especially in Maharastra with Śivājī and his guru, Samartha Guru Rāmdās: 'They organized society according to Hindu ideals, which filled the whole society with moral strength.' In north India 'the great poet Bhūṣaṇ toured the whole of India with Śivājī as a model and brought tremendous awakening to Hindu society . . . Its direct consequence was that the Yavana empire broke into pieces'.[89]

The urge to produce heroic literature remained (cf. 2.2). Biographies of vīr-vīrāṅganās made up a large proportion of literature and journals for children; as long as all anti-British traces were concealed, these patriotic books apparently entered school libraries with relative ease, circumventing colonial censorship on nationalist literature.[90] In the 1910s and 1920s the popular form of drama called Nauṭaṅkī began including more heroic queens and kings in its plots, although not all with overt nationalist overtones.[91]

Heroic narratives naturally centred around the exploits of warriors

---

Culture', *Economic and Political Weekly*, XXIII, 18, 30, April 1988, Women's Studies, pp. 25–33.

[89] See B. Dīkṣit, 'Vīr-śatābdi', in *Mādhurī*, VIII, pt. 2, 3, April 1930, pp. 354–8.

[90] See e.g. *Aitihāsik kahāniyāṁ* (historical stories) by Īśvarīprasād Śarmā. Viyogī Hari's *Vīr satsaī* (1927), a collection of poems of heroic content in Braj, was awarded the Maṅgalāprasād prize in 1928. Another popular collection of *vīr-rasa* poetry for children was Lala Bhagvān Dīn's *Vīr pañcharatna*, Calcutta, Burman Press, 1918.

[91] Hansen, *Grounds for Play*, pp. 108 ff.

and kings. Ballads and tales about them had in the past focussed on rivalry, succession, dispossession, and claims over land, loyalty, and above all, honour.[92] Within the framework of nationalist history, such tales of heroism became suffused with the pathos of Hindu resistance. The paucity of historical sources being a bonus rather than a limitation, historical narratives provided a kind of stage where the painful issues in medieval history could be played out. They thematized heroism and defeat (e.g. Maharana Pratāp), resistance and subjection, good rule versus narrow self-interest (Durgāvatī), self-pride and the loss of honour (*apmān*), communal harmony and treason (Lakṣmībāī), foreign rule and national resurgence (Śivājī); these were the values and questions on the ground, inscribed in the categories of 'we' Hindus and in the long perspective of a national history.

Whereas Maharana Pratāp, Raja Chattrasāl, Śivājī, and Amar Singh Raṭhaur represented evident ideals of masculinity, heroines like Ahalyābāī, Durgāvatī, and Lakṣmībāī transcended gender. They became the perfect nationalist icons for the present, in that they synthesized selfless activism, heroism, wisdom, good rule, freedom, Sarasvatī, and Mother India. Unlike the political ideal of Rāmrājya, the perfect rule of Lord Rām, that of the vīrāṅganā was one of action, mobilizing heroism and self-sacrifice in the cause of a future svarājya. In so far as the warrior queens had fought not for themselves or from lust for power but to defend their kingdoms, and that too on behalf of their sons, they were also sure to be universally acceptable, for they had not overstepped the limits of accepted gender behaviour, of maryādā.[93] *Durgāvatī*, a historical play written by Badrīnāth Bhaṭṭ in 1925 on the Gond queen who defeated Akbar's troops twice before being herself defeated in 1564, is typical of the nationalist shift in the genre. Here the theme of the vīrāṅganā, popular in sāṁgīt and Nauṭaṅkī, is used for a 'serious' play on vīr-rasa intended for reading and not for the stage.[94] It contains the characteristic elements

[92] See for example the story of Amar Singh Raṭhaur, where the conflict between the Rajput underlord and the Mughal emperor is not really the point of the drama, which is rather about Rajput honour and loyalty; or Rani Bīrmati's story, where the heroic self-defence of the Rani against an unspecified Kotwal takes place against the background of succession disputes among Bagheli Rajputs; Lala Nānakchand, *Amar siṃh raṭhaur*, Moradabad, 1910; and Śrīkṛṣṇa Khatrī, *Sāṁgīt bīrmatī*, Kanpur, 1921. Other historical Nauṭaṅkīs by Śrīkṛṣṇa Khatrī related conversely to nationalist heroes such as Chattrapati Śivājī, Maharani Padminī, Rani Durgāvatī; see below.

[93] I owe this point to Sudipta Kaviraj.

[94] Published by Ganga Pustak Mala, Lucknow, it was included in the syllabus for

of the genre: the good, perhaps too merciful, ruler, betrayal, and heroic self-defence before certain defeat. All the categories of the nationalist view of medieval India are present, including Hindu resistance to Muslim expansionism, defeat as a result of betrayal and division, and Rajputs selling out to the Mughals for positions within the empire. Nothing is made of Durgāvatī being a Gond, i.e. 'tribal', queen: she is a 'Hindu' queen to all effect.

Durgāvatī, then, an ideal Hindu ruler and brave warrior, bears the brunt of Akbar's expansionist policy. Though willing to reach a peaceful compromise, she is compelled to defend her reign against the much too powerful Mughal. Her able minister has been made captive in Agra and one of her own courtiers, whom she had treated too mercifully, has betrayed her. Interestingly, Akbar is in the delicate position of being both the just ruler and the main villain; Bhaṭṭ solves the paradox by transferring most of the villainy onto Akbar's minister Asafkhān and by presenting Akbar as a just but ill-advised ruler. While Durgāvatī's indomitable resistance is celebrated with clear nationalist overtones, figures such as Pṛthvīrāj of Bikaner, Bīrbal, Ṭodarmal, and Mānsiṃh give Bhaṭṭ the chance to expound on the theme of Rajputs who sacrificed loyalty to their Hindu 'brothers' for the sake of a foreign ruler (cf. 3.1.1).

The earliest historical novels in Hindi had been translations, mostly from Bengali, where the genre was already flourishing in the 1860s. Bankimchandra's *Durgeśnandinī* (1865) was translated, serialized, and published first in 1882; R.C. Dutt's *Baṅgvijetā* (1874) was serialized in 1879 and published in 1886; his *Mahārāṣṭra jīvan prabhāt* (1878) was first translated around 1889.[95] They aroused great interest among the Hindi literati, especially in the growing publishing centre of Benares. Translations, adaptations, and borrowings from Bengali novels became a practice, so much so that eighteenth-century Bengal, along with earlier Rajputana, became one of the usual backdrops to heroic narratives, as in Kiśorīlāl Gosvāmī's *Hṛdayhārinī* and its sequel *Lavaṅglatā* (1904; comp. 1890–).[96] The astounding success of Devkīnandan Khatrī's romance *Chandrakāntā* (1891), which combined the motifs of Rajput heroism with elements and narrative patterns from the Persian and Urdu

---

Intermediate exams in UP and Punjab. It was reprinted in 1929 and 1933; to my knowledge, it is not now considered a significant work.

[95] Rāy, *Hindī upanyās koś*, vol. 1, pp. 306 ff. For a discussion of these novels, see Chandra, *The Oppressive Present*.

[96] McGregor, *Indian Literature in the Nineteenth and Early Twentieth Centuries*, p. 102.

romance tradition of the *dāstān*, drove historical novelists, geared as they were towards entertainment, to adopt its framework and several of its features.[97] Historical novels turned into romances, with a thin historical backdrop and black-and-white characterizations, and with the Hindu nationalist message as a possible sub-motif. This trend, which continued well into the twentieth century and had illustrious adepts, was exemplified by the historical romances of Kiśorīlāl Gosvāmī.[98] In fact, translations of G.W. Reynolds's *Mysteries of the Court of London* (1850–6) turned these novels into even more sensational dramas, as was the case of Rāmkṛṣṇā Śukla's *Mugal darbār rahasya* (*Mysteries of the Court of Lucknow,* Chand Karyalay, 1928), and Sudarśanlāl Trivedī's *Pyāsī talvār* (*The Thirsty Sword,* 1936).[99] Such romances remained very much the only available kind of historical narrative well into the 1920s and 1930s, even though social novels now occupied centre stage. Although they left almost no trace in literary histories, their popularity testifies to the role such narratives had in propagating a brand of nationalist history that celebrated the inherent virtues of the Hindu community with heroic stories of Rajput kings and queens, and easily adopted the essentialist categories of nationalist discourse. As Ṛṣabhcharaṇ Jain's *Gadar* (*Mutiny*, 1930), one of the very few novels dealing directly with the Revolt of 1857 (by 1930 rechristened 'the first War of Indian Independence') shows, historical novels could effectively combine a strong nationalist message with well-cut, engrossing melodramatic narratives.

When he published *Gadar* in 1930, Ṛṣabhcharaṇ Jain (1912–?) was already well known as a prolific short story writer of the young generation and the author of commercial 'social novels' such as *Bhāī* (1923),

[97] For the tradition of Persian and Urdu dāstān, see Pritchett, *Marvelous Encounters*.

[98] Author of perhaps the first short story in Hindi, 'Indumatī' (*Sarasvatī*, 1900), Gosvāmī was the prolific writer of several historical romances. Among the other practitioners of the genre at the turn of the century were Jayrāmdās Gupta (*Kiśorī vā vīr-bālā*, 1907; *Kaśmīr patan*, 1907; *Vīrāṅganā vā ādarś lalnā*, 1909, etc.), Kārtikprasād Khatrī, Gaṅgāprasād Gupta, and others. The historian Munshi Devīprasād, Brajnandan Sahāy, Bāldev Prasād Miśra, and Thakur Bālbhadra Siṃh were less sensational writers. Interestingly, even literati like Rāmnareś Tripāṭhī and the Miśra-brothers tried their hand at this genre (with *Padmāvatī vā vīrbālā*, 1891; and *Vīrmaṇi*, 1917). See Rāy, *Hindī upanyās koś*, vol. 1, pp. 136 ff; also McGregor, *Indian Literature,* and Kalsi, 'Realism in the Hindi Novel'.

[99] Other historical novels from the post-1920 period include Govindvallabh Pant's *Sūryāst* (1922), Rāmchandra Miśra's *Prempathik* (1926), Bhagavatīcharaṇ Varmā's *Patan* (1927), Jamunādās Mehrā's *Baṅgāl kī bulbul* (1928), Rāmpyāre Tripāṭhī's *Dillī kī śahzādī* (1933); see Rāy, *Hindī upanyās koś,* vol. 2, pp. 123 ff.

Māsṭar sāhab, and *Dillī kā vyābhichār* (*Debauchery in Delhi*, both 1929). In this ostensibly 'original revolutionary novel' (*maulik krāntikārī upanyās*), Jain set out to 'wash the stain' from Azimullāh and other Indians involved in killing English women and children in Kanpur during the events of June 1857. This counter-view of that infamous event in colonial history is framed as a 'true story' told by an old and sick Muslim woman of the narrator's village who turns out to be none other than Azimullāh's mother! Banned on publication, the novel was reprinted several times after Independence.[100]

The narration is articulated in a few strong scenes with plenty of dramatic dialogues. It opens in Bithur, the residence of the dispossessed Maratha Peshwa ruler, where some English sahibs and memsahibs have been invited for a tea party by the Peshwa, Nana Sahib. When news of the mutiny reaches them, the English guests are apprehensive, while the Nana is only disappointed that his party cannot take place. A confrontation ensues between the female guests and Nana's brother, the valiant Rāmchandrarāo, when he stops them from taking forced labour (*begār*) from the villagers and rebukes them. The memsahibs complain to the Nana, who is compelled to punish good Rāmchandrarāo despite Azimullāh's intercession. The first scene thus establishes Azimullāh's righteousness and offers the opportunity for an argument about lawfulness, justice and the moral bankruptcy of the British in India. The second chapter introduces some historical background: while the Nana is presented as the typical flamboyant, good-for-nothing, petty ruler, Azimullāh is the poor but industrious courtier, self-educated and ambitious. On the way back from advocating the cause of the Nana's pension in England, he had stopped in Crimea to see the war and realized that England's might was dependent on Indian resources: 'भारतवर्ष से छीनी हुई रोटी के बल पर ही उन्होंने योरोप-भर में अपना आतंक जमा रखा था' (They held the whole of Europe in fear on the strength of the wealth [lit. the bread] snatched from India). Back in India he started organizing the revolt together with some other Indian 'revolutionaries':

> Work started swiftly. In every city committees were established and propaganda started in secret. Thousands of young men jumped into the ocean of revolution filled with extreme passion. In every cantonment members of such committees infiltrated the army disguised as soldiers and the country made ready to overthrow English rule.[101]

[100] Ṛṣabhcharaṇ Jain, *Gadar*, Delhi, Hindi Pustak Karyalay, 1930; a copy is available in the India Office Library collections in the British Library in London.

[101] Ibid., pp. 45, 47–8.

The vocabulary of nationalist propaganda permeates historical explanation and Azimullāh's actions. In fact, when a 'revolutionary' from Meerut asks Azimullāh why Kanpur did not rise at the same time, the reply is that he restrained soldiers on purpose to avoid a carnage of English civilians and declares: 'Don't worry, brother. Hindostan will definitely be free. These demons will quickly vanish from the land of Bhārat' (p. 60). Why then did Azimullāh, so far innocent and in fact well-intentioned, subsequently order the killing of English women and children captive in the Bibighar in Kanpur? The explanation is provided by the romantic sub-plot, an interreligious and patriotic romance between Azimullāh and Mainā, the Nana's daughter. Mainā is also an archetypal nationalist, who longs for national independence and despises the 'half-naked' English 'sluts' who stroll around as if they were the masters in India. She is Azimullāh's muse, his '*path-pradarśak*' (guide); she loves him, too, because he is a true patriot but will marry him only *after* svarājya is achieved; meanwhile, she agrees to being harassed by an Englishman in order to provoke her loyalist father to anger and revolt. But when Mainā finally refuses to be Azimullāh's wife 'in this life', he becomes the typical *dīvānā* (mad for love), and it is in this deranged state that he takes revenge on the English captives. Thereafter he runs back to Bithur only to find that Mainā has committed satī; there he too jumps on the pyre, after achieving the feat of cutting off his head with his own sword.

The military success of the uprising in Kanpur is shortlived, but long enough to show the possibility of success. Jain's novel dwells little on the description of events: its concern is with the symbolic meaning of this history. Thus a fanciful scene shows General Wheeler, held captive by the Nana, deliver a chivalrous speech in which he acknowledges the Nana's desire to take revenge for the insult on his daughter; all Indians present, Azimullāh included, are moved to tears; the meta-message of this speech is that Jain and Indian nationalists in general respect the military code of honour and have no personal enmity towards the British. The novel's epilogue is a sad elegy:

> What a pity. Again and again the mad worshippers of freedom [*āzādī ke dīvāne*] had to retreat bearing heavy losses; their warm, precious blood could not water the dry plant of independence! That seventeenth of July even the names of thousands of patriots were cancelled, while that of a bloodthirsty and unjust general became immortal in English history. (p. 174)

Although history cannot be changed, the message of the novel is that its meaning can. To that aim, Ṛṣabhcharaṇ Jain *used* historical material imaginatively to contest the message of British historiography and present a nationalist one in the guise of an engrossing costume drama. Although Vṛndāvanlāl Varmā's first novels, such as *Gaṛh kuṇḍār* (1927) and *Virāṭā kī padminī* (1929), were very much in this tradition, his rendition of the equally painful defeat of Rani Lakṣmībāi in the 1857 uprising stemmed from a rather different enterprise.

3.2.2. Vṛndāvanlāl Varmā's Vīrāṅganā

Vṛndāvanlāl Varmā (1889–1973), the most famous and accomplished historical novelist in Hindi of the post-1920 period, started his career with a historical romance on Bundela history, *Gaṛh kuṇḍār*. Indeed, he kept returning to this genre even after he turned to researched historical biographies.[102] It is against this backdrop of historical romances that his *Jhansī kī rānī lakṣmībāī* (1946) and the research behind it acquire exceptional interest.[103] Since it is well documented, it will be interesting to

[102] For details on his life and works, see Appendix.

[103] The plot in a nutshell: the novel opens with an historical overview of the ruling house of Jhansi and its treaties with the British and focuses then on the present ruler, Gaṅgādharrāo, a lover and patron of the arts with little time or patience to rule, keen to keep friendly relations with the British resident. In Bithur, meanwhile, Manu (Lakṣmībāī after the wedding), the thirteen-year-old daughter of Moropant, adviser to the exiled Bajirao Peshwa, grows up with Bajirao's adopted sons, Nana and Rao, and learns military skills as well as reading and writing. She is the only one to remember and believe in the heroic stories of the *Mahābhārata* and the nationalist ideals of Śivājī; she hates the inanity of Indian rulers in their dealings with the British, and is much too outspoken for a girl of her age. Once married to Gaṅgādharrāo, she keeps *pardā* but urges her servants (turned into friends, *sahelīs*) and the women of Jhansi to train in military skills. The women, after some initial hesitation, accept enthusiastically. After the early death of her only son, Gaṅgādharrāo dies, too, in 1853, after having hastily adopted a *dattak* son, who has to be recognized by the Lieutenant-General. Meanwhile, the Company assumes power in Jhansi, while the Rani quietly trains and works at organizing a network with the rulers and people of Avadh, Delhi, and other princely states to fight for svarājya, with the help of Tantya Tope and the Peshwa court. On 4 June 1857, soldiers in Jhansi revolt, and though the Rani herself takes no part in the revolt, she is hailed as queen once the soldiers eliminate all the British officers. When the soldiers leave for Delhi, the Rani is left in charge of the administration and of organizing a new, popular army. Her emphasis on arms, training, and cannons pays off when she has to defend Jhansi from an old claimant to the throne and from an attack from Orchha. They are, however, just small tests before Jhansi is surrounded and attacked by General Rose in 1858. After Tantya Tope's abortive rescue attempt from Kalpi and heroic resistance on the part of the whole population,

delve first into the story of Varmā's engagement with history. Born into a Kayastha family in which one ancestor had died fighting for the Rani, the son of a registrar kanungo, Vṛndāvanlāl Varmā went through the curriculum typical of boys from literate Kayastha families. While at home, he grew up hearing his great-grandmother's tales of the brave, just, and beloved Rani: 'That tradition [of those tales], though wondrous, was also unclear; its outlines were vague and based more on devotion than on truth. Later the study of history and science decreased its value.'[104] Thus, the encounter with 'objective' history at school awakened doubts about those stories, but also strong and angry reactions:

In the 5th and 6th forms we were given E. Marsden's *History of India* in English to study. The book was expensive for boys like me, but I had to buy it anyway. There I read that the Indian people always lost against invaders from cold countries because they belong to a hot country. Now, however, they will never be defeated again because the British belong to a cold country; after they stay here they go back to their cold country, and here they spend the hot season in the hills. When they go back to England, a fresh batch of young Englishmen comes in their place: thus Indians will never be defeated again by anyone. This meant that our country would remain subjected to the British until the end of time. The heroic fight and death of Lakṣmībāi were all worthless. I felt all aflame inside and tore the page out from the book. When I got home my uncle [who paid for his education] found out about the torn book and I got a thrashing. How could even an affectionate man like my uncle bear such a waste of money? He scolded me: 'What is the use of tearing a page from a book where it is written how the British cheated us all? That book must have been printed in thousands of copies . . .' That day my interest in history was awakened. I decided that I would study and research a lot and finally write something to expose those false books. From that day I also started doing more physical exercise—one never knows, if one day I somehow came face to face with an Englishman I wouldn't spare him a sound beating.[105]

Later, after reading Max Müller's *What can India teach us?*, young

---

the Rani has to flee when British troops finally break into the city (thanks to a traitor) and attack the fort. In Kalpi, the Rani tries to reorganize the army of the Nana, and after suffering a defeat in Kalpi, they manage to conquer Gwalior. The hitherto calm Rani is tormented at the prospect of not attaining svarājya in her lifetime until a Baba reminds her that every fight is a step towards the goal. In the ensuing battle against Rose she is killed with the remains of her valorous guard, and her body is cremated before the British can get hold of it.

[104] Author's preface to *Jhānsī kī rānī*, Jhansi, Mayur Prakasan, 1987, p. 1.

[105] Vṛndāvanlāl Varmā, *Apnī kahānī*, Delhi, Prabhat Prakasan, 1993, pp. 14–15.

Vṛndāvanlāl decided to write an Indian history of India himself but could not go beyond the first twenty pages. History could not be argued so easily, he discovered. Thereafter he decided to write historical novels along the lines of Walter Scott's *Ivanhoe* and *The Talisman.* But again, when he started a novel set in Rajputana he realized that he did not know the geography of the place; and when he tried to write one on Rani Lakṣmībāī he realized that he lacked the historical material. His only written source was the Marathi account by D.B. Pārasnīs.[106] It was more accurate than the stories of his childhood but also sided with the British view of 1857 as a Mutiny, and of the Rani as a queen who had fought only to defend her own reign.[107]

Torn between the truth of his grandmother's stories and the truth of historical texts, Varmā could not decide which one was 'true' until, he claims, as a student at the college boarding house in Agra he had a dream in which he was fighting a war for svarājya on the hockey ground on behalf of the Rani! Despite this supra-rational encouragement, Varmā's academic education would not allow him to write only on the basis of that dream, and the whole matter remained in the background until 1932 when he, now a 43-year-old vakil, found at the law court in Jhansi a bundle of 40–50 letters from 1858, addressed by an English soldier to the Lieutenant-Governor: they did not reveal much apart from the fact that the Rani had not fought only for self-defence or because she was compelled by circumstances to do so.

Yet this second revelation in the form of letters giving an eye-witness account led Varmā, already the author of two novels, into a quest that was unprecedented among Hindi writers of historical novels: he was not only going to *use* historical sources in his narrative, he was going to *search* for them. In the process he involved more and more of the inhabitants of Jhansi, living witnesses as well as their descendants, in an attempt to create a sort of community history of the Rani's fight in 1857–8.[108] More documents and accounts confirmed his grandmother's

[106] Reprinted in Hindi as Pārasnīs, *Jhānsī kī rānī lakṣmībāī*, Allahabad, Sahitya Bhavan, 1964; I have unfortunately been unable to see this book.

[107] See author's preface to *Jhānsī kī rānī*, p. 1.

[108] He discovered that a scribe at the Court, a descendant of the Rani's father-in-law, Raghunāthrāo, possessed the diary of Raghunāthrāo's natural son and the chief villain, Alī Bahādur (Pīr Alī) where he disclosed his treacherous role and relationship with Pīr Alī. Once he switched sides to the British, Alī Bahādur had given them some *bayāns* to prove his loyalty; Varmā got hold of them, too. He then found the first of

stories. At this point Varmā was able to refute the 'truth' of colonialist history and find his own way of telling the Indian history of India. A letter from the Rani to a neighbouring Raja asking help for svarājya confirmed Varmā's belief about the core question of his quest, i.e. whether the Rani had fought for her own sake or for the sake of the country. Varmā could thus embed Lakṣmībāī—an icon of the nationalist struggle—into a history of the people of Jhansi and a documented study of the broad historical circumstances.

The novel opens, in fact, with a historical preface introducing the administrative changes during William Bentinck's tenure as Governor-General, when the erstwhile Maratha ruler of Jhansi received the title of Raja. The princely states, their relationship to the East India Company, Dalhousie's paramountcy policy and the Company *bandobast* are discussed critically and with great accuracy. In the princely state of Gwalior at the time of Raghunāthrāo, the Rani's future father-in-law:

> the rule was bad, the administration was bad, but village panchayats worked; the revenue was never fully collected; every villager could be readily defended by his panchayat for its power had not been taken over by the law courts yet. [. . .] Power had not been centralized. People had plenty of opportunities to rely on their own sagacity and valour. Although society was not balanced enough and inequality was evident, economic networks were strong. Wealth would collect in one place and then be shared out again. Each patron supported hundreds of dependents (*āśrit*) closely attached to him; patronage and its beneficiaries were parties in a dynamic relationship.[109]

At the same time, Indian rulers are presented as short-sighted and naive. Raghunāthrāo hopes to keep his kingdom and the favour of the Company by entertaining the local British officers, but they are shown as

---

his living witnesses, a Munshi Jurāb Alī who died around 1936 at the age of 115; he had been a *thanedar* in the service of the British in 1857, and his stories, though he had belonged to the other side, supported those of Varmā's great-grandmother! After finding this living witness, Varmā started to 'bother' all the old men and women of Jhansi, 'but from the enthusiasm and devotion they expressed in telling their stories about the Rani I believe that they did not feel pestered'; ibid., p. 3. He wanted to know about the participation of the people of Jhansi in the resistance, and found out about the various officers, cannoneers, and castes in the Rani's popular army, especially about her legendary women's cavalry. Varmā found further evidence for the minor characters, including Motībāī the actress, while a document of the period proved that the Hindi written a century before was practically identical to present-day Hindi; ibid., pp. 3–4.

[109] Ibid., p. 5.

cunning and far-sighted. A discussion amongst them at the Club seems like a prophecy:

> We need more time. Now we need to get rid of dacoits and riots and increase trade and agriculture. The people will be grateful to us. We shall give petty jobs to the Indians who will learn English and teach them to revere the British. They, in turn, will spread this reverence among the people; the people will always be happy and will not tire of begging from us. Our lads will make sure they will always be in terror of us! That terror will be our only weapon.[110]

Crucial to Varmā's historical vision was the role of human will and intelligence. It was thus important to show not the great Lakṣmībāī, but the gradual transformation of young Manu into Lakṣmībāī. Although not ignoring the theory of predetermination (see Manu's extraordinary *janmapatrī* on p. 26 of the novel), Varmā placed much greater emphasis on the transformation of the spirited, fearless girl into a judicious, restrained, and patient strategist and ruler. The message was thus: Indians were not born slaves or heroes; even a girl can become a heroine by force of will and the intelligent use of her abilities. It is remarkable for a novel about 1857 that the actual description of the fighting, so far the best-documented historically and the most arousing, takes up only the last third of the book. The first two-thirds are devoted to preparations, of Lakṣmībāī for her historical role, of the people of Jhansi to become a popular army, and of the women of Jhansi to become equal citizens of an empowered prajā. In the process, the relationship between ruler and ruled is redefined in participatory and democratic terms.

In a gradual process of self-improvement and self-empowerment Lakṣmībāī changes from a wilful girl (who behaves like a boy) into a dutiful but energetic wife. She first creates a stir by speaking out at her wedding, urging the officiating pandit to tie the knot properly (p. 65). Afterwards, when confined in pardā, she turns the women at court into able fighters. With her husband's death, she changes into a warrior, wearing military attire (p. 199), and a strategist, and prepares her army and weapons while the East India Company rules. After the 1857 uprising she takes her place as a just ruler, a leader of the struggle for svarājya, and finally as a vīrāṅganā, ready to sacrifice her life for the nationalist cause. It is only in these last stages that the Rani acquires a kind of superhuman aura: both the older Nana and Tantya Tope touch her feet as she appears to them in an apotheosis as Bhāratmātā, a nurturing mother to

[110] Ibid., p. 121.

her people, the goddess of independence, and Durga fighting on her vehicle (p. 220).

Varmā's historical imagination is at work in the characterization of the Rani in two specific respects. Firstly, although formally respectful of tradition she is nonetheless more preoccupied with the spirit than the letter of it. Thus she strictly observes the rituals and her dharma (as a wife and then as a widow), but at the same time she introduces changes and widens the scope of *strī*-dharma (cf. 4.4).[111] The women of Jhansi, exemplified by the *bakhśin* (the treasurer's wife), by Jhalkārī the weaver and by the women who gather around the Rani at the two *sindūrotsavs* described in the novel (pp. 92–5 and 324), are at first shocked by the masculine queen, but soon adhere with enthusiasm to her project of total militarization and form a valorous women's army. Much to the surprise of General Rose (p. 343), the Jhansi corps is formed predominantly of Bundelkhandi women from all castes. The freedom and empowerment of women of all castes, one of the elements emphasized by the author (echoing the Rani) as a necessary requisite of svarājya, is represented most clearly by Jhalkārī, the weaver, now an officer and a physical replica of the Rani: 'Had Lakṣmībāī been successful in her struggle for svarājya, Indian women would not be in the pitiful condition many are now in,' comments the author (p. 173). Second, Varmā shows the Rani pushing for a different balance between ruler and subjects. The contrast with her husband, Gaṅgādharrāo, is sharp: while he is a typical extravagant raīs, a lover of theatre, good-hearted but essentially selfish and capricious, she is thrifty, practical, and mindful only of the good of her people (*prajā-hit-chintak*).[112] When she comes to rule on behalf of their adopted son, her rule is reasonable and reformist and seeks consensus. This and the creation of a people's army imply a message of equality and of participation by the common people, the *sarvasādhāraṇ*, one of the tenets of Gandhian nationalism (cf. 5.1 and 5.2). She reminds Tantya Tope several times to look for a base among the people:

> The people are the true force. I believe they are invincible. The Chatrapati [Śivājī] challenged such a huge empire only with the support of the people, not

[111] Ibid., p. 475. The sting is here directed at the United Provinces, the new centre of Hindi culture and the nationalist movement, but very conservative about women's freedom; see Chapter 4 here.

[112] In the novel, Gaṅgādharrāo's passionate involvement with the theatre is not only a nice historical touch, but also illuminates their basic difference, when Lakṣmībāi contrasts his *nāyikā-bhed* with Bhūṣaṇ's heroic poetry; *Jhānsī kī ranī*, pp. 72 ff.

of the kings. . . . The people are our true means. Rajas and Nawabs are worthy for one, maybe two generations; the people's worth, instead, does not wear off generation after generation.[113]

This attitude is reflected also in her respect for all women and for lower castes. When her General Gauskhān voices a dismissive remark about the actress-turned-head-of-intelligence Motībāī, the Rani reflects scornfully: 'Is that prostitute's daughter less self-sacrificing than any respectable woman?! Oh God, social distinctions (*ūṁch-nīch*) even in sacrifice!' To another commander she says: 'How good it would be to have no caste distinctions in our country!' 'It is the God who made them', he answers, and the ensuing silence expresses all the queen's doubts.[114] In his imaginative representation of the Rani as the ideal ruler, then, Varmā expresses not only how things could have been otherwise, but also how he believes modern India should be.

The transformation within Lakṣmībāī is echoed in the people surrounding her: in her maids, in the women of Jhansi at large, and finally in her soldiers and the men of Jhansi, who all turn into an army of heroes. The servants-turned-friends of the Rani are her most immediate replicas: from daughters of an impoverished family to slaves of the queen, they become her sahelīs, her companions, trained in the art of war, and finally shine as vīrāṅgānās, to the extent that each of them at the moment of her death in combat is mistaken for the Rani herself. In his characterization, Varmā makes full use of the imagination to invest even minor characters and ordinary people with a historical vision and to endow their actions with nationalist purposefulness. Their ordinary heroism and historical wisdom redress the balance of defeat. Similarly, prophecies and dreams can frame contingent defeat in the 'long duration' of national resurgence. After a particularly bad day during the siege of Jhansi, the Rani has a dream: 'A fair maiden with beautiful features, large black eyes and a red sari, covered with jewellery, is standing on the ramparts of the fort stopping the fiery cannonballs of the British with her tender hands. "Look, Lakṣmībāī, my hands have turned black from stopping the balls. Do not worry. The goddess of svarājya is immortal" ' (p. 364). Hearing of her dream, the battered townsfolk take heart again. After her last defeat outside Gwalior, Lakṣmībāī can find no rest until a sadhu, Baba Gaṅgādās, prophesizes India's future independence to her: only in this way can she view her own fate and struggle as part of a gradual historical

113 Ibid., pp. 131–2.
114 Ibid., pp. 341, 306.

process whose fulfilment belongs to the future.[115] Thus it is actually the British who are blindly self-confident day-dreamers:

The British saw the smooth and even surface but did not know of the cauldron boiling underneath. They had grabbed India as in a dream, and thought they would keep it in a dream, and the dream would last forever. They never knew or realized that Hindustan may be conquered easily but cannot remain in their grasp for very long. Foreign rulers never took long to conquer this country; they sat on the throne with great pomp . . . but as far as ruling was concerned, it always remained confined to the cantonments. The truth is that it is impossible to rule over an unhappy people, here as everywhere (pp. 205–6).

In a word, the novel reads like a chapter of the Indian history of India, the one Varmā himself wanted to write. It is pervaded by the same feelings the young Varmā had when he reacted to Marsden's textbook, to which it ideally replies. While the assessment of pre-British princely India is balanced and detailed, the indictment of British rule is as well substantiated as it is total. The annexation policy of the East India Company, its tyrannical and suave bandobast, the destruction of panchayats, the enslavement through education, the racial contempt, the innumerable humiliations suffered by Indian subjects, all are taken into account. When the Company takes over the rule of Jhansi in 1854, they dismiss the Raja's small army and dismantle the administration:

Whereas until then hundreds and thousands of literate people could earn a living even on a small salary, now only a few high officers and small jagirdars were employed by the Company at higher salaries. The higher posts were all filled by a handful of Englishmen at exorbitant wages. . . . The entire court was dismissed—poets, artists, *dhrūpad* singers, sitar players, dancers, craftsmen, farewell to all. In its place came the Club, the Dak Bungalow and the *salām* with compulsory prostration for all Indians, high and low.[116]

The burning of Gaṅgādharrāo's library by British troops looting Jhansi in March 1858 is a symbolic climax as it finally explodes the myth of the white man's burden: 'Whatever happened, it inscribed in history with indelible letters the bestiality of those barbarians.' The libraries in Alexandria and Rajagriha were destroyed in a barbaric age, 'but in this age of science and civility . . .'[117] The actual reasons for the Rani's defeat

[115] See also the Rani's prophecies on pp. 356, 373, etc., and Rose's prophecy on p. 403.

[116] Ibid., p. 156.

[117] For the first and last time, the Rani weeps: war is meaningful only to defend one's life and dharma, one's culture and art, she had told her people; now the struggle

belong to history, and there is no tampering with them; but the novelist can write against their grain a narrative of collective heroism, a future envisaged in prophecies and a personal thread of 'ifs', which hint that another history could have happened and could have been told. Colonial subjection, far from being part of a divine plan or of a cosmic cycle, or proof of inherent British superiority, is shown to be the result of accumulated historical circumstances, some of which belong to the sphere of the humanly possible. Heroism, popular participation, a just ruler, and a prophecy allow this novel to carry a positive message even while recounting a painful defeat.

If compared with the work of M. Gupta in neighbouring Chirgaon (3.1.2), Varmā's historical enterprise differs radically. Although both stem from a personal engagement with the past and with nationalist identity, Varmā's history is regionally and realistically rooted in the immediate past and combines family memoirs, the memories of living witnesses and a diverse corpus of official and unofficial documents. It presents ideal characters and a purposeful history, but without gliding uncritically over the social fabric.[118] Although preoccupied with positive self-representation, Varmā's attitude is not normative but critical. Detail and variety do not seem to be in the way of national unity, and each member, each gender, is allowed a voice and participation. The use of mimetic techniques allows the author to give voice to the views of the people in the market place (pp. 139–43), or of the soldiers in the barracks (pp. 225–7) and suggest a participatory, empowering history that prefigures the characteristics of the nationalist struggle. Though relying heavily on the imagination, Varmā's novel is also fundamentally different from mainstream historical romances and tales of vīr-vīrāṅganās: romance features only slightly, and that too by proxy, and is sacrificed to the greater cause of the history of nation. [119]

History and the motif of vīr-vīrāṅganā could be put to different uses

seems useless, until her heroism (*vīrtā*) wakes her up to her duty 'like a tigress'; ibid., pp. 391–2.

[118] There are detailed caste descriptions, and several subplots highlight caste conflicts (some historical) and the way to deal with them: while Gaṅgādharrāo solved one through a despotic ruling (Chapter 8), Lakṣmībāī solves a similarly explosive communal issue (Sunni–Shia–Hindu) concerning rights of way in a procession by listening to the practical advice of a resourceful carpenter; ibid., pp. 280–4.

[119] Two of the sahelīs, along with the actresses-turned-intelligence agents Motībāī and Juhī, once the favourites of the Rani's late husband, carry out chaste romances with the main heroes, but any fulfilment of love is postponed until after svarājya; ibid., p. 381.

even within the same spirit of nationalist celebration. Folk and regional heroes became national heroes, fitted into the categories and the master narrative of Hindu–Indian history, and became examples of martial resistance during the painful medieval and the more recent past; they were now invoked as patrons of the nation. They could be icons of a chivalrous past, models of militant, aggressive Hindu nationalism, or architects of a new and more democratic political order. Even when not actively propounding the stereotype of Muslim villainy, as in the case with narratives which had the British as the enemy, such tales still implicitly confirmed the exclusion of Muslims from the master narrative by accepting its categories and periodization. Thus 'communal harmony' featured at times in works dealing with colonial history, but stereotypes resurfaced as soon as the action took place in the 'Muslim period'. Also, communal harmony was always an additional feature which did not challenge the basic framework of Indian history but only glossed over conflict. The categories implied in this view of Indian history, and its exclusions, were popularized through biographies, readers, plays, novels, ballads, poems, and films in a kind of diffuse historical saṃskāra. The ways in which the Aryan myth and this vision of history conditioned how contemporary society was discussed and imagined, are the subject of the next section.

3.3. The Shape of Society

> A new political caste (jāti) has been formed, the Indian, which will accommodate Hindus, Muslims, Parsis, Jains and Christians for political aims. Likewise, a new *gotra* has to be formed by Brahmans, Kshatriyas, Vaiśyas, Śūdras, and by brahmachāris, gṛhasthas, vanaprasthas, sanyāsīs: they are all Hindus.[120]

This section rests on a simple but, in my opinion, warranted assumption: that in thinking about contemporary Indian society Hindi intellectuals and activists were conditioned by the picture of history they had drawn. The ideals of the Aryan nation and of Vedic society, I argue, provided too powerful a model of society to allow Indian nationalists to think about Indian society, about how it was and how it should be, in any other terms. So much so that even while voicing a critique of Indian society in class terms, socialist leaders, for example, subscribed to this model, either in terms of a cultural ideal (Narendra Dev) or of Sampūrṇānand's 'Vedanta

[120] Mālavīprasād Śrīvāstava, 'Saṅgaṭhan', *Mādhurī*, III, pt. 2, 2, March 1925, p. 201.

socialism' (see 5.3). As in Maithilīśaraṇ Gupta's poem, the Aryan ideal provided not only a source of pride ('we were once the best') but also a grid for comparison with the present; the order and harmony of that past were the ideal to which the splintered and fractious present was negatively compared. This view carried, often very explicitly as we shall see, a value judgement: since Aryan society had originally been harmonious and free from conflict, conflict within Indian society was seen as a mark of decadence and a deviation from the Aryan ideal. In essentialist terms, conflict belonged to the (materialist) West, and harmony to the East. The impact of the historical saṃskāra on thinking about society therefore had important political implications.

Nationalism as a movement and an inspiration had carried a strong element of social critique from the start; as it involved and politicized new and larger strata of Indian society, this element of social critique grew and acquired unprecedented hues. With the Russian Revolution as a fresh inspiration, a class-based interpretation of Indian society and of the leadership of the nationalist movement acquired widespread currency. However, in the view of history mentioned above, social and economic struggles within Indian society were ultimately seen as misguided and spurious. The result was that two sets of tensions emerged in the discourse on society in the Hindi press. One was a conceptual tension between the critique of castes (jātis) as divisive and competitive groups, the defence of varṇa in metaphorical and functional terms (along the terms of the Vedic creation myth of the Puruṣa), and the aspiration to a single, cohesive community (jāti in the singular). The other was also a tension between the normative approach of high caste, often Brahmin, Hindi intellectuals and their saṃskāra of *order*, and the critical voices of activists and writers who took social *justice* as the cornerstone of their vision of society and followed it to radical consequences.

It is much easier to sustain a consensual view of the past than of the present, as Hindi intellectuals and activists discovered while journals of the 1920s resounded with one obsessive call: *saṅgaṭhan*, organization. This call for (self-)organization, whatever the meaning given to the word, expressed a yearning towards larger and more cohesive units, be it at local, regional, or national levels. It also revealed the drive towards a general and comprehensive picture of, and an agenda for, society. Debates on society and social reform in Hindi in this period exhibit both a conceptual effort and a mass-oriented, active, and political edge. While saṅgaṭhan activities were characterized by defensive arguments about Hinduism in danger of extinction, debates over saṅgaṭhan in Hindi journals expressed a positive and constructive search for the wherewithal of social integration and nation building.[121] As the epigraph on saṅgaṭhan at the beginning of this section maintained, for all political purposes the 'category' (jāti) of the nation had to conflate and accommodate all groups; likewise, all Hindus had to feel the affinity of a shared parentage (*gotra*) beside, or instead of, their present one. I shall therefore start by examining how editors and contributors grappled with existing Hindi words and concepts to redefine society in terms closer to the comprehensive English term.

The very semantic indeterminacy about the word 'society' in Hindi debates reveals the tensions behind such attempts at redefinition and at grafting the present ideal of one jāti on to the idealized past of four varṇas. As Kiśorīdās Vājpeyī put it: 'Nowadays people ask: which jāti? It is a mistake. There are four varṇas but one jāti: the Hindu.'[122] Two words were used in Hindi for 'society', samāj and jāti, both with a number of significations and both used as equivalents of the English word. The special issue *Samāj-aṅk* of the journal *Chāṁd* (November 1937) gives a good indication of this semantic indeterminacy: samāj meant a caste or a region (as in 'Mārvāṛ meṁ jātīytā kā rūp' on casteism in Rajasthan),[123] a gender-specific group (as in 'Yukta-prānt kā mahilā-samāj'), or else society as a whole, as in the English term. The editor tried to explain this semantic variance in historical terms: samāj was ideally 'society', and Vedic samāj had been the apex of progress in ancient times, but the present society, *vartamān samāj*, had broken up into a loose amalgam of smaller groups:

> Our society is no more the ancient and well-organized group which controlled political, religious, social, and other institutions. Now various societies [i.e. society in a narrow sense] cannot rule over themselves. At present what we mean

[121] I am not directly concerned here with the political outcomes of this preoccupation, namely the activities of the Hindu Mahasabha and the Śuddhi Sammelan from 1923 onwards; rather, I shall focus on the echo such arguments had in the Hindi press, and the other notions of society that circulated. For Hindu Mahasabha politics, see Baxter, *The Jana Sangha* and Christophe Jaffrelot, *The Hindu Nationalist Movement and Indian Politics*, London, Hurst, 1996. For a typical article on 'Hinduism in danger', see 'Hinduoṃ kā hrās', in *Mādhurī*, I, pt. 2, 4, April 1923 (at the time of the first meeting of the revived Hindu Mahasabha).

[122] Vājpeyī, 'Āryoṁ kī varṇa-vyavasthā', *Mādhurī*, VI, pt. 2, 4, May 1928, p. 540.

[123] See also 'Mārvāṛī samāj aur hindī saṃsār', *Mādhurī*, VI, pt. 1, 5, December 1927, pp. 782–3.

by society is only a particular sampradāy or a caste whose members, spread over a varied geographical area, maintain certain similarities in behaviour and customs (pp. 9–10).

The editorial 'Samāj aur vyakti' also tried, perhaps for the first time, to define society in relation to the individual and not to collective groups, but it kept shifting between possible definitions of samāj: either as a closed, homogeneous sampradāy or as the interdependent ensemble of all individuals, based, at least ideally, upon just economic and gender relations.[124] This semantic indeterminacy reveals the tensions surrounding the general terms of the debate, between the Aryan varṇāśrama system and the present heterogeneous reality, the accommodation of jātis within the four-fold order, and the transition from jāti as localized caste and community to jāti-as-nation.

The journal *Mādhurī* is a good forum for examining debates on society in the 1920s, since the call for the saṅgaṭhan, organization, of the Hindu jāti appeared in every issue. Most contributors to the debate were either Brahmins or Ārya Samājists and held a literal belief in the picture of Indian society as one, orderly *body*, to use the metaphor of the original Puruṣa. 'The only reason why the Hindu jāti has survived through its troubled history is the caste-system, created by our far-sighted ṛṣis and munis to make the Hindu jāti strong (*sabal*), solid (*sudṛṛh*) and well-organized (*suvyavasthit*)', wrote Rāmsevak Tripāṭhī, later editor of Mādhurī.[125] It was a social theory (*kalpanā*) unrivalled in the world, echoed Kiśorīdās Vājpeyī and Balvīr.[126] Such a typically triumphalist opening invariably set the tone and framework for the entire discussion of Hindu society: to talk of Hindu society meant to talk of the varṇa system; even criticism of

[124] The initial definition of society echoes that of a Rousseauvian social contract: 'समाज ऐसे व्यक्तियों का समूह है, जिन्होंने व्यक्तिगत स्वार्थों की सार्वजनिक रक्षा के लिए अपने विषम आचरणों में साम्य उत्पन्न करनेवाले कुछ सामान्य नियमों से शासित होने का समझौता कर लिया।' [Society is a group of people who, in order to publicly protect their individual interests, agree that they will be governed by some common rules which will engender similarity in their dissimilar customs]. It is the existence of commonly agreed codes that transforms any group into a society; *Chāṁd*, XVI, pt. 1, 1, November 1937, pp. 3–4.

[125] Tripāṭhī, 'Hindū-jāti aur varṇa-vyavasthā', *Mādhurī,* V, pt. 2, 4, May 1927, pp. 525–8. The same view was held by Madan Mohan Mālavīya, e.g. in 'Varṇāśram dharma', *Abhyuday,* 1, May 1908, in P. Mālavīya, *Mālavīyajī ke lekh,* Delhi, National Publishing House, 1962, pp. 174–5.

[126] Vājpeyī, 'Āryoṁ kī varṇa-vyavasthā', pp. 534 ff.; Balvīr, 'Sāmājik saṅgaṭhan kā bhārtīy ādarś', *Mādhurī,* IV, pt. 1, 6, December 1925, p. 775.

the division of society into a myriad of jātis led to a positive appraisal of the original varṇas, of which jātis were but a corruption.[127] Thus under the spell of the Aryan myth a once-Brahminical view became universal and dominant when in fact an all-encompassing model was needed.[128] Whether to criticize it or to praise it, Hindi intellectuals always referred to the four-fold classification as the original and essentially Indian model of society; the debate among English-speaking Indian reformers was along much the same lines.[129] Present-day castes were compared or assimilated to the theoretical four varṇas without recognizing the qualitative differences between the two; whenever arguments on contemporary society and the caste system moved to the theoretical ground, caste-as-jāti automatically switched to caste-as-varṇa.

In the public sphere, the defence of varṇa as a category was couched in rational terms. Following an argument disseminated in the Hindi area mainly by the Ārya Samāj, varṇa was explained as an originally flexible category, based not on one's birth (*janma-pradhān*) but on individual deeds (*karma-pradhān*). However, as the Ārya Samāj philosophy graduate Satyavrat Siddhāntālaṃkār argued, a society based only on the division of labour would have bred materialism, unequal distribution of capital and social conflict, as the history of the West showed. Thus ancient 'Indian sociologists' had realized that man is not only an economic being

[127] Satyavrat Siddhāntālaṃkār, 'Hinduoṁ meṁ sāmājik saṅgaṭhan kī kalpanā', *Mādhuri,* VI, pt. 1, 2, September 1927, pp. 224–36.

[128] Much work has been done in the past decade on the colonial construction of 'caste' and its implications. Early orientalists and colonial ethnographers took the traditional Brahmin-centred classification in four varṇas as the original picture of Hindu society. Colonial administrators, called in to settle local caste disputes, objectified jātis into a grid of fixed and standardized categories from a variety of occupational, local, 'fuzzy' and partially mobile identities, and looked for historical genealogies in 'Hindu scriptures', thereby taking a partial and ideal vision of society held by a particular group as the true and complete picture, and turning it into the law. In particular, the 1901 Census tried to fit all local jātis into the traditional Brahmin-centred fourfold classification, thereby initiating frantic manoeuvering for caste ascendancy by caste associations, and also a totalizing conception of caste instead of the earlier, to some extent relatively looser, identities. For an overview and a discussion, see Rashmi Pant, 'The Cognitive Status of Caste in Colonial Ethnography: A Review of Some Literature of the North Western Provinces and Oudh', *Indian Economic and Social History Review*, 24, 2, 1987, pp. 145–62. Also Inden, *Imagining India*.

[129] See Susan Bayly, 'Hindu "Modernizers" and the "Public" Arena: Indigenous Critiques of Caste in Colonial India'; paper presented at the SOAS Conference on the Modernization of Hinduism, London, 1993.

and had created caste to ensure the full development of the individual. By explaining the etymology of varna as *varaṇ karnā*, to choose, Satyavrat defended varṇa on subtler, psychological terms: originally caste was chosen according to one's psychological predisposition (*manovaijñānik pravṛtti*). Closer to the notion of personal dharma (*svadharma*), this interpretation of varṇa loosened it from birth or occupation but reaffirmed it as a rigid category on another basis. Just as one should not escape one's svadharma, one cannot change one's predisposition. And since in Satyavrat's scheme predispositions were also four in number and were partly hereditary, caste by birth, initially criticized, was finally upheld in a subtler, psychologized form.[130]

'Degeneration', along the historical framework outlined earlier in this chapter, was taken as the explanatory device for changes and phenomena in Indian society, too. The proliferation of castes, class and caste conflicts were all explained as resulting from an ignorance of past rules: 'We forgot the rules, we disregarded the system and therefore today we are oppressed, enslaved, poor, helpless, desperate and dependent on others for everything,' wrote Rāmsevak Tripāṭhī.[131] Oppression in the name of caste and internal conflict were not inherent faults of the system but were due to ignorance and corrupted understanding, wrote Kiśorīdās Vājpeyī; division had in fact been brought in by the 'western wind'.[132] The belief that a healthy society was characterized by the absence of conflict was thus a corollary to the defence of varṇa: caste, class, or social conflicts of any other kind were the marks of an unhealthy society and presented a typical picture of Kāliyuga, the dark age. Tulsīḍās' sixteenth-century description of Kāliyuga in the *Rāmcharitmānas* had contemporary echoes for Hindi intellectuals:

> वर्ण धर्म नहिं आश्रम चारी श्रुति विरोध रत सब नरनारी . . .
> शूद्र द्विजन उपदेसहिं जाना मेलि जनेऊ लेहिं कुदाना।

> There are no varṇas, no four *āśramas* left;
> Men and women are keen to refute the *śruti;*
> Śūdras teach knowledge to the twice-born,
> Wear the sacred thread and take corrupt gifts.[133]

The authority of history, of the holy text, and of rational argument combined to give what had been a traditional Brahmin complaint against

[130] Siddhāntālaṃkār, 'Hinduoṁ meṁ sāmājik saṅgaṭhan kī kalpanā', p. 235.
[131] Tripāṭhī, 'Hindū-jāti aur varṇa-vyavasthā', p. 526.
[132] Vājpeyī, 'Āryoṁ kī varṇa-vyavasthā', p. 536.
[133] *Rāmcharitmānas,* VII, 98, 1 and 99, 1; quoted ibid. (incorrect reading).

caste-contamination (*varṇa-saṅkara*) a generalized meaning encompassing all struggle for social change. 'Some Śūdras pretend to become of higher caste by wearing the sacred thread; they are trying to create mixed castes and refusing to adhere to the Vedas and Śāstras, thus drowning the whole Hindu society', wrote Rāmsevak Tripāṭhī placing Tulsīdās' Kāliyuga in the contemporary Indian context.[134] Rāmchandra Śukla's predilection for Tulsīdās rested partly on the view that in Tulsīdās' time, when society (i.e. Hindu society) risked disintegration under the impact of Muslim rule and of different religious reformers, he had 'descended' and 'saved the dharma of the Aryans from disintegrating'. Even now, Indian society and the dharma of the Aryans (Śukla used Aryan and Hindu almost interchangeably) risked disintegration under the pressures of many contrasting forces and the call of several different reformers. With an interesting historical leap, Śukla warned that 'there are many such revolutionaries in Europe. . . . Since the higher classes did not fulfil their duty well, the lower classes were filled with envy, hatred and arrogance; Lenin took advantage of this and became the mahātmā of his time. . . . One should not be deceived by this bestowal of power to the foolish people (*mūrkh jantā*). Leaders who instead act according to the real needs of the people do get their respect'.[135] Thus social order was all about keeping to one's place and one's dharma. Far from being just a great poet, Tulsīdās was a cultural hero who had shown the way to negotiate reform and social order, bhakti and authority.[136] To several Hindi intellectuals of this period, Europe appeared as a large cauldron of unrest, what with World War I, the Russian Revolution, the rise of social democracy in Germany and Italy, and the great strikes and conflicts between capital and labour. As Kiśorīdās Vājpeyī wrote: 'In Europe there are large groupings, especially political ones. Because of these factions a poisonous hatred grows among the people (*prajā-varg*), and it breeds no good consequence. The people (jantā) are harmed by any kind of useless grouping. Therefore, the various conflicts in this country are not caused by the caste-system but by stupidity.'[137]

The ideal Indian society, the varṇa system, seemed instead to ward off the mirage of equality, the danger of class conflict, and the evil of

[134] Tripāṭhī, 'Hindū-jāti aur varṇa-vyavasthā', p. 527.

[135] Śukla, *Gosvāmī tulsīdās*, Benares, Nagari Pracharini Sabha, 1983, pp. 19, 25, 35.

[136] See my 'Tulsidas as a Classic', in K. Snell and M.P. Raeside, eds, *Classics of Modern South Asian Literature*, Wiesbeden, Harrassowitz, 1998.

[137] Vājpeyī, 'Āryoṁ kī varṇa-vyavasthā', p. 537.

materialism, and to reassert India's claim to superiority. The caste-system, in its original, pure form was suggested as the only solution for all conflicts, even for international ones. 'Great thinkers of the West have tried to solve social problems in many ways,' wrote Balvīr, 'but because they lacked the Vedic ideal, at the onset of heavy clouds of adversity their brilliant light died out after a brief glimmer. Unrest continued. The reign of dissatisfaction continued. New movements arose every day'. Nor could Bolshevism or communism, the new stars, succeed, as 'human nature itself is based on natural inequality'. Progress was no cure either, since in its name the blood of workers is sucked everywhere: 'Europe, lost in the fever of materialism, will have to learn the lesson of the ideal society from India, this master of spiritualism, and the civilization of ancient India will rule over the whole earth'.[138] Even an article like Satyavrat's, which started by acknowledging the call for justice made by peasants, untouchables, and non-Brahmins in India and recognizing caste (jāti) divisions to be the main obstacle to svarājya, ended by reaffirming on the theoretical plane that caste (varṇa) was the best system of social organization.[139]

The attack on untouchability and the reactions to it exposed the ambiguity and limitations both in saṅgaṭhan activities and in this discourse of society; and they raised the unspoken issues of power, control, and exploitation. Symbolic acts aiming at assimilating untouchables and Muslim converts into the Hindu fold undertaken jointly by the Ārya Samāj and the reborn Hindu Mahasabha were at first publicly saluted as foretastes of social saṅgaṭhan.[140] But such symbolic acts of reintegration—like purification (śuddhi), temple entry, or allowing untouchables to take water from the common well—rebounded, as they were typically

[138] Balvīr, 'Sāmājik saṅgaṭhan kā bhārtīy ādarś', *Mādhurī*, IV, pt. 1, 6, December 1925, pp. 775, 776 and 779.

[139] Satyavrat Siddhāntalaṅkār, 'Hinduoṁ meṁ samājik saṅgaṭhan kī kalpanā', p. 236.

[140] These activities, as well as the Mahasabha meetings, had an echo in the Hindi press. Rūpnārāyaṇ Pāṇḍey, one of the editors of *Mādhurī*, had previously been the editor of the journal of the Bhārat Dharma Mahāmaṇḍal of Benares; a strong advocate of Hindu saṅgaṭhan, he paid great attention to the subject. Among the many articles and editorials on the subject were Devkīnandan 'Vibhav', 'Hindū saṅgaṭhan', pt.1, *Mādhurī*, II, pt. 2, 3, April 1924, p. 350; Dayāśaṅkar Dube, 'Bhārat meṁ hinduoṁ kī daśā', *Mādhurī*, IV, pt. 1, 2, August 1925, p. 146; 'Hindū jāti kī akṣamtā', *Mādhurī*, I, pt. 2, 2, February 1923, p. 216; Chāndkaraṇ Śārdā, 'Hindū-jāti kī durdaśā ke kāraṇ aur uske nivaraṇ ke upāy' *Mādhurī*, III, pt. 1, 3, October 1924, pp. 290–5.

followed by reparatory measures of self-purification and restrictive statements. These in turn could be used to publicly expose the whole enterprise of caste Hindus as mere hypocrisy. Radical editor Gaṇeś Śaṅkar Vidyārthī reported derisively an incident at Ujhyani village (dist. Badayun), where a group of Chamars had earlier been dissuaded from converting to Islam by being admitted to the village well; however, after this symbolic gesture the wells had been quickly purified with Ganges water and the crisis had reverted to square one.[141] Only a year after the programme of 'purification' of untouchables was launched by the Hindu Mahasabha, its limitations were clearly spelt out: this 'religious duty' involved provisions for the education of untouchables in mixed schools but not in those for Brahmins only; entry into temples was only accorded 'wherever possible according to maryādā'; untouchables were entitled to a separate well in every settlement but not access to the others. Teaching the Vedas, wearing the sacred thread, and dining with untouchables was 'against the Śāstras and lokmaryādā'; conversions to Hinduism were allowed, but not to a particular caste. 'The uplift of untouchables does not mean that people from all varṇas should start eating from their hands. Uplift means to instil in them the taste for cleanliness and purity, to spread education as much as possible, and to think of and tell them ways of increasing their income.'[142] When Congress industrialist Jamnalal Bajaj was interviewed after he had publicly taken food from the hands of some untouchable children in an ashram, he stressed that the *public* question of the removal of untouchability should not be linked to the *private* one of commensality; he had done so once *publicly*, but that would not be his practice.[143] Such incidents and qualifications point to the two different attitudes that I called normative and critical even in matters relating to society and social reform. The normative view, represented by the articles on Indian society quoted above and by Mahasabha leaders like Madan Mohan Mālavīya, embraced a cohesive and orderly *model* of the organizing principles of society but left out the actual norms and customs governing social practice. They spoke of unity, saṅgaṭhan, and gradual reform but stopped short of enforcing a change in social relations. 'Even Madan Mohan Mālavīya, the founder of the movement,

[141] G.Ś. Vidyārthī, 'Hindū raheṁ yā musalmān baneṁ?', *Pratāp*, 1, June 1925, quoted R. Avasthī, *Krānti kā udghoṣ*, vol. 2, Kanpur, Ganesh Shankar Vidyarthi Shiksha Samiti, 1978, pp. 814–17.

[142] Quoted in *Mādhurī*, II, pt. 2, 1, February 1994, pp. 141–2.

[143] *Prem*, II, pt. 2, 1, March–April 1928, pp. 333–4.

will not eat with "lower Mālavīyas",' remarked Janārdan Bhaṭṭ sarcastically;[144] 'Neither can the Gurukul-factory turn a Ḍher into a Brahmin, nor can Mahatma Gandhi bestow a high position on untouchables by adopting a Bhangi girl,' observed a laconic, old Lajjārām Mehtā in 1927.[145] Also, even when caste Hindus argued in favour of a partial reform of untouchability because they needed untouchables for impure jobs, they did so *in the absence* of untouchable interlocutors. By contrast, radical critics highlighted the lack of consistency between the discourse and practice of social reform and the removal of untouchability and were ready to forsake the ideal of social order in favour of a general reshuffling at the hands of the low castes themselves. As G. Ś. Vidyārthī wrote:

An unavoidable consequence will be a powerful wave of consciousness that will rise from all Hindu low castes of northern India which are presently considered worse than cats and dogs; it will be a wave that neither the Śaṅkarāchārya nor Pandit Dīndayāl [of the Hindu Mahasabha] and his friends will be able to stop. They will keep shouting that dharma is lost and sanātan dharma has been destroyed while the wave will pass over the heads of these frogs-in-the-well; it will advance not on the strength of some śloka of the Śāstras, but on the strength of the living inspiration of human dharma.[146]

And Nirālā:

The hope of revival that is colouring our horizon will awaken first of all those jātis which fell asleep first—the śūdra, *antyaj* castes. The signs of awakening that they are showing nowadays are encouraging, while the signs brahmins and kṣatriyas are giving are not signs of awakening but of stupor, they are blabbering in their sleep.[147]

This latter, radical attitude involved a critique of hypocrisy and oppression as structural to the caste system (Premchand) and a discourse of justice and of changed social relations that centred on the lower caste, lower class subject (cf. 5.2). Of course, this was carried out on behalf of the lower caste subjects, not by them: a peculiarity of the Hindi sphere was that the participants in public debates in this period were all from higher caste backgrounds. All critics could do was to suggest

[144] Bhaṭṭ, 'Hindū saṅgaṭhan kā ḍhoṅg', *Chāṁd*, IV, pt. 1, 4, February 1928, p. 438.

[145] Mehtā, 'Hinduoṁ meṁ chuāchūt', *Mādhurī*, V, pt. 1, 6, January 1927, p. 826.

[146] Vidyārthī; 'Hindū raheṁ yā musalmān baneṁ', p. 816.

[147] Essay collected in *Prabandha pratimā* (1940), quoted in Śarmā, *Nirālā kī sāhitya-sādhnā*, vol. 2, p. 239.

identification with the lower caste subject. In a reply to Rāmsevak Tripāṭhī's article quoted above ('Hindū-jāti aur varṇa-vyavasthā'), Santarām, the founder of the Jāt-Pāṁt-Toṛak-Maṇḍal, an anti-caste association within the Ārya Samāj, condemned the hypocrisy of śuddhi and of Tripāṭhī's defence of the caste-system as partial: had Tripāṭhī been a Chamar or a Dong would he have said the same things? 'To say that Hindu society is still alive today thanks to the caste system is like saying that the British rule Indians because they drink wine and liquor.'[148] This strategy of identification, of forcing the reader into another person's place, did not work as well in theoretical debates as it did in literature. In Hindi literature the critique of untouchability produced very powerful works, which also carried a more general argument about justice and individual rights. We need only recall here Premchand's most damning stories about high-caste cruel indifference (*Dūdh kā dam, Ṭhākur kā kuāṁ, Sadgati*), the sensational 'confessions' by Zahūr Bakhś (cf. 4.3), Nirālā's ironic and sensitive sketches *Chaturī chamār* (1935) and *Kullī bhāṭ* (1939), and Nāgarjun's powerful novel *Balchanmā* (1952) in the form of an untouchable's auto-biography.

After the Russian Revolution a radically different vision of society appeared on the Hindi horizon and gained some currency (and some opprobrium) in the public sphere. This vision could also be expressed in terms of saṅgaṭhan, for the call for saṅgaṭhan had also expressed a yearning to accommodate the 'neglected sections' (*upekṣit aṅg*) of society, peasants, workers, untouchables, and women. If radical social reformers had always demanded that social justice be included in the new vision of the nation-to-be, socialism provided a new theoretical framework. In this respect, while Non-Cooperation was a turning point in the political imagination of Hindi intellectuals, the Russian Revolution and the 1919–21 peasant movement in Avadh were, to different degrees, turning points for their social imagination. Whereas national leaders welcomed the October Revolution chiefly as an anti-imperialist struggle, for radical Hindi intellectuals it was a peasants' and workers' struggle against oppressive landlordism and capitalism.[149] 'The age that is coming will be

[148] Santarām, 'Bulbulśāh aur varṇa-vyavasthā', *Mādhurī*, V, pt. 2, 6, July 1927, p. 812.

[149] Kṛṣṇakānta Mālavīya, the editor of *Abhyuday* and *Maryādā*, G.Ś. Vidyārthī and Ramāśaṅkar Avasthī of *Pratāp* and *Prabhā*, Satyabhakta, Rādhāmohan Gokuljī and Rāmchandra Varmā introduced Bolshevist Russia to Hindi readers as a model for the liberation of Indian peasants and workers. See 5.2 here. See also Rāmchandra Varmā's book *Samyavād*, Bombay, 1919, Avasthī's *Rūs kī rājya-krānti*, Kanpur,

the age of peasants and workers', wrote Premchand in 1919 in the path-breaking article 'Old age and new age' (Purānā zamānā, nayā zamānā).[150] Chapter 5 will analyse in greater detail the changing attitudes of Hindi intellectuals towards the peasants, and the role of Congress Socialists in the Hindi area. The Gandhian emphasis on a mass movement and the success of socialism in Russia fostered a view of society that was all-inclusive and egalitarian, where conflict and difference were acknowledged and explained chiefly in economic terms, and where labour was given a particular dignity. It brought about an altogether different ideal of society in Hindi in the 1920s: the critique of caste and class injustice was compounded with visions of future equality and harmony. Some of the first poems on socialism (*sāmyavād*) in Hindi journals, V.B. Talvār remarks, were imbued with this vision: 'The music of bolshevism that echoes in Hindi poems of 1918–20 is a divine tune: bolshevism appears as pure as a mountain stream, as luminous as the light of the sun. It arouses feelings of love and equality. It further shows social inequality, the difference between rich and poor, the exploitation of peasants and workers at the hands of landlords and capitalists, and it prays god and calls on the forces of nature to destroy this system of inequality.'[151] The discourse of Indian society was now articulated in terms of class and class conflict rather than in terms of caste and caste harmony.[152] By the 1930s the arguments and vocabulary became decidedly economic oriented, and the worker—whether peasant or labourer—emerged as the central subject.[153] 'Nowadays there are only two jātis', concluded one socialist pamphlet, 'that of patels, zamindars, thakurs, rajas and nawabs or raīs, contractors, shopkeepers, money-lenders, bankers, house-owners, factory-owners, middlemen, agents, lawyers, officers, and that of the poor—peasants and workers.'[154]

Pratap Press, 1920, and Vināyak Sītārām Sarvaṭe, *Bolśevizm*, Indore, 1921. Cited by Vīr Bhārat Talvār, *Kisān, rāṣṭrīy āndolan aur premchand,* pp. 179–93.

150 Published in *Zamānā* in February 1919, now in Premchand, *Vividh prasaṅg*, vol. 1, Allahabad, Hans Prakasan, 1962, pp. 258–69.

151 Talvār, *Kisān, rāṣṭrīy āndolan aur premchand,* p. 187.

152 We may mention here the articles by Sampūrṇānand: 'Gāndhīvād aur sāmyavād', in *Viśāl bhārat*, April 1936, pp. 413–16; also 'Samājvādī samāj kī kuch viśeṣtāeṁ' and 'Rāmrājya aur sāmyavādī', in *Samājvād kā bigul,* Kashi Pustak Bhandar, Benares 1936, pp. 1–7 and 61–7. See also 5.2 here.

153 See e.g. Prāṇnāth Vidyālaṃkār, *Bhārtīy kisān*, Benares, Rāṣṭrīy Sañjīvanī Granthamālā, vol. 1, 1920; Anon., *Ham bhukhu naṅge kyoṁ haiṁ?,* Kanpur, Kisān Mazdūr Pustak Mālā, 1935.

154 *Ham bhukhe naṅge kyoṁ haiṁ?*, p. 5.

This discourse was certainly important in justifying and popularizing notions of social equality, social and economic justice, and individual dignity. It also appeared to make jātis and varṇas irrelevant by offering a vision of society where caste had no place and no reason to exist. The utopia of Raghupati Sahāy Firāq's story 'Abse sau sāl bād' (A hundred years from now, 1925) presents a completely secular, casteless society of perfectly equal and attributeless individuals. After twenty to twenty-five years of international conflicts (*pralay*), the new society will provide equal rights to all thanks to a welfare state; material progress—jobs, transport, habitation, food—will ensure not only economic welfare but also the right of individual growth for all (after not more than 4–5 hours of work). There will be universal education and new social and gender relations: equal rights for women, even in sexual matters, and free and healthy sexual relations with no need for marriage; a true democracy will nationalize property and do away with class or caste divisions.[155] The disappearance of caste from public discourse in the 1930s as Puruṣottam Agravāl has observed, did not however solve but rather evaded the question: caste was pushed out of secular and socialist discourse but remained crucial to social and political practices.[156] In some cases, adjustments were sought on the ideological level; thus Bhai Parmānand, the Ārya Samājist advocate of śuddhi and saṅgaṭhan, argued that socialism had always existed in India and equality was compatible with the fourfold caste division.[157] Even socialist intellectuals like Narendra Dev and Sampūrṇanand conducted a critique of society in economic terms *at the same time as* they believed in the inherent goodness and harmony of ancient Indian society.[158] So great was the power of the golden image of the Indian past and its perfect social organization.

[155] R. Sahāy Firāq, 'Ab se sau baras bād', in *Mādhurī*, IV, pt. 1, 4, October 1925, pp. 467–71. The picture would probably seem like a true Kāliyuga to more conservative contemporaries, with no social order or hierarchy and free female sexuality!

[156] P. Agravāl, 'Jātivādī kaun', in Rājkiśor, ed., *Harijan se dalit,* Delhi, Vani Prakasan, 1994.

[157] In 'Hindū sāmyavād kyā hai?', *Mādhurī*, VII, pt. 1, 1, August–September 1928, pp. 343–5.

[158] See for example the articles in the collection edited by B.V. Keskar and V.K.N. Menon, *Acharya Narendra Dev. A Commemoration Volume*, New Delhi, National Book Trust, 1971: 'Bhārtīy samāj aur saṃskṛti', 'Bhārtīy dharma' and 'Samājvād kā sāṃskritik ādarś'. In the first two, Narendra Dev explains that harmony (*samanvay*) is the characteristic feature of Indian society and culture; in the third one, he posits class conflict as necessary for self-development; see 5.3 here.

The 1920s, then, witnessed an extensive debate on the shape of society in the name of saṅgaṭhan (self-organization) and mass mobilization. This was both a theoretical effort, prompted by the model of the Aryan ancestors as well as the contemporary example of the Russian Revolution, and a practical one in the midst of religious and political activism. As usual, the writers' saṃskāras (see 1.2.2) left their imprint on the products of social imagination: on the theoretical plane the hold of the fourfold hierarchical model of varṇa was remarkably dominant, even in the open arena of journals. Thus, despite any number of articles on social reform, society was discussed purely in terms of 'Hindu society', and even then only as a degraded version of the original 'Aryan model'. This was both the strength and the weakness of the Aryan and Hindu history outlined in the previous sections—strength, because it did offer a powerful, proud, and pure image of Indian society, superior to the 'West'. That varṇa was a category one step removed from the immediate group identity of jātis was in fact an advantage, for it made the varṇa-based model attractive and available to the larger constituency of caste Hindus. Tellingly, the traditional religious insistence on devotion to Brahmins was largely absent from these articles: 'brahminhood' and 'kṣatriyahood' appear as general, disembodied qualities (*guṇa*) rather than group-specific markers. Finally, placing the discussion on the plane of varṇa allowed ritual practices and actual caste relations to slip out of public discourse. While the varṇa-system provided theoretical order and solutions, the *roṭī-beṭī* (commensality and marriage) system of jātis was largely kept out of public discourse, as would happen later with caste electoral politics. The weakness of this vision of society was that of a normative vision: it rejected criticism, ignored differences of interest or opinion, and introduced a slippage between the ideal self-representation, Truth with a capital 'T', and reality. This slippage worked as a buffer against criticism and new ideas: criticism of the degenerate present could never tarnish the Truth of the ideal.

The example of the Russian Revolution provided a powerful alternative, and socialism a new framework for discussions about Indian society; it also spurred Hindi social thinkers to appropriate socialism as an Indian ideal and find commonalities with Gandhian, and even Vedic, thought. In any case, hardly any time was spent discussing the individual as a social unit. This may signal the empirical acknowledgement of the limited space and meaning of the individual as an independent, attributeless unit in the Indian context, but it also reveals how debates on society usually left empirical individual, ritual, and family concerns out of public discourse. It was only with radical women's journals, as we shall see, that practices of the household and the family, as well as individual feelings and aspirations, were made objects of public scrutiny and linked to the general development of the jāti (as society and nation) and of the individual (see 4.3).

On the practical level, when in 1925 the editor of *Mādhurī* asked 'How much has been achieved in Hindu saṅgaṭhan?' the answer was disappointing.[159] By the end of the 1920s it was clear that even the minor social reshuffling that saṅgaṭhan required for a Hindu jāti to be formed hardly found a consensus. Still, saṅgaṭhan as voluntary youth activism and as social self-advancement proved the success and popularity of the Aryan–Hindu historical saṃskāra outlined in the course of this chapter and gave it a militant edge. A nationalist mythology was in place which provided a powerful self-representation and ensured the ideological cohesion of caste Hindus around a martial, muscular ideal. This new Hindu front was the product of a convergence between the activism, ethos, and social critique of the Ārya Samāj and the political clout and religious conservatism of the Madan Mohan Mālavīya-led Hindu Mahasabha, the same Aryan–Hindu melange characterizing *Bhārat-bhārtī*'s historical message. In fact the Ārya Samāj, in the persons of Lala Lajpat Rai, Svami Śraddhānand (of Gurukul Kangri) and Bhai Parmānand provided the core of saṅgaṭhan activism in north India.[160] Though a new all-encompassing vision of society was not achieved, the call to defensive, anti-Muslim saṅgaṭhan found an easier appeal: heroic examples of Hindu resistance during Muslim rule and Hindu–Muslim riots collapsed the distinction between past and present. The question of Hindu self-defence, which appeared obsessively in the Hindi press throughout the riot-torn 1920s, pushed the issue of societal reorganization aside and defined saṅgaṭhan only in militant terms. This coincided with the call of the Ārya Samāj and the Hindu Mahasabha for the participation of lower castes in Hindu festivals and the recruitment of akhāṛās and volunteer corps,[161] while self-defence squads of students were organized in times of riots.[162] However, as Nandini Gooptu has suggested, common

[159] 'Hindū-saṅgaṭhan kā kārya kitnā huā?', editorial in *Mādhurī*, III, pt. 2, 1, January 1925, pp. 133–4.

[160] See Baxter, *Jana Sangha*, p. 17.

[161] Gooptu, 'The Political Culture of the Urban Poor', pp. 136–7.

[162] E.g. small groups of educated youth were organized into self-defence squads

participation in religious or political activities need not imply that a cohesive sense of communal solidarity was created among various Hindu castes.[163] Radical Ārya Samājists like Bhai Parmānand and Svami Śraddhānand advocated the complete end of the caste system in order to build one Hindu jāti, and associations like the Jāt-Pāṁt-Toṛak-Maṇḍal organized intercaste marriages as a way of breaking caste ties. But the majority in the Hindu front kept the ideological and practical levels of the Hindu 'nation' separate: one was Truth, the other reality. They maintained that the caste system was compatible with Hindu saṅgaṭhan, just as the defence of Hindu interests was compatible with the cause of Indian nationalism.[164] Finally, for all the critiques of jātis, on the practical level castes and caste associations were also accepted as positive foci of social activism, provided they accepted the overall, unifying discourse of the one, national jāti.[165]

---

in the Lucknow riots of 1924 by the Ārya Samāj *pradhān* Rāmsevak Tripāṭhī and by Śrīnārāyaṇ Chaturvedī. The former was the author of several articles mentioned in this section, the latter was at the time principal of the Kanyakubja College; editorial note in *Mādhurī*, II, pt. 2, 3, April 1924, p. 350. The successful recruitment of mostly upper-caste youth by the Rāṣṭrīya Svayamsevak Saṅgh (RSS) in the towns of the province in the 1940s relied initially on the Ārya Samāj network of schools; see Jaffrelot, *The Hindu Nationalist Movement,* pp. 66 ff.

163 Gooptu, 'The Political Culture', p. 140.

164 See 'Indra', 'Hindū saṅgaṭhan kā ādhār', *Mādhurī*, II, pt. 2, 6, July 1924; and Lajpat Rai's presidential speech at 8th A.I. Hindu Mahasabha in Calcutta, 1925, quoted in *Mādhurī*, III, pt. 2, 3, March 1925, in which he upheld the right of Hindus to pursue their own goals while being part of the nationalist movement.

165 See e.g. the appeal to the various groups and castes in *Bhārat-bhārtī, Bhaviṣya khaṇḍ*, stanzas 74–83, pp. 177–9. In this, Hindi intellectuals reflected the pan-Indian trend by which new caste associations (from the late nineteenth century) sought to encompass supra-local groups and networks, to fit into the Brahmin-centred fourfold classification of society—through ritual sanskritization—and to pursue secular values of self-improvement through better education and job opportunities. Caste associations developed between 1880 and 1935 on the basis of the old (and disbanded) panchayats but mirroring (a) the colonial trend toward supra-local caste networks, coalescing castes and sub-castes, and (b) modern associations devoted also to secular values (self-improvement, education) deriving power and authority from the (purportedly) collective general will of caste members. For an overview, see Jackie Assayag, *The Making of Democratic Inequality. Caste, Class, Lobbies and Politics in Contemporary India (1880–1995)*, Pondicherry 1995; also Lucy Carroll, 'Colonial Perceptions of Indian Society and the Emergence of Caste(s) Associations', *Journal of Asian Studies*, 37, 2, February 1978, pp. 233–50; and Pant, 'Cognitive Status of Caste'.

3.4. Conclusion

भारत के बच्चे बच्चे को हम अर्जुन भीम बनाएंगे।
इस देश के बाँके वीरों को शस्त्र विद्या सिखाएंगे।
हैं कतल किये लाखों हिन्दू मंदिर भी सभी गिराये हैं।
जो जुल्म किये हैं दुष्टों ने हम पर उनका मज़ा चखाएंगे।
भारत . . .

रग रग में खून है अर्जुन का हम हनुमान के साथी हैं
पापों की अधर्मी लंका का दुनिया से भ्रम मिटाएंगे।
भारत . . .

We'll turn every child of India into Bhīma and Arjuna / we'll teach the young heroes of this country to fight with weapons.

Thousands of Indians were butchered, temples were destroyed / we'll teach those criminals a good lesson / We'll turn . . .

Arjun's blood is in our veins, we're Hanumān's companions / we'll wipe the blot of sinful Lanka from the earth / We'll turn . . .

(Ārya Samāj bhajan)[166]

This chapter aimed at showing the different aspects of the engagement with history in the Hindi literary sphere, and their implications. We saw how a unified historical identity, a historical saṃskāra, was formed in tandem, but also in competition, with orientalist historiography and provided a crucial component in nationalist ideology. Homogenization, positive self-representation, and the ideals of Hindu valour and militancy were the hallmarks of this saṃskāra, reworked and recreated through both 'high' and 'popular' literature, including songs, religious and theatrical performances, speeches and public *upadeś* (sermons). The role of Ārya Samāj *upadeśaks* (preachers) like Svami Satyadeva Parivrājak or Devīdatt Dvivedī in this respect cannot be overestimated: they aided the widespread circulation of such notions of Indian history, and underlined the relative elasticity with which these notions could be adapted and interpreted for and by local, specific audiences.

A linguistic and conceptual novelty fashioned by Hindi historians and writers was the historical subject 'we', which referred to a cohesive well-defined nation. Colonial historiography was faulted on this point: it was claimed that the history of 'we' as a nation could be traced back from

[166] *Prakāś bhajan satsaṅg*, quoted in Gupta, *Hindī bhāṣa aur sāhitya ko ārya-samāj kī den*, p. 192.

the present day to the Vedic age in one continuous unbroken line. This particular history acquired a new narrative unity and a heroic resonance; also, political and social relations between rulers and ruled and within society were reframed according to general and homogeneous categories: 'we' Hindu'–Indians, 'they' Muslim–foreigners. Any painful and awkward instances, either of defeat or of collaboration, could be dealt with by the appropriate strategies of circumvention or elision.

Literature was the most effective means of disseminating this special vision of Indian history; and the popularity of Maithilīśaraṇ Gupta's *Bhārat-bhārtī*, which was said to be found 'in every house' in the Central Provinces, attests to the enormous appeal of this particular historical saṃskāra. *Bhārat-bhāratī* was a crucial text in the sense that it neatly encapsulated all the leading articles of faith of the new historical imagination: the sense of an undivided past, the glory of the united Hindu nation, the straying from pure Aryan ideals, the consequent decline and decadence of the Hindu nation, the interlude of Muslim rule. Despite critiques by untouchable ideologues and Ārya-Samāj-educated women, this version of Indian history, which was first popularized against a background of political and cultural anti-colonialism, continued to dominate a wide range of nationalist ideologies, from Mālavīya's Hindu conservatism to Narendra Dev's socialism. Crucially, well before Independence this narrative of history became the backbone for other national histories like that of language and literature, and through them it pervaded consciousness in further and more indirect ways than the historical saṃskāra. And while the history curriculum of independent India, at least until the Bharatiya Janata Party (BJP) schools came into being, largely followed the more inclusive and conciliatory framework of Jawaharlal Nehru's *The Discovery of India*, the Hindi literary curriculum closely mirrored the historical saṃskāra outlined in this chapter. This saṃskāra was thus firmly enscribed in the curriculum before Independence and remains so until the present day. Interestingly, in post-Independence literature it has been the so-called regionalist writers, concerned with representing culture and society holistically in a local setting, who have also rejected this nationalist view of history and its categories.

The historical consciousness limned by writers like Maithilīśaraṇ Gupta was also influential in discussions about the reorganization—or, as the buzzword went, saṅgaṭhan—of Indian society in the 1920s. The quest for indigenous models here took a conservative turn as thinker after thinker held up the varṇāśram system as the ideal form of societal organization. The heedless proliferation of castes and exploitation and unrest were seen as a corruption of the orginal perfect model in which conflict and disharmony had been absent. The Russian Revolution of 1917 provided another kind of ideological framework for the discussions on Indian society and introduced and popularized notions of individual rights and social and economic justice; but it, too, could be eventually harmonized with the varṇāśram system, with the notion of a perfectly organized Indian society in the past. Contemporary discussions among Hindi intellectuals did not envisage any other future for Indian society than the one already suggested by imaginings of the past. Potentially explosive issues such as untouchability or women's rights were either evaded or had only limited impact.

What is remarkable about these ideas is their resilience. They not only survived the ideologically turbulent years of the 1920s and 1930s but were carried over into the post-Independence era; in some sense they formed the basis of all debates on the notion of Indian society, both past and present. The historical self-consciousness of the Hindi public sphere was different from similar social and cultural enterprises elsewhere, mainly in the overall conservative, if not entirely status-quo, nature of intellectual opinion. Besides, this historical identity, and the social model it implied, became part of the sanskritization package, and as such appealed to a much greater number of groups and castes than that of its original proponents. The larger consequence of this spread was the serious diminution of critical forces in Hindi society at large and the indirect boosting of the old Brahmanical order, especially, one may add, in educational and literary institutions.

In the next chapter we shall see how the emergence of women's voices in the public sphere both employed and challenged the historical and social vision outlined in this chapter. They also insisted on bringing together the abstract debate and the empirical ground of concrete action and actual reality. We shall see how, by adding a personal and emotional dimension to their claim, and by using the same rational arguments their male counterparts used but with other symbolic referents, women intellectuals argued for a reform of society on the basis of a universal, but gendered, right to individual development and public participation. They in turn would operate some exclusions of their own.

CHAPTER 4

Women and the Hindi Public Sphere

4.1. Education and the Field of Action

Illustration 4.1. The heading of the editorial section in *Chāṁd*. Although *Chāṁd's* editor at this time was a man, the three women busy working suggest that this is a women-only space. Notice the modern and orderly room with electric lights, a spacious desk, and a glass-fronted cupboard.

Source: *Chāṁd*, IV, pt. 2, 5, September 1926, p. 434.

It was only in the 1920s that women's voices began appearing in the Hindi press and in Hindi literature. This was undoubtedly part of the general expansion of Hindi literacy, education and print, and the more widespread participation of people in the nationalist movement after the First World War and the Non-Cooperation movement. Yet women were a special case. Women's access to the public sphere was fraught with peculiar tensions, especially when it concerned 'respectable', upper caste women. Not only were they generally forbidden to appear in public or to interact with men and the outside world because of pardā (seclusion), their lives and roles were also hardly in their own hands. They were controlled at every step by guardians, elders, and families. Women were not only considered dependent individuals but, even more than men, always in relation to some male figure. Even reformers, who since the nineteenth century had advocated some kind of improvement in the status of women as a necessary step for the progress of the nation, envisaged it as a closely monitored process and with the object of making them better wives and mothers.[1] Debates on the 'woman's question', as it was called, were also profoundly affected by the symbolic identification of womanhood with 'Indianness' i.e. with India's peculiar spiritual essence, that which made it superior to and essentially different from the West.[2] Women active in the public sphere whether through print, education, or activism had thus to move within pretty narrow margins and negotiate with both traditional and reformist notions of Indian womanhood.

Yet the same women who were first *granted* controlled access to the Hindi public sphere took up the critical instruments they had acquired to raise questions about themselves, their role and the norms of society, and to undertake public activities in unprecedented ways. In doing so, they were partly shaped by current symbols and notions of Indian femininity (propriety, sevā, maryādā, etc.); at the same time they refashioned these symbols in the new spaces they had access to, whether in literature, in journals, in teaching, or in political activism. This chapter charts the spaces that became available to women and the strategies and idioms they employed to gain a public voice and to expand their horizons and their areas of activity.

[1] For an overview of nineteenth-century debates on, and activities in support of, 'women's reform', see Radha Kumar, *The History of Doing: An Illustrated Account of Movements for Women's Rights and Feminism in India, 1800–1990*, London, Verso, 1993.

[2] Chatterjee, *The Nation and Its Fragments*, pp. 6 ff.

Some limitations remained, as we shall see. Although some of the issues women raised were relevant to women in general, and although nationalist campaigns and peasant movements saw a significant participation of illiterate and rural women, the space Hindi women carved out within the Hindi public sphere was largely an urban and respectable one, and mirrored the class and caste exclusions of the male Hindi sphere.

Women's education is an obvious starting point because it gives an idea of the numbers of women involved and because that is where involvement first started for most of them. The issues at stake were in part different from those examined in the earlier section on education (1.4) but the outcome was the same: education often led to involvement in public activities and in the nationalist movement. Yet, one can argue, even more than schools, it was the women's press that played a crucial role in acquainting women with the world beyond the familiar, with the world of history and with contemporary India (4.2). Women's journals and literature were also crucial in raising questions about the family and about women's status in the family from new angles; most importantly, they argued for the need to acknowledge individual emotions as well as duties, something that received a great deal of attention in the new genre of social novels (4.3). This may account for the great popularity of *Chāṁd* (Allahabad, 1922), the most prominent Hindi women's journal, which became the most widely read Hindi journal generally.[3] As mentioned earlier, the question of women's actual access to the public sphere was not straightforward: if it led to economic independence or political participation, how was it to be compatible with a woman's dharma, her appointed place within the home? Nationalists believed that women would provide moral and numerical strength and were indeed necessary for the nationalist movement to succeed; yet the danger to the 'moral purity' of society was perceived to be great. The last section of the chapter examines the imaginative strategies used by writers to cope with this dilemma.

The Hindi-speaking area had remained largely unaffected by nineteenth-century debates and initiatives for women's education in British India that had taken place mostly in the Bengal and Bombay presidencies.[4] The few schools run by women missionaries had failed to attract girls from Hindu as well as Muslim families, who feared attempts at conversion, and there was otherwise little or no provision for formal education. Private tutors, or women teachers (*ustānīs*) for genteel Muslim

[3] See figures in Table 4.1, p. 64 [1.3.1].

[4] Kumar, *The History of Doing*, especially Chapter 2.

families, though not unheard of, depended on the resources and sensibilities of individual households and were by no means common.[5]

Hindi played a more prominent role in girls' education than in that of boys. Patriotic reformers considered it the ideal language of women's education. Even in the predominantly Urdu-educated Punjab, educational institutions for girls were Hindi-medium, first among them the legendary Kanyā Mahāvidyālay of Jalandhar (est. 1893). In an educated household boys were often educated in Urdu and English and girls in Hindi—the Nehru household being just one such case. This was partly due to the fact that women's education was not intended to be conducive to employment but rather envisaged as an instrument of self-improvement, and partly due to Hindi's association with religion and with devotional texts.

By the 1920s in north India, several educated women had come to the fore and acquired a voice in the male-dominated Hindi sphere. The first stirrings were in the Punjab in the late nineteenth century, thanks to Ārya Samāj educational enterprises.[6] In fact, most of the first vocal and active Hindi-educated women were Ārya Samāj graduates and students. Overall, the situation started to change slowly only in the second and third decades of the twentieth century.

Table 4.1. Girls' schools and pupils in UP*

	Primary		Secondary		College	
	Schools	Pupils	Schools	Pupils	Colleges	Pupils
1913	1067	46,693	85	8290	4	41
1920	1269	43,132	144	15,284	3	49
1930	1723	63,652	2310	33,136	5	155
1940	1724	80,775	432	76,482	13	556

*Sources: for 1913, official report quoted in *Strī-darpaṇ*, XIV, 3, March 1916, p. 178; for the other years *General Report on Public Instruction* for the years 1920, 1930, 1940; OIOLC.

[5] Gail Minault in her recent study on education and Muslim women in north India argues that ustānīs were in fact declining in numbers even though there was growing demand because the network of private charitable endowments (*awqaf*) and patronage which had supported them was crumbling, and it was still unacceptable for women from respectable families to be working for a salary outside the home; G. Minault, *Secluded Scholars: Women's Education and Muslim Social Reform in India*, New Delhi, Oxford University Press, 1998, p. 29.

[6] See Madhu Kishwar, 'Arya Samaj and Women's Education. Kanya Mahavidyalay,

The actual impact and growth of formal schooling were altogether limited. As elsewhere in India, girls' schools in north India were mostly an urban phenomenon, and attendance dropped drastically right at the primary stage as most girls were married or taken out of school before puberty. Figures for the United Provinces compared poorly with Bengal, Bombay, and Madras at the primary stage and became more uniform at the middle and higher stages.[7] All in all, only about 1 per cent of the female population of the United Provinces underwent some formal schooling.[8] In 1920, the proportion of girls to boys, roughly 1/10 at the lower primary stage, plunged to 1/40 at the upper primary stage, 1/200 at the middle stage, and to 1/250 at the high school stage.[9]

Primary education was, without exception in the colonial system, the worst organized and funded, despite the fact that it catered for the largest number of pupils by far. The number of girls' pāṭhśālās kept increasing throughout the two decades under survey, managed predominantly either by local boards or by private individuals with official grants-in-aid. 'Wherever you look', wrote Chandrakumārī Haṇḍu in 1929, 'in narrow lanes, at the edge of open sewers, surrounded by buzzing flies, our delicate maidens (*sukumārī kanyāeṁ*) sit on dirty rags writing on their slates'.[10]

Come, reader, I'll now show you one of these schools. First of all the first form; the teacher says with pride: 'I teach 130 children!' Your clothes are dirty, but what can you do? You get fifteen rupees per month and have to survive on them. You have a long stick in your hand and show your discipline: 'Stand up!,' 'Be quiet.' At this very moment you look like the terrifying image of Kālī and silence descends upon them. The children are dirty, too: their clothes are dirty, their hands are dirty, their faces are dirty, their hair is dishevelled and their frightened faces appear devoid of any sparkle and of the natural joy of children. Their eyes betray no wonder, no playfulness. The teacher says 'Read,' and a child reads out as if she were a lifeless machine.

Jalandhar', *Economic and Political Weekly*, XXI, 17, 26, April 1986, Women's Studies, pp. 9–24.

[7] In 1914, there were a total of 55,049 girls studying in the United Provinces compared to 259,024 in Madras, 220,891 in Bengal, 149,107 in Bombay and 106,100 in Punjab; see 'Bhārat meṁ strī-śikṣā kā prachār', *Strī-darpaṇ*, XIV, 3, March 1916, p. 178. Most of the data and debates on women's education, it should be noted, refer unfortunately only to the United Provinces and, partly, to the Punjab.

[8] Govarddhandās Tripāṭhī, 'Hamāre prānt meṁ bālikāoṁ kī śikṣā', *Chāṁd*, XVIII, pt. 2, 1, December 1940, p. 49.

[9] *General Report* for the year 1921, p. 28.

[10] C. Huṇḍa, 'Hamārī putrī-pāṭhśālāeṁ', *Chāṁd*, VII, pt. 2, 6, October 1929, p. 697.

In the second class, children are committing tables to memory. They all shout '*do dunī chār, do tīy chah, do cauk āṭh*' and not one of them understands what she is saying. Two girls are standing with their faces to the wall: they did not know the lesson by heart. One is sobbing, the other is angry and plotting revenge. She had all the qualities which the country needs: a sharp intellect, a strong sense of purpose and she could not bear injustice. But the master's cruel behaviour is slowly turning her into a stubborn child.[11]

This sorry picture was a far cry from recognizing girls' intellect as a national resource and an instrument for self-development, as nationalist reformers saw it. It reflected both a lack of financial and human resources—trained women teachers were scarce—but also a paradox about the meaning and scope of girls' education. How could educated women turn into school secretaries and manageresses when respectable women were meant to keep pardā, manage the entire household and become the mothers of the nation? The question, as we shall see, was examined in a long series of articles and stories on whether women's education should be role-based or not.

If the bulk of neighbourhood paṭhśālās reflected the uninspiring picture penned above, there were a few more solid institutions that were growing, and in the 1920s started holding intermediate and undergraduate classes.[12] In fact, middle and higher education for girls grew substantially when non-sectarian and non-missionary schools for girls were set up in the 1920s, with the teaching being almost exclusively in the vernacular. The main institutions, which attracted girls also from other provinces, were Kanyā Mahāvidyālay in Jalandhar, Crosthwaite High School (est. 1895) and Prayāg Mahilā Vidyāpīṭh (est. 1922) in Allahabad, Isabella Thoburn school and college in Lucknow (est. 1880s) and Indraprastha Girls' High School and college in Delhi.[13]

[11] Ibid., p. 698.

[12] In 1919 there were only 31 college students at the only girls' college of the Province, Isabella Thoburn in Lucknow. In 1920–1, new intermediate classes were started at three institutions: Annie Besant's Theosophical College in Benares, the Muslim High School in Lucknow, and Crosthwaite High School in Allahabad; *General Report on Public Instruction in the UP, 1918–19*, p. 17; ibid. for 1921, p. 24.

[13] For a detailed study of Kanyā Mahāvidyālay, a product of the Ārya Samāj educational project, see M. Kishwar, 'Arya Samaj and Women's Education'; for Crosthwaite school, see Schomer, *Mahadevi Varma*; for Isabella Thoburn, see the article by Kauśalyādevī, in the women's column 'Mahilā manorañjan' in *Mādhurī*, IV, pt. 1, 6, December 1925. The latter became part of Lucknow University, while classes for Allahabad University were held at Crosthwaite. The decision of the managing committee of Allahabad University, which had so far been co-educational, to have special

The very few early women BAs and MAs, Muslim and Hindu in equal numbers, had belonged to the English-speaking elite, usually the daughters of civil servants or professionals. They were the first ones to be photographed in journals along with public-minded Ranis as 'exceptional women'; their academic achievements were extolled with great pride but they were somehow different, in dress and lifestyle, from the readers' world.[14] The attitude to such women was actually a mixed one of pride, satire, and perceived danger. According to Satyāvatī Devī of the Ārya Samāj Kanyā Gurukul in Saran, women who had reached the top of the English education system had in fact turned their backs on 'Indian civilization'. English education did not inspire patriotism, and 'our women (*strī-samāj*), brought up in the present atmosphere of English education, are getting further and further away from Indian attire and sentiments'.[15] Yet their examination results were published with pride by women's journals.[16]

By the 1920s girls from more ordinary Hindi backgrounds started attending these schools in larger numbers, and it is from these schools that the majority of women in the Hindi public sphere came: Chandrāvatī Lakhanpāl, Mahādevī Varmā, Subhadrā Kumārī Chauhān, Vidyāvatī Sahgal, Tejrānī Dīkṣit, Rāmeśvarī Goyal, etc. (see Box 4.1.).[17] By caste they were almost exclusively Kayastha, Brahmin, Thakur, and Khatri, like their male counterparts; socially they belonged mostly to service families, had a background of active parental or brotherly or conjugal

---

arrangements for female students aroused heated public discussion and provoked two women's meetings in the city. One meeting, apparently more anglicized, objected to the decision arguing that in this way the university was taking a step backwards; the other, presided over by a Mrs Suśīlādevī, supported the decision to have separate teaching arrangements on account of the *present* social situation, in that it would be an incentive to enrol. The editor commented neutrally: 'We are happy that there are enough educated women in our society who can reflect seriously and with full freedom on such matters'; in *Mādhurī*, IV, pt. 1, 1, July 1928, p. 129.

[14] E.g. Miss Nur Jahan Mohammad Yusuf, MA, Vice-Principal of the Lucknow Muslim High School, mentioned in *Chāṁd*: she was awarded a scholarship by the provincial government to pursue educational studies abroad; *Chāṁd*, III, pt. 2, 1–2, May–June 1925, p. 117. *Chāṁd* regularly published pictures and biographies of such women from all over India; the fact that some belonged to one's own province did not make them either more accessible or less exotic.

[15] Satyavatī Devī, 'Striyoṁ ko kaisī śikṣā aur sāhitya kī āvaśyaktā hai?', *Mādhurī*, X, pt. 1, 6, January 1932, p. 788.

[16] See e.g. *Chāṁd*, III, pt. 2, 1–2, May–June 1925, p. 117.

[17] See also biographies in the Appendix.

support, often against the wishes of the larger family, and were pioneers in their own fields. By the late 1920s, when they were being admitted more frequently to D.A.V. Colleges or to Allahabad, Benares and Lucknow Universities for higher degrees, Gandhian nationalism had already affected the code of dress. They could now enter 'the top of the English education system' equipped with homespun Khadi and Indian values.[18]

Although the curricula were different from those of boys' schools, girls were given a fairly comprehensive education: at the Prayāg Mahilā Vidyāpīṭh, for instance, although maths, the 'traditional stumbling block for girls in middle schools', was made optional, girls were taught Hindi, history, geography, and home science, while natural science, religion, English, other Indian languages, as well as music and spinning, were optional subjects. Creativity was also encouraged in writing, and the girls' contributions were published in the school magazine and in other journals.[19]

As Madhu Kishwar has shown in the case of the Kanyā Mahāvidyālay in Jalandhar, even an institution with a culturally conservative view of

[18] Miss Śakuntalā Bhārgava, BA was extolled as one such ideal Indian woman: meeting her 'serious and pure nature' (*gambhīr sāttvik svarūp*) was for the interviewer almost a mystical experience! ('I bowed my head in my mind before that goddess'.) Before being admitted to DAV college in Dehradun in 1925, she had begged her father not to 'clamp her in the shackles of marriage'. With her father's full support, she took the Intermediate examination in 1927, and in 1928 a BA from BHU; at the time of the interview she was studying for an MA in Sanskrit. Her countenance was described as 'very pure, simple and devoid of pretence'; she dressed in Khadi, spent little of her allowance on herself and gave the rest to needy students. Although she did not support 'radical social change' (*sāmājik krānti*) vocally, she was herself 'an image of it'. She had spoken against pardā at the Bhārgava Mahilā-Samiti. 'The importance of Kumārījī lies not only in the fact that she has 'acquired a BA, but that she has established a high model of will-power, character and patriotism (*ātma-bal, charitra-bal aur deśprem*) in front of other women;' *Mādhurī*, VIII, pt. 1, 4, November 1929, pp. 768–70.

[19] S. Agravāl and P.D. Ṭaṇḍon, 'Prayāg mahilā vidyāpīṭh', *Gṛhalakṣmī*, XII, 9, November–December 1921, p. 297. See also Schomer, *Mahadevi Varma*, pp. 215–16. Since *Chāṁd*'s manageress, Vidyāvatī Sahgal, was a former teacher at Crosthwaite, students were encouraged to publish there; Mahādevī's first poems appeared in *Chāṁd* from the very first issue. At Prayāg Mahilā Vidyāpīṭh, with Mahadevī Varmā as principal, literature and creative writing were given a great impulse, and some 'progressive' books like Chandrāvatī Lakhanpāl's *Striyoṁ kī sthiti* (1932, see below) were part of the curriculum. In 1933 the manager, Saṅgamlāl Agravāl, organized the first women's kavi sammelan, which attracted many women who would otherwise not have participated. Both Mahādevī and Subhadrā Kumārī took part, and chair-women became a new fashion at poetry meetings (see 2.4.); ibid., pp. 217–18.

women's role could provide unexpected avenues for public participation during the freedom struggle. One of the aims of the Kanyā Mahāvidyālay was to prepare women preachers (*prachārikās*) for the Ārya Samāj, hence a public role.[20] Later, girl students from the Kanyā Mahāvidyālay were sent to sing songs at the opening session of the historic Lahore Congress of 1919; this would become a typical feature, both at literary and political gatherings.[21] In Allahabad, Crosthwaite and Mahilā Vidyāpīṭh girl students were taken to Anand Bhavan, and Kanyā Mahāvidyālay girls in Jalandhar were regularly taken to the annual sessions of the National Social Conference and the Indian National Congress, where they delivered speeches. Although most girls were married before their schooling was over, in some cases the patriotic atmosphere of the Mahāvidyālay and of Crosthwaite school and the Mahilā Vidyāpīṭh in Allahabad became a prelude to political participation and activity during Non-Cooperation and Civil Disobedience.[22] Even more than Hindi male writers, women writers took an active part in public life, either through constructive work (teaching, social work, etc.) or through direct political involvement (see Box 4.1). The close link between public access and education is further highlighted by the fact that adult women's education expanded noticeably after each wave of the movement.

Box 4.1. Education and Activism

Ārya Samāj women:

Urmilā Devī Śāstrī, Chandrāvatī Lakhanpāl, Rāmeśvarī Goyal, Pārvatī Devī, Vidyāvatī Seṭh, Hukmādevī Gupta, and Satyavatī Viśārda of Jalandhar were all either born to or married into Ārya Samāj families and studied or worked in Ārya Samāj schools. **Chandrāvatī Lakhanpāl** (1904–69) was chairwoman of the Mahilā

[20] Girls were taught the principles and texts of the Ārya Samāj, *sandhyā ucchāraṇ* (utterance of morning and evening prayers), *havan* mantras, the *Rāmāyaṇa*, the *Manusmṛti*, the *Gītā*, and a smattering of the Vedas. This accounts for the learned articles, full of shastric quotations, that women who had been through this curriculum wrote for Hindi magazines; ibid., p. 15.

[21] See Kumar, *The History of Doing*, p. 62. Female pupils singing poems or hymns became a familiar feature at literary meetings.

[22] 'KMV girls and teachers seem to have been the first women political workers that Punjab produced. . . .' National leaders came to speak at both schools, and 'even the buildings, bowers, gardens and pathways on the campus of KMV were named after prominent nationalist leaders'; Kishwar, 'Arya Samaj and Women's Education', p. 18.

Congress Committee in Dehradun; she became Congress Dictator during Civil Disobedience and was jailed for one year; in 1932 she was President of the UP Provincial Political Conference in Agra. **Ūrmilā Śāstrī** (1909–?) belonged to the Mahilā Satyāgraha Samiti of Meerut; she spent six months in jail in 1930 and was elected MLA from Meerut in the 1936 elections. **Vidyāvatī Seṭh** (1889–1974) was the first Hindu girl in the Province to take a BA, in 1917, from Isabella Thoburn College. She resolved to remain an unmarried brahmachāriṇī to devote her life to women's education, and became headmistress first of Mahādevī Kanyā Pāṭhśālā in Dehradun, then around 1920, of the newly founded Kanyā Gurukul (Delhi, then Dehradun) and became politically committed. **Pārvatī Devī** (1888–?) was born into a remarkable Ārya Samāj family from Lyallpur, whose members were all nationalists: one brother was Jaychandra Vidyālaṃkār; she herself was '*prājñā*' (graduate) in Sanskrit. After being widowed, she dedicated her life to women's education and public and political work, first as a teacher and Ārya Samāj preacher, and after 1920 as a Congress activist at the newly founded Svarajya Ashram in Meerut. Arrested for 'inflammatory speeches', she became famous for being given the longest sentence ever to a woman activist, two years. **Rāmeśvarī Goyal** (1911–36) came from a remarkable Ārya Samāj and nationalist Agraval family settled in Jhansi; her grandfather had been principal of the DAV college in Dehradun; her mother, Piṣṭādevī, was a renowned poet and Congress activist in Jhansi and educated all her nine daughters; Rāmeśvarī taught at the Ārya Kanyā Pāṭhśālā in Allahabad until her premature death. **Subhadrā K. Chauhān** (1904–47), educated at Crosthwaite school, Allahabad, became a full-time Congress activist along with her husband, Lakṣmaṇ Siṃh. She first went to jail during a Congress-flag hoisting satyāgraha in 1922; she did Congress propaganda both in Jabalpur, where she lived, one of the few women not observing pardā, and in the countryside: as a consequence, women formed about one-quarter of the Congress in Jabalpur, a remarkable proportion; she took part in all the major campaigns, went to jail several more times and was elected MLA in 1936. **Mahādevī Varmā** (1902–87), also educated at Crosthwaite and with an MA in Sanskrit from Allahabad University, did not take an active political role, but after a visit by Gandhi during a fund-raising tour during Civil Disobedience, she took to wearing khadi and started teaching as a volunteer in two villages outside Allahabad, vowing never to speak English while on Indian soil; she became a renowned poet, refused to live with her husband, and became principal of Prayāg Mahilā Vidyāpīṭh. **Śivrānī Devī** was a child-widow when she became Premchand's second wife; she became involved with Mahilā Congress Samiti in Lucknow, and Premchand was very proud when she was arrested during Civil Disobedience; she also took to writing. **Kamlā Chaudhrī** (1908–70) belonged to the Mahilā Satyāgraha Samiti of Meerut and went to jail in 1930 for six months; she became a member of the Town and Provincial Congress Committee, and of the Constituent Assembly in 1947.[23]

Whatever the actual impact of formal education for girls, the *discursive* importance of the question of women's education was far-reaching and led to a general reflection on women's roles. Education for both boys and girls was considered crucial to counteract cultural colonization and to build a strong and healthy nation. Nineteenth-century debates contrasted the present 'ignorance' of Indian women with their education and high status in India's golden past—but only to stress the importance of education for performing their roles as wives and mothers well.[24] Motherhood was isolated as the central experience of women's lives, and charged with a new nationalist significance: children were no private family affair but were the children of the nation and the makers of tomorrow's India. When, in the early twentieth century, the debate reached the newly forming Hindi sphere, it had already acquired these precise cultural and religious connotations; formal education was to supplement rather than supplant the socialization of girls in patriarchal society.[25] Education for women was planned out by men in accordance with their roles as mothers and housewives (*sugṛhiṇī*); their place should be at home; and their activities and behaviour should be in keeping with the rules of maryādā.

At the onset of the twentieth century, wrote Puruṣottam Dās Ṭaṇḍon in 1916, the debate on whether women should be educated at all, with all

[23] For biographies of the first three, see Appendix. For Urmilā Śāstrī also see *Viśāl bhārat*, II, pt. 2, 3, September 1929, pp. 365–6; and Manmohan Kaur, *Role of Women in the Freedom Movement (1857–1947)*, New Delhi, Sterling, 1986, p. 152. For S.K. Chauhan, Mahādevī Varmā and Rāmeśvarī Goyal see biographies in the Appendix.

[24] See Chakravarti, 'What Happened to the Vedic *Dasi*?' in Sangari and Vaid, *Recasting Women*.

[25] See the essays in Sangari and Vaid, *Recasting Women*.

its speculations about women's education in ancient India, had given way to the question of what kind of education girls should be given.[26] How much of modern education should girls be exposed to? The contrast between the large number of articles in favour of women's education throughout the two decades and the small numbers of pupils shows that girls' education was far from being an accepted or widespread practice. But the second round of debate allowed a larger range of views, with growing numbers of educated girls and women taking part: as we shall see, arguing about education became a way for women to argue for their right to define their own roles.

'The education of each person should keep in mind what he or she has to do when he or she grows up . . . in a word, I believe that the ideal of the whole of women's education should be one of making them into sugṛhiṇīs', wrote Puruṣottam Dās Ṭaṇḍon.[27] Since a woman's true dharma is *pātivrat* dharma, devotion to her husband, education should aim at strengthening that role, not at threatening it. Otherwise, Ṭaṇḍon continued, people would keep preferring non-educated but modest and dutiful women to those who were educated but overlooked their dharma.

Central to this view of role-based education was the preoccupation with male control over feminine subjectivity and with the boundaries of the role, which in Hindi is expressed by the powerful concept of maryādā, propriety, often visualized as a line or boundary. The danger that education would bring with it a sense of self-importance and individual rights was expressed as overstepping maryādā. Answering a Mrs Draupadī who had argued for women's right to freedom, *svatantratā*, in an article on 'Pātivrat' (*Strī-darpaṇ*, November 1913), Brahmadīn Saksenā voiced the worry of such reformers at the idea of individual freedom. What kind of freedom, he asked, unlimited or limited? 'We believe that the first kind of freedom is harmful, for reasons known to all [?!?]. . . . We support limited freedom within maryādā, i.e. *we want to give* as much freedom as is necessary for a woman to become the *arddhāṅginī* or companion of man, and for the happiness of the home.'[28]

This was a view shared by several women as well. Male writers,

[26] P.D. Ṭaṇḍon, 'Strī-śikṣā kī rīti par vichār', *Gṛhalakṣmī*, VII, 3, May–June 1916, pp. 111–13. *Maryādā* (Allahabad, 1910), a journal Ṭaṇḍon was associated with, carried an article on the subject in almost every issue.

[27] Ibid., pp. 111–13.

[28] After all, Saksenā argued, education should always lead to greater happiness; if it led to quarrels or conflicts, it is certain proof that it is wrong; 'Pātivrat dharma aur vartamān śikṣā kram', in *Strī-darpaṇ*, X, 3, March 1914, p. 174, emphasis added.

however, would inevitably stress the controlling role of husbands or male reformers. For example, Ṭaṇḍon designed a curriculum for girls only until the age of 16 or 17: 'After that her husband will probably be her teacher . . . and I think it is best to leave the care of her subsequent and higher education to him.'[29] Ṭaṇḍon's separate curriculum for girls was to take concrete form in the Prayāg Mahilā Vidyāpīṭh. Yet within its limitations, even role-based education became an avenue to emancipation, prompted by the need for women teachers and for employment for unsupported women, and by Gandhi's call to perform political or constructive activities.

The rhetoric of womanhood as motherhood, with its nationalist overtones of the nation as the highest Mother whom everyone was called to serve, provided leeway for unsuspected developments. As we shall see later in the chapter, the rhetoric of service to the Motherland, sevā, became the most powerful tool to break the divide between the 'home and the world' while remaining within the limits of maryādā (4.4.). In a two-part article on the 'need for women's education from a national perspective', Rāmrakh Siṃh Sahgal, the future founder of *Chāṁd*, drew a direct link between the revival of the ancient ideals of Sītā and Sāvitrī and participation in the nationalist struggle. Quoting extensively from *Wake up India* by Annie Besant, Sahgal subscribed to the idea that Indian women were not born ignorant but were bred ignorant: 'Our mothers and sisters should come out in the arena keeping in mind the stories of those heroic women.'[30] By providing critical tools and a sphere of socialization outside the home, girls' schools grew out of the hands of early social reformers into important sites for women to develop a public conscience and in some cases, literary expression and political engagement.

Debates on role-based education also provided a discursive space to argue critically about women's roles and abilities. There were differing arguments about the role, dharma, and nature of women and arguments in favour of a *self-defined* maryādā. For example, the Ārya Samāj reading of Indian history provided an argument in favour of equal education for girls, against traditional customs as man-made, and even for women's right to choose their marriage partner.[31] Questions about women's access to public space and to employment were raised on account of the fact

[29] P.D. Ṭaṇḍon, 'Strī-śikṣā kī rīti par vichār', p. 115.

[30] R.S. Sahgal, 'Rāṣṭrīy dṛṣṭi se strī-śikṣā kī āvaśyaktā', *Strī-darpaṇ*, XXV, 1, July 1921, p. 13.

[31] The author of one such tract recalls that girls were given equal education in the 'Aryan' age, and drew from the familiar examples of Sītā, Sāvitrī, Damayantī,

that respectable employment was a real necessity for many women and could be a form of nationalist sevā. As elsewhere in India, education became a pretext for speaking about burning issues like pardā, mismatched-marriages, dowries, and increasingly, women's rights and economic self-reliance.[32] Those who, like Sahgal, supported the view that education was important *per se* and a means of self-empowerment, argued that women should take education into their own hands and extend traditional roles to the wider arena of society and the nation. Education was thus not plain literacy, but an awakening to self-respect and self-awareness.[33]

The issue of education as a means to employment was hotly debated, as it hit at the heart of women's dependence and home-bound role. It also conjured up the image of the Indian woman's bad 'other': the shameless, flirtatious, and competitive western(ized) woman. Interestingly, reformers and women contributors first introduced it as a solution for 'helpless' (*abalā*) women—widows and women abandoned by their families, often with children—and argued that it was the only respectable alternative to either prostitution or conversion to Christianity or Islam. Faced with these greater dangers, should not women of no means rather seek to support themselves through employment? As proof, *Chāṁd*'s column *Chiṭṭhī-patrī* carried several letters by women, usually educated up to the Hindi Middle examination standard, who asked for help in finding teaching jobs. The editor supported these women vigorously and often carried answers in later issues, giving the names of institutions or of gentlemen

---

Draupadī, etc. to argue against arranged marriages: all these heroines chose their husbands in *svayaṃvaras*. The Puranic ślokas against women's education were men-made, she argued, and the fall continued under Muslim rule; the practice of child marriage, necessary at that time, survived, however, even after the danger had ended. The advent of English education only added fuel to the fire by making a boy's education so expensive that nothing could be spared for girls. Gopāldevī, 'Kyā paṛh-likhkar laṛkiyā kumārī raheṁgī?', *Chāṁd*, V, pt. 2, 6, October 1927, pp. 689–91. See also Subhadrā Devī's dialogue 'Pati-patnī kā kanyā ke viṣay meṁ vārtālāp': here, too, it is the (educated) father who argues in favour of higher education for his daughter, while his wife would like to see her married soon; he also argues in favour of a modified version of svayaṃvar and against pardā, because true modesty, he says, lies within; Subhadrā Devī', 'Pati-patnī kā kanyā ke viṣay meṁ vārtālāp', *Gṛhalakṣmī*, IV, 10, December–January 1914, pp. 519–23.

32 See Veer Bharat Talvar, 'Feminist Consciousness in Women's Journals in Hindi: 1910–20', in Sangari and Vaid, *Recasting Women*.

33 R.S. Sahgal, 'Rāṣṭrīy dṛṣṭi se strī-śikṣā par vichār'.

willing to marry them. It is noteworthy in fact that as a rule, pleading women preferred employment to remarriage, perhaps aware of the social stigma and emotional traumas the latter involved.

The door to activity in the 'world outside' was therefore first opened for women in distress, under exceptional circumstances. Even Prayāg Mahilā Vidyāpīṭh, founded by the first Congress municipal board in Allahabad with Puruṣottam Dās Ṭaṇḍon as chairman, balanced the ideal of an Indian, alternative, role-based education with the practical needs of the students. Although the curriculum differed from that of government schools, students were prepared for the Board of Education's Middle school examinations because of the greater employment value of regular degrees. The Vidyāpīṭh was very successful in combining a focus on cultural identity with flexibility and practical sense. Following the example of the Hindī Sāhitya Sammelan, it started first as an examining institution with sessions twice a year administered in Allahabad and in any centre with at least three candidates.[34] There was no age limit and candidates could take one subject at a time: this formula allowed married girls to take up or resume their studies at home as and when they could.[35] The Mahilā Sevā Sadan, the first teaching and residential wing of the Mahilā Vidyāpīṭh in Allahabad (1930), catered initially to women in need; it hosted mostly widows, girls from impoverished families, and, increasingly, the daughters and wives of men jailed during the nationalist movement.[36]

However, once the issue of employment had been raised, it remained central to women's debates throughout the period, and was argued in all its possible facets: women teachers, doctors, nurses, and lawyers were in great demand; the duty towards the nation was as strong and primary as that towards the family; why limit a mother's love only to her own children, etc. Clearly, participation in the nationalist movement had

[34] 'Gathering together large numbers of women from far away in one place [to teach them] would be very difficult, because of pardah, child-bearing at a young age, and lack of belief in higher education for women. In addition, the cost of attending a teaching university would be prohibitive. Especially in our country, which is so backward socially and economically, giving middle and higher education to as many women as possible at minimal cost can only be accomplished by an examining university;' *Viśāl bhārat*, July 1930, pp. 84–5, quoted by Schomer, *Mahadevi Varma*, p. 214.

[35] It 'recognized the fact that most girls had heavy responsibilities in the home and enabled them to pace their education at their own convenience'; ibid.

[36] For instance, Sampūrṇānand, Lāl Bahādur Śāstrī, and Rajendra Prasad sent their daughters there; ibid., p. 219.

opened a door which could hardly be closed again, and although the primacy of motherhood, the centrality of pātivrat dharma and of maryādā were rarely questioned, the whole definition of a woman's identity and role was at stake.

Perhaps the most comprehensive argument in favour of women's self-definition is contained in Chandrāvatī Lakhanpāl's book *Striyoṁ kī sthiti* (1932).[37] Chandrāvatī, herself educated in Allahabad and Benares, married the Ārya Samāj scholar and professor Satyavrat Siddhāntālaṃkār, taught at Gurukul Kangri, and became a well-known figure in Hindi thanks to *Mādar iṇḍiyā kā javāb* [The Answer to *Mother India*], her reply to Katherine Mayo's *Mother India.* In *Striyoṁ kī sthiti*, the chapter on education opens with an indictment of women's seclusion at home: for her, education was not compatible with the oppressive seclusion of women.

> For centuries the arena of women's activities has been considered the home. Human society did not pause long to consider what their relation was to the world at large. For many, the aim of their life has been to obey their husbands and to bear children. What need is there for education for such things? If they have to study it is enough to study just the amount they need to amuse their husbands. Women should know how to write letters, sew and cook; a woman has no other use.[38]

In her outspoken and persuasive style, Chandrāvatī equated the condition of women with slavery: just as a man could buy a slave and own more than one, a husband in India could buy a wife and keep more than one. 'After keeping women enslaved for centuries and bringing them to their present state, men now say that this is the natural state of women', i.e. that women were naturally dependent on men and would naturally seek their protection (p. 125). To this Chandrāvatī replied that women would still seek marriage, true, but not from a helpless position. She further dismissed the notion of the woman as abalā, physically and intellectually weaker than a man, as a myth: their astounding progress in only two centuries proved that the contrary was true. Given men and women's equality in terms of abilities, to deny them opportunities outside the home amounted to a crime, to enslavement. Thus the curriculum for girls should be comprehensive and on a par with that for boys.

Only at the end did Chandrāvatī raise the issue of the centrality of

[37] Originally published by Gurukul Kangri in 1932, it was subsequently republished by the Ganga Pustak Mala after it was awarded the Seksāriyā and the Sammelan awards in 1934.

[38] Chandravatī Lakhanpāl, *Striyoṁ kī sthiti*, Lucknow, Ganga Pustak Mala, third ed. 1941, p. 123.

marriage: couldn't women be equally, or even more, useful to society otherwise? In any case, they should be allowed not to marry if they so wished. Moreover, employment was useful even for married women since they could share the burden of expenses and provide for themselves in the not-too-rare event of widowhood or abandonment. To deny women education and the right to step out of their homes was an injustice to them and to society. This, concluded Chandrāvatī, was the right way of looking at the question of education from a woman's point of view.[39]

By the 1930s, then, a powerful women's voice on education and the right to self-definition had emerged in Hindi. For the great majority of educated girls, themselves a small minority, marriage continued to be the only end, but the figure of the educated working woman—the unmarried teacher, social worker, or political activist—found a place in the collective imagination and began gaining social acceptance. In fact, a few stories by women authors in the late 1930s featured educated wives feeling trapped at home as in a prison.[40]

All in all, attitudes towards 'educated woman' remained ambiguous. The western-educated woman was the object of disapproval and contempt: as someone who had overstepped maryādā, she had messed up all family and social relations, was bound to end up badly and compared unfavourably with the simple but innocent illiterate girl. This attitude was especially prominent in cartoons, even those in magazines like *Chāṁd* which fervently championed the cause of women's education: whether 'at home' or 'in the world', they seemed to say, women's progress must always carry the brand of Indianness.[41] On the other hand, college girls featured widely in romantic narratives without any moral stigma attached to them: Dhanīrām Prem, Pāṇḍey Bechan Śarmā Ugra, and Nirālā deployed educated heroines as characters who possessed not only 'womanly virtues' but also wit, intelligence, passion and determination.[42] Educated women made more challenging partners to male protagonists, or symbolized the modern sensitive woman, as in Jainendra

[39] Ibid., p. 141.

[40] See Tejrānī Dīkṣit, 'Jvālā', *Chāṁd*, XIV, pt. 2, 2, June 1936, and Tejrānī Pāṭhak, 'Maiṁ kaise haṁsūṁ?', *Chāṁd*, XV, pt. 1, 4, February 1937.

[41] See e.g. Kumārī Chandrakiraṇ, 'Ejūkeṭed vāif', *Chāṁd*, XVIII, pt. 1, 3, August 1940, pp. 194–7. As usual, in this story, too, the cheated husband is as much an object of contempt as the brazen wife. One is reminded of Miss Māltī, the flirtatious England-returned doctor of Premchand's novel *Godān* (1936).

[42] See the witty heroine who rejects the protagonist's ardent love in Dhanīrām Prem's story 'Jalā-bhunā', *Chāṁd*, IX, pt. 2, 4, August 1931; or Ugra's Muslim heroine of a cross-religious love story in Calcutta in *Chand hasīnoṁ ke khuṭūt* (1927); and finally Nirālā's heroines in *Alkā* (1933) and *Nirupamā* (1934–35).

Kumār's *Tyāgpatr* (1937) (see 4.4). The significant presence of school- or college-going female characters in stories and dialogues in women's journals, and in journals generally from the late 1920s onwards, suggests a greater familiarity with the school experience, at least among women contributors, and isolates education as one of the experiences considered crucial in fashioning a feminine subjectivity. In general, educated female characters are bold, speak and argue, have an individual life.

Still, to speak of women's education is to speak of its limitations and exclusions. It remained largely an urban phenomenon, excluding rural women and children of the lower strata and castes completely. Stratification among educated women partly mirrored that among educated males: among them, some educated women of the area were part of the English-speaking elite; Hindu and Muslim female pupils replicated the Hindi–Urdu divide; finally, for many women it was active political participation, and not literacy, which drew them into the public sphere (see 4.2). The rest of this chapter will outline the process by which educated women expanded, challenged, and redefined the role that they had been assigned in the economy of national regeneration. They did so largely through journals, widening in them the range of subjects a woman was meant to know about, by questioning social and moral demands that particularly told on them, and by redefining traditional women's roles and opening up new ones.

4.2. Widening Concerns: Hindi Women's Journals

Women's education, though a major focus of public debate, was such a limited affair that it cannot alone account for the upsurge of women's voices and public involvement in the 1920s and 1930s. Journals and books, reaching out to girls and women educated informally at home or with only partial schooling, significantly supplemented or substituted for formal education. Journals in particular provided a much wider range of information than was available in the curriculum. They were important means of instilling in women public concerns and the sense of a common cultural and political sphere. It is difficult, and in most cases misleading, to call these journals 'feminist',[43] for as we shall see, the strategies and idioms used in championing women's voices and issues differed explicitly from the confrontational attitude of suffragettes in Europe and

[43] See e.g. Talwar, 'Feminist consciousness in women's journals in Hindi: 1910–20'.

America. Besides, as with education and literature for women, journals too were primarily meant to instruct girls on their roles within the household and only gradually widened their concerns.[44] In the process, the boundaries of what was 'useful for women' (*strī-upyogī*) were dramatically redefined.

Strī-upyogī literature[45] was but the last example of a literature of moral instruction that had an old written and oral tradition in India. As historians have recently argued, the peculiarity of nineteenth-century strī-upyogī literature in several Indian languages was that it combined the religious and moral notions and values of strī-dharma with 'new', Victorian values and ideas about domesticity and womanhood that were considered necessary for the reformed household. This involved teaching them virtues like modesty, thrift, pliability, obedience, simplicity, purity, and dedication: making them Indian versions of the Victorian woman. It also involved 'reforming' their language and their forms of entertainment, withdrawing them from participation in the productive process and from holding property rights: in a word, drawing a strong line between the respectable woman in the house (the *bhadramahilā*) and the relatively less shackled and economically independent lower-class woman in the street.[46]

The first Hindi journal edited by women in the twentieth century reproduced this pattern and was explicitly meant as educational material.

[44] E.g. Bhārtendu's *Bālābodhinī* (1874–8), the first women's journal in Hindi, offered a sharp contrast with Bhārtendu's other journalistic enterprises: to female readers the editorial self dispensed information and admonition, economics and *charitras* (biographies of women worthies) as role models but no Braj Bhasa poetry, too dangerously close to śṛṅgāra (the erotic mood) even in its devotional mode, and certainly no discussion of the issues of social reform, many concerning women, that were being so forcefully debated in journals for the general public. Cf. Dalmia, *The Nationalization of Hindu Traditions*, pp. 245 ff.

[45] For the influence of strī-upyogī literature on the development of the Hindi novel, see Kalsi, 'Realism in the Hindi Novel', pp. 27 ff. For a similar trend in Urdu, see Naim, 'Prize-Winning *Adab*'; and Minault, *Secluded Scholars*.

[46] See Sangari and Vaid, *Recasting Women*; Banerjee, *The Parlour and the Street*; Kumar, *The History of Doing*; P. Chatterjee, *The Nation and its Fragments;* Dipesh Chakrabarty, 'The Difference-Deferral of Colonial Modernity: Public Debates on Domesticity in British Bengal', in D. Arnold and D. Hardiman, eds, *Subaltern Studies VIII*, Delhi, OUP, 1994; and K. Sangari, *The Politics of the Possible*, Delhi, Tullika, 1999. In particular, D. Chakrabarty has ingeniously interpreted the term *gṛha-lakṣmī* as a fraught combination of the religious merit of Lakṣmī, the goddess of wealth a bride was supposed to incarnate at home, and the modern nationalist project that saw the house (*gṛha*) as subordinate but part of the project of civil society; ibid., p. 80.

Gṛhalakṣmī ('Lakshmi of the home'—implying a housewife spreading sweetness and light), launched in 1909 in Allahabad by Mrs Gopāldevī and her husband Sudarśanāchārya, a famous Ayurvedic doctor, left little doubt from its name itself about the aims of such education.[47]

Let us examine more closely what strī-upyogī meant for *Gṛhalakṣmī*. Following the principle that education for girls was to be primarily moral and based on their future roles as wives and mothers, *Gṛhalakṣmī* took it upon itself to emphasize the importance of education but also to prepare girls to compromise between their aspirations and the demands of family life.[48] The practical, lower middle class orientation of this education is evident in a dialogue between a mother and daughter on the proper education for girls when the mother remarks that thrift and willingness to learn to do everything are essential because they have no servants. English is part of this education, but without any clear aim or prospect of further and wider reading, employment, or an active public interaction:

> 'Why should I learn English? Will I ever live in England?' [asks the daughter]. 'Of course not [answers her mother] but in order to be able to *answer* properly in case you happened to be in company of some foreigners and they were to ask you questions in their own language.'[49]

The focus, needless to say, was completely on the household; a few curiosities and women's news were the only items about the outside world. A typical issue carried articles, short stories, and many short dialogues with a moral message, a few historical pieces on vīrāṅganās, dialogues on child-rearing, on girls' education and on pardā, articles on strī dharma and pātivrat dharma, on tensions within the family and ways

[47] The journal began with 4000 subscribers, a remarkable figure for a Hindi magazine in those years, and prided itself on surviving on its readership alone. It never recovered from a fire that gutted the office; readership sank to 2500 in 1920 and reached a low of 1000 in 1923 before rising again to about 2000 in 1924, shortly before publication was stopped; see *Gṛhalakṣmī*, XV, 1, March–April 1924, pp. 41–2. In the early 1920s it was mostly written and edited in Gopāldevī's name by Thakur Śrīnāth Siṃh, then a young writer close to the Nehru family who later joined the Indian Press and edited *Bālsakhā* and *Sarasvatī* before launching his own women's journal, *Dīdī*, in the 1940s. Interview with Thakur Śrīnāth Siṃh, Allahabad, July 1993.

[48] Hence every issue carried articles in favour of girls' education, along with just as many on pātivrat dharma and on how education was not to breed conceit; see 'Striyoṁ ko mān karnā anuchit hai', *Gṛhalakṣmī*, IV, 3, May–June 1913.

[49] Pyārelāl Gārg, 'Kyā kyā sīkhnā chāhiye?', *Gṛhalakṣmī*, IV, 3, May–June 1913, p. 149, emphasis added.

of solving them (i.e. by yielding to the elders' wishes), advice on how to avoid bad company and bad reading, etc. The editorial voice was restricted to asking for recipes and contributions from schoolgirls and to suggesting ways of washing clothes.[50] The hybrid idiom of religious merit, of Indianness (versus the West), and of women's equality is exemplified in the advertisement for the first volume of the *Gṛhalakṣmī* granthamālā, *Gṛhiṇī* (*Housewife*):

According to the Hindu scriptures, the relationship between man and wife (*svāmī-strī*) [is such that] they together become one; no difference is left between them; a wife is the companion-in-dharma (*saha-dharminī*) of her husband. But nowadays English education has made Indian husbands degrade their wives from the position of saha-dharminī to that of lover (*praṇayinī*).[51]

The 'Hindu scriptures' are the authority used to advocate equality and companionship between husband and wife, while at the same time distancing oneself from the 'western' notion of companionate marriage based on mutual attraction and affection. All in all, *Gṛhalakṣmī* pursued a moderately educational and reformist mission. Dialogues and articles certainly allowed women and even schoolgirls to gain the unprecedented confidence to speak up publicly, whatever their views. One Kamlā, for example, took on a male voice to point out the dilemma of the 'consequence of women's education'. The male first-person narrator is a university student who was married to an illiterate girl against his will; he then took upon himself the duty of educating her and teaching her to appreciate, if not Milton (in brackets: 'a great English poet'), at least Tulsīdās and Sūrdās. Two years later he has passed his BA and his wife can read and write Hindi well and has learnt a little English. But the result is depicted in a scene in which his wife speaks standard (*śuddh*) Hindi and his mother speaks dialect: when the mother-in-law sees that the daughter-in-law is reading an English book while cooking she starts abusing her and is even more incensed when the daughter-in-law replies respectfully and

[50] See *Gṛhalakṣmī* issue of April–May 1913, IV, 2. In another note on Indian and foreign methods of cleaning pots and pans, *chuāchūt*, pollution by touch, is accepted as matter of fact; ibid., p. 109.

[51] Quoted in *Gṛhalakṣmī*, IV, 2, April–May 1913. The first five titles of the series published up to 1913 included *Gṛhiṇī*, *Choṭī bahū* (*Younger daughter-in-law*), *Lakṣmī-bahū* ('on a young and virtuous daughter-in-law who bears all hardships . . . very useful for schools'), *Prem-latā* ('a novel full of teachings') and *Ādarś bahū* (*The ideal daughter-in-law*).

defends her actions by argument. 'Christānīn' is the final word of abuse.[52] How can the generation gap be filled?

A young 'reader' embraced enthusiastically the reformist goal of role-based education (not to waste time on 'useless and shallow novels and stories') but also looked to European-educated Japan to plead that 'education nowadays must be different'.[53] A Vidyāvatī Devī reported with great enthusiasm the miraculous story of a modern *satī*, fully educated and yet totally devoted to her husband, from Jarauli village (dist. Mainpuri). The report was full of stirring miraculous details and allowed Vidyāvatī to comment: 'Dear women readers! Despite the fact that Kāliyuga is spread all over the earth and no one follows one's own dharma any longer, there are still examples of wifely devotion among the daughters of India'.[54]

By contrast, *Strī-darpaṇ* ('The mirror of women', est. July 1909), edited by the women of the Nehru family (Rāmeśvarī, Rūpkumārī, Kamlā, and Umā) and with a wide and competent range of male and female contributors, was more outspoken in its 'women's view' and in the defence of women's rights. 'It is the only journal which teaches women their rights along with their dharma,' said the publicity in 1919, 'because husbands, brothers and fathers cannot promote the welfare of the country while treating women like animals.'[55]

Compared with *Gṛhalakṣmī*, *Strī-darpaṇ* covered a wider range of issues as strī-upyogī. Apart from the usual fare of articles against pardā, on historical examples of female excellence, and on hygiene and health,

[52] Kamlā, 'Strī-śikṣā kā phal', *Gṛhalakṣmī*, VI, 7, September–October 1915, pp. 357–9.

[53] 'Ek paṭhikā', 'Strī-śikṣā', *Gṛhalakṣmī*, VII, 4, June–July 1916, pp. 175–7.

[54] Two months after she vowed in front of the Ganges that she would become a *satī*, Rāmdevī's husband dies. While she busies herself with preparations her father-in-law is afraid she might fail and invite ridicule upon the family; he is also worried that the police may create a fuss. Rāmdevī herself suggests he call the police, and when they arrive at the appointed time they do not have the courage to stop her. Thousands have come to witness the event from neighbouring villages. Rāmdevī's father-in-law gives her the honour of lighting her husband's funeral pyre; she needs no fire, in fact, rubbing her hands is enough. When the police require the consent of the corpse a voice rises saying 'Yes, come!'. She then disposes of her jewels, leaving them for their two-month-old son, and after she lies on the pyre her clothes burn together with her body, hence keeping her modesty intact. Vidyāvatī Devī, 'Satī samāchār', *Gṛhalakṣmī*, IV, 7, September–October 1913, pp. 377–80.

[55] From the publicity in the journal.

it carried articles *against* role-based education, news of women's achievements in India and abroad, meetings of women's organizations, and both local and international news like the war in Europe, its cost for India and the revolt in China. It looked with great interest at the awakening of women in nearby Bengal and Punjab, and compared it unfavourably with that in the United Provinces. Organizationally, *Strī-darpaṇ* remained a limited family concern, never crossing the threshold of 1000 copies, and belonged to the kind of elite women's movement exemplified by the All India Women's Conference.[56]

It was with the First World War, and then with the nationalist campaigns of 1919–21, that the content of both *Strī-darpaṇ* and *Gṛhalakṣmī* changed considerably. Political news started appearing regularly and both magazines espoused Gandhi's message and the movement wholeheartedly. Articles and speeches by Annie Besant, Sarojini Naidu, and the mother of the Ali brothers began appearing in *Gṛhalakṣmī* from 1918 onwards, and after 1921 the journal published translations of articles and open letters by Mahatma Gandhi. A new editorial column in 1922 carried more political news, which included lobbying by the All India Women's Conference (AIWC) and riots as well as photographs and biographies of women activists. Non-Cooperation made swadeshi chiefly a womanly concern, urging them to come out of pardā to serve the country, and suggesting that deś sevā, service to the country, might be as high a dharma as pātivrat dharma. Yet the journals were reluctant to discount the centrality of pātivrat dharma. To a 'proud woman non-cooperator' who wrote in November 1921 that she wanted to serve Mother India publicly but was hindered by her husband who held different views, the editor of *Strī-darpaṇ* suggested a compromise. While supporting the woman's wish, the editor suggested that she could serve Mother India at home by spinning khadi. Still, strī-dharma was widening its horizons. Also, more and more women contributed, both highly educated and avowedly self-educated. It is difficult now to identify them, for their printed names rarely carried a surname after the dignified appellation of 'Devī'.

The journals grew bolder on the home front, too. A new column of readers' letters opened up a space for 'true stories', and articles by a

[56] In 1923 the journal moved from Rāmeśvarī Nehrū's hands to Kanpur, where it was edited by Sumati Devī and Phulkumārī Mehrotrā, possibly close to the Pratāp Press. For the politics and social composition of the All India Women's Conference, see Geraldine Forbes, *Women in India*, Cambridge: Cambridge University Press 1996; and Kumar, *A History of Doing*.

'newly wedded bride' raised uncomfortable questions about women's subordination to male wishes and male images of real women.[57] The letters in particular, written by women in distress, revealed a less composed female self than that of the women contributors (see 4.3). They did not always meet with the editor's sympathy, and this points to the ambiguity that was typical of moderately reformist or male responses to female emancipation. For example the educated daughter of a Hindi writer from Calcutta complained of her mismatched marriage with a dumb and profligate village boy. She had written to her father asking him to marry her to somebody else or to let her live the life of a widow, but her father's angry reply was that he should never have given her an education since 'the consequence of your education seems to be that you are resolved to disgrace me in front of everyone. Is this the aim of education?'. The editor sympathized with her ill fortune, but also with her father, and urged her to adjust to the fact of her marriage: 'If you leave your husband you might create a scandal among women (*mahilā-samāj*). No such example should be placed before our society; please think it over again.'[58] To an educated Brahmin widow who blamed men for having seduced her, other readers responded by blaming her for her lust and lack of self-control and suggested the example of another 'low-born' woman who had sacrificed her life rather than her honour.[59] The image of the virtuous *and* educated woman, at ease both with her traditional dharma as well as with the new calls of the hour, was not to be tarnished by human weaknesses.

By 1920 a kind of rapprochement was taking place between women's journals and general magazines. On the one hand, women's journals featured a greater number of topical articles and had more established contributors.[60] On the other hand, by the 1920s all mainstream Hindi journals started carrying women's sections, usually with articles

[57] 'Ek nav-vivāhitā vadhu', in *Gṛhalakṣmī*, XIV, 9, November–December 1923; XIV, 11, January–February 1924 and XV, 1, March–April 1924. In 'Hamārī bahueṁ bahut śarmīlī kyoṁ jān paṛtī haiṁ' ('Why do our brides appear so shy?'), for example, she questioned the wisdom of pardā and the highly-valued coyness of young brides and expressed a longing for the unrestrained freedom of her childhood days; *Gṛhalakṣmī*, XV, 1, March–April 1924.

[58] *Gṛhalakṣmī*, XV, 1, March–April 1924, p. 30.

[59] *Chiṭṭhī-patrī*, in *Gṛhalakṣmī*, XIV, 4, January–February 1924; p. 118.

[60] E.g. Viśvāmbharnāth Jijjā, Rāmrakh Siṃh Sahgal, Zahūr Bakhś, Rāmsevak Tripāṭhī, and Śrīnāth Siṃgh.

on problems like pardā, child-widows and education, and with short poems and pieces by women contributors. This was a sign that female readership was being recognized but still as a separate group with special concerns. It was finally *Chāṁd* which not only broke the mould of strī-upyogī literature but also located women's issues at the core of the nationalist quest, just as socialists would do a decade later with peasants and the economic question.

Chāṁd's nationalism started with its perspective: from the very beginning, the awakening and activities of women in the Hindi belt were seen as part of a countrywide, indeed a worldwide, phenomenon. Though most of the longer articles and special issues centred on north Indian women and society, the news section offered information, facts, and figures on women from all over India and abroad as if they were part of the same, irresistible wave. This both legitimized women's initiatives and increased their self-confidence to go further. Also, while addressing educated and newly literate women, *Chāṁd* did not limit itself to issues concerning them but as part of the same project of social and political regeneration also touched on those affecting peasants and workers: all kinds of oppression had to be denounced in the quest for svarājya.[61]

An enterprising Khatri from Lahore, Rāmrakh Siṃh Sahgal (1896–1952), who had a record of involvement with the Congress and of contact with the revolutionary group of Bhagat Singh and Chandrashekhar Azad, began *Chāṁd* in Allahabad in 1922. In size (100 pages) and content, it surpassed all previous women's journals and was more similar to mainstream Hindi literary journals. It incorporated all the columns and features of women's and mainstream magazines (letters, reviews, news, editorials, cartoons, etc.), added plenty of reading material in the form of poems, stories and serialized novels, and launched, with aggressive

[61] See e.g. Rāmeś Prasād, 'Kārkhānoṁ meṁ strī-mazdūr', *Chāṁd*, IV, pt. 1, 4, January 1926, p. 309. Similarly, 'A recent case before the Allahabad High Court has given an important victory to women', wrote the editor when a Koiri woman named Kauliyā was granted maintenance after her husband had 'divorced' her against her will and brought home a Chamar girl. The High Court reversed the decision of the panchayat and of the local magistrate, who had argued that 'men and women of this class (*śreṇī*) do not follow social rules and are naturally cruel; Koiris are not very civilized yet and follow their own social mores.' 'The decision of the first-class magistrate shows clearly that English justice does not care to protect the oppressed women of the Koiri caste,' was the editor's remark; editorial note 'Patnī ke adhikār', *Chāṁd*, VII, pt. 2, 6, October 1929, pp. 735–6.

advertising, a large-scale operation similar to that of *Mādhurī*. It was soon recommended for public and school libraries by the Education departments of the United Provinces, Punjab, Bihar and Rajasthan, and it became the Hindi monthly with the highest readership, jumping from the initial 1000 to 8000 copies in 1927 and to a remarkable 15,000 copies in 1930.[62] With a number of attractive special issues (*Vidhvā-aṅk, Viduṣī-aṅk, Galpāṅk, Achūt-aṅk, Mārvāṛī-aṅk, Kāyastha-aṅk, Rājputānā-aṅk, Samāj-aṅk*, etc.), literary contributions by the best and newest writers, no moral inhibitions against popular fiction,[63] long topical editorials and a strong sense of mission, *Chāṁd* decidedly changed the coordinates of strī-upyogī literature.[64]

Chāṁd accomplished this by breaking the boundaries of 'what women should know' and 'what women should say'. The first move, discussed in this section, encompassed a variety of strategies: first addressing women as protagonists and active subjects of Indian society and of the movement for national regeneration, not only symbolically (as vīrāṅganās and Bhāratmātās) but also as empowered individuals; second, making women equally knowledgeable about all sorts of political, economic, social, and historical questions, with no censorship of any kind; finally, carrying news on women satyāgrahīs and leaders and identifying the journal itself with the nationalist movement. Sahgal's own passionate editorials,

[62] Source: *Statement of Newspapers and Periodicals published in UP*, Government Press, Allahabad, for the relevant years, OIOLC, London.

[63] *Nirmalā* by Premchand was serialized in 1925; Mahādevī Varmā's poems were published from the first issue; Rāmkumār Varmā's poems also appeared regularly; young Chāyāvādī poets like Ānandīprasād Śrīvāstava and Chaṇḍīprasād 'Hṛdayeś' worked on the editorial board ('Hṛdayeś' until his death in 1927) and so did popular writers like G.P. Śrīvāstava, Dhanīrām Prem, and Chatursen Śāstrī. Other assistant editors were Nandkiśor Tivārī and, for a while, Bhubaneśvar Miśra.

[64] The variety and constant attempt at improvement can be gauged by the growing number of miscellaneous columns, starting with *Gharelū davāeṁ* (homemade medicines), *Pāk-śikṣā* (recipes), *Cuṭkule* (jokes), and *Samāchār saṅgrah* (collected news); over the years new columns were started like *Chiṭṭhī-patrī* (letters from the readers), *Sāhitya saṃsār* (book reviews), *Hamāre sahyogī* (articles quoted from other journals) in 1925; *Śānti kuṭir* (spiritual snippets) in 1926; *Vinod vaṭikā* (humorous jokes and stories by G.P. Śrīvāstava) in 1927; *Dubejī kī chiṭṭhī* (very popular humorous letters by Viśvambharnāth Śarmā Kauśik in the style of Bālmukund Gupta's famous 'Śivśambhū ke chiṭṭhe'), *Saṃsār cakra* (news of the world), *Vijñān tathā vaichitrya* (science and curiosities), *Sinemā aur raṅgmañch* (the first column on films in a Hindi journal!), *Dilchasp mukadme* (interesting court cases), *Śrījagadguru kā fatvā* (against religious bigotry), *Kesar kī kyārī* (selection of Urdu verse by 'Bismil' Ilāhābādī) in 1931, etc.

the official bans on the Chand Press and his imprisonment strengthened the identification of the journal and its readers with the nationalist movement.

Chāṁd dedicated more space to news than any other women's journal. Apart from the editorials and the shorter editorial notes, there were separate news sections like *samāchār saṅgrah*, which contained a miscellany of events, laws, public achievements, political gatherings, examination results, and appointments of women from all over India. Naturally, bills concerning women were most closely reported, like the Sarda Bill and the Gaur Bill regarding inter-caste marriages.[65] A sample from the April 1923 issue includes among others information on the Princely States, data on jails and prisoners, on newspapers, on the number of workers in Bombay province, funding for UP municipalities, the Indian police, public debt, and on Indian imports and exports. Scattered among tips on hygiene, such seemingly 'neutral' news contained, in fact, a much wider and more political education than could possibly be acquired through schools—simply by exposing women to news they would not encounter elsewhere. The same issue, in another column, carried news of a case of a doubtful *satī* 'in the kitchen' in a village of district Beinisal; of a widow remarriage in Ambala district; of the election of Umā Nehrū as municipal councillor in Allahabad; on the harassment of peasant women in Mewar state at the hands of Indian soldiers; of a bill against the sale of brides in the Council of State; and of a women's public meeting in Lahore to celebrate Gandhi-day with speeches by Pārvatī Devī, Durgādevī and Pūrṇādevī, with a sale of khadi cloth and fund raising for the Tilak fund in the evening.[66]

Implicit in this uncensored flow of information was the idea, crucial to Habermas' model of the public sphere, that exposure to information itself develops critical attitudes and political consciousness by making public issues the concern of each affected reader. In this way, *Chāṁd* was fostering a civic and political consciousness for women, not unlike that which Mahāvīr Prasād Dvivedī had undertaken in *Sarasvatī* in 1903 (1.3.2).

A powerful notion supporting women's access to the public sphere

[65] See *Samāchār saṅgrah* in *Chāṁd*, VII, pt. 2, 6, October 1929 and VIII, pt. 1, 6, April 1930.

[66] *Chāṁd*, I, 6, April 1923, pp. 350–1. The next issue carried two items on false sadhus who had abducted women; one on a meeting of women of the Socialist and Communist parties of the Ruhr district of Germany; and a foreign astrologer's comment on Gandhi's janma-patrī; *Chāṁd*, I, pt. 2, 1, May–June 1923, pp. 532–3.

was that of sevā-dharma. Sevā, service, bestowed moral capital on, and helped legitimize, women's activities outside the home and redefine their role within the household. The notion of sevā dharma was consistently invoked while redefining women's roles, from housewife to *svayaṃ-sevikā* (volunteer) and to teacher, as we shall see in the final section of this chapter. *Chāṁd* was especially vocal and articulate in this respect. Indian society, wrote the editor of *Chāṁd*, is based on sevā dharma.[67] The caste system in its original form, even the four eras of Indian history, can be read along the lines of sevā and *svārtha*, service and self-interest, as a progression from the former to the latter. The arrival of '*yogeśvar* Gandhi', however, marked a charge of direction: 'We are very happy to see that the goddess of Sevā is coming again into the lap of our beloved Motherland' (p. 8). This primacy of sevā in turn established women as central and active subjects: 'The women of our country have always been committed to sevā-dharma. Truly, a woman's life is the concrete image of sevā' (p. 9).

However, sevā could now be redefined to challenge the traditional division between household and the world: it should not be considered only in practical terms (i.e. housework), and should not be restricted only to the family. After all, Sahgal continued, Sītā was not only Rām's wife, king Daśaratha's daughter-in-law, and queen Kauśalyā's favourite daughter-in-law, she was also Ayodhya's queen, 'the gem of society' (ibid.). In much the same way, to serve only one's husband was harmful, for it bred possessiveness, jealousy, and indifference to the fact that the Motherland, too, had rights over a woman's husband and sons: 'In the old times Gandhārī had blinded herself, nowadays women try to blind their husbands' (p. 11). Thus the entry of women (*ramaṇi-maṇḍal*) into the public sphere was considered both desirable and necessary for the fate of the nationalist movement: 'It is indispensable that they should *enter* the *arena* of sevā' (p. 12, emphases added).

We have to activate women's energy again and apply it for a successful revolution. We envisage an invincible *nārī-maṇḍal* which would set an example and stir the whole country with new ideas, new enthusiasm and pure sacrifice. It will be a golden day for Indian history, when the women (devī) of the Aryan nation, firm in the pursuit of truth, made invincible by their feeling of victory and animated by a disposition to serve, contribute to the progress (*uddhār-sādhnā*) of our society and our country (p. 12).

[67] See 'Sevā-dharma kā ādarś', editorial in *Chāṁd*, III, pt. 2, 1–2, May–June 1925, pp. 3–13. The following quotations are taken from this article, with page numbers in brackets. This argument echoed Gandhi's plea for the participation of women in the movement.

It was thus this idiom of service that allowed women to step out of traditional roles and places without losing respectability. And whenever women took the political initiative, *Chāṁd* applauded. Mrs Dubburi Subbamma, condemned to one year's strict imprisonment for non-co-operation work in 1923, was praised as 'a model for Indian women'.[68]

Before 1930 much of *Chāṁd*'s nationalist message and propaganda was furtive, between the lines, hidden in small news items, with most of the emphasis on social reform. In January 1929 Sahgal announced that he would start serializing the book by the famous Congress activist Pandit Sundarlāl (1886–1981), *Bhārat meṁ aṅgrezī rājya*, an overtly nationalist history of British rule in India. The book was immediately banned[69] and the ban ended the official bonhomie towards the journal: in June 1929 *Chāṁd* was suddenly prohibited in schools and public libraries after having been recommended for years. This was the first of a series of bails and bans[70] which, along with the political weekly *Bhaviṣya,*[71] would bring Sahgal to a financial crisis. Sahgal had long been in contact

[68] *Chāṁd*, I, pt. 2, 1, May–June 1923, p. 532.

[69] P. Sundarlāl, *Bhārat meṁ aṅgrezī rājya:* the publication of this hefty book, which was meant to become a nationalist textbook, was widely publicized in the Hindi press. The ban on it was itself a major political case and put *Chāṁd* on the black list of the government and in the good books of the nationalist movement. The 2000 pre-booked copies printed on 18 March 1929 were immediately proscribed by the UP government, followed a week later by the government of the Central Provinces. Somehow 1700 copies managed to reach the subscribers and only 300 were seized on the railway or at the post office. The government then started a hunt for the remaining copies provoking a countrywide protest. Even Gandhi called it day-light robbery in *Young India* and urged people to resist the humiliation of a house search. Seth Jamnālāl Bajāj was one of those who followed his advice. After the Congress accepted office in the United Provinces in July 1937, Sundarlāl wrote to the new government and the ban was lifted in November 1937. The second edition was not published by the Chand Press, as Sahgal had left the Press long before; this time 10,000 copies of it were published and were sold out even before publication; Gujarati and Urdu editions came out at the same time. See Sundarlāl's preface to the second impression of this edition, published by Triveṇīnāth Vājpeyī at the Omkar Press, Allahabad, 1938 (also of 10,000 copies), copy in the possession of the late Subhadrā Kumārī Chauhān.

[70] Like other Hindi journals, *Chāṁd* was caught up in the repressive policies of the Press Ordinance of 1930: in July 1930 the Chand Press was asked to furnish a bail of Rs 4000 (later reduced to 1000), and the publication of political poems on 'Satyāgrah saṅgrām' and 'Striyoṁ ke ādarś' in August–September 1930 drew a bail of another Rs 1000. Sahgal went to jail, and the May 1931 issue carried a picture of his release.

[71] Started in 1930 for a few months under the editorship of Sundarlāl, with a distribution of 11,000, *Bhaviṣya* also fell victim of the Press Ordinance.

with revolutionaries; in 1931 his sympathies became quite evident, in tune with the sentiments of the people at large, when he published the photographs of those sentenced to death in Sholapur in February 1931 and a special issue on political martyrs, the famous *Phāṃsī-aṅk* (November 1931), which was immediately banned.[72] The new motto of the journal proclaimed: 'Spiritual svarājya is our aim, truth our means and love our method. As long as we remain steadfast in this sacred resolve we do not fear the number and strength of our adversaries.' However, the journal and the press were by now in a financial crisis and in the eye of the storm: and Rāmrakh Siṃh Sahgal was eventually compelled to leave the journal.[73]

What were the reasons for *Chāṁd*'s phenomenal success under Rāmrakh Sahgal? Like *Sarasvatī* twenty years earlier, *Chāṁd* had managed to foster in its readership a feeling of identification with the journal. 'The welfare of women (strī-samāj) depends on our success,' wrote Sahgal after the first six issues in April 1923. He identified *Chāṁd*'s readership as 'the enthusiastic supporters of social reform' and 'the proud souls of women's education'. Women, continued Sahgal, had the duty to foster *Chāṁd* as their own child, and to let it die would be like infanticide: 'If you really want to save the millions of women drowning in an ocean of ignorance; if the heart-rending cries of thirty-five million Indian widows affect you somehow; if you want to destroy the evil customs of child-marriage, dowry, etc., which are eating the tree of Indian society from within, come and join us in the arena.'[74] The response had been indeed enthusiastic, as readership figures and the trust evident from readers' responses suggest. Another strength was the fact that, as we have seen, *Chāṁd* did not limit its audience to educated women (its actual readership) but spoke on behalf of *all* women, from all over the country and from all social strata. It changed the meaning of 'social reform': unlike previous

[72] See *Chāṁd*, VIII, 2, 6, October 1930, and IX, pt. 1, 1, November 1930, especially the editorial on 'Ordinance ṭhag', p. 2.

[73] The crisis led to a confrontation between the two Sahgal brothers: Rāmrakh the editor and daring nationalist and Nandgopāl the manager, sophisticated and on better terms with the British authorities. To save the journal and the publication department, the Chand Press was made into a Limited Company in 1932 with shares of Rs 10. The new board of directors included, apart from the Sahgals, local merchants, professionals and *taluqdars*; seconded by Nandgopāl, it put pressure on the editor to change his policy; a year later Sahgal resigned. From 'The Chand Press, Limited Allahabad. Directors' Report and Balance Sheet for the period ending 31 May 1933', p. 1, and interview with Ashok Saigal, Allahabad, October 1994.

[74] Editorial note in *Chāṁd*, I, 6, April 1923, p. 495.

women's journals it did not want to 'teach' or reform women but to reform 'society' on their behalf. Its approach was thus not the moralizing one of the 'uplift of women', strī-uddhār, but rather a radical critique of society conducted from a strong women's voice. Albeit with a male editor and sub-editors, *Chāṁd* succeeded therefore in becoming an important forum for women's self-awareness and an instrument of politicization within the Hindi sphere.[75]

After Rāmrakh Sahgal resigned,[76] Navjādiklāl Śrīvāstava of *Matvālā* fame became the editor until he was dismissed in September 1935, followed by Mahādevī Varmā (1935–8), and after her, Chatursen Śāstrī. Although they were all able editors, and *Chāṁd* remained a very attractive journal, the magazine lost its political and radical edge. With Mahādevī *Chāṁd* became more of a women's magazine (she insisted on having women contributors) and also a more literary one. Sahgal's ambitious project with its ever-expanding range of concerns now turned into a sophisticated and well-informed journal for educated women, aware of social problems and committed to political freedom but within the limits of a middle class notion of womanliness, in which maryādā was redefined by self-respect (cf. 4.4).

Through *Chāṁd* and the other women's journals we can follow two processes running parallel in the Hindi public sphere. One is the gradual challenge to the category of strī-upyogī, which led to the questioning of male definitions of women. By widening women's concerns to include more and more public issues and by insisting that the totality of women's life was open to debate, journals were crucial in politicizing women. Journals saluted women's empowerment and initiatives as an integral part of the nationalist project. They also helped develop critical tools and a political and historical consciousness through which women could question the double standards of patriarchy and could claim participation

[75] All the readers of *Chāṁd* consulted confirm that *Chāṁd* was prized by the women of the house but read by the whole family, men included. For a positive assessment of the journal see Premchand's note of January 1933, now in *Vividh prasaṅg*, vol. 3, p. 424.

[76] 'I did not start this institution with profit in mind. My only aim was to serve the country and society, and I am pleased to say that I have sincerely fulfilled my vow in the past eleven years—but then I was the sole proprietor. No one had the right to interfere in my policy; I did what I wanted to, and because of my daring I threw hundreds of thousands of rupees into the fire . . .', wrote Sahgal in his resignation note in January 1933 protesting against the 'commercial policy' of the new company directors. Rāmrakh went to Lucknow to revive *Karmayogī*, and *Chāṁd* remained in Nandgopāl's hands. Quoted in Premchand's note in *Vividh prasaṅg*, ibid.

in public life. This process of expansion and radical criticism produced, as we shall see in the following sections, a redefinition of women's roles both within the family and household and in the public domain. The second process, reflected in *Chāṁd*'s development in the 1930s, shows that once however the radical edge was lost, this redefinition of roles amounted to the making of a modern middle class culture, a culture which accepted and reflected class (and caste) exclusions and gender limitations. The change, apparent also in other Hindi mainstream journals, is evident in the language used (a more sophisticated and controlled ārya-bhāṣā), in tastes, more attuned to Chāyāvād and foreign poetry, and in the more limited and abstract range of concerns.[77]

The drastic drop in readership that accompanied this change and the exclusion of the semi-literate, the rural and small-town public, no longer represented on its pages, leaves an open question. Did the choice in favour of sophistication and of a genteel, urban middle-class culture deprive Hindi of its wider role and larger area of influence?

4.3. The Right to Feel

Chāṁd broke the mould of strī-upyogī literature not just by providing political education. Its challenge to social and family norms from a platform of 'basic' human values was even more striking. This involved recognizing women as emotional beings, questioning their home-bound existence, and envisaging new public roles (4.4).

Strī-upyogī literature envisaged women as entirely self-sacrificing, and focused exclusively on their duties and never on their needs. True, even in this way a feminine subjectivity was tenuously acknowledged: at first crudely, through dialogues and rigid juxtapositions of the 'good' and 'bad' daughter-in-law, or sister, this persuasive literature addressed the young female reader and asked her to choose which model to follow, but only so that her character could be trained.[78] Women's journals, we noticed, partly took over this educating role, with both male and female contributors insisting on duties and ideals. Indeed, stressing women's ideals and duties provided a strong plank from which to argue for women's worth and as such remained indispensable even when redefining women's roles (see 4.4). However, by publishing letters and 'true

[77] See Mahādevī Varmā's reflective and balanced editorials, published under the title *Śṛṅkhlā kī kaṛiyāṁ*; see 4.4 here.

[78] It would be hard to understand otherwise the popularity of novels such as those by Nazīr Ahmad; see Naim, 'Prize-winning *adab*'.

stories', journals also provided a space for another voice. *Chāṁd* in particular provided a space where other dimensions of women's lives could be expressed and their emotional needs could be supported. It played an important role in introducing and popularizing a notion of the 'right to feel' which, in turn, highlighted tensions between the individual and society, and requested a renegotiation of social and family norms.

We shall analyse in particular the strategies and arguments by which the 'right to feel' was first introduced and how it gave rise to a genre of sentimental literature that had a lot in common with commercial films. Devalued and marginalized by contemporary literary critics, who deemed it lurid and commercial, this literature nevertheless thematized the tensions between individual aspirations, normative ideals, and social rules in a blend of romance and social critique.

As with other issues concerning women, widows provided a kind of spearhead. The helplessness and commonality of the experience of Hindu widows became a metonymy for the condition of Indian women in general. The pressure to adhere to a life of heavy duties with no emotional bonds or rewards was particularly heavy on them, especially child widows. With a dramatic reversal of fortunes, in upper caste, affluent households, widows became qualitatively different beings from married women, the *suhāgins*. While reformers since the nineteenth century had directed their efforts to the sphere of law and to public demonstrative action,[79] women's journals and fictional narratives explored and thematized this qualitative difference and reclaimed widows as women, or at least as human beings. Hence, while male reformers concentrated on widow remarriage or appealed piously to families to treat widows humanely,[80] women's articles and testimonies spoke of a different agenda. They insisted on the need to retain one's place in one's family; on the need for respectable employment and a place to stay and on the right to keep one's

[79] The question of widows had loomed large in the minds of social reformers since the nineteenth century: for their sheer number, especially in cities like Calcutta and Benares, for the dangers of conversion, abduction (whether forced or consensual) and breach of chastity, and for what has been called a very modern sentiment of outrage; Kumar, *The History of Doing*, Chapter 1.

[80] See Vidyasagar's campaign to lift the ban on widow remarriage in the 1850s; in the Hindi area, in 1915 a section of the Ārya Samāj started in Lahore a Vidhvā Vivāh Sahāyak Sabhā, an association to help widows remarry, which branched out in Benares and Kanpur in the 1920s; it ran an ashram for widows who wanted to remarry, organized their weddings and published a monthly in Urdu, *Vidhvā sahāyak*; see *Chāṁd*, I, pt. 1, 6, April 1923, pp. 532 and 562–5; and VII, pt. 2, 6, October 1929, p. 746.

property; if 'fallen', to receive the same treatment as their male seducers or unlawful partners. Also, emphasizing preventive action, they linked the fate of widows to general women's issues such as child marriage, dowry and mismatched-marriages.

After only six months of publication, *Chāṁd* dedicated its first special issue to the condition of widows and espoused this second approach. 'The aim of this issue is not to shock or to encourage widow remarriage,' wrote Sahgal in the editorial. 'In our society widows are considered useless and harmful. If widows were treated with respect and affection by their families, 75 per cent of them would happily lead a pure life.'[81] The main question is that of the means of subsistence, added one Bhagavatī Devī: the right to divorce is important, and widow remarriage is possible only for young and beautiful child widows, employment is the only alternative to begging and prostitution for other widows and it requires the complete repeal of pardā.[82] *Chāṁd* made public even taboo issues concerning widows—and, by extension, all women—in order to force a rediscussion and redifinition of notions and norms, to justify preventive action (against dowries and child-marriages) and to justify respectable alternatives.

Letters and first-person fictional narratives of widowhood introduced a sense of urgency and a powerful element of personalization. This meant that the reader was forced to confront the cruelty women experienced and to reconsider the common-sense notions that underpinned such cruelty. Besides, life stories legitimized women's voices, the need for kin relationships to be instrinsically affective, and the women's right to suggest solutions to their own problems, thus giving them a new sense of individual worth and emotional life. Such narratives also allowed a bold critique of social and family norms. While looking indulgently at widows' breaches of chastity, *Chāṁd* harshly denounced double standards for men and women: 'Isn't it astonishing that men command child-widows to remain chaste for life when men themselves cannot even keep the vow of monogamy: do men think that women are made of clay or iron?'[83] The 'true stories' of abandonment, sale of brides, polygamy, unlegalized marriages, and sexual relations within the family also

[81] 'Vidhvā-aṅk', *Chāṁd,* I, 6, April 1923, pp. 553, 565–6.

[82] Bhagavatī Devī, 'Nārī-samasyā', *Chāṁd,* VIII, pt. 2, 6, October 1929, pp. 701–3. She ended on a pessimistic note and expressed her disbelief in the possibility of any swift change, since 'Indian women lie in drugged stupor'. The editor disagreed: changes would not take centuries but only a few decades.

[83] Ramāśaṅkar Avasthī, 'Vidhvāoṁ ke do āṁsū', *Chāṁd,* I, 6, April 1923, p. 485.

Illustration 4.2. Heading of the column of readers' letters in *Chāṁd*. The editor is once again depicted as a benevolent woman, to whom the young reader can safely confide.

Source: *Chāṁd*, IV, pt. 2, 6, October 1936, p. 600.

forcefully belied the ideal of the Aryan family. They drew attention to the existence of women's sexuality and emotional needs, often thematizing the thin line between marriage and prostitution, at least from a woman's point of view.

Let us now turn to some of these first-person narratives, first from life and later from fiction. A young Khatri widow of 17 from Delhi, who considered *Chāṁd* her 'guide', wrote in March 1923 of the need to turn the issue into a political one in order to overpower kin resistance:

My father is a firm sanātan dharmī and a member of the Bhārat Dharma Mahāmaṇḍal. But because I was widowed only twenty-one days after my wedding he took pity on me and decided to remarry me. My husband was ill at the time of the wedding (I was 8 at the time, he was thirty-five and already twice a widower). I have studied up to English Middle examination. Our relatives have started cursing my father and threaten to sever all relations with us.

The letter ended with the hope that soon widows like her would be able to bring 'a huge movement in front of Gandhijī and his followers and compel them to keep the pitiful condition of their widowed sisters in mind when they undertake political agitation'.[84]

A woman from Rajputana spoke about the need for a respectable place and employment: a friend of hers, supposedly, a woman of 25 with two children, educated up to the Middle examination, had been abandoned by her husband. She now asked for information about any institution which might shelter her.[85]

A woman from Mathura district raised instead the issue of a daughter-in-law's insecure status even within the household: after her marriage her elder brother-in-law had made advances which she had sternly rebuffed, and thereupon both her husband and mother-in-law had tried to persuade her to give in ('both are sons of my womb', her mother-in-law had said, 'you should consider them one and the same'). The brother-in-law was the family's bread-winner, while her husband was a good-for-nothing fellow who danced with theatre companies.[86]

A 'sister' from a princely state wrote about the need to acknowledge female sexuality: still unmarried after the age of 20 because her parents could not offer enough dowry, she had been unable to 'contain her youthfulness' and had 'married' in secret a boy she fancied. After three happy years she had borne him a child and, forced to leave her parents' house, she had moved in with her lover. Her father and his supporters then persuaded her to move back with them with the promise to marry them properly; they then threw out her lover and now threatened to marry her off to a 40-year-old![87]

An 'unfortunate' Gujarati girl from a trading family, married at 11 into an uneducated and lowly family, voiced a more general critique of women's lack of rights in a Hindu family and raised the issue of women's definition of their own ideals. She wrote of her husband's beatings and general irresponsibility. When her brother had come to take her back he was abused and sent away. 'I have no right to my family property. Hindu society and Hindu law do not help. . . . To serve your husband according

[84] 'Chiṭṭhī-patrī', ibid., pp. 496–7.

[85] 'Chiṭṭhī-patrī', in *Chāṁd*, IV, pt. 2, 6, October 1926, pp. 604–5.

[86] 'Chiṭṭhī-patrī', in *Chāṁd*, XII, pt. 2, 1, May 1934, pp. 99–100. The editor asked 'someone from Mathura' to help her.

[87] Ibid., pp. 100–1. This letter highlighted many social evils—dowry, oppression, etc.—commented the editor (no longer Sahgal); she had erred by marrying in secret but should now stick to her decision and take refuge with the law.

to the tradition of the Vedas is fine, but only when you have chosen him.'[88]

A widowed child-bride from central India, married into a wealthy household, wrote of the desperate helplessness of a widow's fate. The mother of two children, respectively of three years and of four months, she was approached by her younger brother-in-law after the death of her husband. To try and 'protect her virtue' she had even run away once but he had had her abducted; he had then raped her and after 10–15 days handed her to a Muslim ('Yavan') man, who took her in a burqā with him on a train to Bombay. The other passengers in the train had got suspicious and finally managed to save her. She was now sheltered by a very charitable but poor man, but for how long? She was also tormented by the 'well of sin' she had fallen into and was consumed by it day after day.[89]

These are only a few instances, but they testify to Sahgal's skill in making *Chāṁd* a confidante which could be trusted for help and support however 'shocking' one's revelations were.[90] The letters raised a powerful critical voice: they spoke of domestic cruelty and insecurity, of repressed sexuality and of the lack of alternative homes and respectable ways of survival for widows, abandoned wives, and single women. After Sahgal left *Chāṁd*, fewer and fewer letters were published. His intuition that letters created a rapport of mutual trust and support between the journal and its readers and allowed a space for solidarity got lost as *Chāṁd* became a more literary and genteel enterprise.

The persuasive potential of such letters gave rise to a whole genre of fictional letter-confessions with a first-person narrator. In *Chāṁd* these fictional narratives went even further in boldly depicting sensational (and, in a way, titillating) cases concerning women and the family while holding 'society' responsible. The well-cut, melodramatic narrative often had a sentimental sub-plot well as voicing a 'women's critique' of society, echoed and supported by the narrator. Between 1926–7 Zahūr Bakhś (1897–1964), a teacher and prolific writer for children, started writing for *Chāṁd* a series of 'first-person confessions' under the telling title of 'The fire-pit of society'.[91] The first of them, 'How I became a fallen woman?' ('Maiṁ patit kaise huī', *Chāṁd*, January 1926) shows well

[88] *Chāṁd*, XV, pt. 2, 1, May 1927, pp. 86–7.

[89] Ibid.

[90] See in the previous section the letter of a 'fallen' (*patit*) Brahmin widow who was pitied and reprimanded by the editor and readers of *Gṛhalakṣmī*.

[91] Zahūr Bakhś, 'Samāj kā agni-kuṇḍ'; it included also 'Ek musalmān kī ātmakathā' (November 1926), 'Maiṁ musalmān kaise huī?' (December 1926), 'Maiṁ isāī

the sinews of the genre and deserves to be analysed in some detail. The breach of chastity is shown to be but a 'natural' consequence of a mismatched marriage; the girl's feelings are asserted as important and legitimate, and so is her right to define her own strī-dharma; further, her gradual debasement is directly attributed to society's hypocrisy and to the lack of any alternative respectable livelihood for a single woman: thus responsibility is constantly lifted from her shoulders and she is given the chance to express and justify herself.

Bakhś' 'pitiful story' (*karuṇ kathā*) of Kamlā, the daughter of a relatively well-off Brahmin compounder, is told to the narrator 'in her own words'. She was taught how to read and write up to the age of 10; at 14 a marriage was arranged with a suitable boy but negotiations were broken off when the dowry requested turned out to be too high. After her elderly father had retired, embittered by the experience, an aunt (buā) intervened suggesting a 'middle-aged' (50-year-old!) and rich bridegroom, who was ready to pay even for the wedding expenses. The wedding is the first trauma for the girl: 'Everyone around me looked happy but I was sobbing inside the house. No one cared to ask me how I felt!' (p. 276). She displays strong feelings: of anger towards her 'greedy father' and aunt and of disgust towards her ugly husband. At the time of taking leave of her family she begs her mother to keep her even as a servant, but her incensed father warns her not to give vent to her feelings: 'It seems that you will sully the reputation of both families. I warn you, never let a word like that slip out of your mouth or I'll pull your tongue out' (p. 287).

The situation in itself was common enough. But the fact that the story was told from Kamlā's point of view and expressed her feelings provoked in the readers a sense of 'alienation' (the *ostranenie* of the Russian formalists) that forced them to feel the enormity of the injustice done to her. Although formally Kamlā is refused the right to speak, even to feel, the story allows her to express her feelings, both through the story itself (a confession) and through her thoughts and comments on the events. Now, for example, she thinks: 'Very well. Pull out my tongue if you want.

---

kaise huī?' (March 1927), 'Achūt kī ātma-kathā' (May 1927). The common points among them were that the convert or 'fallen' protagonist was unrepentant, and that the downfall or conversion of the individual had been caused by the injustice of Hindu society. Zahūr Bakhś was a pupil of Kāmtāprasād Guru's and taught Hindi at Sagar Municipal Primary School from 1913 to 1948; see Kṣemchandra 'Suman', *Divaṅgat hindī-sevī*, Delhi, Shakun Prakasan, 1981.

But my name is not Kamlā if I don't disgrace you.' She accepts strī-dharma, she adds, but only if it comes from the heart, not when imposed upon her (ibid.).

At her husband's house, her first retort earns her a beating, until a young and handsome cousin of the old bridegroom intervenes in her favour. He, too, was mis-married, to a 5-year-old girl! With only the three of them in the house (husband, cousin, and Kamlā), the cousin is quick to begin his amorous advances. Whereas strī-upyogī literature would have him cast as a villain with the virtuous girl giving up her life in order to keep her virtue, the confession-genre takes quite a different turn.[92] Here the passion between the boy and girl of the same age is but *natural*, and the young bride responds easily and with little guilt: 'Afterwards I felt a little bad, but then I thought that it had been no fault of mine and felt satisfied' (p. 278). The affair grows more and more obvious until the angered husband poisons the cousin in secret; when he threatens Kamlā she leaves for her parents' village, where she moves in with an uncle. This uncle, a widower, has a Thakurain mistress—men are allowed!—who deceives Kamlā and allows her to be raped by a friend of theirs, a young Muslim contractor: thus rape takes place with the consent of the family! A helpless Kamlā accepts her new fate and moves in with the Muslim contractor, thus breaking her dharma; he has another wife, though, who is furious to find Kamlā there when she returns from her parents' house. Kamlā is thrown out of the house under the impassive eyes of her Muslim lover. Instead of going back to her murderous husband she runs away with another young Muslim man to Kanpur, a city of anonymity for them, where they survive by selling off her jewellery. When he finally disappears, Kamlā joins a group of job contractors and in December 1916 leaves with them on a ship to South Africa, where she is signed on as an indentured labourer. A 'loose woman', five times pregnant and with five abortions behind her ('I had forgotten to say this out of shame but now that I am spelling out everything clearly, why hide it?', p. 280) but still attractive, she is noticed there by the white overseer and is gang-raped by him and twelve other men. Too ill to work in the fields, she has to resort to prostitution, pleasing fifteen to twenty men every day. Back in India, now she can only beg in the streets . . .

[92] Alternatively, we may recall the fate of Nirmalā, the heroine of Premchand's eponymous novel (serialized in *Chāṁd* in the same period), who is almost cast aside by her elderly husband because of a suspicion that she may be having a liaison with his elder son (from a previous marriage); in turn, this leads to the son's estrangement and eventually his death. A tragedy.

(1) The old bridegroom thinks nothing of the age difference and marries a young bride.

(2) Attraction is natural between the 'young-blooded' stepmother and stepson.

(3) The old man 'finally goes to hell'.

(4) Once the obstacle is removed, passion overtakes the two young bereaved, who think nothing of the possible consequences.

Illustration 4.3 (1), (2), (3), (4), (5), (6), (7), (8). This unusually long cartoon on the subject of 'mismatched marriages' was accompanied by a verse commentary by *Chāṁd*'s house-poet, Ānandīprasād Śrivāstava.

(5) Soon enough, the stepmother is pregnant and the son denies any responsibility.

(6) The stepmother is thrown out of the house and taken to a place of pilgrimage, where a priest takes advantage of her.

(7) Abandoned yet again, the woman falls prey to a procuress.

(8) Finally, 'Now that she is a prostitute all respect her. Those who threw her out are crazy after her now.'

Source: *Chāṁd*, VII, pt. 1, 3, February 1929, pp. 501–8.

There can be little doubt that this descent into self-debasement, with Kamlā's gradual loss of honour, position, caste, family, dharma, country, freedom and self-respect, and the shocking directness with which it was described, did not fit in the usual canons of 'women's literature'. Yet the moral attached to the story located it within a literature of social reform: 'A promising child of India was sacrificed to the sexual greed of that old wolf! Bribed by money the pandits happily disgraced the holy mantras of the Vedas' (p. 281). The fault was not the girl's, but society's.

By presenting a 'loose woman' as the victim of society, and her confession as a moral tale, such a narrative could first of all break taboos about mentioning the facts and about the parents' involvement in, and responsibility for, the girl's ruin. Second, it allowed the female character to question and judge the system from her position as a 'fallen' woman. This strengthened a point only implied in readers' letters: that it was not only educated and virtuous women upholding 'Aryan' ideals who had the right to speak out. Moreover, whereas the virtuous woman's address was a civilized plea, the fallen woman's one was an indictment, an aggressive confrontation that demanded a response.[93]

More than articles and discussions on social reform, I would argue, it was these hybrid genres (confessions, epistolary novels, social novels),[94] mixing reality with fiction, instruction with entertainment, that allowed taboo issues concerning women to be raised, directly and with the heightenened impact of a melodramatic narrative. The personalization—it was not about 'Indian women', it was about Kamlā, an ordinary girl whom the readers were asked from the beginning to identify with—allowed no critical distance; it asked instead for participation and approval, even along the various turns in Kamlā's downfall. The final comment demanded a public condemnation of domestic cruelty and social hypocrisy.

[93] I am aware that the 'confession' genre, common to commercial literatures in Europe, China, etc., has had different connotations, at times titillating to the point of pornography, at other times politically radical, more often an ambiguous combination of the two. What I am interested in here is the particular meaning such a genre had in the Hindi world of the 1920s. For diverse examples from seventeenth-century France and early twentieth-century China, see Joan De Jean, *Tender Geographies. Women and the Origins of the Novel in France,* New York, Columbia University Press, 1991, and E. Perry Link, *Mandarin Ducks and Butterflies. Popular Fiction in Early Twentieth-Century Chinese Cities*, Berkeley, University of California Press, 1981.

[94] See *Vidhvā, yā abhāginī Kāminī kī ātmakathā*, the novel serialized in *Chāṁd* from April 1923, which also presented information and statistics on widows in India.

Reactions were, predictably, equally strong. It was the aggressive attitude of confrontation and the justification of female sexuality that aroused the strongest objections from those who favoured a conciliatory approach to social reform. It was not only a reluctance to make certain practices public,[95] a fear of spoiling the image of a caring and loving Hindu family and society (especially when there was already a confrontation with the images of western and Muslim societies), but also a resistance to the very strategy of confrontation. Moreover, the fact that the 'social' framework allowed for murky stories of adultery and mesalliances to be presented as women's literature, and also their huge popularity, convinced moralist reformers that it was all a plot to corrupt readers under the cover of social reform.[96]

However, the romantic and sentimental elements in such social narratives grew stronger and stronger, so much so that we can speak of a genre of 'social romances'. Epistolary novels became a popular subgenre which gave vent, through first-person narrators, to a critical female voice and plots justifying feelings and romance. Direct, intimate, and involving, the letter was a perfect form of private expression. It communicated feelings and thoughts that were taboo face to face. In these social romances letters were not only the messengers of love, they also created a private, secluded space where fantasy, the '*mise en scène* of desire', could be played out.[97] But letters also provided an important space for argument and self-reflection: whether addressed to the lover or to a sympathetic friend, they contained arguments in favour of love, reflections

[95] The 'shocking' special issues of *Chāṁd* on Marwaris, Kayasthas, and on Rajputana caused an uproar and a barrage of protests from those influential sections of society and their supporters. The *Mārvāṛī-aṅk* of November 1929, for instance, created such a furore that it led to a defamation case against Sahgal. Ghanshyamdas Birla spurred even Gandhi to write against the issue; Banārsīdās Chaturvedī proposed a motion condemning it at the Hindī Sāhitya Sammelan meeting in Gorakhpur, and Rāmnareś Tripāṭhī came out with a booklet on *Mārvāṛe ke manohar gīt* (Allahabad, 1930) in protest against the 'dirty light' thrown on Marwari literature by *Chāṁd*.

[96] *Ghāsleṭī* literature was the epithet coined by Banārsīdās Chaturvedī, who launched a moralizing campaign in the pages of *Viśāl Bhārat* (cf. 2.3.3); see e.g. Chandragupta Vidyālaṃkār, 'Ghāsleṭ sāhitya', *Viśāl Bhārat*, II, pt. 2, 3, September 1929.

[97] We may contrast these secret letters with the largely formulaic letters of strī-upyogī literature, meant to carry family information and instruction, such as those between Asghari and her father in Nazir Ahmad's *Mirāt-al-urūs* (1869) and between the good daughter-in-law and her father in Pandit Gaurīdatt's *Devrānī jeṭhānī kī kahānī* (1870)—clearly meant to be read out aloud.

on one's own state, along with social commentary.[98] On a formal level, letters, with their multiplicity of points of view, represented the new assumption that individuals could question and change accepted norms and truths, and that new truths and norms needed to emerge out of negotiation, dialogue and argument. It was this combination of elements—romantic fantasy, criticism of norms, renegotiation of roles—that characterized 'social romances'.

For example, *Smṛti kuñj* (*Memories*), an epistolary novel serialized in *Chāṁd* throughout 1926, is presented by the editorial note as a 'beautiful *article* which *describes* the oppression of society'. The novel starts as a straightforward epistolary romance between two middle-class students until we discover that the protagonist, who has just confessed to being in love with her brother's friend, is a child widow. Her feelings, which so far have seemed quite natural, acquire a provocative edge and the romance becomes a melodrama, with 'fiendish society' as the villain which keeps the two lovers apart: 'There is expiation for all sins in Hindu society, but not for this.'[99]

The casting of a widow as heroine is not unusual in such narratives. First, a widow evoked immediate sympathy; second, as mentioned earlier, she could well symbolize the helpless condition of women in general; third, as a marginal character, she allowed the grey area between duty and the 'right to feel' to be explored to maximum dramatic effect.[100] Even when norms did not get broken and the widowed heroine could not fulfil her romantic longings, as in Jainendra Kumār's *Parakh* (1929), the argument in favour of her self-worth and right to feel could be made forcefully. Even then norms were open to discussion. Romance per se clashed with the system of arranged marriages and forced writers to find fictitious ways of letting the romance bloom without turning the lovers into

[98] E.g. Pāṇḍey Bechan Śarmā 'Ugra's sensational romance between a Hindu boy and a Muslim girl in *Chand hasīnoṁ ke khutūt*, one of the bestsellers of 1927. See my 'Reading a Social Romance. *Chand hasīnoṁ ke khutūt*', in Dalmia and Damsteegt, eds, *Narrative Strategies*, Leiden, 1998 and New Delhi, OUP, 1999.

[99] *Chāṁd*, V, pt. 1, 1, November 1926, pp. 48–50, emphases added.

[100] See the fate of Kaṭṭo, the child widow protagonist of Jainendra Kumār's first novel, *Parakh* (1929): moved by her sorry fate and her innocence, Satyadhan at first decides to marry her instead of the wealthy Garimā; he later goes back on his decision, and there is a suggestion that his friend Bihārī might marry her in his stead. In fact, a kind of spiritual union takes place between them, but only to allow Kaṭṭo to pursue her dharma as a servant to Satyadhan and Garimā, and Bihārī to follow his fate as a self-styled renouncer, forsaking his inheritance to embrace the 'simple life' of a peasant.

villains. This meant looking for marginal or extreme situations and characters (widows, good prostitutes, students; and colleges, fairs, trains, parks, etc.), where the scope for individual movement and for individual personalities was fractionally greater.[101]

Social romances struck a balance between plausibility—with conventions fulfilling the readers' expectations of the genre—and artificiality, creating a verisimilar world in which fantastic things may happen and real emotions can be expressed in a setting of realistic details. The story 'Mātṛmandir' by Dhanīrām 'Prem' (1904–79), one of the most popular writers of the day and now virtually forgotten, is a case in point. It blended romance and social critique and used verisimilitude to enhance familiarity and provide the setting for extraordinary events. The female narrator and protagonist, a 16-year-old widow from Aligarh, Phūlmatī, is allowed a successful, if troubled, romance.[102]

When a heavily veiled Phūlmatī gets separated from her heartless mother-in-law at the crowded railway station on their way to Benares and is saved by a young man who buys her a ticket and looks after her during the journey, his kind words are 'the first sympathetic words after years of insults. I felt an unknown joy within me'. (p. 49). In Benares, where the girl is under somewhat less strict control, she meets the young man again at the bathing ghats. He is a college student of her caste and a member of the local Ārya Samāj. Although she remains steadfast to her duties at first and refuses to acknowledge her own feelings, she finally responds to his love: 'My heart had been crushed but it was still a heart. . . . I was a widow but my body was made of flesh and blood. How could I then turn my back on that source of hope?' (p. 58). Back at home, she gives her 'everything' to Murārī, to use the euphemism of the period.[103] The religious books she is given to appease her mind fail to quench her thirst (p. 71), and she is imbued again with the need to live. A happy conclusion to their romance is in sight: Murārī talks of marriage, overcoming her doubts with Ārya Samāj arguments; his resolve weakens when she is found pregnant, and he abandons her though they had agreed to elope. His stern uncle comes instead, bearing a letter in which Murārī admits that he is a coward and will not be able to marry her.

[101] See the talented and educated Kanak, the daughter of a courtesan and heroine of Nirālā's first novel, *Apsarā* (1930).

[102] First published in *Chāṁd*, the story was then included in the collection *Vallarī*, published by the Chand Press in 1932; the page numbers refer to this volume.

[103] 'Why should I lie, I merged myself with Murārī; I had started loving him,' she confesses; ibid., p. 66.

A tragic ending—Phūlmatī heads straight to the river in order to drown herself—is also avoided because of the call to a higher duty, motherhood: the thought of her future baby stops her. Sheltered by an old Muslim woman, Phūlmatī becomes a Muslim after a while, although she keeps to her Hindu customs: 'No, mother, I did not become a Muslim for this [i.e. to remarry]. I converted only to take revenge on the Hindus' (p. 87). Sixteen years later, during a Hindu–Muslim riot, Phūlmatī's child Abdul, a staunch Hindu-hater, takes part in the fighting. A wounded Hindu on the run takes shelter in Phūlmatī's hut—it's Murārī, repentant and himself a widower! As they embrace (he is still her 'god'), Abdul breaks in to find his mother with a Hindu man:

> 'खबरदार! हाथ न चलाना।'
> 'क्यों' 'यह तेरे बाप हैं'
>
> 'I warn you, do not touch him!'
> 'Why?' 'He is your father.' (p. 92)

Father and son are reunited, and the denouement is completed when Murārī's uncle enters, too, fatally wounded by Abdul. He is happy (!) to pay with his life for the injustice that was once committed against Phūlmatī and enjoins them to build with his inheritance a house for unwedded mothers. This is Mātṛmandir: five years later Phūlmatī and Murārī look out of the window of their new home to an idyllic future. The ending is thus both a picture of domesticity (the idyllic couple) and of social reform (Mātṛmandir) and is produced by a blend of personalization, realistic crises, and melodramatic, fantastic reversals.

The social romance was one of the most popular genres of the 1920s and 1930s. Since their popularity extended well beyond the purview of women's journals we must assume, as ever, that there were multiple ways of reading them. And indeed, the pleasures they offered were manifold. Yet there is a thread linking the letters published in *Gṛhalakṣmī* and *Chāṁd* to this fictional genre. At a formal level, we have noted similarities in features like personalization, the uses of the letter, the presence of marginal characters, the indictment of society. At a deeper level, both kinds of texts, despite the obvious generic differences, share two constituent elements.

The first is a critique of public discourse on the Hindu family. At a time when a middle-class morality was gaining currency which did not acknowledge (at least publicly and in principle) polygamy, incest and other illegitimate marriage alliances, and which placed great emphasis on the high ideal of strī-dharma, the letters and novels mentioned here revealed a more fluid and precarious reality for women as wives. Women's letters and narratives showed the underside of strī-dharma and voiced the argument that such a demanding dharma should have certain redeeming conditions attached, namely a recognition of women as human individuals and the right for them to define their own roles and dharma. The ideal was thus reconfirmed, but articles, letters, and fictional texts all expressed the need to renegotiate norms concerning the family and to explore and redefine women's roles and spheres of activity. Women writers in particular did not tire of writing about the humiliation and violence of family discipline.[104]

The second element introduced by letters, both real and fictional, was the notion of a 'right to feel'. At a time when duty and dharma were constantly being reaffirmed and when the erotic and sentimental strands of courtly and popular literature were being criticized, *Chāṁd* and the social romances defended and legitimized individual feelings, both of men and women. A similar emphasis on individual emotions is apparent in the many women poets who came forward and wrote in the Chāyāvād mode. In the case of Mahādevī Varmā, the foremost among them, we can see almost a split between the poetic 'I', involved in an extensive romantic fantasy, and the prosaic 'I' of essays and articles.[105] Thus, if the 'right to feel' points in the direction of a greater individual subjectivity, the various strategies and distancing conventions used in fiction and in poetry suggest that such subjectivity was still highly problematic. Literature, in this respect, provided a safe space for the triumph of individual feelings, but its relationship to reality must be understood to be at best oblique. As with the images of women discussed in the next section or the political stories discussed in the next chapter, literature in this period was 'imaginative'. New figures and relationships could be imagined while remaining within the boundaries of the verisimilar.

4.4. Images of Womanhood

With its gallery of good housewives, mothers, and daughters-in-law, useful literature for women, strī-upyogī *sāhitya*, was all about providing prescriptive role models of womanhood. Such characterizations of

[104] This is a point Sudhā Chauhān made about her mother's writing and wondered why Subhadrā Kumārī wrote about women 'trapped in the cruel family discipline' while she herself enjoyed great freedom and respect from her husband, the Congress activist and playwright Lakṣmaṇ Siṃh Chauhān; Sudhā Chauhān, *Milā tej se tej*, Allahabad, Hans Prakashan, 1975, p. 141.

[105] See Schomer, *Mahadevi Varma*, especially Chapter 9.

'Indian woman' as essentially nurturing, self-sacrificing, and strong were also inflected by the symbolic association with Mother India and, indirectly, with the goddesses Sarasvati and Lakshmi. The trope 'Indian woman' was then juxtaposed with Indian malehood, to the materialist West and to the fickle western woman. When arguing in favour of women's worth, women's journals and literature also exploited this image, but they used it to demand space and respect for women's feelings and their right to enter the public world in suitable roles.

The nationalist movement, and especially Gandhi's particular brand of nationalism, were enormously influential in making this actually happen. As Madhu Kishwar has pointed out, Gandhi had realized in South Africa the vital importance of the cooperation of women in a popular movement. In India, by employing familiar symbols, by devising programmes revolving around the 'seemingly trivial but essential details of daily living' like cloth, salt, and chuāchūt (taboos about bodily contact) that involved women first at home and then also in public, and by envisaging new, brotherly relations between men and women (even husbands and wives), 'he helped women find a new dignity in public life, a new place in the national mainstream, a new self-view and a consciousness that they could themselves act against oppression'. At the same time, his charisma and his idiom 'helped ensure the entry of women into public life without their having to assume a competitive posture *vis-à-vis* men'. Gandhi's charisma, whether in personal contact or from afar, and his saintly persona and authority, proved irresistible inducements to action and to breaking taboos. In fact, although Gandhi was initially reluctant to allow women to take part in salt satyagrahas in 1930, thousands of ordinary women did, in towns and villages.[106] In that, we have seen, they were passionately supported by journals like *Chāṁd.* Finally, women's critical voices and subjective narratives demanded that womanhood be not exclusively defined by male rules.

Given this reshuffling, it is not surprising that women's journals and Hindi literature in this period offer a bewildering variety of female characters. To consider such images is important because they reveal to us the tensions and issues at stake behind the redefinition of womanly roles. By image, then, I do not mean a reflection of 'reality'. Rather,

[106] 'He sought to restrict their participation to mass picketing of drink and drug shops, as to him this was an issue ideally suited to women, not only because they suffered from their husbands' patronage of such shops, but also because the issue was one of purity and of morality;' M. Kishwar, *Gandhi on Women*, Delhi, Manushi Prakashan, 1986, pp. 18–19.

image will be used here to indicate either a role model, aimed at shaping readers' consciousness,[107] or the imaginative space a narrative character provides for shaping a new role (e.g. the svayaṃsevikā, woman volunteer) or for giving new dimensions and new emphases to established ones (e.g. the housewife). As in the case of social romances, internal focalization and a new emphasis on subjectivity allowed the characters' aspirations and feelings to be justified. As we shall see, the idiom of sevā was used very effectively to bestow moral capital (on otherwise unworthy heroines, for example) and to justify women stepping out of traditional roles without losing, in fact gaining, respectability. We can broadly identify five categories of images of women in the works of both male and female writers across several genres: (1) historical women, i.e. vīrāṅganās; (2) traditional heroines like Sita and Savitri reinterpreted in a contemporary light; (3) widows and good-hearted prostitutes; (4) svayaṃsevikās; (5) housewives. All of them were portrayed as having some kind of access to the world outside the home, positively valued as a form of sevā.

There is no need here to dwell at length on the first category (see 3.2). We need only recall that, especially to women readers, vīrāṅganās decried the idea of women as defenceless and weak (abalā). They showed that women had equal intellectual and strategic skills and that women, too, had contributed to national history. As queens, they were depicted as selfless rulers, *defending* a kingdom entrusted to them by others and for the sake of others (male heirs).[108] Although safely too distant in time and rank to provide concrete examples of female leadership, these

[107] Indrani Chatterjee, 'The Bengali Bhadramahila. 1930–34', unpublished M. Phil. thesis, Jawaharlal Nehru University, New Delhi, 1986, p. 57.

[108] Thus Vīr Padmāvatī, the beautiful and talented sister of an impoverished Kshatriya of Bhopal, versed in home sciences as well as in the arts of war, has to don a male disguise and find employment with the Scindia army after being abandoned. After successfully fighting against the British, she is discovered, regains her brother and finds her father and a bridegroom at the Scindia court. Chāṁd Bībī of Ahmadagar, married to Ali Adil Shah of Bijapur, exhibits the same combination of womanly virtues and physical and intellectual training. Her long involvement in public affairs after the death of her husband is described in terms of service: a brave and loyal warrior and a good strategist, Chāṁd Bībī is 'asked' to take part in the succession conflicts in Ahmadabad and defends the kingdom against prince Murad as her duty to her motherland. Depicted as a *kulṭā strī* to the Mughal prince by a traitor, she nonetheless holds her ground with patience (*dhīraj kī mūrti*); Satyavatī, 'Vīr Padmāvatī', in *Gṛhalakṣhmī*, IV, 8, October–November 1913, pp. 398–402; and Gaṅgāśaṅkar Miśra, 'Chāṁd Bibī', in *Gṛhalakṣhmī*, IV, 3, May–June 1913, pp. 126–31.

stories still conveyed the message that women were potentially powerful and able to hold their own in the men's world. 'Khūb laṛī mardānī vah Jhansī-valī rānī' ('She fought like a man she did, the queen of Jhansi') ran a popular song that became the refrain of the most famous poem on Rani Lakṣmībaī by Subhadrā Kumārī Chauhān. At the same time, such heroines still displayed the womanly virtues of sexual and moral purity, self-sacrifice, and a nurturing and kind nature.

Sita had long been considered the quintessential ideal of Indian womanhood. Interestingly, new aspects of Sita were now underlined in order to provide legitimacy to women's participation in the public sphere. 'Until there are satī-women like Sita in India, there will be no Rāmrājya,' Gandhi used to tell women in his speeches and, in the same breath: 'Until women take part in the public (sārvajanik) life of India the country will not progress. Only those women who are pure in body and heart, whose body and heart follow the same goal, can take part in public life'.[109] Thus a strong will and moral purity, conflated in the model of Sita, were to provide a blueprint for women's participation in the movement.[110] Even Krishna's Radha underwent a similar transformation and became the ideal social worker (samājsevikā) in Hariaudh's poem *Priya-pravās* (1914).

In discussions of contemporary society, however, negotiating women's access to the public sphere became more problematic. The existence of pardā, the primacy of wifely dharma, and the negative image of the 'free' westernized woman made even the ideal of 'service to the country' difficult to imagine for urban, respectable north Indian women. New codes of dress and behaviour had to be devised in order to show that the modesty earlier formalized by pardā could now be interiorized.[111] Three images incarnate this change: the widow and/or prostitute, the woman volunteer, and the educated wife, the heroine at home.

In earlier sections I have discussed at length the strategic importance of widows in discussing women's issues: the act of reclaiming good-hearted prostitutes and widows as women mirrored that of re-claiming women as fully-fledged human beings.[112] Provided they made the right

[109] Quoted in the note 'Mahilā-pariṣad meṁ mahātmājī', in *Mādhurī*, III, pt. 1, 1, January 1925, p. 125.

[110] For Gandhi's 'obsession' with moral and sexual purity, see Kishwar, 'Gandhi and Women'.

[111] See Emma Tarlo, *Clothing Matters*, London, Hurst, 1996.

[112] See e.g. Gulāb, the holier-than-thou protagonist of 'Veśyā kā hṛday' (A prostitute's heart) by Dhanīrām Prem, one of the many stories of good-hearted prostitutes.

moral choices and embraced sevā, widows were human potential that could be harnessed to the nationalist cause. Free of domestic responsibilities and in need of some engagement, widows would be ideal for service. As R.S. Sahgal put it, 'we believe that sevā is [the widows'] main field of action (*karmakṣetra*) . . . and the huge potential of our women's energy, now enclosed within four walls, could be unleashed by their example'.[113]

Widows and, to a lesser extent, prostitutes were thus of strategic importance in raising the issue of women's place in the public world, both literally and metaphorically. They posed similar problems for Hindu social reformers: once a woman lost her ritual purity there was literally no place for her in Hindu society. Excluded from the space of the home and from both her natural and acquired family, she found no support, knew no trade, and became easy prey for procuresses. While pathetically showing the cruel rigidity of social and family norms that affected all women, the fate of the lone widow was also a kind of sinister warning to women readers: the same could happen, it was argued, to any woman who by chance or misfortune was left alone out of the sphere of the home. Unable, because of ignorance or pardā, to direct and behave herself in public, she soon got lost.

This set of questions is examined in Premchand's first major novel, *Sevā-sadan,*[114] set in contemporary Benares. Perhaps the first Hindi novel to thematize politics and municipal councils and to include public speeches and meetings, it revolves around one question: where should we keep prostitutes?[115] The question is both literal and metaphorical: in the literal sense, it follows a public proposal to move prostitutes from

---

Gulāb slowly overcomes the righteous disgust young Keśav, the son of a Brahmin priest studying in Lahore, has for her. His hate (*ghṛṇā*) slowly turns into compassion and finally to love. But Gulāb, an icon of sevā, urges Keśav to agree to the match his father has arranged for him in the village, and when he instead resolves to elope with her, she leaves the night before. Her farewell note, in which she writes that she has left to let him follow his duty and that she will love him forever, is the thing Keśav, now a pujārī and married, worships most, 'even more than the image in the temple'. First published in *Chāṁd,* the story appeared later in the collection *Vallarī*, Allahabad, Chand Press, 1932, pp. 97–132.

113 R.S. Sahgal, 'Sevā dharma kā ādarś', editorial in *Chāṁd*, III, pt. 2, 1–2, May–June 1925, p. 12.

114 For a comment on the popularity of this novel, see P. Bakhśī, *Merī apnī kathā,* p. 65. Written in 1917–18 and published in 1919, the first edition sold out within a year. Here page numbers refer to the reprint by Rajkamal Prakasan, Delhi, 1994.

115 Ibid., Chapter 15.

their *koṭhās* in the centre of town to the outskirts, where they would attract fewer clients and 'pollute' the atmosphere to a lesser degree. In a metaphorical sense, it explores the question of space and respectability for ordinary women and for prostitutes. The dilemma of how a 'fallen' woman could be restored to some place within Hindu society is examined through the story of a respectable wife, Suman, who becomes a courtesan (Sumanbāī) after her husband, intolerant of her visits to a neighbouring house, shut her out one night. Social reformers in the city try to find a place for her, but the moment she steps out of her husband's house she also steps out of her socially respectable and ritually pure role as a 'Lakshmi of the house'. The move has disastrous effects not only upon her but upon her whole family: her husband becomes a wandering ascetic, her father commits suicide, and her younger sister is refused as a bride. Her odyssey and only partial retrieval through a new socially useful role—that of manager of an ashram for reformed prostitutes—is long and arduous. In the end, the encounter between Suman and her former respectable friend, Subhadrā, is a thin bridge connecting two separate worlds. Suman is exultant, though: the dire penance she had to endure for her momentary slip is nothing before even the smallest recognition and respect.[116]

Marginal women—widows, former prostitutes, daughters of prostitutes, or girls under duress—were also the first women shown taking up employment outside the home in the name of social and patriotic sevā.[117]

[116] A similar proposition was made by a 'distinguished courtesan' of Benares during an interview published in *Chāṁd*'s special *Veśyā-aṅk* (February 1927) and reprinted in August 1927. There were about a thousand prostitutes living in koṭhīs in Benares, and 10,000 on the street or in 'hotels', she said; 99 per cent were Hindu, many Bengali. The main reasons for prostitution were widowhood and social injustice: 'Young girls from very fine families are thrown out of their houses if only they slightly step over the limit, or they are brought to pilgrimage centres and left there.' At the suggestion that institutions like training ashrams might help prostitutes willing to reform, the courtesan laughed and said: 'If only. But look at how Gandhi's movement collapsed. . . . With only part of the money thus raised you could have set up at least 25 big ashrams for one to ten thousand reformed women.' She was willing to donate money, but what was missing was social willingness to give them 'a place in society . . . and the chance of a life of social service'; 'Veśyāoṁ ke udgār', *Chāṁd*, V, pt. 2, 4, August 1927, p. 455.

[117] E.g. Tārā, the educated and supposed daughter of a prostitute in G.P. Śrīvāstava's *Dil kī āg urf diljale ki āh* (Allahabad, Chand Press, 1936), who in the course of the tortuous plot establishes an abalā ashram and works as a teacher; or Phūlmatī in Dhanirām Prem's story 'Mātṛmandir' (1932); see above 4.3.

This image enabled the fictional possibility of strong women characters, involved in public activity either as self-supporting entrepreneurs or as political activists.[118] It is the (pure) daughter of a sophisticated courtesan who best corresponds to Nirālā's ideal of the 'new woman'—educated, refined, sensitive, independent, and bold—in his first novel, *Apsarā* (1930). A true Chāyāvādī heroine, Kanak fully displays her potentialities of intelligence, initiative, sensitivity, and self-sacrifice in ways that would have been impossible for respectable girls; thereafter she undergoes śuddhi (purification) and becomes a modest Hindu bride. Finally, there is the proud, intelligent, and independent courtesan of a fictive classical past—the heroine of one of the most popular novels of the 1930s, *Chitralekhā* (1934) by Bhagavatīcharaṇ Varmā. Outside the pale of marriage but not of society, Chitralekhā debates, takes decisions and displays all her power in a remarkable trajectory that leads her, like Jainendra Kumār's heroine Kaṭṭo in *Parakh*, to the life of self-sacrifice and dedication to others that she has chosen for herself. Once again the ideal of the self-sacrificing, nurturing woman is confirmed, but this time the role and morality are self-styled.

The figure of the svayaṃsevikā, the nationalist activist, raised very similar issues of public access and individual choice; here, too, the values of sevā and self-sacrifice (tyāg) were invoked, only this time with reference to the empowerment of ordinary women. Not surprisingly, Gandhi's influence is directly mentioned in narratives of svayaṃsevikās, which also highlight the exhilaration and tensions such women felt. Political, economic, and gender issues interlocked in new and interesting ways.

At a very superficial level, fictional images reflected a historical phenomenon, namely the participation of women in nationalist activities. They also worked as propaganda, providing incitement, motivation, and inspiration for women to join the movement. Until 1920, only a handful of educated, upper-caste women from distinguished families had undertaken any kind of public activity in north India.[119] The Non-Cooperation movement of 1919–20 witnessed substantial women's participation for

[118] Tārā is told in *Dil kī āg:* 'Your ashram has shown alone more benefits than scores of Women's Associations, Pardā Clubs and speeches,' p. 271.

[119] As the case of the women of the Nehru family shows, they were the ones who would later move to the highest posts in constitutional politics; see the article by J. 'Nirmal' on women in the UP legislative Assembly in *Sarasvatī*, November 1937, *Kāṅgres ministrī viśeṣāṅk*, pp. 462–4; also Kaur, *Role of Women in the Freedom Movement (1857–1947).*

the first time, especially in Lahore: women held separate public meetings and processions, hawked khadi and lit bonfires of foreign clothes. 'There was a sense of great achievement by women, of new spaces opening up for them.'[120] Significantly, most of the few women active in 1920 later became full-time activists and local Congress leaders (see 4.1). Rural women also took part in peasant protests and attended public meetings.[121] It was the Civil Disobedience movement of 1930, though, that first saw the mass participation of women: a decade of political propaganda and of radical women's journalism as well as the choice of salt, a basic household necessity, as a nationalist issue all contributed to the phenomenon. To manufacture salt in defiance of British laws became a way of 'declaring one's independence in one's daily life and also of revolutionizing one's perception of the kitchen as linked to the nation, the personal as linked to the political'.[122] As Gandhi himself remarked, the movement also had the merit of cutting through class divisions:[123] literate and illiterate women from different backgrounds found themselves rubbing shoulders in processions, picketings, *prabhāt pherīs*, and jails.[124] The sphere of women's political activity extended, as Madhu Kishwar has remarked, from the household to the market, from the street to the jail. Altogether about 3000 women all over India served prison sentences during the Civil Disobedience movement and were celebrated as

[120] Kumar, *The History of Doing*, p. 83.

[121] Rural women 'joined protest activity during certain phases, and their participation brought a new vigour and militance to the movement'; Kapil Kumar, 'Rural women in Oudh 1917–47: Baba Ramchandra and the woman's question', in Sangari and Vaid, *Recasting Women*, pp. 355 ff. The role of women during nationalist and peasant campaigns deserves further study. Madhu Kishwar refers to Raja Rao's novel *Kanthapura* (1937), which shows us 'how the movement looked like and meant to ordinary rural women . . . and suggests why rural women did not come to acquire leadership of the kind that could have influenced the direction of the movement'; Kishwar, *Gandhi and Women*, p. 24.

[122] Ibid., p. 17.

[123] Ibid., p. 19.

[124] Prabhāt pherīs were 'a religious practice familiar and popular among women. In the morning, groups of women would leave their homes and walk to the temple. On the way they would sing devotional songs. But now the songs were changed: political themes were substituted for traditional religious hymns'; V. Agnew, *Elite Women in Indian Politics*, New Delhi, Vikas, 1979, p. 57. Since it was a religious custom, the government was reluctant to prohibit it. However, prabhāt pherīs, especially by young and muscular Congress activists and members of Congress akhāṛās, became an aggressive way of claiming urban public space, and a typical source of communal tension.

national heroines, the new vīrāṅganās, in the Hindi press. Yet, particularly for educated women activists, nationalist work seems to have gone hand in hand, in most cases, with the concern for respectability. Women activists remained generally more restricted in their movements: very few urban, educated women could tour the countryside and establish contact with village women as male activists did.[125] In jail, they remained aloof from lesser activists and common women prisoners.[126] Social divisions persisted in the sharp distinction and discrimination between political prisoners of classes A, B, and C.[127] While this last issue surfaced only in autobiographical writings, perhaps out of a sense of shame, naratives about women volunteers, svayaṃsevikās, emphasized the courage and solidarity of women, and the hostility of men.

Even in literature 1930 marked a watershed. From imaginary characters, removed in time and space or confined to marginal and stigmatized groups, politically active respectable women characters gained greater social acceptance and we find positive images of independent-minded women volunteers. In the short story 'Svayaṃsevikā' (1931) by Rājbahādur Varmā, political sevā is the only way out of the gender, caste, and economic deadlock the protagonist finds herself in. From being a poor and illiterate Paswan (untouchable) servant in a small estate (ṭhikānā) in Marwar, Kesar becomes the captain of a squad of women volunteers during Civil Disobedience in Bombay.[128] Gender and caste oppression

[125] Kishwar, *Gandhi on Women*, p. 19.

[126] When Urmilā Śāstrī, Professor Dharmendranāth's wife and an activist in Meerut, first went to jail in 1930, she complained that the other common inmates were not 'good society' (*acchī sosāiṭī*), and hated their vulgar entertainments: 'There are several kinds of songs and dances, but I had never seen nor heard such obscene songs and dances in my whole life. . . . It is not that I am against *nṛtya-gān* [a sanskritized term, to distinguish "classical" from popular dance], they are high forms of art. They were widespread in ancient India and were especially linked with religion during the Bhakti period. But the kind of song-and-dance I am describing now was really utterly vulgar and obscene, no civilized (*sabhya*) person would have liked it'; Ūrmilā Śāstrī, *Kārāgār*, Atmaram and Sons, Delhi, 1931 (reprint 1980), pp. 37–8.

[127] When Subhadrā Kumārī Chauhān was arrested in 1942, she resented the differential treatment a lot and even more the natural way prisoners accepted the class differences implied. As she later reminisced, A and B class women did not treat C class prisoners very well and refused to share their meals or support C class prisoners' protests; Chauhān, *Milā tej se tej*, pp. 212 ff.

[128] Rājbahādur Varmā, 'Svayaṃsevikā', in *Chāṁd*'s *Rājputānā aṅk*, X, pt. 1, 1, November 1931, pp. 90–9 The issue also contained reports of the peasants' movement in Bijauliya, Mewar, and of their songs; see Āśāsiṃh, 'Jāgrat Rājasthān ke

are here both solved through empowerment by way of nationalist participation.

Initially Kesar is a typical abalā, a weak woman threatened by a young and anglicized (i.e. ruthless and spoilt) Thakur, the master of the estate. She patiently endures overwork, insults, and even beatings, but her self-respect does not allow her to yield to her master's sexual desires, although the ensuing tension puts her whole family in jeopardy. Only nationalism can provide her with a possible way out: her guide is the wife of a purohit who, in her few years at the Ārya-Kanyā Pāṭhśālā in Ajmer, has acquired some education and learnt havan mantras and several Ārya Samāj bhajans. Since the beginning of the salt satyāgraha she has also started reading newspapers and subscribing to the journals *Chāṁd* and *Pratāp*; a picture of Mahatma Gandhi hangs in her room. Kesar visits her occasionally during the year, joins in the bhajans, and listens to stories about Gandhi and the freedom struggle.

At the height of her crisis, when her master's advances have become pressing, Kesar visits the purohit's wife once more. The bhajan she sings has for Kesar a double meaning: Rāvaṇ is both the Thakur and the British, national pride and female honour overlap.

> अरे रावण तू धमकी दिखाता किसे
> मुझे मरने का खौफो-खतर ही नहीं।
> क्या तू सोने की लंका का मान करे
> मेरे आगे वह मिट्टी का घर नहीं।
>
> Who do you think to threaten, Rāvaṇ?
> I am not afraid to die.
> You may flaunt your golden Laṅkā,
> for me it means less than a mud hut.

Kesar is incredulous: how can simple mortals challenge the wicked and powerful? Nothing can overcome the simple strength of honour and dharma, answers the purohit's wife, and 'it is better to lose one's life than to lose one's honour'.[129] Her words inspire Kesar to act. Weeping at length, she pays silent homage to Gandhi's image—they are, the purohit's wife and Gandhi, her real parents—and when at night she receives the

---

katipay gīt', ibid., pp. 113–19. The word used of Kesar is *bandī*, which means both female servant and slave.

[129] Kesar expresses down-to-earth doubts: 'Oh yes, how can slaves dare! Do they have swords or guns? The slightest disobedience and poor women are thrown in jail, forced to pound flour, and those who do not accept losing their honour are marked with a hot iron. What can they do then?' Ibid., p. 96.

final summons from her master instead of yielding, she jumps out of a window in the mansion and runs away on the first train. We see her next at a massive demonstration in Bombay: Gandhi, other leaders, 15,000 male and 3000 female volunteers have already gone to jail, but the enthusiasm of the volunteers and of the crowd has not subsided. Picketing and demonstrations, are exhilarating moments and tests of patience and strategy. Women volunteers have assembled at the house of Hansa Mehta (a historical character) to choose the captain for the day. Several girls volunteer, but it is Kesar *bahin* who is chosen. In only two weeks the leaders have recognized her qualities: endurance, self-sacrifice, and hard work.[130] She has also empowered herself through education: in two months she has learnt to read and write Hindi and a few words of English. Walking in front of her squad in a saffron sari holding the Congress flag, Kesar is truly a new icon of 'Rājput vīrāṅganā'. The Thakur, by chance in Bombay with Kesar's father, sees her picketing a shop. When she starts singing the bhajan the purohit's wife had earlier sung to her, her father is overwhelmed with pride and the Thakur with shame, while cries of 'Mahatma Gandhi kī jay' and 'Kesar bahin kī jay' pierce the sky.

The icon of the svayaṃsevikā is invested with the qualities of sevā, self-sacrifice, modesty, moral and sexual purity, as well as the heroism of the vīrāṅganā; at the same time, political participation is presented here as a way to empowerment, a respectable public role and a source of moral authority. Kesar's flight from sexual, caste, and economic oppression does not lead into prostitution but to a new role, an active and fulfilled life and a political community.

In a later story on a similar theme by a woman writer directly involved in the movement, gender and political issues again overlap; as with peasant activism, political svarājya carried meaning only if also brought about social change: in the case of women, this is equated with gender equality, albeit unsuccessfully. In the story 'Balidān' (Sacrifice, 1937) by Śivrānī Devī, Premchand's widow, a famous and dedicated woman activist believes that partial political empowerment through the electoral victory of 1935 will ensure the empowerment of women.[131] However, after the electoral victory and a parade consecrating her as an icon of Mother India—she is both strong ('it seemed as if Mother India's soul had entered Prabhādevī', p. 112) and fittingly modest (she insists on

[130] 'To keep standing for hours on end in the heat, to work for two days without food or drink, to sleep on the bare ground and endure quietly all sorts of hardships is normal for Kesar;' ibid., p. 98.

[131] Śivrānī Devī, 'Balidān', in *Chāṁd*, XVI, pt. 1, 1, *Samāj-aṅk*, November 1937.

walking along with the others)—there comes disillusionment. Prabhādevī's proposal that women should be granted equal rights in everything including politics, property, society, and religion is heavily defeated in the Assembly by the votes of her fellow Congressmen. As a consequence, Prabhādevī resigns and turns to a 'higher' kind of politics, which incidentally involves a completely female political audience. She will lead a public hunger strike and at a public meeting in a Lucknow park she denounces the rigidity of society. It is as if 'countless unhappy women (*duḥkhinīs*), silent for innumerable years, had started expressing their thoughts through her mouth' (p. 113). She instructs other women volunteers to go to the villages and organize rural women, and all pledge that 'until women are given their proper place [they] will not sleep in peace' (p. 115). The crowd is moved to tears; many prostitutes are in their midst, repentant but afraid to come out. To Gandhi, who eventually pleads with her to desist from the hunger strike (his own weapon, after all), she replies: 'Bapuji, my game is over, I am going. But we have won.' Her funeral, attended by 50,000 people, 'is the funeral of the *Manusmṛti,* too. Everyone said that scores, nay innumerable lives were sacrificed over the *Manusmṛti*' (ibid.). As in social romances, the verisimilar setting allows a fictive character to work as a space for social imagining: he or she may serve as a source of inspiration and persuasion for the readers. In this story, a powerful example of political (and feminist?) propaganda, the protagonist is notably not an exceptional woman: she could be any of the readers, although the absence of any male relative avoids the question of male control of female initiative. Sevā and tyāg, service and self-sacrifice, serve to carry quite a radical message: the issue of women's emancipation is put on a par with national freedom.

'A woman's development should not be confined to the inner quarters (*antaḥpur*)', said writer Uṣādevī Mitrā at a women's meeting in 1931; 'but we should not forget that we can think about "outside matters" only after having properly fulfilled the duties of the home': a woman's highest duty is that of rearing children for service to the Motherland.[132] The existence of positive images of women engaged outside the home should not blind us to the fact that the centrality of the home, of motherhood and wifehood as women's dharma was never challenged openly until, perhaps, the end of the 1930s. Rather, in the Hindi fiction of the 1930s we

[132] Uṣādevī Mitra, 'Striyoṁ kā sthān', speech, place unknown, quoted in *Chāṁd*, IX, pt. 2, 6, October 1931, p. 750. For a similar statement in dialogue form on the household as the real *tapovan* of a wife, see Rāmeśvarī Nehrū, 'Pātivrat dharma', *Chāṁd*, XVIII, pt. 1, 1, 1940, pp. 23–7; also the editorial 'Vivāh aur sāhitya' in *Chāṁd*, V, pt. 1, April 1927, pp. 582–4.

see the image of the housewife, the *gṛhiṇī*, being redefined; she is now invested with emotional and intellectual depth and is shown to have some space for freedom and choice within the household, as well as in her relationship with the outside world and the world of men. With an interesting shift, literature posits the sensitive and aware gṛhiṇī as a fully-fledged individual *subject* who *chooses* the house as her *tapovan*, her 'ascetic grove'. Maybe the reality remained the same—of women ceaselessly adjusting to whatever given situation—but at least literature provided some imaginative space for individual self-determination. Thus characters and narratorial comments indicated that the maryādā of the housebound character was largely self-determined, the result of individual convictions, and not (only) of imposed social norms.

Perhaps the most powerful examples of a new kind of domestic heroine are those created by Jainendra Kumār (1905–88), hailed at the time as 'Hindi's Sharatchandra'. Although one may argue that he provided yet another male picture of womanhood, the popularity of Jainendra and Sharatchandra with generations of both male and female readers proves, for one thing, that it is a picture that held a significant fascination for both sexes.

Sensitive, educated, and loved by her respectful and liberal husband, Sunītā, the protagonist of Jainendra's eponymous novel (1935), still feels unfulfilled. Nothing is wrong on the surface, and her strong-minded devotion to her duty will not allow her even to feel a tinge of regret, but it is as if her potentiality as a woman has not been awakened yet. It is the arrival of a long-lost, eccentric friend of her husband's, Hariprasann, that changes things: Śrīkānt, Sunītā's husband, is all set to normalize him, in other words to find him a job and a wife and to teach him the value of money and the virtues of mundane contentment. Hariprasann has a vague air of danger around him, as he is involved with a group of revolutionaries. Yet Sunītā lets herself be attracted to him (at first in the most indirect way). Even her happy-go-lucky husband encourages their intimacy to the extreme because he feels that she might be more effective than him in leading Hariprasann onto the proper path. In a dramatic climax, left alone with Hariprasann one night, Sunītā agrees to act as the inspiring figure, the icon of Mother India, for his group of young revolutionaries.[133] In the dramatic showdown, her moment of extreme

[133] The reference to Bankim's Devi Chaudhurani is explicit when Hariprasann wants Sunītā to adorn herself for the occasion and says: 'Let the youth of our group see that their Devī Caudhurāni is also a goddess of beauty. Beauty is an aspect of the godhood of god, beauty is power (*śakti*), beauty is the ideal'; Jainendre Kumār, *Sunītā*, Delhi, Purvoday Prakasan, 1990, p. 208.

abandonment—when she is alone and naked in the forest with a stranger!—is the epiphany of her inner strength. Hariprasann, who was actually in love with her, cannot touch her: her maryādā is too strong for him to break through.

Hariprasann is thus instrumental in bringing out Sunītā's strength, her śakti, hidden under the modest and homely attire of the housewife. He is also instrumental in leading Sunītā to explore her identity as a woman beside her role as a wife, and this identity is a wholly spiritual, mystical one:

> We have given the names Hariprasann and Sunītā. These names are not false, but they are only names. Sunītā is a woman [*strī*, we find *nārī* elsewhere], Hariprasann a man (*puruṣ*). If we dig much below those names what is left is only a woman, only a man. Relations and names have a certain existence in our normal behaviour, but if we go deep down in the spirit (*prāṇ*) of creatures it is as if all these things remained on the surface.[134]

Thus, even the conventional image of the housewife could be shown to hide a dimension of universal individuality. In fact, the strength of Sunītā's gendered individual nature is a certain 'naturality', the habit of acting without reflecting too much. Throughout the novel Sunītā displays a remarkable impermeability to influence: her pliancy conceals a patient and inflexible capacity to hold her own ground. As a woman, she *knows* what is right, and she is strong without having to display her power. The latest incarnation of the Indian vīrāṅganā, then, is a quiet and nurturing gṛhiṇī, who from within the home can perform a variety of functions. As Hariprasann challenges her:

> What is the use of a wife who is only faithful to her husband? I need her as an image, who may be unfaithful but is unbending, who will shine among adversities like a flash of lightning in the jungle. I need a mother as well as a slave (*dāsī*). But I need most of all a mantra of enthusiasm, who will have so much love as not to fear violence, who can watch red blood flowing.[135]

In the climax, Sunītā shows Hariprasann that she is all this—transcendent mother, servant, wife, and an individual, too—but without losing her domestic demeanour or her dharma.[136] Jainendra's heroines

[134] Ibid., p. 126.

[135] Ibid., p. 148.

[136] The difference between Premchand's Suman and Jainendra's Mṛṇāl, the aunt who is rejected by her husband in *Tyāgpatra* (The Resignation, 1937), is that Mṛṇāl

are icons of a woman's strength and strong-will behind a demure, unthreatening appearance: the ideal of 'Indian woman' is not questioned, but a strong element of individual choice and self-definition is introduced.

It is interesting that Jainendra's heroines corresponded to the ideal woman as presented by *Chāṁd* when it was eventually forced to describe her in so many words after almost a decade of publication. The fact that *Chāṁd* had refrained from articulating its ideal of the Indian woman had no doubt helped its cause: it had prevented the journal from being labelled as either reformist, radical, social, or political, and it had allowed it to cover a wide range of identities and aspirations, even when its blunt attacks on prominent sections of Hindu society had left many wondering, uncertain about the exact aim of the journal. *Chāṁd*'s ideal, wrote the editor finally, is man–woman equality; *Chāṁd* asks men to respect women, to recognize their '*alaukik śakti*' (supernatural force) and let it develop. The editorial further defined for the first time *Chāṁd*'s ideal woman:

> (1) She should be free from the present ignorance, bad influences and ill feelings; (2) She should be expert in domestic work as well as a faithful and devoted wife (*satī-sādhvī*); (3) She should not observe pardā, but this does not mean that she should go out laden with jewels, unnecessarily attracting men's attention; (4) She should be educated and learned, enough at least to follow the developments of the present age and profit from knowledge; (5) She should be free from the fetters of the present day and should have the full right to express her opinions at home and to realize her aspirations; (6) She should know how to live a life of sevā and sacrifice, and behave affectionately towards her mother- and sisters-in-law at home; (7) She should know how to fight oppression and to defend herself with her own hands; (8) She should keep in good physical health and exercise and walk in the open air; (9) Singing and keeping merry are her ornaments, but only songs that become a respectable woman; (10) She should be as virtuous as a heroic wife and as courageous as a mother of lions (*siṃh-jananī*) and bear sons who will free India from the chains of servitude.[137]

The editorial did not spell out or rule out commitments and public

---

does not let herself be 'saved' nor does she criticize the society which has cast her out for little fault of her own. Mṛṇāl holds to her own truth with no compromise, seeks modest employment, and finally dies quietly in what appears outwardly like a descent into hell.

137 Vṛndāvandās, 'Chāṁd ke prati asantoṣ', *Chāṁd*, VIII, pt. 1, 6, April 1930, p. 700. The quotations that follow are taken from this article.

activities; rather, it took public access, education, and freedom of expression for granted. On the other hand, the focus was clearly on redefined household roles and relationships and on a self-fashioned maryādā. Some space for artistic and emotional expression and initiative fitted into this picture of an educated, aware, and modern middle class woman, as did undoubtedly employment if and when proper.

At the end of the two decades Mahādevī Varmā's overview of the 'modern woman' did include political activists and women teachers. These modern women had recognized their own strength and ability to act and create, although their development had not been matched by an equal effort at adjustment by men.

> Old-fashioned men look down upon them with contempt; modern-minded men support them but are unable to help them actively and the radicals encourage them but find it hard to take them along. Truly, modern women are more alone than old ones.[138]

According to Mahādevī, the danger for the educated woman was to remain caught between two worlds, with 'the call of the new age in front of them, and behind them the burden of several conventions'. What worried her was the fate of women after they came out of their homes during the movement: in the struggle they realized their strength, hardening themselves and opposing male lies about women's frailty and incapacity; however, 'society admires their self-sacrifice but fears their rebellious harshness. You cannot find in them the beautiful and wholesome image of life as before, and even several partisans of modernity look at them with dubious eyes'.[139] Thus the burden of finding a place within the family and social fabric fell again on those women: it was up to them to 'remember their womanhood' while finding different places within society, to face opposition and solitude, and to build bridges of compromise between old and new roles, between themselves and the social world around them. Mahādevī herself, one of the first women to pursue an independent career as a principal of a school and writer in a man's world, appears to have carefully struck a balance between her individual convictions and social expectations.

This chapter has sought to explore what happened when a subject other than the middle class educated male acquired a public voice, and when it moved from being the *object* of public discourse to being the

[138] Mahādevī Varmā, 'Ādhunik nārī kī sthiti par ek dṛṣṭi', in *Chāṁd*, XVI, pt. 1, 3, January 1938, p. 268.

[139] Ibid.

subject of reflection, introspection, and interaction in the public sphere. Although acknowledging the power of the construct of 'Indian woman' for women themselves, we need to go beyond an understanding of women as objects of the 'woman's question' or of patriarchal recasting. Once women had been granted access to public education and public media, some took up the critical instruments they had acquired to raise questions about themselves, their roles, and the norms of society. The process of education, critique, and gradual access to the male-dominated public sphere in many ways mirrored that of Indian intellectuals *vis-à-vis* the Raj. Significantly, women did not use *only* rational arguments but also appealed to justice and feelings, as letters and narratives showed, and carved out new meanings for accepted notions and women's roles (e.g. sevā). Although women's voices were largely shaped by dominant values and expressed them to a certain extent, male and female voices on women's issues differed. In the case of education, men viewed women's education as essentially functional to a reformed household. Women instead emphasized the widening horizon (especially through women's journals) and the individual empowerment education brought about; some further linked education to the issue of respectable employment and took up teaching in the name of 'social service'. As far as the family was concerned, men stressed the value of nurturing and self-sacrificing motherhood, while at the same time they contemplated uplifting ideals of companionate marriage within a careful division of spheres. Women strongly objected to the existing moral double standards for men and women, often offering elaborate historical and social arguments, and denounced the present family structure as cruel and insensitive to women's needs: as the protagonist of one story remarked, she would happily accept strī-dharma but only if it came from the heart, not when imposed upon her. Women's voices emphasized subjectivity and demanded that the family be an affective unit which acknowledged their feelings and their right to belong and to be heard. To be sure, men continued to speak on women's behalf, but now women's points of view had to be reckoned with.

While the gradual entry of women into mainstream media and politics was undoubtedly a significant feature of this period, the importance of women's institutions and spaces such as schools, journals, and picketing lines cannot be overemphasized. Here women's voices could emerge and take 'women's issues' in unforeseen directions and girls could acquire self-confidence and awareness of their own strength. Journals like *Gṛhalakṣhmi, Strī-darpaṇ* and *Chāṁd* gave new meanings to the notion of 'useful for women,' strī-upyogī, and social reform came to mean, certainly in the case of *Chāṁd*, the reform of society on women's behalf. Journals also testify to a diffuse political awareness and nationalism among women beyond the limited pale of women's associations. Finally, through the letters, poetry, and fictional narratives they carried, journals were crucial in establishing a voice and a space for women's subjectivity and emotional life.

Yet women gained more than just a voice and a discursive space. Greater mobility and acceptance of women in public spaces, unthinkable in north India only a generation earlier, were undeniably a fruit of these decades. The gradual spread of education, the impact of the nationalist movement and the greater currency of ideas about social reform were significant factors. Thus the case of women shows that extra-discursive forces are exceptionally important, often decisive, in determining access to, or exclusion from, the public sphere: discursive publicity, i.e. raising the issue in public media, is not enough. Take, for example, the argument that it was not right to marry girls before puberty, as common custom—maintained at least among the upper castes, the protagonists of the public sphere in north India. Such an argument could do little against the social pressure to do so until institutions like girls' schools, other pressures such as a desire for educated wives and even more radical alternatives such as women teaching, writing, and taking part in the nationalist movement, made the idea of marrying a girl after puberty sufficiently 'tame' to be accepted.

Entering public spaces or acquiring self-assurance was fraught with tensions. It certainly did not mean reaching equality. Women's presence in political bodies was often a token one;[140] in offices it was difficult for men to accept women as equal or, even worse, as seniors especially if women were junior in age, and in the household, educated brides were liable to be accused of haughtiness and shamelessness.[141]

The values of 'Indian womanhood'—modesty, sexual chastity, and moral purity; steadfast self-sacrifice and nurturing (whether in sevā or maternity)—were conspicuously present in all the images examined, irrespective of whether they were created by male or female writers and irrespective of the point being pressed. The convention was so strong that, typically, if any of these attributes was missing in a woman's

[140] V. Agnew, *Elite Women in Indian Politics,* pp. 86 ff.

[141] For two powerful examples, see Yaśpāl's character Tārā in *Jhūṭha sac* (1963) and Rājendra Yādav's Prabhā in *Sārā ākāś* (1968, tr. as *Strangers on the Roof*, Delhi, Penguin, 1994), both set around Independence.

character—if a perfect woman slipped out of chastity, if she refused to nurture anyone, if she tried to act like a man, if she overstepped maryādā or moved out of her prescribed area (for which *lakṣmaṇrekhā* is a most evocative term)—then the reader could be sure that either she was not a good woman after all or that something awful would happen to her. In the light of the tensions around women's presence in public spaces, the persistent trope of Indian woman and the concept of maryādā may actually express different objectives. In the case of (most) men, we can speak of 'recasting patriarchy' and a preoccupation with control and containment of women's freedom. For women, we may interpret this 'moral priority' and the subjectively defined maryādā as a source of inner strength (as for Jainendra's Sunītā) or as a strategy to avoid prohibitions, criticism of new roles, and of social change. As Mahādevī's case shows, women leading public lives folllowed a strict code of chastity and respectability, lest they face social criticism and endanger such a choice for other women. Although individually the greater openness of their lives and interaction with men brought about new modes of relationships for educated women, such as literary friendships and political camaraderie, as well as the possibility of love and sexual relations, these had to be kept away from the public gaze. While it can be argued that this kind of self-censorship acted as a limit to openness and debate among women the material presented in this chapter shows that this was only partly the case.[142]

True, *Chāṁd*'s trajectory shows a shift from passionate campaigns on various fronts—against social and caste oppression, for the emancipation of women and of the country—to the crystallizing of a composed, urban, modern middle-class culture that reflected an economically comfortable, educated, high-caste gṛhiṇī identity. *Chāṁd*'s claim to speak for and about *all* women at first had a radical and transformative power: issues like dowry, family oppression, even economic and sexual exploitation, were linked and presented as concerns of all women and of society, not only of an unlucky few. The use of a universal and homogeneous category (strī samāj) in this case increased the provocative impact of the argument. Then, after the editor, Sahgal, left and the provocative edge was lost, the issues raised coincided more accurately with the actual readers of the journal, urban, upper or middle caste women on the way to becoming solidly middle class. The claim to represent all women

[142] The literary friendships of Mahādevī, Subhadrā Kumārī Chauhān, Kamlā Chaudhrī, etc. are well known and documented, while love relations remain rumours.

now silently excluded other women subjects.[143] Mainstream women's journals after Independence became largely vehicles of middle-class acculturation. Yet much had been gained in terms of doors opened, spaces and voices gained, and of a vocabulary of words and images with which to express personal aspirations and negotiate between aspirations, cultural expectations, and social roles.

[143] See G. Pearson, 'Nationalism, Universalization and the Extended Female Space', in G. Minault, ed., *The Extended Family. Women and Political Participation in India and Pakistan*, Delhi, Chanakya Publications, 1981, pp. 175–6.

CHAPTER 5

The Hindi Political Sphere

In the history of political culture in India, the year 1920 marked the beginning of a new phase in the nationalist movement. Mass politics, indigenous languages, popular participants, counter symbols, and counter authority began to play an unprecedented role. The 'public' that was the target of nationalist rhetoric seemed finally to be physically *there*. New leaders and a new Congress party emerged from this phase of the movement, and by the end of the 1930s an indigenous political leadership was ready to inherit the reins of the country.[1] Many of the activists and leaders who emerged in north India during the campaign of 1920 came from the world of Hindi journalism. Writers also believed that they were serving the movement, by fighting with their pens. Literature, the press, and politics were seen as a continuum, a joint effort to liberate the country.

Yet the relationship between the literary and the political spheres was far more complex than most accounts would have us believe. Indeed, as we shall see, it was a difficult and often very bitter one. This had partly to do with the predicament of Hindi as a language, snubbed by non-Hindi politicians and yet picked as the national language. Other difficulties stemmed from the peculiar development of the nationalist political sphere. In order to understand the relationship between the Hindi literary sphere and this expanding political sphere, several angles are needed. First of all, that of 'institutional' spaces and activities, both within and outside the spaces allowed by the colonial state: what I have termed 'constitutional' and 'non-constitutional' domains (5.1). There are several questions to be asked. Who had access to political institutions? Was

[1] For political histories, Pandey, *The Ascendancy of the Congress in the United Provinces*; Sarkar, *Modern India*; Francis Robinson, *Separatism among Indian Muslims*, Cambridge, Cambridge University Press, 1974.

language a barrier and, if so, how was it circumvented? Did 'constitutional' and 'non-constitutional' politics imply two different attitudes to the state and to the public?

The second angle is that of openness in the political sphere (5.2). How open was the Hindi political sphere to the new subejects who joined the movement and brought their own perspectives on svarājya? The question of access and exclusion has already been raised in the previous chapter apropos of women and the public sphere. In this chapter I shall take up the case of peasants (*kisāns*) and peasant activism to examine both their critique of north Indian society and of the Hindi political sphere, and the structural difficulties they faced in making their voice heard. Was a 'subaltern counterpublic' (Nancy Fraser's term) formed by peasants who realized that the nationalist 'we' did not really represent them? Did they form a parallel discursive arena 'where members of subordinate social groups invent and circulate counterdiscourses to formulate oppositional interpretations of their identities, interests and needs'?[2]

The third angle is that of leadership: I shall analyse and compare the profiles of several Hindi political leaders in terms of social background, cultural make-up, connections, and political career (5.3). What interests did they claim to represent? Where did they stand in relation to the Hindi popular public and the state, and to Hindi intellectuals and the literary sphere? This will lead us to the fourth and final angle, that of authority, both cultural and political (5.4). Was the 'moral capital' acquired through writing or through political activism spendable in the public sphere at large? Did political authority acknowledge cultural authority and vice versa? The language controversy of the 1930s provides a good example, for when literary and political figures battled against each other they had to summon all the authority they could in order to overcome their opponents.

5.1. Constitutional and Non-constitutional Domains

How can we get svarājya with the Boards?

Śrīkṛṣṇadatt Pālīvāl

How can we get svarājya by leaving schools?

Sumaṅgal Prakāś's father[3]

[2] Fraser, 'Rethinking the Public Sphere', p. 123.

[3] Śṛikṛṣṇadatt Pālīvāl, 'Kaunsiloṁ dvārā svarājya', *Viśāl bhārat*, February 1936, p. 449; 'Śrī Sumaṅgal Prakāś ke saṃsmaraṇ', in Kṛṣṇanāth, ed., *Kāśī vidyāpīṭh hīrak jayantī. Abhinandan granth,* Benares, Jnanmandal, 1983, p. 185.

In the literary sphere, autonomous activism and institution building went side by side with pressure on, and cooperation with, the colonial state. Literary associations from the nineteenth century onwards not only pursued their autonomous literary agenda; they were also convinced that independent activities were always *best* enhanced by state support—even when the colonial state had long ceased having the semblance of a benevolent agency, the presence of nationalist-minded officers sensitive to the Hindi project always left open a channel of communication. One finds a similar double track in the political sphere. The nationalist movement was concerned both with entering colonial institutions, gradually occupying the state in order to change it from within, and with autonomous activism, mobilizing an increasing number of popular groups, antagonizing the state, and creating a counter authority. Both aspects need to be taken into consideration when analysing the political culture of Indian nationalism.

In this section, then, constitutional and non-constitutional politics signify two styles of politics, of mediating within society and between society and the state. By constitutional politics I mean a political culture that was largely shaped by colonial expectations and by the spaces offered by the colonial state, and which reproduced those expectations in the vernacular. By non-constitutional politics I signify a political culture which tried to grow more autonomously, with an original cultural content and independent institutions that provided spaces where colonial culture could be replaced by a national one. This does not mean that it was not influenced by the colonial context of course, only that in its self-representation it self-consciously emphasized autonomous genealogies and alternative idioms. It was here that non-literate sections of society gained access to the political sphere and made their presence felt to literate elites, as we shall see.

Some of the peculiarities of the state that these political actors had to face need to be recalled.[4] The European bourgeois public sphere described by Habermas struggled to impose an impersonal notion of political power and to gradually transform the absolutist state into a limited constitutional, one, subject to public scrutiny, pressure, and (however partial) influence. The institutions, language, and discourses of the public sphere emerged from the social terrain of this struggle. In India, these institutions and discourses were introduced into a different social universe and

[4] The following discussion is heavily indebted to Sudipta Kaviraj, 'On the Construction of Colonial Power: Structure Discourse Hegemony', in Engels and Marks, eds, *Contesting Colonial Hegemony*, London, British Academic Press, 1994.

under different structural arrangements: they had to contend with different pressures from the British and the colonial state itself, and from different groups of Indian subjects.

The colonial state that late nineteenth- and early twentieth-century Hindi intellectuals faced was an ostensibly benevolent and liberal state which appeared amenable to reasonable arguments and claimed to be equally neutral towards all its Indian subjects. Under colonial rule all Indian citizens, irrespective of status, were subjected to the same set of impersonal laws and public courts: thus any complaint against the law or against other citizens had to take the same form of public procedure through formal complaints and petitions, magistrates, and courts of law.

Yet this state, which swore by liberal principles, pursued interests that were subordinate to those of the mother country even when they differed from the interests of the colonial subjects. The British colonial state in India contended with several conflicting demands of accountability and different needs for legitimacy. First and foremost, it was accountable to the regime in England and to British public opinion. But, and in this lay the first paradox of the colonial state, it was far more powerful than the state was in the mother country, and not bound by the democratic rules, restraints, and demands that restricted elitist politics there. On the other hand it was an *Indian* state, i.e. it had to respond in an intelligible and effective way to the pressures and the social logic of India. In its interaction with the dissimilar and largely unrelated publics of Indian society, and in its discourse of legitimacy both in India and in England, colonial rule adopted different attitudes and idioms. In Sudipta Kaviraj's words, 'In its dialogue with British public opinion it adopted a tone of reasonableness; with the indigenous middle class, it carried on a dialogue through education and legislation; while *vis-à-vis* the sullenly distant popular masses, it adopted primarily a monologue of force.'[5]

Without relinquishing its first vocation of economic extraction, the post-1858 Indian state became more of a 'strong', national state. It intervened to restructure the economy, social processes (through education, bills of social reform, etc.), and relations between the state and society, thus opening new grounds of public confrontation with Indian subjects. Bilingualism—the hierarchy of English and Indian 'vernaculars'—was written into all the relations between the colonial state and its subjects and became duplicated in Indian society. Finally, although power under the colonial regime was public in the sense of being at least a formal and

[5] Ibid., p. 21.

impersonal set of laws and institutions, however iniquitous to large sections of the population, it was heavily 'personified' in local figures of authority—landlords—who usually had at least some control of the impersonal and 'legal' state machinery, the police, and the courts.

However, to the extent that colonial state power was impersonal and public and at least formally not absolute, it potentially implied a democratic discourse which both imperialists and nationalists tried to exploit to different ends.[6] This fostered a culture of petition and of confidence in state patronage that was a direct consequence of state publicity: if the state claimed that its laws applied to all, and that subjects could and should appeal by public means, colonial intellectuals believed that changing the letter of the law would bring about actual change.

However limited, the colonial state did open some spaces for Indian participation and encouraged the formation and expression of 'Indian public opinion' to a certain extent. Indians co-opted through nomination belonged to two groups: they were either 'native chiefs' who were supposed to command the natural obedience of the masses, or western-educated, bilingual civil servants and professionals, often lawyers, who formed a bourgeoning educated public opinion.[7] Since these limited constitutional proceedings were carried on in English, bilingual professionals had an advantage over local notables who did not know the language.[8] They became familiar with the official 'public idiom' both in speech and in writing in order to understand and interact with the state machinery. These first politicians, of whom Madan Mohan Mālavīya is an excellent example, then translated such concepts and language into the vernacular and publicly held the state up against its own rules.[9] This was

[6] See the section on 'The Colonial Context' in Haynes, *Rhetoric and Ritual in Colonial India.*

[7] Restricted franchise structurally limited participation in 'constitutional politics' before 1920 to landed and moneyed elites and to educated professionals, the latter often tied to the former as clients. Being an honorary magistrate or sitting on the local boards became a mark of prestige and a way of securing a new venue of patronage and influence. Nomination was also considered a sign of official benevolence and was one way of showing the kind of 'public commitment' British authorities so appreciated; see Bayly, *The Local Roots of Indian Politics,* and Haynes, *Rhetoric and Ritual in Colonial India.*

[8] Actual participation at meetings was usually low, and it was occasionally remarked that notables or their courtiers who sat on them sometimes did not know English.

[9] E.g. each year the Chairman of the Municipal Board submitted an annual report to the Commissioner for comment (*samālochnā*). In 1920 The Kashi Central

a creative process; in Mālavīya's case, for example, it meant espousing Britain's colonizing mission to demand that the rule of the liberal state be applied to the Indian state, and refuting Indians' incapacity for self-government.[10] He adduced textual evidence to argue that in fact self-rule had existed in ancient India, i.e. that the demand for it by modern Indians was not imitative of British democracy.[11]

Constitutional politicians spoke in the name of the 'general public' (*sarvasādhāraṇ*), yet, as with Hindi reformist intellectuals, the public they claimed to represent was only vaguely defined and intrinsically restricted. As Mālavīya's case shows, constitutional politics raised their claims only in the spaces allowed by the colonial state; even svarājya was envisaged as a gradual reform and paternalistic democracy. Despite the occasionally fiery tones, the kind of popular participation Mālavīya requested was very limited. It was more important that the dialogue and cooperation with the government should not halt. Thus Mālavīya invited the Prince of Wales to BHU in 1929 and conferred upon him a degree *honoris causa* while the Congress in the whole province boycotted the visit and staged black-flag demonstrations.

This style of constitutional politics self-consciously upheld boundaries between different areas of life: there was the official public sphere of the board-assembly-law-court, the civic public sphere, which could overlap with that of the community in religious and political terms, and there was the sphere of the family *birādarī* (brotherhood), each with its distinct idiom, ideology, and behaviour. To take Mālavīya again: in the parliamentary arena he used a strictly constitutional idiom; at the same time he worked to create a Hindu constituency around symbols like the cow and Hindi, and yet he strongly opposed official and unofficial interference with personal and family practices and beliefs (see 5.3).

Successive constitutional innovations, motivated by the twin requirements of financial devolution and the need for a wider circle of Indian collaborators, partially enlarged this constitutional space, first at the local and then at the provincial level. Gradually election supplanted

---

Ratepayers' Association submitted a similar detailed report 'on behalf of the general public' (*sarvasādhāraṇ kī aur se*), which the Benares daily *Āj* translated into Hindi and published over several issues in September. *Āj*, 12, September 1920 and ff.

[10] M.M. Mālavīya, 'Svarājya athvā pratinidhi śāsan-praṇālī', and 'Svarājya kī yogyatā aur uske sādhan', *Abhyuday*, 1907, in P. Mālavīya, *Mālavīyajī ke lekh*, pp. 62 ff.

[11] Mālavīya, 'Svarājya kī kalpanā', *Abhyuday*, 1907, ibid., pp. 121–4.

nomination.[12] However inconsequential, elections turned constitutional politics into more of a political arena and forced candidates to turn to 'the public' and develop proper idioms in the vernaculars, carefully nuanced to match each particular audience.[13] Even 'traditional leaders' favoured by the policy of nomination now had to make active efforts to ensure their erstwhile influence,[14] while separate electorates favoured a politics and idiom of community interests.

When Congress activists and leaders legitimized by the non-constitutional movement were elected to the boards and provincial councils, it was saluted as a popular victory in that they seemed to 'occupy the state'. Although they insisted on certain signs of change (dress, the use of the vernacular, and of course, ideology), Congressmen broadly adapted to the constitutional style. This involved a certain formality of countenance, obeisance to parliamentary rules, and the ability to use the official idiom,

[12] For constitutional reforms, see Sarkar, *Modern India*. Briefly, the 1916 UP Municipalities Act and 1922 UP District Boards Act introduced election at the local level and had important consequences, especially in terms of expectations and opportunities. The 1919 Montagu–Chelmsford constitution introduced partly elective provincial legislatures; despite the extended franchise, its bias in favour of landowning classes ensured the return of a loyal majority. The act also provided representation without responsibility: certain matters remained 'reserved' ('diarchy'); governors had special powers of veto and 'certification' (i.e. to enact legislation refused by the Legislative Assemblies), and ministers were responsible to the governors and not to the assembly; Pandey, *Ascendancy of the Congress Party*, pp. 24 ff.

[13] E.g. it was difficult for C.Y. Chintamani, the renowned editor of *The Leader*, to campaign for a seat in Jhansi in 1920 not knowing any Hindi; finally he had to utter a few sentences in a restricted public meeting just to disavow criticism on this point; Varmā, *Apnī kahānī*, pp. 55 ff.

[14] The real quandaries brought about by this process are poignantly captured in the following incident, reported in the pro-Congress daily *Āj* in 1920 as 'A fight between kshatriyas and non-kshatriyas'. A local zamindar had called a 'public meeting' to ensure peasant support for his anti-Congress candidate, who tried to play the card of the solidarity between rural classes; however, since the meeting was public, it was open to local Congress supporters: one of them stood up in protest and mentioned the satyāgraha Gandhi had undertaken for the peasants in Kheri and Champaran. The villagers started rumbling in agreement. At this point the chairman of the meeting declared it a *private* meeting: 'We have spent Rs 1000' he said, 'this is our *praiveṭ mīṭiṅg*. It is we who decide whether to allow others to speak if we want to.' At this, other local activists stood up in protest and said that it was a public meeting and it was extremely despicable for them to stop or threaten anyone; *Āj*, 22, September 1920, p. 6.

albeit in the vernacular. In fact, the ability to master the idiom of constitutional politics remained a fundamental skill, a symbol of the bilingualism Indian politicians had to command. The first time Sampūrṇānand spoke in the UP Legislative Council after the 1926 elections, he began his speech in Hindi:

The Speaker, Dr Sita Ram, pulled me up, the rule being that unless a member was unable to speak in English, he must use that language. In my heart, I was thankful to the President, because I was anxious that what I was going to say should be understood by the English members opposite. But as a Hindi writer I had to show preference to Hindi. I, therefore, protested mildly against the President's order and continued in English.[15]

In the constitutional arena, then, Hindi was a symbol while English was the language of substance.

Expectations from Congress participation in constitutional politics were always likely to exceed what circumstances allowed. With the emergence of popular, non-constitutional politics led by Gandhi, however, criticism of the boards became structurally different. Whereas earlier criticism tended to focus on individual malpractice, now it was the structure itself that came under fire. Hindi editor and Congress leader Śrīkṛṣṇadatt Pālīvāl noted in 1936 that popular opinion was very much against the Legislative Council, which it 'rightly' considered the 'temple of Māyā':

The Councils are temples of Māyā because ostensibly (*pratyakṣ meṁ*) they are there to help people rule, to put the strings of power in the hands of their representatives; but actually they are there to fulfil the interests of the ruling and capitalist classes! The whole electoral procedure is a demonic Maya (*rākṣasī māyā*) from the beginning to the end. In our country not everybody has yet the right to vote. Those who have it do not control the registration of names. As a result, there is quite a bundle when the list of registers is made. This malpractice has reached its peak in the Municipalities . . .[16]

Besides, constitutional boards only appeared to make power public, in other words transparent and accessible: 'In councils and assemblies one meets power and wealth face to face . . . [but] the rulers' rights are kept safe in a temple where representatives, like untouchables, are denied entry'.[17] Yet, after denouncing the serious limitations on political

[15] Sampurnanand, *Memories and Reflections,* Bombay, Asia Publishing House, 1962, p. 46. It is significant that this major Hindi politician chose to write his autobiography in English, probably aiming at a pan-Indian audience.

[16] Pālīvāl, 'Kaunsiloṁ dvārā svarājya', pp. 449–52.

[17] Ibid.

activity within the assemblies and agreeing with the popular perception that they were a travesty (*svāṁg*), Pālīvāl concluded that to 'enter the enemy's fortress' was a necessary part of the overall strategy for winning svarājya.[18]

Disappointment over the performance of elected Congress boards could even be turned into an indictment of the conflict between 'our boards' and the alien state. When the Benares Municipal Board was threatened (and then met) with suspension for corruption in 1932, Premchand wrote that the boards were still to be valued as a political space open for the public to exercise some degree of activity and power in the administration. Its achievements (e.g. in the field of education) should not be belittled, and enthusiastic non-official members could always open the possibility of reform. 'Whatever progress there has been in Kāśī Municipality', he wrote, 'it has happened during the period of the non-official (*gair-sarkārī*) board, and in my opinion the administration of a non-official board is always the best; at least it is not unrestrained (*niraṅkuś*)'.[19]

Implied in Pālīvāl's critique was the notion that legitimacy rested with the 'people', the 'true' nation shut outside the 'temples of Maya'. Taking on the fictitious persona of a 'shack-dweller' (*jhoṁprā vālā*), editor, poet, and Congress activist Mākhanlāl Chaturvedī voiced a plea to the 'travellers on the national path' (*rāṣṭrīy path ke pathik*) entitled 'Ham jansādhāraṇ haiṁ' (We are the common people). Through mimicry of the stereotypical deferential attitude of the subordinate to the powerful, he measured the distance between constitutional nationalists and the aspirations of common people.

दुखिया की आवाज़। जनसाधारण हैं हम निरे अज्ञान। सेवा करना ही है बस अभिमान। तुम नेता हो आत्मबली मतिदान। हम दुखिया हैं रोते देते प्रान।

This is the voice of a wretched man, a common, ignorant man, only proud to serve. You are the leaders, strongwilled and wise. [. . .]

Your Reform Bill has been passed, very well. We also speak your praise with great joy, but in our huts our wives ask us: 'Will this new law bring us food to fill our stomachs?' We also believe that education is necessary, but education

[18] 'There is no other way. Even Lenin reached this conclusion, even Gandhi has reached it now . . . We neither have or should have any hope in the councils; but we should also stop talking of boycott. Council-entry is a necessary evil, and with this in mind we should put up with them;' ibid.

[19] *Jāgaraṇ*, 21, November 1932, in Premchand, *Vividh prasaṅg*, vol. 2, p. 515. See also Paripūrṇānda Varmā's articles on the history of Kāśī Municipal Board since the Bhagvān Dās-led Congress board of 1923, revealing instances of official responsibility in sabotaging the elected board; *Āj*, February 1933.

cannot fill an empty stomach! . . . Therefore, mahātmās with lofty ideals, we salute you. We thank you, all we have got is tears and we wash your feet with them, but nobody listens to our cry. You are clearing the road at the top. It will take centuries to reach the bottom. We don't have food to eat tomorrow, how can we wait patiently for centuries?[20]

This critique of constitutional politics, and the acknowledgement of the non-constitutional domain as the true sphere of the public, had several implications. First of all, it emphasized the importance of the institutions of the public sphere, from the press to book publishing and education, as *political* activities, and of literary figures as nationalist actors. Writing or teaching were 'constructive' activities and were as important as any other in 'serving' the nation and furthering the cause of the nationalist movement. Premchand's political stories written during the campaigns of 1920 and 1930 provide the ideal example: for the writer they were a way of putting his pen at the direct service of the movement and of propagating its message; for the readers they were a way of making sense of radical political slogans through realistic human stories. Typically they climax at moments of 'conversion' to the nationalist cause, almost helping the reader to take the same step.[21]

Second, non-constitutional politics emphasized the political role of the press as a vehicle of *popular* public opinion. It was especially the duty of the vernacular press to mirror the real nation. The Hindi political press actually changed from being 'journals of ideas' for the educated few to newspapers rooted in local society, reflecting and addressing the 'sādhāraṇ samāj':

Now the time has come for our political ideology and movement not to be restricted to the English-educated, and to spread among the common people (*sāmānya jantā*), and for Indian public opinion (*lokmat*) to be not the opinion of those few educated people, but to mirror the thoughts of all the classes of the country. When we agitate for svarājya we should not forget the principle of a famous political thinker, that democratic rule is actually the rule of public opinion. And one very important way of creating a wide informed public opinion is to use

[20] Mākhanlāl Chaturvedī, 'Ham jansādhāraṇ haiṁ', *Karmavīr*, 14, February 1920, in S. Jośī, ed., *Mākhanlāl chaturvedī racnāvalī*, vol. 2, Delhi, Vani Prakasan, 1983, pp. 13–14.

[21] See 'Lāg dānt' (The Competitors, July 1921), 'Cakmā' (A Little Trick, in *Prabhā*, November 1922); 'Julūs' (The Procession, in '*Haṃs*, March 1930); 'Samar-yātrā' (The Battle March), Benares, Saraswati Press, 1930; the collection *Samar-yātrā* was published in 1930 in the heat of the Civil Disobedience campaign at the specially low price of 2 and a half annas; see *Statement of Publications*, 1930.

Indian (svadeśī) languages along with English for our political interactions and debates.[22]

Hindi editors such as G.Ś. Vidyārthī in Kanpur, Śrīkṛṣṇadatt Pālīvāl in Agra, Mākhanlāl Chaturvedī in Jabalpur, Daśarath Prasād Dvivedī in Gorakhpur, and Bābūrāo Viṣṇu Parāṛkar in Benares (see Box 1.1) were at the forefront of this change. Prosecuted and even jailed when censorship and repression grew stricter during mass campaigns, they often became local heroes. With such events, the press became even more clearly identified with the political movement and it was the Hindi press that first voiced the need to include larger sections of society in the movement, primarily peasants and women (see 5.2 and Chapter 4).[23] 'Let's go to the villages' (*chaliye gāṁvoṁ kī taraf*), urged G.Ś. Vidyārthī: 'Whoever wants to work should turn to the villages. Work in the towns has already been done.'[24] This popular leaning inspired direct criticism of the pre-Gandhian Congress: if it really claimed to be the 'voice of the whole of India' (*saṃyukt bhārat kī āvāz*) 'now . . . those doors must be open which for some reason have been kept closed so far', wrote Vidyārthī.[25]

Another implication of non-constitutional politics was that the politics of the street came to be valued above the 'politics of the library'.[26] Even before 1920 there had been clear signs of dissatisfaction in the United Provinces with the moderate, constitutional Congress of the province.[27] During Non-Cooperation, joining the movement was expressed in terms

22 Vidyārthī's editorial on the forthcoming Lucknow Congress, *Pratāp*, 3, July 1916, in Avasthī, *Krānti kā udghoṣ*, vol. 1, p. 240. See also B.V. Parāṛkar's presidential speech at the Sampādak Sammelan in 1925, quoted in 1.3 in this volume.

23 For an informative study, see Brahmānand, *Bhārtīy svatantratā āndolan*. For information on censorship and repression of the Hindi press after Civil Disobedience, see editorial note in *Sudhā*, IV, 1, 3, October 1930, pp. 434–5.

24 Editorial, *Pratāp*, 19.1.1925; in R. Avasthī, *Krānti kā udghoṣ*, vol. 2, p. 767.

25 G.Ś. Vidyārthī's editorial, *Pratāp*, 11, January 1915; ibid., vol. 1, p. 103.

26 For an excellent example of an early satire on the nature and limitations of constitutional political culture as 'politics of the library', see the fifth scene of Bhārtendu Hariśchandra's play *Bhārat durdaśā* (1880), in Ś. Miśra, ed., *Bhārtendu granthāvalī*, vol. 1, Benares: Nagari Prachārini Sabha, 1974.

27 Hindi editors looked elsewhere, to Bengal and Maharastra, for radicalism and heroic terrorism. Tilak's popularity among students, Hindi scribes and future politicians proves the case; e.g. both G.Ś. Vidyārthī and Narendra Deva claimed Tilak as the greatest political influence before Gandhi; see M.L. Bhargava, *Ganesh Shankar Vidyarthi*, Delhi, Publications Division, Ministry of Information and Broadcasting, 1988, p. 53 and Keskar and Menon, *Acharya Narendra Dev*, p. 25.

of a battle (*laṛāī, saṅgrām*), an arena which one 'jumped into', with akhāṛā-style metaphors. It was there that the nationalist struggle was to be fought. Yet the crowd at nationalist demonstrations awakened mixed reactions, even among Congressmen. On the one hand it was celebrated as a visible symbol of the 'true nation' and its power; from the point of view of the common participants, the experience of the crowd was one of exhilarating empowerment, in which it defied colonial authority and claimed legitimacy and authority for itself 'in the name of' Gandhi and Nehru.[28] In Hindi literature, the crowd is often both the stage for heroic nationalist acts and the audience before which the brutality of the British and their lackeys is exposed.[29] For women in particular, after svadeśī had provided them with ways of being nationalist at home, crossing the threshold to take part in picketing, meetings, and demonstrations was a hugely liberating experience, and it was the presence of a crowd, its emotional charge, and its self-asserted legitimacy, that allowed individual women to take the first step and face the consequences. Similarly, the peasant leader Sahajānand Sarasvatī learned to take advantage of the emotional impact generated by massive peasant rallies and demonstrations. On the other hand, crowds were feared by Congress politicians for their 'unruliness' and their potential to disrupt the exemplary tactics of Congress volunteers, and were sometimes despised for their naiveté. Here elite and popular perceptions tended to come into conflict.[30]

As the concept of svadeśī showed, implicit in the non-constitutional style of politics was the tendency to cross boundaries and conflate publics. There were many ways in which one could be 'nationalist', many possible symbolic changes one could make in things ranging from clothing to speech, work to commensality, relations within the family and with fellow volunteers. The reversal of values that Gandhi's idiom and ideology brought about—the overturned hierarchy and the centrality of the sarvasādhāraṇ, the common people, his emphasis on self-sacrifice over

[28] See Amin, 'Gandhi as Mahatma'; also *Event, Metaphor, Memory, Chauri-Chaura 1922–1992*, Delhi, OUP, 1995.

[29] See for example Premchand's story 'Julūs' (1930) with its different crowds: the well-disciplined body of volunteers, their sympathizers, and the idle passers-by who are transformed into a nationalist crowd by watching the 'martyrdom' of the old Muslim man leading the volunteers at the hands of a cruel loyalist policeman. The same crowd then witnesses the defiant nationalism of the policeman's wife and, ultimately, his own change of heart.

[30] Pandey, 'Congress and the Nation'; Vinita Damodaran, *Broken Promises: Popular Protest, Indian Nationalism and the Congress Party in Bihar*, Delhi, OUP, 1995, p. 230.

worldly success and on 'Indianness' versus modern/foreign culture—enhanced the sense of importance of Hindi activists and intellectuals. At least in words, English was devalued in favour of the vernacular; the very ordinariness of Hindi writers seemed to place them closer to the 'true nation' and give them an advantage in communicating with the masses. In practice, as we have seen, the question of popularity was a thorny one for Hindi writers (2.3.2), for the taste of 'the people' did not match their expectations. They also discovered that Congress rhetoric about the true nation was, in fact, mainly rhetoric. But more on this later in the chapter.

If we compare constitutional and non-constitutional political styles, we notice a number of interesting differences in the relationship between Hindi and English, and in attitudes to colonial and traditional authorities, to the public, to the Hindi literary intelligentsia, and to political and social change. Constitutional politics translated English political vocabulary into Hindi but fostered Hindi as a political language only within a bilingual hierachy; non-constitutional politics tended to refuse (at least symbolically) the bilingual hierachy altogether and to *replace* English with the vernacular. A certain success was achieved in this direction, although in their enthusiasm for Hindi as rāṣṭrabhāṣā, the Hindi intelligentsia fuelled the conflict with Urdu and overlooked the difficulties in actually replacing English at the supra-regional level (5.4). In its relationship with colonial and traditional Indian authorities, despite the occasionally fiery rhetoric, constitutional politics took a mediatory, compromising stance. Non-constitutional politics instead tended to adopt a confrontational attitude and establish counter institutions and figures of counter authority within the movement. Also, whereas constitutional politics upheld boundaries between separate spheres, trying to contain, so to speak, the consequences of political awareness from spilling outside the official or civic domain, non-constitutional politics conflated boundaries and politicized literature, the household, gender, and social practices. Thus while constitutional politicians aimed at political change without social change, at least for the bottom rungs of society, non-constitutional politicians placed social change at the heart of their political agenda. Constitutional politicians tended to accept that the Indian public was divided into hierarchical layers and saw their own role as being mediators between the elites and the masses *as well as* between the colonial state and Indian society, and as educators and guides of the popular public. Politicians and intellectuals who believed in non-constitutional politics saw their own role and that of the nationalist movement as one of 'breaking the chains' within Indian society itself, of forging new relationships, and of empowering new subjects. As we have seen in the case of women and we shall see again in the case of peasants, it was in the non-constitutional domain that these subjects enthusiastically joined the fray, while their constitutional participation and representation remained negligible. 'Tokenism' is the term sometimes used, for example, to describe women's presence within the top rungs of Congress.[31]

These are of course simplifications. In practice the two styles blended and overlapped: constitutional boards became a necessary evil and even Mālavīya envisaged a measure of social change. During the two decades the two streams intertwined; at different times one was more prominent than the other. In the end, bilingualism acted as a kind of bottleneck for vernacular politicians, and parliamentary style was acknowledged as the prerequisite for rule. The trajectory of Congress in the two decades under study in fact shows two opposite but concomitant trends. Non-constitutional politics became an important locus of legitimacy and of osmosis between the literary and the political sphere; it allowed access to new subjects and new publics. At the same time, constitutional politics remained the path to tread. In the Hindi political sphere this is mirrored in the fact that Hindi editor– and activist–politicians did manage to become prominent local and regional leaders. They were also elected to legislative assemblies, often defeating traditional men of influence. Once they became entrenched in the constitutional arena, however, they espoused the logic of constitutional politics and forgot their role as representatives of popular aspirations and public opinion. Historians have explained this trend, particularly evident in the 1930s, as a necessary compromise for a party that aspired to represent all and had to win over influential classes so far loyal to the colonial state. For much of the Hindi intelligentsia, though, the experience was a baffling one, especially at the time of the Congress provincial ministries in 1937: the period of greatest constitutional success was also that of the greatest distance between public opinion and the party. Nowhere is the paradox of these two contrasting trends more evident than in the case of attitudes to peasants and their participation in the nationalist movement.

5.2. Peasants as Subjects

The public of Hindi comprised the whole of north Indian society, especially its bottom rungs: this was perhaps the greatest strength of Hindi's claim *vis-à-vis* English. This claim overlapped in the 1920s with

[31] See Agnew, *Elite Women in Indian Politics*, pp. 86 ff.

the nationalist slogan that the kisāns (peasants) were the true nation and the Congress a kisān Congress. Yet, what happened when peasants actually entered the fray and acquired a voice in the public sphere? In other words, when they turned from objects of nationalist discourse into subjects of political activity? This question is linked to the issue of openness and exclusion in the Hindi public sphere.

Critics of Habermas have pointed out his inadvertent equation of unrestrictedness with equality: the fact that access to the public sphere is not formally restricted to some groups does not mean that all have equal access. Nancy Fraser, for example, has emphasized not only the actual exclusions from the potentially open access to the bourgeois public sphere, something even Habermas conceded was never fully realized in practice, but also the more subtle discriminations that this ostensibly equal discursive interaction implied. Strategies like bracketing status ('as if' it did not exist or count), and protocols of style and decorum in public interaction that are themselves markers of status inequality, effectively marginalized women and members of plebeian classes. The language of political deliberation itself can, by imposing an overarching (and seemingly consensual) 'we', mark subtle forms of control: 'Subordinate groups sometimes cannot find the right voice or words to express their thoughts, and when they do, they discover they are not heard' or else that the 'we' does not really represent them.[32] Under such conditions, Fraser observes, such groups often tend to constitute 'subaltern counterpublics' and form 'parallel discursive arenas' where they may 'invent and circulate counterdiscourses to formulate oppositional interpretations of their identities, interests and needs'.[33]

Without treading too much on ground and arguments already advanced by others,[34] I want to focus here, first, on the bracketing and objectifying strategies of literary and nationalist discourse, and then on their critique by one of the most important and articulate peasant leaders of the

[32] Jane Mansbridge, 'Feminism and Democracy', *The American Prospect,* no. 1, 1990, p. 127, quoted in Nancy Fraser, 'Rethinking the Public Sphere', p. 119.

[33] Ibid., p. 124.

[34] Pandey, 'A Rural Base for Congress' and 'The Congress and the Nation'; Kapil Kumar, *Peasants in Revolt: Tenants, Landlords, Congress and the Raj in Oudh: 1886–1932*, Delhi, Manohar 1984; also 'The Ramcharitmanas as a Radical Text. Baba Ramchandra in Avadh', in S. Chandra, ed., *Social Transformation and Creative Imagination*, Delhi, Allied Publishers, 1984, and 'The Congress–Peasant Relationship in the Late 1930s', in D.N. Panigrahi, ed., *Economy, Society and Politics in India*, Delhi, Vikas, 1985. See also Damodaran, *Broken Promises*.

time, Svami Sahajānand Sarasvatī (1889–1950). Second, I will try to gauge the impact of the peasant critique and peasant activism on the Hindi public sphere. In order to do so, I shall examine literary and political attitudes toward the kisāns before turning to the experience of Sahajānand Sarasvatī, his critique and his agenda. My angle on the 'peasant question' is thus a rather specific one, and my treatment of the material is consequently very selective.

The special *Kisān aṅk* of the influential Allahabad weekly *Abhyuday* (November 1931) provides us with a glimpse of Hindi positions, arguments, and issues related to peasants and peasants' activism. Coming at the end of the Gandhi–Irwin truce and on the eve of the second phase of the Civil Disobedience campaign, the *Abhyuday* issue shows urban Congress intellectuals and politicians espousing wholeheartedly the active participation of peasants in the movement.[35] The nationalist movement, indeed world history, was entering a new phase with new political subjects, they realized. V.N. Tivārī's editorial called it a new chapter in which kisāns were coming to occupy centre stage after being absent 'from the scriptures and histories of India'. The change from a 'non-kisān age' to a 'kisān age' and Gandhian nationalism had brought about a reversal of values and an instability of status: thanks to Gandhi, now 'Congressmen have started to consider rickety village charpoys more high and honourable than a Governor's chair'.[36]

Predictably, the 'kisān age' provoked a wide range of reactions among urban Hindi intellectuals: degrees of enthusiasm varied. The identification of Congress with the kisān should not be taken to mean a 'partiality' in their favour, some said; indeed, Congress was performing a mediating and stabilizing role. As Sardār Narmadāprasād Siṃh put it:

> Congress is actually a peasants' institution (*saṃsthā*). About 70 per cent of its members are kisāns. The tahsil committees, which elect representatives for the higher committees, are completely in the hands of kisāns. Therefore it is only natural that Congress should support the peasants so strongly. It is indeed

[35] 'By reading this issue we guarantee that you will be able to speak confidently on the problem of peasants and to answer forcefully to any question (*muṁh toṛ javāb*)' reads the frontispiece. The issue included articles by '*pūjya* Mālavīyajī', P.D. Ṭaṇḍon, Kṛṣṇakānt Mālavīya (*Abhyuday's* editor), the pro-Congress taluqdars of Kalakankar and Bhadri, Sardar Narmadāprasād Siṃh, Mohanlāl Gautam (secretary of the Kisān Sangh), Lālbahādur Śāstrī (secretary of the Allahabad District Congress Committee), Thakur Śivmūrti Siṃh, Padmakānt Mālavīya, Śrīnāth Siṃh, and V.N. Tivārī, the editor of the issue. *Abhyuday*, XXV, 33, 18, November 1931.

[36] Ibid., p. 9.

praiseworthy that, despite being an institution of the peasants, Congress has not advanced any request on behalf of the peasants moved by partiality (*pakṣapāt*).[37]

The need to contain peasants' initiatives could take the form of a moral appeal. Madan Mohan Mālavīya urged peasant to be fearless, united, just, truthful, and follow dharma: 'धर्म मनुष्य का प्राण है। जिसका धर्म नहीं वह मरे के बराबर है इसलिए तुम अपने धर्म की रक्षा करो। धर्म तुम्हारी रक्षा करेगा।' [Dharma is the life-spirit of man. A man who has no dharma is like a lifeless being. Guard your own dharma and dharma will guard you.][38] Some argued that the struggle of peasants, the 'true nation', was (only?) against the colonial state. P.D. Ṭaṇḍon's article, for example, was a rhetorical ode to the peasant as the 'life energy of our country' and an equally rhetorical appeal to peasants to become martyrs facing police bullets along with Congressmen.[39] While some stated that acknowledging the peasant as subject required working out a nationalist economic and social agenda,[40] others welcomed the overtures of pro-Congress taluqdars as a path to change that would not jeopardize rural and social harmony. Rai Bajraṅg Bahādur Siṃh, taluqdar of Bhadri, for example, wrote that both kisāns and zamindars had been affected by falling prices, and that most zamindars were sorry to be compelled to harass their peasants in order to be able to pay the revenue tax. However, whereas earlier zamindars 'used to consider peasants the source of their wealth', now they considered themselves distinct (*alag*) from the kisāns, and this was the root of the problem. It was sheer folly, and zamindars should quickly realize that peasants were their 'capital', which they should treasure just as a moneylender treasures his.[41] Only the secretary of the Kisān Sangh and future Congress Socialist member Mohanlāl Gautam believed that peasant struggles carried an autonomous political agenda and required an autonomous organization, a position later echoed by the Congress Socialist Party and the Kisān Sabhās. He raised the question of 'which svarājya?' and sketched a vision of a democratic state where peasants, the majority, would rule. Peasants should not be deceived into thinking that all their problems will disappear with svarājya, he wrote; they should instead organize themselves into the Kisān Sangh to be ready to seize power

[37] Narmadāprasād Siṃh, 'Kisān aur congress', ibid., pp. 13–14.

[38] Ibid., p. 1.

[39] Ṭaṇḍon, 'Jīnā ho to marnā sīkho' , ibid., pp.10–11.

[40] Tivārī and Narmadā Prasād Siṃh rebutted fears that peasant activism would lead to a class war by arguing that: 'the zamindari system is itself a class war . . . the present economic basis of society is class war'; ibid., p. 14.

[41] Bajraṅg Bahādur Siṃh, 'Kisān aur zamīndār', ibid., pp. 5–6.

after independence.[42] Thus, when peasants finally came to the forefront of the nationalist movement, reactions differed and touched different layers: symbolic, political, economic. Let us now go briefly into their history.

Surprisingly, for a predominantly rural society and agricultural area, agriculture and the peasantry scarcely featured in the Hindi press before 1920.[43] Debates on the 'drainage of wealth' and the need for the comprehensive progress of the country (*deśonnati*) had already crystallized in Hindi as in other Indian languages by the late nineteenth century, yet the decline in agricultural productivity and rural wealth was touched upon only in the vaguest terms. Commerce and banking featured much more prominently, with arguments about the rich tradition of the Indian trading and banking system, the colonial drainage of wealth, and the expansion of trade and industry as the principal means for national progress. Mahāvīr Prasād Dvivedī was once again a forerunner in Hindi. In what is the first original work of political economy in the language, *Sampattiśāstra* (1907), Dvivedī outlined in a brief section the question of land productivity in terms of capital (*sampatti*) and labour (*mehnat*), and explained the low output of Indian agriculture, compared to that of western countries, with reference to the insecurity of tenure and the drainage of capital. Among the causes of India's economic decline Dvivedī mentioned the '*purānāpan*' (old-fashionedness) of Indians, and their lack of (English) qualities like thrift, self-improvement, cleverness, enterprise, and investment. The book was dedicated to a taluqdar.[44]

[42] Mohanlāl Gautam, 'Kisān saṅgaṭhan', ibid, pp. 15 ff.

[43] The use of the blanket term 'kisān' is of course problematic; it seems that in the eyes of Hindi intellectuals of the 1920s and 1930s, many of them from eastern UP, it indicated the impoverished peasant farmer or tenant, or else the agricultural labourer who had lost his land. Every generalization on the score is problematic, particularly in view of the diverse agrarian systems and relationships in the Hindi area. Certainly Hindi intellectuals, several of them with small landholdings, never considered themselves as kisāns. In fact, any direct family link with the land was hardly ever expatiated upon. Even in Premchand's case, the closeness to the world of the peasant was the result of an active process of affiliation. Rāmnareś Tripāṭhī (1881–1962), Hindi poet and publisher and the path-breaking and invaluable collector of folk songs in Hindi dialects (published in 1930 as *Grām-gīt)*, told the story of how the reality of rural poverty was 'revealed' to him, who after all was *born* in a village in Jaunpur district, by an old woman waiting to sell the wood she had collected by the roadside. This chance encounter and revelation prompted Tripāṭhī to 'explore' the rural world through folk-songs. R.N. Tripāṭhī, *Grām-gīt*, Allahabad, Hindi Mandir, 1930, Preface.

[44] 'Wherever we look we find only signs of despair, very few of hope. The only sign

The impoverished condition of the peasantry began featuring in Hindi first as a subject of poetry, a perfect example of the Dvivedī preference for topical, useful, and moving literature (cf. 2.2).[45] It was the beginning of a trend that saw many established and new poets compose heart-rending poems on the kisān, often taking on the persona of the 'dejected peasant' crying out for sympathy and recognition to educated urban readers (hence the titles: *antarnād, krandan*). The language was usually standard Khari Boli, often in the lofty sanskritized style typical of the Dvivedī poetry: there was no particular attempt to reproduce peasants' speech or the language of folk songs. One notable exception was 'Achūt kī śikāyat' (an untouchable's complaint) in Bhojpuri by an unidentified Hirā Ḍom from Patna, published in *Sarasvatī* in 1914—the only example of a dalit poet (if he was one) in the whole of Hindi literature until the 1980s!

From being part of the background as mute and anonymous servants, peasants inched their way in as objects of literary attention, even though poets were initially apologetic about bringing up such an uninteresting subject.[46] A striking feature of these poems is the impersonation: as in the case of women's confessions, impersonation gave peasants a voice and

---

of hope is that we have encountered a people who are unparalleled for trade and commerce; who have opened the doors to world trade; who have laid down railways throughout the country; who have no lack of capital, and who can never be praised enough for their courage, business skills, effort, and enthusiasm. If we can learn some of their qualities and pay some attention to the improvement of our country's economy we can set right many of our problems' waxed Dvivedī (p. 184). In the best Dvivedī style, the chapter ended with a list of things to do, things which can be done 'even without the help of the king'; M.P. Divedī, *Sampattiśāstra,* Indian Press, Allahabad 1907, p. 185. See also the long list of articles on political and economic subjects in pre-1920 *Sarasvatī*, mostly on trading and banking, in Gauṛ, *Sarasvatī aur rāṣṭrīy navjāgaraṇ*.

[45] Gayāprasād Śukla Sanehī's poem 'Kṛṣak-krandan', published in *Pratāp* in 1913, attracted Dvivedī's attention, and Sanehī became a regular poet for *Sarasvatī.* It was there that his eight-page long poem 'Duḥkhī kisān' under the pen-name 'Triśūl' was published in April 1918; Dhīrendra Varmā, ed., *Hindī sāhitya koś,* vol. 2, Benares, Jnanmandal, 1985, p. 116; see also Talvār, *Kisān, rāṣṭrīy āndolan aur premchand,* p. 112.

[46] We may recall here the debate around the peasants as 'intrinsically' uninteresting characters in Premchand's *Premāśram*, see above 2.3. See Maithilīśaraṇ Gupta's verses concluding the section on *'Kṛṣi aur kṛṣak'* (Agriculture and the peasant) in the second part of *Bhārat-bhārtī*: 'पाठक! न यह कह बैठना-छेड़ा कहाँ का राग है। यह फुल कैसा है कि इसमें गन्ध है न पराग है। है यह कथा नीरस तदपि इसमें हमारा भाग है॥' [Reader! Do not say I have chosen a strange tune, a flower without perfume or pollen. It is an ugly story, but we are part of it.] Gupta, *Bhārat-bhārtī*, p. 98.

forced readers to confront their version of the story, except for the fact that the kisāns in the poems were often silent or reduced to weeping, unable even to tell their own story. As Vīr Bhārat Talvār puts it, peasants were, albeit sympathetically, defined as 'wretched' and 'stupid' (*bechāre* and *mūrkh*), begging or waiting for god's help: impersonations placed the kisān uncompromisingly as the object of an urban, affluent gaze which denied them agency.[47] Even the most vocal and radical poet on the theme, 'Triśūl', wrote in the following terms:

कौन सुनेगा दीन जनों की राम कहानी।
दीनबन्धु भी भूल गए वह बात पुरानी।
रहे बहुत दिन मौन सही सबकी मनमानी।
आँखों से बह गया धैर्य हो-होकर पानी॥
कल न सही तो काल ही किसी तरह कट जाएगा।
रोएंगे कुछ देर तो कुछ तो दुख घट जाएगा॥

Who will listen to the tale of the poor?
Even God, the friend of the poor, has forgotten their old story.
They were silent for long, bore all injustice,
All their patience washed away in tears.
If not tomorrow, Death will surely come;
Weeping will lessen the pain.[48]

Implied in the heart-rending depictions was the notion that the pitiful sight (*karuṇ dṛśya*) of the peasants' plight would be enough to shake affluent town-dwellers out of their indifference and to effect change. Poems combined emotion with economics. In Maithilīśaraṇ Gupta's poem *Bhārat-bhāratī* (1912; cf. 3.1.), the discussion of rural impoverishment on the lines of Dvivedī's argument is followed by a 'jhāṃkī', a tableau, of the helpless plight of the kisāns. The explicit contrast between the plain life of the peasant and the wasteful life of the town-dweller overlaps with lamentations about the happy past and unhappy present. If this provided a powerful positive symbol and gave peasants moral stature, making them the truest representatives of anti-British India and the ideal satyāgrahis, it also helped create an idyllic rural world of the past, easily identified with Kṛṣṇa's pastoral idyll of Braj, where any trace of exploitation or impoverishment was absent.[49] Poet Mukuṭdhar Pāṇḍey spoke

[47] Talvār, *Kisān, rāṣṭrīy āndolan aur premchand*, pp. 147 ff.
[48] *Sarasvatī*, April 1919; quoted ibid., p. 149.
[49] Poet Gopālsiṃh Nepālī wrote in *Sarasvatī* as late as 1932 that in the countryside one found many Tulsīs, Kabīrs, Sūrs, Gopāls, and Gandhis. Here lay the true

with no implications of irony of the expropriation of the peasant's wealth in terms of the peasant's 'generosity' (*audārya*), of his deprivation as asceticism (*tapasyā*), and of his submission to insults as a mark of moral superiority.[50] The gulf between intellectuals and peasants was vast, with the former justifying their ignorance and distance by cloaking peasant hardship in moral clothing.

One can also detect a hiatus between the poetic idealization of peasants and the increasingly stringent political analyses of the reasons behind their impoverishment. From the late 1910s the focus of theoretical discussions shifted from land productivity and drainage of wealth to the peasant as an economic and political subject. Articulated analyses of rural economic conditions in the province were produced in Hindi even before the Avadh movement made it news. The 'intellectual geography' of this awakened interest in peasant issues had its centres in Kanpur, with the Urdu journals *Zamānā* and *Āzād* and the Hindi *Pratāp*; in Allahabad with Kṛṣṇakānt Mālavīya's *Abhyuday* and *Maryādā, Sarasvatī*, C.Y. Chintạmani's *Leader* and Nehru's *Independent*; in Benares with *Āj* and the Jnanmandal Press; and in Indore with the *Hindī Navjīvan* and the Sarasvati Sadan Press. Gaṅgādhar Pant, Dayāśaṅkar Dūbe, Prāṇnāth Vidyālaṃkār, and Ramāśaṅkar Avasthī were the most prominent writers on peasant questions in Hindi; they were also among the first to write about the Russian Revolution and the coming of 'the age of the masses'.[51] 'The much-despised peasants are our true *annadātā* (breadgivers)', wrote Vidyārthī in May 1915, 'not those who consider themselves to be a special kind of people and look down upon those who have to live in toil and poverty as lowly beings'.[52] Gandhi's intervention in Champaran

Bhāratvarṣa of the past and the true Hindustan of the future; quoted in Ś.N. Chaturvedi, ed., *Sarasvatī hīrak jayantī viśeṣāṅk*, Allahabad, Indian Press, 1961, pp. 88–9. Cf. Puru-ṣottam Dās Ṭaṇḍon writing in the special *Kisān aṅk*, of *Abhyuday* in November 1931: 'Our hearts break when we read of the happy condition of villages in the ancient texts of our country, or we read the tales of Gokul and Vrindaban, when we read how happy villagers lived in the Hindu and Muslim periods and compare them with today's sight,' p. 10.

[50] M. Pāṇḍey, 'Kisān', *Mādhurī*, VI, pt. 2, 1, February 1928, p. 333.

[51] See e.g. Gaṅgādhar Pant, 'Avadh ke zamīndār aur kaśtakār', *Sarasvatī*, June–July 1918; also *Pratāp's Rāṣṭrīy aṅk* (Vijayadaśmī, 1917), with an important article under the pseudonym 'Dhruv' on 'Bhārtīy kisān'. For a detailed discussion, see Talvār, *Kisān, rāṣṭrīy āndolan aur premchand*, pp. 110 ff.

[52] G.Ś. Vidyārthī's editorial 'Hamāre annadātā', *Pratāp*, 31, May 1915; also 'Āgāmī kaṅgres', 16, December 1918; in Avasthī, ed., *Krānti kā udghoṣ*, vol. 1, pp. 52, 448.

seemed to open a new chapter marking greater awareness of and interest in rural conditions in the Hindi press. 'For the first time peasants became an issue on a wide scale in the bourgeois public sphere,' and issues directly relevant to them like indebtedness, forced labour, and the general absence of legality were raised and discussed.[53] Explicit parallels were drawn between the awakening Indian peasantry and the successful Russian Revolution, and the need for a broad peasant movement in India was expressed.[54] The agitation in Bijaulia in 1919 and the movement in Avadh between 1920 and 1922 also received wide coverage in the Hindi press, with particular focus on zamindar oppression and peasant demands.[55]

These peasant movements prompted a section of the Hindi nationalist press and some Congress activists to turn decisively towards socialism and engage directly in peasant and labour organization.[56] In Kanpur, the *Pratāp* 'family' founded a Congress ashram at a nearby village, after campaigning with anti-zamindari speeches and agitation in the early 1920s; the ashram provided a training ground for volunteers for the salt satyāgraha in 1930, at a time when trained members of the Hindustani Seva Dal were beginning to work in the villages. In Benares, graduates of Kāśī Vidyāpīṭh like Hariharnāth Śāstrī and Kamlāpati Tripāṭhī and their teachers Narendra Dev and Sampūrṇānand became early Congress Socialist Party members; in 1921 and at the time of Civil Disobedience they toured villages for propaganda. In Bihar, Hindi writers like Rāmvṛkṣa Benīpurī, Rāhul Sāṅkṛtyāyan, and later Vaidyanāth Miśra Nāgārjun became involved in Kisān Sabhā activities. Benīpurī was among the founders of the Congress Socialist Party (CSP) and his weekly *Yuvak* (Patna, 1929) became the CSP organ in Bihar; Rāhul and Nāgarjun later joined the Communist Party. Tracts and articles from the 1930s show the arguments and vocabulary of the peasant issue becoming decidedly socialist and using categories such as labour (mehnat), means of production

[53] *Kisān, rāṣṭrīy āndolan aur premchand*, pp. 108 ff.

[54] See e.g. the articles by R. Avasthī in *Maryādā*: 'Rūsī kisān: āgāmī ādarś' (September 1919); 'Rūsī mazdūr: āgāmī viśvakarmā' (December 1919); 'Rūsī sainik: svatantra rāṣṭrarakṣak' (February 1920); quoted ibid.

[55] *Pratāp*'s coverage of the Avadh movement and of the Munshiganj shootings led to a libel case and a six-month sentence for Vidyārthī that were widely publicized in the press. The photographs of killed and wounded kisāns in *Prabhā* must have left a deep impression and recalled images of Jallianwala Bagh, an epoch-making event in Indian photo-journalism.

[56] Bhargava, *Ganesh Shankar Vidyarthi*, pp. 75 ff.

(*auzār, sādhan*), natural resources (*kudratī cīzeṁ*) and capitalism (*pūñji-vād*). In this perspective peasants and workers—as labourers and producers—appeared as the central subjects, while zamindars and capitalists alike were harmful parasites to be divested of all authority and control:

Nowadays there are only two jātis: that of patels, zamindars, thakurs, nawab-rajas or rais, contractors, shopkeepers, money-lenders, bankers, house-owners, factory-owners and *dalāls* [middlemen, contractors], agents, lawyers and officers, and that of the poor kisāns and *mazdūrs* [workers, labourers].[57]

This view took institutional form in 1934 with the creation of the Congress Socialist Party, whose aims included forming a pressure group within Congress to enact pro-kisān and mazdūr policies, and organizing peasants and workers in the non-constitutional sphere.[58] Significantly, the great majority of Congress Socialist leaders in the United Provinces and Bihar were 'Hindi politicians' like Acharya Narendra Dev, Sampūrṇānand, and J.P. Nārāyaṇ. Although their political loyalty ultimately rested with Congress, they were instrumental in bringing Kisān Sabhās into the Congress fold and mediating between them and the hostile Congress party leadership.

The socialist idea of a society with inherently conflicting interests, however, did not square well with prevailing notions about the harmony of Indian (Hindu) society (cf. 3.3). The ideal of social harmony, placed in either pre-British or in pre-Muslim India, provided, as we have seen, a positive counterpoint both to the present state of Indian society and to modern western societies, torn by social and class struggles. An analogous vision of rural harmony continued to exist in the Hindi public sphere even after the peasant movements of 1920 brought the existence of rural exploitation and peasant grievances out into the open. In this context, the article by leading Hindi critic Rāmchandra Śukla on 'Non-cooperation and non-mercantile classes' (*Express*, Patna, 1921), only recently brought to light, acquires peculiar interest.[59] Śukla's rare foray into direct political comment is particularly relevant because, through a critique of Non-Cooperation, it makes explicit a point of view that was implicit in most

[57] Anon., *Ham bhūkhe naṅge kyoṁ haiṁ?* (1935), p. 5. See also Premchand's last and famous article, 'Mahājanī sabhyatā', written in June 1936, in which he reached a similar conclusion; Premchand, *Maṅgalsūtra tathā anya racnāeṁ* (1946).

[58] See Girja Shankar, *Socialist Trends in Indian National Movement*, Meerut, Twenty-First Century Publishers, 1987.

[59] A Hindi translation in the Gorakhpur journal *Sākṣātkār* has sparked off a debate

articles on 'rural harmony', i.e. the denial that there existed separate and conflicting interests in rural society. The centrality of the small, impoverished zamindar in his argument, rather than of the tenant and labourer, led Rāmchandra Śukla to blame land commercialization for rural distress: 'that hateful mercantilism', which had brought about a dangerous mixture (*saṅkara*, an echo of mixing castes, *varṇa-saṅkara*) of the two neat classes of pre-colonial society, mercantile and non-mercantile, the latter comprising both agrarian and service classes. Earlier each class had kept to its place and had not interfered with the other's sphere: 'In this way, there was complete balance in society . . . Clerical and agrarian classes were content with what they earned according to their position or their share of land.' The interference, along with excessive extraction of land revenue, had ruined 'agricultural classes', zamindars and peasants alike. This analysis provided the background for Śukla's negative assessment of the Non-Cooperation movement, which he interpreted as an attempt by the mercantile class to control the agricultural class. Gandhi's programme he termed 'vague', a 'superficial revolt', 'a mere hullabaloo in which people were taking part thoughtlessly'. Individualism, the product of western education, which 'has filled the minds of our youth with ideas of individual freedom that kill all sense of social and moral discipline', was another factor.[60]

In Śukla's view, then, the tie-up between nationalist volunteers and peasant agitations was extremely suspicious, a step towards social conflict and social chaos, which he uncompromisingly portrayed in terms of Kāliyuga. In this Kāliyuga, spearheaded by the two-headed monster of individualism and capitalism, students would learn to disobey their masters, labourers to disobey their landlords; maryādā would have no place and the result would be total chaos.[61] To maintain the boundaries of maryādā was therefore of utmost importance. The solution to the problem of rural impoverishment lay for Śukla in a programme of economic reform with no social or economic cost: social change would and should be accomplished by mutual goodwill (p. 52). The reluctance to accept social and economic conflict as a feature of Indian society, even

---

over Rāmchandra Śukla's ideology; for lack of either the original article or the translation, I quote here from Talvār's discussion of it in 'Asahyog aur avyāpārik śreṇiyāṁ: rāṣṭrīy āndolan aur rāmchaṇdra śukla', in V.B. Talvār, *Rāṣṭrīy navjāgaraṇ aur sāhitya: kuch prasaṅg, kuch pravṛttiyāṁ*, Delhi, Himachal Pustak Bhandar, 1993.

[60] Ibid., pp. 27–8 and 34–6.

[61] For Śukla's description of Kaliyuga in the context of his appraisal of Rāma, see my 'Tulsīdās as a classic'.

when peasants' grievances were viewed sympathetically, seems to have been widespread in the Hindi public sphere, nationalist or not. In fact, we can read Svami Sahajānand's career as a gradual emancipation from this view of 'rural harmony', a change brought about by his direct involvement with peasants' struggles. As his case shows, a cultural transformation was required before the peasant could be supported as a full political subject.[62] This step involved for Sahajānand the rejection of Gandhian nationalism, a strong critique of Congress as an institution, and the creation of a peasant counter public.

A young sanyāsī who had fled home just before his Matriculation exam, Swami Sahajānand Sarasvatī was first drawn from religious study into 'work for society' (*sāmājik kām*) over an issue of concern to the limited 'samāj' of Bhumihar Brahmins, their claim to Brahmin status. In his own words, 'It is the force of events that inscribes in your mind the importance [of social work], its dignity and the fact that it is a duty. [. . .] Actually, the feeling of *jan-sevā* [service to the people] that arose in my heart was first not one of service to the common people [*jansādhāraṇ kī sevā*]. I thought, why not help the Bhumihar samāj? Then I will go back to the pleasure of my studies and of spiritual knowledge.'[63] Instead, he started reading nationalist newspapers (*Pratāp*) and became a staunch Gandhian, and a Congress activist in Shahabad district.[64] After a year in jail in 1922 he continued Congress and khadi propaganda in Ghazipur and became a member of the UP Congress Committee and All India Congress Committee. His faith in Gandhi was later put on trial many times, especially over the latter's compromising stance on peasant-zamindar relations.[65] Years later Sahajānand urged the kisāns to preserve independent judgement and not to merely 'be infatuated' (*laṭṭū*)

[62] For biographical details, see Appendix; also his autobiography, *Merā jīvan saṅghars*, Delhi, Progressive Publishing House, 1985, and Walter Hauser, 'Swami Sahajanand Sarasvati and the Politics of Social Reform, 1907–50', *Indian Historical Review*, xviii, 1–2, July 1991–January 1992.

[63] Sahajānand Sarasvatī, *Merā jīvan saṅgharṣ*, pp. 97, 101.

[64] Ibid., p. 118.

[65] 'Well, those days I did not know what compromise, reform and revolutionary meant exactly. Nor did I know that Gandhiji was a *samjhautāvādī* (compromiser) and a reformist. I considered him a revolutionary through and through, as many good and reasonable people still consider him even now.' The final disillusionment came after the Bihar earthquake, when Sahajānand, already a peasant leader, witnessed the systematic misuse and profiteering of relief funds by zamindars with the connivance of Congress leaders. When he confronted Gandhi with evidence of this, he received only vague reassurances that the pro-Congress secretary of the maharaja of Darbhanga

with the aura of self-sacrifice around leaders, but rather to test them on the touchstone (*kasauṭī*) of peasants' interests.

> Not to think of one's interests and fall for someone else's sacrifice and believe in what he says with your eyes shut amounts to suicide. We should stop this blind tradition and enquire earnestly into whatever leaders or preachers say, after testing it against our collective interest [of peasants and workers]. Not only that, we should sometimes embarrass leaders who present us with long arguments, as people in Russia and other countries have done from time to time.[66]

His own involvement with kisāns was an extension of his nationalist work. The ashram he had founded at Bihta, near Patna, originally for the religious instruction of Bhumihar children, lay in an area known for zamindar oppression; Sahajānand initially believed that a peasant organization would mediate between tenants and landlords and foster unity for the nationalist movement. The declared aim of the first peasant organization he was involved with, the West Patna Kisān Sabhā (1927; later Bihar Provincial Kisān Sabhā, 1929), was 'to guide the peasant movement in such a manner as to *prevent* landlord–tenant struggle, and to help the Congress in elections to the legislative council'. After the first meeting it was decided that it would not go against Congress on political matters.[67] This first foray also marked Sahajānand's first encounter with the strategies of exclusion that zamindars and Congress leaders practised to neutralize peasants as political subjects. These strategies involved creating bogus peasant organizations, manipulating protocols of public interaction and constitutional politics, domestication in patron–client relationships and appeals to the political primacy of Congress.

Thus, Sahājanand's first task was to oppose zamindar attempts at creating a bogus Kisān Sabhā so that changes in agrarian legislation would favour them. At the public meeting he succeeded in counteracting their considerable personal authority by appealing to rules (*qāydā*) and in-sisting that a widespread public debate be held among peasants in order to elicit their opinion.[68] Local peasants' meetings explaining the effects of the legislation emptied the bogus organization of any authority

---

would redress those complaints. Sahajānand was shocked: 'I realized that he does not know a thing of how the zamindari machinery works! He did not know how they tread on the kisans;' ibid., pp. 224, 259.

66 Sahajānand Sarasvatī, *Kisānoṁ ke dost aur duśman*, Bihta,1942, p. 4.

67 Rakesh Gupta, *Bihar Pesantry and the Kisan Sabha (1936–1947)*, Delhi, People's Publishing House, 1982, pp. 89, 90, emphasis added; Sahajānand Sarasvatī, *Merā jīvan saṅgharṣ*, pp.190 ff.

68 Sahajānand Sarasvatī, *Merā jīvan saṅgharṣ*, pp. 230 ff.

and produced the outcome he desired, but zamindars and their client politicians within Congress were ultimately successful in the constitutional arena and passed the bill in the Legislative Council. On other occasions, when called in for mediation, Sahajānand realized that landlords were only trying to influence his inquiries and silence him into submission.[69] He faced a similar attempt at domestication with the 'nationalist' industrialist Ramkrishna Dalmia.[70]

Sahajānand's role as peasant leader involved touring the province in order to increase peasants' awareness, writing tracts, both addressed to kisāns and to general public opinion on their behalf, and local, intensive campaigns over specific grievances. Gradually his attitude of compromise gave way to an open critique of the zamindari system and of Congress politics. Sahajānand's tracts express this in terms of economic justice and human dignity as fundamental requirements for svarājya. The peasants' own demands were placed forcefully at the centre of the nationalist agenda and laid at the feet of Congress: without fulfilling them, he wrote, it could not be called a kisān Congress. The Kisān Sabhā, the ashram at Bihta, and the printing press thus became institutions of a peasant counterpublic, the centre of a network of activities in the non-constitutional arena.

In *Kisānoṁ ke dost aur duśman* (*Peasants' friends and foes*, 1942), Sahajānand produced a radical critique of the notion of rural harmony

[69] See e.g. the case of a landlord of Gaya, the Raja of Amavan, against whom Sahajānand published the report *Gayā ke kisānoṁ kī karuṇ kahānī*; Sahajānand, *Merā jīvan saṅgharṣ*, pp. 248–50.

[70] Dalmia had set up a sugar mill at Bihta, next to Sahajānand's ashram, in 1932 and tried to influence Sahajānand both through personal pressure and 'traditional' patronage through his family. He first offered unlimited donations for the ashram in exchange for help in getting land for the mill from the local zamindars. Sahajānand's reply was: 'Should I be a servant or a slave of the mill-owners, or become their courtier? I might do it if I consider it my duty, but certainly not for greed for money. I piss on such money.' Ibid., p. 277. Ostensibly, the mill, which had Rajendra Prasad among its directors, was going to be an ideal 'swadeshi mill', with all facilities and fair treatment for the workers and their families. In reality, it started paying peasants even less for their sugarcane than the English mill; Sahajānand then proceeded to organize the local peasants on this issue, and after 'tens of notices and hundreds of meetings' he managed to fetch higher prices for their sugarcane. Subsequent strikes in 1936, 1938, and 1939 again saw Sahajānand take the side of workers and peasants against the 'nationalist' capitalist; ibid., pp. 280–1. Again, despite successful resistance and actism on behalf of the workers 'on the field', Sahajānand was unable to overpower Dalmia in the constitutional or party arena: Dalmia was a major financial contributor for the Congress campaign in the 1937 provincial elections and had his way in choosing Congress candidates; see also Damodaran, *Broken Promises*, p. 62.

from a peasant perspective. First he denied the legitimacy of zamindari with a historical argument, and then denounced the connivance between the seemingly impersonal and impartial power of colonial rule and the violent, unrestrained personal power of zamindars; the zamindari system survived in defiance of all laws only thanks to an excess of violent power and with the active help of the colonial system. 'If the violence and oppression are stopped the zamindari system cannot survive even for one minute.' It was in fact the zamindar, rather than distant colonial rule, that was the real *sarkār* of the kisān; those who hesitated to fight against zamindars did not want to confront this reality.[71]

In Sahajānand's words, the basic difference between the Congress and Kisān Sabhā views on the matter was that 'whereas the Congress sees the economic policy and *roṭī* [bread] reflected through the mirror of politics, and reaches them only through politics, the Kisān Sabhā sees politics in the mirror of economic policy and roṭī and considers it only a medium'.[72] In other words, svarājya had to be framed in terms of economic justice. A Kisān Sabhā slogan said: 'Only a kisān–mazdūr state is the true svarājya.'[73] Sahajānand's words and the slogan contained two predicates: one about the primacy of economic change in defining the agenda of svarājya, the other about full civil and political rights for peasants and labourers.

Sahajānand's recognition of the peasant as subject also led him to a growing awareness of the peasant as a complex category that included impoverished landlords, well-to-do peasants, and landless labourers, subjects with conflicting interests.[74] His understanding of economic and practical issues was coupled with an understanding of cultural and religious aspects. In both, he distinguished between points one could compromise on and basic economic and civil rights that had to be ensured for all.

Finally, Sahajānand came to realize more and more the importance of autonomous peasant initiative and sustained activism. We have already

[71] Sahājanand Sarasvatī, *Kisānoṁ ke dost aur duśman*, pp. 7, 10. For a discussion of the word sarkār, see 5.4.3 n.38 here.

[72] Sahājanand Sarasvatī, *Merā jīvan saṅgharṣ*, p. 324.

[73] Sahājanand Sarasvatī, *Kisānoṁ ke dost aur duśman*, p. 32.

[74] The need to address this question in depth and adjust Kisān Sabhā and nationalist policies accordingly is expressed among others in his pamphlet *Khetmazdūr*, which deals expressly with the need to include rural labourers in the Kisān Sabhā and the problems related to it. Translated and edited with notes by Walter Hauser as *Sahajanand on Agricultural Labour and the Rural Poor*, Delhi, Manohar, 1994.

mentioned Sahajānand's warning that kisāns should subject their avowed leaders to strict control, pointing to a genuine belief in the democratic principle of limited, publicly answerable power. Similarly, he came to the understanding that since one of the greatest strengths of peasants was their number, it was important that they should be *seen*, i.e. physically occupy public space and loudly claim their right of access. The first mass kisān rally at Gaya in 1933 saw hundreds of thousands of peasants cramming the city despite obstruction by the police; in fact, when Sahajānand was issued with a notice under Section 144, and therefore refrained from speaking, he was scolded by kisāns who had assembled in their hundreds of thousands. 'They were right. After all they were my masters, my lords, and they should give orders. I was very happy inside to see that they would not leave anyone alone. See, today they are angry with me. This is right, until they are ready to nag and slap their leaders they will not be free. Therefore that day I welcomed that attitude of theirs with all my heart.'[75] In 1937 and 1938 several mass rallies took place in Patna and other centres at the height of a struggle during the Congress government. For example, during the first parliamentary session peasants went right into the Assembly house in Patna and occupied it for a time to protest against their exclusion from constitutional politics.[76] When Rajendra Prasad told Sahajānand to 'be aware of the mob' after the first mass rallies in Patna, Sahajānand reflected derisively:

> These are the same people who used to call the *kisān samūh* (multitude of peasants) *mass* once. Now it has become a *mob*! These groups of kisāns were *mobs* before, too. For some time they became *masses* for some purpose, and then the *mob* became *mob* again![77]

The emergence of the Kisān Sabhā as an autonomous centre for peasant activism, and its critique of Congress constitutional politics, created a paradox in that once a dividing line between zamindars and kisān was drawn, the ostensible 'kisān Congress' appeared to stand clearly on the other side. It was in fact during the Congress ministry of 1937–9 that the

[75] Sahājanand Sarasvatī, *Merā jīvan saṅghars̤*, p. 263.

[76] G.D. Birla, who was present, commented that 'the rank and file seems to be confusing freedom with indiscipline'; quoted in Sarkar, *Modern India*, p. 364. At the second All India Kisān Sabhā Conference in Faizpur in 1936, for the first time peasants marched 'in a military fashion' through the countryside. This was repeated at all Congress sessions: at the Haripura Congress in Gujarat in 1938, 20,000 peasants marched and held a public meeting in Congress Nagar defying Patel's orders; Sahājanand Sarasvatī, *Merā jīvan saṅghars̤*, p. 325.

[77] Ibid., p. 299, italics in English in the text.

distance between the Congress leadership and Socialists-cum-Kisān Sabhāites was accentuated. On the eve of the elections, Kisān Sabhā candidates were excluded from Congress electoral lists and, to their embarrassment, they had to campaign for Congress zamindar candidates.[78] As Vinita Damodaran remarks: 'The realization that the Congress government was at least willing to protect them as the colonial state had been was a factor that strengthened the psychological and practical position of the landlords immensely.'[79] Later, the spirit of compromise decisively influenced even the drawing up of the zamindari abolition scheme, harking back to a vision of rural harmony and of economic progress without social cost or conflict.[80]

Unanimity was an important political symbol for Congress and for nationalist discourse; it enacted the popular wisdom of the proverb '*ektā meṁ bal*', unity is strength. In the (theoretically) open arenas of the public sphere, however, ideas and slogans were open to criticism and reinterpretation by subjects who wanted to be part of the game. The gradual emergence of peasants as literary, economic, and political subjects was a complex and contradictory process. The nationalist movement and literature included them in order to be truly 'national', and peasants provided, especially for Hindi writers, a symbolic identification with the true nation. Yet even in the 1930s, socialist ideas and radical programmes, advanced both in the press and within Congress, seemed to make little actual impact. As Sumit Sarkar put it: 'The years 1935 and, particularly, 1936 saw the emergence of a pattern in Indian politics which would be repeated often, both before and after Independence. Outwardly, all the signs were of a significant lurch to the Left . . . Yet, in the end the Right within the Congress was able to skilfully and effectively sidestep and

[78] Gyan Pandey, ed., *The Indian Nation in 1942,* Calcutta, P.K. Bagchi, 1988, p. 62; see also Sahajānand Sarasvatī, *Merā jīvan saṅgharṣ,* pp. 242, 292–4.

[79] Damodaran, *Broken Promises*, p. 153. Gyan Pandey remarks about UP around the same time that 'even if socialist slogans were more loudly mouthed, new Congress membership [came] from ranks of rich peasants and small middle landlords . . . Thus, the same year the CSP was formed and gained a substantial following among UP Congress leaders, the UP Congress also restaked its claims to being a landlord-cum-tenant party in the campaign for elections to the central Legislative Assembly'; Pandey, 'Rural Base for Congress', p. 217.

[80] For a discussion of the making of an agrarian programme and the emergence of a consensus around zamindari abolition, see Pandey, 'A Rural Base for Congress'; Shankar, *Socialist Trends in Indian National Movement*; Peter Reeves, 'The Congress and the Abolition of Zamindari in Uttar Pradesh', in J. Masselos, ed., *Struggling and Ruling. The Indian National Congress 1885–1985,* London, Oriental University Press, 1987; Damodaran, *Broken Promises.*

utilize the storm.'[81] Historians grappling with this paradox have put it down to right-wing opposition within Congress and to the restraining influence even leftist national Congress leaders exerted on kisān activism.[82]

From the perspective of the public sphere, we have noticed that the emergence of peasants as political subjects brought about a critique of and challenge to the nationalist vision of Indian society and the idea of 'rural harmony'. The Kisān Sabhā, Sahajānand's tracts, and peasants' campaigns all point to the emergence of a subaltern counterpublic in Bihar with networks and agendas of its own that was yet largely excluded from constitutional spaces, even nationalist ones. We further noticed the defensive strategies the Bihar Congress leadership used to counteract and contain peasants' activities, much more so than in UP, where an organized peasants' movement failed to emerge. These strategies included control over the constitutional arena, arguing for the primacy of the political struggle for independence, the exclusive claim to political leadership for the Congress party and the claim that Congress represented the whole of society. The Congress claim to represent all classes diluted peasant demands and pre-empted their autonomous political legitimacy by calling their movement an economic struggle.[83] Sahajānand, on the other hand, criticized what he called the 'taint of unanimity' within Bihar Congress and spoke derisively of its political culture which discouraged internal dissent.[84] His protracted vocal criticism of the Congress government in Bihar earned him a reprimand from the party and he was eventually expelled as persona non grata in 1940.

Gyan Pandey has argued about Nehru, and we may broaden his

[81] Sarkar, *Modern India, 1917 to 1947*, p. 338.

[82] Pandey, 'A Rural Base for Congress', p. 199.

[83] Thus, peasant struggles in Bihar during the Congress ministry were considered at best narrow, economic struggles, at worst 'anti-national'; Pandey, 'The Congress and the Nation', p. 19. According to Vinita Damodaran: Congress leadership 'increasingly . . . dissociated itself from these popular movements, first by condemning the actions as resulting from the machinations of the Congress socialists, and then actively suppressing them with all the instruments of state repression at its disposal;' Damodaran, *Broken Promises,* p. 10.

[84] Sahājanand Sarasvatī, *Merā jīvan saṅgharṣ*, p. 285. For example, Sahajānand was not included in the Congress inquiry committee on agrarian conditions because, as Rajendra Prasad told him: 'If you were included the report might not be unanimous and we want it to be unanimous, so that it may be valuable and carry some weight. Moreover, if you were included the government and zamindars might raise the cry that it is a report of the Kisān Sabhā. Therefore it is better for you not to be there;' quoted ibid., p. 289.

argument to include Congress Socialist leaders as well, that he moved from an attitude of 'discovery' of the peasantry and keenness to see them as the bulwark of the movement, to one of 'making' the peasantry a part of the nation, subsumed in the overall project.[85] Thus his strong pro-kisān attitude *vis-à-vis* British authorities, landlords, and the Congress Right was combined with a self-appointed role of representation and responsibility. However, the responsibility he felt at first towards the faith (*bharosā*) that peasants had placed in him was later overcome by a responsibility towards law and order and to the 'higher goal' of svarājya. This implied a paternalistic attitude of political guidance, discipline, and education towards peasant masses which Socialist leaders also subscribed to. As Narendra Dev put it: 'These ignorant people trampled upon by tyranny and sunk deep in superstition know only one way out and that is to rush headlong into riotous conduct, and then the Government makes short shrift of them. It is only the revolutionary intelligentsia that can organize them for disciplined action.'[86]

In the constitutional arena, the question of responsibility to the people came second to the logic of governance for the Congress Party. The growing distance between constitutional and non-constitutional nationalist politics, as outlined in the previous section, grew in the 1930s: once in the constitutional arena, pressures from popular activism receded into the background. While local Socialist activists took active part in Kisān Sabhā activities in the non-constitutional arena, and provided much of the local leadership in 1942,[87] peasant organizations were not represented in the Congress leadership. Partial franchise and participation in non-constitutional politics were not enough to ensure for kisāns or their leaders equal access or the right to be heard.

On the other hand, the Kisān Sabhā agenda of dignified survival for all, and its critique of social and economic injustice, made a fair impact on Hindi literature. Earlier attitudes of unthreatening sympathy were replaced by powerful narratives of oppression, struggle, and political awareness. After Premchand, it is noteworthy that it was writers from Bihar who embraced these issues, several of whom were directly involved in Kisān Sabhā activities.[88] The Kisān Sabhā also became an

[85] Pandey, 'The Congress and the Nation'.

[86] Narendra Dev, 'Socialism and the Nationalist Movement', Presidential Address and the First Socialist Conference in Patna, May 1934; in his *Socialism and the National Revolution,* Bombay, Padma Publications, 1946, p. 7.

[87] See Pandey, *The Indian Nation in 1942*.

[88] See for example the work of Vaidyanāth Miśra Nāgārjun, especially his novel *Balchanmā* (1952).

important precedent when peasant struggles resurfaced in the 1970s with the Naxalite movement.

When publicity and public action were taken up by a subordinate subject, the consequences were many and complex. On the part of the peasants and their leaders, there was the attempt to redefine public issues in their own terms and to join hands on the wider stage of public action, initially in the non-constitutional domain, with an awareness of the obstacles involved. Middle class intellectuals' attitudes towards peasant participation varied from enthusiasm to sympathy to unease. Many showed a reluctance to abandon the idea of rural and social harmony, for example: cultural ideas held on to even in the face of a reality of conflict and a commitment to democracy and social justice. This important question is examined in greater detail in the following section, where the impact of cultural ideas upon a number of 'Hindi politicians' from a wide political spectrum is assessed.

5.3. Hindi Politicians

> Just as dawn announces sunrise, the birth of such people [leaders] announces the future rise of the nation. It is they who first dream in their minds of the edifice of the nation and with speeches and articles draw a picture of it to display in front of the general public (sarvasādhāraṇ). And through these speeches and articles they mould whatever elements and strength are needed to build the edifice.
>
> Madan Mohan Mālavīya[89]

The parallel and conflicting agendas of agitation and rule, of political bilingualism and populist rhetoric, of provincial and national aspirations, and finally of Hindi-Hindu cultural affiliation and nationalist openness made 'Hindi politicians' very peculiar political animals. By Hindi politicians I mean here those nationalist political leaders who were active in the Hindi public sphere. Some, like Madan Mohan Mālavīya, realized early on that they needed to address the vernacular public *along with* English-educated Indians and the colonial authorities; for them Hindi was a cultural marker and part and parcel of Hindi-Hindu nationalism. For others, like Gaṇeś Śaṅkar Vidyārthī, Hindi was the 'people's language' (*jantā kī bhāṣā*) and the means to reach the popular public in the non-constitutional arena. All were instrumental in establishing Hindi as a

[89] Mālavīya, 'Rāṣṭra kā nirmāṇ', *Abhyuday,* 1907, in P. Mālavīya, *Mālavīyajī ke lekh*, p. 126.

legitimate language of political discourse and administration. This involved an effort at translation—of English constitutional concepts into Hindi—and also at mediation, working local and more popular symbols and ideas into those concepts, a matter that deserves greater and more specific attention than will be possible here.

Hindi politicians were actively involved in setting up Hindi institutions and the press; at the same time, on the strength of their achievements as local organizers, they were among the first to be nominated to or elected on to constitutional bodies. The most successful Hindi politicians were those who managed to move from the non-constitutional to the constitutional arena. The unofficial authority that 'servants of the country' (*deśsevak*) acquired on the ground thus became an official one as sarkār, government. The repercussions of this on their own political style and on their role in the Hindi public sphere have already been partly covered in the previous sections, and will be discussed more specifically in the following section in relation to Hindi intellectuals. Here a brief overview of five important leaders will allow me to outline some of the peculiar features of Hindi politicians, their attitudes to the state and the public, their understanding of Hindi and of colonial bilingualism, their role and influence in the Hindi public sphere, and their position within the national movement. At least three different axes are necessary: a political axis between right and left, and two cultural axes, one between Hindi and English, which partly overlaps with, but is also distinguished from, another axis between popular and elite. Only in this way can their cultural commonality and the differences in political styles and trajectories emerge. Madan Mohan Mālavīya, Puruṣottam Dās Ṭaṇḍon, Gaṇeś Śaṅkar Vidyārthī, Acharya Narendra Dev, and Babu Sampūrṇānand were not only the most significant Hindi politicians, but they also provide a fair variety of stances.[90]

Madan Mohan Mālavīya (1861–1946) is the appropriate starting point. He was the first Hindi politician in that he was the first to use Hindi

[90] The choice is based partly on their importance, and partly on the variety they offer. Other locally important leaders who played a significant role also in post-Independence politics, would include: Śrīkṛṣṇadatt Pālīvāl, Pandit Sundarlāl, Kamlāpati Tripāṭhī, Lāl Bahādur Śāstrī and Rām Manohar Lohiā in the United Provinces; Seth Govind Dās in the Central Provinces; and Rajendra Prasad and J.P. Nārāyaṇ in Bihar. Ārya Samāj leaders like Svami Śraddhānand and Bhai Parmānand were also important political agitators. Serious monographic studies are still lacking on most Hindi politicians, and so are comprehensive collections of their speeches and writings.

as a language of politics, in public addresses and articles,[91] and because the official recognition of Hindi and the Devanagari script figured on his political agenda as early as 1880.[92] Hindi was for Mālavīya part of his effort at creating and representing a Hindu political constituency, and for this he undertook activities in the public sphere which included Hindu Sabhās, cow-protection, educational facilities for Hindu students, newspapers in Hindi and English, volunteer groups to 'protect Hindus' during festivals and times of crisis, and later śuddhi and saṅgaṭhan.[93] Yet Hindi was for Mālavīya only one of the political idioms at his disposal: he did not question English as the language for addressing colonial authorities and for constitutional politics, nor its pre-eminence as countrywide language in use all over India.

Mālavīya's career started in 1880 with the founding of the Prayāg Hindū Samāj, which rallied against official interference in the local Magh fair. Like its successor, the Madhya Hindū Samāj (1884), the Prayāg Hindū Samāj also campaigned for the issue of Nagari vs Persian script and for cow-protection between 1887 and 1890. The first of a series of organizations that Mālavīya launched in the province culminating in the Hindu Mahasabha in 1923, it was remarkable and new in that it was open to all Hindus and used modern means of communication to appeal to the public and to establish both a local and a wider network. In that it resembled the reformist Ārya Samāj, which also put forward a 'multi-symbol congruence'[94] of language, script, and religion, the first expression of a self-aware modern Hindu identity. Unlike the Ārya Samāj, though, Mālavīya's Sabha upheld religious orthodoxy and took a very cautious view of social reform, and funding for it came not from the community but from rich patrons.[95]

The son of an ordinary Brahmin *vyās* (teacher) of the Ahalyapur area

[91] In the first, and short-lived, Hindi political daily, *Hindosthān* (1883), launched and financed by Raja Rāmpāl Siṃh of Kalakankar (near Allahabad); see R.R. Bhatnagar, *The Rise and Growth of Hindi Journalism*, p. 429.

[92] Remarkable in this respect is his famous pamphlet (in English) on *Court Character and Primary Education in N.-W.P. and Oudh* (1897); for a discussion of it, see King, *One Language, Two Scripts*, pp. 150–2.

[93] For śuddhi (purification) and saṅgaṭhan (organization), see 3.3.

[94] Brass, *Language, Religion and Politics*.

[95] Lütt, *Hindu-Nationalismus im Uttar Pradeś*; Bayly, *The Local Roots of Indian Politics*, especially Chapter four; Brass, *Language, Religion and Politics*, and Sītārām Chaturvedī, *Mahāmanā madan mohan mālavīya*, Benares, Akhil Bhartiya Vikrama Parishad, 1948. Cf. Jones, *Arya Dharm*.

in Allahabad, Mālavīya rose from an ordinary position as Sanskrit teacher at the local Government High School to a prestigious one as advocate to the High Court thanks to powerful patrons.[96] In that respect he provides an early example of the transformation of a 'client' of powerful local patrons into a community politician of independent standing, and of the consolidation of Brahmin authority in modern religious and political terms.[97] His range of idioms and political strategies testifies to his crucial capacity to mediate and adapt to different publics and spheres. Thus he was equally at ease in traditional patron–client relationships with Indian princes and magnates, in the respectful but proud attitude of an educated subject of the empire towards British administrators, and in the powerful role of the political renouncer: selfless public worker, pandit and politician all in one. Above all, he combined to perfection rhetorical, organizational, and fund-raising skills in the public sphere with the rhetoric and strategy of constitutional politics. His titanic effort to raise funds for a Hindu University started with a month-long penance and chanting of the Gāyatrī mantra at Allahabad's chief temple, and took him to princely houses all around India; this developed into life-long relationships of mutual esteem which culminated in a political alliance with the Independent Congress Party and the Congress Nationalist Party in the 1920s and 1930s. In seeking traditional patronage from landed and commercial magnates for educational and Hindu saṅgaṭhan activities, he invested the notion of charity with new nationalist resonances. Charity in this sense was not directed at the local community or at unspecified pilgrims, but at Hindus as members of a homogeneous cultural and political group. While Gandhi's fund raising aimed at erecting a counter authority, in accepting princely patronage Mālavīya indicated to patrons and colonial authorities that his community activities would not disrupt order and hierarchy. In the constitutional arena, he combined the language of representative politics with that of community (jāti), so that the

[96] Thanks to Rāmpāl Siṃh's patronage he supplemented his traditional pāṭhśālā education with a university degree in humanities and law; his first public activities took place under the auspices of his Sanskrit professor, Aditya Ram Bhattacharya; Lütt, *Hindu-Nationalismus,* pp. 148 ff.

[97] Thus he used traditional means of public instruction like stories and sermon to campaign for cow protection, performed public rituals like sacrifices and devised others for political purposes. He himself started performing massive public rituals of initiation (*mantradīkṣā*) of Brahmins, Kshatriyas, Vaiśyas, and Śūdras from 1927 on Dasasvamedha Ghat in Benares, and in 1930 he initiated a large group of Harijans there; Chaturvedī, *Mahāmanā*, pp. 34 ff.

idiom of democratic politics could serve to defend 'Hindu interests'; in the case of separate electorates, for example, he supported the one-man one-vote system because it favoured the Hindu majority.[98]

It is here that the peculiar process of translation and adaptation of concepts of European (English) democracy comes to the surface. Let us take for example Mālavīya's treatment of 'discussion' as a fundamental element of good government. *Prajātantra* here means not exactly 'democracy' but rather a *rājya* (kingdom, rule) in which the subjects, *prajā*, can express their views to the ruler, rājā: 'All these evils disappear when the prajā is given the time to think about and debate those matters . . . The rājā will be informed about the real condition of the prajā and everything will work according to rule.' In this context, 'svarājya means that we may be entitled to think about our government'. To prove that 'the demand for svarājya is not a desire for the *amaṅgal* [calamity] of the kingdom', Mālavīya quoted 'an English politician' on the virtue of discussion:

> Discussion has incentives to progress peculiar to itself. It gives a premium to intelligence. To set out the argument to determine political action with such force and effect that really should determine it, is high and great exertion of intellect. Government by discussion has been [sic] principal organ for improving mankind.[99]

Mālavīya's translation of this passage into Hindi is literal; but after agreeing with the English politician, Mālavīya introduces a qualification: 'If we think even a little, the truth of this statement will be clear, but debate [*vād-vivād*] is an extremely delicate matter.' In order to avoid any *kharābī* (trouble), discussion should be free of partisanship (*pakṣapāt-rahit*) and according to dharma (*dharmapūrvak*), it should display forbearance (*sahiṣṇutā*) and forceful quietness (*śaktipūrvak śānti*); otherwise, 'even a small mistake will produce the opposite effect'. Party factions in India show none of these virtues, he argued. Having set such impossibly high moral standards for political debate, it is easy for Mālavīya to criticize the nature of political debate in India. Since debate is deprived of its practical virtue, any actual debate will fail to match the ideal. In the

[98] M.M. Mālavīya, 'Dharmānusār pratinidhiyoṁ kā chunāv', *Abhyuday,* 19, February 1909, in P. Mālavīya, *Mālavīyajī ke lekh*, pp. 189–91.

[99] M.M. Mālavīya, 'Bhāratvāsī aur deśbhakti', August 1907, quoted ibid., pp. 105, 108–9. Mālavīya's translation reads: 'वाद-विवाद में मुख्य-मुख्य शक्तियाँ हैं जो उन्नति के लिए अत्यन्त उपयोगी हैं। वाद-विवाद से बुद्धि तीव्र होती है। किसी राजनैतिक कार्य का निश्चय करने के लिए उस पर भली-भाँति अपने बुद्धि-बल के द्वारा बहस करना बुद्धि से बड़ा भारी अभ्यास करना है जो कि उसे बढ़ायेगा। वाद-विवाद द्वारा शासन करना मनुष्य जाति की उन्नति करने का मुख्य उपाय है।' Ibid., p. 106.

same article, Mālavīya defines patriotism (*deśbhakti*) as the ability to rise above own's own interests, and *ekmat* (unanimity) is presented as a desirable situation. In Mālavīya's view, then, debate is upheld as a right in order to communicate opinions to the colonial government, while it is simultaneously discredited as lack of patriotism and the source of harmful disagreement when internal to the Indian political sphere. Similarly, his view of political agitation was that of a movement in which the people (prajā) would provide patient and unanimous support while serious, firm and intelligent leaders provided responsible guidance; maryādā acquired strong political connotations in his distinction between gradual and controlled movements (*maryādā-baddh āndolan*) and revolutions and uprisings (*maryādā-viruddh*), which were best avoided.[100]

This is consistent with Mālavīya's view of the public sphere as a national community with one and only one common interest. In his definition, the nation state (rāṣṭra) was synonymous with *unity* transcending different opinions and religions, the common dharma of all. This was the antidote to antagonisms arising from economic disparity, for brotherly love would inspire charity: 'Keep as much as you need for yourself but give the rest to poor brothers. If you do not do so, there is no love in you. Thus you can keep an Annapūrṇā [the goddess of plenty] in each and every house. What is this Annapūrṇā? The spinning-wheel. If every house acquires a spinning wheel poverty will immediately vanish. You know what happiness comes from giving a handful of grain. You wear nice clothes; if you give your old clothes [*utārā huā*] to your poor brother, how happy he will be. How happy will he indeed be if you give him a little food for his child'.[101] It was exactly this view of charity *as* social justice that Sahajānand and radical Hindi writers rallied against (cf. 5.2).

Mālavīya's more immediate concern within the overall national community, the Hindu public, was also envisaged as a compact political community, united in public action but otherwise free to follow customary practices and beliefs. In fact, his brand of politics sought to keep caste and community customs free of official interference and discouraged

[100] M.M. Mālavīya, 'Unnati aur maryādā-baddh āndolan', *Abhyuday*, 1907, ibid., p. 83. See also his public speech published as *Satyāgrah saptāh. Mālavīyajī kā bhāṣaṇ*, Calcutta, Hindi Pustak Agency, 1922, in which he preached a similar self-restraint as the key to a successful political economy. This explains why, if Mālavīya was indeed the first to found a Kisān Sabhā in Allahabad in 1916, it was not to *organize* or *awaken* the peasantry, but to *represent* it in the newly enlarged rural franchise and reserve seats in the legislative councils.

[101] Speech in Benares printed as *Satyāgrah saptāh*, p. 39.

public criticism and discussion on the matter.[102] A fervent believer in the intrinsic goodness of varṇāśram dharma, Mālavīya supported limited reforms concerning widows and untouchability only as a defensive measure against greater evils and greater reforms, and made only token gestures in this regard. 'You may follow restrictions about food, you may not want to eat with your untouchable brothers, but you should consider them your brothers in *social interaction*;' the realm of public interaction thus implied a different protocol of behaviour from that of customary practice.[103]

Finally, as an orthodox Brahmin, a learned pandit, and a professional politician respected by British authorities, as the recipient, conduit, and distributor of considerable financial patronage and as a tireless public worker, Mālavīya embodied several kinds of authority: the traditional authority of the learned and pious Brahmin and expert minister; that of the *rāṣṭrīy sevak*, the selfless and devoted nationalist worker; that of representative and vocal leader of the community *vis-à-vis* the sovereign; and that of the effective man of influence on a personal, local level as well as on the political, constitutional level. His prestige and authority as Hindu leader and Vice-Chancellor of BHU remained high in the Hindi sphere even when his political influence became limited to the right wing of the Congress and his path of gradual constitutional reform became less popular. The first Hindi politician, Mālavīya was also the most 'bilingual' in more senses than one, able to switch idioms and languages according to context. This bilingualism allowed him to acquire the national stature that other Hindi politicians lacked.

A disciple of Mālavīya and himself an advocate, Puruṣottam Dās Ṭaṇḍon (1882–1962) undertook public activism under a similar aegis. He too subscribed to a notion of the politician as a renouncer, partly under the influence of the austere, self-restraining vision of the Radhasoami sect, in which he was reared, and he became popularly known as 'the Gandhi of UP'.[104] In the Hindi public sphere, Ṭaṇḍon's name is linked

[102] Mālavīya passionately opposed the Sarda Bill raising the minimum marriageable age; for critical reports see 'Ārya-vivāh-bil', *Chāṁd*, VII, pt. 2, 6, October 1929, pp. 737–43, and 'Ārya-vivāh-bil', *Chāṁd*, VIII, pt. 1, 6, April 1930, pp. 107–10; see his article 'Varṇāśram dharma', *Abhyuday*, 1, May 1908, in P. Mālavīya, *Mālavīyajī ke lekh*, pp. 174–5.

[103] *Satyāgraha saptāh*, p. 18, emphasis added.

[104] The austere message of the sants, which appealed most to modernizing clerical and small commercial families, gave Ṭaṇḍon a spiritual education, a distaste for modern amenities, and a view of literature as a moral medium. Though Ṭaṇḍon himself

mostly to the Hindī Sāhitya Sammelan, which he controlled for several decades, and to the political struggle for Hindi as a national language. Besides, he was also editor of and contributor to the influential Hindi journals *Abhyuday* and *Maryādā*, and he worked as a local Congress organizer and held several party and elective posts. From municipal councillor and chairman of the municipality he rose to become Parliamentary Secretary (Chief Whip) of the United Provinces Legislative Assembly during the Congress government of 1937–9, where he proved his mettle as a staunch observer of parliamentary rules. He used such positions to further the cause of Hindi, especially in education (cf. 2.5, 5.4). His authority in the literary sphere thus stemmed from his role as head of the chief Hindi literary institution, from his official position, and from his direct access to the national leadership of Congress.

Culturally, Ṭaṇḍon displayed a typical Punjabi Khatri's rejection of Indo-Persian culture in favour of a new affiliation to the 'high tradition' of Indian (Hindu) culture.[105] Although at the head of the Hindi Sāhitya Sammelan for many years, Ṭaṇḍon showed little interest in contemporary secular literature. Despite his commitment to peasant politics and zamindari abolition (see 5.2), he believed uncompromisingly in the 'social harmony' and cultural unity of 'our ancient civilization'.[106] Hindi figured in this picture as a cultural symbol:

> Hindi is the language of svarājya. Our svarājya will not be based on the principle of *Democracy* [in English], but it will protect our ancient civilization, language and the other national components. This is a proven fact (*Yah bāt siddh hī hai*).[107]

A corollary to this, and a view that exercised great influence in the

---

was not an assiduous follower, the influence of the sampradāy can be seen in his austere and non-sectarian religiosity, in his emphasis on simple living, and in his personal interest in Yoga, Tantra and other spiritual practices; see Lakṣmīnārāyaṇ Siṃh, *Rājarṣi puruṣottamdās ṭaṇḍan*, Allahabad, Hindi Sahitya Sammelan, 1982, p. 2. For the Radhasoami sampradāy, see Mark Juergensmeyer, *Radhasoami Reality: the Logic of a Modern Faith*, Princeton, Princeton University Press, 1991.

[105] See Jones, *Arya Dharm*.

[106] Ṭaṇḍon's short essays on 'National literature', 'Philosophy and literature', 'The message of Indian culture', and 'The grove of Hindi literature' in the only available collection of his writings, are exemplary in this respect: the subjects posited are those of literature, philosophy, the nation, and national culture as single abstract entities, which belong to the realm of transcendental value and universal good; J. Nirmal, ed., *Ṭaṇḍan nibandhāvalī*, Wardha, Rastrabhasha Prachar Samiti, 1970.

[107] Ṭaṇḍon's speech at the 10th Hindī Sāhitya Sammelan annual meeting in Patna in March 1921, quoted in *Sammelan patrikā*, VII, 8, April–May 1921, p. 227.

Hindi literary sphere, was Ṭaṇḍon's instrumental and moralistic notion of literature, which has earlier been cited in Chapter 2:

The immortality of national glory (*kīrti*) depends on national literature. National wealth and national literature are mutually dependent. The jāti that wants to make its literature powerful (*śaktiśālī*) must first attempt to become powerful itself . . . Great literature cannot be created by narrow feelings (*saṅkucit bhāv*). No literature can become immortal and worthy of the whole nation's respect if it contains scores of texts full of different opinions . . . Scholars who write disparate texts to spread controversial opinions or particular social beliefs may succeed in their aim, but their works cannot help to produce pure literature (*viśuddh sāhitya*).[108]

Literature, too, could only be envisaged in a holistic national perspective; eclectic personal views were devalued as unnecessarily controversial, impure, and the product of 'narrow feelings'. This instrumental and normative view of literature was not unusual in Hindi, as we have already seen (2.2). However, coming from a political leader of considerable prestige and influence, who was also the foremost political champion of Hindi and leader of the most influential Hindi association, it had a peculiar force: for Hindi writers, as we shall see, it represented the politicians' desire to exercise complete control over literary people and their words, and their indifference to the writers' own efforts. In the person of Ṭaṇḍon a genuinely democratic persuasion coexisted with normative exclusivism. His attitude had a profound effect on the relationship between politicians and writers and on Hindi literature as a whole.

Sampūrṇānand (1891–1969) is perhaps the best example of the successful 'double-track' of Congress politicians and of the cultural make-up of Hindi politicians. He was as comfortable in the politics of the street as in the local constitutional arena of Benares and in the provincial halls of power; he switched easily between English, Hindi, and Urdu but considered Hindi the expression of his cultural identity, and he combined a modern, pragmatic outlook with a deep-seated belief in the classical roots of 'Indian tradition'.

Sampūrṇānand came from an old Benares Kayastha family of average means and education. As he himself put it: 'My early life could hardly have been different from that of any other boy in a lower middle-class family in one of the larger cities in northern India.'[109] His family was

[108] Ṭaṇḍon, 'Jātīy sāhitya', in *Ṭaṇḍan nibandhāvalī*, pp. 74–6.

[109] Sampurnanand, *Memories and Reflections*, p. 1. In his booklet about *Chet siṃh aur kāśī kā vidroh*, (Kanpur, Pratap Press, 1919), Sampūrṇānand mentions that his great-grandfather Sadānandjī was dīvān and companion to Raja Chetsingh.

typical in that it had tried to turn the tide of economic decline in old service jobs by finding new opportunities for employment in the colonial administration through the pursuit of modern education. Sampūrṇānand himself combined a 'scientific mentality' with a personal philosophical and spiritual quest that pulled him away from inherited religious affiliations and took him closer to 'high' scriptural sources, so that he later enjoyed some reputation as a scholar.[110]

Sampūrṇānand, too, like all other Hindi politicians, was connected to Hindi institutions as a teacher and a journalist (see Appendix). He was involved as editor, writer, and teacher in the cluster of educational and publishing activities financed by Śivaprasād Gupta in Benares, Kāśī Vidyāpīṭh, and the Jnanmandal publishing house.[111] His political career largely replicates Ṭaṇḍon's in that he, too, combined brilliant skills as an organizer—particularly precious during frantic political campaigns[112]—with argumentative eloquence and pragmatic skills as a constitutional politician. Like Ṭaṇḍon, he became councillor in the first municipal elections after Non-Cooperation and was particularly active as chairman of the education committee, boosting 'national schools' and commissioning nationalist textbooks (see 1.4). He then easily defeated the Hindu Sabha candidate and was elected to the UP Legislative Council in 1926 and to the provincial Assembly in 1937; he became Education Minister during the Congress provincial government in 1938–9. At the height of the Hindi–Hindustani controversy, his statements and proposals as Education Minister were seen to favour Hindi. The Acharya Narendra Dev committee that he set up to centralize control over primary and secondary schools endorsed Gandhi's Wardha Scheme of Basic Education and a centralized curriculum; it was resisted by Muslim politicians as an instance of Congress pro-Hindi policy, while the Hindi press remained expectant of even more decisive steps.[113] Even more than in the case of

[110] He took a BSc from Allahabad University in 1911; for his spiritual quest see *Memories and Reflections*. Like Ṭaṇḍon, he fostered a more conscious participation in marriage rituals by translating and writing on them in Hindi. At the end of his political career he became Vice-Chancellor of the Sanskrit University in Benares, now named after him.

[111] At Kāśī Vidyāpīṭh he taught philosophy after Dr Bhagvān Dās; for Jnanmandal he published *Antarrāṣṭrīy vidhān* (1924); Sampūrṇānand's younger brother Paripūrṇānand became Ś.P. Gupta's personal secretary.

[112] He was made secretary of the District Congress Committee in 1921, only two years after joining the Congress, and was chosen as the first Dictator for the salt satyāgraha in Benares in 1930; Sampurnanand, *Memories and Reflections*, pp. 25, 53.

[113] As Mukul Kesavan has argued, the Wardha scheme for national education was disliked by UP Muslims for making the vernacular (Hindi, as a rule) the medium of

other Hindi politicians, Sampūrṇānand's authority, originally stemming from his public activism, came to lie in his exercise of political power and patronage (see 5.4), a role he was only to strengthen after Independence. Sampūrṇānand's brand of 'Vedanta socialism' deserves far greater attention than is possible here for its characteristic blend of ideological syncretism and political pragmatism. Like Narendra Dev, Sampūrṇānand was more an intellectual and a leader than a mass organizer: 'strong language' was his most effective tool in fighting Congress right-wingers in the constitutional arena![114] A pragmatist, Sampūrṇānand resigned from the Congress Socialist Party, of which he was a founding member, and fought elections on a Congress ticket, as he did not believe that the Socialist Party had sufficient strength, especially in UP.[115]

The Hindi journalist politician who most believed in the popular potential of Hindi as a political language, and who was most preoccupied with broadening the Hindi public sphere in a popular direction, was Gaṇeś Śaṅkar Vidyārthī (1890–1931). This preoccupation was reflected in Vidyārthī's own activism in the non-constitutional arena: as the founder and editor of *Pratāp*, he introduced a more colloquial language, reported extensively on peasants' and workers' agitation and demands, and actively supported their activities, thus fulfilling B.V. Parāṛkar's aspiration that the Hindi press should express 'the voice of the people' (*jantā kī āvāz*) (cf. 5.1). As a political activist, he was among the first trade unionists in Kanpur and founded a Congress rural ashram in Kanpur district. As a reluctant parliamentarian, he raised questions regarding peasants and labourers within the provincial Legislative Council.[116] Finally, his own anti-elitist image and behaviour reinforced his image as an 'ordinary man'.

Vidyārthī's case shows best how a newspaper could actually become the mediator of popular public opinion, and how the authority of the editor and that of the political leader complemented each other. Although

---

instruction, with textbooks too much concerned with Hindu heroes and Hindu virtues; the scheme's explicit non-violent approach and the schools' name, 'Vidya-Mandir' also, antagonized Muslims. One regional Muslim politician reported that in various parts the 'propaganda for the Wardha Scheme is combined with Hindi Prachar'; quoted in M. Kesavan, 'Congress and the Muslims of UP and Bihar, 1937 to 1939', occasional paper, Delhi, 1990, p. 27.

114 For the ways in which Sampūrṇanand exercised his 'violent'opposition', see his *Memories and Reflections*, pp. 76, 78–81.

115 Ibid., p. 83.

116 See Bhargava, *Ganesh Shankar Vidyarthi*, pp. 93–6; Renuka Khosla, *Urban Politics (with Special Reference to Kanpur)*, New Delhi, S. Chand & Co., 1992.

himself a man of no personal means, Vidyārthī was known as the 'uncrowned king of Kanpur' for the authority he commanded thanks to his public activism, and *Pratāp*'s influence spread far into the rural disticts.[117] In the literary sphere he performed a particularly important role as mediator between literature and nationalist politics: *Pratāp* and the monthly journal *Prabhā* gave prominent space to nationalist poetry, Vidyārthī encouraged many old and young writers, and the *Pratāp* office in the populous Philkhana ward of Kanpur became a veritable literary and political meeting centre. His Kayastha background and secular disposition possibly made Vidyārthī more open to modern tastes and ideas: his reading habits and the books he chose to publish under the Pratap imprint show a preference for political literature and historical novels; he himself translated Victor Hugo's *Ninety-three* into Hindi while in jail. Vidyārthī shared in the strong anti-colonial pride in India's great tradition and entertained high expectations for Hindi as a future 'international language'.[118] Still, that pride was combined with the urge to build a modern Hindi culture that would be different from the past and would include popular subjects, publics, and forms of the language, in order to reflect the 'true' nation.[119]

Finally, Acharya Narendra Dev (1889–1956) was one of the leading Congress Socialist leaders and ideologues both in Hindi and in English. Narendra Dev's more distinguished social standing and educational curriculum make him, with Mālavīya, the most bilingual of the Hindi politicians. His background was different, though, for he came from a distinguished merchant family of Faizabad that had partly made the shift from wealth to culture as the self-defining marker of status.[120] As with

[117] Even in a rural district like Etawah, *Pratāp*'s influence was so great that an official surveyor remarked that, 'we find that in 1929 the political views of teachers of Etawah are moulded mainly by the late Mr Ganesh Shankar Vidyarthi and P. Shri Krishna Dutt Palival—the two Congress leader-journalists of Cawnpore and Agra respectively'; Chaturvedi, *An Educational Survey of a District*, p. 234.

[118] See his presidential speech at the XIX Hindī Sāhitya Sammelan meeting in Gorakhpur in 1930, a few months before he was killed during the Kanpur riots, quoted in Rādhākṛṣṇa, ed., *Gaṇeś Śaṅkar Vidyārthī ke śreṣth nibandh*, Delhi, Atmaram and Sons 1964, pp. 1–2.

[119] See Vidyārthī's editorial 'Rāṣtra kā nirmāṇ' for the special 1915 issue of *Pratāp*, in Avasthī, *Krānti kā udghoṣ*, vol. 2, pp. 977–85.

[120] Narendra Dev came from a wealthy family which had branched out into the professions, acquired zamindaris in the district, and embraced English education two generations earlier. In his childhood he breathed a very cultured and religious atmosphere but one open also to public concerns and politics. His father, Bāldev Prasād,

Sampūrṇānand, Narendra Dev made a personal effort to combine rational knowledge drawn from modern education with allegiance to the Indian tradition as studied from books and documents and imbibed through spiritual encounters; with this went radical politics, born, in Narendra Dev's case, out of a basic concern for justice and the study of socialism.[121] Narendra Dev combined them in practice by being politically active within Congress and the Socialist group, and by teaching ancient history and politics at the national college in Benares, Kāśī Vidyāpīṭh. Thanks to him, Sampūrṇānand, and Śrīprakāś, the Vidyāpīṭh became a cradle of young socialist activists, trade unionists, and future politicians. On the intellectual level, Narendra Dev hovered between a Marxist analysis of the nationalist movement and the agrarian question, a socialist view of society which dismissed caste and social hierarchy, and a cultural affiliation that defined Indian civilization in terms of its basic unity and harmony.[122] If in the Hindi literary sphere Narendra Dev

---

though educated in Persian and English, had studied Sanskrit 'to keep himself abreast of his own culture and religion', enjoyed 'the company of sadhus' (*satsaṅg*), and wrote children's textbooks in English, Hindi and Persian as a hobby. The family library was open to the public and it subscribed to several newspapers. Narendra Dev's subsequent education was in ancient Indian history, archaeology, philology, and epigraphy with Dr Venice and Prof. Norman at Queen's College in Benares before he graduated in law. Narendra Dev, 'My Recollections', in Keskar and Menon, *Acharya Narendra Dev*; see also the recollections of the Sanskrit scholar Gopīnāth Kavirāj, 'Bauddh aur saṃskṛt sāhitya kā vidvān', in the same volume. The shift among Calcutta bhadralok from merchant entrepreneurs who acquired status by the public display of opulence and charity to individuals who set value by culture and public improvement is a point made by Tithi Bhattacharya, 'Defining the Bhadralok through print', paper presented at the SOAS History seminar, December 1998.

[121] In the words of a historian: 'Like so many educated middle-class youth of his generation, Narendra Dev saw in the Kisan's Congress the reconciliation of opposites: the urban Indian's preoccupation with political reform and the rural Indian's preoccupation with agrarian reform;' Harold A. Gould, 'The Rise of the Congress System in a District Political Culture: the Case of Faizabad District in Eastern Uttar Pradesh', in P. Brass and F. Robinson, eds., *The Indian National Congress and Indian Society, 1885–1985: ideology, social structure and political dominance*, Delhi, Chanakya, 1987, p. 269.

[122] See his speeches 'Class Organisations and the Congress' (presidential address at the Gujarat Socialist Conference, Ahmedabad 1935) and 'National Revolution and Socialism' (presidential address at the First All-India Congress Socialist Conference, Patna, May 1934), both offering a class interpretation of the nationalist movement and of the Indian situation, included in Narendra Dev, *Socialism and the National Revolution*; see also the later articles 'Bhārtīy samāj aur saṃskṛti', 'Bhārtīy

was respected as a scholar, in the political sphere his influence was mainly that of a political thinker; as a socialist leader, he devoted more time to writing, party meetings, and exerting pressure in Congress and in the legislative assembly than to organizational work.[123]

The Hindi politicians examined in this section rose as organizers and leaders of public activities of various kinds in the Hindi sphere. Such activism bestowed authority upon them despite their often unremarkable social status; their rise in the Congress went with pragmatic political authority as well as patronage and influence. As politicians, they were largely successful in moving between non-constitutional and constitutional politics. However, the more they became part of the party structure, the more their role as mediators of public opinion shrunk. They were still vocal critics of, and representatives of public opinion against the colonial government but they discouraged dissent and public criticism of the Congress in the public sphere. Though certainly forcing the point, it was against this political culture that Sahajānand spoke so vehemently when he spoke of the 'taint of unanimity'.

What emerges from the overview of their political careers is that, politically, they literally spanned the political spectrum, from Mālavīya's Hindu right to Narendra Dev's socialism. However, the cultural axes of Hindi–English and elite–popular reveal another configuration: despite ideological differences and different roles in the political sphere, all the politicians mentioned so far shared a certain cultural commonality. It is this cultural commonality that makes the category 'Hindi politician' tenable at an important level—that of shared cultural identity. They embraced Hindi as a culturally loaded language, felt a personal affiliation to the 'harmony' of Indian culture, held ancient India and its allegedly homogeneous cultural tradition in high regard, and finally (barring perhaps G.Ś. Vidyārthī) subscribed to a moral view of literature. In this, they reflected the public culture of Hindi that I have been outlining in the course of this book. This showed in their pursuit of Hindi: while upholding Hindi as the political language of the common people, they also viewed it as the daughter of Sanskrit and the vehicle of 'Bhārtīy

dharma', and the broadcast on 'Religious movements as symbols of unity', (November 1950), quoted in Keskar and Menon, *Acharya Narendra Dev*; these emphasize the openness, adaptibility, and progressive tendencies in 'Indian dharma' and culture.

[123] Although his active political career started by speaking and working in villages of Tanda and Akbarpur tahsils during the Avadh movement of 1920–1, and he again toured villages during the salt satyāgraha, his delicate health prevented consistent organizational work.

saṃskṛti', Indian culture. Thus, despite the fact that they were, as 'vernacular' politicians, the best placed to carry forward popular aspirations and democratic demands, culturally they performed a conservative role. Even for leftist Hindi politicians this created a tension between their cultural consciousness and their professed allegiance to social and economic justice.

In fact, the adoption of Hindi and this cultural commonality were backed by varied attitudes to the Hindi–English question and to the cultural and political community that Hindi was supposed to include. For Vidyārthī, Hindi was the antithesis of English in that it addressed and represented a popular public; for Ṭaṇḍon and Sampūrṇānand, Hindi represented 'Indian' (as opposed to 'foreign') culture and was set to replace English as the dominant, countrywide language. The attitude of the more bilingual politicians, Narendra Dev, and in a different way Mālavīya, was more pragmatic, in that English served to address the national audience, while Hindi, in its different language styles, addressed local audiences. They could and would also use Urdu where the local audience was clearly mixed or predominantly Muslim, or when it suited their purpose in other ways. While for them Hindi needed to be on a par with the current national language, English, for others Hindi was to replace English and absorb all its functions. In both cases in legitimizing 'high' Hindi as the national language of power they legitimized themselves as the ruling class inheriting the nation.

Although this cultural consciousness did not necessarily translate into Hindu or elite politics, it nonetheless affected the social and political vision of Hindi leaders.[124] While in Ṭaṇḍon's case it eventually led to conservative politics after Independence, when he took over Mālavīya's mantle in provincial politics, in the case of Sampūrṇānand and Narendra Dev it produced a more subtle hiatus between their political and cultural visions.[125] 'The greatest feature of our culture is how it establishes unity among different systems of life (*jīvan-praṇālī*), and harmony (*samanvay*)

[124] This observation may apply to a large section of the educated Hindi public, which remained broadly loyal to the Congress fold despite holding a culturally conservative 'Hindu' outlook.

[125] As Sampūrṇānand suggested in his article 'Gāndhīvād aur sāmyavād', although class division and class conflict were the main differences between the two ideologies, 'Indian socialists can, if they want to, harmonise socialism with theism and religiosity, i.e. socialism with Gandhism . . . Indian socialism will have a peculiar nature: it will be influenced by Gandhism and by Indian culture, which has given birth to Gandhism, and it will become more spiritual and might even adopt non-violence'; *Viśāl bhārat, Rāṣṭrīy aṅk*, XVII, 4, April 1936, pp. 413–16.

in every field' wrote Narendra Dev; 'the second peculiarity of Indian culture is how it establishes a moral system (*naitik vyavasthā*)', a hierarchy of values with *mokṣa*, liberation, at the top.[126] As we have seen in earlier chapters and especially in the previous section, ideals and values of harmony and unity easily turned from being descriptive to being normative; while not negative in themselves, in presenting Indian culture as a singular block they were easily instrumental in hiding structures of exclusion, hierarchy, and authority. On the political terrain Vidyārthī, Narendra Dev, Sampūrṇānand, and Ṭaṇḍon to a certain extent, challenged the notion of 'social harmony' and maintained that the new times required a new political culture of *prajātantra*, the rule of the people, and that svarājya had no meaning without economic justice. However on the cultural terrain they spoke a language of unity, harmony, and pride in the ancient 'Bhārtīy saṃskṛti'. While politically they carried popular and democratic aspirations, culturally their role was largely conservative. The fact that it was easier to uphold harmony and national unity on the abstract terrain of culture rather than on the fraught one of politics—at a time when national unity was becoming an elusive goal—may explain the ease with which all these politicians embraced it. This holistic ideal was held high as a mirror for the fraught nation to contemplate its own image in. The fact that this ideal became normative, that it censored criticism and exercised exclusion in the literary sphere, did not seem to bother them (cf. 5.4). Vidyārthī's early death leaves the question open as to whether things could have been different, whether a major and popular Hindi politician could have helped put forward a more inclusive and critical Hindi culture.

The limited bilingualism, together with cultural conservatism, of Hindi politicians had another consequence: despite exerting significant local authority and patronage they did not become politicians of national importance. In a way this mirrored Hindi's own predicament. Just as Hindi could not command the same width and breadth of use and of public as English, despite its significant expansion and pervasiveness and despite the fanfare of Hindi propaganda, so also, Sampūrṇānand and P.D. Ṭaṇḍon, the most successful of the Hindi politicians, remained regional leaders, defenders of the vested interests, and of the institutional status of Hindi. And as the centre of power and authority shifted to Delhi, even their cultural role did not develop but formed a kind of cultural entrenchment, a conservative 'Hindī saṃskāra' transmitted through the institutions they had helped found.

[126] Narendra Dev, 'Bhārtīy samāj aur saṃskṛti', in Keskar and Menon, *Acharya Narendra Dev*, p. 253.

The cultural conservatism of Hindi politicians had significant repercussions in the Hindi literary sphere, too. Of the several voices in the Hindi literary sphere, some subscribed to the normative public culture, some were strongly critical, and others claimed autonomy for literary imagination; except perhaps Vidyārthī, Hindi politicians showed a remarkable lack of interest in, and sensitivity to, these varied voices and to contemporary Hindi literary production in general. This indifference caused serious tensions, as the following section will show. Hindi politicians were ideally placed to exercise mediation between the Hindi intelligentsia and public opinion and national leaders. Yet they only worked in one direction, from the latter to the former. This deprived independent Hindi intellectuals of the moral and intellectual authority and political influence they believed they had a right to exercise. Instead, politicians supported with their authority the culturally conservative Hindi intelligentsia and gave them sanction to become the Hindi establishment, at the head of cultural and educational institutions, at the expense of independent voices. By doing so they blocked the way to a further democratization and popularization of Hindi. Literature for them was not a prajātantra, a democracy in which everyone was making a contribution and had a right to express his or her own view, but was a *rājatantra* in which writers were told how to write and were reprimanded if they did otherwise.

5.4. The Question of Authority

The Hindi–Hindustani controversy that raged in the literary and political spheres in the second half of the 1930s can be seen in many ways as the culmination of the processes discussed so far. First, the outcome of the controversy was the climax of the institutionalisation of Hindi as *the* public language of India, in terms of state language (rājbhāṣā) and of national language (rāṣṭrabhāṣā). Second, the public debate in support of Hindi revealed the cultural contours of the Hindi discourse. Third, the controversy identified literary associations (like the Hindī Sāhitya Sammelan) as the source of authority not just in the literary sphere but in the public sphere at large. Finally, the controversy and its resolution expose for us a crisis within the Hindi public sphere over the question of authority.

The question of authority in the public sphere is a complex one. Here, in line with the literary focus of this book, I shall chiefly be concerned with authority in the literary sphere, and consequently with two issues: the first concerns intellectual authority and who it was to be vested in. The second relates to the relationship between political and intellectual authority. These perspectives will guide us in unravelling the meaning of the controversy for the Hindi public sphere and its consequences for the fate of Hindi in independent India. My argument will be that the Hindi–Hindustani controversy strenghtened the links between Hindi politicians and the Hindi establishment at the head of literary associations and educational institutions. They were likely partners as, whatever their political leaning, they shared a certain cultural conservatism, a view of Hindi as a cultural symbol, a normative and moral approach to literature, and an indifference towards contemporary writers. This partnership was fundamental to securing official status for Hindi and counteracting political canvassing for Hindustani at the national level, yet it also undercut the literary and cultural authority of independent writers and critical voices. The cry of 'Hindi in danger' did rally together most Hindi intellectuals and institutions but it also strenghtened normative tendencies and encouraged suspicion towards critical voices.

5.4.1. Hindi or Hindustani?

The Hindī Sāhitya Sammelan (1910) had emerged as the most powerful lobby pressing Congress to establish Hindi as the national language (cf. 2.1). During the Hindi–Hindustani controversy it became the chief site of contention: it was first taken over by pro-Hindustani Congressmen and then was regained by the Hindi side. In the second chapter we saw how literary associations, chiefly the Sammelan, had turned from appealing to the colonial government to lobbying with Congress in the 1920s. We saw how difficult it was for them to switch from the language of scientifically proven advantage and self-improvement that they had used with the colonial government to one of political consensus when they appealed to a national institution like Congress. They also found it surprisingly hard to make themselves heard by Congress leaders (cf. 2.1).

Congress support, which was crucial in securing for Hindi the status of national language, had seemed assured when a triumphant Gandhi sat on the presidential seat of the 8th Hindī Sāhitya Sammelan meeting in Indore in 1918.[127] 'Until all public activities (*sārvajanik kārya*) take place in Hindi the country cannot progress. Until Congress conducts all its

[127] Already in *Hind Swaraj* (1909) Gandhi had expressed himself against English and in favour of Hindi as the national language of India. After he spoke in Hindi at the Congress Session in Lucknow in 1916, Ṭaṇḍon invited him to preside over the 8th Hindī Sāhitya Sammelan in Indore. The huge crowd welcoming him at the station, the enthusiasm of volunteers who carried Gandhi's carriage on their shoulders, the official parade with elephants and horses through the streets of the city, the great tent for ten thousand people, the long and loud clapping when Gandhi took the presidential seat all marked a massive public celebration of both Gandhi and Hindi. The meeting

activities in the rāṣṭrabhāṣā we shall not obtain svarājya', he had said in an interview as early as 1917.[128] Gandhi seemed to incarnate the national aim of the Sammelan to perfection when at Indore he suggested a plan for Hindi propaganda in the south. For this he provided the finance and political blessing, while the Sammelan provided human resources and expertise.[129] In the years to follow, propaganda in the south, especially in Madras, proved to be the most sensational enterprise of the Sammelan and, together with the examinations, the most successful (see 2.4.3). The growing number of south Indians learning Hindi at the Sammelan centres was a concrete example of nation building and binding through language.[130]

Gandhi's view of Hindi differed substantially from that of the Sammelan, though. They agreed that Hindi had to supersede English, but for Gandhi Hindi was the language of village India, a *spoken* language that cut across literacy and script divides: 'I cannot find the softness I find in village speech either in the way our Muslim brothers speak in Lucknow or pandits speak in Prayag. The best language is one which common people can understand; everyone understands village speech.'[131]

---

also provided several Hindi literary people with their first opportunity to hear and meet Gandhi in person; for a description and report on the proceedings, see *Sammelan patrikā*, V, 8–9, March–May 1918, pp. 181–206.

[128] Interview with *Bhāratmitra* correspondent, quoted in *Sammelan Patrikā*, IV, 5 (1917), p. 181.

[129] Gandhi suggested first to Ṭaṇḍon and then to the Sammelan that they set up Hindi teaching classes and instruct Hindi teachers from the south. Before presenting his plan in front of the assembly he had secured the financial help of the Maharaja of Indore, who donated Rs 10,000, and more was promised by other patrons; ibid., pp. 199–202. According to Kaka Kalelkar's memoirs, Ṭaṇḍon was sceptical about the plan at first, but accepted when Gandhi told him with some emphasis that the Sammelan should otherwise withdraw its claim that Hindi could be the national language of India, or he should resign as secretary of the Sammelan; Kaka Kalelkar, 'Rāṣṭrabhāṣā-prachār: gāndhījī aur ṭaṇḍanjī kā sahyog', in *Gāndhī-ṭaṇḍan-smṛti-aṅk, Sammelan patrikā,* LV, 3–4, June–December 1969, p. 25.

[130] Some youths were sent from the south to Allahabad for training, and from Gandhi's ashram Harihar Śarmā was sent to Madras to set up Hindi courses. Gandhi also sent his younger son Devdas (who did not know Hindi at the time) and the experienced preacher Svami Satyadev 'Parivrājak'. In eighteen years 600,000 south Indians were taught Hindi, 42,000 sat for the special examinations, and 600 teachers were trained who worked in 450 centres, all for the limited expense of Rs 6 lakhs; see Gandhi's speech at 24th Indore Hindī Sāhitya Sammelan, 1935, quoted ibid., p. 130. Propaganda work in Tamil Nadu and Andhra was not matched by similar efforts in other provinces.

[131] 'Hindu preachers and Muslim maulvis give speeches in Hindi throughout

He called it Hindi–Hindustani or simply Hindustani whenever he felt that the point about script needed to be made explicitly, especially in the increasingly communalized 1930s.[132]

At first the Sammelan quietly accepted Gandhi's definition, probably only too happy to have found such an influential and popular patron. Gandhi's presidentship of the Hindī Sāhitya Sammelan did seem to put Hindi more urgently on the Congress agenda; the next few annual meetings of the Sammelan were attended by an unprecedented number of nationalist leaders. Yet Gandhi's view of Hindi–Hindustani went completely against fifty years of public efforts for Hindi by the Hindi press and literary associations, not least by the Sammelan. He was invited once again to preside over the 24th meeting in Indore in 1935—undoubtedly to repeat the successful performance of 1918, giving new lustre to the organisation[133] and enhancing Hindi's claim within the Congress; instead Gandhi made the Sammelan formally accept his Hindi–Hindustani definition. Polemics flared up, and many spoke of a 'sudden turn' in Gandhi's policy, even of a betrayal. Yet, even in 1918

Hindustan. And the illiterate people understand them', he wrote in 'Kyā aṅgrezī rāṣṭrabhāṣā ho saktī hai?' (translation of a Gujarati article), quoted in *Sammelan patrikā,* V, 10, June–July 1918, p. 227.

[132] See Lelyveld, 'The Fate of Hindustani'.

[133] Throughout the 1920s there were complaints about the inefficiency, inactivity, and inner squabbles of the Sammelan which left little time or energy for anything else. Ṭaṇḍon, who was the secretary and factotum of the Sammelan for the first ten years, moved to Lahore from 1925 to 1929 to work for the Punjab National Bank; this allowed a rival faction, comprising Rāmjīlāl Śarmā, Lakṣmīdhar Vājpeyī, and other book publishers, to gain control of the managing committee and the main posts: publishers viewed the remarkable growth of the Hindī Sāhitya Sammelan examinations as very profitable if their textbooks were prescribed in the syllabus. In 1927 they tried to take control of the Madras branch and launched a defamation campaign against Harihar Śarmā in order to take over the office; Mālavīya's intervention restored it to Gandhi, to whom he had entrusted it as president of the 9th Hindī Sāhitya Sammelan in Bombay in 1919. Only Banārsīdās Chaturvedī, who had a penchant for noisy controversies, exposed the scheme in print and gave the names of those involved; all other accounts spoke of it as a 'painful incident' or did not mention it at all; see *Viśāl bhārat,* I, pt. 1, 4, April 1928, pp. 457 ff. The furious *dalbandī* (factionalism), as it was called in the press, lasted for over a decade; Rāmjīlāl Śarmā himself died in 1931. In the early 1930s 'Election Sammelans' were squabbles over management posts and a public ritual of speeches and 'lifeless resolutions'. The appointed presidents would give a speech, preside over the proceedings and then be idle for the rest of the year. Since the office was located in Allahabad while presidents belonged to different places, the administration remained in the hands of the secretaries living there; see editorial note in *Mādhurī*, IX, pt. 2, 4, May 1931, p. 603.

when Gandhi had spoken of Hindi he had clearly meant Hindustani, written in both scripts.

Reactions in the Hindi press were extreme. One editorial note in the January 1936 issue of *Sudhā* spoke of it as the Sammelan's pro-Muslim attempt at 'killing Hindi'. With sepulchral metaphors, the editor predicted that all Hindi literature would have to be cremated, since none of it fitted into the Hindustani framework of Gandhi, that 'blind devotee of Muslims'. Because of Gandhi's pious wishes, poor Hindi would have to discard its sumptuous garments to put on an awkward half-rustic, half-Muslim costume; but how could Hindi, Sanskrit's daughter and the language of cow-protecting, non-violent image worshippers who considered India their only land, ever come to terms with the communalist language of cow-eating image destroyers, who considered Arabia and Iran their motherland, and whose foreign culture was violent, brutal, and always harking back to a Muslim empire? Luckily a few patriots like Dr Savarkar were pointing to the right solution: to stop vainly trying to woo Muslims.

A more laconic Devīdatt Śukla, *Sarasvatī*'s editor, commented sarcastically in the July 1935 issue that Hindi speakers had been misguided so far in believing that Hindi had already been accepted as the national language. The honour was to be bestowed on a language which had no literature yet; and if the Hindustani Academy had so far been unsuccessful in establishing its written form, how could the new Sammelan think of succeeding in the same task?[134] Most Hindi intellectuals felt clearly threatened in their own *raison d'être* and in what had been their life-long mission. Their reactions to Gandhi's emphasis on Hindustani may be read in several ways. For example, they believed that for the honour (*pad*) of rāṣṭrabhāṣā, status, and hence a 'high' literature and a 'high' idiom, were more important than popularity. Also, literature expressed the cultural character and pedigree of Hindi; it had also been the main avenue of the writers' self-assertion. In this perspective, the fact that Congress leaders disregarded such efforts and were in fact professedly ignorant about Hindi literature was regarded as suspicious and humiliating. The language controversy thus took the form of a struggle for authority: should it rest with national politicians or with Hindi experts?

The strategy of Congress was to assert its own authority by appropriating the Sammelan and taking over Hindi propaganda.[135] Thus, in the

[134] Editorial 'Sāhitya-sammelan aur hindī kī hatyā', *Sudhā*, IX, pt. 1, 6, January 1936, pp. 692–3. D. Śukla, *Sampādak ke pacchīs varṣ*, pp. 76–7.

[135] At the Nagpur Sammelan of 1936 Gandhi launched a new institution for Hindi

years following the 1935 Indore Sammelan, Congress leaders and activists flocked to Sammelan meetings and were elected presidents.[136] The Hindi world itself split into two camps. In the Hindustani camp, apart from Congressmen like Rajendra Prasad, J. Nehru, Vinoba Bhave, Kaka Kalelkar, Rajagopalachari, Pandit Sundarlāl, and Jamnalal Bajaj, there were intellectuals of mixed Indo-Persian culture, followers of Gandhi and those who did not feel too strongly about the issue anyway, such as Premchand, Dr Tarachand, Jainendra Kumār, and Rāykṛṣṇadās.[137] In the Hindi camp there were Hindi politicians and activists like Ṭaṇḍon, Sampūrṇānand, V.N. Tivārī, Bālkṛṣṇa Śarmā 'Navīn', and those who believed that Hindi had the strength to be open and accommodating, like Śivaprasād Gupta, Bābūrāo Viṣṇu Parāṛkar, Nirālā, and Rāmvilās Śarmā; there were those who subscribed to the notion of Hindi and Hindu history (outlined in Chapter 3) and believed it was now time for Hindi to rule, and those who had devoted their lives to Hindi enterprises, like Lakṣmīdhar Vājpeyī, Śrīnārāyaṇ Chaturvedī, Ambikāprasād Vājpeyī, Viyogī Hari, Kiśoridās Vājpeyī, and Devīdatt Śukla. Despite internal tensions among Hindi supporters about the language policy and the authority of the old Sammelan, they reacted defensively to the attempted takeover. Perhaps for the first time, in fact, nationalist Hindi literati publicly criticised national Congress leaders for their high-handedness. Sammelan meetings between 1938 and 1941, in Simla, Benares, and Abohar, witnessed furious debates and culminated in the successful bid by Hindi supporters

---

propaganda in central India, the Rāṣṭrabhāṣā Prachār Sabhā, to be housed in Wardha. After the takeover of the Sammelan failed, Gandhi preferred to start an autonomous organization for propaganda in the South, the Hindustānī Prachār Sabhā; see Rāmdhārī Siṃh 'Dinkar', 'Hindī-hindustānī vivād', in *Gāndhī-ṭaṇḍan smṛti aṅk*, pp. 36 ff.

[136] In May 1936, Rajendra Prasad presided over the 25th Sammelan meeting in Nagpur, while Kaka Kalelkar presided over the welcome committee, and in April Gandhi inaugurated the new Sammelan library in Allahabad. Young Ajñeya, who was attending a Sammelan meeting for the first time and reported on the proceedings at Nagpur for *Viśāl bhārat*, remarked that 'the first thing to disturb me was that the 'All-India Hindī Sāhitya Sammelan' was neither an all-Indian nor a literary meeting. The atmosphere there was political rather than literary'. What he meant by it, he explained, was not Rajendra Prasad's speech but the atmosphere of intrigue and the presence of political activists rather than literary personalities. Ajñeya, 'Sammelan meṁ kyā dekhā, sunā aur sochā', *Viśāl bhārat*, XVIII, 1, June 1936, p. 674. The next Sammelan meeting in Madras in March 1937 saw again a Congress politician elected as president: Jamnalal Bajaj instead of Maithilīśaraṇ Gupta; see *Chāṁd*, XV, pt. 2, 1, May 1937, pp. 103–5.

[137] Vājpeyī, *Sāhityik jīvan ke anubhav*, p. 83.

to regain control of the associaton.[138] National Congress leaders mostly favoured Hindustani for political reasons, in order not to alienate Muslims; what they had not taken enough into consideration was that the issue of Hindi self-assertion was crucial to the Hindi public sphere and that the institutionalisation of Hindi had already gone a long way and could not be undone. Further, by fighting on the ground of a Hindi organisation they were completely within the Hindi public and press, where opinion in favour of Hindi could easily be mobilized. It was in fact a series of articles in favour of Hindi written in 1939–40 by Congressman Veṅkateś Nārāyaṇ Tivārī, former Chief Whip of the UP Legislative Assembly, that decisively upset the realpolitik of other Congress leaders and upheld Hindi's claim in the political sphere.[139] And it was finally the academic authority of Amarnāth Jhā, Vice-Chancellor of Allahabad University and president of the Sammelan session in Abohar, that settled the tussle within the Sammelan in favour of Hindi and reaffirmed Hindi's claim to be the national language of India. In his speech, Jhā emphatically upheld the original goal of the Hindī Sāhitya Sammelan: 'to spread Devanagari script all over the country and to try to make Hindi the national language'. In this light, the Hindi–Hindustani definition was 'unnecessary': everyone knew that Hindustani was an artificial creation and that Hindi descended directly from Sanskrit. Jhā *personally* liked Urdu poetry, he said, but this did not alter the fact that Hindi and Urdu literature breathed two different atmospheres. Jhā's speech was a resounding success, 'and the supporters of Hindustani saw what the nation really wanted'.[140] The victory within the Hindī Sāhitya Sammelan

[138] The story of those momentous sessions has been told in ample detail in Hindi sources. At the 27th Hindī Sāhitya Sammelan in Simla in 1938 the debate raged furiously for three days. On the fourth day, Śrīnārāyaṇ Chaturvedī of the Hindi camp staged a successful attempt to regain control by having a list of pro-Hindi names accepted for the managing committee, with the tacit support of P.D. Ṭaṇḍon and B.V. Parāṛkar, the appointed president; K. Vājpeyī, 'Hindī gaṅgā ke bhāgīrath', in *Gāndhī-ṭaṇḍan-smṛti-aṅk*, pp. 210–11. At the next session in Benares in December 1939, presided over by Ambikāprasād Vājpeyī, with Rajendra Prasad and Kaka Kalelkar present, Veṅkateś Nārāyaṇ Tivārī gave a powerful speech against Hindustani. Ṭaṇḍon assured the audience that the Nagari script would not be tampered with, and even Rajendra Prasad declared that Hindi would not be harmed; quoted in Śukla, *Sampādak ke pacchīs varṣ*, p. 104.

[139] See e.g. V. N. Tivārī, 'Hindī banām urdū', *Sudhā*, XII, pt. 2, 1, February 1939, pp. 3, 5.

[140] For A. Jhā's speech: *Abohar XXX Hindī sāhitya sammelan kā vistṛt vivaraṇ*, Allahabad, Hindi Sahitya Sammelan, 1941, pp. 19–23. Although he had been a

marked the end of a possible Hindi–Hindustani compromise and the reassertion of the authority of experts and the strategy of committees in dealing with the language question.[141]

The controversy over Hindi–Hindustani may have seemed a trivial one in the minds of nationalists engaged in winning independence for the country. For the Hindi sphere, however, it was an issue that concerned its own existence and development thus far. Passionate 'rational' debates over minute points of style and history reflected a wider and deeper anxiety about the authority of Hindi intellectuals within the nationalist movement and in the future state. Hindi supporters and intellectuals believed that through their long-drawn-out efforts they had earned the right to stake the claim for Hindi as the national language, and for themselves as respected authorities. The Congress stand in favour of Hindustani seemed to belie all this.

Hindi's victory within the Sammelan was a pyrrhic victory, though, one that was repeated in the Constituent Assembly in 1948–50. It foreshadowed the future status of Hindi in independent India. First of all, it was a victory that refused the claims of other subjects and accepted them only as subordinate to the Hindi–Hindu cultural mainstream. In this respect, the supporters of Hindi pursued the same line of competitive self-assertion they had pursued with the colonial administration in relation to Urdu. The hegemonic claim of Hindi over Hindustani, Urdu, and English that would have been impossible with the British government, could be made in the nationalist arena. Yet, by pursuing such an exclusivist concept of rāṣṭrabhāṣā, Hindi supporters effectively weakened its chances of actually replacing English as the language of the nation. In this respect, the fate of Hindi reflected that of Hindi politicians like Ṭaṇḍon or Sampūrṇānand in that its authority remained provincial.

The Hindi victory was also a victory of the Sammelan and reinforced its authority within the literary sphere. It reinforced its hardline language policy within the Hindi literary sphere at the cost of other, more eclectic styles, and its normative view of literature at the cost of independent and

member of the Hindī Sāhitya Sammelan for only one year, Amarnāth Jhā, professor of English and Vice-Chancellor of Allahabad University, was elected president instead of Rajendra Prasad. For reactions: Vājpeyī, *Sāhityik jīvan ke anubhav*, p. 86.

[141] A Lipi-Vistār-Pariṣad, chaired by Kaka Kalelkar, had tried this avenue, and the grammar committee headed by Ṭaṇḍon worked out fanciful grammatical changes, which included abolishing gender for verbal forms and making all words ending in a consonant masculine (!); quoted in *Sudhā*, X, pt. 2, 4, May 1937, p. 359. Again in evidence here is the tendency to solve problems not through open debate but by decree, by the authority of a select committee of 'experts'.

critical views. On the strength of their position at the heads of academic institutions and of textbook production, as ministers and prominent leaders, Hindi intellectuals and politicians managed to impose their version of rāṣṭrabhāṣā and their cultural and historical view as the established one and this remained the case in independent India as well. They also jointly undercut the authority of independent writers. In the following section we shall see how.

5.4.2. A Crisis of Authority

The UP Sāhitya Sammelan meeting in Faizabad in 1937 could well be considered evidence of Hindi's success after decades of struggle: Narendra Dev, the Socialist leader from Faizabad, was chairing the welcome committee; Sampūrṇānand, the new education minister in the Congress government of the province, was to open the art exhibition; P.D. Ṭaṇḍon, the long-standing pillar of the Sammelan and now Speaker of the provincial assembly, presided. There was talk of making Rāmchandra Śukla, the most respected Hindi critic, preside, but in the end he was made to preside only over the proceedings of the literary branch. The audience was large. According to a literary observer, it comprised mostly schoolmasters, subordinate to the new Congress minister, and a sprinkling of local notables loyal to Narendra Dev.[142] Thanks to Nirālā's outspoken comments, however, the celebratory occasion degenerated into a bitter debate over the function of literature, authority, and the relationship between politics and literature. The extraordinary confrontation between a leading Hindi intellectual and leading Hindi politicians shows the extent and nature of the crisis of authority that had intervened.

Nirālā's response is particularly interesting for us. His position as an outsider detached from literary institutions, and his nature, particularly sensitive to questions of prestige and hierarchy, made him one of the very few Hindi writers who thought and wrote at length on these matters and openly criticized esteemed nationalist leaders. This was, we might argue, not because he was the only one to *feel* about the issue but because he was one of the few who questioned and disregarded vested authority, both traditional and nationalist, both political and literary. I do not assume that his reports were 'true' or unbiased; but as far as they were his perceptions, they reveal several critical points that concern us.

[142] The account follows an interview with Nirālā, in *Chakallas*, May–June 1938; quoted in *Nirālā rachnāvalī*, vol. 6, pp. 213–15.

What, then, happened in Faizabad to upset Nirālā so much? Sampūrṇānand was there to open the art exhibition but started speaking freely about poetry. In the beginning, according to Nirālā, he was 'restrained and correct' and accepted that poets had freedom of expression. Eventually, however, he said that 'Poets should give support to politicians'. Nirālā was unable to restrain a loud, irreverent comment: 'Hindi poets are far ahead of politicians.'[143] The first stone was thrown.

The following day was that of presidential speeches. In his impromptu introductory address, Narendra Dev spoke of the 'two great men' (*mahā-puruṣa*) who were gracing the occasion: the 'honourable and revered' Babu Puruṣottam Dās Ṭaṇḍon and the 'respected' Sampūrṇānandjī. Nirālā was appalled: here was Rāmchandra Śukla, a true literary mahāpuruṣa, and Narendra Dev failed even to mention him! This 'inadvertent' slip revealed, according to Nirālā, 'his inner feeling': even a 'generous' politician, a radical and a socialist, unselfconsciously fell into the 'common' mould of paying respects only to powerful people.[144] When eventually Ṭaṇḍon took his presidential seat, he was greeted by loud applause: 'people clapped at seeing their selfless leader grace the high seat of literature.'[145] But when he came forward to deliver his address, he had no prepared speech either. That the speech of the president of the Sāhitya Sammelan was not written showed little consideration, commented Nirālā.[146] In the speech, Ṭaṇḍon mentioned his recent contacts with Mahatma Gandhi, and again and again gave pre-eminence (*prādhānya*) to politics over literature—'as if Sarasvatī [the goddess of literature and learning] were a slave to politics', commented Nirālā.[147] Although he failed even to mention contemporary literature, Ṭaṇḍon nonetheless felt it necessary to urge Hindi writers to 'transcend provincial limits'. This incensed Nirālā: first of all, because he felt that to subordinate literature to politics from the presidential seat of the Sammelan was an insult (*apmān*) to that very seat. Second, because it betrayed ignorance and indifference to contemporary Hindi literary efforts. In a later interview Nirālā clarified his view:

> I can say with full assurance that in this province the contribution literature has made is greater than that of politics. Literary people in this province have been,

[143] Ibid., p. 213.
[144] Ibid.
[145] Ibid.
[146] The speech was on the words Hind, Hindu and Hindi. 'For someone like Ṭaṇḍonjī, who has been for so long the helmsman, the life and soul of the Sammelan, it was hardly a big thing to have an accurate knowledge of those words'; ibid., p. 214.
[147] Ibid.

undoubtedly, much greater people (*baṛe vyakti*) than politicians. True, literary people here have not crossed the Atlantic eight times or the Pacific sixteen times; hardly any of them has had a full European education, but as far as knowledge of reality (*yathārtha jñān*), study (*adhyayan*), activity and sacrifice are concerned, literary people here are ahead of politicians—especially because they are not 'followers', they are 'original'.[148]

We shall come back to these arguments. At the meeting, an exchange ensued between Nirālā and Ṭaṇḍon about the meaning of literature, with Ṭaṇḍon saying that literature always followed politics. The audience, at seeing its leaders questioned and humbled publicly, started abusing Nirālā.[149] As the exchange became more heated, Ṭaṇḍon said that he did not touch literature written by writers who were not of high character (*charitravān*). Nirālā immediately thought of Kalidasa, Tagore, and other not exactly prudish classics: what did such bragging (*ḍaporsaṅkh*) have to do with a literary gathering? He walked out saying 'I am not used to listening to such nonsense.'[150]

Nirālā later pointed out that his opposition was not personal: he respected Ṭaṇḍon's high moral character and selfless public work. He objected to the exclusive use of the word mahāpuruṣa which politicians made. The term itself is interesting and signals an attempt to de-link personal authority from birth, position, or power held. To be a mahāpuruṣa had to do with inner individual qualities or achievements—something Congress leaders and writers had acquired on the field. According to Nirālā, politics and literature deserved equal importance.[151] But at Faizabad, at a literary venue, both politicians and the audience had shown ignorance of and indifference towards literary mahāpuruṣas, despite their contribution. The audience had been readier to listen to the leaders than to Nirālā: political clout and 'high' contacts mattered more than literary achievements.

The second point of contention concerned the autonomy of literature and writers' originality, the sources of personal authority for a writer. According to Nirālā, originality in a writer was itself a political achievement. After all, to enrich Hindi literature by original works of excellence meant contributing to the cultural decolonization of the country. Yet

[148] Ibid. The words in inverted commas are in English in the original.

[149] Nirālā was told to either shut up or go away. He later reflected: 'It is clear whether the people had come there for the sake of literature or for their daily bread; whether politics had made them sensible men or sensible slaves is also clear;' ibid., p. 215.

[150] Ibid., p. 216.

[151] Ibid., p. 214.

Ṭaṇḍon had shown no respect for the autonomy of art. Instead the Sammelan showed that 'Hindi is a puppet in the hands of some non-literary people, not a living goddess in the hearts of her devotees'.[152] What was left in the Sammelan, as Premchand also remarked, was a pompous public ritual that had hardly anything to do with literature. Prevailed upon to take part in the 1934 annual Sammelan meeting in Delhi, Premchand had reported ironically for *Jāgaraṇ:*

This much-publicised conference held this year in Delhi, the capital city of so many rises and falls, has now come to a happy end, as it does every year . . . The disappointment caused by it was similar to that felt by the devout when the Universal Spirit assumes a gross physical form in order to appear before them . . . By lighting bright petromax lamps for four days, by decking the scene with flowers and by singing anthems, the conference has tried to make us believe that Hindi is going to progress by leaps and bounds. . . . The procession started on schedule with tired delegates and some very important persons marching in it . . . The meeting after lunch was characterised by the vigour one usually associates with any meeting held immediately after a meal. . . . How could the anthem sung by girls clad in saffron *saris* possibly fail to enchant those volunteers who had been checking passes with the same alacrity with which a sergeant flashes a warrant of arrest. The portraits of past presidents and the inspirational inscriptions in bold letters which adorned the walls, and the red and blue rosettes pinned to the *kurtas* and jackets of the important persons, were enough to captivate anyone.[153]

The following day at Faizabad, Nirālā tried to regain ground with a speech on the autonomy and importance of the writer. The writer is a seer endowed with a vision that transcends the confines of time and space and the limited horizons of the people, he said. Thus true literature is higher than politics.[154] Politics is necessarily bound by interests—whether individual or national—whereas literature is disinterested and universalistic and aims only at the good (*kalyāṇ*) of man.[155] In the end he sang one of his 'Bādal rāg' poems, written in the early 1920s. In these poems he had used metaphors of gathering clouds and torrential rain to express a yearning for social and political upheaval at the hands of the masses. As on other occasions the force of the poem and his inspiring delivery won over a hostile audience.

A similar confrontation had taken place in December 1935, when Jawaharlal Nehru, invited by the Ratnākar-Rasik Maṇḍal of Benares to receive a letter of felicitation, had delivered a short speech in front of the

152 Ibid., p. 210.
153 Quoted in Rai, *Premchand: His Life and Times*, pp. 302–4.
154 *Nirālā rachnāvalī*, vol. 6, p. 217.
155 Ibid., p. 214.

leading Hindi literary men of Benares: Rāmchandra Śukla, Jayśaṅkar Prasād, Kṛṣṇadev Prasād Gauṛ, and others. In his address, which caused quite a stir in the Hindi press, Nehru said that Hindi had so far produced only courtly poetry, and after svarājya the government would see to it that 300–400 books were translated into Hindi from other languages. Nirālā's response in an editorial was:

> Pandit Jawaharlal Nehru lives in the same place [Allahabad] where the Hindī Sāhitya Sammelan stands, where *Sarasvatī* alone can be called an epoch-making history of Hindi literature. But Panditji has been too immersed in the making of the nation ever to remember the national language or to feel that it was necessary to teach Hindi for the sake of the nation. To our mind, if some of the literary talent Panditji has spent for the nation, a talent which the humble servants of rāṣṭrabhāṣā can hardly grasp, had been spent writing some books in that language, they would understand him very well. Also, Panditji would learn that he could receive much from the very same people he wants to give something to, and that they are much ahead of him in the field of the national language, however much ahead he may consider himself to be in the field of the nation.

If Nehru had been acquainted with Hindi, Nirālā went on to say, he would have realized that Hindi poetry was hardly at the stage of courtly literature any longer, and that all the books he wanted to have translated into Hindi had probably already been translated long ago.[156] To Nehru's suggestion that English, too, should be considered a '*sautelī bhāṣā*' (step-language) of India, Premchand replied: 'In our opinion English has become such an indispensable language under the present circumstances that it hardly needs an association or an institution to help it. Far from being a 'sautelī' language, it is rather a '*paṭrānī*' (head) language and all the other languages of India are reduced to the status of beggars in front of her. The pity is that those who call themselves our leaders are often ignorant of their mother tongue, and the consequences of a society in which its leaders have become so far removed from society that they have no relationship with their language are in front of our eyes.'[157] The superciliousness and ignorance Nehru displayed towards Hindi literature had no correspondence in Bengal, Nirālā told Nehru when they met face to face: there Tagore was as much, if not more, respected than political leaders.[158] Finally, in his editorial Nirālā turned to the literary audience of the Benares meeting:

[156] As quoted in Nirālā's editorial 'Paṇḍit Javāharlāl Nehrū aur Hindī', *Sudhā*, 1 December 1933, in *Nirālā rachnāvalī*, vol. 6, p. 439.

[157] Premchand, 'Bhārtīy sāhitya aur paṇḍit Javāharlāl Nehrū', *Haṃs*, November 1935, in *Vividh prasaṅg*, vol. 3, p. 106.

[158] Nirālā, 'Nehrūjī se do bātem̐' (1936), *Nirālā rachnāvalī*, vol. 6, p. 235. Even Subhash Chandra Bose had not failed to express his condolences at Saratchandra's

The people who remained silent after listening to Panditji's bizarre (*adbhut*) speech must have done so out of civility. Otherwise they could have rebutted such a learned speech! They must have considered it unfitting for their literary disposition to oppose someone they had invited to bestow their respect upon. But we request Hindi literary people that, if they want to avoid being insulted on such matters, to follow this philosophical truth: जो दूसरों को बड़ा मानता है वह दूसरे से छोटा समझा जाता है। (Whoever looks up to someone else will be looked down upon).[159]

The exchange at Faizabad and the 'insult' in Benares pertained to both the representational and discursive aspects of the public sphere: both to hierarchical status and the authority displayed in front of the audience,[160] and to the nature of intellectual authority. When the two aspects overlapped the conflict became sharper.

As Nirālā was painfully aware, it was virtually impossible that an English-educated politician like Nehru would go to a Hindi literary gathering to *learn* or *listen* to something. And if we understand authority as the faculty of being given a respectful hearing, then the hierarchy was only too clear.[161] Nirālā made two attempts to redress the balance and make himself heard with Gandhi and Nehru, and they both went famously wrong. They are reported in two hilarious essays he wrote in 1939. First of all it was virtually impossible for Nirālā, already a famous poet, to have access to Gandhi the political mahāpuruṣa: he was accorded a private audience in Lucknow only when he said he had come to meet Gandhi the president of the Hindī Sāhitya Sammelan.[162] In a spirited

---

death. Nothing similar had happened in Hindi at Prasād's demise, and even Premchand's death had not provoked a suitable condolence motion in the Congress, Nirālā observed. Nirālā's obsessive engagement with Tagore's success and with Bengali critics of Hindi had partly to do with his familiarity with Bengal, and partly with the deference and respect national and Hindi leaders showed towards Bengali literature, a deference that, according to Nirālā, smacked of partiality and resulted from ignorance of Hindi writers' worth.

[159] Nirālā, 'Paṇḍit javāharlāl', p. 439.

[160] On another occasion, at the Delhi Sammelan meeting of 1924, Nirālā, scheduled to recite some of his blank verse, was asked to vacate his 'best seat' (*sabse baṛhiyā kursī*) at the front when the maharaja of Baroda came in for a while. Nirālā vacated the chair. The president, Ayodhyāsiṃh Upādhyāy, stood up 'showing devotion with great humility—his turban folded and his belly and hands outstretched'. At the president's request, Babu P.D. Ṭaṇḍon said a few words in praise of the Maharaja. *Nirālā rachnāvalī*, vol. 6, p. 209.

[161] See D.V.J. Bell, *Power, Influence and Authority*, London, Oxford University Press, 1975.

[162] 'Gāndhījī se bātchīt' and 'Nehrūjī se do bāteṁ', first published in the collection *Prabandha-pratimā* (1940), collected in *Nirālā rachnāvalī*, vol. 6, pp. 224–31 and 231–5. To reach Gandhi's place of stay in Lucknow in 1936 was itself an effort:

conversation which left all others present aghast, Nirālā challenged Gandhi's stance on language and the authority he commanded in the Hindi literary sphere despite his avowed ignorance of Hindi literature. He criticized Gandhi for caring only for 'leadership' (*netṛtva*) and overlooking the natural process by which Hindi and Hindi literature were becoming broad-based and syncretistic in an original, spontaneous way. He also lamented Gandhi's reliance on 'Hindi experts' whose main claim to authority was their very proximity to Gandhi and Tagore. When Nirālā asked him for half an hour in which to recite a few Hindi poems and demonstrate the achievements of contemporary Hindi literature, Gandhi predictably refused for lack of time.[163] That the president of the Hindī Sāhitya Sammelan should not have half an hour to listen to a major Hindi poet only proved Nirālā's point.

Nirālā was very much aware of how such superciliousness towards Hindi writing on the part of respected political leaders harmed the authority of contemporary Hindi writers. He complained about it in several articles, and directly to Nehru at the time of a chance meeting on a train. If only great men like Nehru were to write in Hindi, Nirālā told him, Hindi would greatly profit.

> Hindi writers are common people, fending off the blows of life with one hand while trying to write with the other. Besides, when they write they see great men like you working against them. . . . Thus the people (jantā) consider you, their champions (*pakṣadhar*), their true literary representatives and disregard someone who has been struggling for twenty years in the Hindi literary field. When I started to write I had to face a lot of opposition; now that I am somewhat established, after having fought my opponents and created literature, I find you opposing me in other ways.[164]

In the public and nationalist discourse writers were called to a high task: they were the vanguard of the nation, its critical and imaginative conscience.[165] Nirālā, like most other Hindi writers, fully identified with this role and believed that contemporary Hindi literature had been quite successful in the task. Nirālā himself was acknowledged to have brought about a revolution in Hindi poetry, breaking old conventions in form and

---

finally, while standing on the bridge over the Gomti river, Nirālā saw a goat being carried on a tonga and guessed that it must be Gandhi's goat! Following it, he found where Gandhi was. Ibid., p. 227.

[163] Nirālā, 'Gandhījī se bātchīt', pp. 229–30.

[164] Nirālā, 'Nehrūjī se do bāteṁ', p. 234.

[165] See e.g. V.N. Tivārī, 'Sāhitya aur rāṣṭrīytā', *Sammelan Patrikā*, V, 8–9, 1918; Lakṣhmīdhar Vājpeyī, 'Rāṣṭra ko kaise sāhitya kī āvaśyaktā hai?', *Mādhurī*, X, pt. 1, 1, August 1931; and the editorial 'Rāṣṭra aur sāhitya', *Chāṁd*, XVII, pt. 1, 5, October 1939.

content. Such originality was itself, according to Nirālā, a nationalist achievement, and in this Hindi 'literature was far ahead of politics'; while politicians were constrained by wordly and tactical considerations, literary people moved ahead, breaking new ground not just for themselves but for their readers, too. Instead, when political leaders urged writers not to be courtly, dependent intellectuals anymore, they actually behaved exactly like courtly patrons dispensing patronage and asking for allegiance and deference in return.

It is partly in the context of this avowed role and the dignity of the intellectual that we should understand Nirālā's frustration, particularly at the time when Hindi writers were called, thanks to Hindi rāṣṭrabhāṣā, to new, wider audiences and to an even higher role as 'national writers'. Like most Hindi intellectuals, Nirālā was not prepared to consider even the possibility of English performing such a cultural role: English *had* to be wiped out for any cultural regeneration to take place.

Nirālā's frustration had partly to do with a crisis of authority that was internal to the literary sphere. We have already discussed how critical debates over the nature and function of literature (2.2) and over the nature of criticism itself (2.3) revealed a loss of certainties about the role and rules of literature and a crisis in intellectual authority. These debates were closely related to institutional changes in the literary sphere, a process not too unlike that which had taken place in England in the late nineteenth century. In England, debates over the role of criticism had mirrored a conflict between the originality of the Victorian 'universal man', and of the aesthetic critic, on one side, and the 'rise of the expert' on the other. This was also a contest between individual authority and the authority vested exclusively in the community of experts; and between a common (public) terrain and the specialist, esoteric enclosure of academia.[166] In Hindi, too, the growth of a literary market and a literary public fostered the emergence of independent writers, whose authority

[166] 'Debates about criticism were part of, and were indeed partly caused by, much larger upheavals in British intellectual life. These upheavals were felt in three ways. First . . . in changes in the models of "man", which in many disciplines of knowledge, particularly those in the newly emergent social sciences, were used to underwrite the explanations and the practices. Second, they were felt in *the crisis of intellectual authority* which affected all disciplines of knowledge and which thus profoundly altered the value of particular critical statements. The third . . . was the fact that, along with many other disciplines, criticism became *institutionalized within the universities*: indeed . . . one of the main ends of university reform in the last half of the nineteenth century was to accommodate the growing diversity of intellectual enquiry. More important, along with the process of institutionalization went the companion

stemmed from their creative achievements and their public voice. At the same time, criticism was becoming institutionalized within universities and literary scholars were turning into a professional establishment of university professors. It is common to all nascent professions to try and delimit a particular practice and lay exclusive claim to it: professional knowledge has to be proved valuable and restricted to the 'professionals'.[167] Thus, while writers trod experimental paths, nascent critics attempted to identify and foster particular values considered peculiar to Indian literature (the Romantic idea of the literature of the *Volk*) or useful for the needs of the times. As a result, a crisis ensued between the authority of the independent writer and that vested in the community of scholars, specialists who had the power to decide over the canon.

It was against this institutional authority that Nirālā reacted when he complained about the literary taste of the curriculum and the opposition he had to face from academics.[168] His contacts with the newly born Hindi departments were strained, and his interactions were primarily either with students or *privately* with a few lecturers. However, what Nirālā thirsted for was *public* recognition in the seats of literary authority, and he found that hard to obtain. Over several articles and editorials in the monthly *Sudhā*, he took issue with the authority of professional critics in universities and colleges and with that of the jantā, the people, and the uncriticized popularity of bestsellers. As an iconoclast, he had to challenge the categories invoked as 'natural' by those authorities in order to subvert the consensus of opinion which derived from such categories; in

---

process of professionalization;' Ian Small, *Conditions for Criticism, Authority, Knowledge and Literature in the Late Nineteenth Century*, Oxford, Clarendon Press, 1991, pp. 19–20, emphases added.

[167] By comparison, the process by which professions in Europe sought to acquire status by entering the university as new subjects (and English was one of them) included: '(a) a high degree of generalized and systematic knowledge; (b) primary orientation to the community interest rather than to individual self-interest; (c) a high degree of self-control of behaviour through codes of ethics internalized in the process of work socialization and through voluntary associations organized and operated by work specialists themselves; (d) and a system of rewards (monetary and honorary) that is primarily a set of symbols of work achievement and thus ends in themselves, not means to some other end of individual self-interests;' ibid., pp. 23–4; see also p. 135.

[168] For strong criticism on Chāyāvād, especially from Rāmchandra Śukla, the most influential and respected Hindi critic, see 2.2 here; for the often personal and virulent attacks on Nirālā, see Rāmvilās Śarmā, *Nirālā kī sāhitya sādhnā*, vol. 1. Nirālā resented the fact that Sammelan authorities, so eager to guide students, did not introduce them to the most modern and living literature; *Nirālā rachnāvalī*, vol. 6, p. 211.

the process, he discussed the sources of their authority.[169] Against them he reaffirmed the authority of the original writer.

On the one hand, Nirālā argued against a literal and narrow understanding of 'utility':[170] while new, experimental literature could not be immediately popular with the common readership, it was nonetheless useful in that it refined their tastes and beliefs.[171] True literature eventually 'showed its strength' and stood the test of time; thus writers did move towards the people, but following their own, original paths. On the other hand, at this point in modern Hindi literature, common readers did not take favourably to new writers because they were unprepared and because the literary prachāraks (propagandists), whose duty it was to prepare the ground, were in fact narrow-minded, conservative, and hostile. As a result, common readers were not alerted to writers making the most original contributions. While acknowledging the power of professional critics, Nirālā criticized their attitude:

> The literary horizon of Hindi is very small and most college lecturers do not teach students to fly in the open sky of literature. They want to see them sit in the same nest of literature in which they sit themselves. . . . Most teachers have conservative tastes (*purānī lakīr ke fakīr*), and the few who are new do not favour the new culture. Not everything is bad in the new civilisation, you know; there are many qualities as well. There is a peculiar sparkle in its refinement which makes man's soul as pure as a flower cleansed by a winter morning. But our teachers are unaware of it. This is why their students have their minds stuffed with the same old narrowness. They do not enter the Hindi literary field with lofty literary intentions or with a great new and original talent. They remain confined to visiting the same old koṭhās of nāyikā-bhed and alaṃkāras.[172]

[169] See Bell, *Power, Influence and Authority*.

[170] 'In every literature there are people who consider gross utilitarianism to be the peak (*utkarṣ*) of literature. They say that literature proves to be genuine (*kharā*), useful and valuable as far as its strength lies in the interest of the people (jantā)'. Rather than pitching 'aestheticism' (*saundaryavād*) against 'utilitarianism' (*upyogitāvād*), Nirālā suggested a picture of literature as a tree with many branches. Moreover, one should not confuse *prachalan* (custom) with truth; also, for a writer *prachār* (diffusion) of tastes and beliefs among the people came at a second stage and required considerable effort. Nirālā, 'Sāhitya aur jantā', editorial in *Sudhā*, June 1933; in *Nirālā rachnāvalī*, vol. 6, pp. 501–2.

[171] For the lack of educated readers in Hindi, see Nirālā, 'Sāhitya tathā hamāre lekhakoṁ kā saṅkaṭ', editorial in *Sudhā*, September 1934, reprinted ibid., pp. 468–9.

[172] Nirālā, 'Sāhitya kī vartmān pragati', editorial in *Sudhā*, June 1930; in *Nirālā rachnāvalī*, vol. 5, pp. 460–1. In lamenting the absence of serious literary criticism in Hindi, Nirālā argued along similar lines, and added that 'one feels like tearing

The indictment reveals a competing notion of literature, and is also a cry against marginalization by academia. Although Nirālā's protest was personal, it upheld the authority of the Hindi literary mahāpuruṣa, that humble 'servant of literature' who took the more tortuous, original and problematic way—the way of 'knowledge of reality', of study, action and tapasyā.

5.4.3. Authority in the Hindi Public Sphere

What do these controversies tell us about the crisis of authority in the Hindi public sphere? The absence of both an explicit and direct debate on 'authority' and a direct Hindi equivalent of the word does not imply that the concept itself was absent. Discussions in Hindi groped with an array of existing words and concepts in Indian political culture. Just as sārvajanik did not cover the range and depth of the concept of 'public', the term *adhikār* alone did not express the conflict and crisis of authority. One would have to explore related terms and concepts—such as *pratiṣṭhā* or *prabhāv* (influence)—and how they were subjected to tensions as new sources and forms of authority emerged in the public sphere, something I can only hint at here.

To give one instance, it is useful to keep in mind the various strands of the concept of sarkār, used to indicate the impersonal state, the government in power, and also as an appellation for any person in power. The adjective sarkārī had also the meaning of 'public' in the sense of 'related to the state': a government job is sarkārī naukrī. Particularly when spoken by peasants or generally subordinate classes, the word sarkār demonstrated the overlap of impersonal power and personal power for them, be it in relation to the zamindar, tahsildar, police officer, judge or any educated interlocutor. 'Sarkār' immediately established a personal relation of subordination. Other terms would be svāmī or mālik (lord), which had other overtones, since they are the terms used for God as well. Similarly, *bharosā* (faith, reliance) applied both to God and to subordination to, and protection by, a wordly authority (for bharosā in national leaders see above 5.2.) As Premchand's characters (e.g. Horī in *Godān*) show, the appellation implied an entreaty: Horī never fails to call the zamindar thus, so as to ingratiate him and to request his benevolence and sympathy. Hence, what to the zamindar appeared as a spontaneous (and natural) manifestation of loyalty—along the paternalistic lines of rājā-prajā (king and subject)—was also an attempt to request protection

---

contemporary Hindi criticism to pieces: it is so gross, so lifeless, so far from the human mind'; 'Hindī meṁ ālocnā', *Sudhā*, July 1993; quoted ibid., p. 506.

and reciprocity. It acknowledged that the power of the person above was capricious, that the subordinate had no 'rights' to stand by, and that deference was the best way to make sure that the caprice would turn in one's favour. In educated discourse, sarkār applied both to the impersonal state and to the legally limited government.

Debates in Hindi on Indian political culture centred on the cluster 'rājā–prajā', whether to argue about the existence of contractual or limited sovereignty in ancient India, about mutual relations between rulers and subjects, or about the rights of citizenship and democracy (the 'rule of the prajā', 'prajātantra').[173] Thus zamindars, taluqdars, and conservative intellectuals and politicians emphasised the paternalistic, benevolent aspect of this mutual relationship, while radical intellectuals and politicians underlined the contractual and consensual meaning. According to them, the relationship of sovereignty and subordination existed only as long as the rājā worked for the 'welfare of the people' (*prajā-iṣṭa*): final authority and legitimacy had always rested with the prajā, and they had the right to withhold obedience if the rājā did not perform his duty. Along similar lines one writer, for example, argued that Parliament, the Imperial Council, and the Legislative Council cannot be called public (sārvajanik) institutions precisely because they do not serve the welfare of the public: 'In their decisions they appear to want to harm (*aniṣṭa*) the prajā all the time'. Modern rulers for their part, were 'blinded by the pride of authority (*adhikār-garva*)', by 'greed for fame' (*yaśololuptā*), and by personal enmity.[174]

Authority, in the sense of 'influence' (*pratiṣṭhā, prabhāv*) usually indicated clout and prestige over a limited group of people and in a local arena—be it a jāti, a samāj, a mohallā, or a town. It was connected to status and was used for traditional landed or moneyed elites, 'baṛe vyakti'. As such, it did not enter theoretical political discourse. But did it disappear?

In nationalist political debates in Hindi, patronage and relationships of deference were devalued in favour of an impersonal notion of power and an alternative source of authority in the 'public'. Already, according

[173] E.g. Mālavīya, 'Rāj-dharma', *Abhyuday*, 1908, in P. Mālavīya, *Mālavīyajī ke lekh,* pp. 162-68; 'Indra', 'Prāchīn bhārat meṁ rājnītik svādhīntā', *Mādhurī,* IV, pt. 2, 2, February 1926, pp. 180–6.

[174] Śukdevsiṃh, 'Sārvajanik saṃsthāoṁ kī duravasthā', *Mādhurī*, II, pt. 1, 3, October 1923, p. 264. See also Rāy Bajraṅgbahādur Siṃh, MLC, the taluqdar of Bhadri, 'Talluqedāroṁ kā savāl', *Sarasvatī, Kaṅgres ministrī viśeṣāṅk*, November 1937.

to the moderate reformism of Mahāvīr Prasād Dvivedī, 'good' rulers and administrators were only those who actively served the people and displayed a measure of tyāg (self-sacrifice). Later, one of the cornerstones of Gandhian politics would be to challenge, discredit, and ridicule British authority and to uphold that of the jantā through symbolic reversals of values. A similar shift took place, as we have seen, with the idea of literature as 'service' (2.2). Literary, but especially political activism, sevā, tyāg and achievements thus produced a new kind of personal authority which might enhance social status (as in the case of Motilal Nehru) but was not necessarily connected to it. The majority of Hindi leaders who emerged from the Non-Cooperation and Civil Disobedience movements came from ordinary backgrounds: their authority stemmed from their activities, and wearing khadi, leading a simple, austere life, and being accessible to all became seals of legitimacy (cf. 5.1 and 5.3). They represented an inversion of some traditional marks of aristocratic authority (conspicuous consumption and restricted accessibility) and, at least in the eyes of Hindi intellectuals, marked the Congress mahāpuruṣa, as a 'man of the people'. This kind of authority involved not only a style of living, as we have said, but also an unassuming and approachable attitude. In so far as they embodied this alternative authority, nationalist mahāpuruṣas could be considered the vanguards of the svarājya yet to come.

In the literary field, the discourse and activities connected to the idea of 'the public' engendered a notion of independence and of direct commitment to the people. Writers subscribing to it would keep away from occasions where they might be asked to adhere to customary deference to patrons.[175] In writing, breaking literary conventions became a way of asserting the personal authority of the writer and the individual right to create.

However, parallel to the process of questioning authority and developing alternative sources, there was another 'constitutional' process of consolidation, which led to the formation of a literary establishment and, in the political domain, to the formation of a Congress sarkār. One result was that Congress mahāpuruṣas, whose authority originally stemmed from self-sacrifice and service, fell back into the customary practice of

[175] See Nirālā's experience at the court of Chattarpur, in 'Chatrapur meṁ tīn saptāh', *Sudhā,* July 1928, now in *Nirālā rachnāvalī*, vol. 6, pp. 87–8, and his strong remark that 'the time for Hindi literature has not yet come' when he witnessed deference to important people at the Delhi Sammelan meeting of 1924; *Nirālā rachnāvalī*, vol. 6, p. 209.

personal power. The simple style and tyāg were kept up at the level of appearance and ideology. As the case of the Sāhitya Sammelan showed, when Congress ministers graced public occasions, visited temples, or presided over community functions, they did so with the graciousness and superiority of patronizing sovereigns. When they were not in power, that attitude had seemed a subversive move to infuse such events with nationalist overtones, but now that they were in power it became just a matter of sovereignty and of mutual legitimation.

Nirālā and other Hindi intellectuals noticed all this and wondered. Not only did their own authority as literary figures and mediators of public opinion seem to be curbed and denied, but so did the expectation of a sharing, participatory nationalist authority. The Congress commitment and closeness to the people seemed to have been lost. 'Congress tyranny (*netāśāhī*)' is the term Devīdatt Śukla, the editor of *Sarasvatī,* used in 1939. Similarly, the Congress government in UP was accused of 'overlooking the opinion of the majority' on the issue of Hindi and Hindustani: 'But when did the Congress patriots (deśbhaktas) ever pay attention to the people (jantā)?,' was Śukla's wry comment.[176]

By the end of the 1930s, parts of the more institutionalised Hindi intelligentsia happily secured Congress patronage and some Hindi politicians reached important parliamentary positions. This process favoured reformist and normative tendencies in the literary sphere, affecting the balance of authority within it, the language policy, and the curriculum. Hindi politicians backed the authority of intellectuals entrenched in academic institutions. The potential of Hindi as a popular language, which the popular political press and the most original literary voices developed, was stifled and deprived of authority.

The Hindi political sphere as sketchily analysed in these pages presents several similarities with the literary sphere. Both underwent similar processes of *expansion* and *institutionalisation.* In the political sphere, quantitative expansion to further and lower groups in society involved qualitative changes as well: in language and rhetoric this meant popular idioms and symbols; in nationalist discourse it brought to the fore the critiques and agendas of the different subjects; and in political action it produced a special emphasis on non-constitutional spaces, activities and actors. At the same time, both in the literary and in the political spheres we find a kind of double-track: intellectuals and politicians created separate spaces in opposition and as alternatives to those

[176] Śukla, *Sampādak ke pacchīs varṣ*, p. 117.

of the colonial system, but also worked their way up gradually within the spaces provided by the system. In the first case, the emphasis was on 'breaking the chains', on giving voice to new subjects, and on forging new meaningful bonds. Writing itself was often considered a political act. In the second case the attitude to the public was rather to educate, enthuse, and guide it through responsible leadership, and Hindi became the symbol of Indian–Hindu nationalism and the language of a sub-elite culture. While English–Hindi bilingualism was discarded and delegitimised more radically in the literary sphere, in the political sphere bilingualism remained, at least in practice, the norm, especially in the constitutional arena and in the Congress at the national level. In the case of Hindi politicians, the contradiction between their pledge to Hindi and the practice of bilingualism was solved in a pragmatic way: Hindi was the language they used regionally, and the culturally loaded language, while they used English for national and international politics.

The literary and political spheres also display a similar pattern of exclusion of subordinate subjects. While it is true that urban intellectuals and politicians made space for the peasantry in their view of the public to a certain extent, and that peasants gained some access to the nationalist movement, it was hardly on an equal footing or with a readiness to listen as well as to speak to them. Moreover, the difficulty intellectuals and politicians had in accepting the social conflict that inevitably arose along with peasant activism mirrored on the practical level the widespread and strong resistance to accept internal conflict in debates and in the literary sphere.

As a result, the picture that emerges from the two decades is one of two opposite and concurrent trends: one is a tremendous expansion and the emergence of new, vocal subjects, a vibrant critical and creative urge, and a strong sense of political involvement and cultural responsibility on the part of intellectuals; the other is a cultural and political bottleneck, with a budding literary and political establishment laying exclusive claims to authority and discouraging criticism and dissent.

Afterword

The Hindi world we encountered at the beginning of this book was a heterogeneous one: Hindi as a language was unevenly spread over the geographical and social terrain, there were disparate literary and cultural traditions, and reformist activism and the commercial market were going opposite ways. By the end of the 1930s, we can see the contours of modern Hindi culture as we know it now. Standard Khari Boli Hindi was by then an established public language in civil society, a medium of literature, education, and politics; it was the language of a subordinate elite and of upward mobilization for vast social groups. It has remained so to this day. There are, in fact, many remarkable continuities between processes in the 1920s and 1930s and later developments in independent India, as well as some significant differences, all worth considering.

The decades between 1920 and 1940 were marked, as we have seen, by a dual process of expansion and institutionalization, in the literary as well as in the political sphere. Expansion is what gave these decades an exciting edge, with experimentation, new perspectives, vocal critiques, and the willingness to discuss every thing anew, *nae sire se*, as one would say in Hindi. At the same time, the fact that varied tastes and opinions shared the same space in the pages of journals and were seen as part of a continuum in Hindi literary history helped create a common, uniform saṃskāra, the saṃskāra of the Hindi-educated. It was in this period that the nationalization of religious, linguistic, and literary traditions that Vasudha Dalmia has traced back to the second half of the nineteenth century came to fruition.

The backbone of the now homogeneous Hindi saṃskāra was a Hindi nationalism whose contours and contents have remained remarkably stable in the last eighty years. According to this nationalist discourse, Indian culture, Bhārtīy saṃskṛti, is one, and it mirrors the equally harmonious and unified Hindu–Indian society. P.D. Ṭaṇḍon said in 1947, on the occasion of the first Hindī Sāhitya Sammelan meeting in independent

India: 'If you want to become national (rāṣṭrīy) you have to forsake all attraction (*moh*) to other useless ideas and groups and stand under the banner of one nation, one language, one script, one culture.'[1] As these words make clear, embracing nationalism in this form meant rejecting the plural character of Indian culture. Conflict is contemplated only as something coming from outside, and there is an extreme reluctance to accept and place value on ('useless') self-criticism, dissension, and diversity of any kind. Other constitutive parts of Hindi nationalism are, as we have seen, the historical saṃskāra, with its exclusion of Urdu and Indo-Persian culture as 'foreign', and an emphasis on purity which was expressed in the exclusion of popular and oral traditions, and in the 'normalization' of radical voices (e.g. Kabīr) and of 'vulgar' tastes like the courtly-erotic rīti poetry in Braj Bhasa.

In practice, this moral and normative bias has meant that the encouragement to produce and read Hindi literature has been regularly undercut by exclusions and warnings about what not to read and not to write. It has also created a different way of reading texts within the canon and other literary books: the former are sources of identity, they tell us the Truth about 'who we are', while the latter are read for pleasure: they may speak of the reality around us, but even if this contradicts the Truth, it cannot undermine it. Implied in Hindi nationalism is often, I have argued, a separation between the public idiom and rhetoric of self-representation and other spaces and idioms where different identities, common sense assumptions, tastes, and practices concerning oneself and others can be expressed. As a result, one finds in Hindi an ostensibly secular nationalist self-representation coexisting easily with what Alok Rai has termed 'communal common sense' which, taken in a broad sense, includes assumptions about castes, religious communities, and all sorts of 'Others'. It has also produced remarkable rhetorical strategies, for example in political discourse, in order to speak of entities for long unmentionable in public discourse, such as castes.

The potent efforts to homogenize Hindi and Hindu culture have been so successful in Hindi that even the memory of social, cultural, or historical difference and conflict has been erased in accounts of the nationalist movement and in literary history, and one has to dig into the pages of journals in dusty libraries and tap non-literary sources to unearth any traces of them. In fact, as we have seen, even in the decades between 1920 and 1940 there were many varied forces at work and some processes,

[1] Speech quoted by Narottam Nāgar, 'Svatantra bhārat aur hindī', *Haṃs*, XVIII, 3, December 1947, p. 240.

once set into motion, acquired their own dynamics. For instance, the same literary journals which propagated early varieties of Hindutva and 'Bhārtīy saṃskṛiti' also offered the opportunity for dissenting voices to articulate their claims. Women's journals, which spearheaded a reformed version of femininity, also allowed for emotionality and greater mobility to be expressed, and the nationalist front eventually made more room for them and opened more doors than could have been foreseen originally.

Undoubtedly, one of the reasons for the continuity and success of nationalist discourse in Hindi has been its institutional stranglehold over the transmission of officially recognized knowledge, in other words, over education. Here, the continuity in the syllabus, in the canon, and in the understanding of literary history in the past eighty years is indeed striking. No need for change was felt even after Independence, despite the different political and historical conditions. Marxist (Progressive) critics, too, who have been particularly prominent and active in Hindi ever since the 1940s, have merely enlarged the canon, changed a few stresses (notably on the radical Kabīr), but in broad terms have endorsed Rāmchandra Śukla's understanding *in toto*. This continuity in institutional practice has had some serious consequences. For example, whereas in the early twentieth century the conscious choice for a pure Hindi–Hindu pedigree took place in a contested arena, with Urdu and Indo-Persian culture still at hand, over the following generations the absence of Urdu and Persian from the curriculum has bred a genuine ignorance of Urdu and of the past that is available through Persian texts. The same has happened with oral traditions and morally 'suspect' literary genres, with the result that Hindi academic research has tended to reproduce and reconfirm the canon. All these threads need to be retrieved from the mesh of ignorance and moral bias, and need to be woven together afresh if we want not only a truer picture of north Indian literary culture, but a non-communal understanding of it as well. Finding institutional spaces for this knowledge will, of course, be crucial.

Another reason for the success of the Hindi saṃskāra despite its rigidity has been its role as a vehicle of upward mobilization. In the decades after Independence, lower social groups have sought to acquire it in order to rise socially and economically: proficiency in śuddh Hindi, the language of officialdom, has been an essential requirement for white-collar jobs and for participation in the public sphere. But whereas in the 1920s and 1930 any expansion of the Hindi public sphere to new groups involved them challenging the Hindi saṃskāra from their own respective positions, later opposition either became purely political or was expressed in the same neutral, abstract, and sanskritized language that, as we have seen, carried within itself cultural and social exclusions: the saṃskāra was so strong that it set the ground for its own critics. Rather than expansion, then, the process became one of co-optation and socialization into Hindi's middle-class culture. Thus, although systematically and rightly aggrieved about the predominance of English, Hindi has exercised its own hegemony. It has become, like the class that created it, a middle class culture, the culture of a subordinate but culturally self-satisfied middle class.

Appendix

Biographies

What follows is a series of short biographies of the main Hindi personalities mentioned in the course of the book. Information was collated from a variety of sources, all quoted in the Bibliography. The choice of names was partly dictated by the available information, and partly by the intention of giving as wide as possible a picture of the possible ways of being a 'Hindi intellectual' in this period. Accordingly, I have focused on family background, education, occupation and source of income, social and caste position, mobility and link with the land, literary saṃskāras in the family, participation in the literary sphere, political activism, bilingualism, and relationship with other Indian linguistic areas.

List of Biographies

'Bachchan', Harivaṃś Rāy
Bakhśī, Padumlāl Punnālāl
Baṛathvāl, Pītāmbardatt
Benīpurī, Rāmvṛkṣa
Bhārgava, Dulārelāl
Bhaṭṭ, Badrīnāth

Chaturvedī, Banārsīdās
Chaturvedī, Mākhanlāl
Chaturvedī, Śrīnārāyaṇ
Chauhān, Subhadrākumārī

Dās, Babu Śyāmsundar
Dev, Acharya Narendra
Dīn, Lala Bhagvān
Dvivedī, Mahāvīr Prasād

Gauṛ, Kṛṣṇadev Prasād
Gauṛ, Rāmdās

Goyal, Rāmeśvarī
Gupta, Maithilīśaraṇ
Gupta, Śivaprasād

'Harioudh', Ayodhyāsiṃh Upādhyāy

Jośī, Hemchandra and Ilāchandra

'Kauśik', Viśvambharnāth Śarmā
Kumār, Jainendra

Lakhanpāl, Chandrāvatī

Mālavīya, Kṛṣṇakānt
Mālavīya, Madan Mohan
Miśra, Śyāmbihārī and Śukdevbihārī

'Navīn', Bālkṛṣṇa Śarmā
Nehrū, Rāmeśvarī

'Nirālā', Sūryakānt Tripāṭhī

Ojhā, Dr Gaurīśaṅkar Hīrāchand

Pālīvāl, Śrīkṛṣṇadatt
Pāṇḍey, Rūpnārāyaṇ
Pant, Sumitrānandan
Parāṛkar, Bābūrāo Viṣṇu
Parivrājak, Svami Satyadev
Poddār, Hanumānprasād
Prasād, Jayśaṅkar
Prem, Dhanīrām
Premchand (Dhanpat Rāy)

'Ratnākar', Jagannāth Dās
Raykṛṣṇadās

Sahajānand Sarasvatī, Svami
Sahāy, Śivpūjan
Sahgal, Rāmrakh Siṃh
Sampūrṇānand
'Sanehī', Gayāprasād Śukla
Sāṅkṛtyāyan, Rāhul
Śarmā, Padmasiṃh
Śarmā, Rāmjīlāl
Śāstrī, Hariharnāth
Sītārām, Lala

Śraddhānand, Svami (Mahatma Munśīrām)
Śrīvāstava, G.P.
Śrīvāstava, Navjādiklāl
Śrīvāstava, Pratāp Nārāyaṇ
Śukla, Devīdatt
Śukla, Rāmchandra
Sundarlāl, Pandit

Ṭaṇḍon, Puruṣottam Dās
Tivārī, Veṅkateś Nārāyaṇ
Tripāṭhī, Rāmnareś

'Ugra', Pāṇḍey Bechan Śarmā

Vājpeyī, Ambikāprasād
Vājpeyī, Kiśorīdās
Varmā, Bhagavatīcharaṇ
Varmā, Dhīrendra
Varmā, Mahādevī
Varmā, Babu Rāmchandra
Varmā, Rāmkumār
Varmā, Vṛndāvanlāl
Vidyālaṃkār, Jaychandra
Vidyārthī, Gaṇeś Śaṅkar
Viyogī Hari

'Bachchan', Harivaṃś Rāy (1907–)

Birthplace: Mohallā Mutthiganj, Allahabad.

Education

Educated at the local Municipal school; High School examination in 1925; BA from Kayastha Pathshala and Allahabad University in 1929; dropped out of the MA course in English literature in 1930 to join Civil Disobedience. Enrolled again years later and awarded MA in 1939 (at 32) from BHU; BT from Teachers' Training College, Allahabad in 1939; Ph.D. from Cambridge University in 1954.

Occupation

Teacher, lecturer in English, Hindi officer; poet.

Career

Until 1934 worked irregularly for *Chāṁd, Bhaviṣya,* Abhyuday Press, Pioneer Press, Prayāg Mahilā Vidyāpīṭh, Allahabad Middle school and Agravāl

Vidyālay, where he taught Hindi between 1934 and 1938. First married in 1927 and widowed in 1936. Started writing poetry as a child and shot to fame in 1935 at kavi sammelans with the intoxicating poems of *Madhuśālā*, one of the few collections of Hindi Khari Boli poetry to be truly popular. From 1939 to 1952 he taught in the English department of Allahabad University. Remarried in 1942. After returning from Cambridge in 1955, he was first appointed Hindi producer at Akashvani Radio Centre in Allahabad, then appointed Hindi officer at the Ministry of External Affairs in Delhi in 1955 through his personal contacts with Jawaharlal Nehru. Took part as Indian representative in several international poetry meetings and official trips. Awarded Padmabhushan in 1976. Translated several Shakespeare plays.

Selected Works

Poetry: *Terā hār* (1932); Hindi translation of Omar Khayyam's *Rubaiyyat* (1935); *Madhuśālā* (1935); *Madhubālā* (1936); *Madhukalaś* (1937); *Niśā nimāntraṇ* (1938); *Ekānt saṅgīt* (1939). Autobiography: *Kyā bhūlūṁ kyā yād karūṁ* (4 vols).

Bakhśī, Padumlāl Pannālāl (1894–1971)

Birthplace: Khairagarh, a small town in princely Central India.

Education

Educated at the local Victoria school with Pandit Raviśaṅkar Śukla, who later became Chief Minister of the Central Provinces; failed Matriculation once and obtained a BA in 1922 from Allahabad University.

Occupation

Editor, teacher.

Career

In 1916 became a high school teacher in a town near Khairagarh and contributed occasionally to Hindi journals with articles and translations. His seriousness and wide readings attracted Mahāvīr Prasād Dvivedī, who chose young Bakhśī to replace him as editor of *Sarasvatī* in 1920, where he remained from 1920 to 1925 and again from 1927 to 1929. As his assistant Devīdatt Śukla recalled: 'After Dvivedī left we more or less stopped receiving articles, and we had to write two, three articles for each issue ourselves.' Bakhśī had to face strong opposition in the world of Hindi letters, though his translations and reviews were recognized as being a class of their own. Despite his efforts, Bakhśī resigned in 1925 and once again in 1929 and went back definitely to teaching English in Khairagarh and writing. In 1959 he became head of the Hindi department of Rajnandgaon college.

Selected Works
Essays: *Viśva-sāhitya* (1925).

Baṛathvāl, Pītāmbar Datt (1902–44)

Birthplace: Jaharkhel (Garhwal).

Education
First, traditional Sanskrit education at home, then in Hindi and English at Srinagar Government High School, and at Kalicharan High School and DAV college in Lucknow; BA, MA and LL.B. at BHU. The very first Hindi D.Litt. from BHU in 1934.

Occupation
Lecturer.

Career
A disciple of Śyāmsundar Dās, he worked for several years as director of the Nāgarī Prachāriṇī Sabhā University search for old Hindi manuscripts. First appointed to teach Hindi literature at BHU in 1931, in 1938 he became lecturer at Lucknow University, where he taught until his early death.

Selected Works
Criticism: *The Nirgun School of Hindi Poetry* (in English); *Gosvāmī Tulsīdās* (1925) and *Rūpak-rahasya* (1931) with Śyāmsundar Dās.

Benīpurī, Rāmvṛkṣa (or Rāmbṛkṣa) (1902–68)

Birthplace: Village Benīpur, district Muzaffarpur (Bihar).

Education
Left school in 1920 before taking Matriculation in order to join the Non-Cooperation Movement; passed Hindī Sāhitya Sammelan viśārad exam.

Occupation
Editor, political activist.

Career
Tulsī's *Mānas* awakened Benīpurī's interest in literature and poetry, and he entered the literary field through journalism. Edited many Hindi journals, amongst them several for children: *Taruṇ bhārat* (weekly, 1921), *Kisān mitra* (weekly, 1922), *Bālak* (monthly, 1926), *Yuvak* (monthly, organ of the Bihar Socialist Party, 1929), *Lok saṅgrah* (1934), *Yogī* (weekly, 1935), *Jantā* (Congress Socialist Party weekly, 1937), and *Chunnū-munnū* (monthly,

1950). He was a founding member of the Bihar Socialist Party (1929), and was at first critical of, but then active in, the Bihar Provincial Kisān Sabhā; he also took part in the 1930 and 1942 campaigns and went to jail. Very active in Hindi literary life in Bihar, he was among the founders of the Bihar Hindī Sāhitya Sammelan and its general secretary between 1946 and 1950; was also propaganda secretary of the All-India Hindī Sāhitya Sammelan in 1929. He edited Vidyāpati's poems, wrote a commentary on Biḥārīlāl's *Satsaī*, and a biography of Jay Prakash Narayan. Noted for his floral language and strong sentimentalism.

Selected Works

Sketches: *Patitoṁ ke deś meṁ* (1930–2), *Māṭīkī mūrateṁ* (1941–5). Short stories: *Çitā ke phūl* (1930–2), *Lāltārā* (1937–9), *Qaidī kī patnī* (1940), *Gehūṁ aur gulāb* (1948–50). Historical plays: *Ambapālī* (1941–5), *Sītākī māṁ* (1948–50).

Bhārgava, Dulārelāl (1895–1975)

Birthplace: Lucknow.

Background

Born in the Nawal Kishore family of publishers, originally from Sasni (Aligarh). His father Babu Pyārelāl was more devoted to Urdu and Persian, but Dulārelāl's first wife (who died in 1916) converted him to Hindi.

Education

Only up to Intermediate.

Occupation

Editor and publisher.

Career

In 1922, with the help of his uncle Biṣṇunārāyaṇ Bhārgava, he launched the literary monthly *Mādhurī,* which started a new era in Hindi literary journalism. Himself a poet in Braj Bhasa, with *Mādhurī* Bhārgava helped a Braj Bhasa resurgence; in 1927 he was awarded the first Dev Puraskār for his *Dulāre-dohāvalī* amidst strong controversies. An enterprising editor and publisher, he ventured out on his own with the monthly *Sudhā* and the publishing house Gaṅgā-Pustak-Mālā, devoted only to contemporary Hindi literary works. He published all the most distinguished Hindi writers of the period and gave them high rewards in cash while he kept the copyright. His star seems to have waned at the time of Independence.

Selected Works

Poetry: *Dulāre dohāvalī* (1927).

Bhaṭṭ, Badrīnāth (1891–1934)

Birthplace: Village Gokulpura (Agra district).

Background

Son of the famous Sanskrit and Hindi scholar and commentator Rāmeśvar Bhaṭṭ.

Education

Educated up to to BA.

Occupation

Editor, writer, university lecturer.

Career

Started working for the Indian Press, Allahabad, at Mahāvīr Prasād Dvivedī's behest, in 1916; he was chief editor of the children's journal *Bālsakhā* (1917–19) and contributed regularly to *Sarasvatī*, where he wrote in favour of svacchand poetry in Hindi as early as 1913. Also contributed to a famous humour column in the newspaper *Pratāp* called *Golmālkāriṇī sabhā*. He became the first Hindi lecturer at Lucknow University. Married outside his caste in 1921. Wrote only in Khari Boli, mostly humorous and historical plays.

Selected Works

Plays: *Chuṅgī kī ummīdvārī* (1919), *Chandragupta nāṭak* (1920), *Tulsīdās nāṭak* (1922), *Durgāvatī* (1925), *Vivāh vijñāpan, Miss amerikan* (1929).

Chaturvedī, Banārsīdās (1892–1981)

Birthplace: Firozabad.

Background

Born in an Ārya Samāj family.

Education

Educated up to Intermediate at Agra college; literary education under the guidance of Braj Bhasa poet and scholar Satyanārāyaṇ Kaviratna.

Occupation

Editor.

Career

First started teaching Hindi at Farrukhabad in 1913, then from 1914 to 1920 taught at the Daly College for Indian princes in Indore (where he met Sampūrṇānand). Engaged over the issue of the 'pravāsī bhārtīy', the Indian indentured labourers, especially in Fiji, in 1924 he was sent to East Africa with an Indian National Congress delegation. As secretary of the literary branch of the Hindī Sāhitya Sammelan meeting in Indore in 1918, he met several important literary and political figures. Between 1920 and 1921 he was in Santiniketan with C.F. Andrews, and from 1921 to 1925 he taught at the Gujarat Vidyapith in Ahmedabad; in 1927 he was on the editorial board of *Āryamitra* (Agra) and *Abhyuday* (Allahabad), where he met M.P. Dvivedī, P.D. Ṭaṇḍon, Pandit Sundarlāl, and G.Ś. Vidyārthī. From 1927 to 1937 he edited the monthly *Viśāl bhārat* (Calcutta), the Hindi venture of Ramanand Chatterjee, the renowned editor of the *Modern Review* and the Bengali *Prabasi*. *Viśāl bhārat* became famous for its virulent public campaigns, e.g. against Ugra's *Cakleṭ* and 'obscene literature' (ghāsleṭ sāhitya) and against Nirālā's abstruse style. In 1937 he retired to Tikamgarh (MP), where he directed a local literary institution financed by the local raja and edited the monthly *Madhukar* (1940–52). Nominated member of the Rajya Sabha after Independence (1952–64), his house in Delhi became a centre for Hindi literary people. Thanks to his contacts with Tagore and Gandhi he wielded a certain authority in the Hindi literary world. Known as a prolific correspondent.

Selected Works

Biographies: *Satyanārāyaṇ kaviratna* (1906); *Bhāratbhakta Enḍrūz* (1922). Political and Literary Essays: *Pravāsī bhāratvāsī* (1918); *Rāṣṭrabhāṣā* (1919); *Hṛdaytaraṅg* (1920); *Fijī kī samasyā* (1927).

Chaturvedī, Mākhanlāl (1889–1968)

Birthplace: Village Bavai (dist. Hoshangabad, C.P.).

Background

Born in a poor family of Radhavallabhan affiliation.

Education

Primary education in the village along with Sanskrit at home; Middle examination in 1903 and Normal school examination (for vernacular teachers) in 1904; taught himself English in 1906.

Occupation

Editor.

Career

First appointed teacher at Khandwa Middle School at a salary of Rs 8 per month in 1904, he started editing *Prabhā* (1913, monthly) and writing nationalist poetry under the pen-name 'An Indian Soul', 'Ek bhārtīy ātmā'. He left teaching to join the terrorist movement and became a supporter of Tilak. In Kanpur came in contact with G.Ś. Vidyārthī, met Gandhi in 1917 and resolved to dedicate his life to the welfare of the country. In 1919 he was sent to Jabalpur, where he edited the monthly *Karmavīr* with Mādhavrāo Sapre, Viṣṇudatt Śukla, and Lakṣhmaṇ Siṃh Chauhān. He organized a Provincial Political Assembly in Khandwa and took part in the Nagpur flag satyagraha in 1923, and when Vidyārthī was jailed in 1924 he went to Kanpur to edit *Pratāp*; he was arrested in May 1925 for the first time. In 1926 he was elected to the Legislative Council on a Congress ticket from Mahakoshal. Active in the Madhya Pradesh Hindī Sāhitya Sammelan, he presided over the 1943 All-India Hindī Sāhitya Sammelan. In 1967 he returned the Padmabhushan honour when the Government of India postponed the term by which Hindi was to become the only national language.

Selected Works

Play: *Kṛṣṇārjun yuddh* (1918); Poetry: *Himkirīṭinī* (1941); *Sāhitya devtā* (1941); *Himtaraṅginī* (1949); *Mātā* (1952).

Chaturvedī, Śrīnārāyaṇ (1893–1990)

Birthplace: A village in Etawa district.

Background

Chaturvedī's family, of Ramanuja Vaiṣṇava affiliation, had settled in Etawa district. His grandfather was Sanskrit pandit at the first high school in Etawa, founded after 1857 by A.O. Hume. His father, Chaturvedī Pandit Dvārkāprasād Śarmā, moved to Allahabad in 1892 because of his government job and settled in the same Ahalyapur mohallā where Bālkṛṣṇa Bhaṭṭ, M.M. Mālavīya and, later, P.D. Ṭaṇḍon also lived. After writing two biographies of Robert Clive and Warren Hastings in Hindi, his father was dismissed from government service and survived on his writing.

Education

Educated first at a local pāṭhśālā, where Pandit Sundarlāl was his teacher, then at the Government High School, where Amarnāth Jhā was his school-mate. After the Matriculation exam he enrolled at Ewing Christian College, where he moved from Science to Arts. After some hesitation he then joined the Teachers' Training College in Allahabad, where Mackenzie was principal; later sent by the UP government to London for higher studies in psychology and pedagogy.

Occupation

Civil servant.

Career

After a first stint as a teacher and the Training College, he was appointed to teach in a government school, but joined the Kanyakubja High School in Lucknow instead, and turned it into an Intermediate College. After his sojourn in London he travelled around Europe, America and Japan, and returned in 1928. Appointed Inspector of Schools of Faizabad and Gorakhpur division, he became a highly placed education officer administering a large area of eastern UP. During the provincial Congress ministry he was appointed Education Expansion Officer by Sampūrṇānand. Actively defended and supported the use of Hindi in the education department and in the radio; in 1940 he even launched a journal to this aim, *Ākāśvāṇī*. One of the leaders of the pro-Hindi group in the Hindi–Hindustani controversy, he was also a brilliant cultural organizer and was instrumental in starting kavi sammelans for Hindi propaganda. Entertained excellent relations with the Indian Press, which published all his books, and after his retirement he became the very last editor of *Sarasvatī* (1955–79). His houses in Daryaganj and in Lucknow were meeting places for Hindi literary people and were known as the darbār. He wrote poetry under the pen-name 'Śrīvar'.

Selected Works

Poetry: *Choñch mahākāvya* (1917); Education: *A History of Rural Education in India* (1930); *An Educational Survey of A District* (1935); *Śikṣā vidhān paricay* (1935); Biography: *Samrāṭ pañcham jārj* (1936); Memoirs: *Manorañjak saṃsmaraṇ* (1965).

Chauhān, Subhadrākumārī (1904–48)

Birthplace: A village near Allahabad.

Family

Born in an educated but not affluent orthodox Rajput family which practised pardā.

Education

Educated at Crosthwaite college until Middle examination in 1919; she then joined Annie Besant's Theosophical School in Benares but dropped out in 1921 for the Non-Cooperation movement. In 1920 she passed the Hindī Sāhitya Sammelan prathamā examination.

Occupation

Poet, political activist.

Career

Started writing poetry at the age of six, continued throughout her education and political involvement and was published in the major Hindi journals; her poem 'Jhānsī kī rānī' was one of the most famous poems of the whole nationalist movement. In the year of her Middle school examination, she was married to Lakṣhmaṇ Siṃh Chauhān, who later became a Congress activist and editor, and moved with him to Jabalpur. She was involved in Congress propaganda among women both in the town and in the district, and was one of the few middle class women who did not observe pardā. First arrested during the flag satyagraha in 1923, she was jailed again in 1941 for individual satyagraha. A mother of four, she did not observe chuāchūt and was known for her simple, straightforward manners; her style was equally simple, and she wrote a lot for children, too. Elected member of the Legislative Assembly in 1936. Twice awarded the Seksāriyā prize.

Selected Works

Poetry: *Mukul* (1930), *Bikhre motī* (1932); *Trīdhārā, Sabhā kā khel;* Short Stories: *Unmādinī* (1934) and *Sīdhe-sādhe* (1946).

Dās, Babu Śyāmsundar (1875–1945)

Birthplace: Benares.

Background

Born in a Khatri family; his father was a small cloth merchant who had moved from Amritsar; at his death the burden of the family and of business debts fell on young Śyāmsundar, who 'never lived in a house he owned'.

Education

Received first a traditional guru education, then studied English at the local Hanuman seminary; after passing the Anglo-Vernacular Middle examination in 1890, he enrolled at Queen's Collegiate School, where he passed the Entrance examination in 1892; BA degree in 1897. Refused an offer to enrol for an MA and tried unsuccessfully to enrol in the new Teachers' Training College in Lucknow.

Occupation

Teacher, cultural activist, literary scholar.

Career

After a brief spell at a local press, he became at first Assistant Master, then Assistant Headmaster, at Besant's Central Hindu School in Benares, at a monthly salary of Rs 40. In 1909 he left to work for the State Office of the Maharaja of Kashmir, but returned to Benares in 1912. From 1912 to 1921 he was Headmaster at Kalicharan High School in Lucknow, but after successfully fighting back attempts to turn it into a 'national school' during the Non-Cooperation movement, he resigned. In 1922 he was appointed Head of the newly formed Hindi department at BHU, where he set up the syllabus with Rāmchandra Śukla. One of the founding members of the Nāgarī Prachāriṇī Sabhā (1893), most of his life and activity was devoted to setting up and managing the manifold enterprises of the association: he was chief editor of the monumental dictionary *Hindī śabdasāgar* (1908–29), which employed altogether seventeen people; he was involved in the campaign for the official recognition of Hindi, in Hindi propaganda, in the search for Hindi manuscripts and in all the publication series. He also wrote several textbooks, readers, and manuals for the whole span of the school curriculum. He was on excellent terms with the Indian Press in Allahabad and for some time had all the Sabhā books published there.

Selected Works

Literary criticism: *Sāhityālochan* (1922); *Gadya kusumāvalī* (1925); *Rūparahasya* (1926); *Bhāṣā-rahasya* (1935); Autobiography: *Merī ātmakahānī* (1957).

Dev, Acharya Narendra (1889–1956)

Birthplace: Faizabad.

Background

Born in a wealthy and cultured zamindar family of Faizabad which cherished both Persian and Sanskrit, had received English education for three generations and had branched out in law. His father was active in public life and wrote textbooks in English, Hindi, and Persian as a hobby; the family library was open to the public.

Education

At first educated privately at home, he read Tulsīdās and other Hindi authors before going to school in 1902; he matriculated in 1906 in Allahabad and lived in Mālavīya's Hindu Boarding House with Pandit Sundarlāl at the time of the Swadeshi agitation. After his BA he did an MA in archaeology and ancient history at Benares Queen's College (1913), where he studied Pali, Prakrit, and epigraphy. LLB in 1915.

Occupation
Political activist, educator.

Career
Narendra Dev was attracted to extremist politics (the '*garam dal*') and to the educational ideas of Lala Hardayal and Sri Aurobindo while in Allahabad. Attended all Congress sessions between 1905 and 1908, and rejoined only in 1916. First politically active in Annie Besant's Home Rule league, of which he founded a branch in Faizabad (1915). He dropped his legal practice in 1920. Called to Benares Kāśī Vidyāpīṭh, he taught ancient Indian history, Indian philology, and modern Indian history there, and became first Vice-Chancellor and then Chancellor in 1926. Active during the Non-Cooperation movement in Faizabad in the last phase of the Avadh peasant movement. Personally close to Jawaharlal Nehru. A founding member of the Congress Socialist Party (1934), he was one of its chief leaders in UP. Elected to the Legislative Assembly in 1937, he was put in charge of a committee to reorganise education. Edited the socialist monthly *Saṅgharṣ* from Lucknow from 1939. Confined in 1939–40 during the individual satyagraha, he was arrested in 1942, when Kāśī Vidyāpīṭh was banned and students and professors dispersed in the countryside. After Independence, he became Vice-Chancellor of Lucknow University and BHU.

Selected Works
While in jail, he translated Poussin's French translation of the *Abhidhamma-kosa* into Hindi; his own *Bauddha-dharma-darśan* was published posthumously; Political Essays: *Samājvād kā bigul* (with others, 1940); *Socialism and the National Revolution* (1946).

Dīn, Lala Bhagvān (1876–1930)

Birthplace: Village Barvat, district Fatehpur.

Background
Born in a Kayastha family which had moved at the time of the 1857 rebellion from Raibareilly to Rampur, where they became the *bakhśī* (treasurer) of the local Nawab. His father was an ordinary clerk and was away from home on government errands most of the time.

Education
Educated initially in Urdu and Persian until he moved to Bundelkhand with his father after his mother's death in 1887; he attended a madrasa at Nargaon Cantonment and in 1893 he was admitted to the English school in Fatehpur, where he passed the Entrance examination in 1900. Thanks to a monthly

scholarship of Rs 8 from the provincial government he could enrol at Kayastha Pathshala, Allahabad, but had to leave after the First year examination.

Occupation

Teacher, literary scholar, poet.

Career

First employed as a teacher at the Kayastha Pathshala, then briefly as Persian teacher at the Zenana Mission Girls' High School before joining the State School in Chattarpur, where he taught until 1907. His Hindi saṃskāra came from his grandfather, who was a passionate devotee and read him Tulsīdās' *Rāmcharitmānas.* In Chattarpur he further developed his interest in Hindi literature and in Braj Bhasa poetry thanks to the local public library and learnt prosody from a local pandit; his Braj Bhasa poems were published in the journals *Rasikmitra* and *Raiskvaṭikā* and he himself edited a Braj Bhasa poetry journal from 1905. He learnt the Bundelkhandi language and loved wandering around its hilly regions. Thanks to Śyāmsundar Dās, he obtained a place as Persian master at the Central Hindu School in Benares, and worked as editor of old Hindi texts for the Nāgarī Prachāriṇī Sabhā and on the dictionary *Hindī śabdasāgar*. Around 1915 he started a Hindī Sāhitya Vidyālay to prepare students for the Hindī Sāhitya Sammelan examinations. In 1921 he joined BHU as Hindi lecturer, and taught chiefly rīti poets. Married thrice, the second time to the renowned poet Bundelābālā, and then to her younger sister. Wrote both in Khari Boli and in Braj Bhasa, and was especially skilled at samasyā-pūrtis. Considered one of the few able commentators of Keśavdās.

Selected Works

Poetry: *Vīr pañcaratna* (1918), *Navīn-bīn* (1926); Literary criticism: *Alaṃkārmañjuṣā* (1931), *Vyaṅgyārthamañjuṣā* (1927); ed., *Tulsī-granthāvalī* (1923) with R. Śukla and Brajratnadās; commentaries on *Rāmchandrikā, Kavipriyā, Rasikpriyā,* Tulsīdās' *Kavitāvalī* and *Bihārī satsaī.*

Dvivedī, Mahāvīr Prasād (1864–1938)

Birthplace: Village Daulatpur, district Rai Bareilly.

Background

His grandfather was a learned pandit who recited the Purāṇas to the Bengal army troops; his father was a soldier who took part in the 1857 rebellion and thereafter fled to Bombay, where he worked at the service of a Vallabha Gosvami.

Education

First educated at the village paṭhśālā; in 1877 enrolled at the District School in Bareilly to learn English: he had to take Persian as a subject since Sanskrit was not taught there. After moving to Bombay with his father he learnt Sanskrit, Gujarati, Marathi, Bengali, and English.

Occupation

Telegraph master, editor, literary scholar.

Career

In Bombay Dvivedī initially joined the railways as a clerk and was transferred to Nagpur and Ajmer. After passing an examination he became telegraph signaller, and after a series of transfers and promotions he became head clerk with the District Traffic Superintendent in Jhansi. Meantime he continued studying Sanskrit and old Hindi texts with scholars, and his reviews started being published. One such review of an Indian Press primer caught the attention of its publisher, Chintamani Ghosh, who asked Dvivedī to come and edit the monthly *Sarasvatī*. Dvivedī resigned from his job and joined the Indian Press, although he continued living in Juhi, a village near Kanpur. Under his editorship, the prestige and the importance of the journal grew immensely, and Dvivedī is credited with having formed and standardized modern Hindi prose. His collaboration with the Indian Press resulted in a long series of books and textbooks; in fact, he indirectly guided the Hindi literary policy of the Press as far as books and assistants were concerned, and he was ever grateful to the publisher, Chintamani Ghosh, for the respect he was given. For the Indian Press he translated Bhartṛhari, Kālidāsa, Jayadeva, Jagannātha, etc. into Hindi. His clear and stern views on language and literature earned him enormous prestige in the Hindi literary world, and to have been published in *Sarasvatī* became the seal of recognition. Dvivedī assembled a stable group of contributors, was at the centre of a large network of Hindi scholars and writers, and inspired many of the younger generation. Before he retired he chose his own successor, young P.P. Bakhśī, and also the editor who succeeded him, Devīdatt Śukla. After he retired in 1920, Dvivedī remained a highly respected figure. He moved back to his village, Daulatpur, where he looked after the family fields, opened a public library and an infirmary and served as head of the village panchayat until his death. He also edited his many articles into a number of books. At the XIII Hindī Sāhitya Sammelan meeting in Kanpur in 1923 he presided over the welcome committee, but he generally kept away from Hindi associations and was particularly critical of Śyāmsundar Dās, although he left his books to the Nāgarī Prachāriṇī Sabhā and endowed it with a prize. His last years in the village, without modern amenities, children, or family, were spent in hardship and failing health.

Selected Works

Hindī bhāṣā kī utpatti (1907); *Sampattiśāstra* (1907); *Hindī mahābhārata* (1908). Collections of articles: *Kālidās kī niraṅkuśtā* (1912); *Kālidās aur unkī kavitā* (1920); *Sukavi saṃkīrtan* (1924); *Sāhitya sandarbha* (1928), *Sāhitya sīkar* (1930).

Gauṛ, Kṛṣṇadev Prasād ('Beḍhab banārsī') (1895–1965)

Birthplace: Benares.

Background

His father was head clerk (*munsarim*) at the tribunal in Benares and contributed occasionally to English and Urdu newspapers.

Education

Educated first at Queen's College in Benares and then at Allahabad University, where he acquired an MA in English; he also obtained a Master's degree in political science from Agra University, a BT from BHU and passed the Hindī Sāhitya Sammelan uttamā examination with first class honours.

Occupation

Teacher, writer.

Career

He wrote the first articles while still at school, first in English and then in Hindi, and contributed to K.P. Jaiswal's weekly *Pāṭaliputra* (Patna). Later he wrote humorous articles and poems under the pen-name 'Beḍhab banārsī' and contributed humorous columns to several papers; in 1920 he edited the humorous weekly *Bhūt*, and in 1937 *Khudā kī rāh par*; both ended over personal quarrels despite popular success. In 1938 he launched *Taraṅg*, which also closed down due to financial difficulties. He taught English at DAV college in Benares for many years, was a member of Jayśaṅkar Prasād's circle and defended Chāyāvād poetry. From 1928 to 1930 he was literary secretary of the Hindī Sāhitya Sammelan, and from 1945 to 1948 general secretary of the Nāgarī Prachāriṇī Sabhā.

Selected Works

Poetry: *Beḍhab kī bahak* (1954?), *Kāvya kamal;* Short Stories: *Banārsī ekka* (1930), *Gāndhī kā bhūt, Ṭanāṭan.*

Gauṛ, Rāmdās (1889–1937)

Birthplace: Jaunpur.

Education

First in Benares and Allahabad; in 1903 BA from Muir Central College, Allahabad.

Occupation

Teacher, publicist.

Career

One of the the very few authors of scientific articles and books in Hindi, he taught chemistry in several institutions, including BHU, which he left because of the Non-Cooperation movement. Arrested in 1921, he was fined and sentenced to one year in prison. Later he headed the Science Department of Gurukul Kangri. He was also involved in Śivaprasād Gupta's Jnanmandal Press and instrumental in founding the Vijñān Pariṣad in Allahabad. He wrote in favour of women's education from the pages of *Gṛhalakṣhmī*, and wrote poetry under the pen-names 'Ras' and 'Raghupati'. At Śivaprasād Gupta's request he compiled a massive compendium of Hinduism, *Hindutva* (1938). Also prepared a good critical edition of the *Rāmcharitmānas.*

Selected Works

Philosophy: *Vaijñānik advaitavād* (1920); *Hindutva* (1938).

Goyal, Rāmeśvarī (1911–36)

Birthplace: Jhansi.

Background

Born in a nationalist family, the daughter of a railway officer and of the famous Congress activist and woman poet Pistādevī, who was herself the daughter of the principal of the DAV college in Dehradun.

Education

Studied at Indraprastha College in Delhi; BA from Crosthwaite College and Master's degree from Allahabad University.

Occupation

Poet, teacher.

Career

While still a student, her poems started appearing in *Sudhā* from around 1928, and she was greeted as a promising talent. Also edited the girls' journal *Sahelī* for a short while. She became principal of the Āryakanyā Pāṭhśālā in Allahabad and was also an active Congress campaigner. Married

Prakāśchandra Gupta in 1935. At her death there was a large public commemoration in Jhansi, and her sister in Benares opened a school in her name, which still exists.

Selected Works

Poetry: *Jīvan-svapna* (1937).

Gupta, Babu Maithilīśaraṇ (1886–1964)

Birthplace: Village Chirgaon, near Jhansi.

Background

Born in a merchant family with literary tastes.

Education

Educated at home in Sanskrit and Hindi, and at the local village school. Later taught himself Marathi and Bengali.

Occupation

Poet.

Career

Free from financial worries and the need to work, Gupta devoted himself to poetry: his first Khari Boli poems appeared in a Calcutta magazine, *Vaiśyopkārak,* and then in *Sarasvatī,* where under the guidance and inspiration of M.P. Dvivedī he wrote on historical and mythological themes and illustrated plates of Ravi Varma's paintings. His first long poem, *Raṅg meṁ bhaṅg* (1910) was followed by the great success of *Bhārat-bhārtī* (1912), which sealed his reputation as nationalist poet and as one of the most popular poets of the time. *Sāket*, a mahākāvya retelling the Rāmāyaṇa story, was equally popular and was awarded the Maṅgalāprasād prize in 1932. A friend of Rāykṛṣṇadās and Jayśaṅkar Prasād's, Gupta spent long periods in Benares and was a regular presence at Hindi literary gatherings. His fiftieth birthday was celebrated with the first ever public felicitation for a Hindi living poet in 1936. Hailed as *rāṣṭrakavi*, he became member of the Rajya Sabha in independent India. His brother Siyāśaraṇ Gupta was also a well-known writer.

Selected Works

Poetry: *Raṅg meṁ bhaṅg* (1910); *Bhārat-bhārtī* (1912); *Sāket* (1932); *Hindū* (1927); *Gurukul* (1929); *Dvāpar* (1936), *Jaybhārat* (1952), *Viṣṇupriyā*.

Gupta, Babu Śivaprasād (1883–1945)

Birthplace: Benares.

Background

Born in one of the three most established merchant families of Benares, the Śāh family of Raja Motīchand, originally from Azamgarh, hence the name of 'Azamagarh *gharānā*'; related to Bhagvān Dās.

Education

Studied for a BA at Allahabad University, but was prevented by illness from taking the examination.

Occupation

Philantropist, political activist.

Career

The foremost Congress patron in Benares, he was at the centre of several enterprises in the fields of education, literature, journalism, art, politics, etc. In 1914 he undertook a world tour (narrated in *Pṛthvī pradakṣiṇā*) which took him to Europe, America, Japan, China; on his way back to India in 1916 he was detained in Malaysia for anti-British activities and was released only through the intervention of his uncle Raja Motīchand, Benoy K. Sarkar, and M.M. Mālavīya. In 1917 he founded the publishing house Jnanmandal with a detailed plan to print books of scientific and historical interest in Hindi; the daily *Āj* and the nationalist college Kāśī Vidyāpīṭh (1920) followed, the former as a limited company, the latter as a trust under the pledge that it would never receive government aid. Śivaprasād Gupta was the main patron of Congress activities in Benares, and his generosity toward students, educational institutions, families of jailed Congressmen, Congress funds, revolutionaries, and literary people in need was discrete and unparalleled. A great patron of Hindi, he supported the introduction of Hindi in education and in public administration and always ready to provide nationalist-minded literary people with work; his private secretary was Paripūrṇānand, Sampūrṇānand's younger brother. In 1920 he became an active Congressman and, despite his sympathies for revolutionaries, a follower of Gandhi. During the following decade he was President of the Provincial Congress Committee, All India Congress treasurer, and President of the UP Kisan and Labour Conference (1927). Convicted thrice during Civil Disobedience, he suffered an attack of paralysis in jail. Erected the Bhārat Mātā temple with a huge marble outline of India in 1936.

Selected Works

Travelogue: *Pṛthvī-pradakṣinā* (1924)

'Harioudh', Pandit Ayodhyāsiṃh Upādhyāy (1865–1947)

Birthplace: Nizamabad, district Azamgarh.

Background

Family originally from Badayun, moved to Nizamabad in the fifteenth century, and lived on zamindari, Sanskrit scholarship and priestly duties.

Education

Vidyārambh at five, first at home in Sanskrit and from 1872 at the tahsil school in Nizamabad, where he studied Urdu and Persian. In 1879 he passed the Hindi Middle school examination. After a short spell at Queen's College in Benares to learn English, he passed the Normal school (vernacular teachers') examination in 1887 and the kanungo examination in 1889. Taught himself Bengali.

Occupation

Kanungo, poet, teacher.

Career

Appointed master at Nizamabad tahsil school in 1884 (he had married in 1882), he was noticed by the Education department officer and became a kanungo in 1889; over the years he rose from registrar kanungo to inspector kanungo, for fifteen years touring the neighbouring districts, and then eleven years in Azamgarh. Pensioned by the government in 1923, he was then appointed to teach in the Hindi department at BHU, apparently not too successfully, as Śyāmsundar Dās complained that he would teach only Hindu saṅgaṭhan or his own poetry. Finally he was moved to teach in the Girls' branch of the University (!). His literary education had started at home and then with a local scholar at Azamgarh, who subscribed to Bhārtendu's *Hariśchandra chandrikā* and *Kavivacansudhā*. A great friend of Babu Rāmdīn Siṃh of the Khadagvilas Press of Bankipur, 'Harioudh' was also in contact with George Grierson. He wrote both in Braj Bhasa and in Khari Boli and was often called to attend or preside over kavi sammelans. He was President of the XIV Hindī Sāhitya Sammelan meeting in Delhi in 1924. His long poem *Priyapravās* was widely appreciated and became the object of a controversy when it failed to win the Dev Puraskār in 1927, which went instead to Dulārelāl Bhārgava. His poems were published regularly in all the major Hindi journals. A fervent sanatan dharmi, he was given the title of 'Kavi-samrāṭ' by the Bhārat Dharma Mahāmaṇḍal in 1912.

Selected Works

Novels: *Ṭheṭh hindī kā ṭhāṭh* (1899), *Adhkhilā phul* (1907); Translations: *Rip van ṛinkal* and *The Merchant of Venice* as *Venis kā bāṃkā* (1928). Poetry: *Priyapravās* (1914), *Chokhe-chaupade* (1924) and *Chūbhte chaupade*. Edited *Kabīr-vachanāvalī* (1921) for Nāgarī Prachāriṇī Sabhā. Textbooks: *Bāl-pothī*

(5 vols), *Vernacular Reader* (4 vols), etc. Educational books: *Upadeś kusum, Nīti nibandh.*

Jośī, Hemchandra (1894–?) **and Ilāchandra** (1902–82)

Birthplace: Almora.

Background
Born in a cultured Kanyakubja Brahmin family originally from Jajmau (Kanpur), settled in Nainital; one ancestor had been chief minister to the Raja of Kumaon.

Education
After his MA, Hemchandra went to Europe for further study; he was awarded a D.Litt. from Paris University on economic and political thought in ancient India according to the Ṛgveda. Ilāchandra studied up to high school and taught himself French.

Occupation
Publicists and writers.

Career
Hemchandra acquired a remarkable collection foreign literary works, from which Ilāchandra got his literary education; the latter ran away to Calcutta after his high school. Both brothers were later instrumental in introducing contemporary world literature and literary trends into Hindi, and they acquired a certain reputation for their 'modern' and sophisticated tastes; Hemchandra sent reports and reviews from Europe to Hindi journals. Ilāchandra started writing poetry at an early age, and by the age of 16 he had published with the main Hindi nationalist journals. In 1919 he became a regular contributor of articles and short stories to *Prabhā*, and from 1927 onwards to *Sarasvatī* and *Sudhā.* In 1929 an article in English on 'Recent Hindi literature' published in the *Modern Review* caused a stir for its mordant criticism of contemporary Hindi literature before the English-speaking audience. Until 1936 Ilāchandra led a peripatetic life between Calcutta, Allahabad, and Lucknow; he worked for a while on the editorial board of *Chāṁd*, then became co-editor of *Sudhā* (1929); together with Hemchandra he edited the journals *Viśvavāṇī* (1930) and *Viśvamitra* (1931) in Calcutta. In Allahabad he aso edited *Saṅgam* and *Sāhityakār* for some time, before being offered in 1936 a job as radio producer. Hemchandra contributed to the *Vyutpatti koś* (Etymological Dictionary) of the Nāgarī Prachāriṇī Sabhā. Ilāchandra is credited with having introduced the psychological novel into Hindi, e.g. *Ghṛṇāmay* (1929), *Sanyāsī* (1940).

'Kauśik', Viśvambharnāth Śarmā (1891–1942)

Birthplace: Ambala Cantt., but originally Gangoh (district Saharanpur).

Background

Son of a military storekeeper, he was adopted by his uncle, a lawyer in Kanpur who acquired landed property outside the city.

Education

Educated in Persian and Urdu at school upto Matriculation, and at home in Hindi and Sanskrit.

Occupation

Writer.

Career

Initially wrote Urdu poetry, then shifted to Hindi around 1909 and published short stories in the Kanpur weekly *Jīvan* and a few essays in *Sarasvatī*. After meeting M.P. Dvivedī he was prompted to translate from Bengali and to write original stories; 'Rakṣābandhan' was his first story published in *Sarasvatī*. A prolific author, his short stories appeared regularly in all the major Hindi journals and in book form from Ganga Pustak Mala. Also wrote a life of Rasputin. His humorous column 'Ḍubejī kī chiṭṭhī' appeared in the monthly *Chāṁd*.

Selected Works

Short Stories: *Galp-mandir* (1919), *Chitraśālā* (1924), *Maṇimālā* (1929), *Kallol* (1933). Novels: *Mā* (1929), *Bhikhāriṇī* (1929). Misc.: *Saṃsār kī asabhya jātiyoṁ kī striyāṁ* (1924).

Kumār, Jainendra (1905–88)

Birthplace: Koriyaganj (district Aligarh).

Background

Having lost his father at a very early age, he was brought up by his mother and her brother, the renowned Mahatma Bhagvān Dīn, who had founded a Gurukul in Hastinapur in 1911 and was later involved in Congress activities in the Central Provinces.

Education

First at his uncle's Gurukul, where his name was changed from Ānandī Lāl to Jainendra Kumār. Matriculed from Punjab in 1919 and enrolled in a BSc course at the Central Hindu School in Benares, but left (prompted by his uncle) because of Non-Cooperation. He later attended some courses at the nationalist Tilak School of Politics in Delhi.

Occupation

Writer.

Career

A restless and indecisive youth, after leaving school he moved to Jabalpur, where his uncle was in jail and where *Karmavīr* under Mākhanlāl Chaturvedī had become a sort of ashram for boys who had joined Non-Cooperation. There he started writing reports and helped in his mother's shop. He was arrested during the flag satyagraha in 1923. Not until he published his first novel, *Parakh* (1929, awarded the Hindustani Academy prize in 1931) did he find any stability. Later he grew close to Premchand and along with him supported Hindustani in the Hindi–Hindustani controversy. Greatly influenced by Sharatchandra, he enjoyed a similar reputation in Hindi for his depiction of women's characters and his psychological studies.

Selected Works

Novels: *Parakh* (1929), *Sunītā* (1935), *Tyāgpatra* (1937), *Kalyāṇī* (1939), *Sukhadā* (1953), *Vivarta* (1953), *Vyatīt* (1953), *Jayvarddhan* (1956).

Lakhanpāl, Chandrāvatī (originally Sukla) (1904–69)

Birthplace: Bijnaur.

Background

Born in an Ārya Samāj family, the daughter of Jaynārāyaṇ Śukla, who had translated some *Upaniṣads* into Hindi and wrote original works on sociology.

Education

Educated up to MA in Benares and at Crosthwaite College, Allahabad.

Occupation

Teacher, writer, political activist.

Career

After marrying Satyavrat Siddhāntālaṃkār, Vice-Chacellor of Gurukul Kangri, she taught at the Mahādevī Kanyā Pāṭhśālā and later became Acharya of the Kanyā Mahāvidyālay in Kangri (later Dehradun). She took active part in the Civil Disobedience movement, was chairwoman of the

Mahilā Congress Committee in Dehradun and became a Congress Dictator; she toured the villages until she was arrested and given a one-year sentence. In 1932 she presided over the UP Political Conference in Agra.

Selected Works

Essays: *Mādar indiyā kā javāb* (1927?); *Striyoṁ kī sthiti* (1932, awarded the Seksāriyā prize in 1934); *Śikṣā manovijñān* (1935, awarded the Maṅgalāprasād prize).

Mālavīya, Kṛṣṇakānta (1883–1941)

Birthplace: Allahabad.

Background

A nephew of Madan Mohan Mālavīya.

Education

BA Honours from Allahabad University.

Occupation

Teacher, writer, political activist.

Career

From 1910 to 1935 he edited and managed the very influential political weekly *Abhyuday*, and from 1911 to 1924 the miscellany monthly *Maryādā*; in 1930, when most editors were in jail, his young son Padmakānt edited *Abhyuday*, and took over from him after 1935. Kṛṣṇakānt Mālavīya wrote favourably about the Russian Revolution and communism; he was an active Allahabad Congressman and Hindu Sabha member and was general secretary of M.M. Mālavīya's Independent Congress Party and campaigned for him in the 1926 elections. A municipal councillor in Allahabad, he was also elected to the Legislative Council in 1932 and to the Legislative Assembly in 1936. He went to jail four times between 1920 and 1932, altogether for two- -and-a-half years. He wrote several books, mostly on world politics, and controversial 'useful' books on sexual relations and the family. Known at the time as the 'Kuṁvar Kanhaiyā' of Allahabad.

Selected Works

Useful books: *Sohāg-rāt* (1927), *Manormā ke patra* (1928).

Mālavīya, Pandit Madan Mohan (1861–1946)

Birthplace: Ahalyapur mohallā, Allahabad.

Background

Son of a well-known vyās, an expositor of the scriptures. He changed his name from Mallai to Mālavīya.

Education

Educated first at local Sanskrit pāṭhśālās and then at Muir Central College; BA from Calcutta University in 1884. He had to drop out of the MA course and start teaching Sanskrit at the local Government High School.

Occupation

Lawyer, political activist.

Career

Early public activities included founding the Prayāg Hindū Samāj, with his Sanskrit professor Aditya Ram Bhattacharya and Raja Rampal Singh of Kalakankar (1880); establishing the Bharti Bhavan library (1889) and the Hindu Hostel (1903); and campaigning for cow-protection and for Hindi in the Nagari versus Persian script issue. In 1897 he wrote *Court Script and Primary Education*, and in 1900 he headed the delegation to Antony MacDonnell to press for the recognition of Nagari as an official script in UP. Called by Rampal Singh to edit the first Hindi daily, *Hindosthan* (1877–9), he then went back to study law. His successful career at the Allahabad High Court started in 1893; after Non-Cooperation he only took on a few political cases, as when he defended the accused of Chauri Chaura in 1922. He was also instrumental in starting several influential papers: the weekly *Abhyuday* (1907) and *The Leader* (1909), and the Hindi monthly *Maryādā* (1910). Elected municipal councillor and vice-chairman of Allahabad municipality, in 1903 he was nominated and then elected to the UP Legislative Council; from there he was returned to the Vice-Regal Council, from which he resigned in 1920, though he was initially opposed to Non-Cooperation. After 1920 he was active in politics mainly as a Hindu leader and an ally of landed and industrial magnates. In 1923 he reorganized the All India Hindu Mahasabha; in 1926 he contested elections under the separate banner of the Indian Nationalist Party, and in 1935 with the Congress Nationalist Party. After his life-long dream of building a Hindu University in Benares was realised in 1916, he moved there as Vice-Chancellor of BHU.

Selected Works

Essay: *Court Character and Primary Education in the N.W.-P. and Oudh* (1897).

Miśra, Śyāmbihārī (1873-1947) **and Śukdevbihārī** (1878–1951)

Birthplace: Village Itaunja, district Lucknow.

Background

Born in an eminent and scholarly Kanyakubja Brahmin family which lived off zamindari and moneylending.

Education

After *vidyārambha* at home, both were educated first in Urdu in the village, then at the Church Mission High School in Basti, and finally in Lucknow. Śyāmbihārī first failed his Middle examination, then passed the Entrance exam in 1891 from Jubilee High School, Lucknow. In 1893, he passed Intermediate, in 1895 he was awarded a first class BA [honours] in English from Canning College, Lucknow, and a Master's degree from Allahabad University in 1896. Śukdevbihārī passed his Middle school examination from the Jubilee High School in 1893, and in 1899 was awarded a BA and a gold medal from Canning College. LLB in 1897.

Occupation

Collector and administrator.

Career

Śyāmbihārī became first a deputy collector, then a secretary and dīvān to several princely states; he also served as police superintendent and Collector. From 1924 to 1928 he was Honourable Member of the Council of States, and in 1928 was awarded the title of Rai Bahadur; in 1933 the Maharaja of Orchha gave him the title of Raoraja, and in 1937 Allahabad University conferred upon him an honorary degree. Śukdevbihārī worked first as a lawyer, then as a sub-judge, and finally as dīvān of Chattarpur state, where he invited Hindi writers from time to time. In 1913 he presided at the Kanyakubja Conference in Sitapur. In 1927 he was awarded the title of Rai Bahadur. In 1930, travelled extensively in Europe, and retired in 1931. Both brothers were examiners and members of the senate in several universities. Closely connected to the Nāgarī Prachāriṇī Sabhā, they were in charge of the search for Hindi manuscripts for many years. Their fame relies largely on two works: *Hindī navratna* (1910–11), an anthology with introductions to the 'nine gems' of Hindi literature, and *Miśrabandhu-vinod* (1913), a voluminous compilation of about five thousand Hindi writers and works, based on Śivsiṃh Seṅgar's *Śivsiṃh saroj* (1878) as well as on the catalogues of manuscripts produced by the search; the latter work was criticized by M.P.

Dvivedī and Rāmchandra Śukla. Authoritative critics and reviewers, they also wrote history books in Hindi from English sources, and original historical novels.

Selected Works

Literary history: *Hindī navratnā (1910–11)*; *Miśrabandhu-vinod* (1913).

'Navīn', Bālkṛṣṇa Śarmā (1897–1960)

Birthplace: Village Bhayanam, district Shajapur (Gwalior state).

Background

His father was a poor Vaiṣṇava Brahmin who moved to Nathdwara (Rajputana).

Education

After passing the Middle school examination in English in Shajapur, he moved to Ujjain and attended the high school at Madhav College. After Matriculation, he moved to Kanpur in 1917 to enrol in a BA course at Christ-church College. Left in the final year to join Non-Cooperation.

Occupation

Poet, political activist.

Career

First attended the Lucknow Congress in 1913, where he met G.Ś. Vidyārthī, Mākhanlāl Chaturvedī and Maithilīśaraṇ Gupta; Vidyārthī was especially friendly. Once he moved to Kanpur he became part of the 'Pratāp family' and was introduced to Bhagavatīcharaṇ Varmā, Kauśik, Lakṣhmīdhar Vājpeyī, etc. He wrote both nationalist and love poetry, worked at *Pratāp*, edited *Prabhā* from 1924 and *Pratāp* after Vidyārthī's death in 1931. One short story, 'Santu', was first published in *Sarasvatī* in 1916. Involved in all Congress campaigns with Vidyārthī, Navīn was a follower of Gandhi's and later of Subhash Chandra Bose's. For several years he was member of the UP Provincial Congress Committee. He was also a member of the Constituent Assembly, where he was active in favour of Hindi; elected MP in 1952.

Selected Works

Poetry: *Kusum* (1936); *Apalak* (1952); *Urmilā* (1957).

Nehrū, Rāmeśvarī (1886–1966)

Birthplace: Probably Lahore.

Background

Born in the distinguished Kashmiri Brahmin family of Divan R.B. Raja Narendranath of Lahore, once president of the Hindu Mahasabha and MLA. One forefather had been advisor to Maharaja Ranjit Singh.

Education

Educated at home in Persian and Arabic, and later in English.

Occupation

Political activist, editor.

Career

Married in 1920 to Brajlal Nehru, a nephew of Motilal Nehru's who was Accountant General of the Punjab and later became economic advisor to the Jammu and Kashmir government. From 1909 to 1923 she was founder–editor of *Strī-darpaṇ* with Umā Nehru, Shyamlal Nehru's wife. In 1909 she also founded the Prayāg Mahilā Samiti and campaigned against pardā; both she and Umā were involved in the AIW (Associaton of Indian Women). She was also a member of the Age of Consent Committee in 1926–7, and in 1930 went to the Round Table Conference in London as representative of Indian women. In 1931 she was in Geneva at the League of Nations and toured Europe in 1932. In 1934 she turned to Harijan uplift and in 1935 was elected vice-president of the Harijan Sevak Sangh. In 1937 she visited Australia. From 1938 she continued with Harijan uplift activities in Central India. In 1942 she was put under home arrest (*nazarband*) and subsequently jailed when she violated its rules. The author of several unpublished books, her novel *Sūryadev kā āgaman* was serialized in *Manormā.* After Independence she was engaged in social work.

'Nirālā', Sūryakānt Tripāṭhī (Sūraj Kumār Tevārī)
(1899–1962)

Birthplace: Village Garhakola, district Unnao, in the heart of Avadh.

Background

His father was a petty officer in the army of the small princely state of Mahishadal in Bengal and owned some land and mango groves in the village.

Education

Little formal education; failed Matriculation. Taught himself literary Hindi through journals, chiefly *Sarasvatī* and *Maryādā.* Fluent in Bengali and Sanskrit.

Occupation

Writer, publicist.

Career

After his father's death in 1917, and the death of his wife, brother, and sister-in-law in the influenza epidemic of 1918, he had to provide for himself, his two children, and his nephews. His life was marred by professional instability and the lack of financial security. After a short term in the prince's service, in 1921 he was appointed editor of the Ramakrishna Mission's Hindi periodical *Samanvay* in Calcutta, thanks to a recommendation by M.P. Dvivedī, whose village was near Nirālā's ancestral village. In Calcutta he became acquainted with Hindi literati and joined the '*Matvālā* maṇḍal' in 1923; his first slim collection of poems, *Anāmikā,* appeared in 1922 (reprinted in *Parimal,* 1929). After his first break-up with *Matvālā* in 1924, he took up freelance translation work in Calcutta, then joined *Matvālā* again but also wrote political and topical articles for other magazines. A second break-up with *Matvālā*'s owner was caused by the latter's predilection for 'Ugra', but after a long illness Nirālā returned there, for the first time with a proper salary. A friend of Pant's and Prasād's, he was nonetheless irked by the enthusiastic reception of Pant's *Pallav* (1926) and entered into a bitter argument with him. His popularity among students increased, while he fought against Chāyāvād detractors. For the lack of the formal qualifications, he was at first rejected for a job at *Sudhā*, but then worked in Lucknow from 1930 to 1940, for Dulārelāl Bhārgava's *Sudhā* and Ganga Pustak Mala. In the 1940s he manifested the first signs of mental instability but continued writing. From 1945 onwards he lived alone in Allahabad. The most experimental and wide-ranging of the Chāyāvād poets, and also the author of original sketches, stories, and short novels, he is now considered one of the most prominent Hindi literary figures of this century.

Selected Works

Poetry: *Anāmikā* (1922, later *Parimal*, 1929), *Gītikā* (1936), *Anāmikā* (1937), *Tulsīdās* (1938), *Kukurmuttā* (1942), *Aṇimā* (1943), *Belā* (1943), *Naye patte* (1946). Novels and Sketches: *Apsarā* (1930), *Alkā* (1933), *Chāturī chamār* (as *Sakhī*, 1935), *Kullī bhāṭ* (1939), *Billesur bakarihā* (1942).

Ojhā, R.B. Mahapandit Gaurīśaṅkar Hirāchand (1863–1947)

Birthplace: Rohira village (Sirohi state, Rajputana).

Background

Born in a Brahmin family which had moved from Mewar to Sirohi state in the sixteenth century.

Education

Educated first at home in Hindi, after his *yajñopavīt* he underwent the traditional Sanskrit education in the Vedas, mathematics, etc.; at 14 he moved to Bombay in search of higher educational facilities, and learnt Gujarati for six months before being able to enrol at Elphinstone College; he matriculated from there in 1884. Meanwhile he continued the study of Sanskrit and Prakrit with the famous scholar Pandit Gaṭṭūlāl. Enrolled at Wilson College in 1886, a spell of ill-health interrupted his studies, but until 1888 he remained in Bombay to study epigraphy and ancient history.

Occupation

Museum curator, historian.

Career

In 1888 he was appointed head of the history office of Udaipur state; in 1890 he became director of the newly-opened museum library of Victoria Hall, and in 1908 he was appointed director of the Government Museum in Ajmer, where he remained until his retirement. In 1893 he published the first Hindi book on the subject of ancient scripts (*Prāchīn lipimālā*), which earned him the recognition of scholars and the membership of several scholarly societies; a revised edition came out in 1918. In 1902 he wrote a biography in Hindi of Colonel James Tod and started writing notes on the translation of his *Antiquities of Rajasthan.* Also started publishing an *Itihās granthamālā.* An early member of the Nāgarī Prachāriṇī Sabhā, he edited its journal, the *Nāgarī Prachāriṇī Patrikā*, for several years and published his books with the Sabhā. Edited *Pṛthvīrāj vijay* and *Karamchand vaṃś* and authored several books on various Rajput dynasties. In 1911 he was awarded the title of Rai Bahadur, and in 1928 that of Mahapandit; in 1927 he was President of the Hindī Sāhitya Sammelan, and in 1933 of the Historical branch of the Baroda Oriental Conference; in 1933 he was also presented a huge felicitation volume, *Bhārtīy anuśīlan*, and in 1937 he was awarded the title of Sāhitya Vāchaspati by the Hindī Sāhitya Sammelan and an honorary D.Litt. from BHU. He always wrote only in Hindi.

Selected Works

Historical works: *Solāṅkiyoṁ kā itihās* (1907); *Rājputāne kā itihās* (1923–26); *Madhyakālīn bhārtīy saṃskṛti* (1928).

Pālīvāl, Śrīkṛṣṇadatt (1895–1968)

Birthplace: Village Tanora, Agra district.

Background

Born in a moderately affluent peasant family.

Education

MA in Economics from Allahabad University in 1920; dropped out to join the Non-Cooperation movement. Private study of religious scriptures.

Occupation

Political activist, editor.

Career

Started writing for *Brahmoday*, then went to Kanpur where in 1918 he joined G.Ś. Vidyārthī's '*Pratāp* family'; he edited *Prabhā* under the name of Devadatt Śarmā, and *Pratāp* between 1921 and 1923. Early influenced by Tilak, then by Satyadev Parivrājak, he was involved in the Mainpuri Conspiracy case but was acquitted for lack of evidence. An active Congressman, he moved to Agra, where in 1925 he founded the nationalist weekly *Sainik* (also daily from 1935), which was closed down and fined several times by the censors. In 1923–6 he was member of UP Legislative Council, and in 1928–31 he was member (and later chairman) of the Agra District board. A leader of the Civil Disobedience campaign in Agra district, he was elected on a Congress ticket to the UP Legislative Assembly in 1934 and was the first UP Congress Dictator in 1940, and again went in jail between 1942 and 1945. The leading Congress leader of Agra district, in 1946 he was elected unopposed to the Central Assembly, and was also President of the UP Kisan Congress.

Selected Works

Political works: *Sevā mārg* (1920); *Mārksvād aur gāndhīvād*. Translated Hall Caine's *The Eternal City* into Hindi.

Pāṇḍey, Rūpnārāyaṇ (1884–1958)

Birthplace: Lucknow.

Background

Born in a poor Brahmin family in Lucknow, the son of a Sanskrit scholar.

Education

Orphaned at a young age, he was educated by a local scholar. Studied Sanskrit at Canning College and passed the prathamā examination, but had to start working before he could take the madhyamā exam. Taught himself English, Bengali, Marathi, Gujarati, and Urdu.

Occupation

Translator, editor.

Career

One of the first professional translators and editors in Hindi. Started by translating the Purāṇas and the *Śrīmadbhāgavat* from Sanskrit; then, from Bengali, Kṛttibās' *Rāmāyaṇa* and several Bengali novels and plays, among which Bankimchandra's essays, Tagore's *Āṁkh kī kirkirī* (1919) and *Rājā rānī* (1925), and most of Sharatchandra's novels: all in all, he translated sixty books and wrote fifteen original works. In search of employment, he worked with several journals first with *Nāgarī-prachārak, Nigamāgam-patrikā* (the journal of Bhārat-Dharma Mahāmaṇḍal, which awarded him the title 'Kaviratna'), then with Prasād's *Indu*, with the Indian Press in Allahabad, with *Kanyākubja*, and finally with *Mādhurī*, where he remained, with some gaps, from 1923 to 1935. Stability and fame as an experienced editor brought him some wealth and a lavish style of living. He contributed regularly Braj Bhasa poems and articles to the main literary journals. Also edited *Śivsiṁh saroj* and wrote commentaries on Tulsī's *Rāmāyaṇa* and on *Śivrāj bhūṣaṇ*.

Pant, Sumitrānandan (1900–77)

Birthplace: Kasauni, district Almora.

Background

His father was treasurer of Kasauni state and owned a tea estate; after his mother's early death, he was brought up by his father and grandmother.

Education

First at the village school; in 1912 went to Almora government school to learn English, and in 1918 to Jaynarayan High School in Benares; in 1919 he enrolled at Muir Central College, Allahabad, for a BA, but dropped out in his second year.

Occupation

Poet.

Career

Born in a cultured family, with literary-minded elder brothers, he wrote poetry copiously from an early age. In Benares he first read Sarojini Naidu, Tagore, and the English Romantic poets; thereafter he wrote *Ucchvās* and *Granthi* (1920). In Allahabad his poems started to be published in *Sarasvatī* (the first Chāyāvād poet to be published there) thanks to Bakhśī's personal encouragement, and his poetry collections were published by the Indian Press. He got early recognition, especially after *Pallav* (1926). From 1931 to 1941 he lived in Kalakankar as a guest of the local Maharaja and edited

Rūpābh (1938), a literary journal which acted as a bridge between Chāyāvād and later, Progressive and Experimentalist, poetry. Pant himself moved on to various styles, first under the influence of Gandhi, then of the Progressives, and lastly of Aurobindo Ghosh, a trajectory not untypical of Hindi intellectuals. In 1942 he founded a cultural centre in Almora, Lokāyān, established contacts with Uday Shankar's troupe and wrote poems for one of Shankar's ballets. On that occasion he toured south India and visited Aurobindo for the first time. From 1950 to 1957 he was advisor to All-India Radio. Awarded the Sahitya Akademi Puraskar in 1961.

Selected Works

Poetry: *Ucchvās* (1920), *Granthi* (1920), *Pallav* (1926), *Vīṇā* (1927), *Guñjan* (1932), *Yugānt* (1936), *Yugvāṇī* (1937), *Grāmyā* (1940), *Yugpath* (1948), *Kalā aur būṛhā chāṁd* (1958). Play: *Jyotsnā* (1934).

Parāṛkar, Bābūrāo Viṣṇu (1880–1955)

Birthplace: Benares.

Background

Born in a Maharastrian family; his father had moved to Benares, studied there and become Head Pandit in various government schools in Bihar.

Education

Mostly in Bihar, first in Sanskrit and then in English; Intermediate exam from Tejnarayan College in Bhagalpur. After his father's death he paid for his studies with private tuitions, but after his mother and sister died in a plague epidemic he had to eventually give up his studies.

Occupation

Editor and publicist.

Career

After the death of his mother and sister he went to Calcutta in search of occupation. His first job was with the newspaper *Hindī baṅgvāsī* in 1906; then in 1907–10 he worked for *Hitvārtā*, the Hindi edition of *Hitvādī*, and wrote chiefly political articles and editorials. Meanwhile he attended courses in Hindi and Marathi at the Bengal National College, where he came in contact with Aurobindo Ghosh, its principal, and with his brother Rasbehari Ghosh. In 1910–15 he worked as assistant editor for the daily *Bhāratmitra* with Ambikādatt Vājpeyī. Between 1916 and 1920 he was convicted for political reasons, and in 1920 he returned to Benares, where he joined

Śivaprasād Gupta's nationalist daily *Āj* and made it, together with Śrīprakāś (1890–1971), one of the best Hindi papers. He was arrested and fined Rs 1000 for an article in *Āj* in 1930. When *Āj* was shut during Civil Disobedience, he edited and published the underground cyclostyled bulletin *Rāṇbherī*. Edited the *Premchand smṛti aṅk* for *Haṃs* in 1937. He presided over the First Sampādak Sammelan at the Hindī Sāhitya Sammelan, and Brindaban, and was President of the XXVII Hindī Sāhitya Sammelan in Simla, at the height of the Hindi–Hindustani controversy.

'Parivrājak', Svami Satyadev (alias Sukh Lāl)
(1879–1961)

Birthplace: Ludhiana.

Background

Born in a Thapar family of great religious eclecticism: his great-grandfather had embraced Sikhism, his grandfather was a Shaiva. Although himself a sanātan dharmi, his father sent him to a DAV school and wanted him to join the railways.

Education

Matriculated in 1897 from the DAV school in Ludhiana and gained entrance to the DAV college in Lahore, where he became close to Lajpat Rai. Later he graduated from Central Hindu College, Benares. In 1905–7 he spent two years in the United States at the universities of Chicago and Oregon, studying political science and economics.

Occupation

Preacher, publicist.

Career

After reading Dayānand's biography at school he decided to become a sanyāsī and underwent five years of religious education in Dehradun, Kanpur, and Kāśī. In the 1890s he became an Ārya Samāj preacher (prachārak); his first article in Hindi appeared in *Sarasvatī*. When he decided to go to the United States to cure his eyesight, he collected money for the passage by preaching in Gujarat. From America he corresponded with M.P. Dvivedī, and his reports in *Sarasvatī* became very popular. In the United States he also did fund-raising for his 'downtrodden country'. On his return he first settled in Almora and then in Dehradun, where he was appointed headmaster of the local DAV school. He soon left, however, to launch various educational and publishing enterprises in Calcutta and Benares, and published some nationalist tracts; between 1913 and 1914 he worked as Hindi preacher for the Hindī Sāhitya Sammelan and toured north India. Between 1913 and 1918 he also toured continuously to preach svadeśī and svarājya. In 1918 he was sent to south India to help the Hindi propaganda programme there. In 1923 he left for Germany for further eye treatment, but despite several trips he became blind. He also became attracted to Nazism and wrote favourably about it, and about Hindu saṅgaṭhan, in Hindi journals. After his return he opened an ashram in Jwalapur (Hardwar). Overall a highly original and colourful figure, who inspired many younger minds.

Selected Works

Miscellaneous and political essays: *Rāṣṭrīy saṁdhyā* (1911), *Hindī kā sandeś* (1914), *Satya nibandhāvalī* (1914), *Sañjīvan būṭī* (1915), *Manuṣya ke adhikār* (1922), *Hamārī sadiyoṁ kī gulāmī* (1922), *Saṅgaṭhan kā bigul* (1922), *Qurān meṁ parivartan* (1924); *Bhārtīy samājvād kī rūprekhā* (1939). Travelogues: *Amrīkā digdarśan* (1911), *Merī jarman yātrā* (1924).

Poddār, Hanumānprasād (1892–1971)

Birthplace: Shillong (Assam).

Background

Born in a family of Marwari merchants which moved to Calcutta in 1901.

Education

Educated in Calcutta in Hindi, Bengali, Gujarati, Marathi, and English.

Occupation

Publisher.

Career

In Calcutta he came in contact with Bipin Chandra Pal and Aurobindo Ghosh and took part in terrorist activities from 1910 onwards; in 1916–18 he was jailed for treason and was banned from Bombay. In jail he turned to spiritual matters. Began writing for Hindi journals in 1914. In 1915, after meeting Gandhi, he took the oath of 'serving the country' (deś-sevā). Since 1914 he had started writing articles for Hindi journals. He moved to Bombay in 1918, where he became an ardent follower of Tilak until in 1921 he again turned to religious preaching. With Seth Jaydayāl Goyiṅkā he set up, first in Bombay and then in Gorakhpur, the religious monthly *Kalyāṇ* (1926), which became the Hindi journal with the highest distribution ever and a powerful vehicle for reconfiguring modern Hindu identity. In 1927 he set up the Gita Press in Gorakhpur, and in 1928 the English version of *Kalyāṇ*, *Kalyana*

Kalpataru, came out. In 1929 Gandhi gave a speech at the Gita Press, and Poddār organized the 1929 Hindī Sāhitya Sammelan meeting there. In 1932 he launched *Harijan sevak* with Viyogī Hari and Seth Ghanshyam Das Birla. After Independence he took part in the movement to restore Krishna's 'birthplace' in Mathura. Penned several books and booklets on Hindu culture.

Selected Works

Essays: *Hindū-saṃskṛti kā svarūp; Sinemā manorañjan yā vināś-sādhan; Strī-dharma-praśnottarī* (1926); *Bhakta-bālak* (1930); *Bhakta-nārī* (1930).

Prasād, Jayśaṅkar (1889–1937)

Birthplace: Benares.

Background

Born in a cultured and distinguished Agrawal merchant family which sold scented tobacco for snuff and known as 'Sūṁghnī sāhū'; his father and elder brother were connoisseurs of art and literature. At his father's death in 1901 the family split and business went almost bankrupt. Much of Prasād's life was spent trying to recover the business from debts.

Education

First educated at home by a Braj Bhasa poet; in 1899 he was enrolled at Queen's College, Benares, but attended only up to the 7th grade. After his father's death he started helping with the business at home, and continued to study on his own. He taught himself Sanskrit, which he read widely, Pali, some Urdu, and English.

Occupation

Writer, merchant.

Career

Prasād started writing regularly at fifteen. Much of his life was spent in Benares, apart from a few pilgrimages; a great friend of Rāykṛṣṇadās, and later through him, of Maithilīśaraṇ Gupta, he soon attracted a group of younger writers like Kṛṣṇadev Prasād Gauṛ and Vinod Śaṅkar Vyās. Unhappy with M.P. Dvivedī's policies on Khari Boli poetry, Prasād launched his own sophisticated journal, *Indu* (1909–27), in which he published Rāykṛṣṇadās' poems and his own. Hardly a public person, Prasād was only loosely attached to the Nāgarī Prachāriṇī Sabhā, but nonetheless visited the library assiduously. Although he wrote a lot and regularly in Braj Bhasa, he published only in Khari Boli after 1918. Deeply engaged with ancient history, he wrote copiously about it in the form of learned essays and highly original literary plays. Recognized as the first Chāyāvādī poet after the success of *Āṁsū* (1925), he was published widely in the most prestigious journals. His last few years were devoted to writing his *magnum opus,* the poetic epic *Kāmāyanī,* on the origin of man and civilization after the deluge. He also wrote several short stories and two novels.

Selected Works

Poetry: *Jharnā* (1918), *Āṁsū* (1925), *Lahar* (1933), *Kāmāyanī* (1936). Plays: *Viśākh* (1921), *Kāmnā* (1927), *Janmejay kā Nāgayajña* (1926), *Skandagupta* (1928), *Chandragupta* (1931), *Dhruvasvāminī* (1933). Short stories: *Chāyā* (1912), *Pratidhvani* (1926), *Ākāśdīp* (1929), *Āṁdhī* (1931), *Indrajāl* (1936). Novels: *Kaṅkāl* (1929), *Titlī* (1934).

'Prem', Dhanīrām (1904–79)

Birthplace: Village Dariyapur, district Aligarh.

Education

First at the Atrauli DAV school, then at the Dharma Samaj College and Aligarh Muslim University. Medical degree in 1929 from the National Medical College in Bombay. In 1931 he went abroad to Edinburgh for further medical studies.

Occupation

Medical doctor, writer.

Career

Jailed for one year in 1921 in Aligarh during Non-Cooperation, he established a branch of the Ārya Kumār Sabhā there. Lived and worked as a doctor in England for a few years; after his return, he practised in Bombay and Allahabad and edited *Chāṁd* and *Bhaviṣya* in the 1940s. The author of very popular 'social' short stories and one-act plays, he also wrote two films for Ranjit Movie Company: *Do badmāś* and *Bhulbhulaiyā.*

Selected Works

Short stories: *Prāṇeśvarī* (1931), *Vallarī* (1932), *Prem samādhī, Veśyā kā hṛday* (1933); Political works: *Raṅg aur briṭiś rājnīti, Rūs kā jāgaraṇ;* Biographies: *Vīrāṅganā pannā, Devī jon* (Joan of Arc).

Premchand, (Dhanpat Rāy) (1880–1936)

Birthplace: Village Lamhi, district Benares.

Background

Born in a Kayastha family of clerks and kanungos; his father was a postal clerk in government service.

Education

First in Urdu and Persian with a maulvi in a neighbouring village; then at the Mission School in Gorakhpur where his father was posted, and finally at the prestigious Queen's Collegiate School in Benares, where he passed Matriculation in 1898. Refused free tuition, he had to give up studying. In 1902–4 he attended the Government Teachers' Training College in Allahabad and obtained a BA only in 1919, at the age of thirty-nine, from Allahabad University.

Occupation

Writer, teacher, editor.

Career

His first teaching job was at the Mission School in Chunar in 1899, for Rs 18 a month. After a series of temporary posts and teachers' training, he joined government service. After a brief spell in Allahabad between 1905 and 1909 he taught at the District School in Kanpur and contributed regularly to D.N. Nigam's prestigious Urdu literary journal *Zamānā*; his first story was published in 1907. In 1906 he married Śivrānī Devī, a child-widow; it was his second marriage. From 1909 to 1915 he was appointed sub-deputy inspector of schools in the 'backward' district of Hamirpur. His first collection of short stories (in Urdu), *Soz-e-vatan* (1909), was proscribed; thereafter he changed his pen-name from Navāb Rāi to Premchand. Between 1913 and 1915 he gradually switched from publishing in Urdu to Hindi; his first Hindi story, 'Saut', was published in *Sarasvatī* in 1915. In 1913 he had the first serious bout of an illness that would grow chronic; in 1915 he was allowed to go back to teaching, after he tried unsuccessfully to take over *Zamānā*. Attempts to leave government service for other teaching posts failed and he finally resigned following Gandhi's visit to Gorakhpur. After a short spell at the 'national' Marwari school in Kanpur and at the Kāśī Vidyāpīṭh school in Benares in 1921–3, he started his own printing press, the Sarasvati Press. This did not become a source of independent livelihood, as he had hoped, but of endless financial troubles. In the years to follow, his earnings would chiefly go to pay for the press and for the journals he edited, the monthly *Haṃs* (1930) and the political weekly *Jāgaraṇ* (1932). As a consequence, he had to move to Lucknow and worked first as a literary consultant to Dulārelāl Bhārgava at the Ganga Pustak Mala (1924–5), then as *Mādhurī*'s editor and in the publication department of Nawal Kishore Press (1927–32). Meanwhile he contributed short stories to the leading Hindi journals and wrote several novels. In 1934 he attended the XXIV Hindī Sāhitya Sammelan meeting in

Delhi with Jainendra Kumār, and in the same year he was hired as a script-writer in the Bombay movie industry; neither the job nor the environment suited him. In 1934–6 he became very actively involved in the Hindi–Hindustani controversy in favour of Hindustani. He was also among the founding members of the Bhārtīy Sāhitya Pariṣad, a new all-India writers' association, and handed *Haṃs* over to it in 1935. He presided over the first Progressive Writers' Association in Lucknow in 1936, shortly before his death.

Selected Works

Several collections of short stories; Novels: *Sevā-sadan* (1919), *Vardān* and *Premāśram* (1921), *Raṅgbhūmī* (1925), *Kāyākalpa* (1926), *Nirmalā* (serialised in *Chāṁd* in 1925; published 1927); *Gaban* (1931), *Godān* (1936). Plays: *Saṅgrām* (1923), *Karbalā* (1924). Translated A. France's *Thais* and Gailsworthy and Sharar's *Fazānā-e-āzād* (1925).

'Ratnākar', Babu Jagannāthdās (1866–1932)

Birthplace: Benares.

Background

Born in a distinguished and wealthy family from Panipat district, whose ancestors had been officers at Akabar's court and who had moved first to Lucknow and then to Benares with the decline of the Mughals; the family was known as 'Dillīvāl Agravāl Vaiśya'. His father was a literary connoisseur and a scholar of Persian and Braj Bhasa, distantly related to, and a contemporary of, Bhārtendu Hariśchandra. Poets regularly visited the house.

Education

First in Urdu; BA in 1891 at Queen's College, Benares, with Persian as second language; only started a Master's degree in Persian. Privately studied medieval Hindi poetry, Urdu, Persian, Sanskrit, Prakrit, Apabhramsa, Bengali, Marathi, Punjabi, Ayurveda, astrology, music, history, archaeology, etc.

Occupation

Poet, private secretary of the Maharaja of Ayodhya.

Career

In 1900 he was first appointed Chief Secretary in a small princely state, and in 1902 Private Secretary to the Maharaja of Ayodhya; after the Maharaja's death in 1906, he became Private Secretary to the Maharaja's wife. Mostly occupied with managing work, he had little time for literary pursuits until he retired in 1920, although he was a member of the Kāśī Kavi Samāj. A representative of the old Indo-Persian elite, he first started writing poetry in Persian, then switched to Braj Bhasa and became the most respected Braj Bhasa poet of modern times. After his retirement he became quite active in the Hindi literary scene, regularly attending literary gatherings and kavi sammelans. He presided over the XX Hindī Sāhitya Sammelan in Calcutta in 1922, and in 1925, the first All-India Hindi Kavi Sammelan in Kanpur. His Braj Bhasa poems in a variety of metres, and especially of śṛṅgāra rasa, were regularly published in Hindi journals. He also edited and wrote commentaries on several texts by rīti poets; his commentary to Bihārīlāl's *Satsaī, Bihārī ratnākar* (1922), was widely praised.

Selected Works

Poetry: *Hiṇḍolā* (1894); *Gaṅgāvataraṇ* (1927); *Uddhavaśataka* (1931).

Raykṛṣṇadās (1892–1980)

Birthplace: Benares.

Background

Born in the 'Rāy' family, one of the most established merchant families of Benares, related to Bhārtendu Hariśchandra and Rādhākṛṣṇa Dās. His father was a lover of Sanskrit and of poetry.

Education

Educated first at home, then at Queen's Collegiate School.

Occupation

Poet, art collector, and art historian.

Career

One of the central literary figures of Benares, a connoisseur of poetry and art; at his salon on Ramghat scholars, musicians, writers, and art lovers assembled for half a century. He wrote poetry in Braj Bhasa and Khari Boli from early on, spurred by M.P. Dvivedī and Maithilīśaraṇ Gupta, and published it in *Sarasvatī*. A great friend of Jayśaṅkar Prasād, he helped edit his monthly *Indu* (1909). Very fond of travelling and of exploring artistic and archaeological sites, he assembled a large collections of artefacts which he donated first to the Nāgarī Prachāriṇī Sabhā and then to BHU. He also started a publishing house, Bharti Bhandar, in 1927, with the aim of encouraging cooperative publishing and higher royalties for writers; it was ceded to the Leader Press of Allahabad in 1935 (by then, a Birla concern).

Selected Works

Prose poems: *Sādhnā* (1919), *Chāyāpath, Saṃlāp, Pravāl* (1929). Poems: *Bhāvuk, Brajraj*. Short stories: *Anākhyā* (1929), *Sudhāṃśu.* (1929) Art history: *Bhārat kī chitrakalā* (1939), *Bhārat kī mūrtikalā* (1939).

Sahajānand Sarasvatī, Svami (Navraṅg Rāi) (*ca.* 1889–1950)

Birthplace: Village Deva, tahsil Syedpur, district Ghazipur.

Background

Poor Bhumihar zamindar family.

Education

The first of his family, and one of the first in the village, to become literate, and an exceptionally bright and studious pupil, he first attended the Upper Primary School at Jalalabad in 1899, and after passing the Hindi Middle examination from Ghazipur in 1904 he was awarded a scholarship to continue. Enrolled at the German Mission high school in Ghazipur to study English, he left just before the Matriculation exam in order to become a sanyāsī. The following years were spent on pilgrimage and studying Sanskrit grammar and the śāstras in Benares.

Occupation

Preacher, political activist.

Career

After several years of wanderings and pilgrimages, in 1914 he was called to give speeches and preach at the Bhumihar Brahman Mahasabha in Ballia in support of the Bhumihar claim to Brahminhood. This was the first step of his subsequent career as an activist. He wrote pamphlets and two caste histories to prove the claim: *Bhūmihār brāhmaṇ parichay* (1916), *Brahmarṣivaṃśavistāra*, and a manual on ritual for Bhumihars, but refused to forge a history of Bhumihars in Sanskrit ślokas. Thereafter he resumed his spiritual vocation for a while, but kept abreast of political events. After a meeting with Gandhi in Patna and attending the Nagpur Congress in 1920, he became an active Non-Cooperator in Baksar: used to travelling on foot as a sanyāsī, he toured villages for nationalist propaganda. During his first jail sentence in Ghazipur, Faizabad, and Lucknow, he met other nationalist leaders and 'discovered' the *Gītā*, on which he later wrote a commentary. A founding member, and later president, of the Bihar Provincial Kisān Sabhā

(1929), he also established an ashram at Bihta, near Patna, for Bhumihar boys, which became the centre of his peasant activities. During Civil Disobedience, kisan activities were suspended, to be resumed after it. In the years between 1933 and 1935 he held 120 meetings among peasants, focusing on tenancy reform and rent remission. He also conducted independent enquiries into peasants' conditions in Gaya, Darbhanga and Purnea, was involved in local struggles, and had tense relations with the Bihar Congress leadership. Several close collaborators were Congress Socialist Party members, while he gradually grew closer to the Communist Party of India. By 1944, however, he parted company with the Communists, and tried unsuccessfully to move the BPKS near Congress again.

Selected Works

Autobiography: *Merā jīvan saṅgharṣ* (1985?)

Sahāy, Śivpūjan (1893–1963)

Birthpace: Village Unvans, district Shahabad (Bihar).

Education

First in the village gurudvara and with a maulvi, then in 1903 at the Kayastha Jubilee School in Arrah; matriculated in 1912.

Occupation

Publicist, writer.

Career

The typical uncertain, impecunious, and itinerant freelance Hindi journalist and writer. As a student he started contributing articles to various Bihar journals and was linked to the Arraḥ branch of the Nāgarī Prachāriṇī Sabhā, one of the earliest to be founded. In 1913 he worked for a year as Hindi copyist at the civil court in Benares, then moved to Allahabad, where he wrote and translated; in 1916 he was appointed teacher at his old school, and in 1918 at the Arrah Town School. He kept up literary reading thanks to the Sabhā library. In 1920 he gave up government service and started teaching in a 'national' school in Arrah. In 1921 he edited the journal *Mārvāṛī sudhār* from Arrah and opened a public library in his own village. His literary guru Īśvarīprasād Śarmā advised him to go to Calcutta, where in 1923 he became part of the '*Matvālā* maṇḍal' with Munshi Mahādev Prasād Seṭh, Navjādiklāl Śrīvāstava, and Nirālā, on a voluntary basis; he contributed to other Hindi magazines in Calcutta at the same time. In 1925 he moved shortly to *Mādhurī* under D. Bhārgava, but did not like the professional environment and the hierarchy there. In 1926 he joined the Pustak Bhandar at Laheriyasarai (Darbhanga), the most important Hindi publisher in Bihar, then moved to Kāśī; in 1930 ḥe moved again to Sultanganj (Bhagalpur) to edit *Gaṅgā*, a literary journal, but that, too, did not last long. Bewteen 1931 and 1933 he was back in Kāśī, where he rented a room in Jayśaṅkar Prasād's compound and edited the weekly *Jāgaraṇ*; in 1933 he returned to Laheriyasarai to edit the children's journal *Bālak* until 1939. In 1939 he was finally appointed Hindi professor at Rajendra College in Chapra (until 1949) and became involved with the Bihar Hindī Sāhitya Sammelan; in 1950 he became the first director of the Bihār Rāṣṭrabhāṣā Pariṣad in Patna. Awarded Padmabhushan in 1961, and D.Litt. by Bhagalpur University in 1962.

Selected Works

Sketches: *Dehātī duniyā* (1926); Essays: *Bihār kā bihār; Vibhūti; Grām sudhār; Annapūrṇā ke mandir meṁ.*

Sahgal, Rāmrakh Siṃh (1896–1952)

Birthplace: Village Rakhterha, near Lahore.

Background

Son of a forestry officer.

Occupation

Editor and publisher.

Career

Spent his youth in Jaunpur. At the time of Jallianwala Bagh he was in Jalandhar, where he married Vidyāvatī Devī, who had been educated at the Āryakanyā Mahāvidyālay and later taught at Crosthwaite school in Allahabad. He took part in the Non-Cooperation movement and worked with the Congress in Allahabad; in fact, he was on the first Congress delegation that toured the Avadh countryside at the time of the peasant agitations in 1920, and was in contact with Chandrasekhar Azad and his group. In 1923 he launched *Chāṁd*, with little financial means but with great vision and business skills; it became the journal with the highest sales in the province. After the special issue *Mārvāṛī aṅk* a Marwari youth from Calcutta assaulted him. Helped financially by Seth Rāmgopāl Mohtā from Bikaner, he also established a Mātṛ Mandir for lone mothers and widows in Allahabad, which was also used as a secret meeting place for women revolutionaries like Durgā Bhabhi and Suśīlā Didi. His foray into political journalism, *Bhaviṣya* (1927 ca.) lasted only six issues; after being ousted from *Chāṁd* in 1933,

Sahgal tried establishing a new publishing house in Dehradun, then revived *Karmayogī* in Lucknow in 1938, and the monthly *Guldastā* in 1940. His last days were spent in dire financial straits.

Sampūrṇānand (1891–1969)

Birthplace: Benares.

Background

Ordinary, educated Kayastha family.

Education

Primary education at Harish Chandra School, then at Queen's College, Benares; B.Sc. from Allahabad University in 1911. Teacher's Training TL from Allahabad in 1916.

Occupation

Teacher, political activist.

Career

Started teaching at the 'national' Prem Mahāvidyālay after he vowed that he would never work in government service until svarājya came; he also refused an offer to go abroad because he was 'too orthodox'. After a year at his old school in Benares, he left for the Teachers' Training college. Thanks to a recommendation from the principal, Mr Mackenzie, he was offered a post at Daly College, Indore, where he taught from 1916 to 1918 and met Banārsīdās Chaturvedī. In 1918–21 he became principal of Dungar College, Bikaner. He took part in the 1918 Hindī Sāhitya Sammelan meeting in Indore, where Gandhi was president, and started contributing to Hindi journals. Resigned in order to join Non-Cooperation in Benares and soon became secretary of the District Congress Committee. Briefly edited *Māryādā* in 1921 before going to jail. From 1922 onwards he was member of AICC and professor of philosophy at Kāśī Vidyāpīṭh, along with Narendra Dev, Śrīprakās, and Acharya Bīrbal. Involved in the publication work of Jnanmandal, he published *Antarrāṣṭrīy vidhān* (1924) and *Samājvād* (1936, awarded the Maṅgalāprasād prize). In 1923 he was elected to the Municipal Board and became the chairman of the education committee. In 1926 he was elected member of the provincial Legislative Council from Benares city. The first Congress Dictator during the salt satyagraha in Benares, he was arrested in 1932, and again during the individual satyāgraha in 1939 and in 1942. Three times president of UP PCC, he was also a founding member of the Congress Socialist Party in 1934. Elected again to the UP Legislative

Assembly in 1935, he became the Education minister in the Congress government in 1937–9, and again in 1946. After Independence he was Chief Minister of UP and Governor to Rajasthan.

Selected Works

Political works: *Bhārat ke deśī rāṣṭra* (1918); *Antarrāṣṭrīy vidhān* (1924); *Samājvād* (1936).

'Sanehī', Śukla, Gayāprasād—'Triśūl' (1883–1972)

Birthplace: Village Harha, district Unnav (UP).

Education

Educated until Middle examination in Hindi and Urdu.

Occupation

Teacher, poet.

Careers

Became a Middle School teacher at 16 but continued to study old Hindi, Urdu, and Persian literature. He began publishing poetry in Manoharlāl Dīkṣit's Braj Bhasa poetry journal *Rasikmitra* around 1904, and believed that training was necessary for poetry. His Khari Boli poem 'Kṛṣak-krandan', published in G.Ś. Vidyārthī's *Pratāp* in 1913, attracted M.P. Dvivedī's attention, and he asked Sanehī to write for *Sarasvatī* a poem on 'evil practices' like dowry. This was the first of a long series of poems on social issues and on Puranic characters and episodes in *Sarasvatī.* At Vidyārthī's urge, Sanehī started writing nationalist poems under the name 'Triśūl', while he kept writing on traditional Braj Bhasa themes for Svami Nārāyaṇānanda's *Kavīndra.* After *Kavīndra* closed down, 'Sanehī' himself edited the poetry journal *Sukavi* (1928–50). 'Triśūl's identity remained a mystery until Sanehī left his teaching job in 1921 and moved to Kanpur. One of the most famous nationalist poets of his day, he was instrumental in reviving kavi sammelans for nationalist purposes, and was extremely popular in them.

Selected Works

Poetry: *Prem-pachīsī, Kṛṣak-krandan* (1913), *Rāṣṭrīy mantra* (1921), *Rāṣṭrīy vīṇā* (1922), *Triśūl taraṅg* (1931), *Kalā meṁ triśūl.*

Sāṅkṛtyāyan, Rāhul (Kedārnāth Pāṇḍe, alias Baba Rāmodar Dās) (1893–1963)

Birthplace: Village Pandaha, district Azamgarh.

Background

His maternal grandfather was in the army.

Education

Formal education only upto the Urdu Middle Standard examination; later he underwent Sanskrit education in Benares, Ārya Samāj education at the Ārya Musāfir school in Agra, and Buddhist education in Sri Lanka.

Occupation

Scholar, political activist.

Career

After running away from his grandfather's home he started an itinerant life: travelled first to Benares, then to Calcutta, back to Benares and then off as an ascetic in the Himalayas. He then became a temple mahant under the name Rāmodar Dās; travelled to south India. In 1914 he was in Agra, then as an Ārya Samāj missionary in Lahore. Politically active since 1920, he was first a volunteer in Chapra with flood refugees, and thereafter a Non-Cooperator in Baksar, where he received his first jail sentence and became president of District Congress Committee. After a trip to Nepal he travelled for the first time to Sri Lanka in 1927 for nineteen months, then again was underground in Nepal and went over to Tibet. His first trip to Europe, the Soviet Union, and Asia dates from 1932–3. Active in Kisān Sabhā campaigns in Bihar in 1936, he was jailed during the Congress ministry and, in a famous case, was refused the status of 'political prisoner'; he once again joined the Bihar Congress in 1940 and was jailed between 1940 and 1942. In jail he underwent a new conversion to Communism and became member of the Communist Party; several trips to the Soviet Union followed. The prolific author of over 150 books on ancient Indian history and archaeology, political science, Buddhism, and Communism; the editor and translator of Sanskrit and Tibetan texts; the author of several travel books and of a four-volume autobiography, Rāhul became quite a legendary figure and exercised great allure in the Hindi literary sphere for his vast scholarship and unusual familiarity with Central and East Asia. He was also the author of several children's book and of a few novels. In 1939 he presided over the Bihar Hindī Sāhitya Sammelan, and in 1947 over the All India Hindī Sāhitya Sammelan and the Progressive Writers' Conference; he severed contacts with CPI in 1947 over the question of Urdu.

Śarmā, Padmasiṃh (1877–1932)

Birthplace: Nayak Nagla, district Bijnaur.

Background

Bhumihar family of peasant farmers.

Education

First in Urdu and Persian; Sanskrit (*Aṣṭādhyāya)* at the pāṭhśālā of Pandit Bhīmsen Śarṃa, a disciple of Dayānanda's, in Etawa. He then studied kāvyaśāstra with Pandit Jīvārām Śarmā, and spent two years at the Oriental College in Lahore, where he met Nardev Śarmā. Further studied grammar in Jalandhar with Paṇdit Gaṅgādatt Śāstrī and philosophy in Benares with Kāśīnāth Śāstrī.

Occupation

Scholar.

Career

From 1902 onwards he was preacher for the UP Ārya Pratinidhi Sabhā, and on the editorial board of the journal *Satyavādī,* edited by Munśirāṃ (later Svami Śraddhānand). In 1904 he taught at Gurukul Kangri, and in 1909–17 at Jvalapur Mahāvidyālay, where he edited the journal *Bhāratoday;* for some years he was also secretary of the managing committee of the Mahāvidyālay. A close friend and correspondent of M.P. Dvivedī, he regularly contributed learned essays to *Sarasvatī.* He did not agree, as a purist, with Lala Hansraj's mixed style for Hindi textbooks. In 1918 he was called to work in the publication department of Jnanmandal, Benares; there he published a famous commentary on Bihārī's *Satsaī,* the *Sañjīvan bhāṣya* (1922), which was awarded the first Maṅgalāprasād prize. A close friend of the Urdu poet Akbar Ilahabadi, Padmasiṃh Śarmā is considered the first comparative critic in Hindi. Banārsīdās Chaturvedī and Hariśaṅkar Śarmā were among his disciples. He presided over the XVIII Hindī Sāhitya Sammelan meeting in Moradabad in 1928. In his last years he cooperated with the Hindustani Academy, Allahabad: his speech 'Hindī, urdu, hindustānī' was published in 1932.

Selected Works

Literary criticism: *Sañjīvan bhāṣya* (1922); *Pad-parāg* (1929); *Hindī, urdu aur hindustānī* (1932).

Śarmā, Rāmjīlāl (1876–1931)

Birthplace: A village near Hapur, district Meerut.

Background

Poor but cultured Brahmin family; his father was a scholar of Sanskrit grammar.

Education

English until 5th standard in the village, Sanskrit with a pandit.

Occupation

Publicist, publisher.

Career

Orphaned at a young age, he moved with his family to Hapur in order to get a job. In 1899 he moved to Meerut, found work as a proofreader at the Ārya Samāj press of Pandit Tulsīrām and published two tracts: *Ṭake ser mukti* and *Ṭake ser lakṣmī.* He became an Ārya Samāji and began taking an interest in public affairs. Later he moved to Ajmer for another proofreader's job, and then to Allahabad in 1905, where he was employed by the Indian Press at a monthly salary of Rs 30. Between 1905 and 1913 he worked in the literature department of the Indian Press, writing children's books: e.g. *Bāl manusmṛti* (1907), *Bāl gītā* (1908), *Bāl viṣṇupurāṇa* (1909), *Bāl purāṇa* (1911); and textbooks like *Bālvinod* and *Bālābodhinī* (1912). He also translated I.C. Vidyasagar's *Sītā vanvās* (1909). In 1913 he started his own press, the Hindi Press, which published his own textbooks and the children's journals *Vidyārthī* (1913) and *Khilaunā* (1924). After meeting M.M. Mālavīya he started contributing to *Maryādā* and *Abhyuday.* He was involved in the Hindī Sāhitya Sammelan from the start, and became general secretary from 1923 to 1928; the managing committee led by him tried to oust Harihar Śarmā and take over the Dakṣin Bhārat Hindī Prachār Sabhā. Gandhi and Mālavīya had to intervene in the dispute.

Śāstrī, Harihar Nāth (1904–53)

Birthplace: Village Vajirapur, district Ballia (Eastern UP).

Background

The only son of a sub-inspector of police, Avatār Lāl, from Bihar, he was orphaned at a young age.

Education

Received his first schooling in Chapra, where he passed the High School examination. Went to Benares for further education; in 1921 he joined Kāśī Vidyāpīṭh.

Occupation

Political activist.

Career

Before joining the Vidyāpīṭh he stayed for a short while at the Gandhi ashrams in Patna and in Lahore, where he worked as a teacher and social worker under Lajpat Rai's influence. Was jailed during Non-Cooperation in 1921. After graduating from the Vidyāpīṭh, he worked first as member of Lajpat Rai's Lok Sevak Mandal among untouchables in Benares. Trained with trade union leaders in Bombay at Lajpat Rai's heed, he was sent to work among labourers in Kanpur and lived in the workers' quarter at Gwaltoli. Edited the journal *Mazdūr*. By 1929 he became general secretary of the Kanpur Mazdur Sabha, in 1931–7 was its president. Between 1933 and 1935 he was président of the All India Trade Union Congress, and was also in charge of its UP branch (1929). A founding member of the Congress Socialist Party, he was general secretary of its UP branch in 1934 and opened a branch in Kanpur in the same year. Member of the UP PCC, he was elected MLA in 1937–9. He resigned after Independence on the issue of the Communists' hold over its executive and over AITUC.

Sītārām, R.B. Lala (Avadhvāsī) (1858–1937)

Birthplace: Ayodhya.

Background

Family of Rāmānandī affiliation, originally from Jaunpur.

Education

First taught by Baba Raghunāthdayāl, then learnt Urdu and Persian with a maulvi and acquired Hindi proficiency by reading religious texts. Underwent some formal education, too, and acquired a BA in 1879 before taking an LLB.

Occupation

Civil servant, teacher, translator.

Career

First edited the newspaper *Avadh akhbār* and later taught at Benares Queen's College before becoming headmaster in Sitapur; was later appointed science teacher in Faizabad and then returned to Benares. In 1895 he was appointed Deputy Collector until he retired in 1909. All along he maintained a very close relationship with the Education Department, which he served as examiner and member of the Textbook Committee. He was appointed to write several volumes of *Hindi Selections* (1923) for the first University course in Hindi literature at Calcutta University, and was also involved in the Hindustani Academy, Allahabad. He wrote several textbooks, and poetry under the pen-name 'Bhūp'.

Selected Works

Translations: *Meghadūta* (1883); *Kumārasambhava* (1884); *Raghuvaṃśa* (1885), *Ṛtusaṃhāra* (1893); *Śṛṅgāraṭilaka, Uttararāmacharitmānas, Mālavikāgnimitra, Mṛcchakaṭika, Mahāvīrcharitra, Mālatīmādhava, Hitopadeśa*, etc. as well as some Shakespeare. Historical work: *Ayodhyā kā itihās.*

Śraddhānand, Svami (Lala Munśīrām) (1856–1926)

Birthplace: Talwan, district Jalandhar (Punjab).

Background

Born in a Khatri family, the son of a devout Śaivaite.

Education

Educated in several towns in UP: Benares, Banda, Mirzapur, Benares again and Allahabad; he enrolled at Government College, Lahore for law.

Occupation

Educator, activist.

Career

Munśīrām came early under the influence of Svami Dayānand Sarasvatī, and became president of the Jalandhar Ārya Samāj while starting his law practice. After an extensive fund-raising tour he established a Kanyā Pāṭhśālā in Jalandhar in 1890, which became the Kanyā Mahāvidyālay in 1896, partly thanks to the support of Ārya Samāj women preachers, newly organized into the Strī Samāj. The Kanyā Mahāvidyālay was a pioneering institution in female education and an important instrument of Hindi propaganda in the Punjab. Textbooks were written and an original curriculum was developed. In 1900, in opposition to the compromising and pro-English policy of DAV colleges, Munśīrām founded Gurukul Kangri, first in 1900 in the Vedic pāṭhśālā at Gujranvala and then in 1902 on donated land on the banks of the Ganges near Hardwar; he was its principal from 1902 to 1907. A Mahāvidyālay section was opened in 1907 for Vedic studies, Ayurveda, and humanities (Hindi medium). Initially not involved in politics (unlike DAV college Lahore with its revolutionary circle), the Gurukul grew progressively political. In 1919 Śraddhānand started the nationalist daily *Vijay* under the editorship of his son, Prof. Indra Vidyāvāchaspati (1889–1960), and an Urdu daily, *Tej*, and became involved in Non-Cooperation and Khilafat propaganda. He took saṃnyās in 1917. One of the animators of śuddhi activities within the Ārya Samāj, he held regular śuddhi conferences at the annual Gurukul anniversary celebrations, registered a Bhārat Śuddhi Sabhā in 1911, and renewed activism with the new Hindu Mahasabha in 1923. He was killed by an enraged Muslim in 1926.

Selected Works

Political writings: *Jāti ke dīnoṁ ko mat tyāgo* (1918); *Khatre kā ghaṇṭā* (1926). Autobiography: *Kalyāṇ mārg ke pathik* (1924).

Śrīvāstava, G.P. (1891–1976)

Birthplace: Chapra, Saran district.

Background

His father was a railway clerk, often transferred on duty.

Education

Initial education in Urdu with a maulvi at Chapra; then he followed his father to Gonda and passed the Matriculation exam from there in 1909. In 1910 he took the Entrance examination at Canning College, Lucknow; BA in 1913 and LLB in 1915.

Occupation

Writer, lawyer.

Career

He started by contributing humorous stories to Īśvarīprasād Śarmā's journal *Manorañjan* (Arrah, 1912). A well-known humorous writer, he wrote for all major Hindi journals, especially *Chāṁd* and *Sudhā*. Also translated R.C. Dutt's *The Lake of Palms* (1926). He was awarded a Coronation medal by the government in 1937, and made a public notary of Gonda district.

Selected Works

Short Stories: *Lambī dāṛhī* (1914), *Mār-mārkar hakīm* (1917), *Mardānī aurat* (1920), *Ulaṭpher* (1926), *Dumdār ādmī* (1927); *Vilāyatī ullū* (1932). Novels: *Dilkī āg urf diljale kī āh* (1933).

Śrīvāstava, Munshi Navjādiklāl (1888–1939)

Birthplace: A village near Ballia (eastern UP).

Background

After his father became a sadhu he had to provide for the family from an early age.

Education

Taught himself Hindi, Urdu, Bengali.

Occupation

Publicist.

Career

Forced by need, he moved to Calcutta and first worked as a postman. Thanks to contacts with various printers and journalists he taught himself Hindi, Urdu, and Bengali. Before joining the '*Matvālā* maṇḍal', with Mahādev Prasād Seṭh, Śivpūjan Sahāy, and Nirālā, he worked as a clerk for a soap- and oil-factory; for *Matvālā,* he looked after the accounts and wrote a popular humorous column called 'Matvāle kī bahak'. When Mahādev Prasād Seṭh wanted to move the journal to Mirzapur, he returned to the soap factory and started his own *Mast Matvālā*, but could not support it for long. Left Calcutta for Allahabad, where he edited *Chā̃d* from 1933 to 1935 after Rāmrakh Siṃh Sahgal's departure. After a few other unsuccessful ventures in Calcutta he died in severe penury. A public appeal was launched to raise a subscription for his family.

Śrīvāstava, Pratāpnārāyaṇ (1904–78)

Birthplace: Kanpur.

Background

Born in a wealthy family whose ancestors were officers during the Nawabi period.

Education

First at the Kanpur Ārya Samāj school, where Bhāgavatīcharaṇ Varmā was his classmate; Matriculation in 1921 and BA in 1925 from Christchurch College; in 1927 LLB from Lucknow University.

Occupation

Writer.

Career

While still studying for an MA in 1928, he was offered a post as judge in Jodhpur state but soon returned to Kanpur. In 1924 he started his first novel,

Vidā, an 'original social novel', which received wide acclaim when published in 1929 by the Ganga Pustak Mala with an enthusiastic foreward by Premchand. He then published a series of novels mostly about upper middle-class characters, each time selling the rights to the publisher; none however achieved the success and critical acclaim of the first. A solitary figure, he built a house and lived by writing and by renting out part of it.

Selected Works

Novels: *Vidā* (1929), *Pāp kī aur* (1930), *Vikās* (1938–9), *Vijay* (1937–8), *Bayālīs* (1942?).

Śukla, Devīdatt (1888–1970)

Birthplace: Village Baskar, district Unnao.

Education

Moved in 1908 to Benares to study Hindi and Sanskrit; failed the Intermediate examination.

Occupation

Editor.

Career

While studying in Benares Śukla had two articles published in the *Hindī baṅgvāsī* and in *Bhārat jīvan*, the old Benares weekly. Having failed his Intermediate examination, he applied in vain to *Bhāratamitra* in Calcutta and *Abhyuday* in Allahabad and started working in Benares as an ordinary clerk, first in the office of the Traffic Superintendent and then in that of the Superintendent of Police. He moved to a teaching job in a small town near Kanpur, then to the Education Department of Alwar state. In 1914–18 he travelled further away with a fellow villager to a job in Mahasamund (Central Provinces), but one article in *Maryādā* (in favour of the joint family system) and two (translated) articles in *Sarasvatī* attracted Dvivedī's attention. After he was recalled home to look after the family property, Śukla visited Dvivedī—who lived nearby and knew his uncle—for advice. Dvivedī offered him three potential posts: Śukla chose the one least paid but closest to Divedī, at the Indian Press. His understated style of work and writing, and his readiness to undertake any kind of writing or translation work, won him Dvivedī's favour and that of the publisher, and he rose steadily in the firm, acquiring experience in all aspects of publishing. So much so that when P.P. Bakhśī finally resigned from the editorship of *Sarasvatī* in 1928, Dvivedī suggested Śukla's name instead of looking for a more glamorous editor elsewhere. A typical self-made Hindi publicist, Śukla's presence in the Hindi world was a quiet one: he did not try to use his position in the Press to wield power, nor did he seek self-aggrandizement but took a quiet pride in his work. Until his retirement his abode in Allahabad was a tile-covered room on top of a house in the 'Black Town', where he cooked his own meals. A few photographs show him at home dressed in only a dhotī, and one in meditation covered in ashes—he was a śākta guru—quite a different identity from that in the office.

Śukla, Rāmchandra (1884–1941)

Birthplace: Village Agona, district Basti.

Background

His father was a sadar kanungo, educated at Queen's College, Benares, up to Entrance examination and was fluent in Urdu, Persian, and Sanskrit.

Education

Vidyārambh in Rath, district Hamirpur; in 1898 he took the Middle school examination in English and Urdu from the Anglo-Jubilee School in Mirzapur, and in 1901 the Final examination. At the Kayastha Pathshala in Allahabad he failed both first year (F.A.) in 1901 and the leadership examination in 1902.

Occupation

Literary scholar, university teacher.

Career

In Mirzapur Śuklajī developed literary taste and a knowledge of Hindi, Urdu, Sanskrit, and English thanks to Kedārnāth Pāṭhak and Badrīnārāyaṇ Chaudhrī 'Premghan'. He first joined the collector's office, and then the local Mission School as drawing master. At Śyāmsundar Dās' call he moved to Benares in 1908 to work on the *Hindī śabdasāgar* for the Nāgarī Prachāriṇī Sabhā and was involved in various Sabhā projects, including the *Nāgarī prachāriṇī patrikā*, where he published several scholarly articles and translations. He translated J. Edison's *Pleasures of the Imagination* (*Kalpanā kā ānand*, 1905), Samuel Smiles' *Plain Living and High Thinking* (*Ādarś jīvan*, 1914) and Arnold's *The Light of Asia* in Braj Bhasa verse (*Buddhacharita*,1922). In 1921 he was appointed, with Lala Bhagvān Dīn, as the first Hindi lecturer at BHU; after Ś. Dās' retirement he became Head of the Hindi department. He edited the three volumes of *Tulsī granthāvalī* (1923, with Lala Bhagvān Dīn and Brajratna Dās), the complete works of Jāyasī (1924), and Sūrdās' *Bhramar gīt* (1925) and wrote several textbooks. His history of Hindi literature (1923–9, rev. edn. 1940) is still the standard reference work in Hindi. His essays are collected in *Chintāmaṇi* (2 vols, 1939, 1945).

Sundarlāl, Pandit (1886–1981?)

Birthplace: Village Khatauli, district Muzaffarnagar.

Background

Born in an average Kayastha family, the son of Pandit Totārām, a renowned Ārya Samājist and petty government servant.

Education

Educated first at Saharanpur, then at DAV college, Lahore, where he befriended Lala Hardayal. In Allahabad to study law, he was rusticated in 1906 in a famous political incident and was prevented from taking the LLB examination. He was called 'Pandit' by M.M. Mālavīya and Tej Bahadur Sapru because of his keen interest in, and mastery of, religious scriptures.

Occupation

Political activist, publicist.

Career

He first came under the political influence of Lala Lajpat Rai and helped collect funds for Aurobindo Ghosh and other Bengali revolutionaries in 1905–7. At the 1906 Calcutta Congress he came in contact with Motilal Nehru and became a full-time political worker. In 1909 he founded the political fortnightly *Karmayogī* (18,000 copies), which was forced to close down in 1910 when he was sent to jail. In jail he took saṃnyās as Someśvarānand, and remained a bachelor and a *brahmachārī*. He was also implicated in the Delhi Conspiracy Case with Hardayal in 1913 and went underground between 1912 and 1916. In 1919 he briefly edited R. Sahgal's weekly *Bhaviṣya*, and in 1920 a daily by the same name—which was also forced to close down in 1921. He presided over the UP Provincial Political Conference in Kanpur in 1929, and between 1931 and 1932 he was put in charge of Congress activities in the Central Provinces; in Jabalpur he worked with Mākhanlāl Chaturvedī and Lakṣmaṇ Siṃh Chauhān. He was an excellent public speaker. In the language controversy he fought for Hindustani.

Selected Works

Songs: *Vaidik rāṣṭragīt* (1911, proscribed). History: *Bhārat meṁ aṅgrezī rāj* (1929, banned).

Ṭaṇḍon, Puruṣottam Dās (1882–1962)

Birthplace: Ahalyapur mohallā, Allahabad.

Background

Born in a Khatri family, the son of an ordinary government clerk affiliated to the Radhasoami sampradāy.

Education

First in Hindi with a local maulvi; Middle examination in 1894, Entrance in 1897, Intermediate in 1899 from Kayastha Pathshala with Ramanand Chatterjee as principal. BA in 1904 from Muir Central College, and LLB 1906 and MA in History in 1907.

Occupation

Lawyer, political activist.

Career

Ṭaṇḍon came early under the cultural influence of Bālkṛṣṇa Bhaṭṭ and the political influence of Madan Mohan Mālavīya. After two years of legal practice he joined the High Court in 1908 as Tej Bahadur Sapru's junior and practised until 1920, when he stopped because of Non-Cooperation. Interested in politics from the time of the pre-1900 Nagari campaign, he first took part in a Congress session in 1906 as a delegate. Also edited *Abhyuday* (1910–11) and *Maryādā*, and wrote especially on women's education and Hindi. He was given charge of the Hindī Sāhitya Sammelan right after the first meeting in Benares in 1910, and for years, until the present building was erected, the Sammelan office was in his own house. Between 1914 and 1918, at Mālavīya's heed, he worked as Law minister in Nabha state. In 1918 he presided over Mālavīya's Kisān Sabhā; in 1921 he was jailed for the first time. In 1921 he was also elected chairman of Allahabad Municipality, and was instrumental in establishing the Prayāg Mahilā Vidyāpīth and the Hindī Vidyāpīṭh (1925); the latter, however, did not flourish. In 1923 he presided over the XIII Hindī Sāhitya Sammelan in Kanpur. Refused to join the Hindu Mahasabha. From 1925 to 1929 he accepted a job as secretary of the Ārya Samāj Punjab National Bank in Lahore, where he became member of Lajpat Rai's Servants of the People Society and took over as president in 1928 after Lajpat Rai's death. While in Lahore he was not politically active, but after 1929 he was made President of the Allahabad District Congress Committee during Civil Disobedience and the no-rent campaign and was arrested again after a public meeting. Elected MLA from Allahabad City in 1936, he was made Speaker of the Legislative Assembly during the Congress ministry, and again in 1946. Convenor of the UP Report on Agrarian Conditions in 1936, he was one of the chief supporters of zamindari abolition. At first reluctant to sever Gandhi's relationship with the Sammelan over the Hindi–Hindustani issue, he eventually kept firmly on the Hindi side and accepted Gandhi's resignation. After Independence he took over Mālavīya's mantle as Nehru's chief opponent in the Allahabad and UP Congress; in a famous incident he was elected Congress President in 1951 defeating Nehru, but had to resign under the latter's pressure.

Tivārī, Veṅkateś Nārāyaṇ (1890–1965)

Birthplace: Kanpur.

Education
MA in history from Allahabad in 1910.

Occupation
Editor, political activist.

Career
Joined Gokhale's Sevants of India Society (1910–30) and was active in the Allahabad Congress. From 1914 to 1918 he was general secretary of the UP Provincial Congress Committee, and was member of the UP Legislative Council in 1927–30. In 1921–2 he was sent as secretary of a government of India deputation to British Guyana. He was particularly active during Civil Disobedience and the no-rent agitations in the countryside. He edited *Abhyuday* and *Maryādā* from 1916 to 1917 and again in 1918, and then became the editor of the Leader Press' Hindi weekly *Bhārat*, Allahabad, in 1928–30. A contributor to the Indian Press from 1907, after 1920 he contributed regularly to *Sarasvatī*. Elected MLA in 1937 and again in 1946, he became Parliamentary Secretary (Chief Whip) in the UP Congress ministry of 1937. When Sampūrṇānand refused to establish Urdu as the second official language in the province, raising a storm of protests from the Muslim League, Tivārī wrote a long series of articles in the Hindi press to support him, showing that the 'people's language' was Hindi and not Urdu. In 1953 he became editor of the daily *Jansattā* in Delhi.

Tripāṭhī, Rāmnareś (1881–1962)

Birthplace: Viiiage Koiripur, district Jaunpur.

Background
His grandfather had some land at village Sultanpur, in a small princely state, and worked there for a trader; his father joined the army of Nabha state and rose to the rank of *havaldār*.

Education
First in Urdu at the village until the inspector of schools Rāmnārāyaṇ Miśra (one of the founders of the Nāgarī Prachāriṇi Sabhā) urged him to study Hindi instead. After the Upper Primary examination in the village he went to

Jaunpur to study English at a high school, against his father's wishes, but had to stop after the 9th standard.

Occupation

Publisher, poet.

Career

His first literary exposure was through the Hindi journals subscribed to by the school: *Hindī baṅgvāsī* and *Hindī kesarī; Chandrakāntā* was the first novel he read. After a short spell as a teacher in a pāṭhśāla, he fled to Calcutta for further study. At first he worked as bookseller for the Ārya Samāj preacher Tekchand. Prevented by illness from studying, he was cured only after a long sojourn in Shekhavat (Marwar); there, with the help of Marwari friends, he opened a public library with over 5000 Hindi, Sanskrit and English books, and could study at length. After his father's death in 1915 he returned from Marwar and settled in Allahabad in 1917. He had already written Braj Bhasa poetry under a teacher's guidance; in Allahabad he started the first of his fortunate publishing ventures, *Kavitā-kaumudī*: an elegant and extremely well-produced seven-volume anthology of Hindi, Braj Bhasa, Urdu, Sanskrit, Bengali, and folk poetry. In 1918 he became member of the Home Rule League, and in 1920 he took part in the Non-Cooperation movement and toured the Jaunpur area for the Tilak Swaraj Fund. In 1921 he was fined and jailed for a year. After some indecision, in 1924 he started his own publishing house, Hindi Mandir, and in 1931 he acquired his own press which published literary books, children's books and textbooks, particularly for Sāhitya Sammelan Hindi examinations; he was also involved in the Hindi propaganda scheme in Madras. From 1919 to 1930 he toured all over north India collecting folk songs and produced a three-volume *Grām-gīt* (1930), the first work of its kind in Hindi. A good wrestler and swimmer, he took a five-year brahmacharya vow under the influence of Gandhi and Satyadeva Parivrājak. In 1931 he started editing a children's journal, *Bānar*, which became very popular. Tripāṭhī himself was a respected Khari Boli poet. After selling all his titles to the Sasta-Sahitya-Mandal he retired to Sultanpur, where he had been granted some land; there he built a house and planted an orchard.

Selected Works

Poetry: *Milan* (1928); *Mānasī* (1927); *Svapna* (1929); *Pathik* (1932, Hindustani Academy prize); as editor, *Kavitā-kaumudī* (seven volumes, 1917–24); *Grām-gīt* (1930). Novels: *Vīrāṅganā* (1911); *Vīrbālā* (1911), *Lakṣmī* (1924).

'Ugra', Pāṇḍey Bechan Śarmā (1900–67)

Birthplace: Chunar, district Mirzapur.

Background

Born in an extremely poor and troubled Brahmin family. His father was an addicted gambler and his elder brother a wayward fellow who acted in Rāmlīlā groups.

Education

Only a little primary education in Chunar, as he was expelled from school for rowdy behaviour. Later he partly resumed his education in Benares under B.V. Parāṛkar and Śivaprasād Gupta's tutelage.

Occupation

Writer.

Career

Orphaned early, he grew up under the 'tutelage' of his elder brother, who took him along to play in his Rāmlīlā group in Ayodhya, a difficult experience he later wrote frankly about in his autobiography. After a brief spell in Benares he found himself in Calcutta, where he worked for some time as a shop-clerk. At the time of Non-Cooperation he returned to Benares, joined the movement, and went to jail. In 1920 he wrote a long nationalist poem *Dhruvadhārṇā*, and contributed regularly nationalist stories to *Āj*. While in Benares, he learnt prosody from Lala Bhagvān Dīn. The special issue *Vijayāṅk* he edited of the Gorakhpur paper *Svadeś* was proscribed, and he landed in jail again. Once in Calcutta for a Congress session, he remained there at the *Matvālā* office; the owner Mahādevprasād Seṭh was ritually linked to Ugra's family. There he started writing sensational social novels that, according to a contemporary, 'sold like peanuts'. It was because of his collection of stories about male homosexuality, *Chakleṭ,* that Banārasīdās Chaturvedī launched his campaign against obscene literature. When *Matvālā* faced closure, Ugra moved to Bombay to work for silent films, but earned mostly debts. From Bombay he moved to Indore, where he edited the journals *Vīṇā* and *Svarājya* for some time, and the monthly *Vikram* from Ujjain. From 1945 to 1948 he was again in Bombay, then in Mirzapur until 1950, and after a year in Calcutta he moved eventually to Delhi.

Selected Works

Novels: *Chand hasīnoṁ ke khutūt* (1927); *Budhuā kī beṭī* (1928), *Dillī kā dalāl* (1928); *Chumban.* Short stories: *Chakleṭ* (1927); *Śarābī* (1930); *Ghaṇṭā; Sarkār tumhārī āṁkhoṁ meṁ* (1937); *Jījījī* (1943). Plays: *Mahātmā Isā.* Autobiography: *Apnī khabar* (1960).

Vājpeyī, Ambikāprasād (1880–1968)

Birthplace: Kanpur.

Background

Born in a family of Sanskrit scholars; his father, however, studied only a little mahājanī and went to Calcutta in search of work, first as a clerk and then as a middleman. The family remained in Kanpur.

Education

First in Urdu and Persian with a view to getting a job in the law courts; when one cousin established a school nearby in 1889, he joined it before going to Benares, Calcutta and eventually back to Kanpur District School; matriculated in 1900; one teacher's Hindi primer turned him from Urdu to Hindi.

Occupation

Publicist, political activist.

Career

After some hesitation he first joined Allahabad Bank as a clerk for three years; then, thanks to a relative, he entered the editorial board of the popular Calcutta paper *Hindī baṅgavāsī* and left after learning the rudiments of journalism. Between 1907 and 1910 he taught Hindi to Bengalis and Europeans in Calcutta and edited the journal *Nṛsiṃh*, under Tilak's influence. In 1911 he was offered the editorship of *Bhāratmitra*, and soon launched a daily edition on the occasion of the Delhi Darbar. He was gradually joined by B.V. Parāṛkar, Yaśodānandan Akhaurī, and other literary people, but broke with the managers in 1919 over ideological differences. In 1916 he had established the Calcutta branch of Tilak's Home Rule League; in 1917 he was vice-president of the welcome committee of Calcutta Congress, and in 1921 he went to jail during Non-Cooperation with C.R. Das, Maulana Azad, and others. Between 1920 and 1930 he edited from Benares the political paper *Svatantra*, which became very popular; it closed down when asked to furnish a security of Rs 5000. Between 1904 and 1919 he worked on a project for a Hindi grammar: *Hindī kaumudī*. In 1928 he was made undergraduate examiner for Hindi by Calcutta University, and graduate examiner in 1930. In 1939 he presided over the Hindī Sāhitya Sammelan meeting in Benares at the height of the Hindi–Hindustani controversy. For years he was member of the AICC and, after 1947, of the UP Legislative Assembly.

Selected Works

Linguistic works: *Hindī kaumudī* (1919); *Hindī par fārsī kā prabhāv* (1937; in English as *Persian Influence on Hindi* in 1936). Political works: *Bhārat-śāsan-paddhati* (1923–4); *Hinduoṁ kī rāj-kalpanā*. Others: *Samachārpatroṁ kā itihās* (1953).

Vājpeyī, Kiśorīdās (1898–1981)

Birthplace: Ramnagar, district Kanpur.

Education

Started in 1915 on a traditional Sanskrit curriculum in Brindaban with Kiśorīlāl Gosvāmī, author of popular novels who had opened a press and edited the journal *Vaiṣṇava sarvasva*. Sanskrit Śāstrī degree in 1919.

Occupation

Teacher, scholar, activist.

Career

After his śāstrī degree he moved to the Punjab in 1919, at the time of Jallianwala Bagh. There he started teaching Sanskrit at a Sanatan Dharma High School in Karnal district, and his love for the 'national' language blended with that for 'national freedom'. His manual of poetics with nationalist verses as examples was proscribed by the government (*Rasa aur alaṃkār*, 1931). Involved in Sammelan activities, he published his first Hindi articles on poetry and on grammar (of which he became an expert) in *Mādhurī*. He then decided to quit teaching and become a full-time literary journalist: after an unhappy encounter with *Sudhā's* Dulārelāl Bhārgava he joined *Chāṁd* in Allahabad. Later he resigned after Sahgal had criticized Madan Mohan Mālavīya. After a short spell at *Mādhurī*'s publication department, working on the critical edition of *Śrīmad bhāgavat*, he went back to teach at Hardwar Municipal school (1929–30), where he was expelled for taking part in the Civil Disobedience movement. During the movement he did political work in Agra with Kṛṣṇadatt Pālīvāl and then returned to his job in Hardwar. In 1938 he conducted a public campaign against the naked Naga babas at Hardwar's Kumbha mela. Another public campaign against bribery in government offices cost him his job during the Congress ministry, and only Ṭaṇḍon's intervention reinstated him. Active in Hindi propaganda in Punjab and Kashmir, he organized the 1942 Hindī Sāhitya Sammelan annual meeting at Bhaini Sahab in the Punjab.

Selected Works

Linguistic works: *Rasa aur alaṃkār* (1931); *Hindī śabdānuśāsan; Acchī hindī.* Autobiography: *Sāhityik jīvan ke anubhav aur saṃsmaraṇ.*

Varmā, Bhagavatīcharaṇ (1903–81)

Birthplace: Safipur village, district Unnao; childhood in Patkapur mohallā, Kanpur.

Background

His father was a lawyer in Kanpur.

Education

First at the local Ārya Samāj school, then at the Theosophical School; Intermediate in 1924; BA and LLB from Allahabad University (Holland Hall) in 1928.

Occupation

Lawyer, writer, script writer.

Career

After his father's early death and the death of his mentor in 1920, he had to look after the family under great financial pressure. He came early under the influence of G.Ś. Vidyārthī and published his first poem in *Pratāp* in 1917; among his friends were V. Śarmā 'Kauśik', B. Śarmā 'Navīn', and Ramāśaṅkar Avasthī. Urged by Vidyārthī to read V. Hugo, he also wrote articles on Marx, Mazzini, and prominent French revolutionary leaders for *Prabhā* in 1922–3. Fame as a Chāyāvādī poet came early, and he was published widely in Hindi journals; public recognition first came at the kavi sammelan during the XIII Hindī Sāhitya Sammelan meeting in Kanpur in 1923. His first novel *Patan* (1929) was a flop, but subsequently he became one of the best known and widely read Hindi novelists, and was also a good short-story writer. Once in Allahabad he came in contact with K.K. Mālavīya. After finishing University he tried his hand unsuccessfully at law practice in Hamirpur, then again in Allahabad. Once, short of money, he wrote a collection of poems for Ganga Pustak Mala in one day (called *Ek din*)! After the success of the novel *Chitralekhā* and of the film based on it, he was hired by a movie company in Calcutta as a scriptwriter; later he moved to Bombay but finally settled in Lucknow after 1997, earning comfortably from royalties.

Selected Works

Poetry: *Madhukaṇ* (1932), *Prem-saṅgīt* (1937), *Mānav*. Novels: *Patan* (1929), *Chitralekhā* (1934), *Tīn varṣ* (1946), *Ṭeṛhe-meṛhe rāste* (1946), *Bhūle-bisre chitr* (1959).

Varmā, Dhīrendra (1897–1973)

Birthplace: Bareilly.

Background

Born in an Ārya Samāji Kayastha family of zamindars.

Education

First traditional Sanskrit education; his father wanted to send him to Gurukul Kangri but he finally enrolled at DAV college in Dehradun in 1908 before moving in 1910 to the Queen's Anglo High School in Lucknow (where he was Dulārelāl Bhārgava's classmate). Intermediate in 1916 from Muir Central College; BA in 1918 and MA in Sanskrit in 1921, where he was one of Gaṅgānāth Jhā's favourite students and was awarded a two-year government scholarship for a D.Litt. In 1934 he went to Europe to study phonetics and was awarded a D.Litt. from Paris University for a thesis on Braj Bhasa.

Occupation

University teacher.

Career

Appointed as the first Hindi lecturer at Allahabad University in 1924, he set up the Hindi department there with Devīprasād Śukla (1924–9), and later with former students Rāmśaṅkar Śuka 'Rasāl' and Rāmkumār Varmā. He designed a different curriculum from BHU, more open to modern and contemporary literature, to linguistics and the history of language, and to comparative Indian literature, and he encouraged research in all these subjects. He was linked to the Hindī Sāhitya Sammelan, for which he was examiner, and was a secretary of the Hindustani Academy. In 1935 he became Reader, and in 1945 Professor; until his retirement in 1959 he was Head of the Hindi department and authored several textbooks. He wrote critically about Hindi's claim to rāṣṭrabhāṣā status, and his silence during the Hindi–Hindustani controversy was greatly resented in the Hindi camp.

Selected Works

Linguistics and literary criticism: *Brajbhāṣā vyākaraṇ* (1937); *Aṣṭachāp* (1938). Memoirs: *Merī kālij ḍāyrī* (1951). Essays: *Hindī rāṣtra yā sūbā hindustānī* (1930); *Vichār-dhārā*. Ed. *Hindī sāhitya koś* (1975).

Varmā, Mahādevī (1902–87)

Background

Born in a Kayastha service family originally from Farrukhabad; her father was the first in the family to learn English, after running away from a prospective clerical job to get a BA from Ewing Christian College and an MA in English from Allahabad University. Quite anglicized, he taught Indian princes, first in Darbhanga, then in Bhopal, and finally at the Daly College for princes in Indore; he later became minister of the nearby small state of

Narsinghgarh. He educated all his daughters and later supported Mahādevī's choice of living on her own. Her mother was not educated but was well versed in the religious oral tradition of Vallabha devotion.

Education

Liberally educated at home in literature (both Sanskrit and Braj Bhasa), music and drawing, and composed poetry first as a child. In 1918 she was sent to Crosthwaite College, Allahabad, where she stayed throughout her studies until her BA in 1929 (in 1925 Allahabad University stopped being co-educational), choosing English, philosophy, and Sanskrit as subjects. Subhadrā Kumārī Chauhān and Rāmeśvarī Goyal were her school friends there. She acquired an MA in Sanskrit from the same university.

Career

Started writing as a child, and from 1922 onwards, while still at college, she published her poems in *Chāṁd* and attended selected poetry readings of the Sukavi Samāj; in the beginning she used to write samasyā-pūrtis, then switched to *pragīt* under Pant's influence. Mahādevī got early recognition in the Hindi literary sphere, and her collection *Nīrjā* (1934) was awarded the Seksāriyā award. With Rāmkumār and Bhagavatīcharaṇ Varmā she was considered part of the 'small triad' of Chāyāvād. The unpleasantness of the Lucknow kavi sammelan she presided over in 1937 alienated her from public appearances. Married around 1913, she refused ever to live with her husband afterwards, and he complied. In 1930, she took to wearing khadi and teaching in two villages outside Allahabad, about which she wrote in *Atīt ke chalchitra* and *Śṛṅkhlā kī kaṛiyāṁ*. After a women's kavi sammelan marking the opening of the Mahilā Vidyāpīṭh College in 1932, she was chosen to become its principal. Between November 1935 and July 1938 she edited *Chāṁd*; her *Viduṣī aṅk* was especially praised. She was also instrumental in setting up a 'writers' parliament' in Allahabad, Sāhityakār Saṃsad, with government funds. Thanks to the Vidyāpīṭh she was on good terms with most Congress leaders in the province.

Selected Works

Poems: *Nihār* (1930), *Raśmi* (1932), *Nīrja* (1934), *Dīp-śikhā* (1942). Sketches and essays: *Atīt ke chalchitra* (1941), *Śṛṅkhalā kī kaṛiyāṁ* (1942), *Smṛti kī rekhāeṁ* (1943), *Sāhityakār kī āsthā* (first edn. 1940).

Varmā, Rāmchandra (1889–1969)

Birthplace: Benares.

Background

Born in a Chopra family originally from village Akalgarh, district Gujranvala (Punjab), where all Chopras were called 'Divan' from the time of Maharaja Ranjit Singh.

Occupation

Publicist and translator.

Career

From a very early age he became acquainted with Babu Rāmkṛṣṇa Varmā, the owner of Bharat Jivan Press, started contributing articles to *Bhārat jīvan*, and met Hindi literary people there. He edited *Hindī kesarī* from Nagpur in 1907–8, then started working at the great dictionary project for the Nāgarī Prachāriṇī Sabhā; later he also edited its concise version, the *Saṅkṣipta hindī śabdasāgar* (1933). Closely connected with the Sabhā, he also helped editing the *Nāgarī prachāriṇī patrikā* between 1913 and 1916. Edited the daily version of *Bhārat jīvan* after the First World War started, and took it over at Rāmkṛṣṇa Varmā's death. An extremely prolific translator from English, Urdu, Marathi, Gujarati, Bengali, and Persian and compiler of over sixty Hindi books on a wide range of literary, political, historical, and generally 'useful' subjects. Rāmchandra Varmā exemplifies the kind of strenuous work that was required in order to make ends meet as a Hindi writer. He also edited a Hindi-Urdu dictionary (1936).

Selected Works

Translations: Bernier's travels, S. Smiles' *Thrift* and *Self-Help*, Muhammad Husain Āzād's *Darbār-i-Akbari* (as *Akbarī darbār*, 1924–9), Svami Rāmdās' *Dāsbodh; Chatrasāl* (1919); *Sāmyavād* (1919); *Ham svarājya kyoṁ chāhte haiṁ; Mevāṛ patan* (1928); *Hindū-rājya-tantra* (1928); *Bhāratīy striyāṁ* (1927); *Sāmarthya, samṛddhi aur śānti* (1927); *Goroṁ kā prabhutva; Dharmoṁ kā itihās; Prāchīn mudrā* (1924), *Grāmīṇ samāj*; also translated Sharatchandra's collected works (1936–9).

Varmā, Rāmkumār (1905–?)

Birthplace: Sagar District (Central Provinces).

Background

His father was a Deputy Collector, constantly on transfer.

Education

At first Hindi education at home with his mother Rājrānī Devī, herself a poet. Primary education at various schools in Central India. In 1920 he passed the

Hindī Sāhitya Sammelan prathamā exam with first class marks; while still studying for the Entrance exam he left school in 1921 and started singing and composing songs for prabhat pheris, selling khadi, and giving public speeches. In 1925 he went to Allahabad University; BA in 1927 and MA in Hindi in 1929. Later Ph.D. from Sagar University.

Occupation

Poet, university lecturer.

Career

Published poems from an early age and was very fond of the *Rāmcharitmānas*. His poem 'Deś-sevā' fetched him the Rs 51 Khanna prize in 1922, and R.S. Sahgal asked his poems for *Chāṁd*. Immediately after his MA he was appointed lecturer in the Hindi department of Allahabad University. Widely published in all major Hindi journals, he was considered one of the three 'minor Chāyāvādīs' with Mahādevī and Bhagavatīcharaṇ Varmā. His collection *Chitrarekhā* won the Dev Puraskār in 1935. Authored plays and several textbooks.

Selected Works

Poems: *Vīr hamīr* (1922), *Chittāuṛ kī chitā* (1929), *Añjalī* (1931); *Chitrarekhā* (1935), *Jauhar* (1941). One-act plays: *Pṛthvīrāj kī āṁkheṁ* (1938), *Reśmī ṭāī* (1941), *Rūp-raṅg* 91951). Literary criticism: *Sāhitya samālochnā* (1929), *Kabīr kā rahasyavād* (1930), *Hindī sāhitya kā ālochnātmak itihās* (1939); ed., *Ādhunik hindī kkāvya* (1939).

Varmā, Vṛndāvanlāl (1889–1973)

Birthplace: Ranipur, a qasba near Jhansi.

Background

Born in an established but declining Kayastha family, whose ancestors had once been in the army of Maharaja Chatrasāl and ministers of the state. His father was a registrar kanungo.

Education

First at Lalitpur district school, then after the Middle school examination he enrolled at the high school in Jhansi, where he distinguished himself in English and sports. After a short spell at the kanungo office he joined the Victoria College in Jhansi, and moved to Agra in 1913 to study for an LLB.

Occupation

Lawyer, writer.

Career

A voracious reader with a vivid imagination as well as a passionate sportsman, he started writing very early; his first plays were bought by the Indian Press in 1905 but not published. Thanks to the uncle who sponsored his education, he became acquainted with Bhārtendu's works; as school prizes he read *Ivanhoe* and *Talisman*. He also read Tod, Max Müller, Darwin, and plenty of European literature. In Agra he became acquainted with G.Ś. Vidyārthī and Badrīnāth Bhaṭṭ; with the latter he wrote a humorous column in *Pratāp* called *Golmālkāriṇī sabhā*. Actively involved in public life, he wrote reports for *Pratāp* and campaigned for C.Y. Chintamani's election in 1920 in conflict with local Congress activists. Initiated the cooperative movement in Jhansi in 1924, and in 1936 was elected chairman of the district board. He took part in Congress and Hindī Sāhitya Sammelan meetings. Was a close friend of Vidyārthī and M.Ś. Gupta. He wrote occasionally for most Hindi journals but did not take up writing seriously until 1927 when he became the most popular and original historical novelist in Hindi. He specialised in writing about central India, especially Bundelkhand. A keen hunter and wanderer, he explored the region around Jhansi at length. His works, which span almost four decades, include among others: *Gaṛhkuṇḍār* (1927), a romance with a caste conflict in the fourteenth century as backdrop; *Virāṭā kī padminī* (1929), another romance set in the eighteenth century; *Musāhibjū* (1937), a short novel set around 1800, at the time of the British treaties and annexations; *Jhansī kī rānī Lakṣmībāī* (1946, initially banned in Central India); *Mādhavjī Sindhiyā* (1948); *Mṛgnainī* (1950), one of his most famous works, set in fifteenth- to sixteenth-century Gwalior; *Bhuronvikram* (1955) was an unusual leap in the late Vedic period; *Ahilyābāī* (1955); *Mahārānī Durgāvatī* (1961); and, published posthumously, *Kīcaṛ aur kamal*, on twelfth century Kalinjar, and *Devgāṛh kī muskān*, set in the eleventh century (both 1973).

Vidyālaṃkār, Jaychandra (1896–1977)

Birthplace: Kijkot, district Lyallpur (Punjab).

Background

Born in an Ārya Samāj family in which every member was involved in the nationalist movement: his brothers Dharmachandra, Devachandra, and Indrachandra Nāraṅg founded a publishing house in Allahabad, Hindi Bhavan; his sister Pārvatī Devī took to teaching at an Ārya Samāj school for girls after she was widowed in 1908, and in 1910 she became a public preacher; later she became headmistress of the Vedic Dharma Girls' School in Amritsar and kept contact with revolutionaries in Bengal, the United Provinces, and Punjab.

Education

Graduated from Gurukul Kangri.

Occupation

Historian, college teacher.

Career

Taught first at Gurukul Kangri, then at Gujarat Vidyāpīṭh; in 1921 he was appointed lecturer in history at the National College founded by Lajpat Rai: Bhagat Singh and Sukhdev were among his students. Afterwords he taught at Bihār Vidyāpīṭh from its inception. His *Bhāratvarṣa kī kahānī* (1924) was written especially for children; *Bhārat kā bhaugolik ādhār* (1925) was found objectionable by the police during the Patna Conspiracy Case because it would help revolutionaries identify easy targets in India's communication network; his monumental *Bhārtīy itihās kī rūprekhā* (1934) won the Maṅgalāprasād prize. In 1936, with Rajendra Prasad's help, he founded the Bhārtīy Itihās Pariṣad and was on the editorial board of the monumental *Bhārtīy itihās* in twenty volumes, presided over by Jadunath Sarkar. He went to jail in 1942.

Selected Works

Historical works: *Bhāratvarṣa kā itihās* (1924); *Bhārat kā bhaugolik ādhār* (1925); *Bhārtīy itihās kī rūprekhā* (1934); *Bhārtīy vaṅmay ke amar ratna* (1936).

Vidyārthī, Gaṇeś Śaṅkar (1890–1931)

Birthplace: Kanpur.

Background

Born in an average Kayastha family, his father was a schoolmaster in an Anglo-vernacular school in Gwalior district.

Education

In 1907 he passed the Entrance examination from Christchurch College, Kanpur, and was admitted to the Kayastha Pathshala, Allahabad, where he met Pandit Sundarlāl, but had to leave after a few months owing to financial difficulties.

Occupation

Editor, publicist, political activist.

Career

His first job was at the currency office in Kanpur at a monthly salary of Rs 80. He resigned in 1909. After a short spell of teaching at Rs 20 he was introduced to M.P. Dvivedī and was hired to assist him on *Sarasvatī* in 1911 for Rs 25 per month; meanwhile he accepted an offer from *Abhyuday* in 1912 and moved to Allahabad as assistant editor at Rs 50 a month. After a year's experience there, he returned to Kanpur in 1913 to found the weekly *Pratāp* in the populous Philkhana mohallā with no financial support whatsoever. The first special issue, *Rāṣṭrīy aṅk*, in September 1914, offered 60 pages of articles for 4 annas. The Pratap office became a meeting place for political activists (even revolutionaries like Bhagat Singh) and Hindi literary people. A '*Pratāp* family' was established with Gayāprasād Śukla 'Sanehī' (Triśūl), Ramāśaṅkar Avasthī, Śivnārāyaṇ Miśra (the manager), Bālkṛṣṇa Śarmā 'Navīn', Kṛṣṇadatt Pālīvāl, etc. Further literary friendships included M.Ś. Gupta, V. Varmā, Premchand, Mākhanlāl Chaturvedī and many others. In the 1920s, the Pratap Pustak Mala published political biographies, socialist propaganda, nationalist pamphlets, and song-books. Direct political involvement started when he became a founding member of the Kanpur branch of Annie Besant's Home Rule League in 1916 (Tilak's photo hung above his desk). He then took part in, and reported on, the 1916 Lucknow Congress and organized an Ek-lipi-ek-bhāṣā Sammelan there. Thereafter he became a follower of Gandhi. He gave full coverage to Champaran's enquiry and supported the Kanpur mill strikes in 1919. He was jailed after a libel case following his reports on the Munshiganj police firing on a peasants' meeting. In 1920 he took over the monthly *Prabhā* from M. Chaturvedī. He became convenor of Congress District Conference in Kanpur in 1921, with delegates from villages and wards of the city, and as President of Fatehpur Political Conference in 1923 he was prosecuted for his seditious speeches; at the news of his arrest, most bazaars in Kanpur shut down. While in Naini central jail (1923–4 [*Jel-ḍairī*]) he became a fervent reciter of the *Rāmcharitmānas.* In 1925 he was secretary of the welcome committee of Kanpur Congress. Despite his opposition to Council entry he was selected as Swarajya Party candidate for 1926 elections and was elected with an overwhelming majority. During 1927–9 he was member of the Legislative Council. Involved in political and propaganda work in the district, in 1929 he founded a Congress ashram in Narwal village. As president of the UP Political Conference in Farrukhabad, he urged the adoption of an economic resolution. Killed during the 1931 Kanpur riots.

Viyogī Hari (Hariprasād Dvivedī) (1896–1988)

Birthplace: Chattarpur state (Bundelkhand).

Education

Orphaned at young age, he was educated first at home in Sanskrit and Hindi; in 1915 he matriculated from Chattarpur High School, but had to break off his studies at Intermediate College.

Occupation

Poet, literary activist.

Career

His keen interest in Indian philosophy was cultivated under Babu Gulābrāi's tutelage, who at the time was divan at Chattarpur. A *protegé* of the Rani, Viyogī Hari toured India's pilgrimage places with her. In 1915 met P.D. Ṭaṇḍon in Allahabad and was persuaded to stay and work as volunteer for the Hindī Sāhitya Sammelan and the *Sammelan patrikā* and became one of Ṭaṇḍon's closest assistants. Involved in Sammelan work, he wrote text-books and annotated anthologies for the Sammelan examinations and helped Ṭaṇḍon to found the Hindī Vidyāpīṭh in 1925. On a pilgrimage to south India in 1921, he took saṃnyās and changed his name to Viyogī Hari. He was particularly fond of Tulsī's *Vinaypatrikā*, and wrote a commentary on it and poetry in Braj Bhasa. In 1932 he left literature to work for the Harijan Sevak Sangh in Delhi and edited the Hindi version of *Harijan sevak.* Later he was involved in the *bhūdān* movement. He wrote about forty books in all.

Selected Works

Poetry: *Braj mādhurī sār* (1923); *Vīr satsaī* (1928 awarded Maṅgalāprasād prize); *Viśvadharma* (1930).

Select Bibliography

I. HINDI JOURNALS

I.1. Main Sources

Wherever possible, I have given the dates of change of editorship (not always mentioned in the journal), and the date when the journal stopped publication; the last line shows the issues consulted. All the main sources were collected at the Hindī Sāhitya Sammelan Pustakālay in Allahabad.

Chāṁd (1922–4?): monthly, Allahabad.
Editors:
Rāmrakh Siṃh Sahgal (1922–33),
Navjādiklāl Śrīvāstava (1933–5),
Mahādevī Varmā (1935–8),
Chatursen Śāstrī (1938–).
I, 6 (April 1923) to XVIII, pt. 2, 5 (April 1941).

Gṛhalakṣmī (1909–29): monthly, Allahabad.
Editors: Gopālādevī Prabhākar (Thakur Śrīnāth Siṃh).
V, 2 (April–May 1913) to XV, 6 (August–September 1924).

Mādhurī (1922–50): monthly, Lucknow.
Editors:
Dulārelāl Bhārgava and Rūpnārāyaṇ Pāṇḍey (1922–6),
Premchand and Kṛṣṇabihārī Miśra (1926–31),
Rāmsevak Tripāṭhī (1931–2), Mātādīn Śukla (1933–5),
Rūpnārāyaṇ Pāṇḍey and B. B. Bhaṭnāgar (1935–50).
I, 6 (December 1922) to X, pt. 1, 6 (January 1932).

Maryādā (1910–22): monthly, Allahabad; 1921–2, Benares.
Editors:
P.D. Ṭaṇḍon, Kṛṣṇakānt Mālavīya,

Sampūrṇānand, Premchand (from XXII, 1, October–November 1921).
I, 1 (November 1910) to XXIV, 6 (*caitra* 1979, March–April 1922).

Sammelan patrikā (1913–): monthly, Allahabad.
Editors:
Girijākumār Ghoṣ (1913–14), Viyogī Hari (1924), Rāmkumār Varmā (1927), Jyotiprasād Miśra 'Nirmal' (1940).
I, 6 (February–March 1913 to XXIX, 11–12 [May–July 1942]).

Strī-darpaṇ (1909–28): monthly, Allahabad; from XXIX, 4 (October 1923), Kanpur.
Editors:
Rāmeśvarī, Umā and Rūpkumārī Nehru;
Sumati Devī and Phulkumārī Mehrotrā in Kanpur.
V, 6 (December 1911) to XL, 6 (June 1928).

Sudhā (1927–4?): monthly, Lucknow.
Editors:
Dulārelāl Bhārgava; assistant editors: Rūpnārāyaṇ Pāṇḍey, Nirālā, Ilāchandra Jośī.
I, pt. 1, 5 (December 1927) to XIV, pt. 1, 5 (December 1940)

Viśāl bhārat (1928–38): monthly, Calcutta.
Editor:
Banārsīdās Chaturvedī.
I, 1 (January 1928) to XIX, 1 (January 1937).

I.2. Other Journals Consulted

Āj (1920–): daily, Benares.
Editors: Bābūrāo Viṣṇu Parāṛkar, Śrīprakāś.
Selected issues.

Haṃs (1930–45): monthly, Benares.
Editor: Premchand.
I, 1 (March 1930) to I, 5 (July 1930)

Kalyāṇ (1926–): monthly, Bombay, then Gorakhpur.
Editor: Hanumān Prasād Poddār.
II, 3 (November 1926) to XII, pt. 10, no. 11.

Nāgarī prachāriṇī patrikā (1896–): first quarterly, then monthly, and since 1920 again quarterly, Benares.

Editors:
Śyāmsundar Dās, Sudhākar Dvivedī, Kāśīdās, Rādhākṛṣṇa Dās, Rāmchandra Śukla, Rāmchandra Varmā, Benīprasād, G.H. Ojhā, Chandradhar Śarmā Gulerī, Munshi Devīprasād. At different times, Vāsudevśaraṇ Agravāl, Kṛṣṇadev Prasād Gauṛ, and Sampūrṇānand were also involved.

Prabhā (1913–): monthly, Khandwa (Central Provinces); since 1920, Kanpur.
Editors:
Mākhanlāl Chaturvedī, G. Ś. Vidyārthī, Bālkṛṣṇa Śarmā 'Navīn'.
Selected issues.

Pratāp (1913, 1920): weekly, daily, Kanpur.
Editors: G.Ś. Vidyārthī, Bālkṛṣna Śarmā 'Navīn'.
Selected issues.

Prem (1926–), organ of Prem Mahāvidyālay, monthly, Brindaban.
Editor: Acharya A.T. Gidvāṇī.
I, 1 (1926) to II, pt. 2, 5 (July 1928)

Saṅgharṣ (1937): organ of the Congress Socialist Party, weekly, Lucknow.
Editors: Narendra Dev, Sampūrṇānand.
I, 1 (December 1937) to I, pt. 2, 3 (January 1938).

Sarasvatī (1900–75): monthly, Allahabad.
Editors:
Mahāvīr Prasād Dvivedī (1903–20);
P.P. Bakhśī (1921–5 and 1927–9)
Devīdatt Śukla (1928–46).
1913, 1915–16, 1930–8.

Vidyāpīṭh (1928–): quarterly, published by Kāśī Vidyāpīṭh, Benares.
Editors: Bhagvān Dās, Narendra Dev.
I, 1 (1928) to IV, 1 (1936).

II. ENGLISH OFFICIAL SOURCES, PAMPHLETS AND REFERENCES

Blumhardt, J.F, *Catalogues of the Hindi, Panjabi, Sindhi and Pushtu Printed Books in the Library of the British Museum*, London, Asher, Kegan and Longmans, 1893.

Catalogue of Books Printed in the North-Western Provinces (quarterly publications, variously titled), for the years 1873 to 1875, Allahabad,

Oriental and India Office Library Collections (OIOLC), British Museum, London.

Chand, Tara, 'Some Misconceptions About Hindustani', pamphlet printed at the Leader Press, Allahabad, n.d. but possibly around 1935.

General Report on Public Instruction in the United Provinces of Agra and Oudh (variously title), 1919–27, OIOLC.

Half-Yearly List of Reported Newspapers and Periodicals, Government Press, Allahabad) for the relevant years, OIOLC.

Report of the Working of the Hindustani Academy, United Provinces, Allahabad (1927–39), Allahabad, Hindustani Academy, 1939.

Shaw, Graham, ed., *Publications Proscribed by the Government of India: A Catalogue of the Collections in the India Office Library and Records*, London , India Office Library and Records, 1985.

Shaw, Graham and S. Quraishi, eds, *The Bibliography of South Asian Periodicals: A Union List of Periodicals in South Asian Languages, South Asian Library Group,* Brighton, Harvester, 1982.

Statement of Newspapers and Periodicals Published in UP, Government Press, Allahabad, for the relevant years, OIOLC.

'The Chand Press, Limited Allahabad. Directors' Report and Balance Sheet for the Period Ending 31 May 1933', Allahabad 1933.

The Progress of Education in India, Quinquennial Review, Calcutta, for the years 1917–27, OIOLC.

II.1. Hindi Pamphlets, Official and Unpublished Sources:

47 varṣ ke mukhya mukhya kāryoṁ kā saṅkṣipta vivaraṇ, Benares, Nagari Pracharini Sabha, samvat 1997 (1940).

Anon., *Ham bhukhe naṅge kyoṁ haiṁ?* Kanpur, Kisan Mazdur Pustak Mala, 1935.

Āryabhāṣā pustakālay kā sūchīpatr, vol. 1, Benares, Nagari Pracharini Sabha, 1958.

Asahyog āndolan sambandhī kāśī kī patr-patrikāeṁ, vol. 1, Delhi, Nehru Memorial Museum and Library, 1986, from Abhimanyu Pustakalay, Benares.

Berī, Krṣṇachandra, 'Hindī prakāśan kā itihās', typewritten article, n.d.

Ek-lipi vistār pariṣad - niyamāvalī, Calcutta, n.d., Benares, Aryabhasa Pustakalay.

Hindī sāhitya sammelan kā vārṣik vivaraṇ, Allahabad, Hindī Sāhitya Sammelan, for the years 1910–11, 1911–12.

Hindī sāhitya sammelan kī parīkṣāoṁ kī vivaraṇ-patrikā, saṃvat 1982, Allahabad, Hindi Sahitya Sammelan, 1915.

Hindī-sāhitya-sammelan ke hindī-viśvavidyālay kī parīkṣāoṁ kī vivaraṇ-patrikā, saṃvat 1995–6 [1938–9], Allahabad, Hindi Sahitya Sammelan, 1939.

Nāgarī prachāriṇī sabhā kā vārṣik vivaraṇ, Kāśī Nāgarī Prachāriṇī Sabhā, for the years 1920–1, 1921–2, 1923–4, 1924–5, 1924–5, 1928–9, 1929–30, 1932–3, 1933–4, 1935–6, 1937–8, 1938–9, 1939–40. Benares, Aryabhasa Pustakalay.

Parmānand, Bhāī, *Ārya-samā aur kāṅgres*, Lahore, Akasvani Pustakalay, 1925.

Rāykṛṣṇadās, *Prasād kī yād*. Unpublished manuscript, n.d.

Reports of Hindī Sāhitya Sammelan yearly meetings (variously titled) for: I Benares Sammelan (1910); II Allahabad Sammelan (1912); XIII Kanpur Sammelan (1923); XVIII Muzaffarpur (Bihar) Sammelan (1928); XX Calcutta Sammelan (1931); XXIV Indore Sammelan (1935); XXVII Simla Sammelan (1938); XXX Abohar (Punjab) Sammelan (1941).

Sahajānand Sarasvatī, Svami, *Kisānoṁ ke dost aur duśman*, Bihta, Patna, 1942.

Sampūrṇānand, *Chetsiṃh aur kāśī kā vidroh*, Pratap Pustak Mala no. 13, Kanpur, Pratap Press, 1919.

Satyāgrah saptāh (Mālavīyajī kā bhāṣaṇ), Calcutta, Hindi Pustak Agency, *jyeṣṭ* 1979 (1922).

Sītārām, Lala, *Hindī sarve kameṭī kā riporṭ*, Allahabad, Hindustani Academy, 1930.

Svarājya par mālavīyajī, Kanpur, Pratap Karyalay, 1917.

Tripāṭhī, Rāmnareś, *Mārvāṛe ke manohar gīt*, Allahabad, Hindi Mandir, 1930.

Vidyālaṃkār, Prāṇnāth, *Bhārtīy kisān*, Benares, 1921.

Viśvanāth Prasād, 'Jñānmaṇḍal', typewritten article, n.d.

III. HINDI BOOKS AND ARTICLES

Agravāl, Puruṣottam, 'Rāṣṭrakavi kī rāṣṭrīy chetnā', *Ālochnā*, October–December 1986, pp. 127–36.

———, 'Jātivādī kaun', in Rājkiśor, ed., *Harijan se Dalit,* Delhi, Vani Prakasan, 1994.

———, *Saṃskṛti: varchasva aur pratirodh*, Delhi, Radhakrishna Prakasan, 1995.

Ali, Mushtaq, 'Hindī sāhitya ke itihās meṁ ilāhābād kā yogdān, iṇḍiyan preṡ ke viśiṣṭ sandarbh meṁ', unpublished Ph.D. thesis, University of Allahabad, 1989.

Avadhnandan and Satyanārāyaṇ, *Hindī kī dūsrī pustak,* Madras, Hindi Prachar Pustak Mala, 18th edn, 1939.

Avasthī, Rādhākṛṣṇa, ed., *Krānti kā udghoṣ. Gaṇeś śaṅkar vidyārthī kī kalam se,* 2 vols, Kanpur, Ganesh Shankar Vidyarthi Shiksha Samiti, 1978.

'Bachchan', Harivaṃs Rāy, 'Kavi-sammelan: ek siṃhāvalokan', in A. Kumār, ed., *Bachchan rachnāvalī*, vol. 6, Delhi, Rajkamal Prakasan, third edn, 1987.

Bakhśī, Padumlāl Punnālāl, *Merī apnī kathā*, Allahabad, Indian Press, 1972.

Bhaṭṭ, Badrīnāth, *Tulsīdās nāṭak*, Gokulpura (Agra), Rambhushan Pustakalay, 1922.

———, *Rānī durgāvatī*, Lucknow, Ganga Pustak Mala, 1925.

Bhavānīprasād, *Āryabhāṣa pāṭhāvalī*, 2 parts, Kangri, Gurukul Press, 1927.

Bihār hindī sāhitya sammelan kā itihās (1919–55), Patna, Bihar Hindi Sahitya Sammelan, 1956.

Brahmānand, *Bhārtīy svatantratā āndolan aur uttar pradeś kī hindī patrakāritā*, Delhi, Vani Prakasan, 1986.

Bṛhat hindī koś, eds, K. Prasād, R. Sahāy and M. Śrīvāstava, Benares, Jnanmandal, 1989 (1952).

Chaturvedī, Sītārām, *Mahāmanā madan mohan mālavīya*, Benares, Akhil Bhartiya Vikrama Parishad, 1948.

Chaturvedī, Śrīnārāyaṇ, ed., *Sarasvatī hīrak-jayantī viśeṣāṅk: 1900–59,* Allahabad, Indian Press, 1961.

———, *Manorañjak saṃsmaraṇ*, Allahabad, Indian Press 1965.

Chauhān, Sudhā, *Milā tej se tej,* Allahabad, Hans Prakasan, 1975.

Criticism on the Hindi Reader No. III by Mahavir Prasad Dvivedi, Jhansi, 1899.

Darbār, Gyānvatī, *Bhārtīy netāoṁ kī hindī-sevā,* New Delhi, Ranjan Prakasan, 1961.

Dās, Brajratna, *Bhārtendu maṇḍal,* Benares, Sri Kamalmani-Granthamala-Karyalay, 1949.

Dās, Jagannāth (Ratnākar), comp., *Samasyāpūrti, arthāt kāśī kavisamāj ke dvādaś adhiveśanoṁ par jo pūrtiyāṁ kāśīstha tathā anek deś deśāntar ke kaviyoṁ kī kī huī paṛhī gaī thīṁ*, pt. 1, Benares, saṃvat 1951 (1894).

Dās, Śyāmsundar, *Sāhityālochan*, Benares, Sahitya-Ratna-Mala-Karyalay, 1922.

———, *Hindi Prose Selection* for classes 9 and 10 of High schools, Allahabad, Indian Press, 1929.

———, *Hindī ke nirmātā*, vol. 2, Allahabad, Indian Press, 1941.

———, *Merī ātmakahānī*, Allahabad, Indian Press, 1957.

Devavrat, ed., *Gaṇeś śaṅkar vidyārthī*, Delhi, Atmaram and Sons, 1931.

Dīn, Lala Bhagvān, *Vīr pañcharatna*, Calcutta, Burmen Press, 1918.

———, and R. Gauṛ, *Hindī bhāṣā sār*, prose section, Allahabad, Hindi Sahitya Sammelan, 1927 (1916).

Dvivedī, Devīdatt, *Bhārat kī varṇavyavasthā aur svarājya*, printed by the author, district Fatehpur, Gram Simaura, 1929.

Dvivedī, Mahāvīr Prasād, *Sampattiśāstra*, Allahabad, Indian Press, 1907.

———, *Hindī kī pahlī pustak*, Allahabad, Indian Press, 1911.

Gāndhī-ṭaṇdan-smṛti-aṅk, *Sammelan patrikā*, LV, 3–4, June–December 1969, Allahabad, Hindi Sahitya Sammelan.

Gauṛ, H.P., *Sarasvatī aur rāṣṭrīy jāgaraṇ*, Delhi, National Publishing House, 1986.

Gopāl, Madan, *Bhārtendu hariśchandra*, Delhi, Sahitya Akademi, 1978.

Goyinka, K.K., *Premchand kā aprāpya sāhitya*, 2 vols, New Delhi, Bhartiy Jnanpith, 1988.

Gupta, Lakṣmīnārāyaṇ, *Hindī bhāṣā aur sāhitya ko ārya-samāj kī den*, Lucknow, Lucknow University, 1960.

Gupta, Maithilīśaraṇ, *Bhārat-bhārtī*, 37th reprint, Chirgaon (Jhansi), Sahitya Sadan, 1991 (1912).

Gupta, Manmohan, *Ek krāntikārī ke saṃsmāraṇ*, Allahabad, Indian Press, 1969.

Guru, Kāmtāprasād, *Padya samuchchaya*, Allahabad, Indian Press, 3rd edn, 1934.

'Harioudh', Ayodhyāsiṃh Upādhyāy and Girijādatt Śukla 'Girīś', *Sāhitya-mālā* for classes 5 and 6 (illust.), Benares, Nandkishor and Bros., 1932.

Jain, Ṛṣabhcharaṇ, *Gadar*, Delhi, Hindi Pustak Karyalay, 1930.

Jośī, Śrīkānt, ed., *Mākahanlāl chaturvedī rachnāvalī*, vol. 2, Delhi, Vani Prakasan, 1983.

Kanhāiyālāl, *Rāṣṭrīy śikṣā kā itihās*, Benares, Kashi Vidyapith 1929.

Kapūr, Kālidās, *Hindī-sār-saṅgrah* for classes 4 and 5, Allahabad, Agraval Press, 1933.

———, *Sāhitya-samālochnā*, Allahabad, Indian Press, 1929.

Kauśik, Viśvambharnāth Śarmā, *Chitraśālā*, Lucknow, Ganga-Pustak-Mala, 1924.

Khatrī, Śrīkṛṣṇa, *Sāṁgīt bīrmatī*, Kanpur, 1921.

Kṛṣṇanāth, ed., *Kāśī vidyāpīṭh hīrak jayantī. Abhinandan granth*, Benares, Kashi Vidyapith, 1983.

Kumār, Ajit, *Bachchan rachnāvalī*, vols 6 and 9, Delhi, Rajkamal Prakasan, 3rd edn, 1987.

Kumār, Jainendra, *Parakh*, Bombay, Hindi-Grantha-Ratnakar, 1930 (1929).

———, *Sunītā*, New Delhi, Purvoday Prakasan, 1990 (1935).

———, *Tyāgpatra*, Delhi, Purvoday Prakasan, 1956 (1937).

———, *Mere bhaṭkāv*, New Delhi, Purvoday Prakashan, 1978.

Lakhanpāl, Chandrāvatī, *Striyoṁ kī sthiti*, Lucknow, Ganga Pustak Mala, 1934, third edn, 1941 (first edn Gurukul Kangri 1932).

Lāl, Mukuṭ Bihārī, *Āchārya narendradev: yug aur netṛtva*, Benares, Vishvavidyalay Prakashan, 1987.

Madhureś, *Devkīnandan Khatrī*, New Delhi, Sahitya Akademi, 1980.

Mālavīya, Kṛṣṇakānt, *Sohāg-rāt*, Allahabad, Abhyuday Press, 1927.

Mālavīya, Padmakānt, ed., *Mālavīyajī ke lekh*, Delhi, National Publishing House, 1962.

'Manorañjan', 'Madhuśālā kā sarvapratham sammelan: ek saṃsmaraṇ', in D. Śaraṇ, *Bachchan jī kā jivan tathā vyaktitva*, Kanpur, Sahitya Niketan, 1967, pp. 54–61.

Marsden, E. and Rāmchandra Prasād, *Bhāratvarṣa kā itihās*, Calcutta, Macmillan, 1920.

Milind, Satyaprakāś, ed., *Hindī kī mahilā sāhityakār*, Delhi, Rupkamal Prakasan, 1960.

Miśra, Keśavprasād and Pītāmbardatt Baṛathvāl, *Padya parijāt*, Benares, Nagari Pracharini Sabha, 1931.

Miśra, Kṛṣṇabihārī, *Hindī patrakāritā. Jātīy chetnā aur khaṛī bolī sāhitya kī nirmāṇ bhūmi*, Delhi, Bhartiy Jnanpith, 1985 (1968).

Miśra, Śitikaṇṭh, *Khaṛī bolī kā āndolan*, Benares, Nagari Pracharini Sabha, 1957.

Miśra, Śivaprasād, ed., *Bhārtendu granthāvalī*, vol. 1, Benares, Nagari Pracharini Sabha, 1974.

Miśra, Vidyānivās, ed., *Hindī-may jīvan. Paṇḍit śrīnārāyaṇ chaturvedī*, Delhi, Prabhat Prakashan, n.d.

Motīchandra, *Kāśī kā itihās*, Benares, Visvavidyalay Prakasan, 1962.

Nānakchand, Lala, *Amar siṃh raṭhaur*, Moradabad, 1910.

Nāgar, Amṛtlāl, *Jinke sāth jiyā*, Delhi, Rajpal and Sons, 1973.

Nirālā, Sūryakānt Tripāṭhī, *Nirālā rachnāvalī*, 7 vols, ed. Nandkiśor Naval, Delhi, Rajkamal Prakasan, 1992.

'Nirmal', Jyotiprasād Miśra, *Strī-kavi-kaumudī: hindī meṁ striyoṁ ke kāvya-sāhitya kā vistṛt vivechan*, Allahabad, Gandhi-Hindi-Pustak Bhandar, 1931.

———, ed., *Ṭaṇḍan nibandhāvali. rājarṣi puruṣottamdās ṭaṇḍan ke sāhityik, sāṃskṛtik, rāṣṭrabhāṣā sambandhī tathā anya upyogī nibandhoṁ kā saṅgrah*, Wardha, Rastrabhasha Prachar Samiti, 1970.

Ojhā, Gaurīśaṅkar Hirāchand, *Solāṅkiyoṁ kā prāchīn itihās*, Ajmer, Vedic Karyalay, 1907.

———, *Rājputāne kā itihās*, Ajmer, Vedic Karyalay, 1925.

———, *Madhyakālīn bhārtīy saṃskṛti*, Allahabad, Hindustani Akademi, 1928.

Pāṇḍey, Śyāmnārāyaṇ, *Hāldī ghāṭī*, Allahabad, Indian Press, 1938.

Pant, Sumitrānandan, *Pallav*, Delhi, Rajkamal Prakasan, 1963 (1926).

Prasād, Ratnaśaṅkar, ed., *Prasād vaṅmay*, Benares, Prasad Prakasan, 1990.

Prem, Dhanīrām, *Vallarī*, Allahabad, Chand Press, 1932.

Premchand, *Sevā-sadan*, Delhi, Rajkamal Prakasan, 1994 (1919).

———, *Premāśram*, Allahabad, Hans Prakasan, 1962 (1921).

———, *Nirmalā*, Sadhna New Delhi, Pocket Books, 1990 (1927).

———, *Samar-yātrā*, Benares, 1930.

———, *Mānsarovar*, vol. 7, Allahabad, Sarasvati Press, 1962.

———, *Vividh prasaṅg*, 3 vols, Allahabad, Hans Prakasan, 1980 (1962).

Rādhākṛṣṇa, ed., *Gaṇeś Śaṅkar Vidyārthī ke śreṣṭh nibandh*, Delhi, Atmaram and Sons, 1964.

Rāi, Sujātā, *'Prabhā' aur rāṣṭrīy jāgaraṇ*, New Delhi, Anamika Prakasan, 1989.

Rājkiśor, ed., *Harijan se dalit*, Delhi, Vani Prakasan, 1994.

Rāy, Gopāl, *Hindī upanyās koś*, 2 vols, Patna, Grantha Niketan, 1968.

Rāykṛṣṇadās, ed., *Ikkīs kahāniyāṁ*, Allahabad, Bharti Bhandar, 1941.

Sahajānand Sarasvatī, *Merā jīvan saṅghars*, New Delhi, People Publishing House, 1985.

Sahāy, Śivpūjan, *Smṛtiśeṣ*, New Delhi, Rajkamal Prakasan, 1994.

Saksenā, Rājīv, *Vṛndāvanlāl varmā*, Delhi, Sahitya Akademi, 1985.

Salil, Sureś, ed., *Gaṇeś śaṅkar vidyārthī kī jel-ḍāirī*, Delhi, Pravin Prakasan, 1981.

Sampūrṇānand, Narendra Dev, Śrīprakāś, J.P. Nārāyaṇ, Dāmodar Svarūp Seṭh, Govind Sahāy, *Samyavād kā bigul*, Benares, Kashi Pustak Bhandar, 1936.

Sāṅkṛtyāyan, Rāhul, *Merī jīvan-yātrā*, vol. 2, Allahabad, Kitab Mahal, 1950.

Śaraṇ, Dīnānāth, *Bachchan jī kā jīvan tathā vyaktitva*, Kanpur, Sahitya Niketan, 1967.

Śarmā, Ayodhyānāth and Sadguru Saran, *Sāhitya suman*, 3 parts, Kanpur, Gautam Press, n.d.

Śarmā, Bīnā, 'Pragatiśīl sāhitya ke vikās meṁ "rūpābh" kā yogdān', unpublished M. Phil. dissertation, Centre of Indian Languages, New Delhi, Jawaharlal Nehru University, 1980.

Śarmā, Hemant, ed., *Bhārtendu samagra,* Hindi Pracharak Sansthan, Benares, 1987.

Śarmā, Manu, 'Hindī sāhitya ko kāśī kā den', *Smārikā*, special *Mānas chatuśsatī samāroh*, Benares, January 1974.

Śarmā, Padmasiṃh, *Hindī, urdū, hindustānī*, Allahabad, Hindustani Akademi, 1951 (1932).

Śarmā, Rāmjīlāl, *Bālvinod*, pt. 5, Allahabad, Indian Press, 1910.

———, *Bālābodhinī*, pt. 5, Allahabad, Indian Press, 1912.

Śarmā, Rāmvilās, *Nirālā kī sāhitya sādhnā*, 3 vols, New Delhi, Rajkamal Prakasan, 1969.

———, *Rāmchandra śukla aur hindī ālochnā*, New Delhi, Rajkamal Prakasan, 1973.

———, *Bhārtendu yug aur hindī bhāṣā kī vikās paramparā*, New Delhi, Rajkamal Prakasan, 1975 (1942).

———, *Mahāvīr prasād dvivedī aur hindī navjāgaraṇ,* New Delhi, Rajkamal Prakasan, 1977.

Śāstrī, Chatursen, *Hindū-rāṣṭra kā navnirmāṇ,* Delhi, Hindi-Sahitya-mandal, 1933.

Śāstrī, Ūrmilā, *Kārāgār,* Delhi, Atmaram and Sons, 1980 (1931).

Siṃh, Bachchan, *Āchārya śukla kā itihās paṛhte hue*, New Delhi, National Publishing House, 1989.

Siṃh, Baijnāth, ed., *Dvivedī patrāvalī*, Allahabad, Hindustani Academy, 1954.

———, ed., *Dvivedīyug ke sāhityakāroṁ ke kuch patr*, Allahabad, Hindustani Academy, 1958.

Siṃh, Dhīrendranāth, *Ādhunik hindī ke vikās meṁ khaḍgavilās pres kī bhūmikā*, Patna, Bihar Rastrabhasa Parisad, 1986.

———, ed., Śītlā Prasād Tripāṭhī, *Jānakīmaṅgal nāṭak*, Benares, Nagari Pracharini Sabha, 1996.

Siṃh, Jagmohan and Chamanlāl, eds, *Bhagatsiṃh aur unke sāthiyoṁ ke dastāvez*, Delhi, Rajkamal Prakasan, 1991 (1987).

Siṃh, Lakṣmīnārāyaṇ, *Rājarṣi puruṣottam dās ṭaṇḍan*, Allahabad, Hindi Sahitya Sammelan, 1982.

Siṃh, Nāmvar, *Chāyāvād*, New Delhi, Rajkamal Prakasan, 1955.

———, 'Pantjī kā rūpābh', *Ālochnā*, no. 43, October–December 1977.

———, *Dūsrī paramparā kī khoj*, New Delhi, Rajkamal Prakasan, 1982.

Siṃh, Śiva Prasād, *Itihās timirnāśak*, vol. 3, Allahabad, Government Press, 1874.

Siṃh, Ṭhākurprasād, ed., *Svatantratā saṅgrām ke sainik*, vol. 3, *zilā Ilāhābād*, Allahabad, 1970.

———, *Svatantratā saṅgrām ke sainik*, vol. 11, *zilā Dehrādūn*, Allahabad, 1970.

———, *Svatantratā saṅgrām ke sainik*, vol. 16, *zilā Meraṭh*, Allahabad, 1970.

Siṃh, Tribhuvan Nārāyaṇ, *1921 ke asahyog āndolan kī jhāṁkiyāṁ*, New Delhi, Publications Division, Ministry of Information and Broadcasting, 1971.

Śiśir, Karmendu, ed., *Matvāle kī chakkī*, Hapur, Sambhavna Prakasan, 1990.

Śrīvāstava, G.P., *Dil kī āg urf diljale kī āh*, Allahabad, Chand Press, 2nd edn, 1936 (1933).

Śrīvāstava, Mukundīlāl, *Hindī kī chauthī pustak*, Benares, Jnanmandal, 1925.

Śrīvāstava, Navjādiklāl, *Matvālekī bahak*, ed. Karmendu Śiśir, Hapur, Sambhavna Prakasan, 1988.

Śrīvāstava, Śalīgrām, *Prayāg pradīp*, Allahabad, Hindustani Academy, 1937.

Śukla, Devīdatt, *Kuch kharī-kharī*, Allahabad, Kalyan Mandir 1949.

———, *Sampādak ke pacchīs varṣ*, Allahabad, Kalyan Mandir, 1956.

Śukla, Rāmchandra, *Chintāmaṇi*, 1st part, Allahabad, Indian Press, 1939.

———, *Gosvāmī tulsīdās*, Benares, Nagari Pracharini Sabha, 1983.

———, *Hindī sāhtya kā itihās*, Benares, Nagari Pracharini Sabha, 1990 (1940).

———, *Pratinidhi nibandh*, ed. S. Pāṇḍey, New Delhi, Radhakrishna Prakasan, 1976.

Śukla, Raviśaṅkar, *Hindīvālo, savdhān!* Benares, Nagari Pracharini Sabha, 1947.

Suman, Kṣemchandra, *Divaṅgat hindī-sevī*, New Delhi, Shakun Prakashan, 1981.

Sundarlāl, Pandit, *Bhārat meṁ aṅgrezī rājya*, Allahabad, Omkar Press, 1938 (1929).

Talvār, Vīr Bhārat, *Kisān, rāṣṭrīy āndolan aur premchand: 1918–22. Premāśram aur avadh ke kisān āndolan kā viśeṣ adhyayan*, New Delhi, Northern Book Centre, 1990.

———, *Rāṣṭrīy navjāgaraṇ aur sāhitya: kuch prasaṅg, kuch pravṛttiyāṁ*, Delhi, Himachal Pustak Bhandar, 1993.

Ṭaṇḍon, Puruṣottam Dās, *Ṭaṇḍan nibandhāvalī*, Wardha, Rastrabhasa Prachar Samiti, 1970.

Tripāṭhī, Rāmnareś, *Grām-gīt*, 3 vols, Allahabad, Hindi Mandir, 1930.

———, *Svapnoṁ ke chitr*, Allahabad, Hindi Mandir, 1930.

———, ed., *Kavitā-kaumudi*, 7 vols, Allahabad, Hindi Mandir, 1917–30.

'Ugra', Pāṇḍe Bechan Śarmā, *Chakleṭ*, Calcutta, Tandon Bros., 1953.

———, *Chand hasīnoṁ ke khutūt*, Mirzapur, Bisvim Sadi Pustakalay, 1927.

———, *Dillī kā dalāl*, Mirzapur, Bisvim Sadi Pustakalay, 1927.

Vājpeyī, Ambikāprasād, *Samachārpatroṁ kā itihās*, Benares, Jnanmandal, 1953.

Vājpeyī, Kiśorīdās, *Sāhityik jīvan ke anubhav aur saṃsmāraṇ*, Kankhal, Himalay Agency, 1953.

Varmā, Bhagavatīcharaṇ, *Atīt ke gart se*, Delhi, Rajkamal Prakasan, 1979.

Varmā, Dhīrendra, ed., *Pariṣad nibandhāvalī*, pt. 1, 1929.

———, *Hindī rāṣṭra yā sūbā hindustānī*, Allahabad, Leader Press, 1930.

———, ed., *Hindī sāhitya koś*, vol. 2, Benares, Jnanmandal, 1985.

Varmā, Mahādevī, *Śṛṅkhalā kī kaṛiyāṁ*, Allahabad, Bharti Bhandar, 1942.

———, *Sāhityakār kī āsthā tathā anya nibandh* (originally published as *Mahādevī Varmā kā vivechnātmak gadya*), Allahabad, Students Friends, 1944.

Varmā, Paripūrṇānand, *Bītī yādeṁ*, New Delhi, Purvoday Prakashan, 1976.

Varmā, Vṛndāvanlāl, *Jhānsī kī rānī lakṣmībāī*, Jhansi, Mayur Prakasan, 1987 (1946).

———, *Apnī kahānī*, Delhi, Prabhat Prakasan, 1993 (1962).

Varṣṇey, Lakṣmīsāgar, *Ādhunik hindī sāhitya kī bhūmikā*, Allahabad, Hindi Parishad, 1952.

Vidyālaṃkār, Jaychandra, *Bhārtīy itihās kī rūprekhā*, 2 vols, Allahabad, Hindustani Academy, 1933.

Vidyālaṃkār, Prāṇnāth, *Bhārtīy kisān*, Rāṣṭrīy Sañjīvanī Granthamālā, Benares, vol. 1, 1920.

Viyogī Hari, *Vīr satsaī,* Allahabad, Gandhi-Hindi-Pustak-Bhandar, 1927.

Yādav, Rājendr, *Sārā ākāś*, Delhi, Akshar Prakasan,1968 (English trs. as *Strangers on the Roof*, Delhi, Penguin, 1994).

'Yadavendu', Rāmnārāyaṇ, *Bhārat kā dalit samāj,* Agra, Navyug Sahitya Niketan, 1940.

IV. ENGLISH BOOKS, DISSERTATIONS, ETC.

Agnew, V., *Elite Women in Indian Politics,* New Delhi, Vikas, 1979.

Ahmad, Aijaz, *In Theory: Classes, Nations, Literatures*, Delhi, Oxford University Press, 1992.

Ahmad, Nazir, 'Development of Printing in Urdu, 1743–1857', unpublished M. Phil. thesis, School of Library Archive and Information Studies, University of London, 1976.

Amin, Shahid, 'Gandhi as Mahatma: Gorakhpur District, Eastern UP, 1921–2', in R. Guha, ed., *Subaltern Studies III*, Delhi, Oxford University Press, 1984, pp. 1–55.

———, *Event, Metaphor, Memory: Chauri-Chaura 1922–92*, Delhi, Oxford University Press, 1995.

Anderson, Benedict, *Imagined Communities: Reflections on the Origin and Spread of Nationalism*, Verso, London, 1983.

Appadurai, Arjun, 'Number in the Colonial Imagination', in C.A. Breckenridge and P. van der Veer, eds, *Orientalism and the Postcolonial Predicament,* Philadelphia, University of Pennsylvania Press, 1993, pp. 314–39.

Arnold, David and David Hardiman, eds, *Subaltern Studies VIII*, Delhi, Oxford University Press, 1994.

Assayag, Jackie, *The Making of Democratic Inequality: Caste, Class, Lobbies and Politics in Contemporary India (1880–1995)*, Pondicherry, Pondy Papers in Social Sciences, 1995.

Auerbach, Erich, *Mimesis: The Representation of Reality in Western Literature*, Princeton, Princeton University Press, 1953.

Bagchi, N.G., *Chintamoni Ghosh: The Saga of the Indian Press*, Allahabad, Indian Press, 1984.

Baker, D.E.U., *Changing Political Leadership in An Indian Province: The Central Provinces and Berar, 1919–39*, Delhi, Oxford University Press, 1979.

Banerjee, Sumanta, *The Parlour and the Street. Elite and Popular Culture in Nineteenth-Century Calcutta,* Calcutta, Seagull, 1989.

Barrell, John, *English Literature in History, 1730–80: An Equal, Wide Survey*, London, Hutchinson, 1983.

Basu, Aparna, *The Growth of Education and Political Development in India, 1898–1920*, Delhi, Oxford University Press, 1974.

Baxter, Craig, *Jana Sangha: A Biography of An Indian Political Party,* Philadelphia, Pennsylvania University Press, 1969.

Bayly, C.A., *The Local Roots of Indian Politics, Allahabad 1880–1920,* Oxford, Clarendon Press, 1975.

———, *Rulers, Townsmen and Bazaars*, Cambridge, Cambridge University Press, 1988.

———, *Indian Society and the Making of the British Empire: The New Cambridge History of India*, vol. II-1, Cambridge, Cambridge University Press, 1988.

———, *Empire and Information*, Cambridge, Cambridge University Press, 1996.

Bayly, Susan, 'Hindu "modernizers" and the "public" arena: indigenous critiques of caste in colonial India', paper presented at the conference on 'Vivekananda and the Modernization of Hinduism', London, School of Oriental and African Studies, 1993.

Bell, D.V.J., *Power, Influence, Authority*, London, Oxford University Press, 1975.

Bhargava, M.L., *History of Secondary Education in UP*, Lucknow, Superintendent Printing and Stationery, 1958.

———, *Ganesh Shankar Vidyarthi*, Delhi, Publications Division, Ministry of Information and Broadcasting, 1988.

Bhatia, Tej. K, *A History of the Hindi Grammatical Tradition*, Leiden, Brill, 1987.

Bhatnagar, Ram Ratan, *The Rise and Growth of Hindi Journalism,* Allahabad, Kitab Mahal, 1951.

Bhattacharya, Tithi, 'Defining the Bhadralok Through Print', paper presented at the SOAS history seminar, University of London, December, 1998.

Blackburn, Stuart, 'The Tale of the Book: Print and Storytelling in 19th Century Tamil', in R. Dwyer and C. Pinney, eds, *Pleasure and the Nation: The History, Politics and Consumption of Public Culture in India*, Delhi, OUP, 2001.

Brass, Paul, *Factional Politics in An Indian State: The Congress Party in Uttar Pradesh*, Cambridge, Cambridge University Press, 1962.

———, *Language, Religion and Politics in North India*, Cambridge, Cambridge University Press, 1974.

Brass, Paul with Francis Robinson, eds, *The Indian National Congress and Indian Society, 1885–1985: Ideology, Social Structure and Political Dominance*, Delhi, Chanakya Publications, 1987.

Breckenridge, C.A. and P. van der Veer, eds, *Orientalism and the Postcolonial Predicament,* Philadelphia, University of Pennsylvania Press, 1993.

Calhoun, Craig, ed., *Habermas and the Public Sphere*, Massachusetts, MIT Press, Cambridge, 1992.

Carroll, Lucy, 'Colonial Perceptions of Indian Society and the Emergence of Caste(s) Associations', *Journal of Asian Studies*, 37, 2, February 1978, pp. 233–50.

Chakrabarty, Dipesh, 'The Difference–deferral of Colonial Modernity: Public Debates on Domesticity in British Bengal', in D. Arnold and D. Hardiman, eds, *Subaltern Studies VIII*, Delhi, Oxford University Press, 1994.

Chakravarti, Uma, 'Whatever Happened to the Vedic Dasi? Orientalism, Nationalism and a Script for the Past', in K. Sangari and S. Vaid, eds, *Recasting Women*, Delhi, Kali for Women, 1989.

Chandra, Sudhir, ed., *Social Transformation and Creative Imagination*, Delhi, Allied Publishers, 1984.

———, 'Communal Elements in Late Nineteenth Century Hindi Literature', in M. Hasan, ed., *Communal and Pan-Islamic Trends in Colonial India*, Delhi, Manohar, 1986.

———, *The Oppressive Present: Literature and the Social Imagination*, Delhi, Oxford University Press, 1992.

Chatterjee, Indrani, 'The Bengali Bhadramahila. 1930–4', unpublished M. Phil. thesis, New Delhi, Jawaharlal Nehru University, 1986.

Chatterjee, Partha, *Nationalist Thought and the Colonial World: A Derivative Discourse?*, London, Zed Books, 1986.

Chatterjee, Partha and G. Pandey, eds, *Subaltern Studies VII*, Delhi, Oxford University Press, 1992.

———, *The Nation and Its Fragments*, Princeton, Princeton University Press, 1993.

Chaturvedi, S.N., *The History of Rural Education in the United Provinces of Agra and Oudh (1840–1926)*, Allahabad, Indian Press, 1930.

———, *An Educational Survey of a District*, Allahabad, Indian Press, 1935.

Cohn, Bernard, 'The Command of Language and the Language of

Command', in R. Guha, ed., *Subaltern Studies IV*, Delhi, Oxford University Press 1985, pp. 276–329.

———, 'Representing Authority in Victorian India', in E.J. Hobsbawm and T. Ranger, eds, *The Invention of Tradition*, Cambridge, Cambridge University Press, 1990.

Dalmia, Vasudha, *The Nationalization of Hindu Traditions: Bhāratendu Hariśchandra and Nineteenth-Century Benares*, Delhi, Oxford University Press, 1997.

Dalmia, Vasudha and H. von Stietencron, eds, *Representing Hinduism: The Construction of Religious Traditions and National Identity*, Delhi, Sage Publications, 1995.

Dalmia, Vasudha and T. Damsteegt, eds, *Narrative Strategies*, Delhi, Oxford University Press, 1999.

Damodaran, Vinita, *Broken Promises. Popular Protest, Indian Nationalism and the Congress Party in Bihar*, Delhi, Oxford University Press, 1992.

Dar, S.N. and S. Somaskandam, *History of Benares Hindu University*, Benares, 1966.

Das, Sisir Kumar, *Sahibs and Munshis: An Account of the College of Fort William*, Calcutta, Orion Publications, 1978.

———, *A History of Indian Literature, 1800–1910, Western Impact: Indian Response*, vol. VIII, New Delhi, Sahitya Akademi, 1991.

Das Gupta, Jyotirindranath, *Language Conflict and National Development: Group Politics and National Language Policy in India*, Berkeley, University of California Press, 1970.

DeJean, Joan, *Tender Geographies: Women and the Origins of the Novel in France,* New York, Columbia University Press, 1991.

Dev, Acharya Narendra, *Socialism and the National Revolution*, ed. Yusuf Meherally, Bombay, Padma Publications, 1946.

Devy, Ganesh, *After Amnesia: Tradition and Change in Indian Literary Criticism,* Bombay, Orient Longman, 1992.

Dharwadker, Vinay, 'Orientalism and the Study of Indian Literatures', in C.A. Breckendridge and P. van der Veer, eds, *Orientalism and the Postcolonial Predicament*, Philadelphia, Pennsylvania University Press, 1993, pp. 158–85.

Dittmer, Kerrin, *Die Indischen Muslims und die Hindi–Urdu Kontroversie in den United Provinces*, Wiesbaden, Harrassowitz, 1972.

Dwyer, Rachel and Chris Pinney, eds, *Pleasure and the Nation: The History, Politics and Consumption of Public Culture in India*, Delhi, OUP, 2001.

Eisenstein, Elizabeth, *The Printing Revolution in Early Modern Europe*, 2 vols, Cambridge, Cambridge University Press, 1983.

Eley, Geoff, 'Nations, Publics and Political Cultures: Placing Habermas in the Nineteenth Century', in C. Calhoun, ed., *Habermas and the Public Sphere*, Cambridge, MIT Press, 1992, pp. 289–339.

Faruqi, Shamsur Rahman, *Early Urdu Literary Culture and History*, Delhi, Oxford University Press, 2001.

Forbes, Geraldine, *Women in India*, Cambridge, Cambridge University Press, 1996.

Fraser, Nancy, 'Rethinking the Public Sphere: A Contribution to the Critique of Actually Existing Democracy', in C. Calhoun, ed., *Habermas and the Public Sphere*, Cambridge, MIT Press, 1992.

Freitag, Sandria B., ed., *Culture and Power in Benares: Community, Performance, and Environment, 1800–1980,* Berkeley, University of California Press, 1989.

———, *Collective Action and Community: Public Arenas and the Emergence of Communalism in North India*, Delhi, Oxford University Press, 1990.

———, ed., special issue of *South Asia* on *Aspects of the Public in Colonial South Asia*, XIV, 1, June 1991. ('Introduction', pp. 1–13; and 'Enactments of Ram's Story and the Changing Nature of the Public in British India', pp. 65–90.)

Gaeffke, Peter, *Hindi Literature in the Twentieth Century*, Wiesbaden, Harrassowitz, 1978.

Gandhi, Mohandas Karamchand, *Hind Swaraj*, Cambridge, Cambridge University Press, 1997 (1907).

Ghosh, Anindita, 'Literature, Language and Print in Bengal, *c.* 1780–1905', unpublished Ph.D. thesis, University of Cambridge, 1998.

Gerow, Edwin, *A Glossary of Indian Figures of Speech*, Mouton, Le Hague, 1971.

———, *Indian Poetics. A History of Indian Literature*, vol. 5, fasc. 3, Wiesbaden, Harrassowitz, 1977.

Goody, Jack and Ian Watt, 'The Consequences of Literacy', in J. Goody, ed., *Literacy in Traditional Societies*, Cambridge, Cambridge University Press, 1968.

Gooptu, Nandini, 'The Political Culture of the Urban Poor: The United Provinces between the Two World Wars', unpublished' Ph.D. thesis, Cambridge University, 1991.

Gopal, S., ed., *Selected Works of Jawaharlal Nehru,* vol. 5, New Delhi, Orient Longman, 1973.

Gould, Harold A., 'The Rise of the Congress System in a District Political Culture: The Case of Faizabad District in Eastern Uttar Pradesh', in P. Brass and F. Robinson, eds, *The Indian National Congress and Indian Society, 1885–1985: Ideology, Social Structure and Poitical Dominance*, Delhi, Chanakya Publications, 1987, pp. 242–313.

Grierson, George, *Bihar Peasant Life*, Patna, Government Printing Press, 1885, 2nd edn, 1926 (1885).

Guha, Ranajit, *Elementary Aspects of Peasant Insurgency in Colonial India*, Delhi, Oxford University Press, 1983.

———, ed., *Subaltern Studies III*, Delhi, Oxford University Press, 1984.

———, ed., *Subaltern Studies IV*, Delhi, Oxford University Press, 1985.

———, *An Indian Historiography of India: A Nineteenth-Century Agenda and Its Implications*, Calcutta, K.P. Bagchi, 1988.

Gupta, Rakesh, *Bihar Peasantry and the Kisan Sabha (1936–47)*, New Delhi, People's Publishing House, 1982.

Habermas, Jürgen, *The Structural Transformation of the Public Sphere,* Cambridge, MIT Press, 1989 (original German edition 1962),

Haider, Syed Jalaluddin, 'Munshi Nawal Kishore (1836–95): Mirror of Urdu Printing in British India', *Libri,* XXXI, 3, September 1987.

Hansen, Kathryn, 'The Virangana in North Indian History: Myth and Popular Culture', *Economic and Political Weekly*, XXIII, 18, 30 April 1988, Women's Studies, pp. 25–33.

———, 'The Birth of Hindi Drama in Benares, 1868–85', in S. Freitag, ed., *Culture and Power in Benares,* Berkeley, University of California Press, 1989, pp. 62–92.

———, *Grounds for Play: The Nautanki Theatre of North India*, Berkeley, University of California Press, 1992.

Hauser, Walter, 'Swami Sahajanand Sarasvati and the Politics of Social Reform, 1907–50', *Indian Historical Review,* 18, 1–2 (July 1991–January 1992).

———, *Sahajanand on Agricultural Labour and the Rural Poor: An edited Translation of Khet Mazdoor with the Original Hindi Text,* Delhi, Manohar, 1994.

Haynes, Douglas E., *Rhetoric and Ritual in Colonial India: The Shaping of a Public Culture in Surat City, 1852–1928,* Berkeley, University of California Press, 1991.

Hohendal, Peter Uwe, *Institution of Criticism*, Ithaca, Cornell University Press, 1982.

Horstmann, Monika, 'Towards a Universal Dharma: Kalyāṇ and the Tracts of the Gita Press', in V. Dalmia and H. von Stietencron, eds, *Representing Hinduism: The Construction of Religious Traditions and National Identity*, Delhi, Sage Publications, 1995.

Hudson, William, *Introduction to the Study of Literature*, London, Harrap, 1910.

Inden, Ronald, *Imagining India*, Oxford, Basil Blackwell, 1990.

Jaffrelot, Christophe, *The Hindu Nationalist Movement and Indian Politics*, London, Hurst, 1996.

Joshi, Priya 'Culture and Consumption: Fiction, the Reading Public, and the British Novel in Colonial India', *Book History,* I (1998).

Joshi, Shashi and Bhagwan Josh, *Struggle for Hegemony in India: Culture, Community and Power,* vol. 3, New Delhi, Sage Publications, 1994.

Jones, Kenneth W., *Arya Dharm: Hindu Consciousness in Nineteenth Century Punjab,* Berkeley, California University Press, 1976.

———, ed., *Religious Controversy in British India: Dialogues in South Asian Languages*, Albany, University of New York Press, 1992.

Joshi, P.C., ed. *Rebellion in 1857*, Calcutta, P.C. Bagchi, 1986.

Juergensmeyer, Mark, *Radhasoami Reality: The Logic of a Modern Faith*, Princeton, Princeton University Press, 1991.

Kalsi, Amrik S., 'Realism in the Hindi Novel in the Late Nineteenth and Early Twentieth Centuries', unpublished Ph.D. thesis, Cambridge University, 1975.

Kaur, Manmohan, *Role of Women in the Freedom Movement (1857–1947)*, New Delhi, Sterling, 1986.

Kaviraj, Sudipta, 'The Imaginary Institution of India', in P. Chatterjee and G. Pandey, eds, *Subaltern Studies VII*, Delhi, Oxford University Press, 1992..

———, 'Writing, Speaking, Being—Language and the Historical Formation of Identities in India', in D. Hellmann-Rajanayagam and D. Rothermund, eds, *Nationalstaat und Sprachkonflikte in Süd-und Südostasien,* Stuttgart, Steiner, 1992.

———, *The Unhappy Consciousness: Bankimchandra Chattopadhyay and the Formation of Nationalist Consciousness in India*, Delhi, Oxford University Press, 1994.

———, 'On the Construction of Colonial Power: Structure Discourse Hegemony', in Engels and Marks, eds, *Contesting Colonial Hegemony*, London, British Academic Press, 1994, pp. 19–54.

Kesavan, Mukul, 'Congress and the Muslims of UP and Bihar, 1937 to 1939', Nehru Memorial Museum and Library occasional papers on History and Society, second series, XXVII, 1990.

Keskar, B.V. and V.K.N. Menon, eds, *Acharya Narendra Dev: A Commemoration Volume*, New Delhi, National Book Trust, 1971.

Khosla, Renuka, *Urban Politics (with Special Reference to Kanpur)*, New Delhi, S. Chand and Co., 1992.

King, Christopher R., 'The Nagari Pracharini Sabha of Benares, 1893–1914: A Study of the Social and Political History of the Hindi Language', unpublished Ph.D. Thesis, University of Wisconsin, 1974.

———, 'Forging a New Linguistic Identity: The Hindi Movement in Benares', in S. Freitag, ed., *Culture and Power in Benares*, Berkeley, University of California Press, 1989, pp. 179–202.

———, *One Language, Two Scripts: The Hindi Movement in Nineteenth Century North India*, Bombay, Oxford University Press, 1994.

Kishwar, Madhu, 'Arya Samaj and Women's Education. Kanya Mahavidyalay, Jalandhar', *Economic and Political Weekly*, XXI, 17, 26, April 1986, Women's Studies, pp. 9–24.

———, 'Gandhi on Women', Delhi, Manushi Prakashan, 1986.

Kolff, Dirk H.A., Naukar, *Rajput and Sepoy: The Ethnohistory of the Military Labour Market in Hindustan, 1450–1850*, Cambridge, Cambridge University Press, 1990; reprinted in Delhi, Manushi Prakashan, 1986.

Kumar, Kapil, *Peasants in Revolt: Tenants, Landlords, Congress and the Raj in Oudh: 1886–1932*, Delhi, Manohar, 1984.

———, 'The Ramcharitmanas as a Radical Text: Baba Ramchandra in Avadh', in S. Chandra, ed., *Social Transformation and Creative Imagination*, Delhi, Allied Publishers, 1984.

———, 'The Congress–Peasant Relationship in the Late 1930s', in D.N. Panigrahi, ed., *Economy, Society and Politics in India*, Delhi, Vikas, 1985, pp. 233–54.

———, 'Rural Women in Oudh 1917–47: Baba Ramchandra and the Woman's Question', in K. Sangari and S. Vaid, eds, *Recasting Women*, Delhi, Kali for Women 1989.

Kumar, Krishna, *The Political Agenda of Education: A Study of Colonialist and Nationalist Ideas*, New Delhi, Sage, 1991.

———, *Learning from Conflict*, New Delhi, Longman, 1996.

Kumar, Nita, *The Artisans of Benares: Popular Culture and Identity, 1880–1986*, Princeton, Princeton University Press, 1988.

———, 'Widows, Education and Social Change in Twentieth Century Benares', *Economic and Political Weekly*, 21 April 1991, Women's Studies, pp. 19–25.

———, 'Sanskrit pandits and the modernization of Sanskrit education in the 19th–20th centuries', paper presented at the conference on 'Vivekananda and the modernisation of Hinduism', London, School of Oriental and African Studies, November 1993.

———, 'Oranges for the Girls, or the Half-known Story of the Education of Girls in Twentieth-Century Benares', in N. Kumar, ed., *Women as Subjects: South Asian Histories,* Charlottesville, University Press of Virginia, 1994, pp. 211–31.

———, 'Religion and Ritual in Indian Schools: Benares from the 1880s to the 1940s', in N. Crook, ed., *The Transmission of Knowledge in South Asia*, Delhi, Oxford University Press, 1996.

Kumar, Radha, *The History of Doing: An Illustrated Account of Movements for Women's Rights and Feminism in India, 1800–1990*, Verso, London, 1993.

Landes, Joan, *Women and the Public Sphere in the Age of the French Revolution*, Ithaca, Cornell University Press, 1988.

Lebra-Chapman, Joyce, *The Rani of Jhansi: A Study in Female Heroism,* Honolulu, University of Hawaii Press, 1986.

Lelyveld, David, *Aligarh's First Generation: Muslim Solidarity and English Education in Northern India, 1875–1900,* Chicago, Chicago University Press, 1975.

———, 'The Fate of Hindustani: Colonial Knowledge and the Project of a National Language', in C.A. Breckenridge and P. van de Veer, eds, *Orientalism and the Postcolonial Predicament*, Philadelphia, University of Pennsylvania Press, 1993.

Link, E. Perry, *Mandarin Ducks and Butterflies: Popular Fiction in Early Twentieth-Century Chinese Cities*, Berkeley, University of California Press, 1981.

Lutgendorf, Philip, *The Life of a Text: Performing the Ramcaritmanas of Tulsidas,* Berkeley, University of Caifornia Press, 1991.

———, 'The Quest for the Legendary Tulsīdās', in W. Callewaert and R. Snell, eds, *According to Tradition: Hagiographical Writing in India*, Wiesbaden, Harrassowitz, 1994.

Lütt, Jürgen, *Hindu-Nationalismus in Uttar Pradeś,* Stuttgart, Ernst Klett Verlag, 1970.

McGregor, R.S., 'Bengal and the Development of Hindi, 1850–80', *South Asian Review,* V, 2, 1972.

———, *Hindi Literature of the Nineteenth and Early Twentieth Centuries*, Wiesbaden, Harrassowitz, 1974.

Mahapatra, Pragati, 'The Making of a Cultural Identity: Language, Literature and Gender in Orissa in Late Nineteenth and Early Twentieth Centuries', unpublished Ph.D. thesis, School of Oriental and African Studies, University of London, 1997.

Majeed, Javed, 'The Jargon of Indostan: An Exploration of Jargon in Urdu and East India Company English', in P. Burke and R. Porter, eds, *Languages and Jargons. Contributions to a Social History of Language*, Cambridge, Polity Press, 1995.

Metcalf, Barbara, *Islamic Revival in British India: Deoband 1860–1900*, Princeton, Princeton University Press, 1982.

———, ed., *Moral Conduct and Authority: The Place of Adab in South Asian Islam*, Berkeley, University of California Press, 1984.

Metcalf, Thomas R., *Land, Landlords and the British Raj: Northern India in the Nineteenth Century*, Berkeley, University of California Press, 1979.

Minault, Gail, ed., *The Extended Family: Women and Political Participation in India and Pakistan*, Delhi, Chanakya Publications, 1981.

———, '*Ismat:* Rāshid ul Khairī's novels and Urdu literary journalism for women', in C. Shackle, ed., *Urdu and Muslim South Asia. Studies in honour of Ralph Russell*, London, School of Oriental and African Studies, 1989, pp. 129–38.

———, 'Other Voices, Other Rooms: The View from the Zenana', in N. Kumar, ed., *Women as Subjects: South Asian Histories*, Charlottesville, University Press of Virginia, 1994, pp. 109–24.

———, *Secluded Scholars: Women's Education and Muslim Social Reform in India*, New Delhi, Oxford University Press, 1998.

Misra, B.B., *The Indian Middle Classes: Their Growth in Modern Times*, London, Oxford University Press, 1961.

Mukherjee, Meenakshi, *Realism and Reality: The Novel and Society in India*, Delhi, Oxford University Press, 1985.

Mukta, Parita, *The Community of Mirabai*, Delhi, Oxford University Press, 1994.

Naim, C.M., 'Prize-Winning *Adab*: A Study of Five Urdu Books Written in Response to the Allahabad Government Gazette Notification', in B. Metcalf, ed., *Moral Conduct and Authority: The Place of Adab in South Asian Islam*, Berkeley, University of California Press, 1984.

Nandy, Ashis, *The Intimate Enemy: Loss and Recovery of Self under Colonialism*, Delhi, Oxford University Press, 1983.

Natarajan, S., *A History of the Press in India*, Bombay, Asia Publishing House, 1962.

Nehru, Jawaharlal, *An Autobiography*, Delhi, Oxford University Press, 1998 (1936).

Nurullah, S. and J.P. Naik, *A History of Education in India During the British Period,* Bombay, 1951.

Offredi, Mariola, *I primi cento anni di giornalismo hindi (1826–1926)*, Venezia, ITE, Dolo, 1971.

O'Hanlon, Rosalind, *Caste, Conflict and Ideology: Mahatma Jotirao Phule and Low Caste Protest in Nineteenth-Century Western India*, Cambridge, Cambridge University Press, 1985.

———, *A Comparison Betweeen Men and Women: Tarabai Shinde and the Critique of Gender Relations in Colonial India*, Delhi, Oxford University Press, 1994.

Omvedt, Gail, *Cultural Revolt in a Colonial Society,* Bombay, Scientific Socialist Education Trust, 1976.

———, *Dalit Visions, The Anti-caste Movement and the Construction of An Indian Identity*, New Delhi, Orient Longman, 1995.

Orsini, Francesca, 'Tulsīdās as a Classic', in R. Snell and I. Raeside, eds, *Classics of Modern South Asian Literature*, Wiesbaden, Harrassowitz, 1998.

———, 'Reading a Social Romance: Pāṇḍey Bechan Śarmā Ugra's *Chand hasīnoṁ ke khutūt* (1927)', in V. Dalmia and T. Damsteegt, eds, *Narrative Strategies,* New Delhi, Oxford University Press, 1999.

———, 'Detective Novels. A Commercial Genre in Nineteenth-century north India, in V. Dalmia and S. Blackburn, eds, *New Literary Histories for South Asia* (forthcoming).

Pandey, Gyanendra, 'Mobilization in a Mass Movement: Congress "Propaganda" in the United Provinces (India)', *Modern Asian Studies*, IX, 2, 1975, pp. 205–26.

———, 'A Rural Base for Congress: The United Provinces 1920–40', in D.A. Low, ed., *Congress and the Raj, Facets of the Indian Struggle 1917–47*, London, Heinemann, 1977.

———, *The Ascendancy of the Congress in Uttar Pradesh, 1926–34: A Study in Imperfect Mobilization*, Delhi, Oxford University Press, 1978.

———, 'The Congress and the Nation, c.1917–47', Occasional paper no. 69, Calcutta, Centre for Studies in the Social Sciences, October 1984.

———, ed., *The Indian Nation in 1942,* Calcutta, K.P. Bagchi, 1988.

———, *The Construction of Communalism in Colonial North India*, Delhi, Oxford University Press, 1990.

Pandey, Gyanendra and P. Chatterjee, eds, *Subaltern Studies VII*, Delhi, Oxford University Press, 1992.

Pant, Rashmi, 'The Cognitive Status of Caste in Colonial Ethnography: A Review of Some Literature of the North Western Provinces and Oudh', *Indian Economic and Social History Review*, 24, 2, 1987.

Peabody, Norbert, 'Tod's *Rajast'han* and the Boundaries of Imperial Rule in Nineteenth-Century India', *Modern Asian Studies*, 30, 1, 1996.

———, 'The king is dead, long live the king!: on karmic kin(g)ship in Kota', in S.C. Welch, ed., *Gods, Kings, and Tigers: The Art of Kotah*, Munich, Prestel-Verlag, 1997.

Pearson, Gail, 'Nationalism, Universalization and the Extended Female Space', in G. Minault, ed., *The Extended Family*, Delhi, Chanakya Publications, 1981.

Pinch, William R., 'Historicity and Hagiography in Gangetic India, 1918–36', paper presented at the workshop on 'Vivekananda and the Modernisation of Hinduism', School of Oriental and African Studies, University of London, November 1993.

Prasad, Madhav, 'Cinema and the Desire for Modernity', *Journal of Arts and Ideas*, 25–6, New Delhi, December 1993, pp. 71–86.

Pritchett, Frances W., *Marvelous Encounters: Folk Romance in Urdu and Hindi*, Delhi, Manohar, 1985.

———, *Nets of Awareness: Urdu Poetry and Its Critics,* Berkeley, University of California Press, 1994.

Rahman, Munibur, 'The Musha'irah', in *Annual of Urdu Studies*, 3, 1983, pp. 75–84.

Rai, Alok, *Hindi Nationalism*, Delhi, Orient Longman, 2001.

Rai, Amrit, *A House Divided: The Origin and Development of Hindi/Hindavi*, Delhi, Oxford University Press, 1984.

———, *Premchand, a Life,* Delhi: Oxford University Press, 1991 (tr. of *Kalam kā sipāhī* , Allahabad, Hans Prakasan, 1962).

Raychaudhuri, Tapan, *Europe Reconsidered. Perceptions of the West in Nineteenth Century Bengal*, Delhi, Oxford University Press, 1988.

Reeves, Peter, 'The Congress and the Abolition of Zamindari in Uttar Pradesh', in J. Masselos, ed., *Struggling and Ruling. The Indian National Congress 1885–1985*, London, Oriental University Press, 1987.

———, *Landlords and Governments in Uttar Pradesh: A Study of Their Relations until Zamindari Abolition*, Delhi, Oxford University Press, 1991.

Robinson, Francis, *Separatism Among Indian Muslims: The Politics of the United Provinces Muslims 1860–1923*, Cambridge, Cambridge University Press, 1974.

Sampurnanand [Sampūrṇānand], *Memories and Reflections*, Bombay, Asia Publishing House, 1962.

Sangari, Kumkum, *The Politics of the Possible*, Delhi, Tullika, 1999..

Sangari, Kumkum and S. Vaid, eds, *Recasting Women: Essays in Indian Colonial History*, Delhi, Kali for Women, 1989.

Sarkar, Sumit, *Modern India, 1885 to 1947*, Delhi, Macmillan, 1983.

Schomer, Karine, *Mahadevi Varma and the Chhayavad Age of Modern Hindi Poetry*, Berkeley, University of California Press, 1983.

———, 'Where Have All the Radhas Gone? New Images of Woman in Modern Hindi Poetry', in J.S. Hawley and D. Wulff, eds, *The Divine Consort: Radha and the Goddesses of India*, Berkeley, Berkeley Religious Studies Series, 1983.

Shackle, Christopher, ed., *Urdu and Muslim South Asia: Studies in Honour of Ralph Russell*, London, School of Oriental and African Studies, 1989.

———, and Rupert Snell, *Hindi and Urdu since 1900: A Common Reader*, London, School of Oriental and African Studies, 1990.

———, and Javed Majeed, *Hālī's Musaddas*, New Delhi, Oxford University Press, 1997.

Shankar, Girja, *Socialist Trends in Indian National Movement: Being a Study of the Congress Socialist Party*, Meerut, Twenty-First Century Publishers, 1987.

Shraddhanand, Swami, *Inside Congress,* Bombay, Phoenix, 1946.

Siddiqi, M.H., *Agrarian Unrest in North India: The United Provinces, 1918–22*, New Delhi, Vikas Publishing House, 1978.

Singha, Radhika, Review of *Culture and Power in Benares,* ed. S. Freitag, in *The Economic and Social History Review*, 28, 4, 1989, pp. 466–9.

Small, Ian, *Conditions for Criticism: Authority, Knowledge and Literature in the Late Nineteenth Century*, Oxford, Clarendon Press, 1991.

Stokes, Eric, *The Peasant and the Raj: Studies in Agrarian Society and Peasant Rebellion in Colonial India*, Cambridge, Cambridge University Press, 1978.

Swan, Robert, *Munshi Premchand of Lamhi Village*, Durham, Duke University Press, 1969.

Talwar, Veer Bharat, 'Feminist Consciousness in Women's Journals in Hindi: 1910–20', in K. Sangari and S. Vaid, eds, *Recasting Women*, Delhi, Kali for Women, 1989, pp. 204–32.

Tarlo, Emma, *Clothing Matters*, London, Hurst, 1996.

Tharu, Susie and K. Lalita, eds, *Women's Writing in India*, 2 vols, Oxford University Press, 1993 and 1995.

Thomas, Rosalind, *Literacy and Orality in Ancient Greece*, Cambridge, Cambridge University Press, 1992.

Vedalankar, Shardadevi, *The Development of Hindi Prose in the Early Nineteenth Century (AD 1800–56)*, Allahabad, Lokbharati Publications, 1969.

Viswanathan, Gauri, *Masks of Conquest: Literary Study and British Rule in India*, London, Faber and Faber, 1989.

Washbrooke, David, ' "To each a language of his own": language, culture, and society in colonial India', in P.J. Cornfield, ed., *Language, History and Class,* Oxford, Blackwell, 1991.

Watt, Ian, *The Rise of the Novel: Studies in Defoe, Richardson and Fielding*, Harmondsworth, Penguin, 1979 (1957).

Ziegler, Norman, '*Marvari Historical Chronicles: Sources for the Social and Cultural History of Rajasthan*', *Indian Economic and Social History Review*, XII, 1976, pp. 219–50.

Index